365 Daily Devotions

with *Eric Elder*

365 Daily Devotions with Eric
Copyright © 2020 Eric Elder
All rights reserved.

Interior Layout and Design by Eric Elder.
Cover Photo and Design by Ethan Bliese: ethanbliese.com.
Author Photo by Hayley Breanne Photography: hayleybreannephoto.com.
Cover Photo of Clover Ranch, *A Place to Seek God…and find Him*.

365 Daily Devotions with Eric is one of several inspirational resources produced by Eric Elder Ministries. For more inspirational books, music, and videos, please visit: theranch.org, ericelder.com, and inspiringbooks.com

All devotional books contained herein Copyright © Eric Elder:
Two Weeks with God (1999), *Exodus: Lessons in Freedom* (2005), *Jesus: Lessons in Love* (2007), *Acts: Lessons in Faith* (2008), *Ephesians: Lessons in Grace* (2009), *Nehemiah: Lessons in Rebuilding* (2009), *Israel: Lessons from the Holy Land* (2010), *The Top 20 Passages in the Bible* (2011), *Romans: Lessons in Renewing Your Mind* (2012), *Making the Most of the Darkness* (2014), *15 Tips for a Stronger Marriage* (2014), *Psalms: Lessons in Prayer* (2017), and *St. Nicholas: The Believer* (2014).
All rights reserved.

Unless otherwise noted, all Scripture quotations are from *The Holy Bible, New International Version*. Copyright © 1973, 1978, 1984 by International Bible Society. Used by permission of Zondervan Publishing House. All rights reserved.

Scripture quotations marked (ESV) are from *The Holy Bible, English Standard Version*, Copyright © 2001 by Crossway, a publishing ministry of Good News Publishers. Used by permission. All rights reserved

Scripture quotations marked (NKJV) are from the *New King James Version*. Copyright © 1982 by Thomas Nelson, Inc. All rights reserved. Used by permission.

Scripture quotations marked (KJV) are from *The Authorized (King James) Version*. Rights in the Authorized Version in the United Kingdom are vested in the Crown. Reproduced by permission of the Crown's patentee, Cambridge University Press.

Scripture quotations marked (AMP) are from THE AMPLIFIED BIBLE. Old Testament copyright © 1965, 1987 by The Zondervan Corporation. The Amplified New Testament copyright © 1958, 1987 by The Lockman Foundation. Used by permission.

Scripture quotations marked (NLT) are from *The Holy Bible, New Living Translation,* Copyright © 1996. Used by permission of Tyndale House Publishers, Inc., Wheaton, Illinois 60189. All rights reserved.

ISBN: 978-1-931760-85-0

TABLE OF CONTENTS

Two Weeks with God 5

Exodus: Lessons in Freedom 24

Jesus: Lessons in Love 86

Acts: Lessons in Faith 125

Ephesians: Lessons in Grace 164

Nehemiah: Lessons in Rebuilding 192

Israel: Lessons from the Holy Land 216

The Top 20 Passages in the Bible 286

Romans: Lessons in Renewing Your Mind 321

Making the Most of the Darkness 462

15 Tips for a Stronger Marriage 502

Psalms: Lessons in Prayer 524

St. Nicholas: The Believer 597

Bonus: 12 Tips on Parenting! 652

PREFACE

I love spending quiet time with God every day. It centers me.

For over 30 years now I've been writing down what God has spoken to me during those quiet times with Him. I pray this book encourages you during your own quiet times with Him.

This book contains devotions of various lengths covering various topics. Some have questions for reflection, others have prayers, and still others stand alone. I hope the variety keeps it interesting for you throughout the year!

I'd also suggest one tip in case you find yourself falling behind in your reading. Rather than spending too much time trying to catch up (and possibly giving up reading altogether), just skip ahead to the devotion for the current day and start reading again from there. You can catch any devotions you missed next time around!

Thanks for picking up this book. I pray it blesses you in reading it as it has blessed me in writing it!

Eric Elder

Two Weeks with God

Two Weeks with God

A 14-day devotional to help you clear your mind and focus on God, based on the songs from Eric Elder's CD Clear My Mind

INTRODUCTION

I believe the music from my piano album, *Clear My Mind* (on your favorite music streaming service or on ericelder.com), will go a long way in helping you to clear your mind. Music has a tremendous power to heal our hearts, soothe our souls, and clear our minds.

But I believe this music can help you in another way too: it can bring you into the very presence of God. And I've found that the best way to clear my mind is to spend some time with Him. He promises that whenever we have anxious thoughts, we can bring our requests to Him and He will give us a peace that passes understanding (Philippians 4:7).

God knows you better than anyone else. He knows the depths of what you're going through. He knows where you hurt and how to heal those hurts. There's nothing more soothing or peaceful than to let Him wrap His arms around you and hold you tight.

If that sounds good to you, I'd like to encourage you to go through this devotional. For the next fourteen days you can focus on Him in a way, perhaps, that you've never done before.

By the end of the two weeks, I hope you'll feel better about yourself, about your situation, and about your relationship with God.

Even more, I hope you'll finish with a strong desire to come back to God again and again. Because as much as you might look forward to spending time with Him, He is even more eager to spend time with you. That's why He created you: to fellowship with Him. Always know that He loves you very much.

Enjoy the music—and enjoy your time with God.

DAY 1: MOMENT BY MOMENT   JANUARY 1

I am sometimes overwhelmed by the apparent slowness with which God answers prayer. I wonder how many deep breaths I'll have to take before the answers come. And yet, time after time the answers have come, even if they come gradually, moment by moment.

One of the reasons God takes time to answer our prayers is recorded in the book of Exodus. God told Moses that he would bring his people into a remarkable land, but that it was currently occupied by their enemies. God said, "But I will not drive them out in a single year, because the land would become desolate and the wild animals too numerous for you. Little by little I will drive them out before you, until you have increased enough to take possession of the land" (Exodus 23:29-30).

Because of God's great love for us, He sometimes delays the answers to our prayers so they won't overwhelm us when they come. As the saying goes, "Be careful what you ask for, because you just might get it!" Although we might think we could handle the answer, God knows best and we would do well to follow this advice from Proverbs: "Trust in the Lord with all your heart; and lean not on your own understanding. In all your ways acknowledge him, and he will make your path straight" (Proverbs 3:5-6).

Don't be discouraged if God's answers are slow in coming. God loves you very much. He already sent His Son to die for you. There's nothing He wouldn't do for you. Jesus tells us that everyone who asks receives, and then He adds these touching words: "Which of you, if his son asks for bread, will give him a stone? Or if he asks for a fish, will give him a snake? If you, then, though you are evil, know how to give good gifts to your children, how much more will your Father in heaven give good gifts to those who ask Him" (Matthew 7:7-11)!

The Lord is not slow in keeping His promise, as some understand slowness. The Bible says, "With the Lord a day is like a thousand years, and a thousand years are like a day" (2 Peter 3:8b). Trust Him moment by moment, and soon you'll see the answers to your prayers.

Let Me Pray for You

Lord, I pray for those who need to renew their trust in You today. I pray that You would show them, even this week, that You are answering their prayers moment by moment. Let them know in their hearts that there's nothing You wouldn't do for them, and that if they can trust You with their eternal life, they can trust You for their needs here on earth as well. In Jesus' name, Amen.

Take Time in His Word

"But I will not drive them out in a single year, because the land would become desolate and the wild animals too numerous for you. Little by little I will drive them out before you, until you have increased enough to take possession of the land" (Exodus 23:29-30).

- *Read Romans 8:28. In what things does God work for our good?*
- *Read Ephesians 3:20-21. How much is God able to do for us?*
- *Read John 3:16 and John 15:13. To what length is God willing to go for us?*

Take Time in Prayer

Listen to the song "Moment By Moment" (on your favorite music streaming service or on ericelder.com). Take a few minutes to bring your requests to God. Allow some time for Him to speak to you, too.

After You Pray

By the way, never underestimate what can happen in a moment. The Bible says that a woman who had been bleeding for twelve years touched Jesus' robe and was healed *from that moment* (Matthew 9:22). A boy who had been tormented by demons since childhood had them cast out and was healed *from that moment* (Matthew 17:18). A day will come in the future when a trumpet will sound, the dead will be raised, and we will be transformed into the image of Christ *in a moment, in a flash, in the twinkling of an eye* (1 Corinthians

15:52, KJV and NIV). Keep trusting Him moment by moment, for in one moment you could see the answers to years of prayer!

Lord, I believe You are answering my prayers even now.

DAY 2: YOU ARE THE WAY — JANUARY 2

I recorded these songs on a piano that is very special to me: a restored 1910 "Model B" made by STEINWAY & SONS. I mention this in case you're a piano buff, but also to relate the following story.

One morning as I sat down to play the piano, a ray of light came through the window and illuminated only three letters of the maker's nameplate above my fingers. Highlighted before me were the letters W-A-Y.

I began to write a song about Jesus, who said He was "the way and the truth and the life" (John 14:6). The melody stirred me so much that I played it over and over, singing to Him, "You are the Way, Lord. You are the Way, Lord. You are the Way, Lord. And I will follow, I will follow You."

Later that same day, without prior notice, I was released from my job! At least I thought it was without prior notice. I soon realized that God had shown me in the morning that He Himself was taking me in a new direction. Even though I couldn't see the path ahead of me, I knew which way to go: to follow Christ, the Way. Within a week the path became brighter and brighter.

Although we often want Jesus to show us the whole map at once, He does something even better. He promises to take us there Himself. "Follow me," He said to Peter and Andrew. "Follow me," He said to Matthew. "Follow me," He said to Philip.

Each of these men got up immediately and followed Him. They knew enough about Jesus to know that there was really only one way to go. Peter said it best when Jesus asked the twelve disciples one day if they wanted to leave Him. Peter replied, "Lord, to whom shall we go? You have the words of eternal life" (John 6:68).

When the path ahead looks dark, we can count on Christ to give us light. "I am the light of the world. Whoever follows me will never walk in darkness, but will have the light of life" (John 8:12). He alone is the Way.

Let Me Pray for You

Lord, I pray for those who need direction in their life. I pray that You would go before them and light the path so they can see. I pray that they would stay close to You, and as they do, the path ahead of them would get brighter and brighter. Let them know that You are worthy to follow, for You have the words of eternal life. In Jesus' name, Amen.

Take Time in His Word

"Jesus answered, 'I am the way and the truth and the life. No one comes to the Father except through me'" (John 14:6).

- *Read John 8:12. What promise does Jesus make to those who follow Him?*
- *Read Proverbs 4:18. What happens to the path of the righteous?*
- *Read John 14:1-6. Where will following Jesus ultimately lead us?*

Take Time in Prayer

Listen to the song "You Are The Way" (on your favorite music streaming service or on ericelder.com). Take a few minutes to commit to God that you are willing to follow Jesus wherever He leads you, for He is the Way. Ask Him to light the path ahead of you.

After You Pray

Ultimately, God wants us to follow Jesus not only on earth, but also into heaven. Jesus declared that the only way to come to the Father was through Him: "I am the way and the truth and the life. No one comes to the Father except through me" (John 14:6). When we put our faith in Christ, believing that He died in our place for the sins we have committed, we can be assured that God will take us into heaven. Jesus said, "For my Father's will is that everyone who looks to the Son and believes in Him shall have eternal life, and I will raise him up at the last day" (John 6:40). There's only one sure way to get into heaven on judgment day: put your faith in Christ. And when you stand at the gates, Jesus will say, "Let them in…they're with me."

Lord, You are the Way. I will follow You.

DAY 3: GO INTO ALL THE WORLD   JANUARY 3

There are two things I pray that God would impress on your heart today: 1) that He loves you very much; and 2) that He needs you very much.

First, if you doubt God's love for you, let me tell you again: "God loves you very much." These are more than just words; God has shown us it's true. The Bible says, "God demonstrates His own love for us in this: While we were still sinners, Christ died for us" (Romans 5:8). You are valuable to God. He wouldn't have sent Jesus to die for you if He didn't think you were worth saving. He saved you because He loves you.

Second, God saved you because He has a purpose for your life. Jesus said, "You did not choose me, but I chose you and appointed you to go and bear fruit—fruit that will last" (John 15:16). God has a purpose for our lives: He wants us to bear fruit that will last.

Although God could have used some kind of cosmic loudspeakers to tell everyone in the world about Christ, He has chosen to entrust that job to each of us. Listen to Christ's final words on earth: "Go into all the world and preach the good news to all creation. Whoever believes and is baptized will be saved, but whoever does not believe will be condemned" (Mark 16:15-16). There are people who won't make it into heaven because no one ever told them about Christ. The Bible says, "'Everyone who calls on the name of the Lord will be saved.' How, then, can they call on the one they have not believed in? And how can they believe in the one of whom they have not heard? And how can they hear without someone preaching to them? And how can they preach unless they are sent? As it is written, 'How beautiful are the feet of those who bring good news!'" (Romans 10:13-15).

Wouldn't it be nice to have someone tell you your feet are beautiful? God saved us because he loved us, and also because He needs us to share that love with others. I want to encourage you today to consider sharing the message of Christ with someone else. Think of the joy of seeing someone in heaven because you told them about Christ. And think of the sorrow of not seeing someone there because you didn't.

Let Me Pray for You

Lord, I pray for those who need to know today how very much You love them. I pray Your love would overwhelm them, even now. I ask that You would also show them how very much You need them. Lead them to people who need to know about You, then give them the words to speak. In Jesus' name, Amen.

Take Time in His Word

"He said to them, 'Go into all the world and preach the good news to all creation. Whoever believes and is baptized will be saved, but whoever does not believe will be condemned'" (Mark 16:15-16).

- *Read Ephesians 2:8-10. What has God created us to do?*
- *Read John 15:4-6. What do we need to do so that we can produce fruit?*
- *Read Matthew 25:14-30. Do any talents come to mind that God has given you that He might want you to use for His kingdom?*

Take Time in Prayer

Listen to the song "Go Into All The World" (on your favorite music streaming service or on ericelder.com). Take a few minutes to ask God to reveal His great love to you. Ask Him to bring to mind specific gifts He has given you, and to show you how you can use them to share His love with others.

After You Pray

Our faith can be a very personal thing, but not so personal that others can't see it. Here's how Jesus puts it: "You are the light of the world. A city on a hill cannot be hidden. Neither do people light a lamp and put it under a bowl. Instead they put it on its stand, and it gives light to everyone in the house. In the same way, let your light shine before men, that they may see your good deeds and praise your Father in heaven" (Matthew 5:14-16). If God has lit your lamp, let it shine.

Lord, show me how I can share Your love with others.

DAY 4: STAND ON MEJANUARY 4

The promises God makes in the Bible are rock solid. We can stand on His promises with as much confidence as we can stand on the strongest rock. When doubts or discouragement come against us, we can stand on His word to carry us through. One hymn writer called this "Standing on the Promises of God" (Russell Carter, 1886).

One day, God asked me to do something that surprised me. It wasn't ungodly, but it wasn't what I expected. I wrestled in prayer to find out if He was speaking these words or not. As I often do, I asked God to give me a scripture to back up what He was saying. I asked Him, "Lord, what word can I stand on?" Without hesitation, His answer came back: "My Son, you can stand on Me."

In the Bible, Christ is called the Word (John 1:14). He is as strong as any rock on which we could stand. Another hymn writer wrote, "On Christ the solid rock I stand, all other ground is sinking sand. All other ground is sinking sand" (Edward Mote, 1834).

As I prayed, God brought to my mind other people in the Bible who had also heard perplexing words from God. I thought of Peter, up on a roof, when God asked him to eat food that Peter thought was impure (Acts 10:15). I thought of Abraham when God asked him to sacrifice his son (Genesis 22:2). I thought of Jesus, the night before He died, when He pleaded with God to see if there was any other way (Matthew 26:39).

In each instance, these people submitted their finite wisdom to God's infinite wisdom. As they did, the miraculous occurred. Through Peter's obedience, God brought the message of Christ to the Gentiles. Through Abraham's obedience, God brought forth countless descendants. Through Christ's obedience, God gave all people victory over death, once and for all.

I knew what I had to do that day. With renewed confidence I took my stand on God's Word and soon saw His wisdom prevail in my own situation. If you feel like you're sinking and you need a place to stand, you can always stand on Christ, the Rock, the Living Word.

Let Me Pray for You

Lord, I pray for those who need a solid place to stand. Let them know they can stand on Your promises today. Prove to them that You are faithful to do what You say You will do. Show them that their obedience to You will make a difference in their lives and the lives of others. We ask all these things in the strong name of Jesus, the Solid Rock. Amen.

Take Time in His Word

"The Word became flesh and made his dwelling among us. We have seen his glory, the glory of the One and Only, who came from the Father, full of grace and truth" (John 1:14).

- *Read Matthew 7:24-27. What does a wise person do to build a house that will stand?*
- *Read Isaiah 55:8-11. How do God's thoughts compare to ours?*
- *Read Matthew 26:36-39. How can we apply Christ's example to our own prayers?*

Take Time in Prayer

Listen to the song "Stand On Me" (on your favorite music streaming service or on ericelder.com). Ask God to renew in your heart that His Word is trustworthy. Ask Him to bring to mind a promise that you can stand on today.

After You Pray

If you're looking for a word from God, look in the Bible. It has over 800,000 of them! King David said, "Your word is a lamp to my feet and a light for my path" (Psalm 119:105). The Bible has answers to everyday questions, as well as to eternal ones. If you've been away from the Bible and would like to get reacquainted, You might start in the book of John. Read as much as you can each day, and let God speak to you about your life as well. God speaks in various ways, but He has spoken to me through the pages of the Bible more than any other way. Don't let a day go by without opening this book and asking God to speak to you through it.

Lord, I'm going to stand on Your promises today.

DAY 5: CLEAR MY MIND JANUARY 5

Many people long for a clear mind. At the heart of this longing is a desire for peace. A true peace that lasts. A peace that doesn't fade when the bottle is empty, or when the song is over, or when the world closes in. Believe it or not, such a peace does exist. It's called peace with God, and it's available to every one of us.

The reason we don't have peace with God is because of sin. When we do things that we know He doesn't want us to do, we put a barrier between us and God. Although God is still eager to talk to us, we're no longer eager to talk to Him. Even when He calls to us, we'd rather turn away, and sometimes we run in fear. But we don't have to run away, for God has made a way for us to come back to Him and be clean again. That way is through Jesus. When Jesus died on the cross, He paid the price for all of our sins. When we put our faith in Christ, believing that He has died in our place, God wipes our slate clean. He forgives us so that we can come back to Him with our whole hearts—and with our hearts whole.

God is eager to take us back, like a Father who waits for a lost child to return. Jesus describes our reunion with God like that of a Father whose son ran off and squandered all of his inheritance. When the son returned, ashamed of what he had done, "his father saw him and was filled with compassion for him; he ran to his son, threw his arms around him and kissed him." Then the Father said, "Let's have a feast and celebrate. For this son of mine was dead and is alive again; he was lost and is found" (Luke 15:20, 23-24).

If you'd like this peace, you can have it today by praying a prayer to God. You can let God wrap His arms around you and welcome you back. And even more, when you put your faith in Christ, you will be able to enter heaven and spend eternity with God (1 John 5:13).

When you make peace with God, He clears your name. He separates you from your sins as far as the east is from the west (Psalm 103:12). In fact, He doesn't even remember them (Hebrews 8:12)! And once you know your name is clear, your mind is sure to follow.

Let Me Pray for You

Note: If you've never been at peace with God because of your sins, you can have it today by coming to Him in prayer. Like a father welcoming back his lost son, God will wrap His arms around you and welcome you back, too. And even more, when you put your faith in Christ, you will be able to enter heaven and spend eternity with God. If you would like this peace right now, pray this prayer with me.

"Dear God, I'm sorry for the sins I've committed against You and against others. Thank You for sending Jesus to die for me so I wouldn't have to. I ask for your forgiveness. I ask that Jesus Christ would be Lord of my life. And I ask that You would fill me with your Holy Spirit so that I can follow You with my whole heart. In Jesus' name I pray, Amen."

Take Time in His Word

"Therefore, my brothers, I want you to know that through Jesus the forgiveness of sins is proclaimed to you" (Acts 13:38).

- *Read 1 Peter 3:18a. For what purpose did Christ die for our sins?*
- *Read Romans 5:1. Through whom can we have peace with God?*

- Read 1 John 5:13. Of what can we be assured when we believe in the name of the Son of God?

Take Time in Prayer

Listen to the song "Clear My Mind" (on your favorite music streaming service or on ericelder.com). Ask God to clear your mind and to bring you His peace.

After You Pray

Although peace with God is everlasting, there are times when it comes under attack. Sometimes Satan tries to fill our mind with his lies. Sometimes we have trouble forgiving ourselves. Sometimes the sins of others deeply impact us. Regardless of the cause, the solution is always the same: come to Christ again and again. Jesus said, "Come to me, all you who are weary and burdened and I will give you rest. Take my yoke upon you and learn from me, for I am gentle and humble in heart, and you will find rest for your souls. For my yoke is easy and my burden is light" (Matthew 11:28-30). Come to Christ anytime you need His peace (Philippians 4:6-7).

Lord, You've cleared my name. Now, Lord, please clear my mind.

DAY 6: A GRAND MAN   JANUARY 6

For Father's Day one year I wrote a tribute to my dad. As I recalled various memories of him over the years, I realized what an impact he has had on my life. I wrote this song to go with the tribute to let him know that even though my kids call him Grandpa Bob, he's more than a grandpa. He's a Grand Man.

We all, like Jesus, had an earthly father who raised us. But we all, like Jesus, have a heavenly Father as well. The difference between the two can be, at times, like night and day. As a father to my own children, I am fully aware that no father on earth is perfect! But our heavenly Father is perfect (Matthew 5:48).

Many people, whether they recognize it or not, often view God in the same way they view their earthly father. While sometimes this image we have of God is good, other times it is distorted, and sometimes it is flat-out wrong.

I'd like to encourage you to get to know the God of the Bible, a Father who is good to all and has compassion on all He has made. The Bible says that God is "gracious and compassionate, slow to anger and rich in love" (Psalm 145:8-9). Does that sound like a dad you'd like to get to know better?

At the same time, the God of the Bible disciplines us because of His great love for us. "Our fathers disciplined us for a little while as they thought best; but God disciplines us for our good, that we may share in his holiness" (Hebrews 12:10). Would you like a dad who disciplines you for your own good, and trains you in ways that will bring you peace?

That is the kind of Father we have in heaven. He's the same Father that Jesus called on every time He went to pray. Jesus says that we are His brothers, and that His Father is our Father (Matthew 28:10-12, John 20:17). If you need a fresh view of your heavenly Father, I'd like to encourage you to come to Him in the pages of the Bible. Take a look at the ways God was a good Father to Christ. In the same way, He'll be a good Father to you, too.

Let Me Pray for You

Lord, I pray for those who need to know You as their Father. I pray You would show them what You are like, and that You would correct any wrong thinking they may have about You. And Lord, as they come to see You as You are, I pray they would be filled with the confidence and joy that comes from knowing they are Your child. In Jesus' name, Amen.

Take Time in His Word

"Yet to all who received him, to those who believed in his name, he gave the right to become children of God" (John 1:12).

- *Read Matthew 7:9-11. How does God compare to earthly fathers in this passage?*
- *Read Hebrews 12:5-11. How does God compare to earthly fathers in this passage?*
- *Read John 5:19. Why was it important for Jesus to know His Father well?*

Take Time in Prayer

Listen to the song "A Grand Man" (on your favorite music streaming service or on ericelder.com). Take a minute to thank God for being your Father. Ask Him to make right any of the wrong thoughts you might have about Him as your Father.

After You Pray

God calls us to "'Honor your father and your mother'—which is the first commandment with a promise—'that it may go well with you and that you may enjoy long life on the earth'" (Ephesians 6:2-3). When I wrote a tribute to my dad, it was a great blessing to me as well as to him. I found that the Bible was true when it said that honoring our father and mother is the first commandment with a promise. Honoring our parents is good for them—and good for us. If your parents are still alive, you may want to ask God if there's something you can do to honor them. Then watch the blessings of God pour out on each of you.

Lord, thank You for loving me as a Father.

DAY 7: A DAY TO EXPLORE — JANUARY 7

Congratulations! You've made it to the end of the first week of this devotional! I'd like you to take today to explore the Bible on your own.

Since the day I gave my life to Christ, hardly a day has gone by that I haven't opened my Bible to see what God might have to say to me. It doesn't matter how many times I've read it; God always has something new and fresh to say.

That's because the Bible is not like any other book in the world. The book of Hebrews says, "the word of God is living and active" (Hebrews 4:12). Some days the words seem to jump off the pages as God speaks to me.

It is the best love letter ever written. You could open to any page and you'd see how great God's love is for you. And like all good love letters, this one is worth reading over and over and over again.

So go ahead and explore it today on your own. If your Bible has an index or concordance in the back, look up a topic that's on your mind and see what God has to say about it. Or try reading all the way through one of the shorter books in the Bible in one sitting, like Ephesians or First John.

Whether you're new to the Bible, or you've read it many times, know that God can speak to you every time you open its pages and every time you open your heart to Him.

Let Me Pray for You

Lord, I thank You for telling us so much about You on the pages of the Bible. I thank You that the words are living and active, and that they can speak so personally to each of our hearts. Lord, pour out Your wisdom on those who read Your Word today. And as they get to know You better through these pages, I pray they would want to return to You again tomorrow, and the next day, and every day, for the rest of their lives. In Jesus' name, Amen.

An Online Bible

If you're looking for a Bible online, I highly recommend this one at www.bible.com. It's free, you can read or listen to it online in many languages or you can download it as an app. Enjoy!

DAY 8: I DECLARE — JANUARY 8

One reason the Bible helps so many people is that it tells *real* stories about *real* people who have been touched by a *very real* God. When we read how God worked in the lives of Moses, David, Paul, Esther, Ruth, and countless others, we see how God can work in our lives, too.

In the same way, people can learn from our lives as well. The Bible says, "Declare His glory among the nations, His marvelous deeds among all peoples" (Psalm 96:3).

I wrote this song after my own struggle about whether or not to share with others my own testimony of what God has done in my life. Although I am still self-conscious at times, I have seen God use my testimony for His glory far too often to ever want to hold back if God prompts me to share.

I'd like to encourage you to share your testimony with others, too. Although sharing it may be uncomfortable, you can know that if God is prompting you, He has a purpose for it. There are many hurting people going through the very same things that you've already been through. They need a glimmer of hope that God can work in their lives, too.

The woman at the well didn't have a particularly flattering background, but after she met Jesus, she went back to her town to tell them what He had done for her. The Bible says, "Many of the Samaritans from that town believed in Him because of the woman's testimony…" (John 4:39). The apostle John recorded what Christ had done in his life and the lives of others, "that you may believe that Jesus is the Christ, the Son of God, and that by believing you may have life in His name" (John 20:31).

Peter and John were so excited to tell about Christ, they couldn't keep quiet even when threatened with imprisonment. "Judge for yourselves whether it is right in God's sight to obey you rather than God. For we cannot help speaking about what we have seen and heard" (Acts 4:19-20).

The words of our testimony are like gold to God. When we share them, they can be like gold to others, too.

Let Me Pray for You

Lord, I pray for those whom You have touched, that they would be willing to share with others what You have done for them. Lord, I pray that You would show them, even this week, how their testimony could affect someone else's life. I pray that when they're ready, Your Holy Spirit would lead them in exactly what to say and when to say it. In Jesus' name, Amen.

Take Time in His Word

"Declare His glory among the nations, His marvelous deeds among all peoples" (Psalm 96:3).

- Read Acts 26:1-29. Why was Paul so willing to be honest about what God had done for him?
- Read Revelation 12:10-11. What kind of power does the word of our testimony have?
- Read Mark 5:18-20. What response did the people have when the man who had been demon-possessed told them what Christ had done for him?

Take Time in Prayer

Listen to the song "I Declare" (on your favorite music streaming service or on ericelder.com). Thank God for what He's done in your life. Ask God to put people in your life who might need to hear about what He's done for you.

After You Pray

Every week I receive letters from people on the Internet who have read my testimony and the testimonies of others on our web site called *The Ranch* (www.theranch.org). They often simply need someone to talk to who has struggled with their same struggles. They are looking for hope. When they find a Christian who can point them to God's solution to their problems, they are thrilled, healed and thankful beyond words. If God has helped you through a struggle in your life, would you be willing to share it on the Internet so others could find hope, too? If so, send me your testimony and watch God work through your words.

Lord, help me to share with others what You've done in my life.

DAY 9: TRUST ME   JANUARY 9

This is the first song I ever wrote. I had been asking God what He wanted me to do that day. I was surprised when I thought He said, "Write a song."

Having never written one before, I wasn't exactly sure what to do! I had played the piano most of my life, but I had only played songs that were written down by others. This time God wanted me to write a new song. The Bible says, "He put a new song in my mouth, a hymn of praise to our God. Many will see and fear and put their trust in the LORD" (Psalm 40:3).

On my heart that day was a friend who needed to put his trust in the Lord. He was about to make a decision to leave his wife, but I had pleaded with him that there was another way, the way of Christ.

I had seen God breathe life back into several other marriages as I spoke to them from God's Word, so I knew the words I was speaking to him were trustworthy. Even though he didn't know Christ for himself, I prayed that he would at least trust the words I was speaking to him, for I trust in Christ.

Unfortunately, he chose not to trust Christ nor me. He left his wife, and he left a trail of destruction behind him. But I haven't stopped praying for him, because I know that God answers prayer. Jesus told His disciples that they should "always pray and not give up" (Luke 18:1).

A man named George Mueller prayed for many people during his lifetime who gave their hearts to Christ. His journal records that at the time of his death, there were still three people for whom he had prayed daily, but had not yet accepted Christ. But, on the day of George's funeral, one of them accepted Christ, and the other two did the same shortly thereafter.

We may not always see how God ties up the loose ends of our hopes and prayers for people. But I believe there was a reason that Jesus told his disciples that they should always pray and not give up. One day we'll see why.

Let Me Pray for You

Lord, I pray for those who need encouragement to always pray and not give up. Lord, help them to trust that you do indeed have a plan, and that their prayers are not in vain. Lord, give them favor with those they speak to about You, and let the words they speak come out as if they came straight from You. I pray this in Jesus' name, Amen.

Take Time in His Word

"Then Jesus told His disciples a parable to show them that they should always pray and not give up" (Luke 18:1).

- *Read Luke 18:1-8. What encouragement can you take from this parable?*
- *Read Luke 15:4-10. What happens in heaven when someone who was lost is found?*
- *Read James 5:20. What benefits can come from our influence on others?*

Take Time in Prayer

Listen to the song "Trust Me" (on your favorite music streaming service or on ericelder.com). Pray for someone who needs to know Christ.

After You Pray

God's Word has power not only when we read it, but also when we speak it. The Bible says, "If anyone speaks, he should do it as one speaking the very words of God" (1 Peter 4:11). When we carefully pray about what to say to others, and then ensure that what we say lines up with God's Word, God can use our words powerfully. In one instance, I talked to a man who was separated from his wife. His family and friends told him to divorce her, and he was on the verge of doing just that. When I spoke to him from the Bible, he said, "You're the first person who has told me the Truth!" Within a few months he and his wife were back together again. Your words may be the only the Bible some people will ever hear.

Lord, I am going to pray and not give up.

DAY 10: LORD, I PRAY   **JANUARY 10**

I wrote this song as a lullaby for our children, but it has become a prayer of blessing for our whole family.

I established our nightly prayer routine before I was married. I had heard someone say that he made a commitment to pray with his wife every night before they went to sleep. That way, each of them had received a prayer of blessing every day. I liked the idea so much I began that same week to pray daily with my roommate.

When I got married, I continued those nightly prayers with my wife. Now that we have children, we do the same for each of them at bedtime, placing our hands on their heads and asking God to bless their lives. I believe that our prayers, our verbal blessing, and our physical touch can make a difference.

If you have someone in your life for which you'd like to pray each day, I urge you to consider starting that habit today. Our prayer times with each other can be quiet moments of intimacy in otherwise hectic days.

Some of you may not be in a place where you can pray for someone each day in person. But I can assure you that there is someone who is praying for you. The Bible says that Jesus "is at the right hand of God and is also interceding for us" (Romans 8:34).

By the way, if you have children and want to try singing this song as a prayer over them, here are the words. It simply goes, "Lord, I pray for my children. Lord, I pray for my children. Lord, I pray for my children. Lord, I pray for my children." The next time through, replace the word 'children' with the name of each person in your family. By praying for our children, we can pass onto them the blessings of God, just as Isaac passed them onto his son Jacob, who passed them onto his son Joseph (Genesis 27:25, 48:15).

As you listen to this song, you may also hear a familiar melody in the background. It's a simple reminder of God's great love for us.

Let Me Pray for You

Lord, I thank You for always interceding on our behalf. I pray for those who want to pass on the blessings they've received from You to their families. I ask that You would give them the insight and wisdom to know how to do this in a way that's meaningful to them and honoring to You. In Jesus' name, Amen.

Take Time in His Word

"And he took the children in his arms, put his hands on them and blessed them" (Mark 10:16).

- *Read Mark 10:13-16. How did Jesus bless the children who were brought to Him?*
- *Read Genesis 48:9-20. How did Israel bless his grandchildren?*
- *Read Proverbs 22:6. How can our influence on our children affect them when they are older?*

Take Time in Prayer

Listen to the song "Lord, I Pray" (on your favorite music streaming service or on ericelder.com). Pray, by name, for those you love. Also remember to thank God that Christ is praying for you.

After You Pray

In many of Paul's letters in the New Testament, he prays for the people to whom he wrote and ministered. And at the end of his letters, he would often ask for those people to pray for him as well. If God has blessed you through this ministry, could I ask you to pray for us as well? Here are a few of the prayers Paul asked people to pray on his behalf: "Pray for us that the message of the Lord may spread rapidly and be honored, just as it was with you" (2 Thessalonians 3:1). "And pray for us, too, that God may open a door for our message, so that we may proclaim the mystery of Christ, for which I am in chains. Pray that I may proclaim it clearly, as I should" (Colossians 4:3-4). We know your prayers are heard and answered and we appreciate the time you spend in prayer for us.

Lord, I pray for those I love.

DAY 11: MY LANA   JANUARY 11

One day I read a verse in the Bible that said, "May He give you the desire of your heart…" (Psalm 20:4). Immediately, I knew what my desire was: to marry Lana.

As odd as it seems to me now, this wasn't always my desire. I had dated Lana in college, and we loved each other enough, but I wasn't ready to consider marriage. We moved to different cities and eventually stopped dating.

We still talked from time to time and one day she told me she wasn't really happy in her job. I said I'd pray for her that week. As I prayed, I also sensed that it wasn't her job so much as the fact that God really wanted her to have a husband. So I began to pray that God would send her a husband.

You know the rest! Over the next three months, God put in my heart a love for her like I've never known for anyone else, before or since. I didn't even tell her what was happening to me! At the end of three months of praying, the desire in my heart was so strong that I called her to tell her about it. It turns out that when I called, she had just decided to quit her job, but wasn't sure what to do next. I told her I had an idea!

It was then that I read the verse from Psalm 20. I pleaded with God that He would have her say "Yes!" for she was the desire of my heart. Looking back, I realized that God not only gave me the desire of my heart, but He was the One who put that desire in my heart in the first place.

I've heard this described like a dad who buys his son a blue bicycle for Christmas then hides it in the garage. The dad then spends the next few months showing his son blue bicycles in the stores. By the time the son asks for a blue bicycle for Christmas, the dad is happy to oblige!

I want to encourage you to ask God to fill your heart with His desires so that they may become your desires as well. The Bible says, "Delight yourself in the Lord, and He will give you the desires of your heart" (Psalm 37:4).

Let Me Pray for You

Lord, I pray for those who have been calling out to You for the desires of their hearts. I pray You would put Your desires in their hearts so that their thoughts and prayers will line up with Yours. God, I ask, too, that You would strengthen those who have been waiting for a long time for You to answer their prayers. Let them know that Your promises are true and that You will indeed give them the desires of their hearts. In Jesus' name, Amen.

Take Time in His Word

"May He give you the desire of your heart and make all your plans succeed" (Psalm 20:4).

- *Read Psalm 37:1-9. What does God want us to do while we wait for the desires of our heart?*
- *Read Luke 22:42-43. Who came to strengthen Jesus when He submitted His will to God's?*
- *Read Isaiah 40:29-31. What will God do for those who hope in Him?*

Take Time in Prayer

Listen to the song "My Lana" (on your favorite music streaming service or on ericelder.com). Ask Him to fill your heart with His desires.

After You Pray

If God doesn't give you what you ask for, I believe He has something better in mind. Back in college, Lana sensed that one day we would get married. When we broke up, she was surprised, but felt that if I wasn't the one, God must have someone better in mind for her. During our time apart, I committed my life to Christ. When we got back together, guess what? She got someone better than the Eric she knew! If God would give up His Son for you, you can be sure He wouldn't withhold anything from you unless He had something better in mind. Continue to trust Him. This is one Father who really does know best.

Lord, I pray You would fill my heart with Your desires.

DAY 12: BLESSED ARE YOU JANUARY 12

I have sometimes wondered if God has a unique purpose for my life, a special role for me to play in His world. Last Christmas I saw the answer in the pages of the Bible as I read about Mary when she was chosen to give birth to Jesus.

In God's great plan for the world, He needed a woman to carry His son in her womb. He chose Mary. Her cousin Elizabeth heard the news and exclaimed, "Blessed are you among women, and blessed is the child you will bear" (Luke 1:42)! She was blessed! She had a unique role to fill in God's plan, that of giving birth to the long-awaited Savior.

I began to think about people in the Bible who were called by God for other purposes. Even though God is all-powerful, He has chosen to work through us as His fellow-workers (1 Corinthians 3:6-9).

God needed Moses to lead the slaves out of Egypt (Exodus 3:10). He needed Paul to share Christ with the Gentiles (Acts 13:46). He needed Esther to marry a king to save the

Jews (Esther 4:14). He needed Elijah to speak prophetic words to influence the course of history. Yet listen to what the Bible says about Elijah: "Elijah was a man just like us" (James 5:17).

All the people in the Bible were men and women just like us. And God has created each of us for a unique purpose as well. We really are special! Hallelujah! We're not cookie-cutter men and women made out of gingerbread. Our fingerprints are unique, our voices are unique, our eyes are unique. And God's plans for us are unique.

Paul reminds us that we all have a role to play, just like a body needs various parts to function well. Some of us are eyes, some are ears, and some are hands or feet. "Now you are the body of Christ, and each one of you is a part of it" (1 Corinthians 12:27).

I believe God would say to each one of us, "Blessed are you!" "'For I know the plans I have for you,' declares the LORD, 'plans to prosper you and not to harm you, plans to give you hope and a future'" (Jeremiah 29:11). Let God's unique plans for you sink deep into your soul.

Let Me Pray for You

Lord, I pray for those who wonder if they have a special role to play in Your plan. I pray You would let them know that You do, and that You would show them what that role is. I pray You would also fully equip them to carry out the plans You have for them. In Jesus' name, Amen.

Take Time in His Word

"In a loud voice she exclaimed: 'Blessed are you among women, and blessed is the child you will bear'" (Luke 1:42)!

- *Read 1 Corinthians 12:12-31. Do the parts of the body have unique roles to play?*
- *Read Romans 12:6-8. What are we to do with the gifts God has given us?*
- *Read Esther 4:13-14. Could God have put you into your present position for a unique purpose?*

Take Time in Prayer

Listen to the song "Blessed Are You" (on your favorite music streaming service or on ericelder.com). Ask God to show you how special you are to Him, and to show you your unique role in His plan.

After You Pray

I also believe that God will give us a sense of fulfillment in our unique calling in a way that we won't envy the calling of others. Mary was obviously overjoyed to carry the Son of God in her womb, but I don't think most women would want to trade places with her. There were special demands on her life because of her calling: everything from riding a donkey in her ninth month of pregnancy to watching her son's execution on a cross. God not only called her for that role, but He equipped her uniquely for that role—just like God is calling you and equipping you for yours.

Lord, I believe that You have a unique purpose for my life!

DAY 13: I'VE SEEN THE SUN — JANUARY 13

Not long ago, our family went through a time of transition. While we knew we were following Christ, we were definitely walking by faith and not by sight. All we could see was Christ leading us forward.

Then one morning, I saw the proverbial light at the end of the tunnel. It was actually the sun shining through the window as I read my Bible. As the sun lit up the room, I felt God was telling me that a new day was coming; a day when we would clearly see just where He had brought us.

I began to write a song, "I've Seen the Sun! I've Seen the Sun!" And as I sang, I realized why I was so excited. It wasn't just the fact that the light had broken through. It was the fact that I could now begin to see with my eyes what I had believed in my heart. My sight had finally caught up to my faith.

As I praised God with this song, I raised my voice higher and higher and out came a new refrain: "I'VE SEEN THE SON! I KNOW HIS NAME! HE DIED FOR ME! AND THEN HE ROSE AGAIN! I'VE SEEN THE SON!"

There will be a day when we will see Jesus face to face! (1 Corinthians 13:12, 1 John 3:2). On that day we'll be able to see with our eyes what we have believed in our hearts for so long. We'll be able to say, "He *is* real. He *is* alive. He *really does* care about us. He *really did* come back for us so we could be with Him forever."

John says that we can *know* that we have eternal life if we believe in Christ: "I write these things to you who believe in the name of the Son of God so that you may know that you have eternal life" (1 John 5:13). Faith is no obscure adventure. It is being sure of what we hope for and certain of what we do not see (Hebrews 11:1).

One day our faith and our sight will be the very same thing. What an awesome day that will be! Until then, hold onto your faith—it's worth far more than gold (1 Peter 1:7).

Let Me Pray for You

Lord, I pray for those who need to renew their faith in You today. I pray You would implant a seed of faith deep in their heart so they will never waver again. I pray they would know that You are real, You are alive, and that You really will come back again for them so they can be with You forever! In Jesus' name, Amen.

Take Time in His Word

"I write these things to you who believe in the name of the Son of God so that you may know that you have eternal life" (1 John 5:13).

- Read 2 Corinthians 4:18. On what should we fix our eyes?
- Read 1 Peter 1:7-9. What is the goal of our faith?
- Read 1 John 3:2. Although we don't know everything about the future, what do we know?

Take Time in Prayer

Listen to the song "I've Seen The Sun" (on your favorite music streaming service or on ericelder.com). Ask God to renew your faith. Let Him know you believe that one day you'll see the Son, too!

After You Pray

Just as the sun in the sky is constant and unchanging from day to day, so is the Son of God. He's always there, whether you see Him or not, whether it's cold or hot. It doesn't matter how many clouds may darken the sky. That doesn't change the fact that the sun is still there. If the sun weren't there, you can be sure we'd be flung out of orbit and die instantly. In the same way, Jesus is always there, always strong, always steady, always holding us tight—whether we see Him or not. "Jesus Christ is the same yesterday today and forever" (Hebrews 13:8).

Lord, I look forward to the day when I will see You face to face!

DAY 14: JUST THE BEGINNING   JANUARY 14

I hope you've enjoyed these two weeks with God. I'm sure He's enjoyed these two weeks with you.

Although today is the last day of this devotional, it's just the beginning of your time with God. In fact, this whole life is just the beginning of your time with God. The last line of *Amazing Grace* says it well: "When we've been there ten thousand years, bright shining as the sun, we've no less days to sing God's praise than when we'd first begun" (John Newton, 1725-1807).

These past two weeks were to whet your appetite for more of what God has in store for you. He has so much He wants to do in and through your life that you won't want to miss a day with Him from now on. As Jesus said, "I am the vine and you are the branches… apart from me you can do nothing" (John 15:5).

Stay close to the vine every day. Draw your life from His life, your strength from His strength. Ask Him to fill you with His Holy Spirit from head to toe until you overflow. Don't let a day go by without coming to Him—for His wisdom, for His comfort, for His strength and for His love.

The best way I've found to stay close to God is to stay in the Bible. Go ahead and read the whole thing from cover to cover—then read it again and again and again. There's not a better Book in the world you could spend your time reading. And God promises that when we seek Him, we will find Him, even though He is not far from each one of us (Acts 17:27, Proverbs 8:17).

Let me close our time in prayer.

Lord, I pray that You would bless those who have spent these two weeks with You. I pray that You would draw them to want to spend time with You each day from now on. I pray that You would continue to speak to them and show them the plans You have for their lives. And finally, Lord, I pray that You would fill them with Your peace, Your love, and Your unending joy. In Jesus' name, Amen.

There's More!

If you like this music and devotional, I'd also like to invite you to join me at *The Ranch* at www.theranch.org. It's a spiritual retreat center on the Internet where you can unwind and spend some more time with God. Join me anytime you need a boost in your faith, and invite your friends, too!

Exodus: Lessons in Freedom

50 inspiring devotionals based on one of the most dramatic yet practical books of the Bible

PREFACE

Exodus is one of the most dramatic books in the Bible. Feature films have told various stories from the book of Exodus, ranging from Cecil B. Demille's epic, *The Ten Commandments*, to DreamWorks' animated, *The Prince of Egypt,* to Stephen Spielberg's classic, *Raiders of the Lost Ark.*

But what I like most about the book of Exodus is not how dramatic it is, but how practical it is.

I began this study at a time when I wanted to expand my own ministry. I wanted to learn how God used Moses to set hundreds of thousands of people free. I thought I might learn a few lessons for how God might use me to set others free, too.

I was right. But instead of finding one or two lessons, I found 50!

I began applying these lessons to my own life and ministry and began to see results immediately. These are the lessons that I'll be sharing with you throughout this book—lessons from stories that are over 3,000 years old, and lessons from my own life today; lessons that include some of my favorite Bible stories, and lessons that include some of my favorite personal stories of my own walk with God.

God wants to set you free. He wants to keep you free. And He wants to use you to set others free. May God bless you—and many others—as you read and apply these lessons to your life.

LESSON 1: THE FEAR OF MAN LEADS TO BONDAGE   JANUARY 15

Scripture Reading: Exodus 1:1-14

Could it be that your greatest weakness is actually your greatest strength?

A man came up to me after I spoke at a men's breakfast and said, "Hi Eric, do you remember me?" I strained to put a name with his face, but couldn't do it. When he told me his name, an image from high school immediately flashed across my mind.

We were both freshmen playing flag football in gym class when he got in the way of a senior. This senior knocked my friend to the ground and started pummeling him in the face with his fist. I watched my friend's head bounce up and down on the ground with each pounding.

Why would someone pummel my friend like that? My friend was a big kid, but a nice kid. Even though he hadn't done anything wrong, his sheer size made him appear to be a threat. The pummeling had its effect: my friend never got in this senior's way again, and I made sure I didn't either!

Unfortunately, my friend walked away feeling weak and beaten down when in reality, it was his sheer strength that drew the fire in the first place. When people are fearful of us, or we're fearful of them, it often leads to bondage. Something similar happened to the Israelites. Back in the days of Moses, when the nation of Israel started to grow while they were living in Egypt, the king of Egypt saw their strength and got scared:

"Look," he said to his people, "the Israelites have become much too numerous for us. Come, we must deal shrewdly with them or they will become even more numerous and, if war breaks out, will join our enemies, fight against us and leave the country" (Exodus 1:9-10).

The Israelites were immediately enslaved. For the next 400 years, they were treated as the lowest of the low in Egypt. I'm sure they felt worthless, worn-out and weak. But in reality, it was their great strength that caused the fearful king to put them into bondage. Although they may have felt like the weakest nation on earth, do you remember what God said about them? He called them His "chosen" people, His "treasured possession," and promised that they would become "a great nation." (Deuteronomy 7:6 and Genesis 12:2). This was their destiny. This was their calling. A destiny and calling that the king foresaw and tried to stop.

I got spiritually pummeled a few years ago after speaking as a guest at a local church. I thought the regular pastor would be thrilled when he came back to hear that half a dozen people had put their faith in Christ that day for the very first time. Instead, I got an extremely harsh letter from him a few weeks later saying that one of those people had started going to another church (she wanted to go to a Bible study and her church didn't have one). He blamed me for her leaving and made it clear that he wanted nothing to do with me or my ministry ever again.

For the next few days, I felt like I'd gotten the wind knocked out of me. I felt like I never wanted to speak at another church again. This man was not only an influential pastor in the community, but he was also the president of the minister's association in town. But then God reminded me of my calling, my purpose in life, and what *He* said about me. I was able to shake off the fear of man and stand tall again in the calling of God. That pastor eventually invited me to speak again at his church, and I eventually became president of the minister's association!

But the fear of man almost derailed me from God's plan for my life. I began to look at other areas of my life where I felt weak to see if those areas might really be strengths instead.

Do you feel weak, pummeled or beaten down in certain areas of your life? Could it be that some of those areas might actually be some of your greatest strengths?

Don't let the fear of man keep you down. Ask God what *He* says about you, your gifts and your calling. Listen to what He says, and He will set you free.

LESSON 2: THE FEAR OF GOD LEADS TO FREEDOM JANUARY 16

Scripture Reading: Exodus 1:15-22

I love playing the piano, but I used to be so afraid of playing in front of others that I never wanted to play in public. At home, I could play for hours, loving every minute of it. But in front of others, my brain would check out, and my hands would shake.

Then one day I was reading Jesus' parable about the talents and the three guys who were given different amounts of talents. Two of them made a return on their gifts, but one buried his talent in the ground because he was afraid.

I was convicted. I was letting the "fear of man" keep my talent hidden, when God had given it to me, not just for me but, like all gifts He gives, so that we can bless others.

I had a choice to make: I was going to be guided either by what men might think of me, or by what God might think of me.

The Hebrew midwives in Egypt had a choice to make, too. When the king of Egypt was afraid the Israelites were growing too numerous and might one day leave them, he put them in bondage and ordered the midwives to kill any baby boys as soon as they were born. What could the midwives do? Their hands were tied—or were they? The Bible says:

"The midwives, however, feared God and did not do what the king of Egypt had told them to do; they let the boys live." (Exodus 1:17)

And the results?

"So God was kind to the midwives and the people increased and became even more numerous. And because the midwives feared God, he gave them families of their own" (Exodus 1:20-21).

Although the "fear of man" threatened to keep the midwives in bondage, the "fear of God" set them free. God honored the midwives' healthy fear of Him by blessing them with families of their own and freeing who-knows-how-many children from the grip of death as well.

Instead of succumbing to their honest and understandable fears, God showed them a way around their fears to accomplish what He called them to do: deliver His children.

I found a way around my fear of playing the piano in front of people, too.

One day a friend came to my house and heard a few of the songs I had written. He seemed to be truly touched by the music and thought it would touch others, too. He was a professional musician and asked if he could bring some recording equipment over and record the songs. That was fine with me. I wasn't afraid of making a mistake in front of a machine—just people!

When we finished recording a dozen songs, he gave me a copy of the music. I was amazed by what I heard! I had never heard my songs played before as a "listener." I was always the "player," and my concentration was intensely focused on getting the notes right. For the first time, I was able to truly relax and just listen to the music. And it touched my own heart, too.

I uploaded the songs on the Internet and people began to listen. And they were touched, too, setting them free from worries, tensions, fears and doubts that were keeping them in bondage.

Instead of succumbing to my honest and understandable fears, God showed me a way around my fears to accomplish what He called me to do: deliver His children. And the confidence that has given me has enabled me to play in front of people now, too, not caring so much about the notes I might get wrong, but caring more about the notes God's given me to play.

Is the "fear of man" holding you back from doing some of the very things that God has called you to do, gifted you to do, and equipped you to do? You might want to take a cue from the Hebrew midwives who feared God more than man, and in the process set themselves—and who knows how many others—free.

LESSON 3: A BURNING HEART PRECEDES A BURNING BUSH   JANUARY 17

Scripture Reading: Exodus 2

Do you ever wish God would just show up in a burning bush and tell you clearly what He wanted you to do?

Then I have some good news for you: I believe God wants to do that for you, too! Why? Because while we're looking for a burning bush, God is looking for a burning heart—one that burns with the same desires for which His burns.

When I take a close look at the years leading up to Moses' burning bush experience, I can't help but think that God didn't choose Moses at random. In chapter 2 of Exodus, we read that Moses' heart was bent on rescuing people years before God called him to rescue an entire nation. Three times in the passage preceding the burning bush, we see a burning heart:

1) *He tries to rescue a fellow Hebrew who was being beaten by an Egyptian;*
2) *He tries to rescue two fighting Hebrews from each other;*
3) *He tries to rescue Jethro's daughters from the attacking shepherds.*

Here's a man whose heart was set on rescuing people. So when God was looking for a man to rescue the entire nation of Israel from slavery, to whom did He look? To Moses, a man whose heart was already burning to do the very things that God wanted done.

The lesson for me in this passage is that a burning heart precedes a burning bush. Sometimes we're looking for a burning bush when God is looking for a burning heart. He's looking to see if we're eager to do the things that He wants done. And when He sees a burning heart, He often puts His finger on that person and says, "I choose you for this task because you have shown yourself eager to do the very things I want done."

I remember hearing a pastor from Germany speak to a group of us in the United States, asking if any of us wanted to join him in doing missionary work in Germany. Several hands went up. Then he asked, "Okay, what things have you been doing here in the U.S. with Germanic people?" None of those in the audience had an answer for him. He continued, "When I see that you're working with Germanic people here and that you truly have a heart for them, then let's talk about coming over to Germany and helping me with my work. I want to know that your heart is really in it."

I had some friends who had a heart for Chinese people. They wanted to go to China someday to live and laugh and learn and share with the Chinese. So they started by inviting Chinese people into their home while they lived in the United States. They did this for several years. When God was looking for someone to go to China, whom do you think God called? They eventually moved to China to live among their people God had put on their heart and were able to change even more lives for Him.

When you look at the lives of people like Moses, the Apostle Paul and Joseph, you'll see that while each of them had rather dramatic "burning bush" experiences, their ultimate calling was not radically different from what they had been doing all along: serving God with their whole hearts and doing His will all along the way.

There's good news in all of this for you, too: know that while you're looking for a burning bush, God is looking for a burning heart. In fact, He's actively looking throughout the earth for people whose hearts are fully committed to Him. 2 Chronicles 16:9a says:

> "For the eyes of the LORD range throughout the earth to strengthen those whose hearts are fully committed to him."

God is continually looking at our hearts. Are they fully committed to Him? Are they burning to do the things that He wants done?

If so, know that God wants to strengthen you in the work you're doing. If not, pray that God will set your heart on fire today for the things that fire Him up. Either way, be encouraged! Once your heart is burning for God, He'll see it, and He may even speak to you in your own "burning bush."

LESSON 4: GOD RESCUES PEOPLE THROUGH PEOPLE   JANUARY 18

Scripture Reading: Exodus 3:1-10

Ever wonder why, when God wants something done, He calls on one of us to do it instead of just doing it Himself?

I knew a man who was burdened by the problem of pornography in our country and cried out to God: "Don't You see what's happening? How long are You going to let this go on? When are You going to do something about it?"

Then he heard God speaking those same words right back to him: "Don't you see what's happening? How long are you going to let this go on? When are you going to do something about it?"

The man was so convicted that he started an organization to combat the problem, served on a presidential task force to deal with it, and worked for years to try to set people free from this particular bondage.

As I read about Moses and the burning bush in Exodus, chapter 3, I put myself in Moses' shoes for a minute (except that he had taken his off, of course, as God had told him that he was standing on "holy ground"). If I were Moses, I think I would have been fine with everything God was saying up until the last line. Sentence after sentence, God talked about everything He wanted to do for the Israelites, then the conversation took a sharp turn:

> "I am the God of your fathers…"
> "I have seen the misery of my people…"
> "I have heard them crying out…"
> "I am concerned about their suffering…"
> "I have come down to rescue them…"
> "So now go. I am sending you… to bring my people… out of Egypt"

What?!?! I was with You God up until that last line! If *You're* God, if *You* see their misery, if *You've* heard them crying out, if *You're* concerned about their suffering, if *You've* come down to rescue them, then why don't *You* do it! *You* could do this way better than I could!

No doubt, God was certainly involved. There's no way Moses could have caused the plagues, split the Red Sea, or made the Egyptians gladly give the Israelites all their gold and jewels on their way out of town. But for some reason, God called on Moses to be involved. He told Moses what He was planning to do, then invited Moses to "jump into the story." It's scary, but exciting, that God would let us take part in what He's trying to do on the earth.

The lesson I get out of this is that God likes to rescue people through people. He wants us to be His hands, His feet, His eyes, His ears, His mouth.

A few friends asked me to come pray for a man who was dying of cancer. He was way too young to be on his death bed, and he let me know it. He had a lot of questions for God, saying, "God, what are You doing?" "Why are You doing this to me?" and "Where are You, God?"

I understood what He was saying, but I said, "If you want to know where God is, look around this room! You've got five people standing here by your bedside, praying for you, holding your hand, and talking to you. He's all around your bed! God lives in us and works through each one of us by His Holy Spirit."

Maybe you're reading these words today and thinking, "That's nice for that guy in his bed, but there's no one talking to me. Where is God for me?" Well, I'm talking to you right now! As you read these words, I hope you'll be able to hear the voice of God in them for you, too, because He wants to tell you something, too: "I love you, I care about you, and you know what? I want to use you, too!"

Why does God use people to rescue people? The Apostle Paul says it this way:

> "We are therefore Christ's ambassadors, as though God were making his appeal through us. We implore you on Christ's behalf: Be reconciled to God." (2 Corinthians 5:20).

Let God use you to do His will today.

LESSON 5: LET GOD'S WILL OVERCOME YOUR WON'T JANUARY 19

Scripture Reading: Exodus 3:11-4:31

Have you ever faced a choice between God's "will" and your "won't"? A few years ago I felt God wanted me to go to Israel. I had just quit my job and had about $1,500 in the bank. It wasn't exactly the best time to take a trip! But I couldn't get it off my mind, so I called to find out how much a ticket would be. The answer: $1,498!

Two thoughts went through my head simultaneously, one was mine and one was God's. I said, "God, I don't have enough!" while God said, "Eric, you have just enough!" I knew I had a decision to make. Was I going to follow God's "will," or follow my "won't"?

When God calls us to do something that we're afraid to do, how can we overcome our doubts and fears so they don't get in the way of God's will? God gives us a clue in the story of Moses at the burning bush in Exodus, chapters 3 and 4.

When God spoke to Moses from within the burning bush, it was an experience most of us would envy, hearing God speak exactly what to do, personally and clearly. God said: "So now go, I am sending you to Pharaoh to bring my people the Israelites out of Egypt."

But Moses protested. He had already tried to rescue just a few Israelites and that didn't seem to go too well. So Moses said to God, "Who am I, that I should go to Pharaoh and bring the Israelites out of Egypt?"

He had a good question, one we often ask ourselves when God calls us to do something: "Who am I?"

But God had a good answer, the same answer He often gives to us, an answer that contains some of the most comforting words in the whole Bible: "I will be with you." It's worth repeating over and over. "I will be with you." "I will be with you." "I will be with you."

Knowing that God will be with you can help you submit your won't to God's will. Maybe you've heard these classic lines by an unknown author, but they're worth repeating over and over, too:

A basketball in my hands is worth about $19.
A basketball in Michael Jordan's hands is worth about $33 million.
It depends on whose hands it's in.
A sling shot in my hands is a kid's toy.
A sling shot in David's hand is a mighty weapon.
It depends on whose hands it's in.
Two fish and 5 loaves of bread in my hands is a couple of fish sandwiches.
Two fish and 5 loaves of bread in Jesus' hands will feed thousands.
It depends on whose hands it's in.
Nails in my hands might produce a birdhouse.
Nails in Jesus Christ's hands will produce salvation for the entire world.
It depends on whose hands it's in.

As you see now, it depends on whose hands it's in. So put your concerns, your worries, your fears, your hopes, your dreams, your families, and your relationships in God's hands, because, "It depends on whose hands it's in."

When Moses was convinced that God would be with him, he finally submitted his won't to God's will. God went with Moses to Egypt and together they set the Israelites free. When I was convinced that God would be with me, I finally submitted my won't to God's will, too. God went with me to Israel and we were both tremendously blessed.

God called my wife, our two oldest kids and me to go on a missions trip to Africa. I looked at the cost and said, "God, I can't do it!" To which God seemed to reply, "It's not a matter of whether you can or can't do it, but whether you will or won't do it. Remember, I will be with you and you can do all things through Christ who gives you strength." So we put a deposit down on the trip and prayed for God's will to be done. It was!

Don't let your won't stand in the way of God's will. Remember, God says, "I will be with you."

LESSON 6: THE BATTLE OF FAITH AND FLESH

JANUARY 20

Scripture Reading: Exodus 5

What happens when you step out in faith, thinking you're doing what God wants you to do, but then everything goes wrong?

Don't give up on God too soon! You might find that you're still in the center of God's will—even when everything around you looks worse than ever before.

This happens all the time in the "natural" world. Last summer we hired some guys to fix the broken brick steps that lead up to our house. Within a few days we had a bigger mess than before! The yard was piled with broken bricks and concrete, mounds of sand, bags of cement and stacks of new bricks, not to mention the torn up grass from the backhoe and cement truck. It was a total mess, worse than the one we were trying to fix!

The same thing happened to Moses in Exodus 5, with much more devastating results. He did exactly what God told him to do, asking Pharaoh to let the Israelites go out into the desert for a worship service. The Israelites were thrilled! God had sent a deliverer. But instead of things getting better, things got worse—much worse!

Pharaoh said, "No way!" and ordered the Israelite slaves to continue making the same number of bricks as before, but he'd no longer give them any straw to make the bricks—they would have to find it themselves. The slaves took a beating and they took it out on Moses: "May the Lord look upon you and judge you! You have made us a stench to Pharaoh and his officials and have put a sword in their hand to kill us."

Now Moses faced a battle on two fronts: a battle of faith and a battle of flesh. Although he probably wanted to fight the battle of the flesh first, saving his people from the physical attack coming against them, he knew which battle he had to fight first. He had to fight for his faith—to keep on believing what God had told him. Had he heard from God or not? Had he done something wrong or not? He knew he had to win the battle for his faith first if he was ever going to win the battle of the flesh.

So he did the best thing any of us can do: he returned to the Lord.

He cried out, "O Lord, why have you brought trouble upon this people? Is this why you sent me? Ever since I went to Pharaoh to speak in your name, he has brought trouble upon this people, and you have not rescued your people at all." God answered him, telling him he was right on track and to keep moving forward in faith.

While we were in the middle of our own brick project, I faced another situation that was so frustrating that I wrote in my journal, "I'm pulling my hair out! I want to scream!" I was trying to redesign *The Ranch* website so I could expand it to minister to more people over the Internet. That meant I had to install some new software that I felt God wanted me to use, but I had no idea how to use it. Everything I tried made a bigger mess than before. Instead of making things better, I was making them worse—much worse!

I went outside and looked at the mess in our front yard. I knew that remodeling projects were always like this. When in the middle of it, the mess gets worse before it gets better. I thanked God for the reminder and went back to work.

The website ended up more beautiful and more functional than I could have imagined. Our front steps turned out better than before and the grass began to grow again. These were small victories compared to what Moses finally gained: he was able to set an entire nation free as God had promised.

Just because your steps of faith lead you into worse trouble than before, don't automatically assume that you're out of God's will, or that you've done something wrong. Return to the Lord. Fight the battle of faith first, and the victory in the flesh will follow.

LESSON 7: GOD HELPS US WITH BOTH BATTLES — JANUARY 21

Scripture Reading: Exodus 6

How well do you do on the "Wednesdays" of your life? The way you handle those "hump days" could very well determine what happens with the rest of your week—and the rest of your life!

Maybe it's a marriage that you were really thrilled about jumping into at first, but then starts getting hard. Or maybe it's a baby you've looked forward to having and then it finally comes—along with the dirty diapers, the crying and the sleepless nights. Or maybe it's a Bible study you couldn't wait to start, but then begins to lag and just isn't "speaking to you" anymore. Whatever it is, a "Wednesday" is anything that makes you feel like you just want to throw in the towel and give in.

Moses was definitely having a "Wednesday" in Exodus chapter 6, and the lesson God gave him for how to get through it is a good one for us, too.

Moses had done exactly what God told him to do, asking Pharaoh to "Let my people go." But Pharaoh said, "No," and increased the people's work.

Now Moses was fighting a battle in his flesh *and* a battle in his faith. We find out, in Exodus chapter 6, when Moses returns to the Lord, that God is still with him, ready and willing to help Moses fight both battles. Regarding the battle of the flesh, God says He will help Moses by using His "mighty hand":

> *"Then the LORD said to Moses, 'Now you will see what I will do to Pharaoh: Because of my mighty hand he will let them go; because of my mighty hand he will drive them out of his country'" (Exodus 6:1)*

Regarding the battle of the faith, God tells Moses three things:

1) God reminds Moses that this was His idea, His plan, His covenant (verses 2-5);
2) God reminds Moses that He will be with Moses, that Moses isn't fighting alone (verse 6);
3) God reminds Moses what the outcome will be, what the future holds (verses 7-8).

When you're in the middle of your own battles, be sure to return to the Lord. Let Him speak to you, remind you, reassure you that you're on the right path. If you're not, He'll let you know. But if you are, let Him reassure you that that this is His idea, that He is with you and that He has a plan for your future. These reminders can give you the faith you need to make another push in your flesh, to go another round, to keep moving forward till "Friday" comes.

I had a dream one night where God spoke clearly to me about preaching on the Internet. Even though I thought it would be financially impossible, I saw in the dream an envelope wrapped in a "net"—something that looked like one of those red woven sacks in which they sell grapefruit. There were a few dollars in the envelope and a note saying that the bill had already been paid. I wasn't to worry about the money, but to just keep preaching on the "net."

What did I do when I woke up? I worried about the money! Over time, whenever I "returned to the Lord," He reminded me that this was His idea, that He was with me, and that He had a plan for my future.

Because I returned to Him so many times to get this reminder, I finally took a red mesh grapefruit bag and put it in my bill drawer. Every time I'd worry about the money, I'd open that drawer, see the "net" and immediately sense the peace of God. There was nothing magical about the bag—it was simply a visual reminder of the promises God had made to me—but it helped me get through more than a few of my own "Wednesdays."

Don't let "Wednesdays" get you down. Don't let the rest of your week drop; don't let the rest of your marriage or job or children drop; don't let the rest of your life drop. Return to the Lord. He'll help you fight both battles. Remember: Friday's coming!

LESSON 8: GOD SETS PEOPLE FREE SO ALL WILL KNOW — JANUARY 22

Scripture Reading: Exodus 7-10

People sometimes wonder why God "hardens" Pharaoh's heart in the process of setting the Israelites free from Egypt. Why does God have to do it this way? Doesn't this override Pharaoh's free will, if God is the one who makes Pharaoh's heart hard?

Not at all! A friend of mine compares this to the different effects the sun has on two different objects: butter and clay. What happens when the sun shines on a lump of butter for a few hours? It gets soft. But what happens when the sun shines on a lump of clay for a few hours? It gets hard! The same sun that softens the butter, hardens the clay. The difference is not in the sun, but in the reaction of the objects to the sun.

When God pours out the plagues in Exodus chapters 7, 8, 9 and 10, Moses and Pharaoh have two different reactions. Moses' heart gets softer to God's purposes and Pharaoh's just gets harder and harder.

But there's still a deeper question in this story: Why does God have to bother with Moses, Pharaoh and the plagues at all? If God wants to set the people free, why doesn't He just cut off their chains, open the gates of Egypt and walk the people out? Why, for that matter, does God free anyone the way He does?

Why wait until Daniel's already in the lion's den before saving him? Why wait for little David to come onto the scene before defeating Goliath? Why wait till Jonah's near the bottom of the ocean before sending a whale out to save him?

God tells us the answer in every one of these stories.

He sets people free in a way that the world will know that He is the Lord, so that others will put their faith in Him and be set free, too.

We can read this over and over again in the story of the plagues:

> "...and the Egyptians will know that I am the LORD..." (Exodus 7:5)
> "...by this you will know that I am the LORD..." (Exodus 7:17)
> "...so that you may know there is no one like the LORD..." (Exodus 8:10)
> "...so that you will know that I, the LORD, am in this land." (Exodus 8:22)
> "...that my name might be proclaimed in all the earth." (Exodus 9:16)

We can read this over and over again throughout the Bible.

When God sets Daniel free from the lion's den, He does it in a way that so impresses the king of that land that the king "wrote a letter to all the peoples, nations and men of every language throughout the land…that in every part of my kingdom people must fear and reverence the God of Daniel" (from Daniel 6:25-27).

When God gave David the victory over Goliath, He did it in a way that "the whole world will know that there is a God in Israel" (from 1 Samuel 17:45-46).

When God rescued Jonah from the depths of the ocean, He was able to get His message out to the people of Nineveh so that even the king of that city issued a proclamation to all the people in his land: "Let everyone call urgently on God. Let them give up their evil ways and their violence. Who knows? God may yet relent and with compassion turn from his fierce anger so that we will not perish" (from Jonah 3:7-9).

If you wonder why God does things the way He does, pray that God would soften your heart to the things He's trying to do. Pray that God would soften the hearts of your family and friends to the things He may be trying to do through you. Then trust Him that He really does want to set you and your family and friends free.

God may be waiting for just the right time, just the right place, and just the right circumstances so that others will know that He is the Lord, put their faith and trust in Him, and be set free, too.

LESSON 9: ULTIMATE VICTORY COMES FROM ULTIMATE SACRIFICE   JANUARY 23

Scripture Reading: Exodus 11

How free do you want to be? If you want to get a little bit free, you only have to make a little bit of sacrifice. But if you want to get totally free, you have to make a total sacrifice.

I've ridden on a few swings with my kids before and there's a bit of a thrill that comes with it. But one day I went on a 100 foot bungee swing with them and it was a totally different experience!

After my six year old son and I were pulled half-way up to the top, he asked "Are we there yet?" When we were pulled still higher and higher, he hung onto my arm tighter and tighter. When we got to the top, I counted to three before pulling the cord that would plunge us down the 100 foot drop:

One! Two! Three! Whewwwww! The sense of freedom that came in those next few seconds was overwhelming as we swung down and then back up again over the crowd below us.

Moses had the chance to get a little bit of freedom for the Israelite slaves in Egypt. Pharaoh offered Moses the chance to go into the desert for a few days with just the men. Moses said, "No." Then Pharaoh said Moses could go with the women and children, too, but just leave the animals behind. Moses refused. Each time Pharaoh offered a compromise, Moses held out for total freedom, because that's what God had promised him.

In Exodus chapter 11, God tells Moses that total freedom is just around the corner, but it wouldn't come without cost.

> *So Moses said, "This is what the LORD says: 'About midnight I will go throughout Egypt. Every firstborn son in Egypt will die, from the firstborn son of Pharaoh, who sits on the throne, to the firstborn son of the slave girl, who is at her hand mill, and all the*

firstborn of the cattle as well. There will be loud wailing throughout Egypt—worse than there has ever been or ever will be again. But among the Israelites not a dog will bark at any man or animal.' Then you will know that the LORD makes a distinction between Egypt and Israel" (Exodus 11:4-7).

Ultimate victory comes only from ultimate sacrifice.

None of the Israelites' sons would die in this way, but God called upon them to make a sacrifice, too—of a lamb. When they put the blood of the lamb on the doorframes of their homes, the Angel of the Lord would "pass over" them and not kill their sons, because their sacrifice had already been made.

There are times when something has to die so something else can live.

I heard a woman speak one night about dying to ourselves so that God could live through us. She quoted Madame Guyon, a Christian who lived in France in the 1600's, who talked about this total surrender as "plunging your will into the depths of God's will, there to be lost forever."

I was enthralled by this vision. But a friend of mine, who had heard the same talk, was scared to death by it. He wasn't sure if he could trust God or not and wasn't wanting to take the chance to find out.

I wasn't sure I wanted to do the bungee swing, either, until I saw a sign on the ride that said, "100% safety." That's what I needed to know to enjoy the ride of my life. Maybe you're not sure you want to totally surrender everything in your life to Christ. Let me assure you that based on my experience, the experience of others, and most importantly, the words of God Himself in the Bible, that God is trustworthy. He loves you, cares about you, and has already made the ultimate sacrifice for you. Jesus is *"the Lamb of God, who takes away the sin of the world!" (John 1:29b).*

If you want a little bit of freedom, trust Jesus a little bit. But if you want total freedom, put your faith in Christ for everything in your life. Everything! Then you'll find out the truth of Jesus' words: *"if the Son sets you free, you will be free indeed! (John 8:36)*

LESSON 10: GOD FULFILLS HIS PROMISES IN UNFORGETTABLE WAYS   JANUARY 24

Scripture Reading: Exodus 12

Can you imagine an event so memorable that people would still celebrate it 3,500 years later? Not 35, or 350, but 3,500 years later!?! The Passover was just such an event: the night the Israelites were set free from their bondage in Egypt.

We've already looked at one of the reasons God does things the way He does: so that the whole world will know that He is God, so they will put their faith in Him, too. But in this lesson, we see yet another reason: sometimes God fulfills His promises in a way that is so unforgettable that people will remember it for years to come.

When God called me into full-time ministry, He used a verse about the Passover to confirm it. I was asking God to confirm some things He was telling me were going to happen that day.

Two verses of scripture came to my mind: Genesis 2:3 and Exodus 12:2. I didn't know what the verses said, so I looked up Genesis 2:3. It was about the first Sabbath Day. Assuming I must have heard wrong on that one, I turned to Exodus 12:2, which was about the first Passover. I began to write in my journal, "God, I don't get it," but before I finished the sentence, I felt like God said: "Like the Sabbath and the Passover were markers of special days, so today will mark a special day for you, Eric."

"What will it mark?" I asked.

"The beginning of your ministry," He answered.

God did what He promised to do that day, and within 48 hours I had quit my job and launched out into full-time ministry.

As memorable as that event was for me, it was minuscule compared to what God did for the Israelites on that first Passover night:

> "Each man is to take a lamb for his family...year-old males without defect, and...slaughter them at midnight....take some of the blood and put it on the sides and tops of the doorframes of the houses where they eat the lambs...On that same night I will pass through Egypt and strike down every firstborn—both men and animals—and I will bring judgment on all the gods of Egypt. I am the LORD. The blood will be a sign for you on the houses where you are; and when I see the blood, I will pass over you. No destructive plague will touch you when I strike Egypt. This is a day you are to commemorate; for the generations to come you shall celebrate it as a festival to the LORD—a lasting ordinance" (Exodus 12:3, 6, and 12-14).

And a lasting celebration it has become. When Jesus celebrated the Passover on the night before He died, the tradition was already 1,500 years old. You've probably celebrated it, even if you weren't fully aware of it, if you've ever taken communion, or the Lord's Supper. For it was during the Passover meal that Jesus took the bread and the cup and spoke these words:

> "This is my body, which is for you; do this in remembrance of me...this cup is the new covenant in my blood. Do this whenever you drink it in remembrance of me" (1 Corinthians 11:24-25).

Just as the Old Covenant required a lamb to be sacrificed so the Israelites could go free, the New Covenant has the same requirement so that we can go free, except that Jesus is that lamb. The Bible says, *"For Christ, our Passover lamb, has been sacrificed"* (I Corinthians 5:7).

For all that the Israelites had to go through in Egypt—the hard labor, the waiting, the wailing all around them—their day of freedom was so memorable we still celebrate it 3,500 years later.

Are you waiting for God to do something in your life? Are you wondering why it has to take so long—why your labor might be getting harder not easier? It just might be that God is working things out in such a way that when He does fulfill His promises to you, He will do it in a way that is so unforgettable, that you—and everyone around you—will remember it for years.

LESSON 11: MARK THE DATE   JANUARY 25

Scripture Reading: Exodus 13:1-16

If you could live any day of your life over again—because it was so memorable—which day would you re-live? For me, I'd pick November 19th, 1988, the day I asked my wife, Lana, to marry me. It was perfect in every way, even including the brief rain shower that fell on us while we rode paddle boats at the Houston Zoo.

Some dates are so memorable that we think we'll never forget them. But as time passes, and life takes its unexpected turns, we can sometimes forget, or simply devalue, what God has done for us in the past. And when we forget, we tend to quickly lose ground on any freedom we had gained up to that point.

In the last ten lessons of this study, we looked at how the Israelites were finally able to get free from their bondage. In the next ten lessons, we're going to look at how to stay free, which can be just as important as getting free in the first place.

The first lesson for staying free is this: mark the date. Make a point to deliberately remember, from year to year, just what God has done for you. And not only for you to remember, but as an opportunity to remind those around you what God has done for you, too.

Here's what God told the Israelites to do in Exodus chapter 13:

> "Then Moses said to the people, 'Commemorate this day, the day you came out of Egypt, out of the land of slavery, because the LORD brought you out of it with a mighty hand ... You must keep this ordinance at the appointed time year after year ... In days to come, when your son asks you, 'What does this mean?' say to him, 'With a mighty hand the LORD brought us out of Egypt, out of the land of slavery' ... and it will be like a sign on your hand and a symbol on your forehead that the LORD brought us out of Egypt with his mighty hand.'"

God knew what the Israelites would be facing in the future. He knew that they may one day wonder if they had made the wrong decision, if maybe they should turn around and go back to Egypt, back into bondage. But if they could simply remember this night and the miraculous deliverance they experienced that could only be attributed to the hand of God, they would have the faith to keep moving forward—faith to endure any obstacle in the future.

Some people scoff at holidays, thinking they serve no purpose except to give people a day off of work. But to those who use these "holy" days well, they can be powerful reminders of what God has done and provide "staying power" for those who have been set free.

Here in the United States, we celebrate a holiday called Thanksgiving, a day that was established when the first people who came to this land from overseas wanted to remember all that God had done for them. They had lost much in the process of coming to America, including many loved ones who didn't survive the trip and their first few months here. But rather than despair over what they had lost, they gave thanks for what they had found.

The day before I wrote this lesson was November 19th. Throughout the day, I took time to remember what happened on the day I proposed to Lana. I told my kids about it. I told her brother about it. I told her Dad about it. I bought her flowers. I love to re-live that day in my mind for myself, and out loud for others, because I want to continually remember throughout my life what God has done for me.

Are you struggling to stay free? Wondering if it might be better to head back to Egypt? If so, try taking some time this week to remember some of the things God has done for you in the past. Mark those dates on your calendar. Celebrate them every year. Let them be "like a sign on your hand and a symbol on your forehead" of all that the Lord has done for you.

LESSON 12: GOD'S ROUTE TAKES TIME FOR OUR SAKE — JANUARY 26

Scripture Reading: Exodus 13:17-22

Have you ever been able to see exactly where you want to go, but it seems like it takes forever to get there? The more you walk towards it, the farther away it gets? That may not be an optical illusion. That may just be the hand of God at work.

I've been working on a project for several years. Every once in a while, I think I see the finish line just around the next turn. Then I realize that it wasn't the finish line at all, but just another marker along the way. God urges me on and seems to send me on another lap around the track.

Why does God do that? Isn't He the One who called us to run this race in the first place and holds out the prize for us at the end? In Exodus chapter 13, God gives us at least one of the reasons He holds us back from reaching the finish line too soon.

When God promised the Israelites He would bring them into "the Promised Land," He set them free from Egypt and sent them on their way. But instead of sending them on the straightest route, He deliberately sent them on a much longer route around the desert. He tells us why in Exodus 13:17-18a:

> "When Pharaoh let the people go, God did not lead them on the road through the Philistine country, though that was shorter. For God said, 'If they face war, they might change their minds and return to Egypt.' So God led the people around by the desert road toward the Red Sea."

The Israelites were so fresh out of Egypt that God knew that if they went straight to the Promised Land and had to do battle right away, they might have hightailed it right back to Egypt. God knew that Egypt was a much worse place for them to be and it wasn't where He wanted them to be at all. *For their own protection*, God took them on the longer route.

Oftentimes we get frustrated when we have to take the longer route. We cry out, "God, why is it taking so long for me to get there? Why is it taking so long to restore my marriage that I know You want restored? To get the job that I know you want me to have? To bring back the child that I know You want to bring back? To finish the project that I know You called me to do?"

It might be that God is waiting until we're ready to say with our whole heart: "OK, God, I'm ready to take on this battle no matter what. I'm going to fight for my marriage the way You want me to fight for it. I'm going to fight for my job, fight for my purpose, fight for my calling in life. I want to be able to stand firm in these things, God, so teach me everything I need to know before I get there, because if I get there too soon, I might hightail it back to Egypt."

Proverbs 3:5-6 tells us how we can get this kind of attitude: "Trust in the LORD with all your heart and lean not on your own understanding; in all your ways acknowledge him, and he will make your paths straight."

Sometimes the shortest route in the long run is the longest route in the short run.

Don't be frustrated when God says to take another lap around the track. Don't give up on what God's called you to do. Don't give in to the thinking that you'll never make it. Follow the example of the Apostle Paul: *"But one thing I do: Forgetting what is behind and straining toward what is ahead, I press on toward the goal to win the prize for which God has called me heavenward in Christ Jesus"* (Philippians 3:13b-14).

Tell God: "Father, I'm ready when You are. Whether I reach my goal today or sometime down the road, I'm still going to trust You no matter what. You've brought me this far. I know You'll bring me home."

LESSON 13: STAND FIRM   JANUARY 27

Scripture Reading: Exodus 14:1-14

What can you do when your back is up against the wall, when you can't go forward, and when you feel like God doesn't want you to go backward? Sometimes the best thing to do is the hardest thing to do: to "stand firm."

A few years ago, my family was moving from Texas to Illinois. We had a very short timeframe to sell our house and make the move. As I prayed about it, I felt God wanted us to make the move between February 15th and February 28th, a two week window of time—that was less than two months away.

I was fighting for my faith on this one. I felt I was supposed to sell the house without a realtor, which can often take longer than with a realtor, and I didn't have any time to lose. Then I got a letter from a realtor that almost totally undid my faith. It read:

"It's now been a couple of weeks since you began trying to sell your house by yourself, and for your sake I do hope you will be successful—although the odds are not with you. I say this because currently in this area there are some 470 full-time real estate professionals who are working 7 days a week to sell homes like yours. Yet even with so many professionals on the job, it is still taking an average of 30-120 days to get a listed home sold. Now, if it takes 470 full-time professionals over 4 months to get a house sold, how long will it take you—working part-time by yourself?"

I wondered what to do. It was critical that we sell our house quickly. Then I was reminded of the Israelites in Exodus, chapter 14.

They had just been set free from Egypt when God led them right up to the edge of the Red Sea. Pharaoh had changed his mind again, wondering why he had let his slaves go free. He took his chariots and chased after the Israelites, threatening to put them into bondage again. The Israelites saw their captors coming and cried out to Moses:

> *"Was it because there were no graves in Egypt that you brought us to the desert to die? What have you done to us by bringing us out of Egypt? Didn't we say to you in Egypt, 'Leave us alone; let us serve the Egyptians'? It would have been better for us to serve the Egyptians than to die in the desert!"* (Exodus 14:11-12).

Sometimes we wonder the same thing. We finally get free from something that has enslaved us, then it tries to force its way back into our lives to captivate us again. We panic. We wonder why we ever tried to get free in the first place. But Moses told his people something that helped them stay free, and it can help us stay free as well. Moses answered:

> *"Do not be afraid. Stand firm and you will see the deliverance the LORD will bring you today. The Egyptians you see today you will never see again. The LORD will fight for you; you need only to be still"* (Exodus 14:13-14).

Even Moses couldn't have guessed that God was going to part the Red Sea for them to cross, but he knew that God had brought them this far, and He could bring them home.

In my own small way, I felt like Moses with my back up against the Sea. I was about to panic when I got that realtor's letter. But I decided to "stand firm." As if in confirmation of my decision, I read another story in 1 Kings 18 where God answered the prayers of one man, Elijah, over the misguided prayers of 450 others. It was close enough to my situation up against the 470 realtors mentioned in the letter that it gave me goose bumps!

Three weeks later we had a buyer for the house. We finalized the sale on February 26th and pulled out of town on February 28th.

Standing orders are good orders. If God hasn't directed a change in your plans, the best plan is to "stand firm" in the plan He's already given you.

Don't give in to fear. Stand firm in God!

LESSON 14: TAKE ACTION   JANUARY 28

Scripture Reading: Exodus 14:15-31

In our last study, we took a look at "standing firm" when our back is up against the wall. In this study, we'll look at what to do next, because God doesn't want us to stand still forever. There comes a time when God calls us to take action.

To paraphrase a preacher in the early days of America, who had been praying about what God wanted him to do in regards to creating this new country: "There's a time to pray and a time to act. Now's the time to act!"

Prayer is not a one-way conversation, but is an invitation for God to speak. And when God speaks, we need to do what He says, no matter how trivial a thing He might tell us to do.

God spoke to Moses when Moses' back was up against the wall of the Red Sea. The people had been crying out to Moses, complaining that he had brought them out into the desert to die at the hands of the Egyptians. As the Egyptian chariots quickly approached, Moses told the people to "stand firm," and they would see the deliverance of the Lord.

But then God told Moses what to do next:

> *"Then the LORD said to Moses, 'Why are you crying out to me? Tell the Israelites to move on. Raise your staff and stretch out your hand over the sea to divide the water so that the Israelites can go through the sea on dry ground. …' Then Moses stretched out his hand over the sea, and all that night the LORD drove the sea back with a strong east wind and turned it into dry land. The waters were divided, and the Israelites went through the sea on dry ground, with a wall of water on their right and on their left" (Exodus 14:15-16, 21-22).*

Moses may have thought: *What? Just raise my staff and stretch out my hand over the sea? How could that help!?!* But Moses did what God said to do, and the Lord blew back the waters with His very breath, delivering the Israelites to safety and destroying their captors.

I was farming with my Dad one day when the rain began to fall on our two tractors. I was driving ahead of my Dad, preparing the ground so he could plant the grain behind me. It was critical that we got the crops in the ground that day. We didn't have time for a storm.

As the rain started hitting my face, I stood up on the open-air tractor, held my hand up above my head, and prayed that the rain would stop. Guess what happened? I got drenched! Totally soaked from head to toe! I said, "Okay, God, I don't have control over the wind and rain."

But as I thought about it some more, I said, "Even though I don't have control, God, I believe that You do. I think this is just Satan trying to discourage me. God, I'm going to put my hand back up and keep on praying. I'm going to keep driving and praying until the rain stops, because we need to get Dad's crops in today!"

Although the rain kept pelting me in the face, I held my hand up high. I was still getting soaked for a few more minutes, but by the time I got to the other end of the field and turned around to take another pass, the rain had completely stopped. For the rest of the day, we planted that field as the rain came down in sheets all around us. Even the cars that drove on the road bordering our field had their windshield wipers going all day long, but the rain didn't touch the ground we were planting.

God doesn't always answer our prayers so dramatically, and even when He doesn't, we can be assured that He has something better in mind for us, because God is ultimately FOR us.

But when God *does* tell you to take action, take action! No matter how big or how small that action may be, make sure to get it done. Don't let Satan get you down. Lift your hands to God and press on.

LESSON 15: TAKE TIME TO PRAISE GOD   JANUARY 29

Scripture Reading: Exodus 15:1-21

When you've broken free from something in your life, what's a practical thing you can do to stay free?

One thing is to write down specifically what God has done for you—in a poem, in a song, or just in some words that don't even rhyme. When you take the time to write it down, especially in a way that can be recited or sung later, those words can be a reminder of what God has done for you—and what He's going to do in the future.

I don't think of myself as a poet, but sometimes poems just come out! One came out when I was a senior in college when I was dating Lana. I was working at an office that had an Apple computer called the "Lisa." "Lisa" was Apple's forerunner to the Macintosh and was the first of Apple's computers to have a "graphical user interface," years before Microsoft created "windows."

That's when I fell in love, not only with Lana, but also with Apple computers. I discovered that this computer allowed me to express myself in a poem by drawing pictures next to the text:

"I love your name Lana,
You don't look like a (I drew a picture of a banana).
Your (I drew a picture of her hair) is so curly,
You never look (I drew a picture of a squirrel) -ly."

I'll spare you from having to read the rest of the poem! As goofy as it was, Lana has kept it to this day.

The fact that we take the time to write down something about someone special can have a significant impact on them—and on us.

For the Israelites, when they got free from the Egyptians and made it to the other side of the Red Sea, they seemed to almost spontaneously combust into a song about the experience:

> "I will sing to the LORD, for he is highly exalted. The horse and its rider he has hurled into the sea." (Exodus 15:1)

This goes on for 20 more verses. The song is specifically about their experience, recalling how the water piled up like a wall on each side of them, and then how God blew the water back into place again with His breath, plunging their enemies to the depths like a stone. The song then turns into a song of hope for what God promised to do for them in the future.

Their song was such a powerful reminder of God's deliverance that we still sing some of its refrains today, such as, "And I shall prepare him my heart…" from the song *Exodus XV*.

Just as people love it when we take time to write about how much they mean to us, God loves it, too. One of the reasons is because it takes time to write down the words. In that time, when we recall what God has done for us and what He has promised to do for us in the future, we can find hope to go on. We can remember all that He's done and all that He's going to do. We remind ourselves that we don't really want to go back to our own "Egypt" ever again.

As I wrote this lesson, we were about to celebrate Christmas all around the world. We were getting ready to sing songs about things that God has done throughout the ages, some of them thousands of years ago, and some just a few years ago. I wondered aloud if maybe it was time for a new song, too?

Has God done something in your life that you'd like to remember forever—something that you'd like to pass on to future generations? Or is there someone special in your life who could use a special gift this week? Not a gift from a store, but a gift from a storehouse of love. If so, let it flow! Write a poem to the awesome God we serve—or to someone that you love. If you like music, how about writing a tune, or just humming one that can go along with the poem?

Then give it to your Beloved as a special act of love. They'll keep it forever. And it will help keep you free!

LESSON 16: CRY OUT TO THE LORD   JANUARY 30

Scripture Reading: Exodus 15:22-27

What makes Christmas so special for so many people? I think the answer can be summed up in one word: JESUS. That one word contains more power, more hope and more love than all the other words in the world combined.

Even the word "Jesus" has a significant meaning. It comes from the Greek form of the name Joshua, which means "the Lord saves." So to say that "Jesus Saves" is like saying, in bold and underlined, "The Savior Saves!" It is the saving power of Jesus that makes Christmas so special to me and millions of others around the world.

It is that same Truth that God has been trying to get across to people for thousands of years.

Three thousand years ago there were over 600,000 men, women and children who were on the verge of death in the middle of a desert. They had just lived through some of the most fearful and awesome moments ever recorded in history, and yet they found themselves once again at the edge of calamity.

Having found no water in the desert for three days, they finally found water at a place called Marah—only to discover that the water was bitter and was undrinkable. This was the last straw. They grumbled to Moses, and Moses did the best thing any of us can do in such a situation—he cried out to the Lord:

> "Then Moses cried out to the LORD, and the LORD showed him a piece of wood. He threw it into the water, and the water became sweet" (Exodus 15:25).

Once again, "the Lord saves." There's a big difference between grumbling to others and crying out to the Lord. "Grumbling to others" is giving in to defeat and failure. "Crying out to the Lord" is looking up with hope and anticipation. The people grumbled. Moses cried out to the Lord, and the Lord showed him exactly what to do.

A man here in the U.S., by the name of George Washington Carver, saw poverty and desperation all around him in his home state of Georgia. He cried out to the Lord, asking God to show him the secrets of the universe. God told George that this would be too much for him to handle! So George asked God to show him the secrets of the peanut, an unimportant plant at that time that grew in Georgia. In response to that cry, God showed George hundreds of uses for the peanut, including peanut butter, oils, lubricants, paints and more. George put his wisdom to use and turned the peanut into a $13 million industry for the state of Georgia.

Back to Jesus, I heard from a woman who had grown up as a Buddhist, and who one day she found herself in the blackest of holes. Her marriage, her family, and her life were a total mess. She didn't know what to do. So she did the one thing she hadn't tried before. She called out to Jesus, whom she had heard about on television. Standing in the middle of her living room, she looked up to heaven, with tears in her eyes, and called out to Jesus as loud as she could. With that cry, Jesus totally and completely transformed her life here on earth and gave her a future in heaven, too. You can read her whole story on The Ranch website by going to "Stories" and clicking on "Jesus Get Me Out Of Here!"

I don't know where you are today or what you're going through. But the Lord knows—the Lord who saves, the Lord who took a truly desperate situation and completely turned it around by showing Moses the simplest of solutions—to throw a stick into bitter water to make it sweet.

What do you need from the Lord today? Don't grumble to others. Cry out to the Lord! Listen for His answer, no matter how simple. You might find that the solution is right under your nose. You just need the Lord to show it to you! You'll find out again that the Lord is able to save you and those around you, perhaps even hundreds of thousands around you! Remember what "Jesus" means: "The Lord Saves!"

LESSON 17: TRUST GOD TO PROVIDE SHOWING HE'S THE LORD   JANUARY 31

Scripture Reading: Exodus 16

Want to see the hand of God at work in your life this year? Try this: take time to write down each of your prayers in a journal or on a pad of paper. Then leave some space next to each prayer so that you can come back later to record when, and how, that prayer was answered.

Within just a few weeks, you'll begin to see how many prayers God answers on a regular basis. You'll also see how often He answers those prayers in a way that you'll *know* it was the Lord who answered them. By connecting your prayers to God's answers, you'll both see and know that God's hand is at work in your life.

This is how God said He would answer the prayers of the Israelites when they cried out for food in the desert in Exodus chapter 16:

The LORD said to Moses, "I have heard the grumbling of the Israelites. Tell them, 'At twilight you will eat meat, and in the morning you will be filled with bread. Then you will know that I am the LORD your God'" (Exodus 16:11-12).

Starting the very next day, God gave them manna every morning and quail every night, not as the result of some natural desert phenomenon, but clearly as a result of God delivering on His promise exactly as He told them He would.

One day, God answered one of my prayers in a similarly specific way when I was praying about where God wanted me to live and minister.

I was living in Illinois at the time and had a map of the United States laying out on the table. Just out of curiosity, I closed my eyes and let my finger fall on the map. When I saw that it had landed on Dallas, Texas, I closed the map. I really wasn't wanting to go back to Texas again, since I had just moved back to Illinois from Texas just a few years earlier.

But later that night, as I told a friend on the phone what had happened regarding the map, my friend immediately described to me a picture that God had impressed on his mind when I said the word "Dallas." He described a place called "The Ranch," not the famous ranch from the old TV show "Dallas," but a scene he had never seen before. He told me in detail about the location of the trees, the sunset, some obstacles, a dirt path, a fence, and a river by, next to which stood one solitary tree casting its shadow on the water.

My friend drew what he had seen on a piece of paper. He signed it, dated it and faxed me a copy. Vision or no vision, I still wasn't interested in going to Texas! So I promptly forgot about it…until several months later when I got a phone call from a pastor in Dallas, Texas. He wanted to know if I would be interested in moving to Dallas to serve as the Associate Pastor at his church. I had to pull out my friend's sketch and ask God if there was any connection between the call and my earlier prayer. It turns out there was! You can see the whole story on *The Ranch* website by watching the video for this lesson.

Suffice it to say we ended up moving to Dallas! Exactly one year later—to the day—I found myself standing on the bank of the river outside our new back yard, looking at a scene that had been detailed a year earlier in a drawing I now held in my hand and included the trees, the sunset, the obstacles, the dirt path, the fence, and even the solitary tree casting its shadow onto the water! To top it all off, just behind this scene was a brand new sports rehab center that happened to open that very month called, "The Ranch." (This story was the inspiration for how I decided to call my website *The Ranch!*)

If you want to see the hand of God at work in your life, take time to write down your prayers—then leave room for His answers! When you make the connection between your prayers and God's answers, you'll begin to see clearly that the Lord really is "the LORD!"

LESSON 18: TAKE IT TO THE LORD   FEBRUARY 1

Scripture Reading: Exodus 17:1-7

What can we do when people seem to love us one minute and hate us the next—when we haven't even done anything differently? We can learn a lesson from Moses and do what he did: take it to the Lord.

I remember a man who had heard about some of the things I was doing in my walk of faith with God. He was so impressed that he came over to my house one day said to me: "you're the closest thing to a disciple I've ever seen." Within a month, that same man started to deride and question everything I did. I wasn't doing anything differently, but somehow his perception of me had changed during that month.

People can be fickle—and sometimes with good reason. But we still need to know how to respond to them. Moses had to deal with people's fickle reactions all the time. When things were going great in the camp, the people put their faith in Moses, following him wherever he led. But when circumstances changed, their opinions of Moses changed, even to the point where they wanted to stone him to death.

In Exodus 17, when the people found themselves without water again, they turned on Moses again:

> *"The whole Israelite community set out from the Desert of Sin, traveling from place to place as the LORD commanded. They camped at Rephidim, but there was no water for the people to drink. So they quarreled with Moses and said, 'Give us water to drink.'*
>
> *"Moses replied, 'Why do you quarrel with me? Why do you put the LORD to the test?' But the people were thirsty for water there, and they grumbled against Moses. They said, 'Why did you bring us up out of Egypt to make us and our children and livestock die of thirst?'" (Exodus 17:1-3).*

What could Moses do? Instead of taking it personally, he took it to the Lord—and the Lord answered him.

> *"Then Moses cried out to the LORD, 'What am I to do with these people? They are almost ready to stone me.'*
>
> *"The LORD answered Moses, 'Walk on ahead of the people. Take with you some of the elders of Israel and take in your hand the staff with which you struck the Nile and go. I will stand there before you by the rock at Horeb. Strike the rock, and water will come out of it for the people to drink.' So Moses did this in the sight of the elders of Israel. And he called the place Massah and Meribah because the Israelites quarreled and because they tested the LORD saying, 'Is the LORD among us or not?'" (Exodus 17:4-7).*

This last question is the key question for all of us: "Is the Lord among us or not?" If we can answer that question, we can be dead to compliments and dead to criticism.

When God answered Moses, He clearly told Moses what to do: walk on ahead of the people, take some of the elders with him, along with his staff, with which God had already displayed his power. Then He told Moses: "I will stand there before you by the rock at Horeb."

God said, in effect: "Moses, I am with you. Strike the rock and you'll have water for all the people."

Jesus said similar words to His disciples, words which still apply to all of us who call ourselves His disciples today: *"And surely I am with you always, to the very end of the age"* (Matthew 28:20b).

When we know that God is with us, we can properly respond to people's comments, whether they are compliments or criticism. The key is not in ignoring people's compliments or criticism, but in fully recognizing that God is with us in what we're doing. When we know that He is with us, we will clearly defer people's compliments *and* criticism to Him, knowing that it is God who is calling the shots, not us.

Whether people compliment you or criticize you, don't take it personally. Take it to the Lord, letting Him reassure you that He's still with you!

LESSON 19: TAKE YOUR POSITION AND MAINTAIN YOUR POSITION   FEBRUARY 2

Scripture Reading: Exodus 17:8-16

What difference can it make to those around you whether or not you can "stay up" in your faith? For some people, it may mean the difference between victory and defeat, between staying free and falling back into bondage.

When God calls us to take action, He wants us to take our position, and maintain our position, even when we begin to feel weak. He may even send others to help us so we can continue to stand strong.

In the case of Moses, God sent two men to help him when he was feeling weak. When Moses was wearing out, he lowered his arms, and his army began to lose. But when Aaron and Hur gave him a boost, Moses' army got a boost at the same time. There's a short description of this event in Exodus 17:

> *"The Amalekites came and attacked the Israelites at Rephidim. Moses said to Joshua, 'Choose some of our men and go out to fight the Amalekites. Tomorrow I will stand on top of the hill with the staff of God in my hands.'*
> *"So Joshua fought the Amalekites as Moses had ordered, and Moses, Aaron and Hur went to the top of the hill. As long as Moses held up his hands, the Israelites were winning, but whenever he lowered his hands, the Amalekites were winning. When Moses' hands grew tired, they took a stone and put it under him and he sat on it. Aaron and Hur held his hands up—one on one side, one on the other—so that his hands remained steady till sunset. So Joshua overcame the Amalekite army with the sword"* (Exodus 17:8-13).

It must have seemed odd for Moses to tell Joshua to go into battle while Moses himself went up on a hill, holding his staff in his hands. But they both had their roles to play. They both had to take their positions and maintain their positions for victory to come. Moses needed to keep his staff in the air, and Joshua needed to fight with all his might.

What's the deal with Moses having to hold his arms up in the air? What good could that do? While I'm sure there were supernatural things that God did by having Moses raise his staff, (like turning water into blood and splitting the Red Sea in two), I also think there were some "natural" things that God did through this act, too.

As Joshua and the army looked up to the hill, they could see their leader, Moses, with his staff in his hands raised up to heaven. They could also see if Moses grew weary and lowered his arms. While one movement gave them strength and courage, the other movement led to weakness and discouragement.

Moses, Aaron and Hur all saw the effect this had on Joshua and the army. They knew what needed to be done. When Moses couldn't do it by himself anymore, Aaron and Hur stepped in to lift his hands for him. As they watched Joshua and the army until sunset that day, they saw the result of what they were doing: the Israelites were finally able to overcome the Amalekites.

A famous Christian once told his friend that he didn't want to be a role model for others. His friend said, "It's not a matter of whether or not you want to be a role model. You are a role model. The question is whether you're going to be a good role model or a bad one."

There are times when we may not feel like taking the position God has called us to take. There are times when we may not feel like maintaining the position God has called us to take. We may wish we could go down to fight instead of standing on a hill. Or we may wish we could go stand on a hill instead of going down to fight! But if God has called us to our position, we just need to take it and maintain it.

What position has God called you to take? Take your position and maintain your position—then watch to see the difference it can make in your life, and in the lives of those around you.

LESSON 20: TAKE THE ELDERS WITH YOU — FEBRUARY 3

Scripture Reading: Exodus 17:5-6

Has God ever called you to take a risky step of faith in front of other people? Why does He do that?

I know I'd rather take a risky step of faith when I'm all alone, in private, with no one watching. Sometimes we're able to do that, but there are other times when God calls us to take steps of faith with others looking on.

With today's lesson, we're turning a corner in the book of Exodus. In the first ten lessons, we looked at how to "get free" from the bondages in our life. In lessons 11-20, we covered how to "stay free" once we've gotten free. In the next ten lessons, we're going to look at how to "set others free," a big part of which involves enlisting the help of others.

Take a look at how God begins to do this here in Exodus chapter 17:

> *"The LORD answered Moses, 'Walk on ahead of the people. Take with you some of the elders of Israel and take in your hand the staff with which you struck the Nile, and go. I will stand there before you by the rock at Horeb. Strike the rock, and water will come out of it for the people to drink'" (Exodus 17:5-6).*

Why did God tell Moses to take some of the elders of Israel with him on his way to strike the rock?

Although the text of this chapter doesn't say specifically, we can get an idea of what might be going on by looking ahead at the next few chapters. Moses' father-in-law is about to come onto the scene and tell Moses to divide up the work of leading the people, encouraging Moses to choose leaders over groups of tens, hundreds and thousands to help share the leadership load. The elders that go with Moses to the rock are likely to be some of the same elders who will take on these new roles.

While taking our steps of faith in private may be "safe," taking those same steps in public may be significant in helping others take their own steps of faith down the road.

When I began my Internet ministry, I reached a point where I was overwhelmed with requests for prayer and advice. So I invited some people to help me respond to all the emails that were coming in. One of those who volunteered was a woman from Tennessee who had a heart, and a gift, for helping people. Over the years of helping us, her burden for helping others over the Internet continued to grow.

The week that I wrote this lesson, she launched an Internet ministry of her own. Taking what she has learned about doing ministry over the Internet and combining it with her other God-given gifts and talents, she's now poised to help many more people grow in their faith. Here's part of a note I got from her that week:

"I just wanted to share with you that I got my first prayer request from someone in California. I don't even know how they got my website. I can't tell you how hard that hit me—it was so sudden and I didn't expect to get any hits or prayer requests so soon. It was completely awesome. You should have seen me praising the Lord. All the hard work was worth it! At that moment, the poem on my website came to pass: if I can ease one pain, it will all be worth it!"

The closing of her note tied together this idea of the value of taking others with us while we step out in faith. She wrote: "Thank you for allowing me to volunteer with The Ranch and for encouraging me to reach out to others through your ministry and this one. I don't know where God will take it, but I'm ready! You are my inspiration for my own ministry."

Why does God call us to sometimes take steps of faith with others watching? Perhaps one of the reasons is so that when we walk along with each other, we can encourage each other to keep taking more steps of faith, thus expanding the ministry of "setting others free."

LESSON 21: PUT A SYSTEM IN PLACE — FEBRUARY 4

Scripture Reading: Exodus 18

Feeling overwhelmed with too much to do? Don't despair. Help may be on the way! I was lamenting to a friend one day about all the things I felt God wanted me to do. She asked: "Why would God give you more to do than one person could do?" I knew the answer: He wouldn't. He knows what I can handle and what I can't.

So I knew there were only two options left: 1) Either God *hadn't* given me everything I felt He wanted me to do, and I needed to back out of some of them; Or 2) God *had* given me all the things I felt He wanted me to do, and I needed to find a new way to do them.

It turned out to be some of both. For this lesson, though, I want to focus on the second option. There *are* times when God calls us to accomplish things for Him, that don't require us to do them all by ourselves.

Moses found himself in this situation when leading over 600,000 men, not counting all the women and children, through a desert. Moses' father-in-law, Jethro, saw all that Moses was doing and said:

> *"What is this you are doing for the people? Why do you alone sit as judge, while all these people stand around you from morning till evening?"*
>
> *Moses answered him, "Because the people come to me to seek God's will. Whenever they have a dispute, it is brought to me, and I decide between the parties and inform them of God's decrees and laws."*
>
> *Moses' father-in-law replied, "What you are doing is not good. You and these people who come to you will only wear yourselves out. The work is too heavy for you; you cannot handle it alone. Listen now to me and I will give you some advice, and may God be with you. You must be the people's representative before God and bring their disputes to him. Teach them the decrees and laws, and show them the way to live and the duties they are to perform. But select capable men from all the people—men who fear God, trustworthy men who hate dishonest gain—and appoint them as officials over thousands, hundreds, fifties and tens. Have them serve as judges for the people at all times, but have them bring every difficult case to you; the simple cases they can decide themselves. That will make your load lighter, because they will share it with you. If you do this and God so commands, you will be able to stand the strain, and all these people will go home satisfied."*
>
> *Moses listened to his father-in-law and did everything he said. (Exodus 18:14-24)*

Here was Moses, a man truly called by God to lead the people, yet becoming overwhelmed by taking care of every dispute by himself. Jethro saw that this would eventually wear Moses out—as well as all the people. So Jethro gave Moses some practical advice: "Get help!" Moses did, and he was able to fulfill the call of God on his life in a way that he was able to "stand the strain," and all the people went home "satisfied."

Was Moses called to lead the people? Absolutely. Did that mean he had to meet every need personally? Not at all. While he was still ultimately responsible for the people, he found that by putting a system into place and enlisting the help of others he was able to fulfill the call of God on his life.

If you're feeling overwhelmed with too much to do, it's worth an honest prayer to God: "Am I doing the things You want me to do? And if so, is there another way You want me to do them?" Then listen to His honest answers, which come at times through other people.

Even Moses, as close as He was to God, still allowed God to speak into His life through another human being. God's goal was to meet the needs of the people. Moses' goal was to see that it got done. Take a look at the goal, then look at your role. In the end, I believe God will help you to "stand the strain," and all the people will go home "satisfied."

LESSON 22: LET GOD ESTABLISH YOU IN PEOPLE'S EYES — FEBRUARY 5

Scripture Reading: Exodus 19

How many people will be affected by what you do this week? Chances are, it will be more people than any of us might realize.

We all have a "sphere of influence," people with whom we have contact throughout the week, people who can be influenced by the way we live our lives. It may include people in our own family, people where we work, or people where we just hang out. It may include a bank teller, a postal worker, a doctor, a nurse or a receptionist. It may include people at church, people on the Internet, or people we don't even know, who are watching what we do.

And what we do matters.

Take a look at what happened when Moses was obedient to God's call on his life, taking steps of faith even when surrounded by doubt. When God spoke to Moses from the burning bush, and called him to set the Israelites free, Moses hesitated to believe it. But God assured Moses that he was the man. To confirm it, God told Moses He would give him a sign:

> "I will be with you. And this will be the sign to you that it is I who have sent you: When you have brought the people out of Egypt, you will worship God on this mountain" (Exodus 3:2).

Now if I were Moses, I think I would have been a little bit frustrated that the sign would only come *after* I had taken this huge step of faith! Why would God wait until *after* the Israelites were free, and worshiping Him back at this same mountain, to give Moses "the sign"?

To see why, fast forward several months. In Exodus chapter 19, we see that the sign wasn't just for Moses, but also for those in Moses' new sphere of influence.

When Moses stepped out in faith, and the people came back to the mountain to worship God, that became a sign that anyone could read. As the people gathered there at the foot of the mountain, God told Moses to remind the people:

> "You yourselves have seen what I [God] did to Egypt, and how I carried you on eagles' wings and brought you to myself. Now if you obey me fully and keep my covenant, then out of all nations you will be my treasured possession."

The people heard this and responded together, "We will do everything the LORD has said."

Then God speaks these words to Moses:

> "I am going to come to you in a dense cloud, so that the people will hear me speaking with you and will always put their trust in you'" (from Exodus 19:3-9).

God wasn't done with Moses when they got to the mountain. God still had many years of work ahead for him, and God needed the people to always put their trust in Moses so that they would follow his lead.

Sometimes the signs God gives us are not just for us, but for others to read, too. When we step out in faith, being obedient to what God has called us to do, it releases others to step out in faith and obedience as well.

A few years ago, I felt God wanted me to head up a city-wide outreach here in town. With more than a little fear in my heart, I finally brought up the idea at our local ministers' meeting. Within a year, we had over 200 people involved in planning and pulling off this event.

Looking back, I realized that my stepping out in faith, and doing what God had called me to do, was a catalyst for others to step out in faith and do what God had called them to do.

People are affected by what we do.

What is God calling you to do? Remember that you may not be the only one who is affected by what you do or don't do. None of us live in isolation. In fact, the sign that God gives you to show that He really is with you may just be the sign someone else needs to read! Then they'll be able to see that God is with them, too!

LESSON 23: RULES CAN BE GOOD!   FEBRUARY 6

Scripture Reading: Exodus 20:1-21

How do you like rules? If you're like most people, you probably love rules—for other people, anyway! Rules keep people from stealing our stuff, running into us when we go through intersections, and harming those we love.

But what about rules for ourselves? Many times, we balk at rules. They make us feel restricted and constrained. But the rules God has set into place are the best kind of rules. They're helpful for us *and* for others. Instead of constricting us, they set us free to live the best life possible.

Without rules, I would be like a train without a track, or a kite without a string. If I were a train, I would think that the track was constraining me from going where I wanted to go. But in reality, the track would be the very thing that enabled me to go at all—and to go far and fast! If I were a kite, I would think that the string would be holding me back. But in reality, the tension of the string is the very thing that would help me to go higher and stay up longer than if I were to cut myself loose from it!

Exodus chapter 20 lists the most helpful and enduring set of rules ever given to anyone: The Ten Commandments. Thousands of years later, they still form the basis for many legal systems throughout the world.

> "And God spoke all these words:
> 'I am the LORD your God, who brought you out of Egypt, out of the land of slavery. You shall have no other gods before me.'
> 'You shall not make for yourself an idol in the form of anything in heaven above or on the earth beneath or in the waters below. You shall not bow down to them or worship them; for I, the LORD your God, am a jealous God, punishing the children for the sin of the fathers to the third and fourth generation of those who hate me, but showing love to a thousand generations of those who love me and keep my commandments.'
> 'You shall not misuse the name of the LORD your God, for the LORD will not hold anyone guiltless who misuses his name.'
> 'Remember the Sabbath day by keeping it holy. Six days you shall labor and do all your work, but the seventh day is a Sabbath to the LORD your God. On it you shall not do any work, neither you, nor your son or daughter, nor your manservant or

maidservant, nor your animals, nor the alien within your gates. For in six days the LORD made the heavens and the earth, the sea, and all that is in them, but he rested on the seventh day. Therefore the LORD blessed the Sabbath day and made it holy.'
'Honor your father and your mother, so that you may live long in the land the LORD your God is giving you.'
'You shall not murder.'
'You shall not commit adultery.'
'You shall not steal.'
'You shall not give false testimony against your neighbor.'
'You shall not covet your neighbor's house. You shall not covet your neighbor's wife, or his manservant or maidservant, his ox or donkey, or anything that belongs to your neighbor'"
(Exodus 20:1-17).

Rather than restricting us, these rules free us to live the abundant life God created us to live.

Now step back a minute and look at these rules from God's perspective. Why did He give these rules to Moses at this particular point in the journey out of Egypt? Based on Moses' recent conversation with Jethro, I believe it was God's way to teach everyone His decrees and laws, and to show them the way to live, as Jethro suggested in Exodus 18:20. At this critical point, God gave Moses a detailed set of rules to pass on to others so they could help him lead.

If you're wondering how to lead others better, or if you're wondering how you can live a more abundant life yourself, consider putting a good set of rules into place. A good set of rules, like a train track and a kite string, can often help us go farther and faster, and to fly longer and higher than ever before!

LESSON 24: SHARE WHAT YOU'VE LEARNED WITH OTHERS   FEBRUARY 7

Scripture Reading: Exodus 20:22-23:19

What has God taught you that might be helpful to others? We've all learned things from Him over the years—things we've done wrong, things we've done right, things He's spoken to us or through us.

I was in the midst of writing down some of the things God had spoken to me when I was reading Exodus chapters 20, 21, 22 and 23. When I read about God's conversation with Moses on the mountain, and how God gave Moses the Ten Commandments and the 600+ rules that followed, I saw what God was doing in a new light.

Of course, we're supposed to read what God spoke to Moses during those forty days, and of course, we'll be blessed if we follow that wisdom. But I also saw a new lesson for my life when I stepped back and looked at what God was doing overall. God was pouring out His wisdom to Moses so that Moses could pour it out to others.

The lesson for me was that God has poured out wisdom into our lives, too, and He wants us to pour it out to others.

Up to this point in the story of how God set the Israelites free from Egypt, Moses was the sole judge over the entire nation. Everyone who had a dispute would bring it to Moses to be settled. God would give Moses the wisdom he needed to make a ruling, and Moses would make the decision.

This worked for a time, but eventually it began to wear Moses and the people out. So God, through the words of Jethro, prompted Moses to delegate the work of judging others to several of the other leaders of Israel. Moses would still be available to hear the most difficult cases, but the majority of cases could be decided by these others.

It was at this time—as Moses prepared to delegate these duties—that God called Moses up to the mountain and spoke to him the Ten Commandments and all the rules that followed. As I read through this list of commandments, I could almost picture how the conversation between God and Moses might have gone:

"Moses, do you remember when that bull gored a man to death—the bull that had never gored anyone before? And do you remember how I told you to rule in that situation—that the bull must be killed, but the owner of the bull would not be held responsible? Share that with others.

"And do you remember when another bull gored a man to death, but that bull had a habit of goring people? Do you remember how I told you to rule in that situation—that the bull must be killed as well as the owner, unless those hurt by the goring would accept payment from the owner instead? Share that, too."

Although the actual conversation between God and Moses isn't recorded, the result of what God spoke during those forty days *is* recorded. What should be done when a bull gores someone is clearly spelled out in Exodus 21:28-32.

Maybe God reminded Moses of things that happened in the past, as well as telling him about things that might come up in the future. God spoke to Moses about all kinds of topics one by one, from cases involving adultery, theft and murder, to love, lust and anger. Then God asked Moses to share them with others, which he did.

Now, thousands of years later, we can still read these words of wisdom that came from the mouth of God. They form the foundation of the laws that are currently on the books in country after country. They help us to understand our basic rights, how to get along with each other, and how to better love God and our neighbors.

Think with me for a minute how this lesson might apply to you.

God has spent a lifetime pouring out His wisdom into you. What topics in life has God spoken to you about the most? Or the most often? Or the most clearly? What questions have you struggled with, wrestled through, and found God's answers?

Take time to share what you've learned with others. The answers you've found may set them free, too.

LESSON 25: LITTLE BY LITTLE   FEBRUARY 8

Scripture Reading: Exodus 23:20-33

Praying for anything big to happen in your life? Waiting for God to bring it about? Wondering why it's not coming about as fast as you'd like?

When I get frustrated that I'm not seeing the big, grand vision come together for something that I really think God is putting on my heart, I take comfort from a short passage in Exodus chapter 23. It reminds me that God is able "to do immeasurably more than all we can ask or imagine," as the New Testament says in Ephesians 3:20, but that God doesn't always do it all at once.

Why not? Here's what God told the Israelites, and what He often tells me, too.

As the Israelites approached the "promised land," a huge expanse of property that God promised to give them when they got out of Egypt, God told them that He would drive out the current occupants of the land because of their wickedness and rebellion against Him. But He added:

> *"I will not drive them out in a single year, because the land would become desolate and the wild animals too numerous for you. Little by little I will drive them out before you, until you have increased enough to take possession of the land" (Exodus 23:29-30).*

God was still going to give them their promised land, but little by little, for their own protection, and for the safekeeping of His vision for the land.

Even though there were over 600,000 Israelites at the time, the land was still bigger than they could effectively manage had they gotten it all at once. The land would have become desolate and overrun with wild animals. God, in His grace, was going to wait to drive out the current inhabitants until the Israelites increased enough to take possession of the land.

This is extremely encouraging to me! I don't like to wait for God's promises to be fulfilled—especially when I can see them so clearly, when they look like they're within reach, yet when I can't seem to take hold of them. These verses remind me that God *will* do what He says He will do, but in *His* timing, for *our* good and *for the good of the vision He's given us*.

For many years now I've been praying for a real "ranch," a place where I can invite people to spend time with God, away from the busy-ness of their lives. I've been to just such a ranch with my family—a beautiful private retreat on 240 acres of rolling hills in northern Illinois. Yet as I looked around at the expanse of the property, I couldn't imagine all of the care and maintenance it would take just to put gravel on the back roads every few years, let alone take care of all the cattle, sheep, ducks, fencing and guest homes.

Even though this seems to be exactly what I've been praying for, and continue to pray for, I know that I've not "increased enough to take possession" of the fullness of this vision. That doesn't stop me from asking, and it doesn't stop me from believing that God will someday fulfill the fullness of what He's put on my heart. But it does help me to be thankful—so thankful—that God holds back from giving me what I'm asking for before I can handle it.

Maybe you've been praying for some big things to happen in your life, or a friend's life. Maybe you've wondered why things aren't happening as fast as you'd like, or to the extent that you'd like. Maybe you're getting discouraged and wondering why God is poking around, taking His time, when there are so many things you want to get done—and now!

Take heart from this little passage in Exodus 23. As God Himself says several times in this passage, He *will* do what He promised. There are still things He wants us to do in the meantime. But, for our benefit, and for the benefit of His unfolding vision, He often carries out His will "little by little"—so we won't be overwhelmed by the answer when it does come.

LESSON 26: COME UP TO THE LORD AND WORSHIP FEBRUARY 9

Scripture Reading: Exodus 24

What's the ultimate goal of being set free? What does freedom finally allow us to do, without hindrance?

The answer I've read over and over in Scripture is this: we're set free so we can worship God.

If a person can't worship God, fully from their heart, then they're still in bondage. They may live in a free country, but if they can't worship God, they're not really free at all. On the other hand, they may live in a prison cell, but if they can worship God, they are truly free. The degree of freedom we have in our lives is directly proportional to the degree to which we're able to worship God from our hearts.

This was God's ultimate goal for setting the Israelites free from Egypt. He told Moses to bring the people out into the desert so they could worship Him. He sets us free from sin, not only because it's good and helpful for us, but also so that we can be released to worship Him with our whole hearts.

In Exodus 24, Moses and his people have finally made it out to the place where God told Moses to come. Now they can start doing what they came to do, starting with Moses and some of the other leaders. God calls them up to the mountain to worship. The rest of the people will get their chance soon. But for now, God calls Moses to lead the way:

> "Then he said to Moses, 'Come up to the LORD, you and Aaron, Nadab and Abihu, and seventy of the elders of Israel. You are to worship at a distance, but Moses alone is to approach the LORD; the others must not come near. And the people may not come up with him'" (Exodus 24:1-2).

Moses is about to become their "worship leader."

And what a worship service it is! Take a look at what happens when they come up to the Lord:

> "Moses and Aaron, Nadab and Abihu, and the seventy elders of Israel went up and saw the God of Israel. Under his feet was something like a pavement made of sapphire, clear as the sky itself. But God did not raise his hand against these leaders of the Israelites; they saw God, and they ate and drank." (Exodus 24:9-10).

They saw God—and lived! Then they ate and drank in His presence there on the mountain. Wow! To come into the presence of God, to see Him, to eat and drink and have a party right there at His feet—that's a true mountaintop experience!

The cool thing is, *we* can now do that any day of the week, no matter where we are or what's going on in our lives. We can take a moment, even right now, today, to spend a few minutes in the presence of the Lord, worshiping Him in our hearts.

You may not be able to sing. You may not be able to play an instrument. You may not be able to speak well. But you can do one thing right now that no one can stop you from doing: you can worship God in your heart.

You might not think you can. You might think others are hindering you from it. You might think your circumstances are preventing it. But the truth is, nothing—and no one—can stop you from worshiping God. You can choose right now to worship Him!

Just say, "Father, I want to worship You. I want to be in Your presence. I want to eat and drink and enjoy a few moments with You, right now. I want to worship You!"

If sin is holding you back, confess it. If fear is getting you off track, let the Lord, Your shepherd, lead you beside His still waters. If life is weighing you down, let Jesus pick you up. He offered each of us this promise: *"Come to me, all you who are weary and burdened, and I will give you rest"* (Matthew 11:28).

Come up to the Lord and worship. This is why He set you free!

LESSON 27: GOD CAN SPEAK SPECIFICALLY AND CLEARLY — FEBRUARY 10

Scripture Reading: Exodus 25:1-27:19

Do you ever wonder if God speaks to people? And if so, does He just speak in generalities, giving us good principles to live by, but leaving the details up to us?

I was in a Bible study with a friend who felt that God does speak to us, but only in terms of giving us the "big picture." The specifics were for us to figure out. I understood what my friend was saying—and at times that is certainly true.

But as I've read through the Bible, I've also been struck by how often God speaks to people with very specific instructions—instructions that He wants to be followed precisely—even down to the last "cubit."

Exodus chapters 25, 26, and 27 are prime examples of God speaking specifically and clearly. In the opening words of chapter 25, God tells Moses to collect some very specific items from the people: ram skins dyed red, acacia wood, onyx stones and more. God continues with these words:

> *"Then have them make a sanctuary for me, and I will dwell among them. Make this tabernacle and all its furnishings exactly like the pattern I will show you"* (Exodus 25:8-9).

For the next 89 verses, God gave Moses a detailed description of exactly how to build this tabernacle, and all of the elements within it: the ark of the covenant, the tables, the lampstands, the altars, the oil, the shovels—even the meat forks.

Listen to some of this detail:

> ... *" Make a lampstand of pure gold and hammer it out, base and shaft; its cups, buds and blossoms shall be of one piece with it. Six branches are to extend from the sides of the lampstand—three on one side and three on the other. Three cups shaped like almond flowers with buds and blossoms are to be on one branch, three on the next branch, and the same for all six branches extending from the lampstand"* (Exodus 25:31-33).

> ... *"Make the tabernacle with ten curtains of finely twisted linen and blue, purple and scarlet yarn, with cherubim worked into them by a skilled craftsman. All the curtains are to be the same size—twenty-eight cubits long and four cubits wide"* (Exodus 26:1-2).

> ... *"Build an altar of acacia wood, three cubits high; it is to be square, five cubits long and five cubits wide.... Make a grating for it, a bronze network, and make a bronze ring at each of the four corners of the network. Put it under the ledge of the altar so that it is halfway up the altar"* (Exodus 27:1,4-5).

The detail reminds me of when God told Noah precisely how to build the ark for the animals, describing its dimensions cubit by cubit (a length of about 18 inches).

Why was God so specific? Maybe it was because there had never been a need for a boat like that before. How could Noah have known how many animals would show up? It was better for Noah to follow God's specific instructions up front on how to build the ark, than to try to build it his own way and then have the elephants and hippos and rhinos and giraffes show up!

When we need wisdom, we can ask God for it. He's the Creator of the universe. He knows how every molecule is put together. He knows what needs to be done and how to do it. And He's glad to pour out that wisdom into us.

The Bible says: "If any of you lacks wisdom, he should ask God, who gives generously to all without finding fault, and it will be given to him" (James 1:5).

God *can* speak specifically and clearly. There's no doubt about it scripturally, as in this case from Exodus. Someone might wonder, based on their experience (or lack thereof), if God speaks specifically. But based on Scripture, there's no doubt that He does!

Whatever you're working on right now—a project for work, a new type of ministry, a relationship with a spouse, child or friend—ask God for wisdom on how to proceed. Then listen, and do, what He says.

LESSON 28: GIVE DIGNITY AND HONOR TO THOSE SERVING WITH YOU FEBRUARY 11

Scripture Reading: Exodus 27:20-28:40

What can we do to give dignity and honor to those who serve with us? And what difference can it make when we do?

I once attended a church that was very formal. All the pastors wore black robes. At one point, one of the pastors wanted to start preaching in just his suit, without the robe. He wanted to be less formal so that the people he was trying to reach would feel he was more like them.

But some of the leaders of the church didn't like that idea. It went against their particular view of church life. While the church eventually let him preach without his robe for the first of their three morning worship services, he had to put it on again for the other two services.

I thought the whole debate was somewhat unnecessary as he had a reasonable idea he wanted to implement. But when I read Exodus chapter 28, trying to read it from God's perspective, I was able to see that there *are* times when it's important to do things that will give people dignity and honor for the work they have been called to do.

Here's what God asked Moses to do for his brother Aaron, and Aaron's sons, all of whom God had called to become priests in the tabernacle that they were building:

> *"Make sacred garments for your brother Aaron to give him dignity and honor. Tell all the skilled men to whom I have given wisdom in such matters that they are to make garments for Aaron, for his consecration, so he may serve me as priest" (Exodus 28:2-3).*

Then God described in great detail what the robes and turbans and undergarments should look like.

I don't know what you might think about this idea today, whether or not pastors or priests should wear elaborate robes. But the passage indicates to me that there are times when God asks us to give dignity and honor to the people around us, sometimes in very specific ways, and that God wants us to listen to—and do—what He tells us to do.

I was reading this passage when I was getting ready to launch our newly redesigned website for *The Ranch*. As I tried to think what God might want me to do for those who helped me with the project, I felt He wanted me to have a special online prayer and dedication service for them. So I set a date and time and invited about a dozen people to join me in the chat room.

We had someone from Latvia who had helped redesign the website. We had someone from Denmark who built the software on which the whole system runs. We had someone from Colorado who helps with our prayer ministry and answering emails. We had someone from North Carolina who serves on our board.

I had sent each of them a small bottle of oil, based on a passage we're going to look at next week, but touched on in this passage, so that I could pray for them, anointing and consecrating them for their work of service to God.

I was very hesitant at first, because in some ways, it seemed—well—just very weird to do this over the Internet! I thought it would be hard to really give them dignity and honor like this. But I've also prayed for enough people over the Internet by now to know that prayer has no boundaries.

So as I prayed for each person, I asked them to put some oil on their finger and touch it to their forehead as I typed out my prayers on my keyboard. I later heard back from several of those who came who said that as we prayed together, they had completely broken down in tears, weeping at this special expression of appreciation for their work of service to God.

What about those who work with you? Is there a way that God might want you to give them dignity and honor? I believe that if you'll ask God, He'll answer you. He may not tell you to put a robe on them. But whatever He tells you, when you do it, God will touch people through it.

LESSON 29: ANOINT, ORDAIN AND CONSECRATE THOSE SERVING   FEBRUARY 12

Scripture Reading: Exodus 28:41-29:35

What can we do for the people who work with us to dedicate them—and their gifts and talents—to the Lord? One thing to consider is "anointing" them with oil.

It seems like an ancient practice, anointing people with oil. But one of the most dramatic experiences of my life was an ordination service where I truly felt God Himself was calling me into His service. He used the hands of a pastor to anoint my head with oil, ordaining and consecrating me for the work God had called me to do.

Throughout the Bible, God anointed some of His most powerful leaders with oil for their work of service to Him, like King David, King Saul, and in the passage we're looking at today, the priest Aaron and his sons:

> *"After you put these clothes on your brother Aaron and his sons, anoint and ordain them. Consecrate them so they may serve me as priests"* (Exodus 28:41).

I happened to be in Israel when I read some of these passages about anointing people with oil. It's one thing to read these passages at home. It's another thing entirely to be standing on the spots where these things took place. At one point, I was amazed to think that I was standing at the tomb of Samuel the prophet, the one who walked the very same hills I was walking on when he sought out young David to anoint him as king.

These were real people who had done these things, who lived in real places that still exist today. I wondered what it would be like if God were to send someone to anoint me, right there in Israel, for the work He had called me to do. I had recently quit my job to go into full-time ministry and wondered if God could consecrate me in this specific way, too. So I began to pray that God would send someone. I couldn't believe He did it when it happened the very next day!

I ran into a tour group and began talking to a pastor and his wife. They kept asking me questions about how I had quit my job and gone into ministry. I really didn't want to stand around and chit-chat—I was waiting for God to show up! But as we talked, the pastor asked if I had ever anointed people with oil when I prayed for the sick, as he had found that to be very effective.

I couldn't believe it! I hadn't told him anything about my prayer the day before that God would send someone to anoint me with oil. Yet here was a man standing in front of me who regularly anointed people with oil. I hesitantly asked him if he would pray for me, too, anointing me with oil for the work that God had called me to do. He said he would, and at the next stop on the tour, he'd pick up a bottle of oil at one of the local shops to do it.

So I walked with their group from the Temple Mount, down the Way of the Cross, where Jesus carried his cross to his crucifixion. The tour stopped at the church that now houses the crucifixion site. We bought a little bottle of oil and went into the church to pray.

There, about 20 feet from the foot of the cross which marks the spot where Jesus is said to have died, this man and his wife prayed for me. They anointed me with oil for the work of service God had called me to do. Their prayers were accompanied—at 1:00 sharp—by the loud ringing of church bells overhead, the sounds of a tour group singing hymns, and as sights and smells of burning incense wafted through the room.

I was overwhelmed by the way God had answered my prayers. I'll never look at an anointing service as just an ancient ritual again. It is a powerful means by which God can ordain and consecrate us for our work of service to Him.

God used an earthly man to anoint, ordain and consecrate me for my work, and has since used me to do the same for others. Perhaps God wants to touch those around you in a similar way, praying for them that they would use their gifts and talents to bear much fruit for Him.

LESSON 30: MULTIPLY FREEDOM BY INVOLVING OTHERS — FEBRUARY 13

Scripture Reading: Exodus 18:17-19

What could you do to lighten the load of all that God wants you to do? As a summary of the last nine lessons, here's a short list of some of the things God had Moses do to lighten his load. These things not only lightened his load, but they allowed God to accomplish through Moses all that God wanted to do. Maybe they could help you to accomplish more, too.

1) *Delegate. Jethro helped Moses to see that Moses would only wear himself out unless he involved others in the work.*
2) *Write it down. God helped Moses to write down what he had already learned from God, and would need to know in the future, so that Moses could share this wisdom with others.*
3) *Trust God's timing. God showed Moses a huge vision for what He wanted to do through Moses, but God also told him that it wouldn't happen overnight, but rather, little by little.*
4) *Listen for God's specific instructions. God spoke in specific detail about how God wanted the people to do the work—and Moses listened.*
5) *Give dignity and honor to those serving with you. God showed Moses not only specific ways to involve others, but also how to give them dignity and honor for their work.*

By putting a system in place, Moses was able to multiply the number of people who could experience the freedom God had in mind for them, including us today who still benefit from those words. Moses still had meaningful work to do, but he was relieved from having to do it all himself.

As I wrote this lesson, I had just returned from a missions trip to Africa. My wife and I had been wanting to do something to help the people of Africa in some way, but we had no idea what to do. The problems facing that continent are overwhelming. But after voicing our desire to each other and to God, God showed us a way that we could help. He invited us to join a missions trip to Swaziland to plant hundreds of small vegetable gardens in people's backyards.

The project was simple enough in theory, but took a huge amount of planning and effort to make it work in practice. We certainly couldn't have done it alone. Thankfully, we didn't have to.

God raised up people to help in dozens of ways: donors who funded the trip, drivers who helped us get through the mountains, pastors who went ahead of us to prepare the people for what we were going to do, translators who helped us interact with the local people, administrators who handled the logistics for our team, and secretaries who arranged hundreds of details during the week.

If we had tried to do this alone, the five of us who went from Streator might have planted five or ten gardens the whole week. But, by involving others, God was able to use our team of 80 volunteers, working alongside the beautiful people of Swaziland, to plant and distribute over 8,000 of these small vegetable gardens. Over the past few years, thousands of volunteers, on dozens of similar trips, have been able to plant and distribute hundreds of thousands of these life-giving gardens.

I often think that I'm the one that has to accomplish the whole vision that God puts on my heart. While I'm willing to do the work, I get overwhelmed because there's too much work to do. The truth is there *is* too much work to do—at least for one person. But by involving others, we can finish the work together.

If you feel overwhelmed by the visions that God has put on your heart, remember that Moses needed help, too. Remember Jethro's words to Moses:

"What you are doing is not good. You and these people who come to you will only wear yourselves out. The work is too heavy for you; you cannot handle it alone. Listen

now to me and I will give you some advice, and may God be with you..." (Exodus 18:17b-19a).

Moses took Jethro's advice by involving others—and God *was* with him. May God be with you, too.

LESSON 31: GOD WANTS TO MEET WITH US AND SPEAK TO US   FEBRUARY 14

Scripture Reading: Exodus 29:36-46

There's nothing better than to be with someone you love, spending an extended period of time with them, day and night. Over the next ten lessons we're going to focus on worshiping God, and what it feels to be in love with, and spend extended time with Him.

Since I first read about prayer and fasting in the Bible, I've tried it for various amounts of time. Why would I want to give up food to pray for a day, or five days, or ten, twenty or forty days? It's not because I like giving up food. I don't! But I love being with God. I've found that when I empty myself of the things of the world, it makes more room in my life to be filled with the things of God.

In Exodus 29:38-56, God told the Israelites to make a sacrifice to Him every day in the morning, and every day in the evening at the entrance to the Tent of Meeting. There He would meet with them and speak to them.

> *"This is what you are to offer on the altar regularly each day: two lambs a year old. Offer one in the morning and the other at twilight....a pleasing aroma, an offering made to the LORD by fire. For the generations to come this burnt offering is to be made regularly at the entrance to the Tent of Meeting before the LORD. There I will meet you and speak to you; there also I will meet with the Israelites, and the place will be consecrated by my glory"* (Exodus 29:38-39, 41b-43).

This is why God set the Israelites free, so He could meet with them and speak to them. It's the same reason He set you and me free, so He could meet with us and speak to us.

Thankfully, we don't have to wait till Sunday, or any special time of the year. We can meet with God every morning and every evening. And God *wants* to meet with us, live with us and speak to us.

When I first became a Christian, I began a habit of setting aside time every morning and every evening to spend time with God. I would wake up early, take my Bible and a journal, and spend time with God before I went to work. Then in the evenings, I would take time to read more from the Bible, or another Christian book—something that would focus my thoughts on Him again at night.

I've found that whenever I've regularly done this over the years, it has helped me to sandwich in my day, between waking up and going to bed. I'll get my marching orders in the morning, then recap the day again in the evening. It can be hard to keep this schedule, and there are times when I haven't kept it up. But reading this passage has reminded me again of the value setting aside time twice a day to intentionally be with God.

A number of godly men and women over the years have made this a regular practice in their lives. Saints of the past, and saints of today, have written daily devotionals for this purpose with titles like Charles Spurgeon's *Morning and Evening*, or Joyce Meyers' *Starting Your Day Right: Devotions for Each Morning of the Year* and *Ending Your Day Right:*

Devotions for Every Evening of the Year. You can sign up at various websites on the Internet, like www.crosswalk.com, and receive a devotional twice a day by email.

It's not always easy to carve out time to spend time with God. But it's so worth it. Sacrificing this way for God is like a lucky honeymoon couple going to Hawaii for a week. They don't get in the plane because they want to sit in a cramped seat for hours on end. They do it because when they get there, they'll get to spend uninterrupted time with their beloved, day and night.

Take time today, and every day—even twice a day—to get away with your Beloved. He wants to meet with you and speak with you.

LESSON 32: MAKE A PLACE TO MEET WITH GOD TWICE A DAY   FEBRUARY 15

Scripture Reading: Exodus 30:1-16

Last time we looked at making a time to meet with God twice a day. Today we'll look at making a place to meet with God twice a day, a place where we can truly "worship" Him.

In Exodus 30, God asked Aaron to build an altar for burning incense. This was to be a fragrant offering to God, twice a day:

> *"Make an altar of acacia wood for burning incense. … Aaron must burn fragrant incense on the altar every morning when he tends the lamps. He must burn incense again when he lights the lamps at twilight so incense will burn regularly before the LORD for the generations to come" (Exodus 30:1,7-8).*

I know I'm not Aaron, but as I read this passage, I was trying to think of a way that I could do something similar every morning and every evening as part of my own quiet time with God.

Although my piano's not made of acacia wood, I decided that I could use it as an altar. This wasn't to be a thing that I could worship, but a place where I could worship, a place where I could send up my own fragrant offering to the Lord. As Aaron tended the lamps every morning and every evening, I thought I could light a candle there by my piano, too. Then as I would play the piano, or sing a song, or put my Bible on the front of the piano and read some scripture from it, I would have a visual reminder that these moments were dedicated to God.

After doing this for several weeks, I found out that lighting the candle reminded me to focus on Him, making this a special time of personal worship. This wasn't to be a time to ask God for things, but a time to make a fragrant offering of my life to Him, serving Him, pleasing Him and spending time with Him.

The lit candle reminded me that my quiet time isn't just a time to be alone. *It's a time to be with God.*

It's amazing how that simple act of lighting the candle twice a day, and playing a song, let me know if I had truly spent time with God during the day. I would sometimes think, "Oh, yeah, I read my Bible this morning," or "I thought about God as I got out of bed," or "I prayed about something as I jumped in the car." The candle helped me to focus not just on thinking "about" God, but being "with" God.

Do you have a place where you can go to worship God? A quiet spot in your house, or somewhere else, where you can meet with Him, twice a day? My wife, Lana, put a chair in a closet several years ago and goes in there from time to time when she needs an extra special time with God. Although there's barely enough room for her feet in the closet, it's enough room for her to cozy up with her Bible and journal and focus solely on Him.

Some of my friends have a special desk where they sit on a straight back chair to help keep them awake and focused. Others sit at their kitchen table, or on their front porch when the weather's nice, or jump in their truck with the motor turned off. Some keep a Bible and notepad by their bed so they can spend time with God the first and last thing every day.

One of the best places I've found in my busy house is in the bathtub! With the bathroom fan running and the curtain pulled, this drowns out many of the other sounds and distractions in the house. I've accidentally baptized a couple of Bibles doing this. But the time with God is awesome!

If you don't already have a place, consider finding one where you can spend time with God every morning and every evening. Try several places! This is not only to help you form a lifelong habit of a daily quiet time with God, but can also help you experience changes in your life, and your relationship with Him, as a result of the time you spend together each day.

LESSON 33: CLEANSE AND CONSECRATE YOURSELF FOR WORSHIP   FEBRUARY 16

Scripture Reading: Exodus 30:17-38

Today I'd like to talk about why we sometimes aren't able to fully come into worship. We want to worship God, but we're held back by something.

Exodus 30 gives us a clue about one of the things that can hold us back—and how to get past it. There was something that Aaron and his sons were to do every time they came into the place of worship, and something that would happen if they didn't:

> *"Then the LORD said to Moses, 'Make a bronze basin, with its bronze stand, for washing. Place it between the Tent of Meeting and the altar and put water in it. Aaron and his sons are to wash their hands and feet with water from it. Whenever they enter the Tent of Meeting, they shall wash with water so that they will not die'" (Exodus 30:18-20a).*

They were to wash their hands and feet in water from a bronze basin whenever they entered the place of worship. If they didn't, they'd die! It seems like God was pretty serious about getting clean before coming into His presence!

Sometimes we get pretty lax about coming into the presence of God. I know I do. I love to be able to come to God *Just as I Am*, like the famous song that's sung at Billy Graham crusades. But this passage is a reminder to me that if I'm ever finding it hard to fully enter into worship, it would be good to look and see if there's anything in my life that might need cleansing—not physically with water, but inwardly in my heart or life.

I've had guys share with me that they're struggling in a relationship with their wife. I'll sometimes ask them if there's anything they haven't told their wife, anything that they might have done to sin against her. Oftentimes, they'll say, "Yes." It's no surprise then that they find their relationship with their wife has cooled off. Who wants to be around someone else when they've sinned against them and haven't confessed it?

One man told me he was struggling with intimacy with his wife. Then he also told me he was struggling with homosexual pornography. I asked him if he had ever talked to his wife about this struggle. "Of course not!" he answered, "it would hurt her too much if I told her."

I told him, "Buddy, it's hurting her too much now, every day, and it's playing out in every part of your relationship with her. It's not going to hurt her more by telling her, it's going to finally help you, and her, start to get the healing you both need." I'm fully aware that there are better and worse times for confessing these things, and there are better and worse ways to communicate the truth. But ultimately, it is the truth that will set us free.

It's similar in our relationships with God. Sometimes we have sin in our lives, sins against Him, and we don't really feel like spending time with Him. We don't feel like worshiping Him. But if we would confess our sins to God, and come clean to Him, we'd be much more eager to come into His presence.

Confession is critical, especially to God. It shows God, or the other person, that you really do care about your relationship with them. Rather than driving them away, it usually draws them closer to you.

If there's anything on your heart that you want to confess to God, maybe you'd like to take some time right now to get things right with Him again. It might only take 30 seconds after you finish reading this note to just talk to Him and say, "I'm sorry for what I've done. I pray that You'd forgive me." It might take a few hours or days. But whatever it takes, do it. Come clean. The cleansing you'll feel afterwards can make the worship you experience later all the more sweet.

And here's an encouraging promise from God's Word:

> *"If we confess our sins, he is faithful and just and will forgive us our sins and purify us from all unrighteousness" (1 John 1:19).*

LESSON 34: GOD CHOOSES AND EQUIPS PEOPLE TO DO HIS WORK — FEBRUARY 17

Scripture Reading: Exodus 31:1-11

If you feel like you're not very gifted or skilled, or if you wonder if God's going to use you in any special way, today's lesson is for you. God *does* choose and equip people to do His work.

In the last few chapters of Exodus, God has gone into considerable detail telling Moses how to make all kinds of things for the place of worship: the tapestries, altar, utensils, incense and oils. Now God tells Moses how it would all get done: God had chosen and equipped people to do His work:

> *"Then the LORD said to Moses, 'See, I have chosen Bezalel...and I have filled him with the Spirit of God, with skill, ability and knowledge in all kinds of crafts—to make artistic designs for work in gold, silver and bronze, to cut and set stones, to work in wood, and to engage in all kinds of craftsmanship. Moreover, I have appointed Oholiab...to help him. Also I have given skill to all the craftsmen to make everything I have commanded you'" (Exodus 31:1-6).*

What was the very first thing with which God had filled Bezalel? The Spirit of God. It's encouraging to me to know that when God calls us to do something, He will, first and foremost, fill us with His Spirit so we can do it.

I remember praying for a man on the night he gave his life to the Lord. As we talked, he told me he had really wanted to read his Bible, but in the 50+ years he had been alive, he had never been able to do it. So I prayed with him: "Lord, fill him with Your Spirit so that he can do the things he wants to do."

I left my Bible with him and the next day he started reading it. Then he bought his own Bible and kept reading it. Within a few weeks, he had finished the New Testament, so he went back to the Old Testament and read it, too. Then he started reading the whole thing all over again and began passing out Bibles to all his friends. Now he's a pastor of a church!

If you feel like you're not able to do what God's called you to do, ask Him again: "Father, fill me with Your Spirit so I can do the things You want me to do."

But God didn't stop there with Bezalel. God also filled him with "skill, ability and knowledge in all kinds of crafts." God also said He'd send yet another man, Oholiab, to help Bezelel, along with many other people to help them both. God equipped all of them with various skills, abilities and knowledge to do His work.

Asking God to equip you isn't a "magical" prayer. I've anointed my hands with oil and prayed that God would help me to play the piano better. After washing off my hands, I sat down to play again—and it sounded just like it did before! But over time, God has answered that prayer by giving me more and more opportunities to play and lead worship and develop my skills.

Now this is just a guess on my part, but where do you think all those Israelites got their skills, abilities and knowledge to do all kinds of intricate work with gold, silver and bronze? Remember that they had just been slaves in Egypt, working for kings who were later buried in those incredible pyramids. Have you ever seen the coffins or other things they've brought out of Egypt, like King Tut's headpiece, or the other intricate carvings found in his tomb? Who worked on all that stuff? It's probably fair to say that a number of the slaves helped to carry out the details of that elaborate work.

I wonder if the Israelites might have felt that all those years were wasted, making images of someone else's gods. But now, God was calling them to use their gifts and skills for Him, to make a place of worship that far surpassed anything they had ever done before.

Keep praying that God will fill you with His Spirit, giving you skills, abilities and knowledge that you can ultimately use for Him.

LESSON 35: OBSERVE THE SABBATH   FEBRUARY 18

Scripture Reading: Exodus 31:12-18

How would it feel if your boss came to you this week and said, "Why don't you take a day off this week. It's no problem. You've worked hard, just go home and get some rest." I think that would feel great!

The truth is, that's what God says to us every week.

Even when God gives us a huge task to do, He still wants us to be sure to take a break every seven days, just like He wanted Moses and the Israelites to take a break when they had a huge task before them.

In the chapters leading up to Exodus 31, God has laid out in detail all the work that the Israelites would need to do to build their house of worship. The work would take many months to complete. But at the end of everything God called them to do, God closed with these words:

> *"For six days, work is to be done, but the seventh day is a Sabbath of rest, holy to the LORD. Whoever does any work on the Sabbath day must be put to death. The Israelites are to observe the Sabbath, celebrating it for the generations to come as a lasting covenant. It will be a sign between me and the Israelites forever, for in six days the LORD made the heavens and the earth, and on the seventh day he abstained from work and rested"* (Exodus 31:15-18).

God Himself took a break at the end of a long, hard week of creating the universe, and we've been on a seven-day calendar ever since. Like so many of God's laws, the penalty of death wasn't meant to be mean, but to emphasize just how critical this law would be to our own well-being. God knows how we're wired. He's the One who wired us! He knows that we need a rest every seven days, and He's thrilled to give it to us.

I grew up on a farm in Illinois, and my Dad worked as hard as anyone I knew. But not on Sunday. It didn't matter if there was still work to be done or not, or whether it was raining or sunny, Dad took off—and we did, too. It was great! (As a side note: the Sabbath for Jews is from sunset on Friday through sunset on Saturday, whereas the early Christians began to celebrate the Sabbath on Sunday, the "Lord's Day," which is the day Jesus rose from the dead.)

One Sunday night, my wife Lana began to make a big lasagna dinner for some guests we were having over for dinner on Monday night. I didn't think it was a very good way for her to spend her "day off." But when we were talking about it with a friend a few weeks later, our friend asked Lana if making the lasagna dinner brought "rest to her soul." Lana said it really did, because she was able to enjoy the whole process of making the dinner while I watched the kids.

For Lana, making that lasagna dinner was truly relaxing and restful. I had to wonder if Jesus wasn't smiling at me and my legalistic view of the Sabbath. The religious leaders of Jesus' day looked at what He was doing as breaking the Sabbath rules, too, like healing others, or allowing His disciples to gather food from the fields (Matthew 12:1-14). But rather than breaking the law, Jesus was revealing the heart of the law, a law which was designed to bring true "rest to our souls," a kind of rest which Jesus still offers to all who come to Him as well:

> *"Come to me, all you who are weary and burdened, and I will give you rest. Take my yoke upon you and learn from me, for I am gentle and humble in heart, and you will find rest for your souls. For my yoke is easy and my burden is light"* (Matthew 11:28-30).

What about you? What would you do this week that would truly bring rest to your soul? God may be eagerly waiting and hoping you'll do that very thing, too!

LESSON 36: PEOPLE WILL WORSHIP, BUT WHAT?   FEBRUARY 19

Scripture Reading: Exodus 32:1-6

As human beings, we want to worship something. We desire to worship, we're wired to worship, and we will worship. But what will we worship?

One of my missionary friends says that his definition of missions is to help people turn away from worshiping anything that was pulling them away from God, so that they could worship the One True God. It isn't a matter of whether or not people will worship, but a matter of who or what they will worship.

Exodus 32 gives us one of the clearest pictures of this truth in the Bible.

While Moses was spending forty days and nights in the presence of God, getting the detailed plans for what God wanted them to do next, the Israelites were growing impatient down at the bottom of the mountain. They went to Moses' right-hand man and brother, Aaron, saying,

> "Come, make us gods who will go before us. As for this fellow Moses who brought us up out of Egypt, we don't know what has happened to him" (Exodus 32:1b).

Now Aaron, having seen all the great signs and wonders that God had just finished doing for the people, should have naturally said something like this: "Didn't you see that pillar of fire? That cloud of smoke? Those Egyptians smashed by the waves of the sea? What are you thinking?" But that's not what Aaron said. He said:

> " 'Take off the gold earrings that your wives, your sons and your daughters are wearing, and bring them to me.' So all the people took off their earrings and brought them to Aaron. He took what they handed him and made it into an idol cast in the shape of a calf, fashioning it with a tool. Then they said, 'These are your gods, O Israel, who brought you up out of Egypt.' ... Afterward they sat down to eat and drink and got up to indulge in revelry" (Exodus 32:2-4, 6b).

The people grew impatient waiting for what God had in mind for them. God knew it was in their hearts to shape and fashion things out of gold. He had a blueprint in mind for them that was about to blow them away with the magnificence and awe of it and would inspire in their hearts for impassioned worship. But instead, they chose to put their God-given skills to use in ways that took them further from God, instead of drawing them closer to Him.

I had a friend who told me about her 32-year old daughter who had decided to pursue a lesbian relationship. My friend asked me how she could continue to show love and acceptance to her daughter, without approving of the relationship. She especially wondered how she could possibly ask her daughter to give up this relationship, when it seemed like this was the first time her daughter had been happy in her entire life. What could I say?

I told her: "Your daughter may be really happy for the first time in her life. It sounds like she's found someone who loves and accepts her. There's nothing wrong with a loving and accepting friendship—we all need those. But it's the sexualization of that friendship that isn't what God wants for her. If she thinks what she has now is good, imagine what God has in store for her! God says He can do immeasurably more than all we can ask or imagine."

I know in my own life I was happy, having fun, and thought I was doing fine—until I put my faith in Christ. But when I started reading the Bible, I saw that God had more in store for me. What I was doing would never bring me to that point, and would probably destroy me, like it eventually destroyed the Israelites. Many of them died as a result.

Looking back on my life, the happiness I experienced then pales in comparison to what God has given me now. I was trying to meet my valid needs, but in invalid ways.

We're all going to worship something. It's a valid need we all have. But only by worshiping the One True God can we truly satisfy that need, for our benefit, and for His.

LESSON 37: WE CAN TURN PEOPLE BACK WHEN THEY TURN AWAY — FEBRUARY 20

Scripture Reading: Exodus 32:7-14

Have you ever tried to help someone out with their life, only to see them turn away from God? You wonder if they'll ever turn back around? You think to yourself, "Man, I could really help that person if they would just let me."

I want to encourage you that all is not lost when our friends, family, or co-workers turn away from God. Even though they may be quick to turn away from God, we can turn them back. We have the power of the Living God in our lives to help turn their lives around.

Take encouragement from what happened to Moses in Exodus chapter 32. When God and Moses finished talking on the mountain, God gave Moses a heads-up about what was going on back at camp. God said:

> "Go down, because your people, whom you brought up out of Egypt, have become corrupt. They have been quick to turn away from what I commanded them and have made themselves an idol cast in the shape of a calf. They have bowed down to it and sacrificed to it and have said, 'These are your gods, O Israel, who brought you up out of Egypt'" (Exodus 32:8-9).

If you've followed the story of these people up to this point, what do you think you would do with them now? They've just seen miracle after miracle after miracle of God working in their lives. They've just been set free from 400 years of bondage in slavery. Yet here they are, a short time later, and again, they're turning their back on God.

Here's what God thought of doing at this point:

> "I have seen these people," the LORD said to Moses, "and they are a stiff-necked people. Now leave me alone so that my anger may burn against them and that I may destroy them. Then I will make you into a great nation" (Exodus 32:10).

Moses may have felt the exact same thing. But when Moses heard what God was about to do, something clicked within Moses. He said, in effect, "No, God, don't do it!"

Moses didn't plead the innocence of the people, like we might try to do regarding our friends, saying, "It's just a calf, they'll turn back. Let 'em go, it's no big deal." Moses didn't try to argue on the people's behalf based on their merit, but based on God's promises:

> "O LORD," he said, "why should your anger burn against your people, whom you brought out of Egypt with great power and a mighty hand? Why should the Egyptians say, 'It was with evil intent that he brought them out, to kill them in the mountains and to wipe them off the face of the earth'? Turn from your fierce anger; relent and do not

bring disaster on your people. Remember your servants Abraham, Isaac and Israel, to whom you swore by your own self: 'I will make your descendants as numerous as the stars in the sky and I will give your descendants all this land I promised them, and it will be their inheritance forever.' " Then the LORD relented and did not bring on his people the disaster he had threatened (Exodus 32:8-14).

Something similar happened back in Genesis chapter 6 when God threatened to destroy the earth with a flood. But on account of Noah, God gave humanity another chance.

While it's true that people can be quick to turn away from God, it's also true that we can turn them back. We have the power of the Living God with us to help turn their lives around.

We can stand in the gap for them. We can pray for them. We can listen to them, speak the truth to them, and show love to them. Remember that God is *"not wanting anyone to perish, but everyone to come to repentance"* (2 Peter 3:9b).

Call out to God on their behalf, saying, "God, please spare my daughter from the bad decisions she's made. Spare my son, my boss, my mother, my father, my brother, my friend. Have mercy on them Lord, not because of their goodness, but because of Yours. In Jesus' name, Amen."

LESSON 38: WE MUST DEAL WITH SIN WITH A HEART LIKE JESUS FEBRUARY 21

Scripture Reading: Exodus 32:15-35

If we want to help set others free from sin, at some point we must deal with their sin. But the way we deal with it makes all the difference in the world.

We can learn a lesson from the way Moses dealt with the sin of his people when they created a golden calf and began to worship it.

Moses was hot with anger at their sin, and God called Moses to administer justice to the people. But even in Moses' righteous anger, he only took things as far as God told him to—and no further. Even more important, he showed his true heart for God and for the people, by offering his own life as a willing sacrifice in their place.

Take a look at what Moses said the day after he had to administer God's justice to the people:

"The next day Moses said to the people, 'You have committed a great sin. But now I will go up to the LORD; perhaps I can make atonement for your sin.' So Moses went back to the LORD and said, 'Oh, what a great sin these people have committed! They have made themselves gods of gold. But now, please forgive their sin—but if not, then blot me out of the book you have written'" (Exodus 32:31-32).

Moses had done what God had told him to do, but his words reveal the heart from which he had done it. He admitted that the people had sinned, not glossing over it, not trying to minimize it, but acknowledging that it was great indeed. But he also called on God to forgive their sin, adding that if God wouldn't forgive them, then to please blot his own name out of God's book.

Moses was able to effectively execute justice because he was also willing to take the same punishment upon himself as what might have come to those who had sinned. He didn't come against them as one who was merely outraged by their actions, even though he *was* outraged. He came to them as one who was also willing to stand in the gap for them.

Doesn't that sound like someone else in the Bible? It sounds to me like Jesus.

It sounds exactly like what Jesus did for us when he willingly died on the cross. He hadn't done anything wrong. In fact, He had done everything right. But because of His great love for us, He was willing to take upon Himself the punishment that we rightfully deserved for our sin.

This is the kind of heart that God wants us to have when He calls us to deal with other people's sin: a heart full of love. I've been in situations where I haven't had this kind of heart. But I've known that I've needed to do whatever it took to get this kind of heart before I would be able to effectively confront the sin in another person's life.

Even though we can't die in the place of others, as Jesus did, we can have hearts that are willing to do so. We can have the same kind of heart that Jesus had. We can walk with people through their struggles. We can talk with them as they try to find their way out. We can listen to them as they anguish over the very real, and sometimes very precious things they may need to leave behind in order to get free. We can ask God's forgiveness for them, even when they repeatedly make mistakes on their road to recovery.

The Bible says that Jesus is the only one who can condemn any of us, but instead of condemning us, He's sitting at the right hand of God, praying for us (see Romans 8:34).

That's the kind of heart God wants us to have for others when we deal with their sin. A heart that can feel the pain that God feels when people sin, but a heart that is also willing to stand in the gap for them when they do. God wants us to deal with sin from a heart full of love—a heart just like Jesus.

LESSON 39: MEETING WITH GOD   FEBRUARY 22

Scripture Reading: Exodus 33:1-17

For me, one of the most encouraging things to read about in the Bible is when people meet with God. It's amazing to me that God not only met with people in the Bible, but that He also wants to meet with us.

One of those biblical meetings occurs in the middle of Exodus chapter 33, which describes how Moses would often meet with God.

> "Now Moses used to take a tent and pitch it outside the camp some distance away, calling it the 'tent of meeting.' Anyone inquiring of the LORD would go to the tent of meeting outside the camp. And whenever Moses went out to the tent, all the people rose and stood at the entrances to their tents, watching Moses until he entered the tent. As Moses went into the tent, the pillar of cloud would come down and stay at the entrance, while the LORD spoke with Moses. Whenever the people saw the pillar of cloud standing at the entrance to the tent, they all stood and worshiped, each at the entrance to his tent. The LORD would speak to Moses face to face, as a man speaks with his friend. Then Moses would return to the camp, but his young aide Joshua son of Nun did not leave the tent" (Exodus 33:7-11).

This passage is tucked in the midst of a very difficult time in the life of the Israelites. God was really angry with them for what they had just done, by turning away from Him. After dealing with their sin, God told them to go ahead of Him into the promised land. Then God added, *"But I will not go with you, because you are a stiff-necked people and I might destroy you on the way" (Exodus 33:3b).*

The people were distressed to hear this. So Moses did again what was apparently something he had been doing already on a regular basis. He went out to meet with God in the "tent of meeting."

I think many of us go through times when we feel like God is really close to us, then go through other times when we feel He is far from us. There are many reasons for this kind of ebb and flow in our relationship with God. But I know for me, if God seems distant, I want to make sure it isn't because I have become "stiff-necked," like God described had happened to the people in this passage. I want to make sure my neck is well-lubricated, and fully turned towards Him.

I remember an author who described a time in his own life when he was feeling empty in the things he was doing for God. He realized that he was using his own skills and abilities more and more to serve God, but relying on God less and less. In order to regain His full reliance on God to do what God had called him to do, he realized he needed to turn back to God again in a personal relationship that was real and vibrant.

As part of his personal renewal, he made a commitment to himself to write out his dialog with God daily, filling at least one page of a notebook per day. By intentionally carving out time to be with God again, he was able to recapture the joy and fullness of serving Him.

We don't have to deliberately sin to feel like God is distant. But sometimes through our busy-ness, laziness, or plain neglect, we can find ourselves farther and farther from the one true relationship that matters most: our relationship with God.

God wants to meet with us. And when we put our faith in Christ, God promises to send His Holy Spirit to not only meet with us, but to live within us (see Romans 8:11), and to speak with us, too:

> *"But when he, the Spirit of truth, comes, he will guide you into all truth. He will not speak on his own; he will speak only what he hears, and he will tell you what is yet to come" (John 16:13).*

God wants to meet with you, too. Take time to meet with Him today.

LESSON 40: WE'RE SET FREE TO WORSHIP   FEBRUARY 23

Scripture Reading: Exodus 33:11

We've reached lesson 40 of this 50 lesson study of the book of Exodus. Before we head into the final 10 lessons of this study, I'd like to remind you of the purpose of "the Exodus," of getting free, in the first place.

God sets us free so we can worship Him. We don't have to wait till we die and go to heaven to be in the presence of God. We don't have to wait till we get to the end of some spiritual journey to be with Him. We don't even have to wait one more minute.

We can worship God in our hearts right now. We can spend time in His presence, commune with Him, at any given moment.

There's a little passage tucked in Exodus 33 that reminds me of this. The Bible says that when Moses would want to spend time with God, he would go to the "Tent of Meeting," and God would meet with him there. But then the Bible adds these words:

> "Then Moses would return to the camp, but his young aide Joshua son of Nun did not leave the tent" (Exodus 33:11b).

I try to picture what it would be like to be a young aide to Moses, the great deliverer of the people of Israel. What would it be like to walk beside him into the tent of meeting, and watch him as the Lord would, *"speak to Moses face to face, as a man speaks to his friend"* (Exodus 33:11a)?

I think it would be awesome! Apparently, so did Joshua. Since Moses was the leader of the nation, he had to then go back to the camp to deal with the issues of the day. But not Joshua. Joshua stayed. He wasn't about to leave that tent. He was going to stay right there in the presence of God.

Although they hadn't reached the promised land yet, they could still spend time in the presence of God. Although they hadn't resolved all of the problems and struggles of life, they could still worship Him. Although they were still in the midst of one of the worst struggles of their nation, this didn't deter Joshua from spending time in the "tent of meeting." Rather than deterring the people, it probably drove them even deeper into the presence of the Living God.

Sometimes we think that we have to reach a certain place in our freedom before we can fully worship God. We think that we have to get free of a particular sin or be fully restored from a broken relationship. Or we wonder if we might never really be able to worship God here on this earth, but will only get to *truly* enter His presence when we die.

But this passage in Exodus, as well as many others throughout the Bible, encourage me that we can, at any moment, step into the presence of God. Sure, it's a lot easier to step into His presence when we're not weighted down with sin and strife and struggle. That's why God wants us so desperately to throw off anything that might entangle us.

And yet, sometimes, it's the very act of coming into His presence that helps us to finally surrender our grip on those things that are holding us back, letting God Himself take the weights off of our shoulders. As Joshua would later find out, when Moses died and Joshua had to take over the leadership of the entire nation, those regular moments in the presence of God would prove invaluable to his own effectiveness as a leader.

Whether there's peace all around you, or strife swirling out of control, I'd like to encourage you to step into God's presence sometime today, even right now if you can. Like Joshua, maybe you can just stay there and linger awhile with God, like a honeymoon couple enjoying some intimate moments together.

Worshiping God is one of the most glorious, life-giving, and life producing acts in which we can engage. It's the reason God set us free in the first place. Why not take a little time to just step into His presence today?

LESSON 41: ASK GOD TO SHOW YOU HIS GLORY   FEBRUARY 24

Scripture Reading: Exodus 33:18-23

I'd like you to listen in to a conversation that took place several thousand years ago between God and Moses. In this conversation, you'll learn something about what it's like to have an intimate relationship with God, and what you can do to take that relationship even deeper.

The conversation takes place in chapter 33 of the book of Exodus. Moses has just been pleading with God to come with him on the next leg of his journey.

> The LORD replied, "My Presence will go with you, and I will give you rest." Then Moses said to him, "If your Presence does not go with us, do not send us up from here. How will anyone know that you are pleased with me and with your people unless you go with us? What else will distinguish me and your people from all the other people on the face of the earth?"
> And the LORD said to Moses, "I will do the very thing you have asked, because I am pleased with you and I know you by name."
> Then Moses said, "Now show me your glory."
> And the LORD said, "I will cause all my goodness to pass in front of you, and I will proclaim my name, the LORD, in your presence" (Exodus 33:14-19a).

What's amazing to me about this conversation is that throughout this whole journey called "the exodus" from Egypt, Moses has been walking with God, talking with God, and seeing God work in various ways. And yet, here in chapter 33, Moses is still asking to see more and more of God. He says to God, "Now show me your glory."

One of the lessons I get out of this conversation is that no matter how close we are to God, or how close we have been in the past, we can always go deeper with Him. There's always more to learn about Him. There's always more that God wants to reveal to us about Himself, if we're willing to ask.

Maybe this is one of the reasons God makes it possible for us to spend eternity in heaven with Him when we put our faith in Christ, because it will take that long to get to know Him as deeply as possible.

This idea of spending time with God so that we can get to know Him more is a huge part of what it means to experience His "glory." If you look closely at the conversation, you'll see that God says that He knows Moses by name. He knows who Moses is. He knows what makes Moses tick. He knows his *name*. So when Moses asks to see God's glory, God replies, in essence, "All right, I'll show you *My* name, too. I'll show you more of who I am." God knows Moses, and Moses wants to know God.

In the purest sense, this is at the heart of what it means to be intimate with someone else: to reveal more of yourself to them, and to invite them to reveal more of themselves to you.

In fact, the Hebrew word often used in the Bible to describe the conception of a child is "yada," which means "to know." When the Bible says that "Adam knew Eve," it means that they were so intimate that they conceived a child! (see Genesis 4:1, NKJV) Interestingly, this same word "yada" is used to describe the intimacy that takes place when we worship God, an intimacy in which we reveal more of ourselves to Him, and He reveals more of Himself to us.

God invites us to be intimate with Him, to worship Him with our entire beings. He wants us to love Him with all of our heart, soul, mind and strength, not rushing through these moments of intimacy, but taking the time to reveal ourselves to each other.

No matter how close to, or far away from God you might feel, take some extra time today to ask Him to reveal more of Himself to you. Ask God to show you His glory.

LESSON 42: ABSORB THE NAME OF THE LORD — FEBRUARY 25

Scripture Reading: Exodus 34:1-7

If God wore a name tag, I think today's scripture passage would be on it. A person's name often reveals something about who they are. This was especially true in biblical days. The name "Moses," for instance, meant "drawn out of the water," which describes exactly how he was rescued from the Nile River by one of Pharaoh's daughters.

God's name reveals to us who He is, too. So when Moses says to God in Exodus 34, "show me Your glory," God responds by saying that He would cause His "name" to pass in front of Moses, thus revealing to Moses more about who He is. Here's what God says:

> "Then the LORD came down in the cloud and stood there with him and proclaimed his name, the LORD. And he passed in front of Moses, proclaiming, 'The LORD, the LORD, the compassionate and gracious God, slow to anger, abounding in love and faithfulness, maintaining love to thousands, and forgiving wickedness, rebellion and sin. Yet he does not leave the guilty unpunished; he punishes the children and their children for the sin of the fathers to the third and fourth generation'" (Exodus 34:5-7).

God's name tag would read something like this: "Hello, my name is… Compassionate. Gracious. Slow to Anger. Abounding in Love and Faithfulness. Forgiving, Yet Just."

To me, it's an Old Testament description of what Christ came to demonstrate for us in the New Testament. The prophet Jeremiah later tells us that God is going to make a new covenant with the people, not one written on tablets of stone, but one that would be written on people's hearts. Not a covenant where the children would have to pay for the sins of their fathers, but one where each person would be called to account for their own sins.

Some people think that God is portrayed in the Old Testament as being easily provoked to anger. But the way I read it, I see God as incredibly compassionate, gracious and slow to anger. If you read the Bible from beginning to end, you'll see a repeating pattern of God drawing people to Himself, then people turning away. God draws them back, then they turn away. He draws them again, then they turn away again. At some point, if God is a "just" God, He must eventually punish sin.

But if God were merely "just," He would have wiped out the entire planet long ago. In fact, way back in Genesis chapter 6, just six chapters into the history of man, God was tempted to do just that because of the wickedness of the people. But God relented and gave mankind another chance. And another. And another. The fact that any of us are still alive today is a testimony to God's compassion, grace, and ability to be slow to anger. The fact that God sent Jesus to die, so that anyone who would put their faith in Him would be saved from the punishment of death, shows that He is still willing to go to incredible lengths to be forgiving, yet just.

I've heard the difference between justice, mercy and grace described by the different possible reactions of a man who had caught a thief trying to steal a brand new Harley-Davidson motorcycle from his garage. If the owner grabbed a gun and shot the thief, or escorted him to jail, that would be justice. The thief was stealing his stuff, and stealing is wrong, so justice requires some kind of penalty.

But if the owner said, "I'm just going to let you go and walk out of here now. Even though what you've done is wrong, I'm not going to touch you, just go," that would be mercy.

But if the owner turned around, went back into the house and got the keys to the Harley, came back and handed them to the thief, signed over the title to him, and handed him $100 to put gas in it, that would be grace.

And that's what God has done for us through Christ:

> "But God demonstrates his own love for us in this: While we were still sinners, Christ died for us" (Romans 5:8).

Take time to absorb the name of the Lord, realizing how incredibly loving and gracious He is. Then remember to extend that same love and grace to others.

LESSON 43: WORSHIP AND WONDER — FEBRUARY 26

Scripture Reading: Exodus 34:8-10

I've had moments in my life where something will happen and I'll think, "Wow, that was the presence of God passing right in front of me."

I don't always sense His presence like this, but when I do, I'm usually taken aback by it, and I'm not quite sure how to react. It's overwhelming, on one hand, to realize that God has just passed by. But it's often such a small thing, on the other hand, that alerts me to His presence, that it makes me stop and think, "Was that really God?"

I love how Moses responds when the presence of God passed by Him in Exodus chapter 34:

> "Moses bowed to the ground at once and worshiped. 'O Lord, if I have found favor in your eyes,' he said, 'then let the Lord go with us. Although this is a stiff-necked people, forgive our wickedness and our sin, and take us as your inheritance.' Then the LORD said: 'I am making a covenant with you. Before all your people I will do wonders never before done in any nation in all the world. The people you live among will see how awesome is the work that I, the LORD, will do for you'" (Exodus 34:8-10).

Moses' response was immediate: he bowed down and worshiped, "at once."

The night before I wrote this lesson, I had one of those moments where I felt God's presence passing by.

All week I had been thinking about an illustration of what grace looks like that I had read twenty years ago in Victor Hugo's book, *Les Miserables*. In the book, a thief takes refuge in the home of a bishop, who was the first person who offered the thief a meal and lodging since his escape from prison. As they prepared for bed that night, the bishop handed the thief a silver candlestick to light his way to his bedroom for the night.

In the middle of the night, the thief's heart became hard again and he took the opportunity to escape while he still could, stealing the silver utensils that they had used for dinner as he left the house. But early the next morning, the police caught the thief and brought him back to the bishop's house. The bishop exclaimed, "Oh, you are back again! I am glad to see you. I gave you the candlesticks, too, which are silver also, and will bring forty francs. Why did you not take them?"

The thief was stunned, as were the police. The bishop added solemnly, "Never forget you have promised me you would use the money to become an honest man," which is exactly what happened.

I remembered that picture of grace from Hugo's book and wanted to share it with others, but didn't know where in my house to find the book I had once read. The night before I was to write this lesson, my 8 year-old son and I were reading from another book, a large collection of short stories, when my son said, "I'd like to just flip through the pages and pick a story with my fingers." He ran his fingers through the 832 page book and opened it. I stared in disbelief at the title of the story in front of my eyes. It was called, *The Good Bishop*, and it gave a short, 3-page summary of this very incident with the candlesticks from Victor Hugo's book, *Les Miserables.*

I felt as if the presence of God had just passed by.

I wanted to bow down and worship. Not just because God had found the story for me that I had been looking for, in a place where I never would have looked for it, but because earlier in the day I was wondering why some of the "big" things I've been praying about have not yet been answered.

I was reminded that God is not just in the big things—and He's not just in the little things. God is in *every* thing.

The next time God passes by, what will your response be? I'm praying that more and more, my response will be like that of Moses, to bow down at once, and worship.

LESSON 44: OUR ROLE AND GOD'S ROLE   FEBRUARY 27

Scripture Reading: Exodus 34:11-28

We're going to look in this lesson at something that puzzles a lot of people, including me. Sometimes we wonder how much we have to do for God, and how much He's going to do for us. It's hard to find the balance. The truth is that we both have roles to play. God has things He wants us to do, and then there are things He says He'll do.

A quick look at Exodus chapter 34, verses 10-28, when God made a covenant with the Israelites, shows these two roles. If you take a look at that passage, you'll see that God says there are things He's going to do, and then He says there are things He wants them to do.

Here are a few things that God says He's going to do for them:

- *He'll do wonders never before done in any nation of the world (verse 10)*
- *He'll drive out the nations ahead of them (verse 11)*
- *He'll enlarge their territory (verse 24)*

And here are a few things that God wants them to do:

- *Obey what He commands (verse 11)*
- *Don't make cast idols (verse 17)* (I think this was just a reminder about the golden calf, "That was a bad move guys, don't ever do that again, OK?")
- *Celebrate the feasts and make sure to rest every seventh day (verses 18 and 21)*

I think this is helpful for our own understanding of how we interact with God.

Sometimes we might sit back and mistakenly say, "It's all in Your hands God. I'm not going to do a thing. I'm leaving it all up to You." There are times when it's important to simply pray, and pray, and pray. But prayer is a conversation with God, and oftentimes during those conversations, God tells us things that He wants us to do. In those times, we've got to do our part.

Other times, we might mistakenly think that we've got to do everything. We think that if we don't do it, it won't get done. We act as if God's not likely to do *anything* for us. We forget that God has a huge role to play in everything we do. In the case of the Israelites, God's role was to do certain things, like performing wonders never before done in any nation of the world, driving out nations before them, and enlarging their territory—little things like that.

So there are often these two things going on at the same time: things God will do, and things He wants us to do. We need to trust God to do His part, and we need to do our part to the best of our ability.

There's a final point in this passage that I don't want you to miss. God ends His conversation with Moses with these words:

> *"Then the LORD said to Moses, 'Write down these words, for in accordance with these words I have made a covenant with you and with Israel.' Moses was there with the LORD forty days and forty nights without eating bread or drinking water. And he wrote on the tablets the words of the covenant—the Ten Commandments" (Exodus 34:27-28).*

Moses had just finished two back-to-back 40-day fasts. He had totally emptied himself so he could be totally filled with God. The words that God spoke to Moses in those quiet times together turned out to be some of the longest lasting words in the history of the world: the Ten Commandments. Three thousand years later they are still some of the most talked-about and cherished words ever written.

Our quiet times with God have power. This Exodus study is proof of that to me. It was during my own 40-day fast, almost three years before writing this devotional, that I first took the notes from the book of Exodus that have resulted in this study. What we do in our quiet times with God can have an effect days, months and even years into the future.

God wants us to spend time with Him, and to act on what He tells us to do during that time. God will do His part. He just wants us to do ours.

LESSON 45: SPENDING TIME IN GOD'S PRESENCE CHANGES US   FEBRUARY 28

Scripture Reading: Exodus 34:29-35

If you've ever read through the book of Psalms, you may have noticed that King David doesn't always go into God's presence with a really happy attitude, but he usually comes out with one.

Just flip through the Psalms and see how many times this happens. Psalm 4, for instance, starts with, "Answer me when I call to you, O my righteous God. Give me relief from my distress; be merciful to me and hear my prayer" (verse 1), but it ends with, "I will lie down in peace, for you alone, O LORD, make me dwell in safety" (verse 8).

Over and over the pattern repeats. David starts out pretty angry with God, and angry with the people around him, but he ends up by praising God and trusting Him completely. Why?

Because spending time in God's presence changes us. Sometimes we don't even notice the change, but others do. And when they notice the change in us, it changes them, too.

Take a look at the change that took place in Moses when he spent time in God's presence. In Exodus chapter 34, the change was so visible, it was reflected in his face:

> *"When Moses came down from Mount Sinai with the two tablets of the Testimony in his hands, he was not aware that his face was radiant because he had spoken with the LORD. When Aaron and all the Israelites saw Moses, his face was radiant, and they were afraid to come near him. But Moses called to them; so Aaron and all the leaders of the community came back to him, and he spoke to them. Afterward all the Israelites came near him, and he gave them all the commands the LORD had given him on Mount Sinai. When Moses finished speaking to them, he put a veil over his face. But whenever he entered the LORD's presence to speak with him, he removed the veil until he came out. And when he came out and told the Israelites what he had been commanded, they saw that his face was radiant. Then Moses would put the veil back over his face until he went in to speak with the LORD"* (Exodus 34:29-35).

Here's a man with a super-tan! Moses had just asked God in Exodus chapter 33: "Show me your glory." Later, when Moses came down from the mountain, he had God's glory all over him! He was so radiant, so physically changed, that he had to put a veil over his face when he talked to other people!

Spending time in God's presence changes us. The more time we spend with God, the more we're changed we'll be—physically, emotionally, spiritually—in all kinds of ways. Whenever we ask to see God's glory, we shouldn't be surprised to find that His glory is reflected in us.

What causes the moon to shine so bright? It's the reflection of the sun. There's nothing inherent in the moon to make it light up the night. That's what God wants to do through each one of us. He wants us to spend time with Him, absorbing His glory, so we can go out and reflect the light of His Son into the darkness of the world around us.

Moses wasn't even aware how his time with God had changed him. But others were. The glory that covered Moses was certainly for Moses' benefit, but it also overflowed to all of those around him.

If you'll diligently spend time with God, you'll start to see that the overflow from your time with Him will naturally touch other people. Although this may not be your main purpose for spending time with God, He can use the overflow of your experience to "prime the pump" for others.

Spending time in God's presence changes us. Although you may come into His presence tired, angry, frustrated or broken, chances are good that a little time with the Creator of the universe, the One who gave you life and breath, will give you new life, too. He'll restore you, encourage you, strengthen you and help you to put your trust in Him more and more.

LESSON 46: MAKE THE CALL TO ALL WHO ARE WILLING AND SKILLED   MARCH 1

Scripture Reading: Exodus 35:1-36:7

If God has put a vision on your heart to do something for Him, I want to encourage you today to take a step of faith: make the call to all who are willing and skilled to help you do what God wants done.

If you're like me, asking for help is one of the hardest parts of carrying out God's will. But I'm encouraged by what I read in Exodus chapter 35. Here we see that Moses has come down from the mountain with a detailed vision in mind for what God wanted him to do next: to build an incredible place of worship for God. Now, it's time for Moses to ask the people for their help, to see if they will provide the resources and the labor to make it happen. How will he ask them? And how will they respond? Let's take a look:

> *"Moses said to the whole Israelite community, 'This is what the LORD has commanded: From what you have, take an offering for the LORD. Everyone who is willing is to bring to the LORD an offering of gold, silver and bronze; blue, purple and scarlet yarn and fine linen; goat hair; ram skins dyed red and hides of sea cows; acacia wood; olive oil for the light; spices for the anointing oil and for the fragrant incense; and onyx stones and other gems to be mounted on the ephod and breastpiece. All who are skilled among you are to come and make everything the LORD has commanded...'" (Exodus 35:4-10).*

He calls on all who are willing and skilled to "give" to the work and to "get involved" in the work. Now let's look at the response:

> *"Then the whole Israelite community withdrew from Moses' presence, and everyone who was willing and whose heart moved him came and brought an offering to the LORD for the work on the Tent of Meeting, for all its service, and for the sacred garments. ... All the Israelite men and women who were willing brought to the LORD freewill offerings for all the work the LORD through Moses had commanded them to do" (Exodus 35:21, 29).*

In the end, God had stirred the hearts of so many people that they had to be restrained from giving any more!

> *"Then Moses gave an order and they sent this word throughout the camp: 'No man or woman is to make anything else as an offering for the sanctuary.' And so the people were restrained from bringing more, because what they already had was more than enough to do all the work" (Exodus 36:6-7).*

When I first read this passage, I wondered what that must feel like, to see people give and get involved to such an extent that they had to be restrained from giving any more. But when I came back to this passage again to teach it to others, I was in the middle of raising funds for five of us to go on a missions trip to Africa. Up to that point, I had often questioned if we'd be able to raise enough for even one of us to go, let alone five.

I took encouragement from this passage and kept pressing on. In the final weeks before our trip, I found myself having to tell people to not give any more to the trip, for we had already raised all that we needed for all five of us to go.

We can sometimes look at a passage like this, and even hear a story like I just told, and be either discouraged or encouraged, wondering why it's not happening to us, or looking forward to when it will happen to us.

My encouragement to you is to make the call. Make the call to all who are willing to help you carry out the vision that God has put on your heart. As Christians, God has entrusted us with great visions, great plans and great ways to reach the world for Him. God wants us to step out in faith, make the call, and ask people to give and get involved in doing what God wants done. Make the call!

LESSON 47: DO THE WORK   MARCH 2

Scripture Reading: Exodus 36:8-39:32

I don't know about you, but there are times when I've planned, prayed and gotten things ready to take on a huge project, but by the time it comes to do the work, I'm already exhausted! I feel like a woman who's nine months pregnant, but when it comes time to push, I don't have the strength.

When we feel like we can't push any farther, that's often when we need to push the most. That's often the culmination of all that we've worked so hard to achieve up to that point. If we stop pushing at the moment of delivery, we're going to shortchange, and possibly even abort, the whole plan.

We've come to that point in the book of Exodus, too. We're on Lesson 47 out of 50. With just three lessons to go, the people are finally ready to do the work that God had given Moses such a detailed vision for back on the mountaintop. Take a look at just a few of the verses as the work begins:

> *"All the skilled men among the workmen made the tabernacle with ten curtains of finely twisted linen and blue, purple and scarlet yarn, with cherubim worked into them by a skilled craftsman. All the curtains were the same size—twenty-eight cubits long and four cubits wide. They joined five of the curtains together and did the same with the other five. Then they made loops of blue material along the edge of the end curtain in one set, and the same was done with the end curtain in the other set. They also made fifty loops on one curtain and fifty loops on the end curtain of the other set, with the loops opposite each other. Then they made fifty gold clasps and used them to fasten the two sets of curtains together so that the tabernacle was a unit" (Exodus 36:8-13).*

The description of all the work continues in similar detail for another three chapters. Sometimes we can skip over these details in the Bible, but this is the foundation for what God called them to do. They came out of the desert to worship God, and now they're building a place of worship to do it.

When I studied this passage initially, I heard about a songwriting contest. I had written a song about five years earlier that I really liked and had put a lot of time into, but never recorded it. The contest turned out to be just the thing I needed to finally spur me on to do the work and get it recorded. Although I didn't exactly have the time to mess with this kind of thing, I felt like I needed to follow through on all the work I had previously done on the song.

So I stepped out of my comfort zone and sent an email to a woman in California. I loved her voice, but didn't have any money to pay her for this project. I asked her if she'd still be willing to record the song for this contest, anyway. Amazingly, she said, "Yes," and asked some of her friends to help her record it.

It turned out to be a beautiful recording, and although we didn't win the contest, I was so thankful to have it recorded. When I called to thank her for her work on it, she said, "Oh, no, thank you! Thank you for asking and letting me do it!" She told me how the song had really ministered to her that week as she worked on it. Had I not "made the call" to get the work done, the song still wouldn't be recorded, and those involved would have missed out on the blessing it turned out to be to them as well.

I know how hard it can be to "do the work" when the time finally comes to do it.

But for whatever project God's given you, don't lose heart. Don't lose strength. This final push could be what finally delivers your "baby." Many people will be blessed through your work, including those who work on it with you!

So don't give up. Don't give in. Don't stop pushing now. Do the work! And get it done!

LESSON 48: FINISH THE WORK   MARCH 3

Scripture Reading: Exodus 39:33-40:33

We're just around the corner from the end of this study of the book of Exodus. Appropriately, then, this lesson is called, "Finish the Work."

Today is "payday" for Moses and for all the people traveling with him. They're about to reach the culmination of all that they've worked for, and all that they've been set free for: to worship God.

The details of their work, as listed in Exodus chapters 39 and 40, might seem trivial, dull and something to skip over to someone just skimming through the Bible. But if you've ever worked on a building project yourself, you know that when the end of the project starts coming into view, those days can be some of the most exciting and beautiful days of the entire project!

Can you imagine what the people who were building this place of worship must have thought as they saw it all finally coming together? They've just carved all these beautiful things, gilded them with gold, and decorated them with all kinds of precious stones. They've just crafted beautiful works of art that were conceived in the very mind of God Himself.

Then they started bringing them forward to Moses, letting him look over each item to see that it was finished exactly as God had described them to him on the mountain. They begin to put it all together, standing each piece up in its place. They light the lamps, burn the incense, and put the tablets of stone, the very words of God, into the ark of the covenant, and Wow! The work is finally complete!

The whole process concludes with these words:

> "So all the work on the tabernacle, the Tent of Meeting, was completed. The Israelites did everything just as the LORD commanded Moses….And so Moses finished the work" (Exodus 39:32, 40:33b).

What a powerful moment! Have you ever heard about something called the "212 Principle," popularized in a book by Mac Anderson and Sam Parker? At 211 degrees Fahrenheit, water is hot, but at 212 degrees, water boils. And when water boils, you get steam, and steam can power a locomotive. Although there's only one degree of difference between 211 and 212, that extra degree can be enough to take all the previous effort over the top!

I don't know what kind of project you might be working on right now. I don't know if you're at 211 degrees, or 150, or 98.6! But I do know that we all have a tendency to wear out when we're working on a project, even a project that God has clearly called us to do. We can get to the point where we're not sure if we can take one more step. We're not sure that we can raise the temperature one more degree. But let me encourage you that if God's called you to do it, keep on doing it!

The American inventor, Thomas Edison, worked non-stop for several years to perfect the light bulb. He tested over 6,000 materials to use for filaments—everything from bamboo to cedar to hickory. After thousands of tests and a pile of failed materials that stacked up outside his house high enough to reach his second floor window, Edison finally hit upon a material that burned long enough, and bright enough, for commercial success: carbonized cotton.

Edison's perseverance paid off, not only for himself, but for all of us who have benefited from his perseverance. Edison said, "Many of life's failures were men who did not realize how close they were to success when they gave up."

The Apostle Paul, who knew how hard it was to persevere in the work of the Lord year after year, even in the face of endless persecution, hardship and personal suffering, still had enough confidence in the end result of that perseverance that he wrote to the people living in Galatia: *"Let us not become weary in doing good, for at the proper time we will reap a harvest if we do not give up" (Galatians 6:9).*

Don't become weary in doing good! Finish the work! At the proper time, you will reap a harvest, if you do not give up.

LESSON 49: THE GLORY OF THE LORD COVERS THE WORK   MARCH 4

Scripture Reading: Exodus 40:34-38

We've come to the last five verses, and the spectacular conclusion, of the book of Exodus. Take a look at what happens when Moses finishes the work:

> *"Then the cloud covered the Tent of Meeting, and the glory of the LORD filled the tabernacle. Moses could not enter the Tent of Meeting because the cloud had settled upon it, and the glory of the LORD filled the tabernacle. In all the travels of the Israelites, whenever the cloud lifted from above the tabernacle, they would set out; but if the cloud did not lift, they did not set out—until the day it lifted. So the cloud of the LORD was over the tabernacle by day, and fire was in the cloud by night, in the sight of all the house of Israel during all their travels" (Exodus 40:34-38).*

What is it that Moses sees that so fills the tabernacle that he can't even get into it? The glory of the Lord—the very thing that Moses had asked to see back in Exodus 33:18 when he said, "Now show me your glory." But this time, Moses wasn't the only one who got to see it—everyone got to see it!

There's a lesson here for me, for you and for everyone who does their work as if working for the Lord: when you've finished the work, been obedient to the vision, and brought it to its conclusion, the glory of the Lord can finally come down on your work in a way that everyone can see it.

I've had some experiences in my life where I've sensed the presence of God in a way that I can only describe as "the glory of the Lord." I'm not an expert in the glory of the Lord, but from what I've read in the Bible, from what I've learned from other Christians, and from what I've experienced in my own life, the glory of the Lord seems to be actual "stuff," like the air we breathe. It's real, physical and tangible. It can be seen, sensed and felt.

I've sensed it during worship, when one time I was just singing to God in what seemed to be a normal, enjoyable worship experience, and all of a sudden, the presence of the Lord was so real and tangible that I felt like I couldn't move if I wanted to. And I didn't want to! I wanted to stay in His presence as long as I possibly could!

I've sensed it during my quiet times, when once I was sitting back on my couch, writing in my journal, and suddenly felt like melted butter was being poured into my chest. Maybe it was the oil of the Holy Spirit, if that sounds more palatable, but whatever words I would use to describe it couldn't do justice to what I felt during those precious minutes with the Lord.

I'd love to be able to finish a project and see the glory of the Lord come down and cover it in a way that everyone could see it, so that I couldn't even stand up anymore! At that point, I wouldn't care! If my purpose in doing all that I do is to worship the Lord, as was the case for the Israelites, then who cares if He bowls me over when it's done, and I'm laid out flat on the floor in His presence? That's right where I'd want to be anyway! I wouldn't want to go anywhere else!

If the Lord picked up and moved, I'd want to pick up and move with Him, like the Israelites who followed Him. I wouldn't want to stay back! I'd want to be with God!

My prayer for you as you work on your own projects for the Lord, and even as you come to the end of this study with me, is that when you've finished the work, been obedient to the vision, and brought it to its conclusion, that the glory of the Lord would show up in such a way that you, and everyone else, can see it.

Now, may the Lord show you His glory!

LESSON 50: FREE TO WORSHIP   MARCH 5

Scripture Reading: Exodus 3:12

Thanks for taking the time to go through this study of the book of Exodus with me. I've learned a lot from the story of how God set the Israelites free, and I hope you have, too.

As we close out our time together, I'd like to remind you of three key points from this study that apply directly to each of our lives.

1) God set the Israelites free so they could worship Him—and that's the same reason He set you free, too.

This reason is stated throughout the book of Exodus, from the first time that God called to Moses from the burning bush: *"When you have brought the people out of Egypt, you will worship God on this mountain'"* (Exodus 3:12b).

To the words Moses spoke to Pharaoh: "Go to Pharaoh and say to him, 'This is what the LORD says: Let my people go, so that they may worship me'" (Exodus 8:1b).

To the concluding scene of the entire book, when the glory of the Lord descended on the place the Israelites built to worship Him: *"Then the cloud covered the Tent of Meeting, and the glory of the LORD filled the tabernacle" (Exodus 40:34).*

To be truly free means to be able to worship God with your whole heart. If you can worship God with your whole heart, regardless of whatever else might be going on around you, you're free! But if you can't worship God in your heart, for whatever reason, you're still in bondage, and God wants to set you free.

If that's the case, you might want to review these lessons again to look for ideas to help you get fully free.

2) God helped the Israelites to stay free—and He wants to help you stay free, too.

God's help included a system of rules to keep the Israelites, and each of us, from plunging back into bondage again. These rules are summarized in the Ten Commandments:

> *"You shall have no other gods before me...*
> *You shall not make for yourself an idol...*
> *You shall not misuse the name of the LORD your God...*
> *Remember the Sabbath day by keeping it holy...*
> *Honor your father and your mother...*
> *You shall not murder.*
> *You shall not commit adultery.*
> *You shall not steal.*
> *You shall not give false testimony against your neighbor.*
> *You shall not covet..." (from Exodus 20:1-17).*

Rather than restricting us, these rules free us to live the abundant life God has created us to live.

Again, if you've gotten free in the past, but are struggling to stay free now, you might want to review these lessons again for more insights on how to restore the freedom you once had.

3) God invited Moses to take part in His plan to set others free—just like God is inviting you to take part in it, too.

Hundreds of years before Moses was even born, God had a plan for setting the Israelites free. God told Abraham:

> *"Know for certain that your descendants will be strangers in a country not their own, and they will be enslaved and mistreated four hundred years. But I will punish the nation they serve as slaves, and afterward they will come out with great possessions"* (Genesis 15:14).

And that's exactly what happened. God had a plan in mind for setting His people free, and He called on Moses to help Him with that plan.

God has a plan for setting others free, too, and He's called on you and me to help Him with that plan.

What's His plan? God knew that our sins would enslave us—and eventually kill us. So God sent Jesus, His Son, to die for our sins so we could be free to live with Him forever:

"For God so loved the world that he gave his one and only Son, that whoever believes in him shall not perish but have eternal life" (John 3:16).

After dying for our freedom, and rising again from the dead, Jesus asked His followers to do one more thing:

"Go into all the world and preach the good news to all creation" (Mark 16:15).

He's inviting you into His plan. Won't you join Him?

Jesus: Lessons in Love

30 inspiring devotionals based on the greatest "lover" of all time, Jesus Christ

INTRODUCTION TO "JESUS: LESSONS IN LOVE" - THE GREATEST COMMANDMENT
MARCH 6

Scripture Reading: Matthew 22:37-39

I've been wrestling with something I recently heard, and I'd like to share it with you. I wonder if it affects you like it affects me:

"If you're not close to people who are far from God, you're probably not as close to God as you think you are."

I don't know about you, but that makes me squirm a little bit. I've been a Christian for over twenty years. I run an Internet ministry that reaches thousands of people a month. I've been the president of our local ministers' association for several years. But if I were to judge my relationship with God by how close I am to people who are far from Him, I don't know that I'd score very high.

I want to win people to Christ. I want to make a difference in the world. But I can't say that I always want to do what it takes to love people the way Christ loved them.

I was reading a letter recently from a man who actually had Jesus over to his house for dinner. It was written by a man named Matthew. He was a tax collector who lived at the same time as Jesus.

It must have been as much of a surprise to Matthew as it was to everyone else in town when Jesus walked up to Matthew and said, "Follow me." Matthew ended up hosting a banquet at his house for Jesus.

The religious leaders were outraged. They questioned some of Jesus' followers:

"Why does your teacher eat with tax collectors and 'sinners'?"
On hearing this, Jesus said, "It is not the healthy who need a doctor, but the sick. But go and learn what this means: 'I desire mercy, not sacrifice.' For I have not come to call the righteous, but sinners" (Matthew 9:9-13).

I love Jesus' response. But it nails me as much as it nailed the religious leaders of that day. I don't want to be a Pharisee, a Sadducee, or any other kind of "-see." I want to be like Jesus.

I want to learn how to love God more. I want to learn how to love people more. And I want to learn how to love myself more.

These are, according to Jesus, the greatest of commandments:

"'Love the Lord your God with all your heart and with all your soul and with all your mind.' This is the first and greatest commandment. And the second is like it: 'Love your neighbor as yourself'" (Matthew 22:37-39).

Jesus gave us the best example for how to live out these commandments. That's why I'm going to be reading Matthew's letter again and again in the days ahead. Matthew covers the life of Jesus in 28 chapters, from the foretelling of His birth to His death and resurrection. Not only did Matthew have Jesus over for dinner, but he went on to spend the next three years of his life with Jesus, day and night.

Matthew watched how Jesus loved people, healed people, forgave people, taught people. Matthew watched as Jesus prayed to God, pleaded with God, submitted to God. Matthew watched as Jesus responded to His critics, walked away from His critics, and was eventually killed by His critics. And Matthew watched as people loved Jesus, adored Jesus, and gave up their lives for Jesus.

I love Matthew's letter for a number of reasons, not the least of which is that I put my faith in Christ twenty years ago while reading about Him in Matthew's letter. I'm so thankful that Jesus went out of His way to love people who didn't yet believe in Him, who didn't yet trust in Him, who didn't yet live their lives for Him.

I'm so thankful because I'm one of those people. And I want to be just like Him.

I hope you'll join me in the days ahead as I take a closer look, page by page through Matthew's letter, at how we can all be more like Jesus, starting next time with Chapter 1.

I also want to encourage you to read each day's Scripture Reading in your own Bible in addition to my devotional for that day. I've limited myself to touching upon just one thought in each chapter of Matthew, but there's so much God may speak to you about other subjects in your life. When you're done reading all the daily Scripture Readings, you'll have read through the entire book of Matthew.

And finally, I've included a prayer at the end of each devotional to help you focus your own prayers by praying them along with me. Here's today's prayer.

Prayer: Father, help me to be more like Jesus so that I can love You, love others and love myself more. In Jesus' name, Amen.

LESSON 1: HOW TO BEGIN LOVING OTHERS MORE   MARCH 7

Scripture Reading: Matthew 1

Jesus told a story about two people...one who loved much, and one who loved little. It's a story that I'm particularly interested in because I want to learn how to truly love God and love others more. But how? Where do I start in my desire to be more loving? I believe Jesus tells us in this story.

He told it while at a dinner party at the home of a religious leader. A woman who had lived a sinful life came into the house to find Jesus. She fell at His feet, weeping and wetting His feet with her tears, then pouring some perfume on His feet and wiping them with her hair.

The man who had invited Jesus to dinner was outraged, not so much at the woman, but at Jesus, who would allow such a sinful woman to touch Him. So Jesus said to the man:

"Simon, I have something to tell you."

"Tell me teacher," he said.

"Two men owed money to a certain moneylender. One owed him five hundred denarii, [a denarius was a coin worth about a day's wages] and the other fifty. Neither of them had the money to pay him back, so he canceled the debts of both. Now which of them will love him more?"

Simon replied, "I suppose the one who had the bigger debt canceled."

"You have judged correctly," Jesus said.

Then he turned toward the woman and said to Simon, "Do you see this woman? I came into your house. You did not give me any water for my feet, but she wet my feet with her tears and wiped them with her hair. You did not give me a kiss, but this woman, from the time I entered, has not stopped kissing my feet. You did not put oil on my head, but she has poured perfume on my feet. Therefore, I tell you, her many sins have been forgiven—for she loved much. But he who has been forgiven little loves little" (Luke 7:40-47).

Here's what I get from this story: the amount of love we have for God and for others is directly related to how much we have been forgiven. If we have been forgiven much, we will love much, but if we have been forgiven little, we will love little.

So how can I begin to grow in my love for God and for others? Sin more, so I can love more? I don't think so! I think the place to begin is to realize how very much we have already been forgiven.

How much is that? Enough for God to send Jesus to earth to die in our place for the sins we've committed.

This is where the book of Matthew starts. After giving us a detailed genealogy of where Jesus came from, Matthew tells us what Jesus came for. The angel who spoke to Joseph said it best:

"Joseph son of David, do not be afraid to take Mary home as your wife, because what is conceived in her is from the Holy Spirit. She will give birth to a son, and you are to give him the name Jesus, because he will save his people from their sins" (Matthew 1:20b-21).

Jesus came to save us from our sins. God loved us so much that He didn't want us to die because of all that we had done wrong. If our sins were serious enough for Jesus to have to die for them, they must be terribly grievous to God. And if that's true, then each of us have already been forgiven much.

We don't have to sin more to be forgiven of more in order to love more. We just need to realize how much we've already sinned, how much we've already been forgiven, and how much we've already been loved by God. Once we realize that, I believe that love will naturally flow out from within us, like tears mixed with perfume and poured out at Jesus' feet.

Prayer: Father, help us realize how much You've loved us and forgiven us, so that we can love You and love others more. In Jesus' name, Amen.

LESSON 2: SEEING PEOPLE AS GOD SEES THEM   MARCH 8

Scripture Reading: Matthew 2

Part of loving others involves seeing people as God sees them. Sometimes that takes more effort than other times!

One of the hardest, but most rewarding, parts of my ministry, is listening to people as they share some of their deepest personal sins they've committed, and listening to the pain that it's caused them, God and others. It's hard, because I'm torn between wanting to cry and wanting to run away as they pour out things that are truly unsettling. But it's rewarding, because I know that their confession often leads to greater healing than they've ever known before. As the Bible says:

> "Therefore confess your sins to each other and pray for each other so that you may be healed" (James 5:16a).

But in the midst of listening to people confess their sins, I'm also torn in another way: I'm torn in my feelings towards them as people. I want to love them, but because of what they're telling me, I sometimes wonder how I can. How can God do it? How can He continue loving people, knowing what they've done? And how can I?

Matthew 2 gives me a clue: God loves people because He sees their lives from beginning to end. He created them. He knows them intimately. And He sees them not only for what they are, but also for what they are to become.

The verses in Matthew 2 show us how much care God took to see that Jesus was born, in the right place, at the right time, and how much God was involved in moving Jesus through those early years of His life in ways that kept Him alive and on course to fulfill the purposes for which God sent Him to earth.

- Micah foretold, hundreds of years before Jesus was born, that Jesus would be born in Bethlehem (see Micah 5:2).
- Hosea foretold that Jesus would later return from Egypt, saying, "Out of Egypt I called my son" (Hosea 11:1).
- Jeremiah foretold that there would be suffering back in Bethlehem on account of Christ, saying there would be "weeping and great mourning" (Jeremiah 31:15).

If God knew these things about Jesus' life, but no one else's, I might not be convinced that God takes the same care with each of us. But God knows each of us just as intimately and has unique purposes for each of our lives.

- David says: "All the days ordained for me were written in Your book before one of them came to be" (Psalm 139:16b).
- God told Jeremiah: "Before I formed you in the womb I knew you, before you were born I set you apart; I appointed you as a prophet to the nations" (Jeremiah 1:5).
- Isaiah said: "Before I was born the Lord called me; from my birth he has made mention of my name" (Isaiah 49:1b).

And God foretold the births of people like Isaac and John the Baptist, even before they were conceived:

- *"Then the LORD said, 'I will surely return to you about this time next year, and Sarah your wife will have a son'" (Genesis 18:10).*
- *"Your wife Elizabeth will bear you a son, and you are to give him the name John" (Luke 1:13b).*

God knows each one of us, intimately, and He loves each one of us, even when we mess up terribly. I think part of the reason is that He has the ability to see our lives from beginning to end.

That's a good reminder for me when I see someone in the midst of their sin. If I can see them as God sees them, then I'll be much more likely to truly love them, and to truly help them get back on track with God's plans for their lives.

Although I don't naturally have the ability to see people as God sees them, I know God can give me that ability if I ask Him for it, the ability see people as He sees them, so I can love them as He loves them.

Prayer: Father, help me see people as You see them, so I can love them as You love them. In Jesus' name, Amen.

LESSON 3: LOVING OTHERS AS GOD LOVES THEM   MARCH 9

Scripture Reading: Matthew 3

I have a question for you. There's a point in Jesus' life where God's love for His Son, Jesus, is so full, that God speaks these words from heaven so that all those around Jesus can hear:

"This is my Son, whom I love, with Him I am well-pleased."

The question is this: At what point in Jesus' life does God speak these words? Was it:
A) After Jesus had just healed someone who was sick?
B) After He walked on water?
C) After He had raised someone from the dead?
D) After He had preached a life-changing message to a massive crowd?
E) None of the above.

If you answered, "E) None of the above," you're right. The point at which God vocalized His tremendous love for His Son wasn't after Jesus did any of these things. It takes place before every one of them. In fact, it takes place before Jesus did even one recorded miracle, or one recorded act of service to anyone else. It takes place in Matthew chapter 3, when Jesus came to John to be baptized by Him:

"As soon as Jesus was baptized, he went up out of the water. At that moment heaven was opened, and he saw the Spirit of God descending like a dove and lighting on him. And a voice from heaven said, 'This is my Son, whom I love; with him I am well pleased.'" (Matthew 3:16-17).

God loved Jesus right from the beginning of Jesus' ministry, not just at the end of it. What does this say about God's love for us and for others? Is God's love the same for us, or was it different for Jesus, because Jesus was, after all, sinless!

As a father myself, I believe God's love for us begins way before we would even think it would. My oldest daughter turned sixteen this weekend. I remember the sense of love I began to feel for her in those first moments after her birth, and then in those first days, those first weeks, and those first months as a baby. Right from the start I felt an overwhelming love for her, even though she hadn't yet done one spectacular thing for me or for anyone else. In fact, about all she did was eat, sleep, cry, and make messes that we had to clean up. But my love for her was unmeasurable.

I'm sure my love for my daughter is just a fraction of the kind of love God has for each one of us. Even before we could ever possibly do one miracle in His name, or one act of kindness, or one good deed for someone else, God loves us.

Even when all we can do is eat, sleep, cry, and make messes that He has to clean up, God loves us. Even though we're not anywhere close to being sinless, like Jesus was, God loves us. The Bible says:

> "But God demonstrates his own love for us in this: While we were still sinners, Christ died for us" (Romans 5:8).

God loves us, even though we sin. That's why He sent Jesus to die in our place. God isn't waiting for you to do something spectacular before He loves you. He loves you right now, this very minute.

If we want to love others the way that God loves them, then we need to set our hearts on loving them before they ever do even one good deed. We need to commit to loving them even when all they might do is eat, sleep, cry, and make messes that we have to clean up. We need to keep loving them, even when they sin. For when we can have a love like that in our hearts for others, then we'll be able to truly begin to love them as God loves them.

Prayer: Father, help me to have a heart like Yours, a heart that loves others for no other reason than the fact that You created them and that You love them, even when they mess up. In Jesus' name, Amen.

LESSON 4: WHAT WOULD JESUS PREACH   MARCH 10

Scripture Reading: Matthew 4

Jesus preached many things, but in Matthew chapter 4, I'm struck by one of the very first messages Jesus preached. While it was a message of love, Jesus didn't start off with the words, "Love one another," or "Do to others what you would have them do to you." Here's the way Jesus began his preaching ministry:

> "Repent, for the kingdom of heaven is near" (Matthew 4:17).

To some people, that may not sound like a very loving message for the beginning of a ministry. But from God's point of view, it's one of the most loving messages we could hear ourselves, or share with others: "Repent, for the kingdom of heaven is near." Just as John the Baptist pleaded with people to repent, to turn away from their sins, Jesus continued preaching this same message after John was put in prison.

Jesus, of all people, knew how destructive sin is in people's lives. It's so destructive that God sent Jesus to die for our sins so that we wouldn't have die for them ourselves. But even though Jesus would eventually pay the ultimate price for our sins, He still called for people to repent. Why? Because Jesus knew that our sins don't only affect us for our eternal life, but they also affect us for our life here on earth.

If the Bible is true when it says that "the wages of sin is death" (Romans 3:23), as I believe it is, then calling people to turn away from their sins so that they can have life is one of the most loving messages we could ever share. It's a message that applies to believers and non-believers alike.

All people, long-time Christians included, can be caught up in all kinds of sin. Sometimes it's easy to fall into thinking that it's OK to keep on sinning since we know that Jesus will forgive us of our sins when we ask Him. While that's true, it's also equally true that He calls us to repent of our sins. While Jesus' death spares us from the eternal consequences of our sins, He also wants to spare us from the earthly consequences of our sins.

Every sin we commit takes one more notch out of our lives. Sin destroys our relationships with God and with others. Sin keeps us from seeing clearly, acting appropriately, and experiencing the abundant life that God wants us to live.

If we want to love others like Jesus loved them, it seems that we need to be willing to preach to others like Jesus preached to them. We don't have to preach in a way that is "holier than thou," and God wants us to be wise about where, when, and with whom we share any words from Him. But if we want to have true concern for others, one of the best ways to show them that we really care for them, and love them, is to share the message of repentance with them.

The book of James is one of the most compassionate books in the whole Bible, calling believers to put their faith into action on behalf of others. In addition to calling us to do things like feed and clothe those in need, James ends his book with these words:

> "My brothers, if one of you should wander from the truth and someone should bring him back, remember this: whoever turns a sinner from the error of his way will save him from death and cover over a multitude of sins" (James 5:19-20).

The next time I'm afraid to approach someone regarding their sins, I need to remember that this is one of the most loving things I could ever do for them. If I want to truly walk as Jesus walked, I need to be willing to preach as Jesus preached. In doing so, I may be able to "save them from death and cover over a multitude of sins."

Prayer: Father, help me be willing to preach the message of repentance where, when, and to whom You call me to preach it, as a way of truly expressing Your love towards them. In Jesus' name, Amen.

LESSON 5: GETTING TO THE HEART OF LOVE — MARCH 11

Scripture Reading: Matthew 5

I tried pole vaulting back when I was in Junior High. The goal was to take a long pole in your hands, then run with all your might and plant the end of the pole in a box just in front of a bar raised high on two other bars in front of you. All I remember was that when I tried it, I felt an incredible jolt when I planted the pole in the box. Not only did I not make it over the bar, I didn't even make it off the ground!

I've since learned that part of the trick is getting the pole to bend properly. As the pole bends, it transfers all of the energy of the runner into the pole, which then helps to propel the runner up and over the bar at the top.

I bring this up because I sometimes feel the same kind of jolt when I read Jesus' words in Matthew chapter 5 about how to love others. I want to love others, and I think I'm a loving person much of the time, but as I read what true love really involves, not only do I not think I'm making it over the bar, I'm not even sure I'm making it off the ground.

The reason I feel this way is because Jesus gets to the heart of love in this passage. Rather than lowering the bar for all of us, Jesus raises it...or more accurately, He shows us what's really involved in loving others.

He gives several examples:

> *"You have heard that it was said to the people long ago, 'Do not murder, and anyone who murders will be subject to judgment.' But I tell you that anyone who is angry with his brother will be subject to judgment" (Matthew 5:21-22).*
>
> *"You have heard that it was said, 'Do not commit adultery.' But I tell you that anyone who looks at a woman lustfully has already committed adultery with her in his heart" (Matthew 5:27-28).*
>
> *"Again, you have heard that it was said to the people long ago, 'Do not break your oath, but keep the oaths you have made to the Lord.' But I tell you, Do not swear at all...Simply let your 'Yes' be 'Yes,' and your 'No,' 'No'; anything beyond this comes from the evil one" (Matthew 5:33-34, 37).*

Then He concludes with these astounding words:

> *"You have heard that it was said, 'Love your neighbor and hate your enemy.' But I tell you: Love your enemies and pray for those who persecute you, that you may be sons of your Father in heaven. He causes his sun to rise on the evil and the good, and sends rain on the righteous and the unrighteous. If you love those who love you, what reward will you get? Are not even the tax collectors doing that? And if you greet only your brothers, what are you doing more than others? Do not even pagans do that? Be perfect, therefore, as your heavenly Father is perfect" (Matthew 5:43-48).*

Talk about raising the bar! It's hard enough to be consistent in loving my wife, my family, and my friends. But to love my enemies, too? That's impossible! Or at least it would be without Christ.

When we let the love of Christ flow through us to others, all things are possible. He's able to transfer all of His energy and love into us, and then propel us over even the highest bar. And you know what? When we're able to get our hearts right and let Christ work through us to love even our enemies, imagine what kind of love we could show to those who already love us!

Rather than giving us an impossible task, Jesus shows us that true love comes from Him, then flows out to others. Let His love flow through you today.

Prayer: Father, pour out Your love into my heart again today so that I can love others the way You want me to...even my enemies. In Jesus' name, Amen.

LESSON 6: DOING A HEART CHECK	MARCH 12

Scripture Reading: Matthew 6

There are times when we need to show people that we love them. It's important that we let them know, in tangible ways, that we appreciate them, care for them, and are willing to do anything for them.

I remember talking to a husband who was about to get a divorce from his wife because she wanted them to move across the country, but he didn't want to. I asked him: "If someone were threatening your wife's life, would you be willing to die for her?" "Yes," he answered, "I would." So I added, "If you're willing to die for her, would you be willing to live for her?" He recommitted his life to Christ and to his marriage and they were soon reconciled to each other.

This kind of tangible expression of our love can make or break a relationship.

But there are other times when God calls us to do our acts of love in secret, in ways that only God Himself can see. Jesus tells us the reason why in Matthew chapter 6:

"Be careful not to do your 'acts of righteousness' before men, to be seen by them. If you do, you will have no reward from your Father in heaven. So when you give to the needy, do not announce it with trumpets, as the hypocrites do in the synagogues and on the streets, to be honored by men. I tell you the truth, they have received their reward in full. But when you give to the needy, do not let your left hand know what your right hand is doing, so that your giving may be in secret. Then your Father, who sees what is done in secret, will reward you" (Matthew 6:1-4).

This passage serves as a "heart-check" for me. When I'm considering doing some "acts of righteousness," or "acts of love," I always want to check my motives. Am I wanting to do these things out of an attempt to love others more? Or out of an attempt to get others to love me more? These are two very different things.

To reiterate this thought, Jesus gives us a second example that applies when we pray for others:

"And when you pray, do not be like the hypocrites, for they love to pray standing in the synagogues and on the street corners to be seen by men. I tell you the truth, they have received their reward in full. But when you pray, go into your room, close the door and pray to your Father, who is unseen. Then your Father, who sees what is done in secret, will reward you" (Matthew 6:5-6).

As if to underscore it one more time, Jesus gives us a third example, too:

"When you fast, do not look somber as the hypocrites do, for they disfigure their faces to show men they are fasting. I tell you the truth, they have received their reward in full. But when you fast, put oil on your head and wash your face, so that it will not be obvious to men that you are fasting, but only to your Father, who is unseen; and your Father, who sees what is done in secret, will reward you" (Matthew 6:16-18).

Each of these examples remind me that there are times when our giving, our praying, and our fasting are to be done in secret, with no thought of the fact that others may never know who gave to them, prayed for them, or fasted on behalf of them. These are good reminders to me to check my heart even when I feel prompted to express my love in a more visible way. I need to always be sure that my motivation is to truly show others how much I love them, rather than trying to get them to love me more.

God promises that He will not leave our good deeds unrewarded, but by promising to reward us Himself, it frees us from trying to get our rewards from those we're trying to love. It's this kind of heart-check that will help us to truly love others more.

Prayer: Father, help me to keep my heart in check, so that I can truly express my love for others in ways that truly blesses their lives. In Jesus' name, Amen.

LESSON 7: GOLDEN LOVE   MARCH 13

Scripture Reading: Matthew 7

One year ago this weekend, I was headed to the African country of Swaziland. Eighty of us from the U.S. were on a missions trip to work side-by-side with the people of Swaziland to plant thousands of vegetable gardens near their homes.

On the trip, I met a man who helped me see what it takes to live a life of sacrificial love. He was a pastor who had worked with this organization for over a year, helping to plant gardens throughout the country with dozens of teams that had come over to help.

One day, I was looking at a map of Swaziland with him. The map showed which areas of the country had already been planted, and which areas still needed to be planted. We were planting in one of the last areas remaining in the country, but I noticed there was still one more area yet to be planted. I asked him about it, and he said that the one remaining area was the village where he lived.

I couldn't believe it. I turned and looked at him and said, "You've been bringing teams over here, helping people plant all over the country, but you haven't brought a team to help you plant in your own village yet?"

He replied, "We have a saying here in Swaziland: 'We would rather starve than let our guests go hungry.'" He went on to explain: he wanted to make sure that all of the other areas were served first, then he would bring a team to his own area. I about burst into tears on the spot. It still makes my eyes water just thinking about it.

There's a verse of scripture in the middle of Matthew chapter 7 that people refer to as "The Golden Rule." (And it's not, "He who has the gold makes the rules"!) Jesus included these words in his sermon on the mount, saying that they sum up the teachings that God had given up to that point:

> *"So in everything, do to others what you would have them do to you, for this sums up the Law and the Prophets"* (Matthew 7:12).

Do to others what you would have them do to you. It seems like such a simple thing…and sometimes it is. If a storeowner gives you too much change at the store, you can hand back the extra change, because that's what you would want a customer to do if they came into your store. Or if you notice someone who needs money for a worthy project, you might give it to them because you know that if you needed money for a worthy project, you'd want them to help you.

But sometimes it's a much harder thing to do. Sometimes, as in the case of this pastor from Swaziland, allowing others to go ahead of you can literally mean death for someone you love.

How can anyone live that kind of life? How can anyone have that much love for others, that they would let someone in their own family perish so that someone else might live?

How? God gave us the ultimate example of just such a love when He allowed His own Son, Jesus, to die in our place. When Jesus called us to "do to others what you would have them do to you," He was calling us to do something that He Himself would soon be doing to the fullest extent, giving of His own life so that we could live.

Last time I mentioned that God wants us to be willing to live for others. This time, the call is to be willing to die for them, too. Jesus calls us to be willing to do both. When our hearts are at that point of willingness, we'll know that we have achieved the greatest love possible.

We'll have a love like that of Christ Himself who said, and then later exemplified for us, these words:

> "Greater love has no one than this, that he lay down his life for his friends" (John 15:13).

Prayer: Father, help me to do for others as I would have them do for me. In Jesus' name, Amen.

LESSON 8: LOVE THAT HEALS — MARCH 14

Scripture Reading: Matthew 8

Do you know someone who's sick? I'd like to encourage you to pray for them.

Our prayers do make a difference. When Jesus walked the earth, He was moved with compassion for those around Him, healing those who needed healing. If we want to express the love of Christ like He did, one of the things we can do is to try to alleviate the pain and suffering of those we come in contact with, too.

Take a look at what Jesus did for three people in Matthew chapter 8 who were sick: First, there's the man with leprosy who came to Jesus and said,

> "Lord, if You are willing, You can make me clean." Jesus reached out His hand and touched the man. "I am willing," He said, "Be clean!" Immediately he was cured of his leprosy (Matthew 8:2-3).

Second, there's the army officer who came to Jesus asking for help.

> "Lord," he said, "my servant lies at home paralyzed and in terrible suffering." Jesus said to him, "I will go and heal him" (Matthew 8:5-7).

When the officer protests Jesus' offer to come to his house in person because he feels he doesn't deserve to have Jesus come under his roof, Jesus sees the officers' faith and declares:

> "Go! It will be done just as you believed it would" And his servant was healed at that very hour (Matthew 8:13).

Third, there's Peter's mother-in-law, lying in bed with a fever. When Jesus came into Peter's house, Jesus saw her, touched her hand, and the fever left her. She got up and began to wait on Jesus (see Matthew 8:14-15).

These are just a few of the many acts of healing that Jesus did for those around Him. While there are many more recorded in the Bible, these are enough for me today to recognize that one of the ways we can express love to others is through healing.

I don't know what you've experienced when you've prayed for people to be healed. I've prayed for people who have been surprisingly healed, and I've prayed for others who have unfortunately died. But I come back to the fact that God is a healing God, and that Jesus regularly and consistently healed those He came in contact with. So I've continued to regularly and consistently pray for those around me to be healed, and I've seen people healed time after time.

I also take encouragement from all of the prayers that have gone before me for diseases that were once thought to be fatal and incurable. I think about diseases that here in the U.S. were once devastating, like polio, which in 1952 was out of control, crippling 21,000 people a year, mostly children, and killing 3,100. Then came doctors Salk and Sabin who searched for a solution to this epidemic and found them by producing the injectable and oral polio vaccines.

Whenever I pray for people with cancer, or other fatal, crippling or incurable diseases, I also pray that God will reveal the cure to someone, to some researcher, or even to me or to my children. God has answered such prayers in the past, and God will answer such prayers in the future. Our prayers are never in vain, when we put our faith in the God who heals and put our trust in Him with the timing and the outcome.

Pray for those around you to be healed. Type out your prayers in an email to them. Give them a call and pray for them over the phone. Take a cue from Jesus: when someone stops to tell you about their sickness, take a minute right then and there to pray for them.

There's no doubt when I read the Scriptures that one of the ways that Jesus expressed His love to others was through healing. Maybe that's a way you can express your love to others, too.

Prayer: Father, help me to pray for those who are sick, and to keep praying for them, that they would be healed in Jesus' name, Amen.

LESSON 9: BRING YOUR FRIENDS TO JESUS   MARCH 15

Scripture Reading: Matthew 9

Do you have some friends who could use a touch from Jesus? I'd like to encourage you to bring them to Him today.

Whether they need healing, a change of heart, a change of lifestyle, or a change in their eternal destination, Jesus can do it. I know, because He did it for me when I was reading Matthew chapter 9, twenty years ago. Now I want to bring as many people as I can to Jesus so He can do the same things for them.

Look with me at what Jesus did in Matthew chapter 9 when some people brought their friends and family members to Jesus:

First, we have the men who brought their paralyzed friend, lying on a mat, to be healed by Jesus. The Bible says that "when Jesus saw their faith," He healed the paralytic and forgave him of his sins. The man took up his mat and went home, and the crowd was filled with awe and praised God (see Matthew 9:1-8). Note what it was that triggered Jesus' action in this passage: it says that He did these things for the paralytic "when Jesus saw THEIR faith."

Next, we have Matthew, the author of this book of the Bible, who had Jesus over to his house for dinner. It seems that Matthew also invited many of his fellow tax collectors and other "sinners" to eat with him and Jesus and the disciples. Even though Jesus was criticized by some people for going to the house of someone like Matthew, Jesus made it clear that these were exactly the people He came for. In response to these critics, Jesus said, "It is not the healthy who need a doctor, but the sick…For I have not come to call the righteous, but sinners" (see Matthew 9:9-13). Jesus wants us to invite Him over to meet our unsaved, and perhaps unwholesome, friends!

Third, we have the father, Jairus, who couldn't bring his dying daughter to Jesus, so Jairus brought Jesus to her. When Jesus got to his house, the girl had already died. Those in the house told Jairus, "Your daughter is dead. Why bother the teacher [Jesus] any more?" Ignoring what they said, Jesus told Jairus, "Don't be afraid; just believe." Then Jesus walked into the house, took the girl by the hand and said, "Little girl, I say to you, get up!" Immediately she got up and walked around (see Matthew 9:18-26 and Mark 5:22-43). Even though the girl wasn't able to come to Jesus herself, her father was still able to bring Jesus to her.

Do you see the influence each of these people had on their friends and family? By bringing their friends and family to Jesus, or bringing Jesus to them, their friends and family were healed, changed, forgiven and given a new life! How would you like to be used by God like that? You can! Even today, this week, this month!

Bring your friends to Jesus or bring Jesus to them. With Easter just around the corner, you've got a perfect opportunity to invite your unchurched friends to church. This is a time when they may be most likely to attend, if at all. It's a time when they can hear the story of the resurrection and begin their journey with the Living God.

One of the people who played a crucial role in my own salvation was my cousin who invited me to her church when I moved to her city. Within a year of attending her church, I put my faith in Christ.

Maybe that's what God wants to do through you, too? He's looking for people to join Him in His work. As Jesus said at the end of this chapter:

> "The harvest is plentiful but the workers are few. Ask the Lord of the harvest, therefore, to send out workers into his harvest field" (Matthew 9:37-38).

Want to be one of those workers? Bring your friends to Jesus!

Prayer: Father, help me have the courage to step out and bring my friends to Jesus, so He can touch their lives as He's touched mine. In Jesus' name, Amen.

LESSON 10: PERFECT LOVE DRIVES OUT FEAR — MARCH 16

Scripture Reading: Matthew 10

I had a chance to go to Israel in 1995 and stand in front of a cross that many believe marks the spot where Jesus died. As I stood on that hallowed spot, I couldn't help but drop to my knees and say, "Thank You!" over and over for what Jesus had done for me.

When I finally stood up, I walked back across the room to talk to the man who had brought me to this place. Although he was my host for the week, he wasn't a believer. In fact, he had made it quite clear that he was opposed to the gospel of Jesus Christ, and to Christianity as a whole.

But as I returned to him from the foot of the cross, I couldn't help but tell him why I had dropped to my knees. I couldn't help but tell him about this Man, Jesus, who loved me so much that He was willing to die in my place for the sins that I had committed. I couldn't help but tell him that I was alive because Jesus died.

I was so overwhelmed with God's love that it drove out my fear.

There's a passage in Matthew 10 where Jesus tells his disciples to go into the surrounding communities and preach about the kingdom of heaven, heal the sick, raise the dead, and drive out demons. Jesus told them that even though He was sending them out like sheep among wolves, that they didn't have to be afraid:

> "Do not be afraid of those who kill the body but cannot kill the soul. Rather, be afraid of the One who can destroy both soul and body in hell. Are not two sparrows sold for a penny? Yet not one of them will fall to the ground apart from the will of your Father. And even the very hairs of your head are all numbered. So don't be afraid; you are worth more than many sparrows" (Matthew 10:28-31).

I remember many times during my trip when fear crept up on me. I remember walking down a long corridor in an airport in Germany, late at night and all alone, to board the plane to Israel. At the end of the corridor was a guard behind a bulletproof glass with a gun pointed at me through a tiny hole. I began to question why I had come when the words from a *VeggieTales* video came to mind. I began to sing under my breath, "God is bigger than the boogie man...He's bigger than Godzilla and the monsters on TV..." God filled me with His peace.

I remember being afraid when I pulled up to the house where I was going to stay. The people I was going to stay with were relatives of someone I knew here in the States, but I knew they might be openly hostile to Christ. A wave of fear passed through me as I stepped out of the car to greet the eldest member of this extended family. In that moment, God reminded me of some verses from the Bible:

> "When you enter a house, first say, 'Peace to this house.' If a man of peace is there, your peace will rest on him; if not, it will return to you. Stay in that house, eating and drinking whatever they give you... Do not move around from house to house" (Luke 10:5-7).

I happened to remember the traditional greeting meant "Peace be with you," so I put out my hand and said, "Salam aleikum." I didn't know what he might do. He took hold of my hand and shook it firmly, saying, "wa-aleikum-as-salam," which means, "and peace be with you." I was suddenly at peace again and knew that I was right where God wanted me to be.

Jesus said, "perfect love drives out fear" (1 John 4:18). Call on God's perfect love to fill you today. As He does, boldly share the love that He's poured out on you with others.

Prayer: Father, fill me with Your perfect love that drives out fear, so that I can boldly share about Christ with those I love. In Jesus' name, Amen.

LESSON 11: LOVING OTHERS THROUGH THEIR DOUBTS   MARCH 17

Scripture Reading: Matthew 11

What do you do when someone you love begins to have doubts about God? Or when they've never put their faith in Him at all? One of the best things you can do is to love them through their doubts.

Take a look at how Jesus did this in Matthew chapter 11. In this chapter, Jesus actually deals with three different categories of doubters, using three different approaches.

The first category is made up of what I would call "honest doubters"—people who want to believe, but because of circumstances or sincere challenges to their faith, they're looking for answers to help them overcome their unbelief.

As surprising as it may seem, John the Baptist may have been one of these men. Even though John is the one who baptized Jesus, who proclaimed, "Look, the Lamb of God, who takes away the sin of the world!" (John 1:29b), when John landed in prison, he sent disciples to ask Jesus, "Are you the one who was to come, or should we expect someone else?" (Matthew 11:3).

Jesus didn't rebuke John for the question, but instead simply said,

"Go back and report to John what you hear and see: The blind receive sight, the lame walk, those who have leprosy are cured, the deaf hear, the dead are raised, and the good news is preached to the poor" (Matthew 11:4-5).

Then Jesus commends John to the listening crowd:

"Among those born of women there has not risen anyone greater than John the Baptist" (Matthew 11:11).

Sometimes people need a gentle reminder of all that Christ has done, and continues to do, even if they aren't seeing it right then in their own life.

The second category is made of up what I would call "skeptical doubters"—people who stand back and cross their arms while they look at the facts, seeing if they line up with their preconceived notions of what a man of God should or should not do. In their attempts to be "wise," they can sometimes shut out the possibility of faith because Jesus doesn't meet their expectations.

Jesus pointed out the dilemma of such expectations by saying,

"John came neither eating nor drinking, and they say, 'He has a demon.' The Son of Man [Jesus] came eating and drinking, and they say, 'Here is a glutton and a drunkard, a friend of tax collectors and 'sinners.' But wisdom is proved right by her actions" (Matthew 11:18-19).

Sometimes people need to hear a wise response that challenges their assumptions and gives them true wisdom so they can put their faith in Christ.

The third category is made up of what I would call "stubborn doubters"—people who don't want to believe regardless of the evidence. Jesus sharply rebukes those who lived in the cities where He performed most of His miracles by saying,

> *"Woe to you, Korazin! Woe to you, Bethsaida! If the miracles that were performed in you had been performed in Tyre and Sidon, they would have repented long ago in sackcloth and ashes." (Matthew 11: 21-22).*

But even in this sharp rebuke, I don't think Jesus was wasting His breath. Sometimes people need a strong wake-up call to get them thinking clearly again and respond in faith.

The best way to help people who have doubts is to love them through it, whether that love takes the form of a gentle reminder, a wise response, or a sharp rebuke.

Jesus concludes by calling us all to put our complete trust in Him:

> *"Come to me, all you who are weary and burdened, and I will give you rest. Take my yoke upon you and learn from me, for I am gentle and humble in heart, and you will find rest for your souls. For my yoke is easy and my burden is light" (Matthew 11:28-30).*

Jesus wants you to come to Him today, putting your complete trust in Him, and encouraging others to do the same.

Prayer: Father, I'm going to put my complete trust in You today, and I ask that You would help to encourage others to do the same. In Jesus' name, Amen.

LESSON 12: LOVE DOES WHAT'S RIGHT   MARCH 18

Scripture Reading: Matthew 12

How many times have you pulled back from loving others because doing so might bring on some unwanted consequences? Is it OK to pull back sometimes because of the threats? Or should we always press ahead regardless of the threats?

These are questions Jesus faced on a regular basis. And it's encouraging to me to see that He handled different situations differently.

Let's look at just two of these situations from Matthew 12. The first deals with whether or not Jesus would heal a man, even though doing so might cost Jesus His life.

> *"Going on from that place, He went into their synagogue, and a man with a shriveled hand was there. Looking for a reason to accuse Jesus, they asked Him, 'Is it lawful to heal on the Sabbath?' He said to them, 'If any of you has a sheep and it falls into a pit on the Sabbath, will you not take hold of it and lift it out? How much more valuable is a man than a sheep! Therefore it is lawful to do good on the Sabbath.' Then He said to the man, 'Stretch out your hand.' So he stretched it out and it was completely restored, just as sound as the other. But the Pharisees went out and plotted how they might kill Jesus" (Matthew 12:9-14).*

Jesus was facing a setup, and He could have backed away because of the threat. But rather than backing down, and leaving the man's hand shriveled, Jesus put His love for the man ahead of His own life. He did what was right, even when threatened. That's a bold kind of love.

But in the next situation, Jesus takes a different approach:

"Aware of this, Jesus withdrew from that place. Many followed Him, and He healed all their sick, warning them not to tell who He was" (Matthew 12:15).

Matthew says this was to fulfill what the prophet Isaiah said:

"He will not quarrel or cry out; no one will hear His voice in the streets. A bruised reed He will not break, and a smoldering wick He will not snuff out, till He leads justice to victory" (Matthew 12:19-20).

Jesus could have backed off at this point and stopped healing people all together. But instead, He continued to heal many, even though it was no longer in the open, and even with a warning telling people not to tell others who He was. He showed the same bold love, but with a different approach.

There are times when we need to openly challenge irrational thinking. But there are other times when we need to simply do what's right in quiet. In either case, the bottom line is still this: to continue loving others and doing what God has called us to do, rather than backing off because of people's threats.

I faced a dilemma one day when I was asked to lead worship at our church. In putting together the set of songs for that morning, one song stood out in my mind above all the others. I knew it would be the song where people would really meet God in the worship time. But the very next day, I got a note from someone who for some reason felt compelled to tell me there was one song we should never sing in church. It was the very song I planned to do, but hadn't even told anyone I was doing!

It wasn't a life-threatening dilemma, but it was a real one. Would I continue with the worship set as I had planned, knowing how powerful it could be? Or would I back down and try to please this person? I decided to do the song, and it was powerful.

We all face similar dilemmas every day. Will we give up because of someone's threats? Or will be go forth and do what's right, trusting God to work out the details? In all cases, I pray we will always put love first, not the threats.

Prayer: Father, help me to always move forward in love, doing what's right, even when threatened. In Jesus' name, Amen.

LESSON 13: LOVING OTHERS THROUGH PARABLES   MARCH 19

Scripture Reading: Matthew 13

The sun and the wind decided to have a contest one day to see which of them was the strongest. When they saw a man walking down the street wearing a warm winter coat, they agreed that whoever could get the man's coat off would truly be the strongest.

The wind thought this would be a piece of cake, so he began to blow with all his might. But the harder he blew, the tighter the man held onto his coat. Eventually, the wind gave up, and the sun took a turn. The sun came out from behind a cloud and began to shine brighter and brighter. As the man got hotter and hotter, he finally took off the coat of his own accord. The wind had to concede that the sun was indeed stronger.

When trying to get your family and friends to put their faith more fully in God, which approach do you think would work best? To blow harder and harder like the wind, or to shine brighter and brighter like the sun?

I had to use this illustration one day to help a friend. Although he meant well, his actions toward others often had the effect of repelling them from what he wanted them to do, rather than drawing them to do it of their own accord. I could have just told him directly what was happening, but I felt by using a parable, he might be able to see better what was really happening.

Jesus knew the power of parables, too, telling them often. Matthew includes seven of Jesus' parables in Matthew chapter 13: the parables of the sower, the weeds, the mustard seed, the yeast, the hidden treasure, the pearl, and the net. Matthew says:

> "Jesus spoke all these things to the crowd in parables; he did not say anything to them without using a parable" (Matthew 13:34).

Why did Jesus use so many parables? When asked this question by His disciples, Jesus replied, in part: "Though seeing, they do not see; though hearing, they do not hear or understand" (Matthew 13:13). When confronted directly, people's defensiveness can sometimes cloud their thinking to words that could otherwise be truly helpful. People can often see a point better when it is illustrated as an external reality first, then they can apply the principle to their own lives internally.

The prophet Nathan used this approach when speaking to King David when David committed adultery with another man's wife. Nathan said:

> "There were two men in a certain town, one rich and the other poor. The rich man had a very large number of sheep and cattle, but the poor man had nothing except one little ewe lamb he had bought. He raised it, and it grew up with him and his children. It shared his food, drank from his cup and even slept in his arms. It was like a daughter to him.
> "Now a traveler came to the rich man, but the rich man refrained from taking one of his own sheep or cattle to prepare a meal for the traveler who had come to him. Instead, he took the ewe lamb that belonged to the poor man and prepared it for the one who had come to him."
> David burned with anger against the man and said to Nathan, "As surely as the LORD lives, the man who did this deserves to die! He must pay for that lamb four times over, because he did such a thing and had no pity."
> Then Nathan said to David, "You are the man!" (2 Samuel 12:1b-7a).

Through this story, David was finally able to see the truth of what he had done, leading him to true repentance.

The next time you have to approach someone with something that might be hard to share directly, try using a parable, an illustration or a story. Rather than blowing harder and harder like the wind, try shining brighter and brighter like the sun!

Prayer: Father, give me wisdom to know how to approach those I love, so that they may hear Your truth in a way that moves them to action. In Jesus' name, Amen.

LESSON 14: BALANCING LOVING ACTIONS WITH LOVING PRAYERS   MARCH 20

Scripture Reading: Matthew 14

How do you balance the time you spend loving others with your actions and taking time alone to pray? How do you meet the needs of others and still have time alone with God? One way is to follow the example of Jesus in Matthew chapter 14. Although Jesus was regularly among the multitudes, He also regularly withdrew to solitary places to pray.

In this passage, Jesus and His disciples were inundated with people who needed them. In fact, Mark says that "so many people were coming and going that they did not even have a chance to eat," so Jesus said to the disciples,

"Come with me by yourselves to a quiet place and get some rest" (Mark 6:31).

It was also at this time that Jesus truly needed some time alone with His Father. John the Baptist had just been beheaded—John, who was Jesus' cousin, Jesus' baptizer, Jesus' forerunner in calling the people to repentance, and Jesus' predecessor in giving his life for the kingdom of God.

But as Jesus tried to withdraw to a quiet place, the inevitable happened. When His boat landed, the people had already beaten him to the spot on foot. Mark says,

"When Jesus landed and saw a large crowd, he had compassion on them, because they were like sheep without a shepherd. So he began teaching them many things" (Mark 6:33).

It was in this context that Jesus performed one of his most famous miracles. It had been a long day of ministering to the people and the disciples finally said to Jesus,

"Send the crowds away, so they can go to the villages and buy themselves some food" (Matthew 14:15b).

I can almost read their thoughts between the lines: "and maybe we'll finally get a chance to eat, too!" That's why they came out to this solitary area in the first place!

There were over 5,000 people there, and all the disciples could find were five loaves of bread and two fish. Jesus looked to heaven, gave thanks, the food turned out to be enough for everyone, with twelve basketfuls left over…one for each of the disciples!

Now fast forward a few hours, and we find that Jesus was finally able to get alone to pray. He sent the crowds home satisfied and sent the disciples on ahead by boat to their next stop. After praying, Jesus was able to perform another of his most famous miracles: He walked across the water to rejoin them in the boat.

It's interesting to me that two of Jesus' most famous miracles were done for the sake of expediency, not for the sake of wowing the people! While Jesus obviously made it a priority to be with people and love them as much as possible, He also made it a priority to take time alone to pray. Through those prayers, God was able to accomplish things that would otherwise have been humanly impossible.

Elijah did some of his most impressive miracles for the sake of expediency, too, such as splitting a river in two so he could cross over on dry ground. He didn't do this to impress anyone; he simply had places to go and people to see before he was taken to heaven (see 2 Kings, chapter 2).

Has God given you seemingly impossible tasks? Do the needs around you overwhelm your human abilities to meet them? Let me encourage you to take time alone to pray. I've heard several spiritual men and women say, "I have so much to do, I don't have time NOT to pray." They realize that it is only through prayer that they will be able to accomplish all that God has put on their hearts to do.

No matter what else you have to do today, make sure you take time to pray.

Get alone with God, the Creator of time itself. He'll show you how to make the most of the time He's given you, even accomplishing things that seem humanly impossible!

Prayer: Father, give me supernatural wisdom to know how to do all that You've put on my heart to do. In Jesus' name, Amen.

LESSON 15: LOVING OTHERS WITH PERSISTENT FAITH   MARCH 21

Scripture Reading: Matthew 15

Have you ever felt like God is ignoring your prayers? Or when you share your hopes with others, they tell you not to bother God with the request? Or when God does answer, it's not really the answer you're looking for?

Or possibly worst of all, have you ever poured out your heart's desire, only to be rebuked so sharply that you wished you had never asked at all?

If so, I want to encourage you not to give up on your prayers too quickly. God may still have something in store for you.

Take a look at a real live woman who came to Jesus with a request in Matthew chapter 15.

This woman must have heard or seen some of the miracles that Jesus had done, for she came pleading to Him to heal her daughter.

> *She cried out, "Lord, Son of David, have mercy on me! My daughter is suffering terribly from demon-possession."*

But look at what Jesus did next. The Bible says, "Jesus did not answer a word." Wow! Not a word! This is pretty shocking, considering all that Jesus did for so many people. Yet it looked like He was just going to ignore the woman completely. But as shocking as that was, look at what Jesus' disciples did next. The Bible says,

> *"So his disciples came to him and urged him, 'Send her away, for she keeps crying out after us.'"*

Wow! As if it weren't bad enough to be ignored, the ones who claimed to be followers of Jesus came and told her to get lost, too.

So Jesus finally breaks His silence. But when He does speak, it's hardly the answer the woman was looking for. Jesus says,

"I was sent only to the lost sheep of Israel."

She was a Canaanite, not a Jew, not one of the "lost sheep of Israel." What? Jesus, of all people? Not being willing to help someone, regardless of who they were?

Imagine the thoughts that could have gone through her mind, thoughts that might go through our minds too if we were in her situation: "I should have known better. I don't know why I thought Jesus would ever want to help someone like me. I'm sure He does love some people, but probably not people like me." Had the woman given up there, the story might have ended very differently. But she didn't. She persisted in her faith. She came to Jesus and knelt before Him:

> "Lord, help me!" she said.

Then came what could have been the worst blow of all: Jesus replied,

> "It is not right to take the children's bread and toss it to their dogs."

I don't know if Jesus was just testing her faith here, or trying to teach something to the disciples, but whatever the reason, she may have been wishing by this point that she had never asked at all.

But she didn't. She had a daughter that she loved, a daughter that desperately needed healing. She tossed aside whatever feelings she may have had and held firm in her faith. She knew she could trust Jesus' heart. She knew she could trust His character. She knew she could trust Jesus to do what's best.

> She replied: "Yes, Lord, but even the dogs eat the crumbs that fall from their masters' table."

And Jesus honored her persistent faith.
He answered,

> "Woman, you have great faith! Your request is granted." And her daughter was healed from that very hour.

Jesus is trustworthy, even when He's silent. Jesus is trustworthy, even when others may tell you to go away. Jesus is trustworthy, even when you may not like the answers. Jesus is trustworthy, even when your hopes are dashed, and you wonder if you should have ever asked at all.

Persist in your faith, especially on behalf of those you love. As you do, I pray that you'll eventually hear Jesus say to you, too: "You have great faith! Your request is granted."

Prayer: Father, increase my faith so that it persists even in the face of silence, frustration or discouragement, all so that I can see Your will done here on earth. In Jesus' name, Amen.

LESSON 16: LOVING OTHERS BY DYING TO SELF MARCH 22

Scripture Reading: Matthew 16

A friend was praying with me one day when she said something so profound, I wrote it down. I didn't even fully understand what she was saying at the time, and I'm not sure I completely understand it still! But I knew that what she said contained a truth that I needed to hear and explore. She said:

"Beware of unbroken men and beware of unbrokenness in yourself."

She was concerned that there may be people who would want to exploit some of my gifts that God had given me for their own purposes, rather than His purposes. And she was concerned that because of my own wants and needs and desires, that I might be swayed to believe and follow those who wanted to put my gifts to use.

I understood the concern, but I still had a lot of questions. What is an "unbroken man"? What does "unbrokenness" look like? How should I respond when presented with various opportunities to use my gifts?

There's a passage in Matthew 16 that sheds some light on this for me. It begins with Jesus warning the disciples:

> *"Be on your guard against the yeast of the Pharisees and Sadducees" (Matthew 16:5b).*

Jesus goes on to explain this in a way that the disciples could understand that they were to beware of the teaching of the Pharisees and Sadducees, the religious leaders of the day.

While the Pharisees and Sadducees claimed to follow the teachings of God and may have at times been sincerely trying to follow Him, they often succumbed to protecting themselves and their traditions rather than giving their lives truly for others. In a sense, they were still "unbroken men," men who still seemed to "have it together" and were trying desperately to "keep it together," when in reality, they would have been better off realizing that they didn't have it together at all, and it was only God who could hold them together.

But within the very same passage, Jesus shows that it wasn't only the Pharisees and Sadducees that the disciples needed to be on guard against, but themselves as well, their own thoughts and desires. Jesus shows how quickly we can go from following God's thoughts and desires to following our own when He asks the disciples who they think He is.

Simon Peter answered: "You are the Christ, the Son of the living God" (Matthew 16:16). Jesus commends Peter by saying, "Blessed are you, Simon son of Jonah, for this was not revealed to you by man, but by my Father in heaven," and then by describing the powerful role Peter will play in building God's kingdom on earth and in heaven.

But in the very next passage, as Jesus explains that He will soon suffer, die and be raised to life again, Peter exclaims: *"Never Lord! This shall never happen to you!"* Look at what Jesus says to Peter this time:

> *"Jesus turned and said to Peter, 'Get behind me, Satan! You are a stumbling block to me; you do not have in mind the things of God, but the things of men.'" (Matthew 16:23).*

Within a span of only a few minutes, Peter went from being commended for expressing a truth that he had received from God, to being condemned for expressing a falsehood that came from his own thinking.

How can we guard against "unbrokenness," against harmful thoughts and teachings, whether in others or in ourselves? Jesus tells us one way in the next sentence:

> *"Then Jesus said to his disciples, 'If anyone would come after me, he must deny himself and take up his cross and follow me. For whoever wants to save his life will lose it, but whoever loses his life for me will find it'" (Matthew 16:24-25).*

If our thinking is based on trying to save ourselves, protect ourselves, defend ourselves, it may be our undoing. While it's not always wrong to save, protect and defend ourselves, it is if it keeps us from doing what's right.

Instead of trying to "keep it together," my prayer is to realize how truly broken I am. In the end, it's by putting my full faith and trust in God that I will truly be able to "keep it together."

Prayer: Father, help me to trust You fully, so that I can love others fully, without regard for my own life. In Jesus' name, Amen.

LESSON 17: LOVING OTHERS BY INCREASING OUR FAITH   MARCH 23

Scripture Reading: Matthew 17

I've mentioned before how our faith can affect those we love. Today I'd like to talk about increasing our faith, so we can affect others even more.

Take a look at the example in Matthew chapter 17. A man comes with his son to Jesus to ask Jesus to pray for the boy. The man says:

"Lord, have mercy on my son," he said. "He has seizures and is suffering greatly. He often falls into the fire or into the water. I brought him to your disciples, but they could not heal him" (Matthew 17:15-16).

So Jesus heals the boy in a moment. The passage continues:

Then the disciples came to Jesus in private and asked, "Why couldn't we drive it out?"
He replied, "Because you have so little faith. I tell you the truth, if you have faith as small as a mustard seed, you can say to this mountain, 'Move from here to there' and it will move. Nothing will be impossible for you" (Matthew 17:20-21).

It seems like Jesus is being incredibly blunt. But it also seems that the reason He's being so blunt is because what He's saying is—to Him—simply an established fact: If you have faith as small as a mustard seed, you can say to this mountain, 'Move from here to there' and it will move. Nothing will be impossible for you.

If it's such a fact, why don't we see it in action? The truth is, we do.

I was reading a few years ago about the power of the atomic bomb that was dropped on the city of Hiroshima, Japan. Even though an atom is one of the smallest of particles in the world, when split, an atom can produce enough energy to level an entire city within seconds. The same atomic power is at work every day at a nuclear plant near my house, powering our entire city, giving power to even the computer I'm using to type these words.

When Jesus says that something as small as a mustard seed has enough power to move a mountain, we tend to think He's exaggerating. And yet the truth is that something even smaller than a mustard seed can move a mountain—or several—in an instant.

Faith in Jesus is powerful. It can move mountains. It can bring healing. It can bring repentance. It can bring new life.

Jesus didn't rebuke the demon-possessed boy, or his father, for their lack of faith. But Jesus rebuked the disciples for theirs. They had seen the power of God at work all around them, yet they faltered when putting that faith in action.

I falter, too. I don't want to, but I do. I get tired. I wonder if my prayers will ever be answered. I wonder if my faith will ever make a difference.

It's at those times that I need to renew my sense of faith and wonder in the power of Jesus Christ. It's at those times when I need to reread the stories recorded in the gospels of Matthew, Mark, Luke and John to get a fresh perspective of what faith can do. It's at those times when I need to remind myself of what the early followers of Jesus did in His name, as recorded in the book of Acts.

When I do, I'm encouraged to put my faith in Christ again, to put my faith in the power that is available to all of us who believe in His name. Power that can move mountains. Power that can restore marriages. Power that can revive broken bodies. Power that can bring people and situations and circumstances back to life.

If you need a boost in your faith today, this week, this month, read and reread what Jesus and His followers did in Matthew, Mark, Luke, John and Acts. Then put your faith to work on behalf of those you love. When you do, as Jesus promised, "Nothing will be impossible for you."

Prayer: Father, open my eyes to see what's possible when I put my faith in You, then increase my faith so I can watch You do it. In Jesus' name, Amen.

LESSON 18: LOVING OTHERS WITH FORGIVENESS   MARCH 24

Scripture Reading: Matthew 18

One of the best ways we can express love to someone is to forgive them.

I can think of no greater expression Jesus made of His love for me than to forgive me of my sins. And it's because of His forgiveness of me that I'm able to forgive others.

Listen to how Jesus describes this connection between His forgiveness of us, and our forgiveness of others, as recorded in Matthew 18:23-35:

> "Therefore, the kingdom of heaven is like a king who wanted to settle accounts with his servants. As he began the settlement, a man who owed him ten thousand talents [that is, millions of dollars] was brought to him. Since he was not able to pay, the master ordered that he and his wife and his children and all that he had be sold to repay the debt.
> "The servant fell on his knees before him. 'Be patient with me,' he begged, 'and I will pay back everything.' The servant's master took pity on him, canceled the debt and let him go. "But when that servant went out, he found one of his fellow servants who owed him a hundred denarii [that is, a few dollars]. He grabbed him and began to choke him. 'Pay back what you owe me!' he demanded.
> "His fellow servant fell to his knees and begged him, 'Be patient with me, and I will pay you back.'
> "But he refused. Instead, he went off and had the man thrown into prison until he could pay the debt. When the other servants saw what had happened, they were greatly distressed and went and told their master everything that had happened.
> "Then the master called the servant in. 'You wicked servant,' he said, 'I canceled all that debt of yours because you begged me to. Shouldn't you have had mercy on your fellow servant just as I had on you?' In anger his master turned him over to the jailers to be tortured, until he should pay back all he owed.
> "This is how my heavenly Father will treat each of you unless you forgive your brother from your heart."

Jesus calls us to forgive others. This doesn't mean that we excuse them, agree with them, or ignore them. It means we forgive them. It means that we acknowledge that what they've done has hurt us, whether intentional or not, whether justified or not. It hurt. Once we acknowledge that we've been hurt, then we can forgive.

When I'm working through forgiving someone on my own, I'll sometimes write out the specific offenses I feel a person has done to me, line by line:

"He made a decision that cost me x amount of dollars"

"He made me feel demeaned and humiliated by the way he spoke to me"

"He spoke negatively about me to others, possibly turning them against me, too."

Then I'll go through each offense, line by line, and I'll speak words of forgiveness, out loud, just for myself and God to hear. (I'll decide later whether or not it would be helpful to speak these words to someone else…only after I've truly forgiven them from my heart.) I'll say:

"I forgive him for making a decision that cost me x amount of dollars"

"I forgive him for making me feel demeaned and humiliated by the way he spoke to me"

"I forgive him for speaking negatively about me to others, possibly turning them against me, too."

It's never easy, and I don't rush through it, because I want to make sure that my heart is right. But when I'm done, I know that I've at least begun to do what's right. Being specific helps me deal with each issue, one by one, and when I've finished going through the list, I'll throw it away. As Paul says in 1 Corinthians 13:4-5, "Love…keeps no record of wrongs."

Whatever method you choose, choose to forgive. According to Matthew 18:32-35, you'll find that when you "forgive your brother from your heart," you'll release two people from potential torment: the other person…and yourself.

Prayer: Father, help me to forgive others as You have forgiven me. I pray this in Jesus' name, Amen.

LESSON 19: LOVING OTHERS THROUGH GIVING   MARCH 25

Scripture Reading: Matthew 19

What hinders you from following Jesus completely? There's a story in the Bible about a rich young man who faced this question. He had kept the commands of God. He didn't murder. He didn't commit adultery. He didn't steal, didn't give false testimony, honored his father and mother, and loved his neighbor as himself. He asked Jesus,

> *"What do I still lack?"*
> *Jesus answered, "If you want to be perfect, go, sell your possessions and give to the poor, and you will have treasure in heaven. Then come, follow me."*
> *When the young man heard this, he went away sad, because he had great wealth.*
> *(Matthew 19:18-21).*

The young man had done so much for God, yet there was still something that held him back. It makes me wonder what I might still be holding back. What is hindering me from following Jesus completely?

I remember when I felt like God was calling me into full-time ministry. I wanted to do it, felt called to do it, and was willing to give up almost anything to do it. But as I prayed through the costs, one stood out above all the others. Lana and I had saved up enough money to put a down-payment on our first house, a beautiful little house with a white picket fence. I loved that little house. I knew that if I went into full-time ministry, I might have to give it up.

As I prayed, I sensed God asking me, "Eric, do you love people more than things? Or things more than people?" I knew what I had to do. I offered the house up to God as well. Although He let me keep it for another year, I eventually had to give it up when I accepted a call to serve a church in another state. I still miss that little house, but I'm thankful that I didn't let it hold me back from doing what God called me to do.

I don't think God is as concerned about the possessions we own as He is about the possessions that own us. What is it that keeps us from following Christ completely? What holds us back from moving forward?

In order to hold on tight to God, letting Him take us wherever He wants us to go, we may have to let go of other things in our life. We may be holding onto good things, even godly things. But if they hinder us from following Christ completely, we're better off letting them go and grabbing onto Him.

Jesus concludes this passage by reminding His disciples that whatever they've given up to follow Him will not go unnoticed. Peter said to Jesus, "We have left everything to follow you! What then will there be for us?"

Jesus answered:

> "I tell you the truth, at the renewal of all things, when the Son of Man sits on his glorious throne, you who have followed me will also sit on twelve thrones, judging the twelve tribes of Israel. And everyone who has left houses or brothers or sisters or father or mother or children or fields for my sake will receive a hundred times as much and will inherit eternal life" (Matthew 19:28-29).

A hundred times as much! Wow! God has so much in store for us, we can't even imagine! If what's holding us back seems so huge, imagine getting back a hundred times more! It's almost incomprehensible.

But we can't receive what God has in store for us when our fists are clenched around something else. When we open our hands to give, we're also opening them to receive.

Open your hands today. Let God use you, and what He has given you, to bless others. Then let Him bless you back in return. As Jesus told His disciples earlier: "Freely you have received, freely give" (Matthew 10:8b).

Prayer: Father, open my heart and my hands to give to others as You have called me to give, so that I may bless them, bless You, and even receive a blessing in return. In Jesus' name, Amen.

LESSON 20: BECOMING A GREAT LOVER — MARCH 26

Scripture Reading: Matthew 20

Want to become a great lover? Not just the romantic kind, but a great lover of people in general? Jesus tells us how in Matthew chapter 20.

> "…whoever wants to become great among you must be your servant…" (Matthew 20:26b).

If we want to become great, we must serve others.

This is a principle Jesus taught often. It's a principle that seems to defy reason, yet we recognize its truth when we see it in action.

Mother Teresa became great, winning the Nobel Peace Prize in 1979. Yet she never sought the prize. She sought to serve others. As she saw the suffering and poverty outside the school where she taught in Calcutta, India, she sought and received permission to leave the convent school and devote herself to working among the poorest of the poor. The more she served, the more awards and distinctions she was offered, many of which she politely declined, as that was not her purpose in serving.

Jesus explained this principle to his disciples after the mother of James and John came to Jesus. She asked that Jesus would let her sons have the highest positions of honor, to sit at Jesus' right and left when He came into His kingdom. Jesus told them they didn't know what they were asking for, and that those places belonged only to those for whom they had been prepared by His Father.

Jesus explains more about this principle as the passage continues:

"When the ten heard about this, they were indignant with the two brothers. Jesus called them together and said, 'You know that the rulers of the Gentiles lord it over them, and their high officials exercise authority over them. Not so with you. Instead, whoever wants to become great among you must be your servant, and whoever wants to be first must be your slave— just as the Son of Man did not come to be served, but to serve, and to give his life as a ransom for many' " (Matthew 20:24-28).

If you want to become a great lover, serve others. Although I mentioned this principle was not just about becoming a great romantic lover, the same truth applies to romance.

I've written a book called, *What God Says About Sex*. In it, I describe one of my own epiphanies regarding how God might want to use me to bless my wife, Lana. There are times when I'll look at her and ask myself, "If God were here right now, what would He do to bless her? How would He want me to use my hands, my words, my eyes, my ears, and my heart to bless her in a special way?"

Sometimes I'll sense that God wants me to caress her forehead, stroke her hair, or give her gentle kisses on her lips and cheeks. While it's nearly impossible for me not to take pleasure in this, too, my honest motivation at times like these is not to satisfy my own desires, but to let God work through me to satisfy hers.

Becoming a great lover of people, whether it involves romantic love or not, requires that we truly serve them. Bruce Wilkinson, in his book, *A Life God Rewards*, writes, "True good works are always focused on sincerely trying to improve the well-being of another."

What can you do today that would truly improve the well-being of someone you love? Is there a word you can offer, a card you can send, an email you can write? Is there something practical you can do, a trip you could make for them, a hand you could offer?

Even though you may not be seeking a reward for your good deeds, the truth is you will be rewarded for loving others. Jesus said, *"I tell you the truth, anyone who gives you a cup of water in My name…will certainly not lose his reward"* (Mark 9:41).

God wants us to become great lovers. He has shown us how. Now it's up to us to follow through.

Prayer: *Father, help me today to become the great lover You want me to be by serving others. In Jesus' name, Amen.*

LESSON 21: LOVE FOLLOWS THROUGH — MARCH 27

Scripture Reading: Matthew 21

There are times when I'll be at a store with my kids and they'll ask me if we can buy something. If I know there's a special occasion coming up, like Christmas or a birthday, I might tell them, "No, we can't get that today." Then I'll go back to the store later and get what they asked for. When they finally get it, they're thrilled, and quickly forget that I had ever said no.

On the other hand, there are times when my kids will ask me for something and I'll say, "Yes, we can get that sometime." But if we never get around to getting it, they end up disappointed and frustrated, no matter how many times I might have said, "Yes, we can get that sometime."

In comparing the power of actions versus words, Ralph Waldo Emerson said: "What you do speaks so loudly that I cannot hear what you say."

Jesus sums up this idea in a parable in Matthew chapter 21. Jesus said:

> *"What do you think? There was a man who had two sons. He went to the first and said, 'Son, go and work today in the vineyard.'*
>
> *"'I will not,' he answered, but later he changed his mind and went.*
>
> *"Then the father went to the other son and said the same thing. He answered, 'I will, sir,' but he did not go.*
>
> *"Which of the two did what his father wanted?"*
>
> *"The first," they answered.*
>
> *Jesus said to them, "I tell you the truth, the tax collectors and the prostitutes are entering the kingdom of God ahead of you. For John came to you to show you the way of righteousness, and you did not believe him, but the tax collectors and the prostitutes did. And even after you saw this, you did not repent and believe him"* (Matthew 21:28-32).

I love this story because it reminds me the importance of following through on our promises.

If we say we love God, but never repent, or never believe Him, then what good is it to say that we love Him? If we say we love our family or friends, but never follow through with the things that we promise to do for them, what good is it to say that we love them?

Jesus explained earlier the importance of letting our "Yes" be "Yes" and our "No" be "No." But here, Jesus goes to the heart of the issue. In the end, what we do matters even more than what we say.

It is what we do that will have lasting impact on those we love. It is what we do that will demonstrate our deep love and commitment to God. It is what we do that reveals how deeply committed we are in comparison to our verbal commitments of love.

This applies to everything from keeping a wedding vow to keeping a promise to a friend that we'll be at their house at 10:00. In the end, it's what we do that will speak more about our love for them than what we say.

What can you do today to follow through on a commitment you've made to God or to someone you love? How can you differentiate yourself from the religious leaders of Jesus' day who claimed to love God, but didn't follow through on what they said?

Maybe keeping your commitment is something as simple as making a phone call, filling out a job application, or keeping an appointment. Maybe it would mean taking the "next step" in a bigger issue, like saving a bit of money each week to reduce an overwhelming debt, or telling a trusted friend about a habit that's got a choke-hold on you, or opening up to your spouse about a struggle that's been keeping you from true intimacy. You may not be able to tackle the whole thing in a day, but you might be able to take a step towards it.

God wants us to follow through in our love for Him and others. In the end, it is our actions that will declare our love the loudest.

Prayer: Father, show me what I can do to follow through on my commitments to love You and love others more. In Jesus' name, Amen.

LESSON 22: THE ULTIMATE GOAL OF LIFE   MARCH 28

Scripture Reading: Matthew 22

For Harry Potter fans, the week I wrote this devotional was one of the biggest doubleheaders of all time: the fifth movie came out the weekend before, and the seventh, and final, book in the series came out the following weekend.

Here's what I wrote:

Whatever you think of the various themes in the Harry Potter series, there's one theme that seems inarguably good: the theme of sacrificial love. In the first book, readers found out that Harry's parents, and his mother in particular, loved Harry with such a deep and sacrificial love, that even the most vile person on earth couldn't break through it to kill him. Even though Harry's parents died in the process, they succeeded in demonstrating their profound love for Harry.

Now, in the seventh and final book, readers are about to find out the answer to the question that has persisted throughout the entire series: what's going to happen to Harry Potter in his final conflict with evil? Will he live or not? It's almost guaranteed that either Harry will die, his archenemy will die, or both of them will die.

But there's another question I think readers will get an answer to this week. Although some people say there's no such thing as a dumb question, I still think that some questions are better than others! If we ask the wrong question, we'll often come to the wrong conclusion. Asking the right questions is key to life.

Beyond the question, *"Will Harry live or not?"* I think readers will find the answer to an even more important question: *"Will Harry love or not?"* In other words, "Will Harry Potter demonstrate his love for others as it was demonstrated by his parents to him?" The answer to these two questions could be entirely different, regardless of whether Harry lives or dies.

If the test of success in life is dependent on whether we live or not, none of us will pass! But if the test of success in life is whether we love or not, then all of us will have an equal chance of passing, regardless of whatever else we may do in life.

People asked Jesus all kinds of questions—some to trap Him, others to trick Him. But one man asked Jesus a question that was so wise Jesus said to him, "You are not far from the kingdom of God."

The question was this: "Of all the commandments, which is the most important?"

"The most important one," answered Jesus, "is this: 'Hear, O Israel, the Lord our God, the Lord is one. Love the Lord your God with all your heart and with all your soul and with all your mind and with all your strength.' The second is this: 'Love your neighbor as yourself.' There is no commandment greater than these" (Mark 12:29-31 and Matthew 22:37-40).

The man had asked the right question. And Jesus gave a brilliant response.

We may have heard Jesus's answer so often that we don't realize the incredible power of His words. Jesus says that the goal of everything in life—everything—boils down to whether or not we love God with all our heart, soul, mind and strength; and whether or not we love others as ourselves. Love is the ultimate goal of life.

Will Harry Potter live or not? I don't know. I'm curious, but I'm even more curious if Harry Potter will love or not. Will he demonstrate his love to others as it has been demonstrated to him? The answer to that question will determine the success or failure of Harry Potter's life. And it's the same question that will determine the success or failure of our lives.

Will we love God and others as God has loved us? Will we succeed in life, by demonstrating our love for others as Christ demonstrated His when He gave His life for us? If our answer to these questions is a resounding "YES!" then it won't matter what else we might do in life. We will have succeeded in the ultimate goal of life, the goal of love.

Prayer: Father, help me demonstrate my love for You and others as You have demonstrated it to me. In Jesus' name, Amen.

LESSON 23: LOVING PEOPLE, NOT JUST WORDS   MARCH 29

Scripture Reading: Matthew 23

The day I put my faith in Jesus was the same day I put my faith in the Bible, from which I learned about Jesus. I fell in love with both on the same day.

When people talk about how much they love the Bible, they're not just talking about a book from which they've learned much, they're also talking about a Person from whom they've learned much.

I suppose it's like a young lover who takes a picture of his beloved out of his wallet and tenderly kisses the image. It's not the picture that the young man's in love with, but a person whose image is represented by the picture. If his love for the picture ever began to surpass his love for the person, then we'd know that something had started to go wrong.

Believe it or not, the same thing can happen to those of us who love the Bible. When our love for the Word of God begins to supersede our love for God—and our love for the people of God about whom the words were written—then we know something has started to go wrong.

Jesus criticized the religious leaders of His day for this very thing. They claimed to love the Word of God, and even gave the appearance of following the commands found in it to the "T." But Jesus saw their hearts; He saw that they weren't motivated by their love for others, but by how they appeared to others. It was a subtle difference that produced drastically different results than God had intended.

Jesus didn't condemn these leaders for what they were teaching, for they were teaching the Word of God. But He did condemn then for how they put those words into practice. He said:

> *"The teachers of the law and the Pharisees sit in Moses' seat. So you must obey them and do everything they tell you. But do not do what they do, for they do not practice what they preach. They tie up heavy loads and put them on men's shoulders, but they themselves are not willing to lift a finger to move them. Everything they do is done for men to see…" (Matthew 23:2-5).*

Jesus goes on to denounce the actions of those leaders in some of the strongest words in the Bible, calling them hypocrites, snakes, vipers, and sons of hell. Yikes! I don't want to be like that! I hope you don't either! So what can we do instead?

Jesus tells us in the same passage. For starters, we're to do the opposite of what the teachers of the law and the Pharisees were doing! He doesn't want us to just preach to others, but to practice what we preach. When we give godly advice to others, we're not just to walk away and say, "I've told you what to do, now good luck." He wants us to at least lift a finger—and more—to help them to do it.

If someone's struggling with an addiction, rather than just telling them it's wrong, offer to be their accountability partner. If someone's considering a divorce, rather than just telling them to try to work it out with their spouse, help them to work it out with their spouse. If someone's going under financially, rather than just telling them to work out a budget, help them to work out a budget. I'm preaching to myself, too! It's often easier to tell people what they should do than to help them to do it, which is why I'm studying these "lessons in love"!

Our motivation in sharing God's Word must always be love—saying and doing things that will truly benefit those we're trying to help, whether anyone sees our good deeds or not.

If we claim to love the Word of God, we must also love the people of God about whom the words are written. To do anything less would be like falling in love with a piece of paper with some ink on it.

Prayer: Father, help me to love Your people, remembering that Your words were written because of Your great love for them. In Jesus' name, Amen.

LESSON 24: DON'T LET YOUR LOVE GROW COLD — MARCH 30

Scripture Reading: Matthew 24

Jesus tells us many things that will happen as the time gets closer to His return. Most of them I can't do anything about: famines, earthquakes, wars and rumors of war.

But there's one thing Jesus mentions in Matthew chapter 24 that I can do: don't let my love grow cold. Jesus says:

> *"Because of the increase of wickedness, the love of most will grow cold, but he who stands firm to the end will be saved" (Matthew 24:12:13).*

I can see how our love could grow cold. As the world approaches its grand finale, with rampant, widespread destruction, it would be easy to become embittered, frustrated, heartsick and fearful. I can see how people could turn away from God and turn away from each other.

But Jesus gives us the key to surviving those times. And it's really the key to surviving whatever we're facing right now, too. The key is this: "Don't let your love grow cold."

When your love grows cold, the end really has come. When your love grows cold, that's the end of joy, the end of relationships, the end of happiness, the end of hope. At all costs, whatever it takes, we need to keep our love alive. Our love for God, and our love for others.

I was speaking to a group one time about what to do when people treat us poorly. The answer, I suggested, was to "Love 'em more." What should we do when people run away from us? "Love 'em more." What should we do when people break our hearts and disappoint us? "Love 'em more."

One of the people in the group came up to me the next day. She said she loved that message on "Love me more." Whenever people would treat her poorly, she'd remind them that they're supposed to "Love me more." She was joking, of course, having gotten the two key letters backwards, turning "em" into "me." It's a minor change with major ramifications. When things get rough in relationships, we expect others to "Love me more." But what God calls us to do is to "Love them more," or as I put it, "Love 'em more."

This is a message that we don't have to wait to put into practice until the end of the world as we know it. It's a message that we can start practicing today, so when the end comes, we'll be ready. In fact, we're closer to Jesus' return today than ever before. We're not lacking in famines, earthquakes, wars and rumors of war. If there's a time to put our love into practice, we need to start "practicing" now.

None of us know when the day of His return will come. Although there will be signs, it will come suddenly. People will be eating and drinking as usual, marrying and giving in marriage up until that day. *"Two men will be in the field; one will be taken and the other left. Two women will be grinding with a hand mill; one will be taken and the other left"* (Matthew 24:40-41).

The grand finale of life will come upon us in an instant. What can we do about it? 1) Don't be surprised when these things happen. Jesus says, *"but see to it that you are not alarmed. Such things must happen, but the end is still to come"* (Matthew 24:6b). 2) Don't let your love grow cold.

How can we keep our love from growing cold? By fanning the flames of our love.

When people hurt you or mistreat you, "Love 'em more."

When people leave you or forsake you, "Love 'em more."

When people sin against you or hate you, "Love 'em more."

Just like Jesus did for us when people hurt and mistreated Him, left and forsook Him, sinned against and hated Him. He just loved 'em more.

Even to the very end, the thing that will save the day will be love. As wickedness increases all around us, we need to do what Jesus did: "Love 'em more."

Prayer: Father, help me to love others more, even as—and especially when—we see the end approaching. In Jesus' name, Amen.

LESSON 25: LOVE IS PREPARED   MARCH 31

Scripture Reading: Matthew 25

I was reading the Parable of the Talents one day when my life took a radical turn. The parable is a story in Matthew chapter 25 where Jesus tells about a man who gave three of his servants varying amounts of talents—a unit of money that was worth more than $1,000.

You're probably familiar with the story: the man gave the first servant five talents, the second servant two talents, and the third servant one talent. Then the man went on a journey.

Quite a while later, the man came back to see what each servant had done with his talents. Two of the servants had put their talents to use, making a good return on the man's investment. Each was rewarded by their master with these words:

"Well done, good and faithful servant! You have been faithful with a few things; I will put you in charge of many things. Come and share your master's happiness!"

But the third servant had buried his talent and was rebuked as wicked and lazy. Even what he had was taken away from him, and he was thrown out into the darkness.

Of course, after reading the story, I wanted to be like the first two servants, not like the third.

Wondering how I was doing with the "talents" God had given me, I began to write a question in my journal. "Lord, am I using the gifts you've given me?" I was surprised when the answer I heard back was a clear and simple, "No."

Wow! I thought I was doing pretty good! I was working hard at my job, involved in some Bible studies at church, and so on. But I knew that if this really was God speaking to me, I wanted to listen up. I didn't want to be like the wicked, lazy servant in the story who didn't put his talents to use.

"Lord, what do you want me to do?" I wrote.

I felt God answered: "I told them to make a return on what I gave them."

So I began to list out a few of my talents, asking God how I could make better use of them for Him. One week later, I quit my secular job and went into full-time ministry.

Jesus told two other parables in Matthew chapter 25, both of which talk about preparing for Christ's return. Jesus doesn't want us to be surprised when that day comes. He doesn't want us to fall asleep waiting for His return. He doesn't want us to bury our talents in the ground. He doesn't want us to neglect the needs of those around us.

He wants us to put our gifts to use to the fullest, to be ready when He comes back.

It doesn't mean we all need to be in "full-time ministry." But it does mean that we're to use the gifts He's given us to work towards His purposes on the earth. Whether it's giving food to the hungry, drinks to the thirsty, or clothes to the naked. Whether it's looking after those who are sick, visiting those who are in prison, or caring for our children or parents. Whether it's cooking or sewing, teaching or preaching, singing or praying.

When Jesus comes back, He wants us to be prepared for His return. Not because He wants us to work our way into heaven. But because He wants us to make a good return on His investment. He's given us all kinds of gifts, and He wants us to use them to the fullest, to accomplish all that He has created us to do.

Take inventory of some of the gifts God has given you. Ask Him how you can use those gifts for Him. Let's pray that one day we'll all hear Him say, "Well done, good and faithful servant! You have been faithful with a few things; I will put you in charge of many things. Come and share your master's happiness!"

Prayer: Father, help me to make a good return on the gifts You've given me, for my sake, for Yours, and for those who will be touched as a result. In Jesus' name, Amen.

LESSON 26: LAVISH LOVE   APRIL 1

Scripture Reading: Matthew 26

I've read the story in Matthew chapter 26 many times about the woman who poured out a jar of very expensive perfume onto Jesus's head. I've always been impressed by the woman's action, and by Jesus's response to it.

But it wasn't until recently that I've seen the story from God's perspective, which has deepened my appreciation for it even more.

In case you haven't read it, or just need a refresher, here's the story:

> *While Jesus was in Bethany in the home of a man known as Simon the Leper, a woman came to him with an alabaster jar of very expensive perfume, which she poured on his head as he was reclining at the table. When the disciples saw this, they were indignant. "Why this waste?" they asked. "This perfume could have been sold at a high price and the money given to the poor."*
> *Aware of this, Jesus said to them, "Why are you bothering this woman? She has done a beautiful thing to me. The poor you will always have with you, but you will not always have me. When she poured this perfume on my body, she did it to prepare me for burial. I tell you the truth, wherever this gospel is preached throughout the world, what she has done will also be told, in memory of her"* (Matthew 26:6-13).

I love this woman's lavish love for Jesus. I'm sure she knew the value of her gift. She didn't see it as wasteful, but as totally appropriate for the one who was to receive it.

I also love Jesus's response to this gift. He wasn't bothered that someone poured out such a lavish expression of love upon Him. He was, after all, the one who turned water into wine —and not just any wine, but the best. He understood what it meant to lavish love upon others.

But what I love even more about this story is the lavish love of God for His Son displayed in this act. From God's perspective, it's almost as if God wanted to pour out a special measure of His love to Jesus, so He moved on the heart of a woman who had a very expensive jar of perfume, allowing her to be His hands to His Son. He put in her heart the willingness to pick up her alabaster jar and pour it out on Jesus's head.

God knew what Jesus was about to undergo. Jesus knew what He was about to undergo. If there was ever a time where Jesus might have doubted His Father's love for Him, it was in the upcoming days of mocking, beating, and being nailed to a cross. This demonstration of love was as if God wanted to assure Jesus of His love yet one more time, moving on the heart of a woman who could pour out just such an expression. It was an act of lavish love, not only from the woman, but from God Himself, given through the woman.

Why is this so important to point out? Because God may want to do the same thing through you for others. He may want to show someone His lavish love, and in order to do that, He may move on your heart to display it. We all have an alabaster jar of some kind. It may not be an expensive perfume, but it may be just as valuable to the person receiving it.

Maybe it's a gift of time, of attention, of writing a song, of serving with our hands. Maybe it's a gift of money, giving something that may or may not mean much to us, but will certainly mean something special to the recipient. Maybe it's a gift of an item, an object of value, something that would mean the world to someone else.

Sometimes love is outlandishly lavish. But sometimes, from God's perspective, it's just the kind of love that He wants us to pour out on others.

Prayer: Father, help me to be willing to show Your lavish love to others, demonstrating Your love for them in tangible ways. In Jesus' name, Amen.

LESSON 27: A TALE OF TWO DEATHS — APRIL 2

Scripture Reading: Matthew 27

Two of the most famous deaths ever recorded take place in Matthew chapter 27. Interestingly, even though these two men had starkly different lives and deaths, the way each of them died was a reflection of the way they lived. And in their deaths, there's a lesson for how we can live and die better, too.

The chapter opens with the death of Judas, the disciple who betrayed Jesus with a kiss. His sad death is a reflection of his sad life. Just days before, he had watched contemptuously as a woman poured out a jar of expensive perfume onto Jesus's head. He complained, *"Why wasn't this perfume sold and the money given to the poor? It was worth a year's wages."*

The Bible goes on to say, "He did not say this because he cared about the poor but because he was a thief; as keeper of the money bag, he used to help himself to what was put into it." (John 12:5-6).

It was this event that caused Judas to go to the chief priests and ask, "'What are you willing to give me if I hand him over to you?' So they counted out for him thirty silver coins. From then on Judas watched for an opportunity to hand him over" (Matthew 26:15-16).

It was almost as if following Jesus was simply a means to an end for Judas. As long as the money was coming in, he was glad to follow. But when he saw this "wasteful" display of money by the woman, and Jesus's apparent indifference to the finances involved, Judas began to look for another way to profit from the situation.

Sadly, when he realized his mistake, betraying an innocent man to death for thirty pieces of silver, it was too late. He couldn't live with what he had done, so he took his own life. It seems that money was what Judas lived for, and money was what Judas died for.

Contrast this story with the other story of death in this chapter, the death of Jesus.

Having been betrayed by Judas, Jesus was taken to be sentenced. Yet when accused, the Bible says, "But Jesus made no reply, not even to a single charge—to the great amazement of the governor" (Matthew 27:14).

Jesus knew what He had to do. Although He had agonized in prayer, asking God if there was any other way to do what He had to do, Jesus was willing to follow God no matter what. Jesus had always lived for others. Now He was about to die for others, too.

Taking His last breath on the cross, Jesus called out in a loud voice, *"Father, into your hands I commit my spirit"* (Luke 23:46).

The deaths of these two men couldn't have been more different. Judas took his life because of sin. Jesus gave up His life because of love. The difference can be seen when looking into their hearts.

When you look into the heart of love, you'll find selflessness. When you look into the heart of sin, you'll find selfishness.

If we want to love like Jesus loved, we've got to live like Jesus lived—then be willing to die like Jesus died. In doing so, we'll find true life. As Jesus Himself said,

> "For whoever wants to save his life will lose it, but whoever loses his life for Me will find it" (Matthew 16:25).

I pray that when people look into your heart and mine, that they'll see that our hearts are willing to die for the same things that we're willing to live for.

I pray that our hearts would overflow with a love that is eager to live for others, give to others, and even to die for others when that time comes.

I'm not expecting to die anytime soon, and you may not be either. But I pray that when that day comes, our deaths would be a reflection of our lives, a reflection of the heart of Jesus.

Prayer: Father, help me to give up my life of selfishness so that I can give out a life of selflessness. In Jesus' name, Amen.

LESSON 28: FIT FOR WHAT? — APRIL 3

Scripture Reading: Matthew 28

Why do we go to church? Read the Bible? Pray? Listen to sermons? Read devotionals?

Why? To grow. To be stronger in our faith. To help us through difficult times. To find God's answers for specific questions on our heart. Certainly it's for each of those things.

But there's more! God has more in mind for us from all of our reading, studying and praying than simply our own spiritual growth. He wants us to be spiritually fit. The question is, fit for what?

Jesus tells us the answer in Matthew chapter 28, verses 18 through 20. In this passage, often referred to as "The Great Commission," Jesus gives His final instructions to His disciples—instructions that apply to us today as well, as followers of Jesus Christ. Jesus said:

> "All authority in heaven and on earth has been given to me. Therefore go and make disciples of all nations, baptizing them in the name of the Father and of the Son and of the Holy Spirit, and teaching them to obey everything I have commanded you. And surely I am with you always, to the very end of the age" (Matthew 28:18-20).

If all of our reading and studying and praying was solely to help us grow for our own sakes, we'd be like a body builder who works out for years to compete in a contest, but never actually uses his muscles to lift anything "in the real world." They would certainly be fit, but fit for what?

I'm not against bodybuilding, and I wish I had some of those muscles myself! But in reading Jesus' words, I'm convicted that sometimes we as Christians can focus so much on the workout that we forget why we're working out.

Our spiritual workouts may include Bible studies, quiet times, and memorizing scripture, all of which are great and helpful in their own right. But in the end, Jesus wants us to put what we've learned into practice, serving others as He served them. Baptizing others as He baptized them. Teaching others as He taught them.

How can we do that today? How can we use our gifts to make disciples of all nations? How can we encourage people to get baptized? How can we teach others to obey all that Christ has commanded us?

The list is endless of how God creatively uses people to join Him in His work.

I know a woman who wondered how God could use her to fulfill this command. She liked to swim…but what could she do with that? Then a neighbor boy asked her if she would teach him how to swim in her backyard pool. She agreed to do it, on the condition that he memorize a Bible verse every time he came for a lesson. He did it, loved it, and soon brought his friends. They, too, began taking swimming lessons and memorizing Scripture. Within a few years, this woman was holding her swimming classes at a public pool, because over a hundred kids were coming each day to learn how to swim and memorize Scripture.

I have an aunt who loves to cook, but how could that help fulfill The Great Commission? Over the years, she has hosted hundreds of pastors, Bible teachers, missionaries, students, neighbors, friends and relatives in her home, giving them a physical, as well as a spiritual lift as they've come through her home.

How might He want to use you this week, this month, this year? What do you love doing? What do you have a passion for? What are you skilled at that could be tweaked, even just a little, to help bring others into the kingdom of God?

God has gifted you, certainly because He loves you, but also because He wants to love others through you.

Keep asking God how you can get into the best spiritual shape possible. He wants each of us to be as fit as we can be…fit for all that He wants to do through us in the days ahead.

Prayer: Father, help me to find creative ways to put my spiritual fitness to use for You and Your kingdom. In Jesus' name, Amen.

CONCLUSION: THE GREATEST OF THESE — APRIL 4

Scripture Reading: 1 Corinthians 13:1-13

Today we've come to the end of our study of the book of Matthew. I hope you've enjoyed learning how to love God, love others, and love ourselves more by seeing how Jesus did each of those things.

Here are some of the things I've learned about love from the life of Jesus, one from each of Matthew's 28 chapters:

1) Those who have been forgiven much love much
2) Love starts by seeing others as God sees them
3) Love continues by seeing how much God loves people even before they were born
4) Love sometimes requires that we call people to repent from things that are destroying them
5) We're called to love everyone, even our enemies

6) We're called to make sure our motives are right, by sometimes doing loving acts in secret
7) The Golden Rule is still golden: God wants us to do to others as we would have them do to us
8) We can love others by praying for their healing
9) We can love others by bringing them to Jesus
10) We can let God's perfect love drive out our fears
11) We can love others by helping them through their doubts
12) Love requires us to do right, even when threatened
13) People sometimes respond better to our loving words when spoken in parables
14) Love is balanced between prayer and action
15) Love often requires persistence
16) Love often requires dying to our own desires
17) Love often requires asking for more faith to see the lives of our friends changed
18) Love forgives
19) Love gives
20) Love serves
21) Love follows through
22) Our success in life is not determined by how long we live, but by how much we love
23) Our love for God's Word should be directly related to our love for God's people
24) When tempted to let our love grow cold, we must determine to love others more
25) Love is prepared
26) Love is lavish
27) Love is sacrificial
28) Love goes to the ends of the earth

There's a lot we can learn from reading the Bible. There's a lot we can learn from praying. But in the end, all of our reading and praying won't matter unless we express what we've learned in love. Theology matters, but only to the extent that it influences our ability to love.

I love the way Oliver Thomas puts it: "Authentic religion is not a theology test. It's a love test."

If what we learn doesn't influence what we do, all of our learning is in vain.

The Apostle Paul expressed it well when he wrote:

> "If I speak in the tongues of men and of angels, but have not love, I am only a resounding gong or a clanging cymbal. If I have the gift of prophecy and can fathom all mysteries and all knowledge, and if I have a faith that can move mountains, but have not love, I am nothing. If I give all I possess to the poor and surrender my body to the flames, but have not love, I gain nothing" (1 Corinthians 13:1-4).

Paul continues his passage on love by giving one of the most useful summaries of love found not only in the whole Bible, but perhaps in all the writings of the world. He continues:

> "Love is patient, love is kind. It does not envy, it does not boast, it is not proud. It is not rude, it is not self-seeking, it is not easily angered, it keeps no record of wrongs.

Love does not delight in evil but rejoices with the truth. It always protects, always trusts, always hopes, always perseveres. Love never fails" (1 Corinthians 13:4-7).

Paul concludes his famous passage on love by expressing the greatest things God looks for in a person, the greatest measure of every one of our lives. The same words that I'd like to conclude with as well:

"And now these three remain: faith, hope and love. But the greatest of these is love" (1 Corinthians 13:13).

Prayer: Father, help me to keep love at the forefront of everything else I do in life. In Jesus' name, Amen.

ACTS
Lessons In Faith

Acts: Lessons in Faith

30 inspiring devotionals based on the lives of the very first followers of Christ

INTRODUCTION TO "ACTS: LESSONS IN FAITH"   APRIL 5

Scripture Reading: Acts 27:25

One of my favorite lines about faith comes from the movie *The Incredibles*.

There's a scene where a mom and her kids are on a plane that's about to be blown apart. The mom calls on her daughter to put a shield around the plane, something bigger than she's ever done before. The daughter panics and in her doubt, she can't do it. The plane explodes, but not before the mom grabs her kids to parachute into the water below.

Later, when the daughter apologizes, her mom responds:

"It isn't your fault. It wasn't fair for me to suddenly ask so much of you. But things are different now. And doubt is a luxury we can't afford anymore, sweetie. You have more power than you realize. Don't think. And don't worry. If the time comes, you'll know what to do. It's in your blood."

There are times in our lives when it's OK to doubt. But there comes a time in each of our lives where "doubt is a luxury you can't afford anymore." You either believe or you don't, and the outcome depends on what you choose to believe. The truth is, as a Christian, you do have more power than you realize. When you put your faith in Christ, God puts a seed of faith within you. It's in your blood.

My goal in the coming weeks is to strengthen your faith, to help you believe that God is who He says He is and that He will do what He says He will do.

If you've already put your faith in Christ, I want to strengthen the faith that's already within you. If you haven't yet put your faith in Christ, I want to help you get to the point where you *can* put your faith in Him.

I want to get you to the point where the Apostle Paul was at the end of the book of Acts.

Like the mom and her kids in *The Incredibles*, Paul was on a ship that was about to be blown apart. Hurricane force winds had pummeled his boat for days. The other men on the ship had given up all hope of being saved. But just as the men think all is lost, Paul stands up and says:

> "...keep up your courage, because not one of you will be lost; only the ship will be destroyed. Last night an angel of the God whose I am and whom I serve stood beside me and said, 'Do not be afraid, Paul. You must stand trial before Caesar; and God has graciously given you the lives of all who sail with you.' So keep up your courage, men, for I have faith in God that it will happen just as He told me" (Acts 27:22-25).

And it did.

That's the kind of faith God wants you to have, a faith that says, "I have faith in God it will happen just as He told me." In the coming weeks, I want to walk with you through the book of Acts, chapter by chapter, taking a look at the various ways faith expressed itself in the lives of the very first followers of Christ. Sometimes God called them to wait. Other times He called them to stand up. Still other times He called them to speak, to pray, to give, to heal, to raise people from the dead.

My hope and prayer is that God will use this time to increase your faith to the point where you can say, like the Apostle Paul, "…for I have faith in God that it will happen just as He told me."

I also want to encourage you to read each day's Scripture Reading in your own Bible in addition to my devotional for that day. I've limited myself to touching upon just one thought in each chapter of Acts, but there's so much God may speak to you about other subjects in your life. When you're done reading all the daily Scripture Readings, you'll have read through the entire book of Acts.

And finally, I've included a prayer at the end of each devotional to help you focus your own prayers by praying them along with me. Here's today's prayer.

Prayer: Father, I pray that You would fill me with faith in the days ahead, a faith that can say, "I have faith in God that it will happen just as He told me." In Jesus' name, Amen.

LESSON 1: FAITH WAITS   APRIL 6

Scripture Reading: Acts 1

I think it's ironic, but fitting, that the very first thing Jesus tells His disciples to do in the book of Acts isn't an "act" at all. He tells them to "wait."

> *"On one occasion, while He was eating with them, He gave them this command: 'Do not leave Jerusalem, but wait for the gift my Father promised, which you have heard me speak about. For John baptized with water, but in a few days you will be baptized with the Holy Spirit'" (Acts 1:4-5).*

Wait. Wait for the gift of the Holy Spirit. You see, without God, what's the point of going on? If God's called you to wait, waiting can be just as much an act of faith as doing. And *not* waiting can be your downfall.

When God promised to give Abraham many descendants, Abraham got impatient and got his wife's servant girl pregnant instead. God said that their child Ishmael would have descendants galore, but that he would always be in hostility towards his brothers. When Abraham and his wife eventually had a child of their own, God blessed that child, Isaac, with many descendants, too. But unfortunately, the hostility between those two brothers has carried on for generations, even to this day, as present-day Muslims claim Ishmael as their forefather and present-day Jews claim Isaac as theirs.

God honors His promises, but there's a price to pay for not waiting.

It's hard to wait, I know. But I want to encourage you today, if God's called you to wait, wait.

I remember one of the times when I was waiting on God. I felt that God had called me to go to Israel. Even though I didn't know why, but I sensed it was important, so I went. After a few days of looking around Jerusalem, I began to wonder if God was ever going to show up at all. What was I waiting for anyway?

As I laid on my bed, I read this verse from Psalm 27:14:

> "Wait for the Lord, be strong and take heart and wait for the Lord."

But I read it in the Amplified Bible, which gives even more detail about what the Hebrew and Greek words in the Bible mean. I love the way the Amplified Bible puts it:

> "Wait and hope for and expect the Lord; be brave and of good courage and let your heart be stout and enduring. Yes, wait for and hope for and expect the Lord" (Psalm 27:14, AMP).

It changed my whole perspective. Instead of waiting idly and wondering if God would ever show up, I began to look forward to what God was going to do. The next day, God did show up in a powerful way. I met a pastor on the temple mount who was also visiting in Israel. He prayed for me that day, anointed me with oil, and spoke a prophetic word over me about my future life and ministry, including much of what I'm doing today.

The difference between waiting idly and waiting expectantly is the difference between sitting at home alone, wondering if anyone's ever going to stop by, and sitting at home, waiting for the most important person in your life to walk through that door at any minute, because they called ahead and told you they were on their way.

If you're not convinced that it's worth it to wait, here are a few benefits of waiting: You'll sleep better, feel better, think clearer. You'll be more content, less frustrated, kinder, gentler, more patient, more gracious. You'll grow stronger, live longer, stand firmer. Here's how the Bible puts it in Isaiah 40:31:

> "But they that wait upon the LORD shall renew their strength; they shall mount up with wings as eagles; they shall run, and not be weary; and they shall walk, and not faint" (Isaiah 40:31, KJV).

If God's called you to wait, wait. Wait for the Lord. "Yes, wait for and hope for and expect the Lord" (Psalm 27:14, AMP).

Prayer: Father, help me to wait on You with expectancy, looking forward to what You're going to do at the end of the wait. In Jesus' name, Amen.

LESSON 2: FAITH ACTS   APRIL 7

Scripture Reading: Acts 2

There's a scene in the movie *Spider-Man 2* where Spider-Man is swooping from building to building when suddenly he has a web failure. He crashes into the alley below, looks at his hands and says, "Why is this happening to me?"

He wonders if he's losing his power. But it's not true. He still has the same power he's always had since he first got bitten by that supercharged spider. *It's in his blood.* What he lacks is *faith*. He's had some bad things happen to him and he's ready to give up. He just wants to go back to being Peter Parker, a normal guy with a normal job.

But after a pep talk from his Aunt May, Peter goes back to being Spider-Man. From the top of a building, he takes a flying leap over the edge, yelling, "I'm back! I'm back!"

Seconds later, he looks down, panics, and plummets into the cars parked below. He stands up gingerly and says, "My back. My back."

I guess he still has a ways to go! But he's *working* on it, something that I want to encourage you to do today, too.

I've heard it said that faith is like a muscle, it gets stronger the more we exercise it. There was another Peter who exercised his faith on a regular basis, Peter the Apostle, the one who stepped over the edge of a boat to walk on water, but seconds later, looked down, panicked and began to sink. This is the same Peter who stood by Jesus the night he was arrested, saying he'd die for Jesus, but then denied that he even knew Jesus three times before the morning.

Some people criticize Peter for his lack of faith, but the truth is, he's the only one who stepped over the edge of the boat and got to experience walking on water, even if only for a short time.

On the day of Pentecost, when Jesus sent the Holy Spirit to empower the disciples as He promised He would, the Bible says:

"Then Peter stood up with the Eleven, raised his voice and addressed the crowd: 'Fellow Jews and all of you who live in Jerusalem, let me explain this to you; listen carefully to what I say…'" (Acts 2:14).

Peter's message was so powerful that three thousand were baptized and put their faith in Christ as a result.

How did Peter go from denying Christ to proclaiming His name to thousands? In short, he got his faith back. He'd seen Jesus raised from the dead, he waited when Jesus told him to wait, and he "got a dose of the Holy Ghost." The combination was powerful, and when God told him to act, Peter stood up and boldly told the people gathered what he knew about Jesus.

Peter exercised his faith on a regular basis. And God wants us to do the same, even when asked to do a "little thing"—bring a meal to a friend, visit someone in a nursing home, send an email to someone who needs encouragement, speak the truth in love, encourage your co-workers to do what's right, instead of what's safe, easy or more profitable.

God told a poor widow to gather empty jars from her neighbors so He could fill them with oil. God did the miracle, but she had to gather the jars (see 2 Kings 4). God told Naaman to wash seven times in the Jordan River, something Naaman thought was too small to make any difference. But Naaman did it, and God healed him (see 2 Kings 5).

Jesus told the disciples they'd be His witnesses to the ends of the earth. When the day of Pentecost came, all Peter had to do was stand up and tell them what he knew about Jesus. God brought people from the ends of the earth to him (see Acts 2:5-12).

If God's calling you to act, act—even if it's just a little thing.

Prayer: Father, help me to wait when you say "Wait," and to act when you say "Act," so I can accomplish all You want to accomplish through me. In Jesus' name, Amen.

LESSON 3: FAITH HEALS APRIL 8

Scripture Reading: Acts 3

I'd like to talk about healing today, but before I do, I'd like to say a word to those of you who may have lost someone close to you, whether recently or in the past.

I know what it's like to lose someone you love. I believe there are times to pray that God will take your loved ones home to heaven where there will be "no more death or mourning or crying or pain…" (Revelation 21:4). For the Christian, the moment we pass from this life to the next will be the greatest and most miraculous healing any of us will ever experience.

But there's also a time to pray with all the strength and faith you have for God to heal someone, here and now, in the name of Jesus, and that's what our passage is talking about today.

In Acts chapter 3, Peter and John came across a man who was crippled from birth. The man asked Peter and John for money, to which Peter responded:

> "Silver or gold I do not have, but what I have I give you. In the name of Jesus Christ of Nazareth, walk" (Acts 3:6).

Peter took the man by the hand, the man's feet and ankles became instantly strong, and he began walking and jumping and praising God.

It was a powerful scene—so powerful that people came running from all over to see what had happened. Peter said:

> "Men of Israel, why does this surprise you? Why do you stare at us as if by our own power or godliness we had made this man walk? … By faith in the name of Jesus, this man whom you see and know was made strong. It is Jesus' name and the faith that comes through Him that has given this complete healing to him, as you can all see" (Acts 3:12, 16).

Faith heals. In this case, I think it's interesting that it doesn't seem to be so much the faith of the man who was healed that made the difference. He was just asking Peter and John for money. It seems to be the faith of Peter and John that made the difference. They were the ones who had the faith to say to the man, "In the name of Jesus Christ of Nazareth, walk." They were the ones who reached out and pulled the man to his feet. It's a testimony to me of the power of the faith of a friend.

And you can be that friend when you pray for those around you.

There was a time when I would tell someone I'd pray for them, then walk away and pray later when I got home alone. While that was a good thing to do, Jesus said, "For where two or three come together in my name, there am I with them" (Matthew 18:20).

I have no doubt that if Jesus were standing right there with me as I prayed for you, that He would reach out and touch you with His power. And Jesus tells us that when we come together in His name, He will be right there with us. Knowing this truth increases my faith tremendously.

So I've found it to be more powerful, and more meaningful to the person for whom I'm praying, to stop and ask them, "Can I pray for you right now?" If they agree, which almost always happens, then I say a prayer with them right there, whether in a hallway or in a store or at a restaurant. It's a simple thing that doesn't have to draw attention, but simply bowing our heads and praying at the time the need is expressed. Aside from being powerful and meaningful, it also helps me to remember to pray so I don't forget by the time I get home!

For some of you, I want to go further and encourage you not just to pray for your family and friends to be healed in Jesus' name, but to pray for them out loud and in front of them. I know this may be foreign territory for some of you, but it's a great way to exercise your faith. It can be as simple as this, "Father, heal my friend. In Jesus' name, Amen." Not only will you become stronger in your faith, but so will your family and friends.

As James said,

> "...pray for each other so you may be healed" (James 5:16b).

So whether in private or out loud, exercise your faith today! Pray for those around you to be healed in Jesus' name.

Prayer: Father, give me the faith to believe in Your power to heal and to pray that my family and friends will be healed. In Jesus' name, Amen.

LESSON 4: FAITH SAVES　　　　　　　　　　　　　　　　　　　　　APRIL 9

Scripture Reading: Acts 4

When people say they're "saved," what do they mean? And what exactly are they saved from?

To say you're saved means more than just the fact that you're a Christian. It means you've been saved *from* something. Specifically, it means you've been saved from hell, both the literal hell that Jesus talked about when people are separated from God for all eternity, and the practical hell that you can experience here on this earth when you continue to follow your own sinful ways.

To someone who isn't "saved," the word seems to be either offensive or just plain laughable. But to someone who *is* "saved," the word is full of life, because they know what would have happened to them had Jesus not come to save them.

I read this week that one of the candidates running for office is being questioned because their pastor "preaches hell for anyone who doesn't believe in Jesus." I guess when you put it that way, it does sound rather offensive. But the truth is, it's the same message that Jesus preached. (Good thing He isn't running for office—He'd probably get crucified again!)

Some people, unfortunately, think that Jesus is out to get them, that He came to condemn them for what they've done. But Jesus didn't come to condemn you. He came to save you. He even says so in His own words:

> "For God did not send His Son into the world to condemn the world, but to save the world through Him. Whoever believes in Him is not condemned, but whoever does not believe stands condemned already because he has not believed in the name of God's one and only Son" (John 3:17-18).

So, yes, there is hell to pay if you don't believe in Jesus. But no one's going to hell because they haven't believed in Jesus; they're going to hell because of their sins, which is a completely different reason altogether. Whenever you sin, it separates you from God. And without a savior, you'd be separated from God forever. That's hell. That's the fate from which Jesus came to save you.

When the Apostles Peter and John were arrested for preaching that Jesus could save people from their sins, they didn't back down even when threatened with death. In Acts chapter 4, they spoke boldly about the fact that Jesus alone had the power to save:

> "Salvation is found in no one else, for there is no other name under heaven given to men by which we must be saved" (Acts 4:12).

Faith saves. One of my favorite scenes in the *Indiana Jones* series is when Indy comes to the edge of a cliff and can't see any way across to the cliff on the other side. With a look of exasperation, he says, "It's a leap of faith!" With his enemies pressing in from behind and no other way forward, he takes a giant step into what looks like thin air in front of him, only to find that he has stepped onto a solid rock bridge that had been camouflaged from view. Indy's "leap of faith" had saved him.

Jesus wants to save you from more than just a bad ending to the movie of your life. He wants to save you from hell, both here on earth and on into eternity.

When Jesus died on the cross, He extended an invitation to every person in the world who had strayed from God to come back to Him. The price for our sins had been paid. But reconciliation is a two way street. Just because one party wants to be reconciled with the other doesn't mean they *are* reconciled. Both parties have to agree to it.

Jesus has done His part. Now He's waiting for each person to respond individually. And the way you respond is by faith.

If you've never put your faith in Christ to save you from your sins, I pray you'll do it today. He'd love to say to you what He said to the woman who wiped His feet with her tears:

> "Your sins are forgiven. Your faith has saved you; go in peace" (Luke 7:48,50).

Prayer: Father, forgive me for the sins I have committed, too, as I put my faith in Christ. In Jesus' name, Amen.

LESSON 5: FAITH OBEYS   APRIL 10

Scripture Reading: Acts 5

I'd like to talk today about my all-time favorite Super Hero, if you could call Him that. His name is Jesus Christ and He's the best example of our topic today, "Faith Obeys."

I can't think of anyone who epitomizes obedience more than Jesus on the night before He died when He prayed: "...not My will, but Yours be done" (Luke 22:42).

But just because Jesus was the Son of God, it doesn't mean that He didn't agonize over the choices He made, just like the rest of us do. Luke says that Jesus was in such anguish over His decision that night that, "His sweat was like drops of blood falling to the ground" (Luke 22.44b).

I guess it's not really fair to compare Jesus to other Superheroes like Superman or Spider-Man, because Jesus *was* the Son of God. He had access to powers they could never have imagined. But at the same time, Jesus was also fully human—more *real*, and more *like us*, than Superman or Spider-Man ever were.

The Bible says that Jesus had real flesh and blood (Hebrews 2:14), was born as a baby (Luke 2:7), was scolded by his parents (Luke 2:48), and grew in wisdom and stature (Luke 2:52). He experienced love (John 11:5), anger (Mark 3:5), joy (Hebrews 12:2), betrayal (Luke 22:48), temptation (Hebrews 4:15) and pain (Matthew 27:46). He bled (John 19:34), He cried (John 11:35), He suffered (Hebrews 13:12) and He died (Mark 15:39).

The more that I can envision Jesus as a real human being, the more I can envision that I can really do what He did, as He said I could do when He said, "I tell you the truth, anyone who has faith in Me will do what I have been doing" (John 14:12).

That includes being obedient to God, regardless of the consequences to us personally. Peter and John found that same strength to obey God, even when threatened with death, as we can see in Acts chapters 4 and 5. After calling on the name of Jesus to heal a man who had been crippled for over forty years, Peter and John were commanded by the religious leaders to stop speaking or teaching at all in the name of Jesus. Peter replied,

> *"Judge for yourselves whether it is right in God's sight to obey you rather than God. For we cannot help speaking about what we have seen and heard…We must obey God rather than men!" (Acts 4:19-20, 5:29).*

When faced with death, Peter and John had to make a choice. These weren't idle threats. The religious leaders had already shown their resolve to follow through on their threats by putting Jesus to death.

But Peter and John also knew what Jesus had called them to do. They had just seen Christ perform a miracle through them when they called on His name. So they responded with the only response that made sense to them: "…we cannot help speaking about what we have seen and heard."

If God is calling you to stop a relationship that you know is destroying you, stop it, even if it seems too hard or too complicated. If God is calling you to stay in a marriage that you'd rather get out of, stay in it. If God is calling you to another job, take it, but if He's calling you to stay in your current job, don't leave. If He's calling you to stop a bad habit that's killing you, stop it, and if He's calling you to start a good habit that will save you, start it!

God gave Peter and John the strength to do what they needed to do, just like He gave Jesus the strength to do what He needed to do—just like He'll give you the strength to do what He wants you to do, when you put your faith in Christ.

Prayer: Father, help me to do all that You're calling me to do today, to obey Your will, not my own, and not the will of others, but Yours alone. In Jesus' name, Amen.

LESSON 6: FAITH FILLS — APRIL 11

Scripture Reading: Acts 6

I suppose you've heard what happens when you sing a country music song backwards, right? You get your car back, you get your dog back, you get your wife back.

Well today, I want to talk about how to get something else back: I want to talk about how to get your faith back — how to get your faith back if you've lost it, how to find it for the first time if you've never found it before, and if you've already found it, how to help others find their faith, too, so that they can truly become filled with faith, or "faith full."

There's a scene in the movie *The Chronicles of Narnia* where Lucy and her brothers and sister finally all stumble into the land of Narnia when they're trying to hide in an old wardrobe. Lucy had discovered Narnia before, but when she told her family about it, they made fun of her, they got mad at her, and they told her to stop imagining things. But now they all see it with their own eyes and finally believe. I love that moment of discovery, when people go from doubt to faith, from unbelief to belief, from questioning what others have told them to believing it with they're whole heart, soul, mind and strength.

Acts chapter 6 describes one of the early believers named Stephen in a way that I'd love to become as well. Acts says that Stephen was:

"a man who was full of faith and of the Holy Spirit" (Acts 6:5).

That's what I think God wants each of you to be: men and women who are full of faith and of the Holy Spirit. Men and women who are so filled with faith that it overflows from within you and onto those around you.

But how can we get to the point where we're "faith full"? How can we help other people discover what we've found to be true?

Here are three things I'd recommend:

1) Read your Bible. The Bible contains story after story of people who have put their faith in God and become filled with faith as a result. When you read their stories, it will help to increase your faith as well.

Today's a good day to read John chapter 20, for instance, where it describes three sets of people at the moment when they went from doubt to belief, who got to see Jesus raised from the day on that first Easter morning and in the days immediately following His resurrection. The Apostle John says he wrote these stories for you: "Jesus did many other miraculous signs in the presence of his disciples, which are not recorded in this book. But these are written that you may believe that Jesus is the Christ, the Son of God, and that by believing you may have life in His name" (John 20:30-31).

2) Research your Barriers. If you've got questions that are keeping you from fully believing what God has said in His Word, take time to get your questions answered so you can move forward in your faith.

This is what Lee Strobel did when his wife told him she had become a Christian. Lee was an atheist and the legal affairs editor for the *Chicago Tribune*. He decided to use his journalism and legal training to thoroughly investigate Christianity, hoping to liberate his wife from this cult! But his plan backfired when he found more evidence that supported the resurrection than he ever imagined, and he ended up putting his faith in Christ.

3) Reconnect with your Brothers and Sisters in Christ. God doesn't want you to go it alone. He wants you to help each other, to bear each other's burdens and to sharpen each other like iron sharpens iron.

C.S. Lewis, who wrote *The Chronicles of Narnia* and other great Christian works, went to Oxford College as an atheist. But after reading books by George McDonald and others he admired and discovered were strong Christians, he turned from atheism to believing there must be a God. But it was when he began to meet with other Christians in person, like fellow student J.R.R. Tolkien who later wrote *The Lord of The Rings*, they challenged his thoughts and ideas. After talking with his friends till three in the morning one night, Lewis went home and the next morning went from just believing in God to becoming a Christian.

Read your Bible. Research your Barriers, and Reconnect with your Brothers and Sisters in Christ.

These aren't the only way to become filled with faith, but they're certainly good things to do, even if you're a strong believer, because they can help you keep up in the faith that you've already come to believe in your heart.

Prayer: Father, thank You for giving me so many examples of people who have put their faith in You. Help me to keep putting my faith in You, and to help others put their faith in You, too. In Jesus' name, Amen.

LESSON 7: FAITH SPEAKS — APRIL 12

Scripture Reading: Acts 7

There are times when God wants you to hold your tongue. For instance, when Jesus healed two blind men, He told them sternly, "See that no one knows about this" (Matthew 9:30). And when Jesus brought Jairus' daughter back from the dead, Jesus gave strict orders not to let anyone know about it (Mark 5:43).

But there are other times when God wants you to speak. For instance, when Jesus cast the demons out of the man named Legion, Jesus told him: "Return home and tell how much God has done for you" (Luke 8:39a). Or when Jesus healed ten men of leprosy on the road to Jerusalem, He told them: "Go, show yourselves to the priests" (Luke 17:14b).

So there are times when God wants you to hold your tongue, but there are also times when God wants you to speak. And when God calls you to speak, He wants you to be ready. The Bible says, "Always be prepared to give an answer to everyone who asks you to give the reason for the hope that you have" (1 Peter 3:15).

I'd like to give you three ideas today to help you speak when God calls you to speak. I've pulled these ideas from the story in Acts chapter 7 where God called Stephen to speak. Stephen spoke boldly, even though it was dangerous to do so. When Stephen was arrested and had to defend himself, he gave one of the boldest speeches in the Bible. Because of it, he was stoned to death, but his words were not in vain.

Here are the three things that I noticed Stephen did, and we can do, when God says to speak:

1) *Don't be afraid.*
2) *Pair up your words with Scripture.*
3) *Trust God to use His Word to transform lives.*

First, don't be afraid. Jesus had already forewarned His followers before He died that they would be arrested and flogged and persecuted. Jesus told them: "So do not be afraid of them. There is nothing concealed that will not be disclosed or hidden that will not be made known. What I tell you in the dark, speak in the daylight; what is whispered in your ear, proclaim from the roofs. Do not be afraid of those who kill the body but cannot kill the soul. Rather, be afraid of the One who can destroy both soul and body in hell" (Matthew 10:26-28).

Although Stephen could have been afraid that day, he didn't let it keep him from speaking.

Second, pair up your words with Scripture. Stephen might also have worried about what he was going to say to his accusers, but Jesus had already told His followers: "But when they arrest you, do not worry about what to say or how to say it. At that time you will be given what to say, for it will not be you speaking, but the Spirit of your Father speaking through you" (Matthew 10:19-20).

God did give Stephen words to speak. *His* Word. When Stephen spoke, he paired up his own words with Scripture to support what he was saying. Stephen quoted from Genesis, Exodus, Deuteronomy, Amos and Isaiah. When Stephen spoke, God spoke His Words through Stephen. This is one of the reasons it's so important to read your Bible, study your Bible and memorize your Bible. When you know God's Word, it helps you to infuse your words with His.

Third, trust that God will use His Word to transform lives. The Bible says that one of the men who heard Stephen speak that day was Saul, who at the time gave approval to Stephen's death. But if you keep reading in Acts, you'll see that Saul became a Christian himself shortly thereafter. Jesus changed Saul's name to Paul, and Paul went on to write much of the rest of the New Testament, including the letters to the Romans, Corinthians, Galatians, Ephesians, Philippians, Colossians and more.

Even though Stephen died, God used his words that day to reach many lives, including ours over 2,000 years later! As God said, "My word…will not return to Me empty but will accomplish what I desire and achieve the purpose for which I sent it" (Isaiah 55:11).

When God calls you to speak, speak. Don't be afraid. Pair up your words with Scripture. And trust that God will use His Word to transform lives.

Prayer: Father, help us to speak when you say, "Speak." In Jesus' name, Amen.

LESSON 8: FAITH EXPLAINS   APRIL 13

Scripture Reading: Acts 8

If God has given you a special gift to help people understand the Bible, I'd like to encourage you today to use that gift. You may not even realize it's a gift. You may think that reading and understanding the Bible just comes naturally to you. But I'd like to show you what a gift it really is.

In Acts chapter 8, an angel of the Lord told Philip, one of Jesus' disciples, to go to the road that leads down from Jerusalem to Gaza. Along the way, Philip encountered a man from Ethiopia who was sitting in his chariot reading from the book of Isaiah.

The Ethiopian was an important official in charge of the treasury for Candace, the Queen of Ethiopia. He had been to Jerusalem to worship and was now on his way back home. The Spirit told Philip to go near the man's chariot, and when he did, he heard the man reading from Isaiah the prophet. Philip asked: "Do you understand what you are reading?" To which the Ethiopian replied:

> *"How can I, unless someone explains it to me?" (Acts 8:31)*

So the Ethiopian invited Philip to come up and sit with him. Philip began with that very passage of Scripture and told the man the good news about Jesus.

As they traveled together along the road, the Ethiopian understood so well that he said, "Look here is water. Why shouldn't I be baptized?" So the Ethiopian stopped the chariot, was baptized, and went on his way rejoicing!

God had given Philip special insight into the Scriptures. He had exposed him to the teachings and the life of Jesus in a way that Philip was able to help someone else understand why Jesus had to come and die.

The Ethiopian was smart (he was in charge of the Queen's treasury). He loved God (he was just returning from a lengthy trip to worship in Jerusalem). And he was eager to learn spiritual truths (he was reading the book of Isaiah). But he still needed someone to explain the Scriptures to him. So God sent Philip to do just that.

Faith explains. When God gives you the faith to believe and to understand what He's done through Christ, He wants you to share what you've learned with others.

I remember flying to California one time, hoping to share with someone I knew there about what Christ had done for me. But even though I tried to bring up the topic throughout the weekend, God never opened the door for me to walk through and share. As I flew home, my plane made a stop in another city before I reached home. A man boarded the plane, sat down next to me, and proceeded to open up a brand new Bible to the first page of the New Testament.

I glanced up to see his face and couldn't believe it! It was a friend of mine from college who had been involved in some of the same things that Christ had eventually delivered me from! He was just as shocked to see me as I was to see him. When I asked about the Bible, he said his mother was worried about him so had bought this Bible for him. He thought he'd give it a try and had sat down to open it for the very first time. I knew what God wanted me to do.

We spent the rest of the flight talking about his life and talking about the Scriptures. I started with the passage where he had opened his Bible and I explained how Christ had delivered me from the very things with which my friend still struggled.

Although I don't know what happened to him after we left the plane, I do know that God answered my prayers to be able to share what was on my heart. And He answered my friend's prayers (or at least his mother's!) that someone would help him to understand what he was reading.

If God has given you the ability to understand the Scriptures, know that it's a gift, and know that God wants you to use that gift to explain those Scriptures to those around you.

Prayer: Father, help me make the most of every opportunity You give me to explain to others what You've revealed to me. In Jesus' name, Amen.

LESSON 9: FAITH SURRENDERS   APRIL 14

Scripture Reading: Acts 9

There are times when I'll be singing a song of worship to God when my arms almost automatically begin to rise up. Almost without thinking I'll find myself with my arms fully outstretched above my head in praise to God. It's a beautiful time of both reaching out to God and completely giving myself to Him—an act of surrender, you might call it—with my hands up in the air, nothing to hide and gladly submitted to the Lordship of Christ.

I remember a similar moment when I put my faith in Christ at 23, having taken control of my own life for those years and seeing where I ended up, then finally yielding to Christ to let Him call the shots from then on. It was no longer a hard thing to do, but joyous, yielding myself completely to God's will and purposes.

The Apostle Paul experienced his own profound moment of surrender on the road to Damascus.

Even though Paul was extremely religious, he didn't believe in Christ. He was committed to imprisoning—and even killing—those who did. He had gotten permission from the high priest in Jerusalem to go to Damascus and take prisoner those who belonged to what was then called "the Way."

Here's what happened to Paul that not only changed the course of the rest of his trip, but also the rest of his life. In this passage, Paul is still called Saul, as Christ had not yet given him his new name:

> "As he neared Damascus on his journey, suddenly a light from heaven flashed around him. He fell to the ground and heard a voice say to him, 'Saul, Saul, why do you persecute me?'
> 'Who are you, Lord?' Saul asked.
> 'I am Jesus, whom you are persecuting,' He replied. 'Now get up and go into the city, and you will be told what you must do'" (Acts 9:3-6).

When Paul got up from that experience, he was physically blinded. Those traveling with him led him into Damascus, where he stayed for three days, neither eating nor drinking.

During those same three days, a believer in Damascus named Ananias faced his own moment of surrender.

He had already put his faith in Christ, but when the Lord, in a vision, called him to go and pray for Paul to receive his sight back, Ananias wrestled with what he was going to do. He had heard reports about what Paul had done to believers in Jerusalem. He knew Paul had authority from the chief priests to do the same in Damascus. Faced with this extremely tough dilemma, Ananias chose to surrender to the will of God:

> "Then Ananias went to the house and entered it. Placing his hands on Saul, he said, 'Brother Saul, the Lord—Jesus, who appeared to you on the road as you were coming here—has sent me so that you may see again and be filled with the Holy Spirit.' Immediately, something like scales fell from Saul's eyes, and he could see again. He got up and was baptized, and after taking some food, he regained his strength" (Acts 9:17-19).

From that day on, and for the rest of his life, Paul went on to preach boldly in the name of Christ. He wrote much of the New Testament, which has affected literally millions of lives in the 2,000 years since then.

Thank God that Paul surrendered his will to God's. And thank God that Ananias surrendered his will to God's, too.

Faith surrenders. Whether you're still just considering putting your faith in Christ for the first time, or whether you've been a believer for years, I want to encourage you today to surrender whatever's left of your will to the will of God. Is there something God is calling you to do? Somewhere He wants you to go? Someone He wants you to talk to? Something He wants you to give to Him?

Lift up your hands and take hold of His. Lift up your heart and give it to Him. Give up your will and get into His. Whatever you're planning to do, wherever you're planning to go, it will pale in comparison to what He wants to do in and through you.

Prayer: Father, give me the faith to surrender my will to Yours. In Jesus' name, Amen.

LESSON 10: FAITH GIVES — APRIL 15

Scripture Reading: Acts 10

What prompts you to give? When you see a need around you, what is it that causes you to want to reach out and help? For me, I've found that when my faith is strong, my desire to give is strong. But when my faith is weak, my desire to give is weak. It seems that the more I'm able to trust God with my life and my resources, the more I'm able to let go of the things that I would otherwise try to hang onto.

Faith gives. And when God sees our faith and our giving, He loves to bless us back in return.

Take a look at what happened to a man in the Bible named Cornelius when he gave to others in response to his faith. Cornelius was a commander in the Roman army and even though he wasn't Jewish, he was a devout and God-fearing man who prayed to God regularly and gave generously to those in need. Here's what happened to him as recorded in Acts chapter 10:

> *"One day at about three in the afternoon he had a vision. He distinctly saw an angel of God, who came to him and said, 'Cornelius!'*
> *"Cornelius stared at him in fear. 'What is it, Lord?' he asked.*
> *"The angel answered, 'Your prayers and gifts to the poor have come up as a memorial offering before God. Now send men to Joppa to bring back a man named Simon who is called Peter. He is staying with Simon the tanner, whose house is by the sea'"* (Acts 10:3-6).

Cornelius sent for Peter, who came in response to a vision of his own that God had given him. Peter shared with Cornelius the good news about Christ. Cornelius and the large crowd who came to his house to see Peter were baptized with water and the Holy Spirit.

God honored Cornelius' prayers and gifts. They had made their way up to God as a memorial offering to Him. And God poured out his blessing back on Cornelius.

Faith gives and God sees those gifts. They are a natural response to the faith that God wells up inside of you. Your giving is a practical way to love God and love others.

I remember telling some friends about all that God had been doing in and through my life one time. When I finished, one of the people listening to me reached into his pocket and pulled out all the money he had. He put it in my hand.

I was totally caught off guard. Why was he giving me money? I had just been telling them about what God was doing in the world and in my life. I knew this man didn't have money to spare. I tried a few times to put it back into his hands, but he wouldn't take it. One of my other friends finally pulled me aside to the kitchen and said to me, "He's giving that money to God, not to you. As you're telling him about the power of God to work in people's lives, God's working on his heart, and this is the way he wants to respond. Please don't try to stop what God is doing in his life by giving the money back."

This man was growing in his faith as he listened to my stories, and his desire to do something in response swelled up within him. When God increases our faith, he also increases our desire and willingness to give.

Are there needs around you that God might be prompting you to support with your prayers and gifts? Is God trying to increase your faith so that when a need arises, you'll be able to meet it with both your faith and your giving?

God wants you to be devout and God-fearing like Cornelius, praying and giving generously to those who have needs. When you do, know that God will not overlook your prayers and gifts. He loves to bless the hearts of those who bless His heart, just like He blessed Cornelius and everyone who came to his house to hear the good news about Christ.

Prayer: Father, increase my faith and increase my willingness to give at the same time. In Jesus' name, Amen.

LESSON 11: FAITH INCLUDES — APRIL 16

Scripture Reading: Acts 11

Some people think that Christianity is exclusive. They think that because Christ said that people must believe in Him in order to come back to the Father that Christianity excludes people. The truth is, Christianity is not exclusive, but incredibly inclusive. It's open to all people, of all ages, from all races and all nationalities.

The story of Peter and Cornelius in Acts chapters 10 and 11 shows us just how inclusive Christianity really is. Peter was a Jew and one of the closest follower of Christ, but God sent Peter to Cornelius, who was not Jewish, to tell him the good news about Christ. Peter went, but not without some having to triple check with God beforehand. The Bible says that as Peter was praying one day, he had a vision from God:

> "He saw heaven opened and something like a large sheet being let down to earth by its four corners. It contained all kinds of four-footed animals, as well as reptiles of the earth and birds of the air. Then a voice told him, 'Get up, Peter. Kill and eat.'
> 'Surely not, Lord!' Peter replied. 'I have never eaten anything impure or unclean.'
> The voice spoke to him a second time, 'Do not call anything impure that God has made clean.'
> This happened three times, and immediately the sheet was taken back to heaven" (Acts 10:11-16).

As Peter was wondering about the vision, some men arrived at his door, asking if he would come with them to see Cornelius, a man who was a Roman soldier, but who was devout and God-fearing, prayed regularly and gave generously to those in need.

Realizing the vision was from God, Peter went with them, shared the good news of Christ with Cornelius and all those at his house, and they were all baptized in both water and in the Holy Spirit.

Peter realized God's desire to keep the Jewish people holy by not interacting with non-Jews was for their protection, but not for the exclusion of others. It was a way to keep the Jews pure, not keep others out. Others have always been welcome, and now, through Jesus, the way was made clear for them. When Peter told the other disciples what had happened, they praised God saying, "So then, God has granted even the Gentiles repentance unto life" (Acts 11:18b).

I used to think Christians were being prideful and arrogant when they claimed that you had to believe in Christ in order to come to God. But I learned that it was not Christians who made that claim, but Jesus Himself. Just before His death and resurrection into heaven, Jesus told His disciples how to get where He was going:

> *"You know the way to the place where I am going….I am the way and the truth and the life. No one comes to the Father except through me" (John 14:4,6).*

There was no pride or arrogance in what Jesus said, but simple, humble truth. Christ went on to demonstrate His love for us and the truthfulness of what He said when He died for our sins and opened the way for anyone who believed in Him to come back to God, free, clean and forgiven.

Peter shared this good news on another occasion to a crowd of thousands who had gathered from all over the world. During his message, Peter made this bold claim about Jesus: "Salvation is found in no one else, for there is no other name under heaven given to men by which we must be saved" (Acts 4:12). When the people heard it, rather than turning their backs and responding with disgust at Peter's arrogance, over 3,000 of them turned their hearts towards Christ, putting their faith in Him, and being baptized in His name.

Faith includes, as Cornelius and his entire household discovered.

If you've never put your faith in Christ, I encourage you to do it today. If you know someone who needs to put their faith in Christ, invite them to come to Him today. He is the way and the truth and the life, and His way is open to all.

Prayer: Father, thank You for sending Jesus as the way back to You. Help me invite others back, too. In Jesus' name, Amen.

LESSON 12: FAITH PRAYS　　　　　　　　　　　　　　　　　　　　　APRIL 17

Scripture Reading: Acts 12

If you need something supernatural to happen, do something supernatural: pray.

Prayer is not just quiet meditation. It's not just thinking through your thoughts on your own. Prayer is having a conversation with the God who created you, who knows you better than anyone else, and who can act in ways that are both natural and even "super" natural.

One of the most dramatic answers to prayer is recorded in Acts chapter 12. I'd like to share it with you today to encourage you to pray earnestly for situations in your life for which there appear to be no earthly answers.

Here's the background for this story: After Saul stopped persecuting the early Christians, they finally enjoyed a time of peace and continued to grow in numbers. But then King Herod took up the persecution again and began to arrest some of those believers putting a man named James to death with the sword. When Herod saw that this pleased some of the Jews, he put Peter in prison, too, planning to put him on trial after the Passover.

Things looked bleak for Peter. There was little hope for him after what had just happened to James, but those early believers weren't hopeless. They did what they could: they prayed.

The Bible says, "but the church was earnestly praying to God for him" (Acts 12:5). Look what happened when they did:

> *"The night before Herod was to bring him to trial, Peter was sleeping between two soldiers, bound with two chains, and sentries stood guard at the entrance. Suddenly*

an angel of the Lord appeared and a light shone in the cell. He struck Peter on the side and woke him up. 'Quick, get up!' he said, and the chains fell off Peter's wrists.
"Then the angel said to him, 'Put on your clothes and sandals.' And Peter did so. 'Wrap your cloak around you and follow me,' the angel told him. Peter followed him out of the prison, but he had no idea that what the angel was doing was really happening; he thought he was seeing a vision. They passed the first and second guards and came to the iron gate leading to the city. It opened for them by itself, and they went through it. When they had walked the length of one street, suddenly the angel left him.
"Then Peter came to himself and said, 'Now I know without a doubt that the Lord sent his angel and rescued me from Herod's clutches and from everything the Jewish people were anticipating'" (Acts 12:6-11).

Faith prays. It may seem obvious that when people are filled with faith, they pray. But interestingly, it may not have been their great faith that drove them to prayer, but perhaps that they had nowhere else to turn. When Peter showed up later that night at the door of a house where many believers were gathered in prayer for him, the people didn't even believe that it was really Peter at the door. When a servant girl came to tell them Peter was there, they told her, "You're out of your mind!" (Acts 12:15). They didn't believe her until Peter kept knocking and they finally opened the door for him. Then they saw for themselves and were astonished.

I love stories like this where God acts in such a way that it even astonishes those who are praying. We may think we're full of faith, but when God answers remarkably like this, we realize just how little faith we had going into our prayers. But nonetheless, they were praying "earnestly."

That's the kind of faith I want for you today. A faith that will pray earnestly. A faith that will pray trusting that God is ultimately in control, but that still prays with full hope and expectation for God to do a miracle.

There's no shame in praying, just power. Abraham Lincoln confessed, "I have been driven many times to my knees by the overwhelming conviction that I had nowhere else to go."

Faith prays. If you need something supernatural to happen, do something supernatural. Pray, and pray earnestly.

Prayer: Father, give me the faith to pray earnestly for Your will to be done here on earth as it is in heaven. In Jesus' name, Amen.

LESSON 13: FAITH FASTS   APRIL 18

Scripture Reading: Acts 13

One of the best ways I've found to intensify, deepen or accelerate my prayers is to fast—to go without food for a period of time so I can focus more intensely on praying.

I don't remember hearing much about fasting when I was growing up. I don't know if it was because I was just a child, or because those around me didn't fast, or because those who did fasted in a way that didn't draw attention to their fasting. But I do know that when I began to read the Bible as an adult, I was surprised by the number of references to prayer and fasting throughout both the Old and New Testament. Moses, David, Elijah, Paul and Jesus Himself are just a few of the many who fasted.

As I read other Christian books, I was surprised to find that many people throughout history, including leaders of major Christian movements also fasted: Luther, Wesley, Finney, Edwards, Booth, to name just a few. I also found that many of the Christian leaders that I knew and respected living today also fasted with profound results.

After reading so many inspiring stories, I decided to try it myself. Now, after twenty years adding fasting to my prayer life at various times, whether for a few days or for several weeks at a time, I can confirm that some of the most significant words I've heard from the Lord have come during those times of prayer and fasting. God has spoken to me about all kinds of things, from who to marry to how to expand my ministry. It seems that when I empty myself physically, I'm able to fill up more spiritually.

Acts chapter 13 records how the earliest Christians fasted and prayed, and how God spoke to them during their fast:

"While they were worshiping the Lord and fasting, the Holy Spirit said, 'Set apart for me Barnabas and Saul for the work to which I have called them.' So after they had fasted and prayed, they placed their hands on them and sent them off" (Acts 13:2-3).

This was the beginning of Saul's (also known as Paul's) missionary journeys. The believers were gathered in prayer, worshiping the Lord and fasting, when God spoke to them through His Holy Spirit that He wanted two of them to set off in a new direction. While this may have seemed like simple next steps for Barnabas and Paul, it began a whole new life of travel and ministry for them. These trips resulted in new church starts in city after city. Because of the prayers and fasting of those early believers, God charted a new life course for Paul, one which took him through to the end of his life.

If you're asking God for direction in your life, for wisdom about how to move forward, for answers as to the next steps you should take, consider intensifying your prayers with fasting. If you're praying for situations that seem to have hit a roadblock and you don't know how to go any further in your prayers, try fasting to break through that barrier.

When Jesus' disciples were praying for a boy who was having seizures and suffering greatly, their prayers didn't seem to help, so they came to Jesus for help. Jesus drove out the demon that was affecting the boy and he was healed from that moment. When the disciples later came to Jesus in private and asked why they couldn't drive it out, He said,

"Because you have so little faith. I tell you the truth, if you have faith as small as a mustard seed, you can say to this mountain, 'Move from here to there' and it will move. Nothing will be impossible for you. But this kind does not go out except by prayer and fasting" (Matthew 17:20-21).

It seems from this passage, and from many others in the Bible, that fasting adds a dimension to our faith and to our prayers that is not available without it.

If you want to intensify, deepen or accelerate your prayers—and fill up more spiritually at the same time—try fasting!

Prayer: Father, help me to grow in my faith, even through fasting and prayer, so that I can see Your will done here on the earth. In Jesus' name, Amen.

LESSON 14: FAITH PERSISTS — APRIL 19

Scripture Reading: Acts 14

There are times when all of us face obstacles that seem just too big to get past. Times when we're ready to throw in the towel. Times when we want to give up and to walk away from the things we feel God has called us to do.

If you're facing times like that today, I want to encourage you to press on, to be persistent in your faith. Don't give up now. Now's the time to let God work through you in a way that you can shine for Him.

Michael Jordan was an incredible basketball player. But the crowds didn't come to watch him walk onto an empty court and shoot free-throws for an hour and a half. They came to watch him shine in the face of opposition. They came to watch him take the ball from one end of the court to the other, making his way through opponents who were doing everything they could to stop him.

When someone would try to steal the ball, Michael would dribble behind his back. When someone blocked his way forward, Michael would spin his way around. When someone would try to block his shot, Michael would leap into the air beyond their reach, swishing the ball through the net on his way back down.

The times Michael Jordan shone the brightest were the times when his opposition was the most intense.

Paul and Barnabas in the book of Acts remind me of Michael Jordan. When God sent them out to win the world for Christ, they went from city to city, winning converts all along the way. But they weren't shooting free-throws on an empty court. One of the reasons they shone so bright was because their opposition was so intense. In city after city, they were spoken against, thrown out of town, and even stoned and left for dead.

In the city of Iconium, many people came to Christ. But others began to stir up trouble for Paul and Barnabas. Rather than running away, they pressed on. The Bible says:

> "So Paul and Barnabas spent considerable time there, speaking boldly for the Lord, who confirmed the message of his grace by enabling them to do miraculous signs and wonders" (Acts 13:4).

Instead of throwing in the towel, Paul and Barnabas decided to stay even longer. When the people of Iconium eventually made a plan to kill them, they escaped. When the people of Lystra stoned them and left them for dead, they recovered and went right back into the city. When they had finished making their way through city after city, they didn't just call it quits. They turned around and went right back through each of the cities where people had tried to kill them before, strengthening the believers they had won in those cities, and encouraging them to remain true to the faith.

When the opposition came, Paul and Barnabas dribbled behind their backs, spun around the opposition, and leapt into the air as they swished the ball through the net on their way back down.

Faith persists. It doesn't give up and go home just because an opponent shows up on the court. That's the time when faith shines. That's the time when the crowds go wild for Christ. That's the time when God Himself will cheer you on, sending His Holy Spirit to do things through you that you could never have done on your own.

I don't know what kind of opposition you're facing today: problems with your marriage, your money, your ministry, your ideas. Problems with your health, your plans, your future, your dreams. Problems with your family, your friends, your parents, your kids. Problems with your business, your home, your life, your career.

But whatever you're facing right now, I want to encourage you to press on. Press on in your faith. Fix your eyes on Jesus, the author and perfecter or your faith, who for the joy set before Him, endured the cross (see Hebrews 12:2).

Press on, as Paul did, toward the goal to win the prize for which God has called you heavenward in Christ Jesus (Philippians 3:14).

If God has called you to it, press on through it!

Prayer: Father, help me to be persistent in my faith, to press on to win the prize for which You have called me heavenward in Christ Jesus. In Jesus' name, Amen.

LESSON 15: FAITH PURIFIES — APRIL 20

Scripture Reading: Acts 15

If you've ever read *Macbeth* by Shakespeare, you may remember the scene where Macbeth's wife rubs her hands together over and over, trying to wash out an imaginary stain. What she was really trying to do was to "wash her hands" of a plot that she and her husband had planned to kill King Duncan. Even though the stain is imaginary, it represented something very real that she had done.

Many people have felt what Lady Macbeth felt. They've done something they can't take back. No matter what they do, they can't get clean. They can't purify themselves. Maybe you're in that situation yourself today or know someone who is.

The truth is, you can't purify yourself. You can't wash, cleanse or save yourself from your own sins. But the good news is that Jesus can. And the way He does it is through faith.

It might seem odd that a mere thought—putting your faith in Christ—could open the floodgates of cleansing that you need. But it's not just the thought that brings the cleansing. It's Christ who brings the cleansing. It's Christ, who died on the cross to take your sins upon Him so you could be clean, if you'll just believe Him and put your faith in Him.

Some people wring their hands over what they can do to be clean. The earliest Christians made it clear that of all the things someone might try to do, the one necessary ingredient is faith.

One of the times the disciples had to address this issue head on is recorded in Acts chapter 15. Here's a portion of how the issue came up and how the disciples responded:

> *"Some men came down from Judea to Antioch and were teaching the brothers: 'Unless you are circumcised, according to the custom taught by Moses, you cannot be saved.' This brought Paul and Barnabas into sharp dispute and debate with them. So Paul and Barnabas were appointed, along with some other believers, to go up to Jerusalem to see the apostles and elders about this question.... Then some of the believers who belonged to the party of the Pharisees stood up and said, 'The Gentiles must be circumcised and required to obey the law of Moses.'*
> *"The apostles and elders met to consider this question. After much discussion, Peter got up and addressed them: 'Brothers, you know that some time ago God made a*

choice among you that the Gentiles might hear from my lips the message of the gospel and believe. God, who knows the heart, showed that He accepted them by giving the Holy Spirit to them, just as He did to us. He made no distinction between us and them, for He purified their hearts by faith. Now then, why do you try to test God by putting on the necks of the disciples a yoke that neither we nor our fathers have been able to bear? No! We believe it is through the grace of our Lord Jesus that we are saved, just as they are" (Acts 15:1-2,5-11).

When it came down to it, Paul, Barnabas, Peter and the elders agreed: it is "through the grace of our Lord Jesus that we are saved" and that God "purified their hearts by faith."

I remember when my wife Lana was baptized. As she came up out of the water, she said that as the water dripped off her, she felt like her sins were being washed away. That's the kind of cleansing that Lady Macbeth longed for, but never experienced, because she never put her faith in Christ.

If that's the kind of cleansing that you're longing for, you don't have to wring your hands over and over. You can experience it, too, when you put your faith in Christ.

Confess your sins to Him and let Him wash you in His grace, removing your sins "as far as the east is from the west" (Psalm 103:12). As the Bible promises: "If we confess our sins, He is faithful and just and will forgive us our sins and purify us from all unrighteousness" (1 John 1:9).

Let Him purify you today, by faith.

Prayer: Father, I confess my sins to You and put my faith in Christ, asking that You would cleanse me, wash me and purify me from all unrighteousness. In Jesus' name, Amen.

LESSON 16: FAITH SINGS   APRIL 21

Scripture Reading: Acts 16

When you're down, singing is probably one of the last things you feel like doing. But it could be the very thing you need to bring you back up.

Singing is an expression of faith that you can exercise anytime, anywhere and with powerful results, as can be seen in Acts chapter 16. Even after being beaten and severely flogged earlier in the day, Paul and Silas sang at midnight in their prison cell. God heard their song and set them free.

Paul and Silas had been sharing about Christ in the city of Philippi (to which Paul later wrote his letter to the Philippians) when they ran across a slave girl who was possessed by an evil spirit by which she predicted the future. Paul cast the spirit out of her, causing her owners to realize that they were going to lose any future profits from the girl's unusual abilities.

The owners of the girl seized Paul and Silas and brought them to the authorities, rallying the crowds against them as well, saying that they were throwing the city into an uproar. Paul and Silas were stripped, beaten and severely flogged, then put in the inner cell of the prison with their feet in the stocks.

Even after such a grueling day, listen to what the book of Acts says Paul and Silas did that night:

> "About midnight Paul and Silas were praying and singing hymns to God, and the other prisoners were listening to them" (Acts 16:25).

They prayed and sang hymns to God. I can understand their praying, but it's hard to imagine they had the strength, let alone the desire, to sing. But the fact that they were praying and singing makes me think that their prayers were more expressions of faith to God rather than frustration with God; prayers of trusting in God rather than interrogating God. Listen to what happened next as they expressed their faith in this way.

> "Suddenly there was such a violent earthquake that the foundations of the prison were shaken. At once all the prison doors flew open, and everybody's chains came loose" (Acts 16:26-34).

Faith sings. And when faith sings, God responds. God not only set Paul and Silas free, but He set all the other prisoners free who were listening to them sing. If you continue reading the passage, you'll find that God even set the jailer free, the one who had been holding them in their prison!

I was listening to a well-known, elderly pastor who talked about those times in his life when he was the most down. He said that the only thing that he had found that could consistently lift his spirits was to sing praises to God. As he sang, his spirits would lift, and he could see clearly again that God was in control of his life and circumstances.

King David did the same. As you read through many of his songs, which are recorded in the book of Psalms (which means "songs"), you'll see that he's often quite downcast as he begins singing, but by the end of the song, God has lifted his spirits and set him free.

Psalm 5, for instance, starts with the words, "Give ear to my words, O LORD, consider my sighing. Listen to my cry for help, my King and my God, for to You I pray" (Psalm 5:1-2).

But by the end of the song, David is singing out his praises to God, "But let all who take refuge in You be glad; let them ever sing for joy. Spread your protection over them, that those who love Your name may rejoice in You. For surely, O LORD, you bless the righteous; you surround them with your favor as with a shield" (Psalm 5:11-12).

There's power in singing; power to lift us up and set us free, power to set those around us free, and even power to set those who are holding us in bondage free. If you need a lift today, express your faith to God with a song!

Prayer: Father, help me to sing to You, even when it may be the last thing I may want to do, so that You can set me free. In Jesus' name, Amen.

LESSON 17: FAITH EXAMINES APRIL 22

Scripture Reading: Acts 17

I've spent the last few weeks in and out of doctors' offices and the hospital with my Dad, trying to discover the source of some recent health problems.

Like many people, my Dad doesn't really like doctors, hospitals or anything to do with examinations. He'd rather live with some minor discomfort than subject himself to the tests that are needed to find out what's really wrong. Unless he's in dire pain or distress, why rock the boat?

But as I went with him and helped him to see why the doctors wanted to do the tests they did, he consented. In the end, it turned out that my Dad just needs a shot once a month. It's a simple solution, but if left uncorrected, could have led to his death.

For some people, reading the Bible sounds about as fun as going to see the doctor. If you're not in dire pain or distress, why rock the boat?

Why? Because the Bible is filled with simple solutions to some of our biggest problems that, if left uncorrected, could lead to our death, both here on earth and eternally.

For people who are eager to live life to the fullest, doing a careful examination of their life from time to time is one of the smartest things they can do. They're like the Bereans mentioned in the Bible, the people who lived in a city in Greece called Berea who did another kind of examination, but one that was just as life-changing.

When Paul went to the Bereans to tell them that Jesus was Christ, he found that they were more noble than the people of other cities he had visited:

> "Now the Bereans were of more noble character than the Thessalonians, for they received the message with great eagerness and examined the Scriptures every day to see if what Paul said was true" (Acts 17:11).

The Bereans were eager to hear about Jesus, to find out if He really was the Savior, the Messiah, the Christ. They wanted to find out the truth, because they knew how important that truth would be to them. So they examined the Scriptures every day to see if what Paul was telling them was true.

The reason I like the Bereans so much is because I was one myself. Although I had gone to church all my life, I never really read the Bible on my own until my mid-20's. I began attending a church where they had a class called the Berean Class. When I asked why they called it that, they told me the story of the Bereans in the Bible who eagerly examined the Scriptures every day to see if what they were being taught was true.

So I went out and bought a Bible filled with helpful study notes. I began to read it, and really enjoyed it! The more I read, the more eager I was to keep reading! I began to discover that all that I had been taught about the Bible was true. One day, I finally put my faith in Christ. It turned out to the be single most important turning point of my life, literally saving my life here on earth and for eternity.

Paul went to many cities and reasoned with many people from the Scriptures, explaining and proving that the Christ had to suffer and rise from the dead. "This Jesus I am proclaiming to you is the Christ," he said (Acts 17:3b). As a result, many believed, both Jews and Greek, men and women.

Faith examines. If you're curious about the Bible, about Jesus, or about any of the hundreds of other topics addressed in the Bible, from relationships to healing, from sexuality to eternal life, I'd encourage you to read the Bible for yourself. Examine it. Study it. Eagerly receive the message contained within it—and believe it.

You may find you just need a shot of B12, or you may need some serious, but life-saving surgery. Either way, when you examine the Bible like the Bereans did, you'll find that it contains the words you need to live the fullest life possible here on earth—and in heaven, too.

Prayer: Father, help me to eagerly examine Your Word daily to find out for myself that the words are true. In Jesus' name, Amen.

LESSON 18: FAITH WORKS

APRIL 23

Scripture Reading: Acts 18

A friend once asked me, "Do you think God wants everyone to quit their job and go into full-time ministry?"

I thought it was a great question, because the answer can affect your view of ministry—and of work in general.

First, there's no doubt that God wants more people to go into full-time ministry. When Jesus was going from town to town, preaching and healing people, the Bible says "when He saw the crowds, He had compassion on them, because they were harassed and helpless, like sheep without a shepherd. Then He said to His disciples, 'The harvest is plentiful, but the workers are few. Ask the Lord of the harvest, therefore, to send out workers into his harvest field'" (Matthew 9:36-38).

Jesus saw the overwhelming needs of the world and asked His disciples to pray for more workers. Many of those disciples themselves had heard Jesus' call to "Follow Me," something which often required them to leave their profession, whether fishermen or tax collectors.

On the other hand, God has created, gifted and skilled each of us to do meaningful work, whether it's in full-time ministry or not. Work is a blessing from God, not a curse as some people think. Even before the first man sinned, the Bible says that God put him in the Garden of Eden with a specific task in mind:

> *"The LORD God took the man and put him in the Garden of Eden to work it and take care of it" (Genesis 2:15).*

Of course, after Adam sinned, God did tell him that from then on his work would be very hard, with much sweat and toil (see Genesis 3:17-19). But the work itself was not a curse. God wanted Adam to work the land from the very beginning and to eat the fruit that came from it.

The Apostle Paul seems to have grasped both of these aspects of work. He applied himself to both jobs God had called and gifted him to do: at times doing the spiritual work of preaching and encouraging people in their relationship with Christ, and at times doing the practical work of making tents, a profession that met his own needs and the needs of those around him. In Acts chapter 18, we read that Paul went to the city of Corinth for a year and a half, staying with some fellow tentmakers there named Aquila and Priscilla:

> *"Paul went to see them, and because he was a tentmaker as they were, he stayed and worked with them. Every Sabbath he reasoned in the synagogue, trying to persuade Jews and Greeks" (Acts 18:1-4).*

Even though Paul was free to earn his living from his preaching (as he wrote later in 1 Corinthians 9), he was also free to earn his living from making tents. It wasn't the source of his income that directed Paul's work, but serving the Lord in all that he did. As Paul wrote later to the Christians in Ephesus, some of whom were slaves and some of whom were free:

> *"Serve wholeheartedly, as if you were serving the Lord, not men, because you know that the Lord will reward everyone for whatever good he does, whether he is slave or free" (Ephesians 6:7-8).*

The truth is that everything we have comes from God. As King David said in his prayer of thanksgiving to God: "Everything comes from You, and we have given You only what comes from Your hand" (2 Chronicles 29:14).

A friend of mine, who started a business in a country that doesn't officially allow Christian missionaries, says that his work is 100% business and 100% ministry. I think that's a good way for all of us to view our work, whether that work is seemingly secular or religious.

Be open to God's call to ministry. The harvest is plentiful but the workers are few. But also be open to using whatever gifts and skills God has given you to meet the life needs of those around you. Whatever you do, work as if you were serving the Lord. You'll be rewarded when you do.

Prayer: Father, help me to hear Your call on my life and to follow it with my whole heart wherever it leads. In Jesus' name, Amen.

LESSON 19: FAITH BAPTIZES   APRIL 24

Scripture Reading: Acts 19

Of all the things Jesus could have said in His final words to His disciples, He included baptism as one of the top three. Jesus said:

> *"Therefore go and make disciples of all nations, baptizing them in the name of the Father and of the Son and of the Holy Spirit, and teaching them to obey everything I have commanded you" (Matthew 28:19-20a).*

Go and make disciples… baptizing them… and teaching them to obey My commands. What is it about baptism that gives it such a priority?

I think John the Baptist may have said it best when He said: "I baptize you with water for repentance. But after me will come one who is more powerful than I, whose sandals I am not fit to carry. He will baptize you with the Holy Spirit and with fire" (Matthew 3:11).

There's something empowering that happens when a person is baptized in the name of the Father and of the Son and of the Holy Spirit. It's the empowerment of the Holy Spirit—the empowerment to carry out all of the rest of the things that Christ has called us to do.

When the Apostle Paul left Corinth and went to Ephesus, the Bible says:

> *"There he found some disciples and asked, 'Did you receive the Holy Spirit when you believed?*
> *They answered, 'No, we have not even heard that there is a Holy Spirit.'*
> *So Paul asked, 'Then what baptism did you receive?'*
> *'John's baptism,' they replied.*
> *Paul said, 'John's baptism was a baptism of repentance. He told the people to believe in the one coming after him, that is, in Jesus.' On hearing this, they were baptized into the name of the Lord Jesus. When Paul placed his hands on them, the Holy Spirit came on them, and they spoke in tongues and prophesied. There were about twelve men in all." (Acts 19:1b-7).*

When these Ephesian believers were baptized, God empowered them to do things that they weren't able to do before—supernatural things that only the Holy Spirit could have done through them.

Christ calls us to be baptized, and yet there are many people who have never taken this step to be baptized. As a result, they're missing out on many things, one of which is the supernatural ability to do things they could never have done on their own.

I know because I was one of those people. I had put my faith in Christ and repented of my sins, but I didn't follow it up with the step of baptism. A friend asked me to consider it, so I studied the Scriptures and asked others who had been baptized about their experiences. But it took me another two years to finally get around to it.

One day I was asking Christ to do more in me and through me when I felt Him asking me if I had been obedient to the things He had already asked me to do. I had to answer, "No," and baptism was at the top of the list.

I knew that if I wanted to ask God to do more in my life, I needed to be obedient to the things He had already asked me to do. So I was baptized. The next day, God empowered me to do supernatural things that I could never have done on my own.

Faith baptizes. Throughout the book of Acts, when people put their faith in Christ, they got baptized as well, whether it was the 3,000 who believed on the day of Pentecost (Acts 2:37-41), the Ethiopian eunuch (Acts 8:34-38), the Apostle Paul (Acts 9:18-19), Cornelius and his friends and relatives (Acts 10:44-48), the jailer and his family (Acts 16:29-34), the many who believed in Corinth (Acts 18:8), or the dozen who are mentioned in today's passage (Acts 19:1-7).

If you feel God prompting you to be baptized, I want to encourage you to do it. It's not only part of being a Christian, it's also part of receiving the empowerment of God to do all He wants to do in you and through you.

Prayer: Father, thank You for Your Holy Spirit and for the empowerment that comes through Him. In Jesus' name, Amen.

LESSON 20: FAITH RESURRECTS — APRIL 25

Scripture Reading: Acts 20

Some people think they have power when they can take a gun and shoot someone dead. But I think that someone has power if they can take someone who's been dead and bring them back to life. Now that's power!

You can read about at least ten resurrection stories in the Bible, stories where someone has been physically dead and then been raised back to life.

- *Elijah raised the son of the widow (1 Kings 17:17-22)*
- *Elisha raised the son of the Shunamite woman (2 Kings 4:32-35)*
- *Elisha's bones touched a dead man who was raised back to life (2 Kings 13:20-21)*
- *Jesus raised a widow's son (Luke 7:11-15)*
- *Jesus raised Jairus' daughter (Luke 8:49-56)*
- *Jesus raised Lazarus after Lazarus was dead for four days (John 11:1-44)*
- *God raised Jesus from the dead (Matthew 28:5-10)*

- God raised many others from the dead at the same time He raised Jesus (Matthew 27:50-53).
- Peter raised Tabitha from the dead (Acts 9:38-40)
- Paul raised Eutychus from the dead (Acts 20:9-12).

Let's take a look at this last story, since we're looking today at Acts, chapter 20. As the Apostle Luke tells the story, Paul was speaking late into the night in the city of Troas. He was to leave early the next morning, so he stayed up all night speaking to the people:

> "Seated in a window was a young man named Eutychus, who was sinking into a deep sleep as Paul talked on and on. When he was sound asleep, he fell to the ground from the third story and was picked up dead. Paul went down, threw himself on the young man and put his arms around him. 'Don't be alarmed,' he said. 'He's alive!' Then he went upstairs again and broke bread and ate. After talking until daylight, he left. The people took the young man home alive and were greatly comforted" (Acts 20:9-12).

Faith resurrects. Not just a spiritual resurrection that will happen when those who believe in Christ will be raised to new life in heaven, but faith that even resurrects people who have died and then come back to life here on earth.

This doesn't mean that just because we have faith in Christ, we can, or even should, raise everyone who dies back from the dead. God *does* have a plan and He's limited *all* of our life spans for a reason.

But it does mean that all of us who have put our faith in Christ—and have been filled with, and empowered by, His Holy Spirit—have access to the same life-giving power that raised Jesus from the dead. Paul, who raised Eutychus from the dead, also wrote:

> "But if Christ is in you, your body is dead because of sin, yet your spirit is alive because of righteousness. And if the Spirit of Him who raised Jesus from the dead is living in you, He who raised Christ from the dead will also give life to your mortal bodies through His Spirit, who lives in you" (Romans 8:10-11).

Paul was sharing a spiritual truth, but it's a physical truth as well. Paul knew from his own experience that the Spirit of God could literally bring people back from the dead.

If God calls you to pray for someone to be raised from the dead, by all means and by faith, do it! But God also wants you to use that power of faith to pray life back into all kinds of situations and circumstances in the world around you.

If you're a believer in the Lord Jesus Christ and you need God to breathe life into something you're facing today, call on the power of God's Holy Spirit that lives within you—the same Spirit who raised Christ from the dead.

If you've never put your faith in Christ to forgive you of your sins, do it today. You will be raised to a new life with Him here on earth, and you can be assured that you'll be raised to an eternal life with Him in heaven.

Prayer: Father, fill me with Your Holy Spirit—the same Spirit who raised Christ from the dead—and give me the faith to call on Your Spirit to pray life into everything around me. In Jesus' name, Amen.

LESSON 21: FAITH DIES
APRIL 26

Scripture Reading: Acts 21

I remember the fear that came over me when I read the headline in our college newspaper that Congress had reinstated the draft and all men my age were to report immediately to serve in the military.

I couldn't believe it. I'm not against serving in the military, but I had been considering studying abroad in the coming year, but I hadn't made up my mind yet. Traveling alone, the cost of the program and other fears held me back from making a decision. But now, with the possibility that I might have to go into the service, and might even die doing it, my fears of studying abroad paled in comparison.

As I headed to the men's showers that morning, I was still shaking my head in disbelief when someone else walked in and commented on the article. He asked if I noticed the date on the paper. It was April 1st—April Fool's Day here in the U.S. The whole article was a hoax.

Even though my heart rate began to slow down, my mind was just getting started. Having faced the possibility of death, I felt now that I was given a new shot at life. I decided that day to study abroad and the following year I did.

Facing death has a way of waking us up and bringing us back to life. Jesus said it like this:

> "For whoever wants to save his life will lose it, but whoever loses his life for Me will find it" (Matthew 16:25).

The Apostle Paul had an abundant life, in large part, I believe, because he was willing to lose his life at any moment. Although he certainly didn't have a death wish, he wasn't afraid to die for Christ, either.

In Acts 21, Paul was warned by men and by the Holy Spirit that if he continued on his journey to the city of Jerusalem, he would be bound in chains when he got there. Paul's friends pleaded with him not to go to Jerusalem, but Paul replied:

> "Why are you weeping and breaking my heart? I am ready not only to be bound, but also to die in Jerusalem for the name of the Lord Jesus" (Acts 21:13).

Paul went on to Jerusalem and was indeed bound and put into prison. The rest of the book of Acts documents his travels from prison to prison as his case was appealed to higher and higher authorities all the way to Caesar in Rome. Although the book of Acts ends before the end of Paul's life, church tradition tells us that Paul was eventually beheaded in Rome for his faith.

There are times when God calls people to use their faith to raise the dead, as Paul had just done for Eutychus in Acts 20. But there are also times when God calls people to use their faith to be ready to die, as Paul was ready in Acts 21. But how can the same faith lead to two such different results? Paul tell us in Romans 14:7-8:

> "For none of us lives to himself alone and none of us dies to himself alone. If we live, we live to the Lord; and if we die, we die to the Lord. So, whether we live or die, we belong to the Lord" (Romans 14:7-8).

It was Paul's willingness to die for Christ that allowed him to live for Christ so boldly. Some thought he was foolish to go to Jerusalem when he was warned about what awaited him there. But as another missionary named James Elliot wrote: "He is no fool who gives what he cannot keep to gain that which he cannot lose."

God has many things He wants to do *for* you by faith. But God also has many things He wants to do *through* you by faith—for others.

How would it change your life if you were truly willing to die for Christ? If you truly no longer feared death? According to the Apostle Paul, the missionary Jim Elliot, and even Jesus Christ Himself, it's only when you're ready to lose your life for Christ that you will truly find it.

Prayer: Father, help me to be ready to die for Christ so that I can truly live for Him. In Jesus' name, Amen.

LESSON 22: FAITH TESTIFIES   APRIL 27

Scripture Reading: Acts 22

Has God touched your life in a special way? If so, that's part of your testimony—and God loves it when you testify to others about what He has done for you.

But I also know it can be hard to share your testimony. When I first put my faith in Christ, I was asked to share my testimony with my singles class at church. "No way," I thought! It wasn't that I didn't want to talk about what God had done, but I didn't want to talk about what I had done. I was way too embarrassed to talk about the sin from which God had delivered me.

Yet over the years, as I've shared my testimony with more and more people, I've seen God give hope, encouragement and eternal life to others. Some people who hear my story are encouraged because they've struggled with some of the same things with which I've struggled. Others are encouraged because they realize that the God who could deliver me from the depths of my sin can deliver them from the depths of theirs.

The Apostle Paul had a lot of good reasons not to share his testimony with others. Not only did he have to share some difficult things about himself personally, but he also faced the real possibility of being killed every time he shared it. While Paul could have been afraid for his life, he wasn't afraid to testify about what Christ had done for him. As a result, he brought encouragement and eternal life to many.

When Paul's friends warned him not to go to Jerusalem because he might be bound and possibly killed, Paul went anyway, regardless of the outcome to his own life. Starting with the very first day he was bound in Jerusalem, look at how many times Paul was able to share his testimony:

- *Paul testified to the crowd in Jerusalem (Acts 22:1-21),*
- *he testified to the chief priests and religious leaders in Jerusalem (Acts 23:1-10),*
- *he testified to Governor Felix in Caesarea (Acts 24:1-26),*
- *he testified to Governor Festus and King Agrippa in Caesarea (Acts 26:1-32),*
- *and he testified to the people in Rome while awaiting to testify to Caesar (Acts 28:28-31).*

Paul could have been killed for his testimony, but he wanted to use every opportunity he could to share this new life he had found with others.

One of the things that helped me overcome the fear of sharing my testimony was to stand in the middle of a cemetery and think about what it meant from an eternal perspective. In the end, what did it matter if I lost my pride—or even my life—by sharing my testimony? If God could use it to do for others what He had done for me, it would be worth it.

That perspective has given me a tremendous freedom to be able to share my testimony when God wants me to share it. I'm still careful and prayerful about it, but my focus now is more on how it will affect those who hear it than on how it will affect me. Even Jesus spoke about the importance of timing when He told His disciples, "I have much more to say to you, more than you can now bear" (John 16:12). We still need to be in tune with what our listeners need to hear.

But whatever the timing, know that the words of your testimony are like gold to God and that they have tremendous power. The Bible says:

"They overcame him by the blood of the Lamb and by the word of their testimony; they did not love their lives so much as to shrink from death" (Revelation 12:11).

It's by the blood of the Lamb—Jesus—and by the word of your testimony that you can overcome Satan. When you share your testimony, you can give hope, comfort peace, strength, encouragement and life to those who are losing theirs.

What has God done for you that could bring hope and eternal life to others? Reread Paul's simple testimony in Acts 22, then consider sharing your testimony with others, too.

Prayer: Father, give me the faith to share my testimony with others. In Jesus' name, Amen.

LESSON 23: FAITH KEEPS A CLEAR CONSCIENCE — APRIL 28

Scripture Reading: Acts 23

A man who once walked across the entire United States said that the hardest thing about his walk wasn't the mountains, or the extreme weather, or any of the things I would have expected. He said the hardest part of the walk was the sand in his shoes.

The little grains of sand didn't seem like a big deal at first, but over time, the sand would build up and lead to blisters, infections and ongoing pain.

It can sometimes be the same way with sin. It may not be the big sins that threaten to undo you, but the little ones—a lie here or there, a lustful thought towards a co-worker, a glance from time to time at pornography. Because of God's grace, He doesn't blast at every wrong turn. But over time, those "little" sins build up and lead to a bigger problem.

The man who walked across America said that he learned to regularly empty out the sand from his shoes *before* it became a problem. Today, you may find that your conscience is being pricked about some "little" sins in your life that God wants you to give up. If so, I'd like to encourage you to follow those promptings, take off your shoes, and empty out the sand before it leads to a bigger problem.

The Apostle Paul knew the value of keeping a clear conscience. He would regularly do whatever it took to ensure that he was honoring God and others with his thoughts and actions. And the payoff was huge.

In Acts 23, when Paul was arrested and brought before the highest religious leaders in Jerusalem, Paul was asked to speak on his own behalf. He began by saying this:

"My brothers, I have fulfilled my duty to God in all good conscience to this day" (Acts 23:1b).

Even though the charges against Paul could have cost him his life, his conscience was clear. He had gone out of his way when he first entered Jerusalem to enter into the strict purification rites of the Jewish people. He wanted to honor both God and those who lived in that city (see Acts 22:17-26).

So when the accusations came, Paul was able to say with full confidence that his conscience was clear. By the end of Paul's testimony, at the end of chapter 23, the commander overseeing Paul's case concluded that there was "no charge against him that deserved death or imprisonment" (Acts 23:29b). Paul survived another day and went on to minister for many more years.

Your faith can help you in so many ways, one of which is to keep your conscience clear.

I've heard it said that "a clear conscience makes a soft pillow." God gave you a conscience for a reason: not to make you feel guilty, but to keep you headed in the right direction. Like the sensitive nerve endings on your fingertips that keep you from burning your hand on a hot stove, your conscience serves to warn you from burning yourself in other ways. Not only will you sleep better with a clear conscience, but it can also save your life, your marriage, your job, your reputation, your ministry and your good witness.

As the Apostle Peter said, "Live such good lives among the pagans that, though they accuse you of doing wrong, they may see your good deeds and glorify God on the day he visits us" (1 Peter 2:12).

Faith keeps a clear conscience. Is there sand building up in your shoes today? Take time to empty them out.

If you've sinned, confess it to God and then to a trusted friend. If you're caught in some lies, come clean today by telling the truth. If you've started a habit that's taking you where neither you nor God want you to go, give it up today. If you're in a relationship that's crossing lines that should never be crossed, break it off now before it destroys you and those around you.

May we all get to the point where we can say like Paul, "My brothers, I have fulfilled my duty to God in all good conscience to this day" (Acts 23:1b).

Prayer: Father, help me to empty my shoes of the sands of sin in my life before they bring me down completely. In Jesus' name, Amen.

LESSON 24: FAITH FLEES   APRIL 29

Scripture Reading: Acts 24

I often think of someone who is filled with faith as someone who can tough out any situation, who can stand firm in the face of adversity, who never walks away from a fight when their faith is at stake. But as I read through the book of Acts, and other books in the Bible, I see that there are times when it's simple wisdom to walk away—or to run—when God wants to keep you from a dangerous situation.

For all the times when the Apostle Paul stood his ground, took a beating, and faced death, there were other times when he slipped away from those who intended to harm him.

When Paul first put his faith in Christ on the road to Damascus, the Jews there conspired to kill him. But when Paul learned of their plan, the believers in Damascus "took him by night and lowered him in a basket through an opening in the wall" (Acts 9:25).

Paul had to flee again when he came to Jerusalem. More than forty men had taken an oath not to eat or drink until they had killed Paul. When the son of Paul's sister heard about the plot, he warned Paul. Paul sent the young man to the commander of the centurions who immediately gave these orders:

> "Get ready a detachment of two hundred soldiers, seventy horsemen and two hundred spearmen to go to Caesarea at nine tonight. Provide mounts for Paul so that he may be taken safely to Governor Felix" (Acts 23:23b-24).

In cases like these, Paul fled for his life. Because he did, God was able to use him for many more years to testify to kings, governors and even us today who still read letters that he wrote after he fled.

There are even times when Jesus fled from those who meant Him harm. One day, when Jesus had so angered the Pharisees in Jerusalem, they picked up stones in order to stone Him to death. But John tells us that "Jesus hid Himself, slipping away from the temple grounds" (John 8:59b).

On another occasion, Jesus' words so infuriated the people in the synagogue that Luke tells us, "They got up, drove Him out of the town, and took Him to the brow of the hill on which the town was built, in order to throw him down the cliff. But He walked right through the crowd and went on his way" (Luke 4:29-30).

While there may be times when your faith will help you to go to the cross like Jesus did (see 1 Peter 2:23), or face beatings and imprisonment like Paul often did, there may be other times when your faith will help you to flee from situations that are potentially dangerous, just like both Paul and Jesus did.

The key is to walk so in tune with God that you know when to stand and when to run. There's nothing disgraceful about saving your life when God doesn't want you to die. There's nothing cowardly about fleeing from a potentially harmful situation when God doesn't want you to be harmed. Walking away, slipping through the crowd or fleeing for your life could be the most faith-filled thing you could do.

There may be times when it's more productive to walk away quietly from your boss who is treating you in a demeaning way, or to slip away for a time from an angry spouse while they take time to cool down, or to disengage from a conversation with someone that may be more destructive than constructive.

The ultimate goal in knowing what to do in situations like these is not to protect your pride or to defend things in which you strongly believe, but to follow God at every turn.

That's why it's so important to stay close to God, to cultivate your prayer life and to deepen your relationship with God and His Word. By doing so, God can more clearly point you in the direction He wants you to go, whether it's to stand firm or to flee. Whatever He calls you to do, know that He'll give you the faith to do it.

Prayer: Father, help me to stay so close to You that I can know which way to go every step of the way. In Jesus' name, Amen.

Eric Elder

LESSON 25: FAITH APPEALS

APRIL 30

Scripture Reading: Acts 25

Some people think that when Christians are challenged, they should roll over and play dead—to "turn the other cheek" at all times. Oftentimes that's exactly what we're supposed to do as a way of submitting to one another and honoring those in authority over us.

But then there are other times when we, as followers of Christ, are called to defend ourselves, to take authority over wrongs that have been done to us, and to appeal to higher authorities. These, too, are biblical teachings.

Throughout the book of Acts, Paul takes care to walk through this maze of when to stand firm and when to run, when to submit to others and when to defend himself against them. In Acts chapter 25, Paul takes his boldest stand against the false accusations that were made against him: he appeals to Caesar. Paul says this to Governor Festus who was hearing his case:

> "I have not done any wrong to the Jews, as you yourself know very well. If, however, I am guilty of doing anything deserving death, I do not refuse to die. But if the charges brought against me by these Jews are not true, no one has the right to hand me over to them. I appeal to Caesar!" (Acts 25:10-11).

Appealing to Caesar was no small deal. Caesar was the king, the highest authority in the entire Roman Empire, and his decision would be final—and possibly fatal. The appeal would be costly in terms of time and travel to Rome. In Paul's case, the trip itself was almost fatal, and Paul was under house arrest in Rome for at least two years waiting for Caesar to hear his case.

But there was nothing ungodly nor disgraceful about Paul's appeal. He knew he was innocent, and he knew God wanted him to continue to testify about Christ in Rome. At the very beginning of Paul's trials back in Jerusalem, the Lord stood near to Paul one night and said, "Take courage! As you have testified about me in Jerusalem, so you must also testify in Rome." While it took great courage to appeal to Caesar and be sent to Rome, he was also simply following the clear command of the Lord.

When Paul appealed, Governor Festus conferred with his council and declared: "You have appealed to Caesar. To Caesar you will go!" (Acts 25:12).

Here in the U.S., an appeal is simply another step in the legal process. It's not a sign of defying authority, but a way of following the steps that the authorities have set up, realizing that different people come to different conclusions, even based on the same evidence.

I'm amazed at the number of cases that are decided in the U.S. Supreme Court by a 5 to 4 decision. These are the some of the brightest and most highly trained people in the country regarding the law, yet they still reach completely opposite conclusions. While it could make some people cynical of the process, it makes me thankful for it, that our country has made a way to give us as many chances as possible to prove our innocence, or for someone else to prove our guilt.

There are times when your faith in Christ will compel you to submit to a decision that's wrong, regardless of whether you simply believe it is wrong or whether it's in fact wrong. It can be simple prudence and godliness to submit to someone's decision, whether it's a judge, a boss, a spouse, a parent or a friend.

But there are other times when your faith in Christ will compel you to appeal a wrongful decision, to respectfully call upon someone else to step in and hear your case.

In the end, God Himself is the One who will ultimately decide your case. So the important thing is to stay as close to Him as possible and follow His wisdom for whether He wants you to pursue or drop any appeal here on earth. Maybe He'll say to you what He said to Paul: "Take courage! As you have testified about me in Jerusalem, so you must also testify in Rome" (Acts 23:11).

Prayer: Father, help me to hear from You if there's ever a time You want me to appeal a decision that's been made. In Jesus' name, Amen.

LESSON 26: FAITH MODELS — MAY 1

Scripture Reading: Acts 26

The great evangelist H.A. Ironside was interrupted one time by the shouts of an atheist. The atheist yelled, "There is no God! Jesus is a myth!" and finally, "I challenge you to a debate!"

Ironside responded, "I accept your challenge, sir! But on one condition. When you come, bring with you ten men and women whose lives have been changed for the better by the message of atheism. Bring former prostitutes and criminals whose lives have been changed, who are now moral and responsible individuals. Bring outcasts who had no hope and have them tell us how becoming atheists has lifted them out of the pit!

"And sir," he concluded, "if you can find ten such men and woman, I will be happy to debate you. And when I come, I will gladly bring with me two hundred men and women from this very city whose lives have been transformed in just those ways by the power of the gospel of Jesus Christ."

Ironside knew that atheism doesn't change lives. Jesus changes lives.

If you're a Christian, your testimony is like gold to God. The story of how you came to Christ, how He forgave you of your sins and how He gave you the assurance that you will live with Him forever will speak volumes to those around you.

You may not consider yourself a great evangelist. You may not feel like there's much in your life that others would want to emulate. But the truth is that when others see your changed life, it can lead them to put their faith in Christ, too.

The Apostle Paul knew the power of a testimony. He shared it on many occasions, one of which is in Acts chapter 26 when he was on trial in front of Governor Festus and King Agrippa. After hearing Paul's story, King Agrippa said to Paul,

> "Do you think that in such a short time you can persuade me to be a Christian?"
> Paul replied, "Short time or long—I pray God that not only you but all who are listening to me today may become what I am, except for these chains." (Acts 26:28-29).

Paul didn't claim to be perfect. But he *did* claim to be changed. He claimed to have had an encounter with the Risen Christ that transformed his life and then he prayed that all who were listening to him would become what he was.

Faith models. Just like a fashion model wears cool clothes to show others what their life might become like if they put on the same thing, a Christian model is one who shows others what their life might become if they put their faith in Christ.

I had a friend who was living an immoral lifestyle. I knew that if he kept it up, it could kill him. I knew because I had lived a similar life, until I put my faith in Christ. I prayed with him one day that he would become what I had become, a Christian. It wasn't that I thought I was perfect. I wanted him to follow me, because I followed Christ.

Paul called others to follow his lead when he said in 1 Corinthians, "Follow my example, as I follow the example of Christ" (1 Corinthians 11:1). It's not prideful to ask people to become what you've become. It's simply faithful.

An athlete once told his coach he didn't want to be a role model. His coach said, "It's not a question of whether you want to be a role model or not. You're already a role model. The question is whether you'll be a good one or a bad one."

You're already a role model, too, whether you're a Christian or not. If you're a Christian, God wants you to model your faith, to let others see it in your life, to let them hear it from your lips—that Christ has truly forgiven you, changed you and given you the assurance that you'll live with Him forever. If you're not a Christian, my prayer for you is the same as Paul's, "that not only you but all who are listening to me today may become what I am..."

Prayer: Father, give me the faith to model my life in a way that leads others to Christ. In Jesus' name, Amen.

LESSON 27: FAITH WARNS   MAY 2

Scripture Reading: Acts 27

Is there anyone in your life who could use a good warning right about now? Someone who is straying from God's path and needs help finding their way back? Or someone who is headed for danger—and even trying to take you along?

If so, I want to encourage you today to give them a godly warning about what lies ahead. As hard as it may be, know that even if they don't listen to you right now, your warning may help them to listen closer in the future.

I'm sure it took a lot of faith for the Apostle Paul to warn those around him of the danger facing them in Acts chapter 27. After all, Paul was hardly in a position of authority over any of them, being himself a prisoner on board a ship bound for Rome. Yet after his first warning proved to be true, even those who had authority over Paul began to regard his advice as if their lives depended on it—because it did!

Take a look at the first warning Paul offered when he foresaw the winter storms which loomed ahead:

> *"'Men, I can see that our voyage is going to be disastrous and bring great loss to ship and cargo, and to our own lives also.' But the centurion, instead of listening to what Paul said, followed the advice of the pilot and of the owner of the ship. Since the harbor was unsuitable to winter in, the majority decided that we should sail on, hoping to reach Phoenix and winter there" (Acts 27:9-12a).*

So much for Paul's warning! But it wasn't wasted. When the wind whipped up with hurricane force and the crew had to let the storm drive them along in a direction they hadn't planned to go, the crew eventually began to listen to Paul. He stood up before them and said:

"'Men, you should have taken my advice not to sail from Crete; then you would have spared yourselves this damage and loss. But now I urge you to keep up your courage, because not one of you will be lost; only the ship will be destroyed. Last night an angel of the God whose I am and whom I serve stood beside me and said, 'Do not be afraid, Paul. You must stand trial before Caesar; and God has graciously given you the lives of all who sail with you.' So keep up your courage, men, for I have faith in God that it will happen just as he told me. Nevertheless, we must run aground on some island'" (Acts 27:21-26).

From that point on, the crew listened to everything Paul said. When some men tried to escape in a lifeboat, Paul warned the centurion that they must stay with the ship or be lost. The centurion brought them back. When all aboard had not eaten for fourteen days, Paul encouraged them to finally eat some food as they were about to be saved, but would need the remaining food to survive.

In the end, their ship ran aground on a remote island and was blasted apart by the pounding waves. But just as Paul had foretold, all 276 of the men on board survived.

I would love to be able to speak to others with the confidence which came from the faith that Paul had when he said, "So keep up your courage, men, for I have faith in God that it will happen just as he told me." I pray for that kind of faith for myself, and I want to encourage you to pray for it for yourself as well.

Faith warns. Even when your warnings may not be heeded the first time, they might still be necessary to help others believe in what you say the next time…and the next…and the next. If there's someone in your life who needs a good warning today, ask God if you're the one to give it to them.

If there's someone in your life who is headed in the wrong direction, or even to hell, ask God to give you the faith to point them in the right direction today.

Prayer: Father, help me to have the faith to give godly warnings to those who need it today. In Jesus' name, Amen.

LESSON 28: FAITH SUPPLIES   MAY 3

Scripture Reading: Acts 28

One of the natural responses that often bursts forth when someone's faith increases is the desire to give. Those who are touched by a message of faith often respond by giving back to those who touched them.

When I first put my faith in Christ, I was so moved that I instinctively began to support the church where I was saved. As I began to hear about missionaries who were taking the same message that touched me to others throughout the world, my natural response was to give. I wanted everyone to experience the same thing that I had experienced.

I still do. It's not that I feel that I have to give. It's simply the response of my heart to what God is doing in my life. I also believe that the increased desire to give comes from my increased trust in God; that He will continue to supply all of my needs, even as He uses me to help to supply the needs of others.

Those who were touched by the ministry of the Apostle Paul on the island of Malta had a similar response of giving.

Paul, along with his shipmates, had been shipwrecked on the island. The islanders showed unusual kindness to Paul and the others by building a fire for them because it was raining and cold. When a viper bit Paul on the hand as he threw some brushwood into the fire, the islanders thought Paul must have been guilty of a deadly crime: even though he had escaped from the shipwreck, they thought he would now die from the snakebite. When Paul didn't die, the islanders changed their minds and thought he was a god!

Even though Paul wasn't a god, God still had work to do through Paul. Paul and the others were invited into the home of Publius, a chief official of the island. When Paul found out that Publius' father was sick in bed with fever and dysentery, Paul went to see him, "…and after prayer, placed his hands on him and healed him. When this had happened, the rest of the sick on the island came and were cured" (Acts 28:8-9).

While Paul's faith in Christ allowed him to do many miracles in Jesus' name, look at the response of faith that took place among the islanders who were touched by these miracles. The very next sentence of the story says:

> "They honored us in many ways and when we were ready to sail, they furnished us with the supplies we needed" (Acts 28:10).

Faith supplies. When God works in powerful ways, people naturally want to respond in kind. They want to give freely to others as others have given freely to them.

In this way, Paul and the crew were able to go onto the next leg of their journey to Rome, where God had told Paul he would have to testify before Caesar. God had provided everything Paul needed to get as far as Malta. When the supplies ran out, God provided still more through those believers who had just been touched by God through Paul's ministry.

Supplying the needs of others is a natural response of faith.

Have you been touched in a special way through someone's ministry? Maybe someone in your local church, which nourishes you and perhaps your family? Maybe someone who has stopped by to pray for you? Maybe someone who has sent you a special gift or card or email or text message when you needed it? Maybe a ministry on the TV, or radio, or even this one on the Internet, that God has used in a special way to reach out to you to help you to increase your faith?

If so—and if God is causing your faith to well up within you with the desire to give—I encourage you to respond in faith and give. It's a way to not only help that person or that ministry on the next leg of their journey, it's a way to let them know that your heart is going with them as well. As Jesus said, "For where your treasure is, there your heart will be also" (Luke 12:34).

Prayer: Father, show me how to respond in faith to those who have touched my life for You. In Jesus' name, Amen.

CONCLUSION: THE POWER OF FAITH — MAY 4

Scripture Reading: Matthew 17:20

At the end of the book of Acts, you'll see that Paul finally made it to Rome. He stayed there for two years awaiting his trial before Caesar, living in his own rented house under house arrest. He welcomed all who came to see him, preaching boldly about the kingdom of God and teaching about Christ.

And that's where the book of Acts ends.

In some ways, it seems like the book ends in mid-sentence—like there's a page or two still missing. What happened to Paul? Did he ever make it to his trial? Was he ever able to testify before Caesar?

Even though the Bible doesn't record what happened next, I believe that Paul *did* make it to his trial and that he *did* get to testify before Caesar. Why? Because the same God who brought Paul this far had also told Paul that he would one day testify in Rome. Back in Acts 23, when Paul was first arrested in Jerusalem and when many were plotting to kill him, God said to Paul:

> "Take courage! As you have testified about Me in Jerusalem, so you must also testify in Rome" (Acts 23:11).

Then again in Acts 27, when Paul's shipmates were about to give up hope that they would ever be saved from the storm, an angel of God spoke to Paul again, as Paul told the men:

> "Last night an angel of the God whose I am and whom I serve stood beside me and said, 'Do not be afraid, Paul. You must stand trial before Caesar; and God has graciously given you the lives of all who sail with you.' So keep up your courage, men, for I have faith in God that it will happen just as He told me" (Acts 27:23-25).

That's the kind of faith I've been praying for myself and for you as well all throughout this study, the kind of faith that says, "I have faith in God that it will happen just as He told me." Because I know, like Paul knew, and like Christ knew, that when you have faith in Christ, nothing will be impossible for you.

In the mid-1900's, there was a woman who did all kinds of miracles in the name of Christ, seeing people saved, healed and delivered from various addictions. When asked what kind of gift God had given to her to be able to do so many things, she said she didn't have the gift of evangelism or healing or prayer. She said she had the gift of faith. And with faith, all kinds of things are possible.

We've seen through the book of Acts how faith helped these earliest of believers to do all kinds of things. We've seen that faith waits, acts, heals, saves, obeys, fills, speaks, explains, surrenders, gives, includes, prays, fasts, persists, purifies, sings, examines, works, baptizes, resurrects, dies, testifies, keeps a clear conscience, appeals, models, warns and supplies. And I have a feeling that's just the beginning.

The truth is the book of Acts really is unfinished. Jesus is still alive. He's still working through people today. And He still wants to work through you. You may be surprised at what you can do when you put your faith in Him. For all the incredible things that Jesus did, here's what He said you could do if you had faith in Him:

> "I tell you the truth, anyone who has faith in Me will do what I have been doing. He will do even greater things than these, because I am going to the Father" (John 14:11-12).

As we finish this study together, my prayer is that the following words of Christ would echo in your ears in the days ahead, words that will give you the faith to do all that Christ still wants you to do:

"I tell you the truth, if you have faith as small as a mustard seed, you can say to this mountain, 'Move from here to there' and it will move. Nothing will be impossible for you" (Matthew 17:20).

Prayer: Father, give me the faith to move mountains and more. In Jesus' name, Amen.

EPHESIANS
Lessons In Grace

Ephesians: Lessons in Grace

20 inspiring lessons based on one of the most grace-filled books in the Bible

INTRODUCTION: THE GRACE OF AN AMERICAN IDOL　　　　　　　　　　　　**MAY 5**

Scripture Reading: Ephesians 3:18-19

Even if you've never watched *American Idol*, you may still have heard of Adam Lambert. He competed in the grand finale of this nation's most famous singing contest.

Besides having an astounding voice, there's another thing that stands out to me about this top contender: his consistent graciousness.

When complimented by the judges for an outstanding performance, Adam readily offers his thanks to those in the band who helped make it possible. When asked by the host how he'll be adding his own spin to a famous song, Adam compliments the one who wrote the song, saying that it was so well-written there's little he could add to make it better.

It seems that almost every time a compliment comes his way, Adam steers the praise towards those around him.

While not many of us will ever be able to sing like Adam Lambert, we can all take a lesson from this other facet of his life that has helped to make him so incredibly successful: his graciousness towards others. Does this mean we should follow his example in everything he does? Of course not! We all do some things that are more honoring to God than others. But his graciousness is something we would all do well to emulate.

When your thoughts, words and actions are filled with grace, people are naturally drawn towards you. They're more likely to listen to what you have to say, to do what you ask them to do, and to become all that they can become. God wants you to be grace-filled, not only because it will enhance *your* life, but because it will enhance the lives of those around you as well.

God knows what a blessing graciousness can be because He's been showering people with grace throughout human history. He knows that the best way to express His love to others is to overwhelm them with His grace.

God's grace has helped transform countless lives, turning some of the most sour, bitter and angry people into people who are the most joy-filled, happy, and delightful people I know. I've also seen how those who don't understand God's grace, or who find it hard to understand or receive, also find it hard to express grace to others in meaningful or practical ways.

As for me, well, I guess I'm somewhere in between! I'd like to be more consistently gracious, but I'm not there yet. Sometimes I'm just too self-focused. Sometimes I become critical of others, forgetting how much grace God has already showered upon me.

Sometimes I'm just not thinking, and ungraciousness slips out when I should have been gracious instead. Whatever the reason, I know that I have a lot to learn and a lot of room to grow.

So in the coming days, I'm going to be taking a closer look at the book of Ephesians, and I'd be glad for you to take a look along with me. Even though the book is only six chapters long, Ephesians is one of the most grace-filled books in the whole Bible. The Apostle Paul, who wrote the book originally as a letter to the Christians in the ancient Greek city of Ephesus (now modern-day Turkey), filled his letter with grace both in words and tone.

From the opening words to the closing line, Paul uses the word "grace" a dozen times, encouraging the Ephesians to understand and receive God's grace for themselves and then to extend it to others. He prayed for them the same prayer that I'll be praying for you, and for myself, in the weeks ahead:

> "…that you, being rooted and established in love, may have power, together with all the saints, to grasp how wide, and long and high and deep is the love of Christ, and to know this love that surpasses knowledge—that you may be filled to the measure of all the fullness of God" (Ephesians 3:18-19).

I'm looking forward to this study of the book of Ephesians. I pray that God will overwhelm you with His grace, and that you'll find it the most natural thing in the world to pour it out on others as well.

If you've never read the book of Ephesians before, I think you'll find it to be filled with both grand thoughts about God and practical suggestions for your life. For those who have read it before, I think you'll be amazed at how many of the most famous verses in the Bible are found in this very short book.

At the top of each devotional, I've included a Scripture Reading that I encourage you to read on your own, as I don't include the full text of Ephesians in this book. When you're finished reading each of these Scripture Readings, you'll have read through the entire book of Ephesians.

I've also included a prayer at the end of each devotional that you can use to pray along with me. I hope this helps you to begin a quiet time of prayer with God in response to what you've read. To get you started, here's today's prayer:

Prayer: Father, thank You for the graciousness that we've seen displayed in the lives of others, and thank You for the graciousness that You've showered upon us. Help us, Lord, to be filled so much with Your grace that it flows out to those around us as well, blessing them—and ourselves—along the way. In Jesus' name, Amen.

LESSON 1: GRACE BEGINS WITH A THOUGHT — MAY 6

Scripture Reading: Ephesians 1:1-2

Some people think that being kind and gracious is a sign of weakness, but the exact opposite is true. The measure of graciousness in your life is the true measure of your strength.

According to the 19th century British hymn-writer, Frederick W. Faber:

> "Kindness has converted more sinners than zeal, eloquence, or learning."

Being kind and gracious towards others, even when they give you no reason to be kind to them, can have a greater and longer-lasting impact on their lives than perhaps anything else you could offer them. But where does grace begin? Where can you start if you want to be more gracious in your life? The answer I've found is this: grace begins with a thought.

One of my favorite birthday presents was a bottle of water. What I loved so much about this present wasn't just the water itself, but the thought behind it.

It started years earlier when I was on a business trip to New York. During a meeting, someone at the table asked if I'd like anything to drink. I didn't want to be a bother, and I didn't want them to have to spend anything on me, so I just said, "Sure, I'll take some water."

But a few minutes later, this man came back with a cold bottle of the most incredible water I had ever tasted in my life. I had no idea water could taste so good! It turned out to be a bottle of Evian mineral water, imported from the mountains of France.

When I came back from that trip, I went to the store to see if I could get some more bottles of that water. I went into sticker shock at the price. I decided I didn't need to relive that experience bad enough to pay that much. But I must have mentioned it to my family, because when my birthday came around, my oldest son, who was still pretty young at the time, went out and bought me a few bottles of Evian water.

I asked my wife if she told him to get it for me, but she didn't. He just thought of it himself.

I was touched. It wasn't like I talked or dreamed about this water all the time. But here my son had made a mental note of something that was special to me, and when a special occasion arose, he went out and got it for me. It wasn't an expensive gift as far as gifts go—even though it was expensive as far as water goes! But what made it so special was the thought that went into it.

And that's where grace begins: with a thought.

In the book of Ephesians, the Apostle Paul opens with these words:

> "Paul, an apostle of Christ Jesus by the will of God, To the saints in Ephesus, the faithful in Christ Jesus: Grace and peace to you from God our Father and the Lord Jesus Christ" (Ephesians 1:1-2).

Paul wished for them to have God's grace and peace in their lives, and he meant it! He backed up his graceful thoughts towards them by writing the letter. Perhaps the most gracious thing about this whole letter is that Paul took time to write it at all!

Here he was, bound in chains as a prisoner in Rome. But rather than focusing on himself and his own problems, he took the time to send a letter to those who needed some encouragement in their lives. That one act of kindness is still impacting lives today, as we're still reading and learning from the words that Paul took the time to write almost 2,000 years ago!

If you want to grow in graciousness towards others, the best place to start is with a thought. Take some time to let your thoughts roam through different ways you could express grace to those around you. Pick up a pen. Pick up a phone. Pick up a bottle of water.

It doesn't take much to be gracious, but it does take some thought. Give it some thought today. You'll be blessed—and you'll be a blessing—when you do.

Prayer: Father, thank You for the kindness that You've shown to me, and I pray that You'd help me to show it to others. Give me Your thoughts to know how I can be a blessing to those around me today. In Jesus' name, Amen.

LESSON 2: GOD'S GRACE IS GLORIOUS AND LAVISH — MAY 7

Scripture Reading: Ephesians 1:3-23

Have you ever tried to describe something incredible—a beautiful sunset, a magnificent canyon, a massive mountain—but your words seem to fall flat? No matter how hard you try to describe it, you know that the only way others will be able to catch a glimpse of what you're trying to describe is if they can somehow experience it themselves?

It seems that this is what the Apostle Paul may have felt as he tried to describe God's grace in the book of Ephesians. As much as Paul tried to describe it, as both "glorious" and "lavish," Paul knew that the best way for the Ephesians to fully understand what he was saying was for them to experience it themselves. So he prayed:

> "I keep asking that the God of our Lord Jesus Christ, the glorious Father, may give you the Spirit of wisdom and revelation, so that you may know Him better. I pray also that the eyes of your heart may be enlightened in order that you may know the hope to which He has called you, the riches of His glorious inheritance in the saints, and His incomparably great power for us who believe" (Ephesians 1:16-19).

Paul prayed that the "eyes of their heart" would be enlightened, that they would be able to know God—and God's plans for them, and God's inheritance for them, and God's power for them—not just in their heads, but in their hearts.

It's a prayer that I know God answers because I've seen Him answer it in my own life, and because I've seen Him answer it when I've prayed it for others.

The most memorable time I watched God answer this prayer was when I was praying for a woman who was dying of cancer. She believed in her head that God loved her, but because her battle with cancer had taken up so much of her life, she had trouble believing it in her heart. I went to see her to pray for her healing, but when we finally sat down to pray, I asked her what she would like me to pray for her. She said simply that she'd like to hear God's voice, to hear him speak directly to her heart. She said she had been a Christian for so many years, yet she had never heard God speak to her personally.

It wasn't that she hadn't read the Bible or hadn't been to church. She had done both all her life. It was just that she didn't feel that what she had read about God's love and grace applied to her *personally*.

All I could do at that point was to pray. To pray that God would open the eyes of her heart. To pray that God would speak to her in a way that she could understand it and believe it personally, not just in her head, but deep inside her heart. So we prayed, and I went back home.

I got a call from her a few days later. She told me that she was sicker than she had ever been in her life. But she went on to say that even though she felt sicker than ever before, she felt, for the first time in her life, that God had truly spoken to her. She could hardly describe it, but she said that she went to a special church service that weekend and the speaker was talking about God's lavish love from the book of Ephesians. And for the first time in her life, she felt that God was speaking those words directly to her.

In the weeks that followed, she and her husband took communion together every day, experiencing a sweet fellowship with each other and with the Lord until the day finally came that He took her home to commune with Him forever. God had answered her prayer.

If you'd like to experience God's love and grace in a personal way, not just in your head, but deep inside your heart, let me encourage you to pray. Pray that God would open the eyes of your heart, that you may know Him better. Let Him pour out His glorious and lavish grace on you today.

Prayer: Father, thank You for giving me a glimpse of Your glorious and lavish grace. Thank You for telling me about it through the words of the Bible and through the words of those who have experienced it themselves. I pray that You would open the eyes of my heart so that I could know You better. Help me to experience Your glorious and lavish grace in a fresh way today. In Jesus' name, Amen.

LESSON 3: GOD'S GRACE IS A GIFT   MAY 8

Scripture Reading: Ephesians 2:1-10

Have you ever been able to tell someone some good news? It feels great, doesn't it? I was able to be the bearer of good news to someone this week, and it was a lot of fun.

Someone had heard about our upcoming trip to Israel this fall and wanted to surprise one of the worship leaders at their church with a gift: an all-expense paid trip to come with us to Israel.

The donor of the trip wanted to remain anonymous and asked me to call the recipient to tell him about the gift. When I made the call, this worship leader was overcome to the point of tears, unable to believe what he was hearing. He had told me before that he desperately wanted to come with us, but it would take a miracle.

When I told him his miracle had just happened, he asked, "Are you sure they wanted to give it to *me*? I don't deserve it! How could I ever pay them back?"

I told him he didn't have to pay it back. It was a gift. He didn't even have to deserve it. All he had to do was to receive it. If he wanted to go, all he had to do was say, "Yes." Through tears, he said, "Yes, I want to go!" And now, he's on his way!

Moments like these help me to understand God's gift of grace a little better.

When God offered me the gift of grace, to forgive me of my sins and give me the gift of eternal life, my reaction was much like this worship leader's: "Are you sure He wants to give it to me? I don't deserve it! How could I ever pay Him back?"

But God's gift of grace was just that—a gift. I didn't have to pay it back. I didn't even have to deserve it. All I had to do was receive it. If I wanted to be forgiven, saved, born again and given a new life—both here on earth and in heaven forever—all I had to do was to receive it by faith. Through tears, I said, "Yes, Lord, I believe." And now, I'm on my way!

The Apostle Paul gave a beautiful description of how all of this works in his letter to the Ephesians. He wrote:

> *"As for you, you were dead in your transgressions and sins, in which you used to live when you followed the ways of this world and of the ruler of the kingdom of the air,*

the spirit who is now at work in those who are disobedient. All of us also lived among them at one time, gratifying the cravings of our sinful nature and following its desires and thoughts. Like the rest, we were by nature objects of wrath. But because of His great love for us, God, who is rich in mercy, made us alive with Christ even when we were dead in transgressions—it is by grace you have been saved. And God raised us up with Christ and seated us with Him in the heavenly realms in Christ Jesus, in order that in the coming ages He might show the incomparable riches of His grace, expressed in His kindness to us in Christ Jesus. For it is by grace you have been saved, through faith—and this not from yourselves, it is the gift of God—not by works, so that no one can boast. For we are God's workmanship, created in Christ Jesus to do good works, which God prepared in advance for us to do" (Ephesians 2:1-10).

Paul reminded the Ephesians—and us—that God's grace is a gift.

You may feel like you don't deserve it, that your sins have pulled you down too far to receive God's wonderful gift of grace. But that's exactly why God sent Jesus to earth—not to condemn you for your sins, but to free you from them, inviting you to live with Him forever.

If you've never received God's gift of eternal life, it can be yours today. When your faith touches God's grace, the transaction is complete. Eternal life becomes yours. It's a gift that really is meant for you.

Prayer: Father, thank You for loving me even though there are times when I'm sure I've been unlovable. I'm sorry for the things I've done wrong in my life, and I want to thank You for sending Jesus to die in my place. Fill me with Your Holy Spirit. and help me to live my life for You from this day forward. In Jesus' name. Amen.

LESSON 4: GOD'S GRACE DRAWS YOU NEAR — MAY 9

Scripture Reading: Ephesians 2:11-22

God's grace is like a powerful magnet: it draws you close to Him. No matter how far away you may feel from God, God can still draw you near.

There's an old joke that says that the Prime Minister of Israel came to visit the President of the United States in his office one day. The Prime Minister noticed a red telephone on the President's desk. When the Prime Minister asked about it, the President said, "Oh, that's my direct line to God."

After a few minutes, the Prime Minister asked if he could use the phone. The President said, "Sure, but don't talk too long, because it's pretty expensive from here."

A few months later, when the President of the United States went to visit the Prime Minister of Israel in *his* office, he noticed the Prime Minister had a red phone on *his* desk, too. When the President found out that the phone did the same thing as his phone back home, he asked the Prime Minister if he could use it for just a few minutes.

The Prime Minister said, "Sure, and you can talk as long as you want! From here it's a local call."

While God does seem to have a special place in His heart for Israel, the truth is that no matter where you live in the world, you can talk to God anytime, for as long as you want. Every call to God is a local call when you place that call through Jesus Christ.

As the Apostle Paul wrote in his letter to the Ephesians, Christ destroyed the dividing wall that once separated the Jews from the Gentiles (or "non-Jews"), as well as the wall that once separated all people from their Creator. Now anyone can come near to God through Christ. Paul said:

> "Therefore, remember that formerly you who are Gentiles by birth…were separate from Christ, excluded from citizenship in Israel and foreigners to the covenants of the promise, without hope and without God in the world. But now in Christ Jesus you who once were far away have been brought near through the blood of Christ.
>
> "For He Himself is our peace, who has made the two one and has destroyed the barrier, the dividing wall of hostility…. He came and preached peace to you who were far away and peace to those who were near" (Ephesians 2:11a, 12-14, 17).

God's grace draws you near. It doesn't matter how close or how far away you may feel you are, His grace can draw you in.

The first time I went to Israel, I stayed with a Muslim family on the West Bank. They were incredibly gracious and treated me like a king.

But as I thought about how close they lived to the paths where Jesus once walked and ministered and died, I also thought about how far away they were from the peace that Christ offers to all who put their faith in Him.

Even though I lived over 6,000 miles away from this land where Christ called His home, God's grace was still powerful enough to reach out to me on the other side of the world and draw me close to Him. He's not far from any one of us. As Luke, the writer of the book of Acts, says:

> "From one man He [God] made every nation of men, that they should inhabit the whole earth; and He determined the times set for them and the exact places where they should live. God did this so that men would seek Him and perhaps reach out for Him and find Him, though He is not far from each one of us" (Acts 17:26-27).

God is not far from you today. It doesn't matter where you were born or where you live. What matters is that you keep putting your faith in Christ, realizing that it was God's grace, demonstrated in Christ, that destroyed the dividing wall of hostility between you and God.

Reach out today and give Him a call. And feel free to talk as long as you want! No matter where you are, it's always a local call.

Prayer: Father, thank You for sending Jesus to bridge the gap between me and You, and between me and my fellow believers. Lord, I pray that I would be able to experience just how near You are to me today, sensing Your presence as close as the very air I breathe. Lord, help me to reach out to You today. In Jesus' name, Amen.

LESSON 5: GRACE GROWS BEST IN WINTER — MAY 10

Scripture Reading: Ephesians 3:1-13

When you're going through tough times, it can be hard to see God at work in your life. Sometimes you begin to question whether He's really paying attention to your prayers. Sometimes you begin to question if He's even there at all.

If you're going through a tough time in your life right now, I want to encourage you that God is hearing your prayers. He does care. And He really is there. You may even find that God is at work doing the most important work He's ever done in your life.

It was at such a time as this that Samuel Rutherford, a Scottish minister who was imprisoned for his faith back in the 1600's, wrote to a friend about a truth he had discovered during that extremely difficult time. He wrote:

> "I see that grace groweth best in winter."

When I think of the people I know who are among the most gracious, I realize that they are often the people who have been through some of the hardest circumstances in life.

The Apostle Paul was one of those people. Even though he was frequently beaten, robbed, imprisoned and left for dead, Paul didn't let those things crush his spirit. Instead, he put his faith in Christ even more. The more he suffered, the more he seemed to grow in grace.

Listen to how Paul described himself, both in terms of his own feelings of brokenness, and the grace that God had given him in his life:

> "Although I am less than the least of all God's people, this grace was given me: to preach to the Gentiles the unsearchable riches of Christ, and to make plain to everyone the administration of this mystery, which for ages past was kept hidden in God, who created all things" (Ephesians 3:8-9).

Compare this description of himself with two other descriptions he gave in two of his other letters.

The author J.I. Packer notes that in Paul's first letter to the Corinthians, written about 54 AD, Paul referred to himself as "the least of the apostles" (1 Corinthians 15:9). By the time he wrote his letter to the Ephesians, about 7 years later in 61 AD, Paul called himself "the least of all God's people" (Ephesians 3:8). But by the time he wrote his letter to Timothy, about 4 years after that in 65 AD, Paul described himself as the "chief of all sinners" (1 Timothy 1:15).

As Paul continued to walk with God through all those years of suffering, he went from considering himself as the least of the apostles, to the least of all God's people, to the chief of all sinners. It seems that the closer he got to God, the more aware he became of his own sinfulness. No wonder his letters are so filled with grace, using the word "grace" over 80 times throughout his letters in the New Testament. He truly saw God's grace at work in his own life and wanted to extend that grace to all those around him.

Paul knew the secret of how to handle suffering: keep looking up. Keep trusting in God to work things out for His glory. Paul said as much to the Ephesians, encouraging them to keep coming to God freely and confidently, not being discouraged by Paul's own sufferings:

> "In Him and through faith in Him we may approach God with freedom and confidence. I ask you, therefore, not to be discouraged because of my sufferings for you, which are your glory" (Ephesians 3:12-13).

Paul saw that his suffering was not in vain, but would serve God's purpose in the end. As he wrote in his letter to the Romans:

> "And we know that in all things God works for the good of those who love Him, who have been called according to His purpose" (Romans 8:28).

Whatever you're facing today, keep putting your faith in Christ. Keep trusting Him that He will work all things for your good as you continue to love Him, no matter how hard it may seem at the time. Grace, it seems, truly does grow best in winter.

Prayer: Father, thank You for Your grace that You have showered upon me, even in the difficult times. I pray that You would help me to see that You're still at work in my life, even when things look like they're falling apart. Help me to keep turning to You during this time, growing closer to You and growing deeper in Your grace. In Jesus' name, Amen.

LESSON 6: HOW MUCH ARE YOU WORTH? — MAY 11

Scripture Reading: Ephesians 3:14-19

How much do you think you're worth? It depends on who you ask, and what they're counting.

If you were to ask an accountant, you'd find out that your worth could be extremely low or extremely high, depending on your assets. Michael Jackson, who created some of the most memorable music in history, was once asked by a reporter: "How much do you think you're worth?" Jackson replied, "It's way up there." Michael was counting the value of his accumulated wealth, including his 50% ownership of the entire Beatles music collection.

If you were to ask *Wired* magazine, you'd find out that you're worth about $45 million. That's because they're counting the value of the organs, tissues, and fluids that make up your body, assuming it were legal to sell them on the open market (which it's not). According to hospital and insurance estimates, your bone marrow alone is worth about $23 million, based on 1,000 grams at $23,000 per gram. One lung would be worth $116,400, a kidney $91,400 and a heart $57,000.

If you were to ask the U.S. Bureau of Chemistry and Soils, you'd find out that your net worth is just under one dollar. That's because they're counting your worth in terms of the market value of the chemicals and minerals that make up your body, including 65% oxygen, 18% carbon, 10% hydrogen, 3% nitrogen, and trace quantities of silicon, copper, aluminum, arsenic and so on.

But if you were to ask God, the One who created you and loves you more than anyone else in the world, you'd get an answer that blows all the others away.

That's because God counts your worth in terms of how much He loves you. But calculating God's love for you is nearly impossible. The Apostle Paul tried to express how much God loved the people in Ephesus, but he knew they would hardly be able to comprehend it. So he got down on his knees and prayed that they would have the power to grasp just how much God loved them. Here's what he wrote:

> "For this reason I kneel before the Father, from whom His whole family in heaven and on earth derives its name. I pray that out of His glorious riches He may strengthen you with power through His Spirit in your inner being, so that Christ may dwell in your hearts through faith. And I pray that you, being rooted and established in love, may have power, together with all the saints, to grasp how wide and long and high and

deep is the love of Christ, and to know this love that surpasses knowledge—that you may be filled to the measure of all the fullness of God" (Ephesians 3:14-19).

How much are you worth? If you were to calculate it according to God's love for you, you'd find out that the answer is much closer to Michael Jackson's than any other: "It's way up there!"

When God created you, and the world in which you live, He spared no expense, lavishing His love on you with all kinds of colors, flavors, sights, sounds, attractions and delights.

And when God saw that you were going astray, He spared no expense to get you back, paying more to save you than just $1 dollar, or $1,000 dollars or $45 million dollars. He paid more than an arm and a leg. He even paid more than what many consider the ultimate price—giving up His life for you. He went even further than that, and sacrificed the life of His most beloved Son, Jesus Christ.

And when Jesus died for you, He didn't do it because He had to, He did it because He wanted to. He did it because He loves you, because He considers you to be His friend.

"Greater love has no one than this," Jesus said, "than He lay down His life for His friends" (John 15:13).

You're worth more to God than you might even be able to comprehend. But still I pray that God will give you the power today to grasp just how "wide and long and high and deep is the love of Christ" … for you.

Prayer: Father, I pray that You would give me the power today to grasp how wide and long and high and deep is the love of Christ for me. I pray that You would help me to give up my simple thoughts that maybe You don't love me because of what I have or don't have, or what others say or don't say about my worth, but to realize just how vast and complex and astounding is Your love for me. I pray that You would overwhelm me with Your love today in a way that I can see it, sense it, know it, and believe it, deep in my heart. In Jesus' name, Amen.

LESSON 7: HOW MUCH CAN YOU IMAGINE?   MAY 12

Scripture Reading: Ephesians 3:20-21

Have you ever found yourself to be a little disappointed with God, wondering why He hasn't answered your prayers in the way you thought He might?

You may *want* to pray in faith, but you also want to pray realistically. So how can you pray in a way that expresses your faith and trust in God, without being disappointed if you don't see the answers in the way that you expected?

For me, I've found that even if I overreach in my prayers, asking and expecting more from God in the short run than He actually provides, I know that in the long run He can still answer my prayers in a way that goes beyond anything I could have asked or imagined.

Back when I used to work as a computer analyst for a large company, I heard a professional technology forecaster say that the trouble with technology forecasting is that people often vastly *overestimate* the short-term impact of new technologies, but vastly *underestimate* their long-term impact.

My own experience with the Internet was a prime example. When I saw a demonstration of the very first web browser, Mosaic, the presenter pulled up a page on his computer with a picture of three doors on it. As he clicked on each door, it pulled up a web page from a computer in Germany, then a page from a computer in another country, and finally a page from a computer in a third country. Everyone in the room was amazed. I began to imagine all kinds of possibilities of what could be done with such an easy-to-use worldwide network.

Yet with all the potential I could see or imagine for the Internet on that day, it paled in comparison to what the Internet has become today. It actually took several years for my initially high, short-term expectations of the Internet to finally become a reality within our company. But I could never have imagined the long-term impact the Internet would have on my own life in the future, forming the foundation for the rest of my life's work and ministry.

I think the same applies to our expectations of God. There are times when we tend to overestimate how God will answer our prayers in the short-term. But we vastly underestimate how God will answer our prayers in the long-term. While we may be disappointed in the short-term answers to our prayers, the long-term answers often go way beyond all we could ask or imagine.

In reading through one of my prayer journals from a few years ago, I ran across some disappointing days when I was trying to figure out how to fund the renovations at our Clover Ranch retreat house. When a job opportunity came up, I decided to apply, take on a second job, and put all the money I made at that job into the repairs on the house. When that job fell through even before I got started, I was disappointed.

But within a few months, God brought someone who not only donated enough to put a new roof on the house, but to completely redo the bathroom, the kitchen, and replace all the windows! I wrote in my journal that it was "beyond what I could imagine." My disappointment with God in the short run was replaced by amazement with God in the long run.

The Apostle Paul said it like this:

> "Now to Him who is able to do immeasurably more than all we ask or imagine, according to His power that is at work within us, to Him be glory in the church and in Christ Jesus throughout all generations, for ever and ever! Amen" (Ephesians 3:20-21).

The next time you set out to ask God for something, ask boldly. But remember what God told the prophet Isaiah:

> "As the heavens are higher than the earth, so are My ways higher than your ways, and My thoughts than your thoughts" (Isaiah 55:9).

By doing so, you can pray in faith and pray realistically, trusting God to answer in His way and His timing—and believing that He can do "immeasurably more than all you could ask or imagine."

Prayer: Father, thank You for Your Word, which says even more than I would expect it to say. Thank You for Your grace and mercy that allows us to come before You with our requests. And Lord, increase my faith so that I can come to you with boldness and confidence, trusting that You can indeed do more than all I could ask or imagine. In Jesus' name, Amen.

LESSON 8: EXTEND GRACE TO YOUR FELLOW BELIEVERS — MAY 13

Scripture Reading: Ephesians 4:1-6

Have you ever known people who can show incredible grace to those they hardly know, but who seem to withhold that grace from their fellow believers? I heard a joke that directly illustrates this problem:

> I was walking across a bridge one day, and I saw a man standing on the edge, about to jump off. So I ran over and said, "Stop! Don't do it!"
> "Why shouldn't I?" he said.
> I said, "Well, there's so much to live for!"
> He said, "Like what?"
> I said, "Well, are you religious or atheist?"
> He said, "Religious."
> I said, "Me too! Are you Christian or Buddhist?"
> He said, "Christian."
> I said, "Me too! Are you Catholic or Protestant?"
> He said, "Protestant."
> I said, "Me too! Are your Episcopalian or Baptist?"
> He said, "Baptist!"
> I said, "Wow! Me too! Are you Baptist Church of God or Baptist Church of the Lord?"
> He said, "Baptist Church of God!"
> I said, "Me too! Are your Original Baptist Church of God or are you Reformed Baptist Church of God?"
> He said, "Reformed Baptist Church of God!"
> I said, "Me too! Are you Reformed Baptist Church of God, Reformation of 1879, or Reformed Baptist Church of God, Reformation of 1915?"
> He said, "Reformed Baptist Church of God, Reformation of 1915!"
> I said, "Die, heretic scum!" and I pushed him off.

That joke was voted the best religious joke of all time in an online poll a few years ago, probably because it hits so close to home for so many people. Maybe you've seen it happen yourself, where people who are otherwise extremely close to each other in their thoughts and beliefs let something *comparatively* minor cause a sharp disagreement.

God reminds us in the book of Ephesians that He's extended incredible grace to us all, and He wants us to extend that same grace to our fellow believers. The Apostle Paul wrote:

> "As a prisoner for the Lord, then, I urge you to live a life worthy of the calling you have received. Be completely humble and gentle; be patient, bearing with one another in love. Make every effort to keep the unity of the Spirit through the bond of peace. There is one body and one Spirit—just as you were called to one hope when you were called—one Lord, one faith, one baptism; one God and Father of all, who is over all and through all and in all" (Ephesians 4:1-6).

Paul says something similar in his letter to the Galatians:

> "Therefore, as we have opportunity, let us do good to all people, especially to those who belong to the family of believers" (Galatians 6:10).

I know of a man who built one of the largest churches in India. A friend who knew him said that one of the reasons for his success was that he never, ever spoke a negative word against anyone or any church who was working in that country in the name of Christ, even if he disagreed with their doctrine or approach. As a result of his true graciousness, he was able to build bridges with many people, expanding the kingdom of God at every turn.

Jesus alluded to the same idea one day when the Apostle John came to Him and said:

> "Teacher, we saw a man driving out demons in Your name and we told him to stop, because he was not one of us."
> "Do not stop him," Jesus said. "No one who does a miracle in My name can in the next moment say anything bad about Me, for whoever is not against us is for us. I tell you the truth, anyone who gives you a cup of water in my name because you belong to Christ will certainly not lose his reward" (Mark 9:39-41).

The next time you're tempted to push someone off the bridge who is otherwise extremely close to you in their thoughts and beliefs, don't do it! Extend to them the same grace that God has extended to you. Give them a cup of cold water, in Jesus' name, making every effort "to keep the unity of the Spirit through the bond of peace."

Prayer: Father, thank You for reminding me to seek unity with my fellow believers, rather than trying to find fault with them. Help me to be truly gracious today, and truly forgiving, when I run across those who approach their faith and life different than I do. Help me focus on our shared love for You and extend the same kind of grace to them that You've extended to me. In Jesus' name, Amen.

LESSON 9: USE YOUR GIFTS TO SERVE OTHERS — MAY 14

Scripture Reading: Ephesians 4:7-16

I once belonged to a church that had 3,500 ministers! That's a lot of ministers! But it wasn't because they had 3,500 people on staff. It was because they considered every member a minister. They expected and encouraged every member to minister to others, to serve others, with the particular gifts that God had given them.

That was the church where I finally decided to put my faith in Christ. It wasn't just because of the great sermons, or the powerful Sunday School lessons, which were important. It was also because of the various members who reached out to me, who invited me to Bible studies in their homes, who prayed for me, and who served me—ministered to me—in various other ways.

When the truth of God's love for me in Christ finally broke through to my heart and mind, I decided to devote the rest of my life to serving Him, too. That didn't mean that I went immediately into "professional" ministry. It meant that I had now become the three-thousand, five hundred and first minister at that church, using the gifts God had given me to minister to others.

This is how the Bible describes ministry. While there are certainly specific gifts—or "graces," as the Bible sometimes refers to them— that are given to some to preach or teach, to prophesy or evangelize, or to oversee the workings of the church, these gifts are simply a means to an end: to equip the rest of God's people for works of service.

Here's how the Apostle Paul puts it in Ephesians chapter 4:

> *"But to each one of us grace has been given as Christ apportioned it.... It was He who gave some to be apostles, some to be prophets, some to be evangelists, and some to be pastors and teachers, to prepare God's people for works of service, so that the body of Christ may be built up until we all reach unity in the faith and in the knowledge of the Son of God and become mature, attaining to the whole measure of the fullness of Christ" (Ephesians 4:7, 11-13).*

The Apostle Peter puts it like this, in 1 Peter chapter 4:

> *"Each one should use whatever gift he has received to serve others, faithfully administering God's grace in its various forms. If anyone speaks, he should do it as one speaking the very words of God. If anyone serves, he should do it with the strength God provides, so that in all things God may be praised through Jesus Christ" (1 Peter 4:10-11a).*

When I first put my faith in Christ and received the gift of eternal life, I was surprised to find out that God still had more gifts to give me! I thought eternal life was enough! But it wasn't enough for God. He still had more He wanted to do in and through me, so He poured other gifts into my life, gifts that were not just for me, but to equip me to serve others.

If you've already received the gift of eternal life by putting your faith in Christ, God still has more He wants to do in and through you, too.

For some of you, God has called you, gifted you, and equipped you with the ability to teach, preach, evangelize, prophesy and oversee His work here on the earth. If so, God wants you—*He needs you*—to use those gifts to equip others, "to prepare God's people for works of service."

For some of you, God has called you, gifted you, and equipped you with gifts of faith, mercy, encouragement, serving, giving, leadership, administration—and the list goes on and on (just read Paul's letters to the Corinthians, chapters 12 and 13, or to the Romans, chapter 12, for more about spiritual gifts and how to use them). But all gifts are given for the same reason, "so that the body of Christ may be built up until we all reach unity in the faith and in the knowledge of the Son of God and become mature, attaining to the whole measure of the fullness of Christ."

Your church doesn't have just one minister, or two, or ten or twenty. Every member is a minister, when you use your gifts to serve others.

Prayer: Father, thank You for giving me the gift of eternal life, and thank You for going further and giving me even more gifts beyond that! Help me to think of ways today to use the gifts You've given me to serve others. Help me to not neglect those gifts, but to put them into practice so they can grow better and stronger, not only for my sake, but for those You want to touch through me. In Jesus' name, Amen.

LESSON 10: FORGIVE AS CHRIST HAS FORGIVEN YOU   MAY 15

Scripture Reading: Ephesians 4:17-32

One of the things I've noticed about gracious people is that they often have an incredible capacity to overlook the faults of others and focus on their strengths instead. I suppose it's the same way that God looks at us, even if we don't always perceive it that way.

While it might seem that gracious people could be simply unaware of just how sinful others can be, usually just the opposite is true. Gracious people, like God, often seem to understand sin and just how destructive sin can be. But just like God, they also understand something else. They understand just how powerful forgiveness can be.

As a result, when faced with a sin in someone else's life, those who are filled with grace make a conscious decision to choose forgiveness over anger, blessing over cursing, and compassion over destruction.

The Apostle Paul understood these choices as well. In his letter to the Ephesians, he urged them to give up their thoughts of anger, rage and malice, and to extend forgiveness, grace and kindness instead. He wrote:

"'In your anger do not sin': Do not let the sun go down while you are still angry, and do not give the devil a foothold… Do not let any unwholesome talk come out of your mouths, but only what is helpful for building others up according to their needs, that it may benefit those who listen. And do not grieve the Holy Spirit of God, with whom you were sealed for the day of redemption. Get rid of all bitterness, rage and anger, brawling and slander, along with every form of malice. Be kind and compassionate to one another, forgiving each other, just as in Christ God forgave you" (Ephesians 4:26-27, 29-32).

Forgiveness is at the heart of grace. It's what makes Christ Himself so gracious. The Bible says that Christ didn't wait for us to turn from our sins before He was willing to die for us, but rather,

"While we were still sinners, Christ died for us" (Romans 5:8b).

That's grace. That's forgiveness. That's what God has done for us in Christ. And that's what God wants us to do for others.

Being gracious isn't about ignoring, or excusing, other people's sin. Being gracious is about forgiving other people's sin—because God, in Christ, has forgiven you of yours.

In Matthew 18, Jesus tells the parable of the unmerciful servant. In the story, Jesus tells about a king who forgives one of his servants of a huge debt. But when that servant goes home and demands repayment of a debt that one of his fellow men owed to him, the king had the unmerciful servant thrown into prison, saying that he wouldn't get out until he paid back all he owed. Jesus' ends the story with these words:

"This is how My heavenly Father will treat each of you unless you forgive your brother from your heart" (Matthew 18:35).

If someone has wronged you, God understands. He knows the hurt and pain that sin can cause. But He also knows how heavy it can be to carry around the burden of anger, as well as the burden of what's been done to you. You don't have to carry both. Let go of the anger, and let God heal the hurt.

When Jesus taught His disciples how to pray, he included these words: "Forgive us our debts, as we also have forgiven our debtors" (Matthew 6:12). Then He added these sobering words:

> "For if you forgive men when they sin against you, your heavenly Father will also forgive you. But if you do not forgive men their sins, your Father will not forgive your sins" (Matthew 6:14-15).

If anyone understands forgiveness, it's Christ. And if anyone can help you to forgive others when they've sinned against you, it's Christ, too. Let Him help you to forgive. Let Him show you what true grace is about by teaching you how to extend it to others. Then one day, when others look to you and say, "How can you be so gracious!?!" you'll be able to say, "Because Christ has been so gracious to me."

Prayer: Our Father in heaven, hallowed be Your name, Your kingdom come, Your will be done on earth as it is in heaven. Give us today our daily bread. Forgive us our debts, as we also have forgiven our debtors. And lead us not into temptation, but deliver us from the evil one, for Yours is the kingdom and the power and the glory forever. Amen. (from Matthew 6:9-13)

LESSON 11: LIVE A LIFE OF LOVE   MAY 16

Scripture Reading: Ephesians 5:1-18

I love the title of today's message: "Live a Life of Love." That phrase is full of alliteration, …all the "L's" and "v's" and "f's" combine to make it just roll off your lips: "Live a Life of Love."

I remember back in college I thought I was doing just that. I thought I was living a life of love, enjoying my friendships to my heart's content, and loving others as best I knew how.

But when the pain of the inevitable broken relationships finally caught up with me, I realized that I wasn't really living a life of love. It was more like a life of lust, and for some reason, that phrase just doesn't have the same ring to it.

I found out why, a few years later, as I began to read the Bible for the first time as an adult. I finally saw that I had been crossing boundaries in my relationships that God never intended for me to cross. I began searching the Scriptures for everything else that God had to say about love and life, and I was amazed at what I discovered.

As I stepped into God's plan for my life in this area, I found that His way of loving was way better than anything I had imagined. I was so thankful that I took the time to discover what He said about these things instead of just following my own plans.

So now, when I see others heading down the same path that I had been on, I want to warn them, encourage them, help them to get back onto God's path. I want to share with them the same things that the Apostle Paul shared with the Ephesians when he said:

> "Be imitators of God, therefore, as dearly loved children and live a life of love, just as Christ loved us and gave Himself up for us as a fragrant offering and sacrifice to God. But among you there must not be even a hint of sexual immorality, or of any kind of

impurity, or of greed, because these are improper for God's holy people. Nor should there be obscenity, foolish talk or coarse joking, which are out of place, but rather thanksgiving.... For it is shameful even to mention what the disobedient do in secret" (Ephesians 5:1-3).

Paul encouraged the Ephesians to live a life of love, but to do so in a way that didn't have even a *hint* of sexual immorality. And God wants us to do the same.

I read this week about a governor who lived his life according to this approach…at least, most of the time. But once a year he'd take a trip with some friends to "let steam out of the box." Those annual outings eventually undid him. What started as seemingly innocent fun turned into sharing his email address with a stranger, then meeting up with her again in the future. It eventually turned into a full-blown affair—and a full-blown nightmare. The relationship resulted in the destruction of his marriage, his career, and his relationship with God.

While I know that God can still work in his life to sort things out, to bring some good out of all the bad that's been done, I also know that it didn't have to be this way. God wasn't trying to "box him in" by saying he shouldn't have even a hint of sexual immorality. God was trying to help him "live a life of love," one that would truly lead to the abundant life that God intends for you and me, too.

Maybe you're like me and you're wondering if you may have crossed some lines that God never intended for you to cross. If so, I'd encourage you to take a close look at God's Word so you can find out for sure. As Paul said to the Ephesians:

"Live as children of light….and find out what pleases the Lord… Therefore do not be foolish, but understand what the Lord's will is" (Ephesians 5:8b, 10, 17).

Find out what pleases the Lord and take time to understand what His will is. Then you'll truly be able to "live a life of love."

Prayer: Father, thank You for giving me life, and thank You for showing me how to live a life of love—through Christ. I pray that You would help me to give my life to others, just as He gave His life for me. Lord, help me to drop anything in my life that has even a hint of sexual immorality in it, and help me to never cross any boundaries that You don't want me to cross. In Jesus' name, Amen.

LESSON 12: LET YOUR HEART SING — MAY 17

Scripture Reading: Ephesians 5:19-20

When I think of gracious people, it seems like they're often walking around with a song in their hearts. Whether any songs actually come out of their mouths or not, it seems like their words are practically musical, as if they're flowing out from songs being sung deep within them.

The Apostle Paul encouraged the Ephesians speak to each other with songs, too. He wrote:

"Speak to one another with psalms, hymns and spiritual songs. Sing and make music in your heart to the Lord, always giving thanks to God the Father for everything, in the name of our Lord Jesus Christ" (Ephesians 5:19-20).

There's something about singing that brings joy to the surface. And there's something about having a song in your heart that spreads joy to those around you.

I have a nine-year-old son who can sing about anything. He'll sing about brushing his teeth, or a bumblebee he just saw, or a trip he's about to take. Whatever the topic, he's glad to sing about it. Sometimes he doesn't even have words for his songs—he'll just start humming a tune as he's walking around or riding in a car, letting the music flow from within him.

What has struck me about his singing is that whenever he sings, he's happy. It's not like he's always happy before he starts singing. But once he starts, his whole outlook and disposition changes. The songs themselves seem to bring joy into his heart and life.

I decided to try it myself this week when I was riding with some of my kids in the car. Every once in a while, I'd need to remind them to talk nicer to each other, or to act more sweetly. So I began singing my reminders to my kids rather than speaking. Even though I didn't have much of a tune to what I was singing, the words came out much more pleasant and brought more smiles. It's hard to be angry when you're singing! It was a good lesson for me.

And it was a good reminder of the power of these verses from Ephesians. If you can try to keep a song in your heart, giving thanks to the Lord for all things, you'll be more gracious, more cheerful, more helpful, and get a better response from those around you. It doesn't mean that you have to sing about everything that comes into your mind, or else the person at the drive-up window might start to wonder about you. But it might just bring a bigger smile to your face and the faces of those around you to *think* about singing whatever you're going to say, even if you don't actually sing it.

My family and I were in a nursing home this week visiting a close friend who's is in the final days of her life. Although she wasn't able to respond much, she seemed to perk up when we sang a song or two for her. We didn't sing any big or fancy songs, just some songs that we all happened to know and that we sometimes sing as prayers before we eat. Maybe you've heard of the "Johnny Appleseed" song or the "Superman" prayer. They're simple, but thankful songs.

Even though they were just simple songs, they seemed to lift the spirits of everyone in the room, even in the face of impending death. Songs have a way of helping us refocus our thoughts and reframing our situations, especially songs of thanks and praise to God.

If you need a lift in your spirit today or want to give a lift to the spirits of those around you, try singing a song. Make some music in your heart and let it flow out of your mouth. Even if you don't feel much like singing, you may find that singing is exactly "the cure for what ails ya'."

If you need some ideas where to start, take a look at the book of Psalms, which means "songs." Try speaking or singing the words to one of the Psalms out loud. Then consider sharing those words with those around you and see what a blessing it can be.

Prayer: Father, thank You for encouraging me to sing and make music in my heart to You. Help me to sing to You in a way that blesses You, blesses those around me, and blesses my own heart as well. Lord, fill me with Your Spirit again today, the Spirit that bring music to my life. In Jesus' name, Amen.

LESSON 13: SUBMIT TO ONE ANOTHER — MAY 18

Scripture Reading: Ephesians 5:21-33

One of the hardest things to do in life is what Paul asked the Ephesians to do in Ephesians chapter 5. Paul wrote:

> *"Submit to one another out of reverence for Christ" (Ephesians 5:21).*

It may not sound that hard. In fact, it probably sounds quite reasonable. It's like listening to Jesus, and nodding in agreement, when He says, "Love one another" (John 13:34). Of course we should love one another. That's the most reasonable thing in the world to do. But it took on a whole new meaning when Jesus defined what it meant to "love one another." Jesus said:

> *"Greater love has no one than this, that he lay down his life for his friends" (John 15:13).*

When your life is at stake, it's no longer quite as simple or convenient to "love one another." It's especially hard when the other person you're supposed to be loving just happens to be a jerk. But Jesus went beyond just loving his friends. The Bible says that Jesus laid down His life even for those who were sinning against Him. Paul wrote:

> *"Now, most people would not be willing to die for an upright person, though someone might perhaps be willing to die for a person who is especially good. But God showed His great love for us by sending Christ to die for us while we were still sinners" (Romans 5:7-8, NLT).*

It's the same thing with submission. It might sound easy enough to "submit to one another." But the truth is, none of us want to submit to anyone! It goes against human nature. It goes against "free will." It goes against the "rugged individualism" that many people think made our country so great.

But by submitting to one another, by surrendering your will to someone else's, you're demonstrating your love to them in one of the greatest ways possible. While it may be one of the most difficult things to do in life, it's also one of the most gracious. And it can turn your relationships around in a heartbeat.

I got a call one night from a couple who was having a knockdown, drag-out fight. I had only recently met them, and the wife said she was trying to decide if she should call me or call the police. When I got to their door and heard them fighting inside, I was wondering myself if she should have called the police instead!

But when we all sat down to talk, it turned out that the husband truly loved his wife, and the wife truly loved her husband. But their lives were so busy that when the husband wanted to spend more time with his wife, he expressed it in anger and frustration at their schedule, and she gave it right back to him with frustrations of her own. It quickly became a battle of the wills, and the fighting escalated from there.

I asked the wife if she believed her husband truly loved her, and if she could see that his anger grew out of an honest desire to spend more time with her, and she said, "Yes." I asked the husband if his wife were in danger, would he willingly give up his life for her, and he said, "Yes."

Then I shared with them the next words that Paul wrote to the Ephesians:

> "Wives, submit to your husbands as to the Lord....Husbands, love your wives, just as Christ loved the church and gave Himself up for her..." (Ephesians 5:22, 25).

That truth helped them through another night. I'm thankful to say it's now been over fifteen years since that night, and they're still together and serving the Lord. It's hard work to submitting to one another, surrendering your will to someone else's. But the benefits to you, to others, and to the Lord far outweigh the work involved.

Submit to one another out of reverence for Christ. Lay down your life for those you love—and even for those who are sinning against you. As you do, I pray that God's love and grace will flow from you to them—just as it flowed from Christ to you.

Prayer: Father, thank You for challenging me to submit to one another out of reverence for Your Son. Lord, even though I know it's hard, I pray that You would give me Your Spirit to help me to do it, for I want to be as gracious and loving as I can be, and I want to honor You in all I do. In Jesus' name, Amen.

LESSON 14: SUBMIT TO ONE ANOTHER - PART 2   MAY 19

Scripture Reading: Ephesians 6:1-4

When the Apostle Paul told the Ephesians to "submit to one another out of reverence for Christ," he followed it up with several practical examples for how to do this in real life. In chapter 6, Paul described how children and parents can "submit to one another":

> "Children, obey your parents in the Lord, for this is right. 'Honor your father and mother'—which is the first commandment with a promise—'that it may go well with you and that you may enjoy long life on the earth.'
> "Fathers, do not exasperate your children; instead, bring them up in the training and instruction of the Lord" (Ephesians 6:1-3).

It's hard being a parent. But it's hard being a child, too.

Maybe you heard about the man who observed a woman in the grocery store with a three-year-old girl in her basket. As they passed the cookie section, the little girl asked for cookies and her mother told her, "No." The little girl immediately began to whine and fuss, and the mother said quietly, "Now Jane, we just have half of the aisles left to go through—don't be upset. It won't be long now."

Soon, they came to the candy aisle and the little girl began to shout for candy. When told she couldn't have any, she began to cry. The mother said, "There, there, Jane, don't cry—only two more aisles to go and then we'll be checking out."

When they got to the checkout stand, the little girl immediately began to clamor for gum and burst into a terrible tantrum upon discovering there'd be no gum purchased. The mother said serenely, "Jane, we'll be through this checkout stand in 5 minutes and then you can go home and have a nice nap."

The man followed them out to the parking lot and stopped the woman to compliment her. "I couldn't help noticing how patient you were with little Jane. It's quite commendable," he remarked.

The mother replied, "I'm Jane. My little girl's name is Tammy."

It takes a lot of patience to be gracious, especially between children and parents. Yet Paul tells us there's value in doing so.

For children, Paul points out that obeying your parents is the first of the Ten Commandments with a promise: "that it may go well with you and enjoy a long life on the earth." Not only do things go better for you, but children someday may grow up to have children of their own and realize that "what goes around comes around." I've heard it said that "diaper" spelled backwards is "repaid!"

For parents, Paul says not to exasperate your children, meaning not to irritate them so much that that they become enraged. "Instead," Paul says, "bring them up in the training and instruction of the Lord." King Solomon knew the long-term benefits of training a child in how to live a godly life. He said:

> "Train a child in the way he should go, and when he is old he will not turn from it" (Proverbs 22:6).

And some of you may find yourself in the same place that my wife and I are in right now: taking care of both your children and your parents at the same time, as Lana's parents have moved in with us as their health has started to decline. Even after all these years as children and as parents, we're still in the process of learning what it means to "obey your parents in the Lord," and to "not exasperate your children."

Some days it means holding your tongue when you'd rather talk back. Other days it means speaking the truth in love when you'd rather not talk at all. At times it means serving a meal and cutting up someone's food. At other times, it means training someone else how to make a serve a meal and cut up their own food. Quite often it means surrendering your will to accommodate someone else's. But occasionally it means exerting your own will for the benefit of everyone involved.

Submit to one another out of reverence to Christ. You'll be blessed—and so will those around you—when you do.

Prayer: Father, thank You for reminding me to how to submit to one another out of reverence for Christ, especially to those closest to me. Help me to know how to apply these words in practical way today, whether that's honoring my parents and or training my children in Your ways, or both. Lord, help me to do these things in a way that blesses You, blesses them, and blesses me as well. In Jesus' name, Amen.

LESSON 15: SUBMIT TO ONE ANOTHER - PART 3   MAY 20

Scripture Reading: Ephesians 6:5-9

When Paul encouraged the Ephesians to "submit to one another out of reverence for Christ" (Ephesians 5:21), he gave them three practical examples for how to do this: one for husbands and wives, one for parent and children, and one for masters and slaves.

While the terms "masters" and "slaves" may not apply to many people today, the terms "employers" and "employees" certainly do. And Paul's words to the Ephesians are just as fitting for these types of working relationships, too. Listen to Paul's words, and see how they might apply to you today:

> "Slaves, obey your earthly masters with respect and fear, and with sincerity of heart, just as you would obey Christ. Obey them not only to win their favor when their eye is on you, but like slaves of Christ, doing the will of God from your heart. Serve wholeheartedly, as if you were serving the Lord, not men, because you know that the Lord will reward everyone for whatever good he does, whether he is slave or free.
> "And masters, treat your slaves in the same way. Do not threaten them, since you know that He who is both their Master and yours is in heaven, and there is no favoritism with Him" (Ephesians 6:5-9).

I don't know about you, but I've had a fair share of bosses in my lifetime. Some of which I had great respect for, and others of which I had very little respect for. But as I look at Paul's words, he never said anything about whether or not a master was worthy of respect, but that we were to treat them with respect, obeying them just as we would obey Christ.

I know from experience just how hard that can be. But I also know from experience just how beneficial that can be, often doing more for my working relationships than I could have imagined.

In one instance, I had a boss who didn't like me from day one—and he let me know it. He had heard I was some kind of go-getter and he wasn't about to let me go anywhere. Things went from bad to worse.

One day he asked me to do yet one more thing that I felt was about to push me over the edge. It wasn't immoral or unethical—he simply asked me to fill out a survey that the company had distributed, asking employees to fill it out voluntarily and anonymously. But since I was out of town when the survey was distributed, he sent me a copy and told me I had to fill mine out and fax it back to him by the following day.

I took issue with his request, since it was supposed to be voluntary and anonymous. By mandating that I fill it out, and then fax it back with my phone number right there on the fax, it would violate both of those conditions.

But after making my case, he still held onto his position, and I held onto mine. Late that night, Paul's words to the Ephesians came back to me, to "obey your earthly masters with respect and fear...just as you would obey Christ." Even though I disagreed with his approach, I filled out the survey and faxed it back to him so it would be on his desk in the morning.

Our whole relationship turned around that day. My boss became my biggest champion from that day forward and for the rest of my career at that company. It was a lesson that proved once more that God's words spoken through Paul were true, that God really will "reward everyone for whatever good he does." And it was a lesson that helped me when I later became an employer myself—and a husband and a father.

Submitting to one another really does work! It demonstrates a graciousness on your part and can make your relationships flow better all around—whether they're between husbands and wives, parents and children, or "masters and slaves." Don't miss out on the reward God has for you! Submit to one another out of reverence for Christ!

Prayer: Father, thanks for the reminder to submit to those with whom I work, whether I work for them or they work for me. Help me to be gracious in my relationships with each person in the workplace, so that Your blessings would flow to us and through us. Help me in all my relationships to submit to one another out of reverence to Christ. In Jesus' name, Amen.

LESSON 16: OVERCOME YOUR ENEMIES WITH GRACE — MAY 21

Scripture Reading: Ephesians 6:10-18

One of the best ways to overcome your enemies is to make them your friends.

I made a friend like this back in college. When we were taking an English Literature class together, it seemed like we were always at odds. I was always defending King Arthur as the hero of the books, and she was always defending Queen Guinevere. In class, it seemed like we'd never agree on anything.

But one day we both showed up for tryouts at a college musical. We realized we had more in common than we thought, and both of us softened up in our approach. That softening had such an effect on our friendship, that a few years after college was over, she even agreed to sing at my wedding.

There are times when God calls you to overcome your enemies by destroying them so completely that they no longer have an effect on your life. But there are other times when God calls you to overcome your enemies by winning them over with your love, realizing that the battle may not be against them, but against spiritual forces that may be turning them against you.

The Apostle Paul talks about these battles in his letter to the Ephesians, and the kinds of weapons that God gave them to fight these battles. You might call these "weapons of grace," weapons that can turn your enemies into your friends!

Listen to these words as Paul describes this spiritual "armor of God."

> "Finally, be strong in the Lord and in His mighty power. Put on the full armor of God so that you can take your stand against the devil's schemes. For our struggle is not against flesh and blood, but against the rulers, against the authorities, against the powers of this dark world and against the spiritual forces of evil in the heavenly realms. Therefore put on the full armor of God, so that when the day of evil comes, you may be able to stand your ground, and after you have done everything, to stand. Stand firm then, with the belt of truth buckled around your waist, with the breastplate of righteousness in place, and with your feet fitted with the readiness that comes from the gospel of peace. In addition to all this, take up the shield of faith, with which you can extinguish all the flaming arrows of the evil one. Take the helmet of salvation and the sword of the Spirit, which is the Word of God. And pray in the Spirit on all occasions with all kinds of prayers and requests. With this in mind, be alert and always keep on praying for all the saints" (Ephesians 6:10-18).

The next time someone comes against you, speaks against you, or tries to overpower you, go ahead and put on your battle gear. But instead of gearing up with all your usual defenses, try some of God's. To paraphrase the Apostle Paul:

Be truthful. Be righteous. Be eager to share the gospel of peace. Keep up your faith. Keep in mind that Jesus has already saved you. Speak the truth in love. And keep on praying, continually.

These are God's weapons of grace, weapons that you can use to defend yourselves, and disarm your opponents, oftentimes with a greater impact than physical weapons could have.

It was through Jesus' love and grace that He turned you from being His enemy to being His friend (see Romans 5:10 and John 15:15). So it shouldn't be surprising that God wants you to use these same weapons to overcome your enemies, making them your friends as well. It may not happen overnight, but over time you may just find their hearts softening towards you, as the real enemy, the power of darkness, has to flee when the light turns on.

Remember that your battle is not against flesh and blood, but against spiritual forces in the heavenly realm. In a spiritual battle, you need spiritual armor, which is much softer and more gracious than physical armor, but in the end, is much stronger and more powerful.

Put on your spiritual armor today. Clothe yourself with truth, righteousness, peace, faith, salvation, God's Word and prayer. Let God's love flow through you to those around you and watch what happens.

Prayer: Father, thank You for reminding me that the battles I face aren't always against an enemy I can see, but against spiritual forces in the heavenly realm. Help me to put on my spiritual armor of love and grace today so that I can overcome those who are against me—and even make them my friends. In Jesus' name, Amen.

LESSON 17: GRACE IS "OTHERS-FOCUSED"   MAY 22

Scripture Reading: Ephesians 6:19-22

I'm sitting today with one of the most gracious women I know. It's not my wife, although she's quite gracious. And it's not anyone particularly famous, except to her family and to those of us who know her well.

Her name is Mary Lou Schrock, and she was a lifetime friend of my Dad's until he passed away earlier this year. She stepped back into his life about nineteen years ago, filling a void that was left after my mom passed away. Mary Lou has been like a second mother to me, coming to our kids' birthday parties, spending countless hours with my Dad during days of sickness and health, and spending Christmas mornings with our family year after year.

She's invested her life in taking care of others. But in recent years, she's had to let others take care of her. If she had a choice, I'm sure she'd gladly switch roles. That's just the kind of woman she is. And that's one of the things that makes her so gracious as well. Whether she was baking a meal for someone, or helping out at the nursing home, or writing a card to send to someone who needed a lift, she was always thinking of others.

In a way, she was very much like the Apostle Paul, who displayed a similar quality of graciousness. From the beginning of his letter to the Ephesians until the very end, he was always "others-focused." I can't imagine it was easy, though.

As a prisoner in Rome, I'm sure he could have written thousands of words talking about himself, complaining of the false accusations made against him, the unjust beatings he'd had to endure, or the hardships of life as a prisoner in the first century A.D. But instead, he wrote thousands of words talking about *them*, focusing on *their* lives, *their* trials, and *their* relationships with God.

The only time he asked for anything for himself was at the very end of his letter. And even then, his only request was for them to pray that he would be able to fearlessly proclaim the message of Christ to others, the very thing that landed him in prison in the first place. He wrote:

> *"Pray also for me, that whenever I open my mouth, words may be given me so that I will fearlessly make known the mystery of the gospel, for which I am in chains. Pray that I may declare it fearlessly, as I should" (Ephesians 6:19-20).*

Paul was already on trial for proclaiming the good news about Jesus Christ, and he was awaiting a very likely death sentence for it. Yet he called on the Ephesians to pray that God would help him to keep proclaiming the message of Christ without fear. To the end, even when asking for prayer for himself, Paul remained steadfastly committed to others. And God wants us to remain "others-focused" as well.

This doesn't mean that you can't talk about yourself, your problems and your needs. But it does mean that you should be thoughtful about when and how you share those needs. You don't want to be like the woman who said: "Enough about me. Let's talk about you. What do *you* think about me?"

As "others-focused" as he was, Paul knew that it was also important to let others know how he was doing, too. So at the end of his letter, he wrote:

> *"Tychicus, the dear brother and faithful servant in the Lord, will tell you everything, so that you also may know how I am and what I am doing. I am sending him to you for this very purpose, that you may know how we are, and that he may encourage you" (Ephesians 6:21-22).*

Paul didn't ignore himself and his needs completely. But he was gracious enough to know there was an appropriate time and place to share those needs. And God wants us to do the same.

God wants us to be people who are "others-focused" to the core, people who regularly spend time thinking about the needs of others and how to meet those needs. He wants us to be people like Mary Lou, people who invest their lives in ways that will bless those around us.

Prayer: Father, thank You for helping me see that grace is "others-focused." I pray that You would help me to be so focused on others that my life and my problems will fade in comparison. Help me to be filled with Your grace to such an extent that I would gladly pour it out on others, regardless of the cost to me personally. Let me be a good ambassador for You, and a good messenger of Your grace to those around me. In Jesus' name, Amen.

LESSON 18: HOW GRACIOUS IS GRACIOUS ENOUGH? — MAY 23

Scripture Reading: Ephesians 6:23-24

As we come to the closing words of Paul's letter to the Ephesians, I'd like to touch on the idea of just how gracious we have to be in order to be "gracious enough." Just how much grace has God shown to us? And how much grace does He want us to show to others?

One of my favorite quotes on this topic goes like this:

> *"Sometimes you have to be overly gracious in order to be gracious enough."*

When I think of that quote, I think of a woman named Jean. Jean is a businesswoman from England whom we met on a missions trip a few years ago. She helped us out shortly after that trip by coming to a retreat center we're renovating here in Illinois called Clover Ranch. She came to help us with some interior decorating.

But when she arrived, it became clear that the house needed much more than a coat of paint and some pretty pictures. While she was taking a bath one day, the pipes burst in the upstairs bathroom, pouring water down into the kitchen below. While replacing those pipes, it became clear that the wiring had to be redone as well. We ended up gutting both the bathroom and the kitchen entirely, starting again from scratch. Then the rain came, and we realized that water was coming in around many of the old windows and they would have to be replaced before we could even think about any interior decorating. The house was a mess and she hadn't even gotten to start on what she initially came to do.

In spite of all of this, Jean was a trooper. We invited her to stay in our own home during all of this, but like the loyal captain of a ship, she wanted to stay with her vessel. She continued to live at Clover Ranch, without a functional kitchen or bathroom, except for a sink and a shower stall in the basement and accompanied by a host of crickets and spiders and other creatures that seemed to thrive in the chaos of the reconstruction.

Through it all, Jean was not just gracious. She was *overly gracious*. She talked about how thankful she was to be out in the country, to have time to think and pray, and to be part of helping us out with this project.

While Lana and I felt bad that she had to live in such an inhospitable situation, Jean's grace helped ease our burden. She expressed over and over that she truly wanted to help us out. The only reason we could even possibly believe her was that she was consistently overly gracious. If she had just said, "It's OK, don't worry about it," that would have been gracious. But we would have still felt miserable for what was happening. Yet because of her overflowing graciousness, we were finally able to believe that she was sincere in her thankfulness and solid in her belief that God had placed her right where He wanted her to be for that season of her life.

Through her words and actions, Jean taught us the value of being overly gracious. Just saying a kind word or two doesn't always get the message across. Sometimes we need to be overly gracious, as God has been with us, in order for others to truly believe that we're sincere.

Like the Apostle Paul, who used the word *grace* a dozen times in his letter to the Ephesians, and another seventy-five times in his other letters in the New Testament, it may seem like we would never be able to talk about grace enough, to demonstrate it enough, to live it enough, or to truly express it enough so that others would be able to believe it and receive it.

But if we keep trying, if we keep sharing, if we keep expressing God's grace to others as if *God Himself* was expressing *His grace through us*, then perhaps others would begin to believe us. Just maybe they'd begin to realize how much we love them, and how much God loves them. Just maybe, by being "overly gracious," we'd finally be able to be "gracious enough."

Prayer: Father, thank You for being overly gracious with me. Thank You for expressing Your grace to me in a way that I could believe it and receive it. Now, Lord, help me to do the same in sharing Your grace with others. In Jesus' name, Amen.

CONCLUSION: HAVING A GRACE-FILLED HEART — MAY 24

Scripture Reading: Ephesians 6:24

As I was writing these messages about grace, someone asked me if I had any ideas for how they could have a more grace-filled heart—a heart that would help them to appreciate others more instead of complaining, to forgive instead of holding grudges, and to love instead of being angry.

Here's a summary of what I shared in response, taken from things I've learned from the book of Ephesians and other places in the Bible. I thought you might like to read them, too, as a summary of our study together:

1) Practice continual forgiveness. Forgiveness is the heart of the gospel, as Jesus forgave us even while we were still sinning against Him. It's the heart of showing grace towards others as well. As Paul said, "Be kind and compassionate to one another, forgiving each other, just as in Christ God forgave you" (Ephesians 4:32). By choosing to forgive others, as God has forgiven you, you'll be well on your way towards having a grace-filled heart.

2) Fill your mind with the things of God. Paul wrote to the Philippians: "…whatever is true, whatever is noble, whatever is right, whatever is pure, whatever is lovely, whatever is admirable—if anything is excellent or praiseworthy—think about such things" (Philippians 4:8). By reading God's Word daily, memorizing verses of scripture, and meditating on what you're reading, you'll find that God will begin to fill your mind with His thoughts, His ideas and His point of view on whatever you're facing. Keep filling your heart and mind with the things of God as much as possible, every day, several times throughout the day. This will pay off with huge dividends for you and for those around you, both in the short-term and in the long-term.

3) Keep asking yourself, "What Would Jesus Do?" (WWJD). This is a simple, but helpful reminder to try to think and act and speak as Jesus would. It's not just an intellectual exercise. It's a practical way to accomplish God's work here on the earth. When Jesus went back to heaven, He sent His Holy Spirit to live inside us so that we could be His body—His hands, His feet, His eyes and ears and voice to those around us. Paul wrote to the Corinthians, "Now you are the body of Christ, and each one of you is a part of it" (1 Corinthians 12:27). As a believer in Christ, God wants to work through *you* as if Jesus Himself were doing the work—because He is!

4) Pray at all times. As Paul said to the Ephesians: "And pray in the Spirit on all occasions with all kinds of prayers and requests" (Ephesians 6:18). By praying throughout the day, seeking His will and listening for His voice, you'll be able to stay focused on what God wants at all times. It's like walking through the day with a friend—and even better—because Jesus is a friend who knows everything! So as you walk or sit or talk or think, keep on praying and talking to God at all times. It'll be both a joy to you and a practical help to those around you.

5) "Be quick to listen, slow to speak and slow to become angry" (James 1:19). This practical reminder from James will help you to spiritually "count to 10" before responding to others. While it doesn't say you can't get angry, or you can't ever say anything with which others might disagree, it does say to wait to speak until after you have listened carefully—meaning "with care" and "fully." When you do this, your words will simply come out

better, expressing more love and grace, even when speaking things that may be hard to hear.

While having a grace-filled heart can take a lifetime, the Bible is full of practical steps that you can take right now to have an impact right away. That's the beauty of God's Word! It starts working as soon as you apply it to your life, and it keeps on working to the end. Put it into practice today, and may God fill you with His grace as you do.

As Paul said in his closing line to the Ephesians:

"Grace to all who love our Lord Jesus Christ with an undying love" (Ephesians 6:24).

Prayer: Father, thank You for this study of Paul's letter to the Ephesians. Thank You for the wisdom that You poured into him, and thank You for preserving that wisdom in this letter so that we can learn from it even 2,000 years later. Continue to give us a desire to learn all we can from Your Word, so that we can fill our hearts with Your grace, and then share it with others. In Jesus' name, Amen.

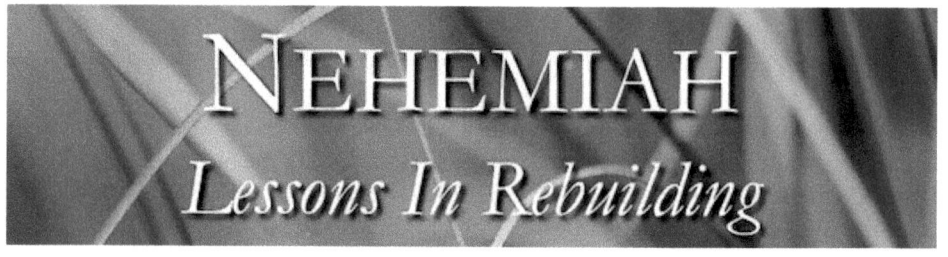

Nehemiah: Lessons in Rebuilding

15 inspiring devotionals based on one of the most ambitious rebuilding projects of all time

INTRODUCTION TO "NEHEMIAH: LESSONS IN REBUILDING" — MAY 25

Scripture Reading: Nehemiah 6:15-16

Is there something broken in your life that you'd like to fix, but don't know how? A broken marriage, a failing business, a dying relationship? Or is there something that's fallen apart that you'd like to rebuild: a house, a church, a ministry, a career? If so, then you'll love to learn some lessons in rebuilding from the biblical book of Nehemiah.

Nehemiah took on a rebuilding project that seemed imposing, impractical and nearly impossible. But when he told God what he wanted to do, and God gave him the green light to do it, God walked him through every step of the project. With God's help, Nehemiah and his people rebuilt a wall around the entire city of Jerusalem.

People told Nehemiah it was impossible; people tried to stop his work; people threatened his life. But Nehemiah pressed on. After many months of planning, praying, fighting and building, the work was finally complete. When all the surrounding countries, including his enemies, saw what Nehemiah had done, they also knew *how* he got it done. The book of Nehemiah says:

> "...they realized that this work had been done with the help of our God" (Nehemiah 6:16).

If you'd like to learn how Nehemiah did it, and how God helped him along the way, I invite you to join me in learning about this great rebuilding project as recorded in the book of Nehemiah. If you've got something on your heart that you want to rebuild, I'd like to encourage you in the weeks ahead to do it.

Here's a simple truth: if it matters to you, it matters to God. God cares about the details of your life. He cares about the things that you care about. That doesn't mean that He always wants you to head out and do whatever you want to do. Our plans are not always His plans.

But if He doesn't want you to do it, He'll let you know, if you're willing to listen. God has redirected many people's good plans so He can do something better through them, (see 2 Samuel 7, for instance, where King David wanted to build a house for God, but God wanted to build a house for David).

But if God *does* want you to go forward with your plans, He'd love to help you succeed. He is undoubtedly *for* you. He created you, He loves you and He has an incredible plan for your life. You could say He has a "vested" interest in you, because He's in-vested so many gifts and skills into your life because He has so many things He wants to do through you.

The hardest part of starting a project is often believing that God really wants you to do it; that He really cares, and that He'll really help you every step of the way. Once you know that, you're half-way there! After that, it's just a matter of figuring out the details of how to proceed. I hope this study encourages you on both levels, giving you both the confidence to believe in the project that's on your heart, and giving you the practical steps to do it.

Nehemiah followed a series of practical steps to rebuild the wall around Jerusalem, steps which you can follow to rebuild the things in your own life that need rebuilding. It involved much prayer, much planning, many people and fair amount of hard work. But He didn't have to do it alone: God helped him all along the way.

By the end of this study, I hope that you'll have the confidence and the tools that you need in order to reach the goal that Nehemiah reached as recorded in Nehemiah 6:15:

"So the wall was completed…" (Nehemiah 6:15).

Those words are stated with such simplicity that they could never do justice to the work involved, nor the accomplishment that was achieved. But they are stated in a way that when I hear them, I'm inspired that what Nehemiah was able to accomplish, I just might be able to accomplish, too, with God's help. My prayer is that they inspire you as well.

As we go through this study, I'll include a Scripture Reading to go with each devotional. I hope you'll read these passages along with what I write, because I can only touch on one or two thoughts in each devotional, but God has so much He wants to say to you! By the end of the study, when you're finished reading each of these Scripture Readings, you'll have read through the entire book of Nehemiah.

I've also included a prayer that you can pray with me at the end of each devotional. I hope this helps you to begin a quiet time of prayer with God in response to what you've read. Here's today's prayer:

Prayer: Father, open my eyes to see what Nehemiah saw that helped him to accomplish what was on his heart, and help me learn how to do the same. In Jesus' name, Amen.

LESSON 1: SIT DOWN AND WEEP   MAY 26

Scripture Reading: Nehemiah 1:1-4

Where do you start to rebuild something in your life that's been broken? Whether you're trying to rebuild your marriage, family, city, nation, house, career, business, or whatever's important to you that's been lost, where can you possibly begin to undertake such an overwhelming project?

The best place to start is where Nehemiah started: he sat down and wept. When Nehemiah heard that the people in Jerusalem were in distress and the wall around their city was in ruins, the very first thing he did—before he prayed, before he ran back home, before he lifted even one stone to try to fix it—he sat down and wept.

Here's how Nehemiah says it, as recorded in the Bible:

> "In the month of Kislev in the twentieth year, while I was in the citadel of Susa, Hanani, one of my brothers, came from Judah with some other men, and I questioned them about the Jewish remnant that survived the exile, and also about Jerusalem.
> "They said to me, 'Those who survived the exile and are back in the province are in great trouble and disgrace. The wall of Jerusalem is broken down, and its gates have been burned with fire.'
> "When I heard these things, I sat down and wept" (Nehemiah 1:1b-4a).

When something has fallen apart in your life, the best first step you can take toward rebuilding it is to sit down and weep over what's been lost, to let the depth of the destruction sink deep into your soul. Without a full understanding of what's been lost, it's very hard to take the steps you need to take to reclaim it. But once you grasp what's happened, along with all of its implications, God can use that understanding to help you take the rest of the steps you need to reverse what's been done.

I remember when I first heard about a couple who was going through adultery. I was stunned, shocked and numbed by what I'd heard. I could sit with them and listen, I could pray for them, but I felt helpless about what else I could really do. It wasn't until several days later that the full weight of what I had heard finally hit me, along with all of its implications. When it did, I just sat down and wept, and wept and wept.

There was something about the tears that brought me to the place where I knew I had to do something to intervene in this situation. I knew that no matter what it took, I needed to step in and do what I could to help repair what had been broken. While people usually see tears as a sign of weakness, it was—ironically—the tears that gave me the strength to do what I needed to do.

What is it in your life that's been broken that you desperately wish could be repaired? What is it that you've lost that you wish you could restore, and how badly do you want to see it restored?

The best first step you could possibly take is to sit down and weep.

The rebuilding project I'm working on right now is the restoration of the farmhouse where I grew up. Our ministry bought it a few years ago to turn it into a personal retreat for people who want to renew their relationship with God. But the project didn't start with tearing down walls, or sanding the floors, or even signing the papers at the bank. It started one day when I visited the farm after it had fallen into disrepair.

I just knelt down on the grass and wept, praying that God would someday restore it, remembering these words from 2 Chronicles:

> "If my people, who are called by my name, will humble themselves and pray and seek my face and turn from their wicked ways, then will I hear from heaven and will forgive their sin and will heal their land" (2 Chronicles 7:14).

It turned out to be the best first step I could take. And, if you follow Nehemiah's example, it could be the best first step you can take as well: to simply sit down and weep.

Prayer: Father, help me to weep over what's been lost, and give me Your strength to rebuild it again. In Jesus' name, Amen.

LESSON 2: GET UP AND PRAY

Scripture Reading: Nehemiah 1:4-11

There's a scene in the middle of the classic Christmas movie *It's A Wonderful Life* that I hardly noticed in all the years that I've watched it—until I became a Christian, that is. The message of the movie is so powerful, I missed the fact that the whole chain of events that takes place throughout the movie starts with a prayer.

When George Bailey, the character played by Jimmy Stewart, finds himself at a loss for what to do next, he prays:

> "God...God...Dear Father in Heaven, I'm not a praying man, but if You're up there and You can hear me, show me the way. I'm at the end of my rope. Show me the way, God."

And God does.

There's a time to weep over the losses in your life, but there's also a time to move forward. And the best way to move forward is to get up and pray. Although you may feel like George Bailey at times, not even sure if God's there and listening at all, I assure you He is. God is there and God does care. Knowing that can make all the difference in your prayers.

If you think of prayer as just a time to be alone, or a time to talk to yourself and try to work things out on your own, then you may not have much incentive to pray at all. But if you truly believe that God is there, and that when you talk, He listens—and responds—then turning to prayer takes on a whole new meaning.

When the prophet Nehemiah suffered a great loss in his life, he sat down and wept, but the next thing he did was to get up and pray. Listen to the words of Nehemiah, and his prayer, as recorded in Nehemiah chapter 1:

> "When I heard these things, I sat down and wept. For some days I mourned and fasted and prayed before the God of heaven. Then I said:
> 'O LORD, God of heaven, the great and awesome God, who keeps His covenant of love with those who love Him and obey His commands, let Your ear be attentive and Your eyes open to hear the prayer Your servant is praying before You day and night for Your servants, the people of Israel. I confess the sins we Israelites, including myself and my father's house, have committed against You. We have acted very wickedly toward You. We have not obeyed the commands, decrees and laws You gave Your servant Moses.
> 'Remember the instruction You gave Your servant Moses, saying, 'If you are unfaithful, I will scatter you among the nations, but if you return to me and obey my commands, then even if your exiled people are at the farthest horizon, I will gather them from there and bring them to the place I have chosen as a dwelling for My Name.'
> 'They are Your servants and Your people, whom You redeemed by Your great strength and Your mighty hand. O Lord, let Your ear be attentive to the prayer of this Your servant and to the prayer of Your servants who delight in revering Your name. Give Your servant success today by granting him favor in the presence of this man'" (Nehemiah 1:4-11).

Nehemiah knew that God was there, that God was listening, and that God knew best what to do next. Nehemiah mourned, fasted and prayed. He confessed his own sins, as well as those of his countrymen. And he reminded himself—and God—of God's promises, asking for God's favor as he moved forward.

I don't know whether you're more like George Bailey, who didn't think of himself as a praying man, or more like Nehemiah, who prayed regularly, or somewhere in between. But I do know that whoever you are, you can pray to your Father in heaven and He will hear you—and He will respond. That prayer could very well be the one that starts the whole chain of events of the rest of your life.

Come to God today and pray, even if it's as simple as saying, "I'm at the end of my rope. Show me the way, God." And He will.

Prayer: Father, I'm at the end of my rope and I don't know what to do next. I confess my sins to you. Show me the way, Lord, and help me to know what to do next. In Jesus' name, Amen.

LESSON 3: ACKNOWLEDGE YOUR POSITION — MAY 28

Scripture Reading: Nehemiah 1:11b

If God has called you to rebuild something in your life, do you have any idea why He called you to do it? Why He didn't call on someone else?

Maybe you don't feel particularly qualified to undertake the project God has put on your heart. If so, I'd like to encourage you to take a closer look at a few of the reasons God may have called you, *specifically*.

Nehemiah may have thought that he was an unlikely candidate to rebuild the wall around Jerusalem. As far as we know, he wasn't an architect, a bricklayer or a gate builder. He was, as he tells us at the end of Nehemiah chapter 1, a cupbearer:

"I was cupbearer to the king" (Nehemiah 1:11b).

As cupbearer to the king, Nehemiah was a servant in the king's court, serving the king his wine. Yet God called him to undertake one of the greatest rebuilding projects documented in the Bible. He may have wondered why God called him specifically, too. In fact, just a few verses later, when Nehemiah approached the king with his idea, Nehemiah says,

"I was very much afraid" (Nehemiah 2:2b).

He had a lot to fear as a servant to a king in a foreign land. Yet there was something about Nehemiah's position that made him a more likely candidate than even he may have realized. As cupbearer, Nehemiah was in a highly trusted position. The king literally had to trust his cupbearer with his life, because anyone might try to poison him at any time. The cupbearer helped to keep the king alive.

As you can read throughout the rest of the book of Nehemiah, you'll see that God used the trust that Nehemiah had earned to give him great favor with the king. God moved on the king's heart to provide Nehemiah with the resources he needed to rebuild the wall, to send him letters of safe passage back to Jerusalem, and to eventually appoint Nehemiah as the governor of the rebuilt city.

So even though Nehemiah felt "very much afraid," God had very good reasons for choosing him! Nehemiah acknowledged his position, both the fear he felt and willingness he showed to use whatever favor God had given him to advance this project.

Queen Esther faced the same dilemma when her people were about to be destroyed. As wife of another king, she was in a unique position to ask him to overturn a wrongful law of the land. Yet, she also knew that approaching the king with such a request could mean death for her if the king felt insulted by her approach. Still, Esther's cousin Mordecai reminded her of her unique position, saying,

> "And who knows but that you have come to royal position for such a time as this?" (Esther 4:14b).

So Esther acknowledged her position, recognizing both the incredible *impossibility* and the incredible *possibility* of what God had laid before her. In the end, she concluded that she would go to the king no matter what, saying,

> "And if I perish, I perish" (Esther 4:16b).

God used both her humility and her unique position to save the lives of her people.

Maybe you feel like there's no way you can move forward with what God's called you to do. But know this: if God has put a special project on your heart, know that He has a very good reason for choosing you! And if you look closely at some of His reasons, they may just give you the confidence you need to move forward, too.

Maybe it's simply because you have a stronger desire to see it succeed than anyone else. Maybe it's because the project involves people or places close to you, so you have a greater vested interest in the outcome than anyone else. Maybe it's because of the unique position God has given you in life, a position that gives you access to resources others may not have.

Whatever the reasons, acknowledge your position, recognizing both the incredible impossibility and the incredible possibility of what God has laid before you. Then ask Him for help to move past your fears and move on with the task at hand.

Prayer: Father, help me to see why You have called me, specifically, to this task. Give me insight so that I can get the courage I need to move past my fears. In Jesus' name, Amen.

LESSON 4: FIND YOUR RESOURCES — MAY 29

Scripture Reading: Nehemiah 2:1-10

Has God called you to do something that's bigger than you can pull off yourself? Then it's time to call on Him to help you find the resources you need from somewhere else.

It's hard to ask for help, though. But the good news is that when you ask God first, He'll show you who to ask next. Listen to this conversation that Nehemiah had with King Artaxerxes, just after Nehemiah had been praying to God about rebuilding the wall around Jerusalem:

> "In the month of Nisan in the twentieth year of King Artaxerxes, when wine was brought for him, I took the wine and gave it to the king. I had not been sad in his

presence before; so the king asked me, 'Why does your face look so sad when you are not ill? This can be nothing but sadness of heart.'
"I was very much afraid, but I said to the king, 'May the king live forever! Why should my face not look sad when the city where my fathers are buried lies in ruins, and its gates have been destroyed by fire?'
"The king said to me, 'What is it you want?'
"Then I prayed to the God of heaven, and I answered the king, 'If it pleases the king and if your servant has found favor in his sight, let him send me to the city in Judah where my fathers are buried so that I can rebuild it.'
"Then the king, with the queen sitting beside him, asked me, 'How long will your journey take, and when will you get back?' It pleased the king to send me; so I set a time.
"I also said to him, 'If it pleases the king, may I have letters to the governors of Trans-Euphrates, so that they will provide me safe-conduct until I arrive in Judah? And may I have a letter to Asaph, keeper of the king's forest, so he will give me timber to make beams for the gates of the citadel by the temple and for the city wall and for the residence I will occupy?' And because the gracious hand of my God was upon me, the king granted my requests. So I went to the governors of Trans-Euphrates and gave them the king's letters. The king had also sent army officers and cavalry with me" (Nehemiah 2:1-9).

Even though Nehemiah was "very much afraid," God opened a door for him with the king, and Nehemiah walked through it. I can't guarantee that God will send a king to give you what you need, but it may surprise you who God does put in your path.

I was afraid to ask for help when we began renovating Clover Ranch, but I knew there was no way we could do it on our own. So when I asked God for help, He began to put me in touch with people who had the resources I needed to move forward. One person knew about plumbing and came along to help; another knew about electricity and offered a hand.

At one point, God brought someone with significant resources at their disposal, but I was too afraid to ask for their help. I didn't want to seem presumptuous. I didn't want to jeopardize our new friendship. I didn't want to hear another "No," as I had often heard before. But God reminded me that this was His project, not just mine. So I asked—and God answered. It turned out to be the most significant contribution to the project to date.

There's a story told about Mother Teresa, who went walking door-to-door to raise money for her orphans. At one door, when she asked for help, a man spat in her face. She took her habit, wiped her face clean and said,

"Well, that's for me. That's for my humility. Now how about something for the children?"

The man gave her some money.

If God has put a project on your heart, remember that He wants you to succeed even more than you do. My prayer for you is that when God opens a door in front of you, you'll have the courage you need to walk through it and find the resources you need.

Prayer: Father, help me to find the resources I need to accomplish what You've put on my heart. When it just seems too overwhelming for me to do on my own, give me the boldness to ask for help. In Jesus' name, Amen.

LESSON 5: EXAMINE THE SITUATION   MAY 30

Scripture Reading: Nehemiah 2:10-16

There will come a time when it's important to enlist the help of others to do all that God has called you to do. But there's also a time when you need to talk to God, and God alone, about your project, letting Him help you to examine the situation at hand so you can take the next steps together.

Nehemiah reached this point when he arrived in Jerusalem. There were already a couple of people who had heard about what he wanted to do, and they weren't happy about it. Nehemiah says:

> "When Sanballat the Horonite and Tobiah the Ammonite official heard about this, they were very much disturbed that someone had come to promote the welfare of the Israelites" (Nehemiah 2:10).

So Nehemiah took his next steps alone. He had heard about the condition of the walls surrounding Jerusalem from others, but now was the time for him to see the site for himself. He went at night, taking with him only a few trusted friends. Here's how Nehemiah describes it as chapter 2 continues:

> "I went to Jerusalem, and after staying there three days I set out during the night with a few men. I had not told anyone what my God had put in my heart to do for Jerusalem. There were no mounts with me except the one I was riding on.
> "By night I went out through the Valley Gate toward the Jackal Well and the Dung Gate, examining the walls of Jerusalem, which had been broken down, and its gates, which had been destroyed by fire. Then I moved on toward the Fountain Gate and the King's Pool, but there was not enough room for my mount to get through; so I went up the valley by night, examining the wall. Finally, I turned back and reentered through the Valley Gate. The officials did not know where I had gone or what I was doing, because as yet I had said nothing to the Jews or the priests or nobles or officials or any others who would be doing the work" (Nehemiah 2:11-16).

As important as it would soon be for Nehemiah to tell others about his plans, it was also important that he see for himself the extent of the work involved beforehand. So Nehemiah examined the situation, looking over his project from one end to the other and getting a good grasp of what needed to be done.

I remember hearing about a couple who had gotten a divorce. God put it in my heart to pray that they would be reconciled. But as I talked to others, I heard something totally different: their family didn't want them to be reconciled, their friends didn't want them to be reconciled, and neither the husband nor wife wanted to be reconciled!

I had to go back to God and listen carefully to what He wanted me to do for them, which was to continue to pray for their reconciliation. So I kept up with what God had put in my heart to do until one day, to the shock of their family and friends, and even to themselves, they were finally reconciled and remarried to each other once again. *(If you'd like to hear more of their story, you can watch it on The Ranch website at www.theranch.org, called "It's Never Too Late.")*

The time will come when it's wise and critical to involve others. But there are also times when you need to spend time with God, and God alone, as you honestly examine the situation.

It could be easy to get discouraged at this point, with so much to do and with others possibly opposing your efforts. But I'd like to point you back to something Nehemiah said as he set out to examine the situation in front of him. He wrote:

> "I had not told anyone what my God had put in my heart to do for Jerusalem" (Nehemiah 2:12b).

Nehemiah knew that rebuilding the walls wasn't just a good idea, it was God's idea—an idea that God had put in his heart. Let God encourage you today as you carefully examine the situation at hand. Let Him show you what needs to be done next. Then trust Him to walk beside you as you move forward, every step of the way.

Prayer: Father, I come to You today to ask for Your help as I examine the situation in front of me. Let me see the full scope of what needs to be done so I can know what to do next. In Jesus' name, Amen.

LESSON 6: GATHER OTHERS TO HELP — MAY 31

Scripture Reading: Nehemiah 2:17-20

Do you ever feel like you're all alone in the world? That no one else cares about the things that God has put on your heart? That if anything is ever going to get done, you're going to have to do it yourself?

This is one of Satan's best strategies to discourage you: to make you feel isolated, alone, without help and without hope. Let me assure you today, you're not alone. There's always hope. And God wants to help you more than you know. The Bible says:

> "For the eyes of the LORD range throughout the earth to strengthen those whose hearts are fully committed to Him" (2 Chronicles 16:9).

Nehemiah knew the importance of spending time alone with God. Up to this point, Nehemiah had only told a few trusted friends about his plans, even inspecting the walls of Jerusalem at night so he could see for himself what needed to be done. But when it was time to begin the work, he gathered others to help: the Jews, priests, nobles, officials and all the others who would be doing the work. When the time was right, Nehemiah told the others of his plans, as recorded in Nehemiah chapter 2:

> "Then I said to them, 'You see the trouble we are in: Jerusalem lies in ruins, and its gates have been burned with fire. Come, let us rebuild the wall of Jerusalem, and we will no longer be in disgrace.' I also told them about the gracious hand of my God upon me and what the king had said to me.
> "They replied, 'Let us start rebuilding.' So they began this good work" (Nehemiah 2:17-18).

There were still naysayers who opposed the work: Sanballat the Horonite, Tobiah the Ammonite and Geshem the Arab. They mocked and ridiculed the Israelites, but Nehemiah simply replied:

> "The God of heaven will give us success. We His servants will start rebuilding, but as for you, you have no share in Jerusalem or any claim or historic right to it" (Nehemiah 2:20).

Nehemiah was ready to move forward—no matter what—and God moved on the hearts of others to help him along the way. There may be naysayers in your life who aren't lifting a finger to help you right now. But that doesn't mean you have to go it alone. Gather others to help: pastors, spouses, friends, relatives, volunteers, paid workers, youth groups. If you get a "No" from one or two or three or more, just keep asking others, or come back to the same ones at a later time.

I remember asking one man to share his testimony at an event we were putting on in town. I really felt God had prompted me to ask him. He said, "No, there's no way I could do that." I went home and prayed again, and God kept putting his name on my heart. I went back to him the next week and asked him again. Without batting an eye, he said, "Sure, I'd be glad to do it!" His testimony turned out to be one of the highlights of the event.

I couldn't count the number of times I've felt like I was all alone in what God had called me to do. But the truth is, I also couldn't count the number of times God has sent people to help me to do what He's put on my heart to do. It's taken persistence, time and a continual realization that there's no way I would be able to do it on my own. That, plus knowing that God is for me—not against me—in the plans that He's put on my heart, has helped me to continue to gather others to help along the way.

Don't let Satan keep you down. Don't give in when he tries to magnify the negative and minimize the positive in your life. Keep coming back to God and let Him strongly support you in what you're doing. Take courage from the story of Nehemiah and keep asking others for help. I pray for you that like Nehemiah, "the God of heaven will give you success."

Prayer: Father, help me know who to ask for help. Help me have the wisdom and the discretion to ask those who can truly help with my situation. In Jesus' name, Amen.

LESSON 7: START REBUILDING   JUNE 1

Scripture Reading: Nehemiah 3:1-32

You know how to eat an elephant, right? One bite at a time. It's the same with any big project that God has called you to do. While it may seem overwhelming, there comes a time—after all the thinking and planning and praying—that you just have to take the plunge and start rebuilding.

Nehemiah and his friends were finally ready to take the plunge themselves in Nehemiah chapter 3, when they began to rebuild the walls around Jerusalem, section by section and gate by gate.

Nehemiah gives a detailed description of all they did, starting with the work of Eliashib the high priest and his fellow priests:

> "Eliashib the high priest and his fellow priests went to work and rebuilt the Sheep Gate. They dedicated it and set its doors in place, building as far as the Tower of the Hundred, which they dedicated, and as far as the Tower of Hananel. The men of Jericho built the adjoining section, and Zaccur son of Imri built next to them. The Fish

Gate was rebuilt by the sons of Hassenaah. They laid its beams and put its doors and bolts and bars in place. Meremoth son of Uriah, the son of Hakkoz, repaired the next section. Next to him Meshullam son of Berekiah, the son of Meshezabel, made repairs, and next to him Zadok son of Baana also made repairs..." (Nehemiah 3:1-4).

This detailed description of the work continues for the rest of the chapter. They repaired the Jeshanah Gate, the Broad Wall, the Tower of the Ovens, the Valley Gate, the Dung Gate. They worked on the Fountain Gate, the wall of the Pool of Siloam, and up to the House of the Heroes. They continued on to the Water Gate, the Horse Gate, the East Gate, the Inspection Gate, and the Sheep Gate. As you read the report, you can tell this is one of the largest building projects undertaken in the Bible. And many of the gates in Jerusalem today still have these same names!

You could say it all started back when God first put the idea into Nehemiah's heart. But the work of his hands was just as important.

After thinking and planning and praying about your own project, you may have some good ideas for what needs to be done. But sometimes it's taking that first step of actual work that's the most important. They say that a journey of a thousand miles begins with a single step, and today may be the day for you to take yours.

What specific action step can you take today to advance the project that God has put on your heart? If you've been blocked at various points along the way, what other steps can you take in the meantime? If you're waiting on God, that's fine. But if He's waiting on you, then you'd better get going!

When I first began my Internet ministry, I went to pick out a computer. I had just quit my job and didn't have a computer of my own, so I needed to get one to begin the work. So I shopped and shopped, checking prices and features, trying to find just the right one.

At one point, I felt like God was saying: "I've called you to walk alongside Me in this, but My stride is long, so you'd better get going if you want to keep up!" I knew I'd better get moving! Twelve years and several computers later, I still have more steps to take to keep up with all that God wants me to do. I just need to keep moving forward, too, step by step.

Have you ever seen a round tuit? If not, join the club. They must be pretty rare, though, and they must be pretty valuable, too, because when people talk about the big dreams they want to accomplish in their lives, they often add, "But I've just never gotten a round tuit."

Maybe today's your lucky day and you'll finally get "a round tuit" for yourself! Look around and see what specific steps you can take today toward fulfilling the dream God has put on your heart. Then take it!

Prayer: Father, I want to keep up with You and Your plans for my life. Help me to take whatever steps I need to take today to advance the project You've put on my heart. In Jesus' name, Amen.

LESSON 8: PRAY AGAINST OPPOSITION — JUNE 2

Scripture Reading: Nehemiah 4:1-5

Has anyone ever laughed when you told them about your "good idea"? It can be disheartening, but it doesn't have to destroy your plans. Just keep going back to the Lord in prayer, putting your hope and trust in Him.

I remember someone laughed at me when I told them I wanted to start a ministry on the Internet. She said, "But not everyone has a connection to the Internet!" I already had doubts of my own, and her comments didn't help.

But in the same instant, God brought to mind the incredible potential He had shown me for the idea. I had put a great deal of thought into how it could work, and I knew the idea had merit. More importantly, I felt God had His hand in the idea. Somehow I found the courage to respond to her remark by saying, "You're right, not everyone has a connection to the Internet yet. But I'll start with the 30 million that are connected and work my way up from there!" (That was back in 1995 when the Internet was just taking off for public use. As I write this, there are now over 1.5 billion people connected to the Internet—and counting!)

It's hard to face opposition to your ideas especially when you're just getting started. But by going back to the Lord in prayer, He can help you through it.

People laughed at Nehemiah and his fellow Jews when they had the "good idea" to rebuild the wall of Jerusalem, too. Here's what a couple of people said to them as they began rebuilding:

> "When Sanballat heard that we were rebuilding the wall, he became angry and was greatly incensed. He ridiculed the Jews, and in the presence of his associates and the army of Samaria, he said, 'What are those feeble Jews doing? Will they restore their wall? Will they offer sacrifices? Will they finish in a day? Can they bring the stones back to life from those heaps of rubble—burned as they are?' Tobiah the Ammonite, who was at his side, said, 'What they are building—if even a fox climbed up on it, he would break down their wall of stones!'" (Nehemiah 4:1-4).

Nehemiah and his fellow Jews may have had their own doubts, too, but they didn't let the ridicule discourage them. They simply went to the Lord in prayer. They prayed:

> "Hear us, O our God, for we are despised. Turn their insults back on their own heads. Give them over as plunder in a land of captivity. Do not cover up their guilt or blot out their sins from your sight, for they have thrown insults in the face of the builders" (Nehemiah 4:4-5).

It was a pretty strongly worded prayer, but the fact is they prayed. They put their hope and trust in their God to vindicate them in their cause. You may prefer to pray as Jesus prayed, asking God to bless those who don't yet understand what you're attempting to do, "Father, forgive them, for they do not know what they are doing" (Luke 23:34). In any case, turn to the Lord in prayer.

God vindicated Nehemiah, and time after time, God has vindicated me. Sometimes He even blesses those who have previously laughed at my ideas in ways they couldn't have imagined.

When I used to work for a secular company, I promoted a project that would allow the employees to work from home. This was before the idea of "telecommuting" had caught on, and very few people had such an opportunity. One man in my company told me point blank it was dumb idea and would never work. But I went forward with the project and ten of us moved home to test it out. Within six months it was shown to be so successful the company allowed more people to apply to do the same.

This man who had laughed at my idea decided to apply. He moved back to his own hometown, about four hours away from where he worked, and he later told me what a blessing it was to him and his family, and how thankful he was that our project had proved him wrong.

The next time someone laughs at your "good idea," just turn your heart back to God in prayer.

Prayer: Father, help me have the wisdom to pray to you when others laugh at what You've called me to do. Bless them, Lord, even in spite of what they are saying. In Jesus' name, Amen.

LESSON 9: WORK WITH ALL YOUR HEART — JUNE 3

Scripture Reading: Nehemiah 4:6

I was praying about my goals for the new year when I felt God saying to me, "Finish the ones from last year." Three projects popped into my head that I've been working on but haven't finished yet. I wrote those down as my "new" goals for this year— to finish the old ones!

It's easy to look at what's "undone" in your life, but it's just as important to look at what has been done already, to see just how far God has brought you.

Nehemiah paused in the midst of his story about rebuilding the walls around Jerusalem to take note of what had been accomplished so far. It's just one sentence, but it's worth noting what he says:

> "So we rebuilt the wall till all of it reached half its height, for the people worked with all their heart" (Nehemiah 4:6).

The people had worked with all their heart and now the wall was half-way finished. I don't know if you're the type of person who sees half a glass of water as half full or half empty. But today I want to encourage you to look at the projects you're working on as half full. I also want to encourage you to dive into the rest of the project with all your heart.

In the movie, *Fireproof*, there's a scene where the husband in the movie confesses that he was just going through the motions of trying to save his marriage, but that his heart wasn't really in it. Through prayer and a realization of just what this meant to him and his family, he was able to get his heart back in the game. Rather than working out of duty, he began to work "with all his heart" like those in Nehemiah's story did. From that moment on, the husband's work changed from a chore to a passion and ended up saving his marriage in the end.

One way to help get your heart back in the game is to think about how far God has brought you already.

I like to keep a prayer journal and I often want to dive in by writing out all the questions that are on my mind, asking God for His help in walking me through each day. But some time ago I decided to make it a habit to always begin my journal with the words, "Father, thank You..." and then write down several things for which I was truly thankful. God will often bring to mind things He's done for me, and the progress He's helped me to make so far. Once I see the glass as half full, it prepares my heart to be ready to do whatever God says to fill the rest of the glass.

What has God brought you through this past year? What has He helped you to accomplish? What projects, goals, ambitions, dreams, desires were you able to start? You may want to sit down for a few minutes today and just thank God for the progress you've made up to this point. You may even want to write down some of the things He's walked you through that you never thought you'd be able to do. Once you see how far you've come, God can give you the heart to keep moving forward. Then work at it with all your heart. As the Apostle Paul told the Colossians:

> "Whatever you do, work at it with all your heart, as working for the Lord, not for men, since you know that you will receive an inheritance from the Lord as a reward. It is the Lord Christ you are serving" (Colossians 3:23-24).

Whether you're moving forward with brand new goals, or moving forward to finish some old ones, remember that God really is for you in accomplishing what He's put on your heart to do. He wants you to succeed at it. He wants to walk with you through it. He wants to help you day by day. So take some time to remember what God has done for you so far, then "work with all your heart" to finish the good work He's put on your heart to do.

Prayer: Father, thank You for all you've helped me to accomplish this far. I pray that You would help me to "work with all my heart" to finish the work You've put on my heart. In Jesus' name, Amen.

LESSON 10: DON'T BE AFRAID — JUNE 4

Scripture Reading: Nehemiah 4:7-14

Many times in the Bible, when things were getting tense, someone would often show up on the scene and say the words, "Don't be afraid."

What I've found interesting in reading through these stories is that the person speaking is not saying, "There's nothing to fear." They're saying, "Don't be afraid," even though the danger is very real. Real threats are at hand. Real attacks are on their way. Real lives are at stake. It's not like telling your kids to go back to bed because there's no such thing as monsters. In these stories, the "monsters" are very real, just like they may be in your life right now, too.

So, if the danger is real, why would God send angels or others to tell people, "Don't be afraid?" The reason is that even though the danger is real, so is God. As someone has said, "Don't tell God how big your storm is. Tell the storm how big your God is."

When Nehemiah and his people faced life-threatening attacks in Nehemiah chapter 4, Nehemiah said:

> *"Don't be afraid of them. Remember the Lord, who is great and awesome..."* (Nehemiah 4:14a).

If you look at the threats that were being made against Nehemiah and his people, you'll see that Nehemiah wasn't trying to discount the threats, or make light of them, or say that they didn't exist, like fairy-tale monsters in a closet. He wanted to remind them to remember the Lord, the one who had called them to this project in the first place.

As you read the story, you'll see that the situation looked bleak—and it was bleak. When those who opposed the rebuilding of the wall around Jerusalem heard that the repairs had gone ahead and that the gaps were being closed,

> *"...they were very angry. They all plotted together to come and fight against Jerusalem and stir up trouble against it"* (Nehemiah 4:7b, 8).
>
> *"The people in Judah said, 'The strength of the laborers is giving out, and there is so much rubble that we cannot rebuild the wall.' Also our enemies said, 'Before they know it or see us, we will be right there among them and will kill them and put an end to the work.' Then the Jews who lived near them came and told us ten times over, 'Wherever you turn, they will attack us'"* (Nehemiah 4:10-12).

It was in the midst of these very discouraging times that Nehemiah took bold action and spoke bold words:

> *"Therefore I stationed some of the people behind the lowest points of the wall at the exposed places, posting them by families, with their swords, spears and bows. After I looked things over, I stood up and said to the nobles, the officials and the rest of the people, 'Don't be afraid of them. Remember the Lord, who is great and awesome, and fight for your brothers, your sons and your daughters, your wives and your homes'"* (Nehemiah 4:13-14).

I'm not here today to tell you there's nothing to fear. Real attacks may come. There is fighting throughout the world, and even Israel is under attack once again. For you, it may be that your finances are crumbling. Your health may be failing. The adulteress who threatened your marriage may be back in the picture. But as real as those threats may be, I want to tell you today that God is just as real. I want to tell you today: "Remember the Lord, who is great and awesome, and fight for your brothers, your sons and your daughters, your wives and your homes."

When fatigue sets in, remind yourself that "this matters."

As the Lord told Jehosephat:

> *"Do not be afraid or discouraged because of this vast army. For the battle is not yours, but God's"* (2 Chronicles 20:15).

As the Lord told the Israelites through the prophet Isaiah:

> *"Do not be afraid, for I am with you."* (Isaiah 43:5a).

As the Lord told Daniel:

"Do not be afraid, Daniel. Since the first day that you set your mind to gain understanding and to humble yourself before your God, your words were heard, and I have come in response to them" (Daniel 10:12).

Don't be afraid. Remember the Lord, who is great and awesome. Keep putting your trust in Him.

Prayer: Father, thank You for promising to never leave me nor forsake me. Help me to remember You today so that I don't have to be afraid. In Jesus' name, Amen.

LESSON 11: FIGHT FOR WHAT YOU HOLD DEAR   JUNE 5

Scripture Reading: Nehemiah 4:14-23

One of the most powerful scenes in the *Lord of the Rings* trilogy comes in the final movie, when Aragorn implores his men not to give in to fear, but to fight for what they hold dear. Riding his horse back and forth in front of his troops, Aragorn calls out:

"I see in your eyes the same fear that would take the heart of me. A day may come when the courage of men fails, when we forsake our friends and break all bonds of fellowship, but it is not this day. An hour of woes and shattered shields, when the age of men comes crashing down! But it is not this day! This day we fight! By all that you hold dear on this good Earth, I bid you stand, Men of the West!"

If you find yourself overwhelmed by fears today, don't let them take your heart! If God has called you into this battle, don't give in to your fears. Fight for what you hold dear. Fight for your faith. Fight for your marriage. Fight for your children, your business, your friends, your family, your neighbors, your ministry, your health, your career.

Fight the way Nehemiah encouraged his people to fight when they came under attack: Nehemiah called out:

"Don't be afraid of them. Remember the Lord, who is great and awesome, and fight for your brothers, your sons and your daughters, your wives and your homes" (Nehemiah 4:14).

Nehemiah didn't discount that the battle was real. He encouraged the people to remember the Lord who had called them into this battle in the first place. But Nehemiah didn't stop there. He didn't throw up his hands in despair and act as if the battle would go away on its own. He called on his people to prepare for battle.

He called for half the men to keep on working, and he equipped the other half of the men with spears, shields, bows and armor to stand guard behind the workers. He had those who carried materials do their work with one hand and hold a weapon in the other. And he had those who worked with both their hands still wear a sword at their side.

He had a man stay with him at all times who could sound a trumpet. He knew that the work was extensive, and the workers were widely separated from each other, so he told them,

"Wherever you hear the sound of the trumpet, join us there. Our God will fight for us!" (Nehemiah 4:20).

Even though Nehemiah fully trusted that God would fight *for* them, he still armed his people so that God could fight *through* them. If God has called you into this battle, He's certainly willing to fight for you. But don't be surprised if He chooses to fight through you, too!

Nehemiah and his people worked from the first light of dawn till the stars came out, and they stayed inside the city at night. Neither he nor his brothers nor the guards with him even took off their clothes. Each had their weapon, even when they went for water.

Nehemiah's plan worked, and God's plan kept moving forward. The same wisdom that worked for Nehemiah can work for you, too. Look to the Lord and follow His lead.

Work with one hand and hold a weapon in the other. If the work is too extensive and spread out, sound the trumpet and call for help. Work all day, but stay in at night. Don't let your guard down, even when you go for water.

A day may come when the courage of men fails…but it is not this day! This day we fight! Don't give in to fear. Don't give up on the work God has called you to do. And don't turn your back on the battle, either. At the risk of sounding repetitive, I want to repeat Nehemiah's quote just one more time!

> *"Remember the Lord, who is great and awesome, and fight for your brothers, your sons and your daughters, your wives and your homes."*

Don't give in to fear. Fight for what you hold dear!

Prayer: Father, help me to fight the good fight of faith today. Help me to look to You so that I can follow Your lead. Show me what I can do today to fight for what I hold dear. In Jesus' name, Amen.

LESSON 12: HELP THOSE WHO ARE HELPING YOU — JUNE 6

Scripture Reading: Nehemiah 5

There was a creative ad campaign a few years ago called, "Don't Almost Give." Its purpose was to raise people's awareness of the needs around them, encouraging people to help meet those needs.

One ad showed an elderly woman sitting alone in her chair, staring blankly ahead. The narrator said,

> *"This is Sarah Watkins. A lot of people almost helped her. One almost cooked for her. Another almost drove her to the doctor. Still another almost stopped by to say 'Hello.' They almost helped. They almost gave of themselves. But almost giving is the same as not giving at all."*

The series of ads concluded with the words,

> *"Remember all those times you almost helped? You meant to, but somehow you forgot. You were too busy, and it slipped your mind. Well, it's only human, this almost giving. But if you almost gave, there's a good chance everybody else almost gave, too. Don't almost give. Give."*

In the story of Nehemiah, there was a point where Nehemiah became aware of the needs of those who were helping him rebuild the wall around Jerusalem. When Nehemiah recognized their need, he didn't just "almost give." He gave, in terms of both his personal resources and his influence over others, to help ease their burden.

Nehemiah found out that the Jews who were working with him were having to mortgage their fields, their vineyards and their homes just to get food to survive. They were selling their sons and daughters into temporary slavery until they could pay off their debts. Unfortunately, it was their fellow Jews who were buying these slaves and charging interest on the loans.

When Nehemiah heard these things, he was angry. The Jewish law was clear that while there was nothing wrong with lending money to their brothers in need, the Jews were not to charge interest to their fellow Jews, which they were doing. And by holding their property as collateral, those who needed the money could not continue making a living. So Nehemiah gathered the nobles who were making these loans and told them:

"What you are doing is not right. Shouldn't you walk in the fear of our God to avoid the reproach of our Gentile enemies? I and my brothers and my men are also lending the people money and grain. But let the exacting of usury [charging interest] stop! Give back to them immediately their fields, vineyards, olive groves and houses, and also the usury you are charging them—the hundredth part of the money, grain, new wine and oil" (Nehemiah 5:9-11).

The people responded:

"We will give it back. And we will not demand anything more from them. We will do as you say" (Nehemiah 5:12).

Nehemiah also agreed to ease their burden by not collecting the tax that was due to him to meet his own needs during the entire time that he served as their governor. Instead, Nehemiah regularly had a hundred and fifty Jews and nobles eating around his table, as well as those from surrounding nations. Nehemiah did this from his own resources, because the demands on his people were so heavy.

Because of the nature of my work, I often have to call on others to help me do what God has put on my heart to do. Nehemiah's actions are a helpful and necessary reminder to think about ways I can practically help those who are helping me, both for their own sake, and for the sake of the project that God has called us to do together.

If there are people helping you do what God has put on your heart to do, I'd like to encourage you to take some time in the coming days to listen to their hearts. See if they have needs that you could help meet, whether directly or through your influence, then do what you can to meet those needs.

Don't almost give. Give. Help those who are helping you so that together you can do all that God has called you to do.

Prayer: Father, show me the needs of those who are helping me so that I can help them as well. Give me the resources and influence to help meet their needs in practical ways so that together we can accomplish all that You've put on our hearts to do. In Jesus' name, Amen.

LESSON 13: DON'T GIVE IN — JUNE 7

Scripture Reading: Nehemiah 6:1-4

Some people will try to discourage you from reaching your dreams because they love you, they care about you, and they don't want to see you get hurt in pursuing something that may never happen.

But others will try to discourage you because they're afraid you might actually accomplish what you've set out to do. They're not interested in your future, your success, your well-being. They're interested in their own dreams and goals and will do whatever they can to stop you from achieving yours.

Nehemiah faced his share of opposition. But one group opposed him throughout his project because they were afraid he'd actually accomplish what he had set out to do. They tried to lure him away from his project, calling out to him:

"Come, let us meet together in one of the villages on the plain of Ono" (Nehemiah 6:2).

But Nehemiah saw through their plan. He knew they meant to harm him, not help him. So he sent messengers to them with this reply:

"I am carrying on a great project and cannot go down. Why should the work stop while I leave it and go down to you?" (Nehemiah 6:3).

Those who opposed Nehemiah didn't just ask him to leave the work and meet with them once or twice. Four times they tried to lure him away. And four times, Nehemiah gave them the same answer: "Why should the work stop while I leave it and go down to you?"

Sometimes it may seem impolite if we don't respond to all of our critics. We feel we need to explain ourselves to them, hear them out, and negotiate with them through our disagreements. But sometimes we just need to follow Nehemiah's example. You don't negotiate with a wolf.

Even Jesus warned his disciples:

"I am sending you out like sheep among wolves. Therefore be as shrewd as snakes and as innocent as doves" (Matthew 10:16).

When others want you to give up on your plans, give careful thought to their reasons. Is their advice really for your benefit, or simply for their own? While it's important to listen to those who truly care about you and who care about what you feel God has called you to do, it can be just as important to ignore those who don't care about you, who care mainly about their own plans instead.

I was hard at work renovating our Clover Ranch retreat center one day when a man came by and asked if I would be willing to sell the place. He wasn't a wolf, but he also wasn't aware of what God had spoken to me about the project. He said he'd had his eye on the property for some time and would really like to buy it if I'd like to sell it. His offer was tempting. I was starting to wear out from working on the project myself. It would be much easier, I thought, to just give in and sell the place to him.

I talked to my Dad later that day and mentioned this man's offer. My Dad said, "Don't sell it to him. You've put in too much work into it to sell it off now." His words woke me up to the reality of the situation, and to the vision that God had put on my heart for the project in the first place. My Dad was right. The project had been a lot of work, but this wasn't the time to give in. This was the time to press on and finish what God had put on my heart to do.

There are times when you might be tempted to give in to the demands of others. You may even see their offer as a welcome relief at the time, getting you out of more hard work. But if God has put this project on your heart, don't even go there. Don't give up. Don't give in. Don't go down and meet with those who would try to distract you from what God has called you to do, especially wolves who don't have your best interest at heart.

Don't give in. Keep pressing on with all that God has put on your heart to do.

Prayer: Father, help me to not give in to the demands of others who don't have my best interest at heart. Help me to put Your priorities ahead of even my own, so that I can finish the work You've called me to do. In Jesus' name, Amen.

LESSON 14: DON'T FALL FOR LIES — JUNE 8

Scripture Reading: Nehemiah 6:5-14

The Broadway musical, *Wicked*, tells the "untold" story of the witches of Oz. Using some creative storytelling, the show's writer convinces the audience that the Wicked Witch of the West was really just misunderstood, and that the supposedly "good" Wizard of Oz was really the one who was "wicked."

By the end of the show, the audience is cheering for the green witch's success, and hoping for the wizard's defeat. It's a compelling story that shows the power of words to sway people's thoughts, portraying that which is evil as good, and that which is good as evil.

Satan knows the power of words, too. But when he speaks, he doesn't just use "creative storytelling" to entertain an audience; he uses outright lies to destroy people's lives. Satan is so adept at lying that Jesus called him both "a liar" and the "father of lies." Jesus went on to say that lying is such an innate part of Satan's character that, "when he lies, he speaks his native language" (John 8:44b).

I think it's critical that you're aware of this, because Satan wants to lie to you, too, especially when you're doing the work of God. Sometimes he'll spread lies about you and your work, and sometimes he'll lie to you directly to entice you to give up on your work and give in to his plan.

What can you do to defend yourself when Satan attacks you like this? What can you do to combat the lies he throws at you?

You can do what Nehemiah did: don't fall for the lies; confront them with the truth.

When Nehemiah was nearly finished rebuilding the wall around Jerusalem, his opponents brought on their fiercest attack. They began to spread lies about Nehemiah to others, sending an "open" letter to Nehemiah that said:

> *"It is reported among the nations—and Geshem says it is true—that you and the Jews are plotting to revolt, and therefore you are building the wall. Moreover, according to these reports you are about to become their king and have even appointed prophets to make this proclamation about you in Jerusalem: 'There is a king in Judah!' Now*

this report will get back to the king; so come, let us confer together" (Nehemiah 6:6-7).

What could Nehemiah do? He could have panicked, even if it wasn't true, and tried to meet with them so word didn't get back to the king. But doing so would have sent him directly into the trap they were setting for him. So Nehemiah sent a reply back that said:

> "Nothing like what you are saying is happening; you are just making it up out of your head" (Nehemiah 6:8).

Rather than being intimidated and giving up on the work, he prayed to the Lord,

> "Now strengthen my hands" (Nehemiah 6:9b).

Nehemiah's opponents even hired some prophets to speak lies directly to Nehemiah, telling him that people were coming to kill him, warning him to run and hide inside the temple walls, thus causing him to sin and discredit his name. But Nehemiah saw through those lies, too, saying:

> "Should a man like me run away? Or should one like me go into the temple to save his life? I will not go!" (Nehemiah 6:12-13).

Is Satan trying to lie to you today, whether in your head or by using someone else's words? If so, I want to encourage you: don't fall for the lies; confront them with the truth. Confront them with the Truth of God as spoken in His Word and the Truth of God as spoken by His Holy Spirit to your heart.

There's power in words, but there's even more power in God's Word. Don't let Satan call "wicked" that which God calls good. Keep reminding yourself of God's Word. He loves you (John 3:16). He's for you, not against you (Romans 8:31). He wants to give you a future and a hope (Jeremiah 29:11). Don't fall for lies! Confront them with the truth! As you'll find out in the next message, when the attack is fiercest, you may be closer to victory than you think!

Prayer: Father, help me to confront the lies of Satan with the Truth of Your Word. Remind me of that Truth when I need it, and help me to speak that Truth, to myself and to others, so that I can see Your victory in the end. In Jesus' name, Amen.

LESSON 15: THE WALL IS COMPLETE! — JUNE 9

Scripture Reading: Nehemiah 6:15-19

Just when Nehemiah's storm seemed the darkest, a ray of light broke though. In the face of death threats and lies, Nehemiah finally achieved what he had set out to do.

The description of it is tucked in the middle of the book of Nehemiah, in the middle of a chapter. But those two simple lines must have spoken volumes to Nehemiah, just as they did to the surrounding nations:

> "So the wall was completed on the twenty-fifth of Elul, in fifty-two days. When all our enemies heard about this, all the surrounding nations were afraid and lost their self-confidence, because they realized that this work had been done with the help of our God" (Nehemiah 6:15-16).

After all his prayers, tears and hard work, Nehemiah finally saw the fruit of his labor.

The completion of the wall didn't mean that his life's work was over: he continued to serve as the governor over that region for another twelve years. And it didn't mean that his battles were over: he would still have to deal with his opponents from time to time.

But the completion of the wall did mean that Nehemiah, with God's help, was able to accomplish the monumental work that God had put on his heart. He was able to do what others thought was impossible. And he was able to take part in God's plan to continue His mission in the world: in this case, the restoration of the Israelites to the holy city of Jerusalem.

Now that the wall around the city was restored, Israelite families could begin moving back into Jerusalem, rebuilding their homes and rebuilding their lives. The rebuilding of the wall was an achievement in and of itself, but it was a means to an end for God's overarching plan.

When God calls you to work on a project, I think it's helpful to keep in mind both the project itself, and the future purpose for which God called you to it.

When God rebuilt the marriage of a couple whom I had been talking to and praying with for some time, I watched in amazement as God not only restored their marriage, but went on to redirect the husband into ministry, becoming a pastor and building up a new church in his city that reached out to his ethnic group. He and the church then went on to begin a missions outreach back to their home country.

The restoration of their marriage was critical, and no small feat on its own. But it served as a launching pad for what God had in mind for their lives once their marriage was restored.

As for me, as I write this, I'm still working on my renovation project at our Clover Ranch retreat. It's taken way more than fifty-two days, and some days I wonder if it will ever be done. I was having that feeling this week again as I was putting a third coat of stain on some wood trim that will be used around the doorways and windows in the kitchen. I was starting to wear out, thinking that I still have two coats of varnish to put on after this third coat of stain finally dried.

But when I looked at the wood again, it crossed my mind of just how long it had taken for the tree to grow that I was now staining. I was thankful that I didn't have to grow the tree from scratch as well!

In view of how long God has been at work trying to reach the people I'm hoping to reach through this retreat center, I realized that my little time spent on it is just a drop in the bucket. It's an important project, but it's just one more step in the series of steps that God has been taking all along to see His work complete.

Don't be discouraged if it takes longer than fifty-two days to complete your project. Rather, be encouraged by the story of Nehemiah and by what God can do once your project is finished. Also, be encouraged by the Word of God, which says in the book of Galatians:

> *"Let us not become weary in doing good, for at the proper time we will reap a harvest if we do not give up" (Galatians 6:9).*

Before I close for today, I'd like to say a word to those of you who have worked your hardest at something and yet, for various reasons aren't able to see the work finished. In the words of one wife who was trying her best to restore her relationship with her husband, she said:

> "...even if there is no happy ending for our marriage, I will not regret the stand I have taken. I will know that I made the right decision and followed the only course possible for me. I will have done all that I could."

God knows your heart, and He'll honor your heart as you honor His. Don't give up. Don't give in. Keep pressing on with what God has called you to do. Whatever the outcome, you *will* reap a harvest at the proper time, if you do not give up.

Prayer: Father, thank You for Nehemiah's example of what it means to keep pressing on, and thank You for helping him to accomplish that which you put on his heart to do. Father, help me to do the same, for Your sake, and for the sake of those who will be affected by my work both now and in the generations to come. In Jesus' name, Amen.

CONCLUSION: MAINTAINING WHAT YOU'VE BUILT — JUNE 10

Scripture Reading: Nehemiah 7-13

I was working on a project one day and called a friend for help. I told him I was reading the directions and he said, "The first thing to do is to throw away the directions!" He offered to come and help me himself.

I appreciated his offer, but I soon found out he had only done this once before and the project was bigger than he thought. I decided it was time to pull out the directions again!

Perhaps the best advice I can give you for how to maintain what you've worked so hard to build is this: Read the directions! Pull out a copy of God's Word and do what it says. The same directions that helped you to rebuild what's broken in your life can help you maintain what you've built.

This is exactly what Nehemiah did when they finished rebuilding the wall around Jerusalem. Nehemiah assembled all the people in one place and had Ezra the scribe, along with the Levites, read and explain God's Word to the people. Nehemiah says:

> *"They read from the Book of the Law of God, making it clear and giving the meaning so that the people could understand what was being read" (Nehemiah 8:8).*

The rest of the book of Nehemiah describes the effects God's Word had on the people—the same effects it can have on you:

1) It caused them to weep for what they had lost, due to their own sins and the sins of their fathers. Nehemiah says,

> *"For all the people had been weeping as they listened to the words of the Law" (Nehemiah 8:9b).*

God knew how the wall fell into disrepair in the first place, and He knew how to put it together again.

2) It caused them to praise God for what He had done. Nehemiah knew they were heartbroken over what had been lost, but he lifted their spirits by telling them,

> *"Go and enjoy choice food and sweet drinks and send some to those who have nothing prepared. This day is sacred to our Lord. Do not grieve, for the joy of the LORD is your strength" (Nehemiah 8:10).*

God wanted them to know what had gone wrong, but He also wanted them to get up and move on.

3) It caused them to recommit their future to God. The people said,

"In view of all this, we are making a binding agreement, putting it in writing, and our leaders, our Levites and our priests are affixing their seals to it" (Nehemiah 9:38).

After rebuilding the wall, they wanted to rebuild their lives in a way that honored God.

4) It caused them to dedicate the work to God. The party they held to dedicate the wall was so exuberant that Nehemiah said,

"The sound of rejoicing in Jerusalem could be heard far away" (Nehemiah 12:43b).

They marked the occasion with an all-out celebration, dedicating the work of their hands into God's hands.

Nehemiah did it, and so can you. He set out to achieve what God had put on his heart, then he followed through with the hard work to get it done. Even though the project seemed imposing, impractical and nearly impossible, God helped Nehemiah all along the way. God provided Nehemiah with the wisdom, resources, strength and people to pull it off, just like God will do for you when He gives you the green light to do something for Him.

The same God who helped Nehemiah will help you, too. God loves you. He is *for* you. And He wants you to succeed, not only for Your sake, but for His sake, and for the sake of all those who will be touched by the work of your hands in the future.

Just because our study of the book of Nehemiah is finished, it doesn't mean that your study of God's Word has to stop here. Don't throw out the directions just because the project is finished! Keep reading and rereading God's Word every day for the rest of your life!

I pray that as you read it, like Nehemiah, you'll find that the joy of the Lord is *your* strength as well.

Prayer: Father, thank You for giving me Your Word to help me rebuild my life and maintain what I've rebuilt. Lord, help me to keep reading and rereading Your Word, and in so doing, help me to find that Your joy is my strength. In Jesus' name, Amen.

Israel: Lessons from the Holy Land

30 inspiring devotionals based on the land where Jesus walked

WELCOME TO ISRAEL!   JUNE 11

In the lessons ahead, I'd like to take you on a "devotional tour" of the Holy Land. My goal is to help bring the Bible to life in a way that you may have never experienced before. We're going to look at the places where Jesus walked and taught and ministered, as well as the places where many other famous stories from the Bible took place.

I pray that these devotionals will not only give you a deeper appreciation for this land that "the Lord your God cares for" (Deuteronomy 11:12), but that it will help you to grow closer to Christ—and stronger in your faith in Him.

I've included a short video (1-2 minutes, usually) with each lesson to give you a feel for what these places look like, taken while I guided a group through Israel in 2009. We'll start today in Jerusalem with a look at the Garden Tomb. Without further ado, welcome to *Israel: Lessons from the Holy Land!*

INTRODUCTION: TURNING SAD ENDINGS INTO NEW BEGINNINGS

There's a spot in Jerusalem where you can walk inside a tomb from the time of Christ. As you walk in, you can imagine what it must have been like for those who walked into Jesus' tomb on that first Easter morning, when the angels greeted them with these words:

> *"Do not be afraid, for I know that you are looking for Jesus, who was crucified. He is not here; He has risen, just as He said. Come and see the place where He lay"* (Matthew 28:6).

If you'd like to take a minute (well, about a minute-and-ten seconds), you can walk into the tomb with me and see it for yourself. Then read on to see why the story of what happened that first Easter morning is perhaps the most significant event that's ever taken place in the entire history of Israel.

Watch "What Happened at the Garden Tomb?" (or on ericelder.com).

What I love about the Easter story is that just when it looked like all hope was lost, God showed up and showed the disciples that the death of Jesus wasn't the end—it was just the beginning of something even better.

In a matter of days, the disciples went from thinking that their hopes and plans and dreams for the future had been dashed forever, to seeing that God had bigger hopes and plans and dreams for them than they could have ever imagined!

You can almost see their faces light up as God opens their eyes to the truth. Watch what happens as Jesus reveals Himself to two of the disciples as they walk along the road:

> Now that same day two of them were going to a village called Emmaus, about seven miles from Jerusalem. They were talking with each other about everything that had happened. As they talked and discussed these things with each other, Jesus Himself came up and walked along with them; but they were kept from recognizing Him.
> He asked them, "What are you discussing together as you walk along?"
> They stood still, their faces downcast. One of them, named Cleopas, asked Him, "Are you only a visitor to Jerusalem and do not know the things that have happened there in these days?"
> "What things?" He asked.
> "About Jesus of Nazareth," they replied. "He was a prophet, powerful in word and deed before God and all the people. The chief priests and our rulers handed Him over to be sentenced to death, and they crucified Him; but we had hoped that He was the one who was going to redeem Israel. And what is more, it is the third day since all this took place. In addition, some of our women amazed us. They went to the tomb early this morning but didn't find His body. They came and told us that they had seen a vision of angels, who said He was alive. Then some of our companions went to the tomb and found it just as the women had said, but Him they did not see" (Luke 24:13-24).

Take a look at the disciples' faces when Jesus first walks up and starts talking to them. The Bible says, "They stood still, their faces downcast." I don't know how exactly Jesus was able to hide His true identity from them, but I do know that it's hard to see when our faces are downcast. But look at what happens as the story continues.

> He said to them, "How foolish you are, and how slow of heart to believe all that the prophets have spoken! Did not the Christ have to suffer these things and then enter his glory?" And beginning with Moses and all the Prophets, He explained to them what was said in all the Scriptures concerning Himself.
> As they approached the village to which they were going, Jesus acted as if He were going farther. But they urged Him strongly, "Stay with us, for it is nearly evening; the day is almost over." So He went in to stay with them.
> When He was at the table with them, He took bread, gave thanks, broke it and began to give it to them. Then their eyes were opened, and they recognized Him, and He disappeared from their sight. They asked each other, "Were not our hearts burning within us while He talked with us on the road and opened the Scriptures to us?"
> They got up and returned at once to Jerusalem. There they found the Eleven and those with them, assembled together and saying, "It is true! The Lord has risen and has appeared to Simon." Then the two told what had happened on the way, and how Jesus was recognized by them when He broke the bread (Luke 24:25 -35).

The disciples went from downcast to delighted, and as they did, their hearts began to burn within them. They were eager to learn everything they possibly could from this Man who was walking with them, so much so that they "urged Him strongly" to stay with them. Then, when Jesus took the bread, gave thanks, broke it and began to give it to them, their eyes were opened to the Truth. Even though Jesus disappeared in that moment, their excitement about what they felt didn't disappear. They got up at once and ran to tell the others the good news: This wasn't the end at all, but just the beginning of something new!

There are times when you may feel like God, or people, or life itself has pulled the rug out from under you. It may seem like all your hopes and plans and dreams are crashing down around you. You might wonder how you'll ever be able to get back up again. But I want to encourage you to do what the disciples did as they walked along the road. They stopped looking down and they started looking up. They looked up to the One who held their life in His hands—the same One who holds your life in His hands—the One who gives each one of us "life and breath and everything else" (Acts 17:25b).

What may look like an ending to something in your life may in fact be just the beginning of something entirely new, something even bigger and better and more remarkable than you ever could have imagined. And if you think that's just wishful thinking, just remember the Easter story, and remember the God who specializes in turning sad endings into new beginnings!

Let's pray...

Father, thank You for the reminder that You can take the sad endings in our lives and turn them into new beginnings. Open my eyes that I may see just what you have in store for me. In Jesus' name, Amen.

LESSON 1: WHERE DID ISRAEL GET ITS NAME?   JUNE 12

On the pages ahead, I'd like to take you on a "devotional tour" of the Holy Land. In each lesson, I'll be asking (and answering) a question about Israel and some of the major events that have taken place there. My goal is to give you both a history lesson and a faith lesson: a history lesson about this land that is so precious to God, and a faith lesson that you can apply to your own life today.

I'd like to start with a foundational question: "Where did Israel get its name?"

To check your answer, keep reading on, or take a look at the short video clip at the link below that I recorded on the coast of the Mediterranean Sea, at the western edge of Israel.

Watch "Where Did Israel Get Its Name?" (or on ericelder.com).

So where did Israel get its name? Israel was named after Abraham's grandson, Jacob, whom God later renamed "Israel."

Jacob got this new name after an all-night wrestling match with an opponent whom Jacob comes to believe is God Himself. At the end of the struggle, Jacob's opponent declares, "Your name will no longer be Jacob, but Israel, because you have struggled with God and with men and have overcome" (Genesis 32:28). "Israel" means struggles, or strives, with God.

So the land of Israel was named after the man who lived there. His twelve sons and their families became the twelve "tribes" of Israel and spread out to live throughout the land. The Bible says that the borders of Israel at that time extended from the desert in the south to Lebanon in the north, and from the Euphrates River on the east to the western sea, or Mediterranean, on the west (see Deuteronomy 11:24 and Joshua 3:1-4).

The land of Israel was actually promised to Jacob's grandfather, Abraham, years earlier, which is why the land of Israel is often referred to as the "promised land."

What I love about reading these passages in the Bible is that they are continual reminders to me that God keeps His promises, whether they are to all of humanity, as in the case of God's promise to Noah that God would never again destroy the earth with a flood, or to a particular nation, as in this case of God's promise to the Israelites that He would bring them into this land, and then bring them back again if they were ever taken away. When God makes a promise, He keeps it!

Here's the original promise that God made to Abraham way back in the twelfth chapter of the Bible, about 4,000 years ago. God said to Abraham:

> "Leave your country, your people and your father's household and go to the land I will show you. I will make you into a great nation and I will bless you; I will make your name great, and you will be a blessing. I will bless those who bless you, and whoever curses you I will curse; and all peoples on earth will be blessed through you" (Genesis 12:1-3).

So Abraham obeyed and went. And when Abraham got there, God gave him this promise:

> "Lift up your eyes from where you are and look north and south, east and west. All the land that you see I will give to you and your offspring forever. I will make your offspring like the dust of the earth, so that if anyone could count the dust, then your offspring could be counted. Go, walk through the length and breadth of the land, for I am giving it to you" (Genesis 13:14-17).

God also forewarned Abraham that his descendants one day would be strangers in another country and enslaved for four hundred years, but afterward they would return to the promised land. This took place when a famine came upon Israel, and Israel's sons moved to Egypt to get food. As the sons' families grew in number, they were enslaved by the Egyptians for fear that they would become too powerful.

Four hundred years later, God sent Moses to set the Israelites free and return them to their homeland. God reminded the Israelites of His promise, saying to them as they approached the promised land:

> "Every place where you set your foot will be yours: Your territory will extend from the desert to Lebanon, and from the Euphrates River to the western sea" (Deuteronomy 11:24, and again in Joshua 1:3-4).

Almost a thousand years later, the Israelites were taken captive again, this time to Babylon. But again, God promised that one day they would return to their land. God told the prophet Jeremiah to buy a field in Israel, even though they were about to be taken away, to let the people know that one day they would return again and that,

> "Houses, fields and vineyards will again be bought in this land." (Jeremiah 32:15).

They did return about seventy years later. Another five hundred or so years later, Jesus was born in Israel. Except for a few years when Jesus was young, when his parents took Him to Egypt to protect Him from King Herod, Jesus spent His entire life and ministry in the land of Israel.

And when Jesus comes back again, He'll return to the land of His birth, to Israel.

God keeps His promises!

From Genesis to Revelation, God talks about His promises regarding both the land and the people of Israel. It is a land that is truly precious to God. The Bible says,

> "It is a land the LORD your God cares for; the eyes of the LORD your God are continually on it from the beginning of the year to its end" (Deuteronomy 11:12).

And it's a land that reminds us that God keeps His promises, whether they're made to all of humanity, or to particular nations, or to individual people like you and like me.

God loves you, He cares about your life, and He wants to see you accomplish all that He has prepared in advance for you to do. If God has made you a promise, hold onto it! God keeps His promises.

Let's pray:

Father, thank You for the promises that You have made throughout history, and the promises that You have made to us in our lifetime. Lord, help us to remember Your promises, and to hold onto them tightly, knowing that You will always keep them. In Jesus' name, Amen.

LESSON 2: WHAT HAPPENED IN CAESAREA? JUNE 13

Today we're headed up the coast of the Mediterranean Sea to the city of Caesarea. Why Caesarea? Because something remarkable happened there about 2,000 years ago. To see what happened, take a look at the short video clip below, then read on to see how this story can apply to your life today.

"Watch "What Happened in Caesarea?" (or on ericelder.com).

So what happened in Caesarea? This is where Peter preached the good news about Jesus to Cornelius. And what makes it so remarkable? Because this is where God made it crystal clear that Jesus didn't come just as a Savior for the Jews, but for *anyone* who would believe in Him.

The other thing that's remarkable about this story is the way God spoke to Peter and Cornelius. God spoke in a way that was very specific, helping each of them know exactly what God wanted them to do next in their lives. Wouldn't all of us love to have God do that for us! The truth is, He can, and often does, and if we read the story carefully, we can see some clues as to why God spoke to these two so clearly.

Here's how God spoke to Cornelius:

> *At Caesarea there was a man named Cornelius, a centurion in what was known as the Italian Regiment. He and all his family were devout and God-fearing; he gave generously to those in need and prayed to God regularly. One day at about three in the afternoon he had a vision. He distinctly saw an angel of God, who came to him and said, "Cornelius!"*

> Cornelius stared at him in fear. "What is it, Lord?" he asked.

> *The angel answered, "Your prayers and gifts to the poor have come up as a memorial offering before God. Now send men to Joppa to bring back a man named Simon who is called Peter. He is staying with Simon the tanner, whose house is by the sea"* (Acts 10:1-6).

And here's how God spoke to Peter:

> *About noon the following day as they were on their journey and approaching the city, Peter went up on the roof to pray. He became hungry and wanted something to eat, and while the meal was being prepared, he fell into a trance. He saw heaven opened and something like a large sheet being let down to earth by its four corners. It contained all kinds of four-footed animals, as well as reptiles of the earth and birds of the air. Then a voice told him, "Get up, Peter. Kill and eat."*
> *"Surely not, Lord!" Peter replied. "I have never eaten anything impure or unclean."*
> *The voice spoke to him a second time, "Do not call anything impure that God has made clean."*
> *This happened three times, and immediately the sheet was taken back to heaven. While Peter was wondering about the meaning of the vision, the men sent by Cornelius found out where Simon's house was and stopped at the gate. They called out, asking if Simon who was known as Peter was staying there.*
> *While Peter was still thinking about the vision, the Spirit said to him, "Simon, three men are looking for you. So get up and go downstairs. Do not hesitate to go with them, for I have sent them" (Acts 10:9-20).*

Did you catch why God spoke the way He did to Cornelius? And why God might have spoken to Peter the way He did?

In Cornelius' case, the Bible says, "He [Cornelius] and all his family were devout and God-fearing; he gave generously to those in need and prayed to God regularly." The angel then says very specifically: "Your prayers and gifts to the poor have come up as a memorial offering before God." Then the angel proceeds to share with him what to do next.

And as for Peter's case, his story begins with the words, "Peter went up on the roof to pray." It was during that time of prayer that God spoke to Peter and revealed to him what he needed to do next, too.

Prayer in its most basic form is having a conversation with God. Sometimes it may feel like it's only a one-way conversation, but I've found that the more I pray, and the more that I wait for and listen for and expect Him to answer, the more I actually hear God speak to me in return! It's not rocket-science, but it does take is faith. And in Cornelius' example, he didn't rely on his faith alone, but he was continually demonstrating his faith in God by his good deeds. He was putting his money where his mouth was, so to speak. Or, as Jesus said it: "For where your treasure is, there your heart will be also" (Matthew 6:22).

The beauty of this story is that God was not only moved by the prayers and gifts of these men, but God answered their prayers in a way that went beyond either of their expectations. For Cornelius, it opened up a whole new understanding of who God was and what He could do next to come into a more full and right relationship with Him. And for Peter, this opened a whole new door of ministry that he would have never realized even needed to be opened without his prayers and God's response, that God wanted him to proclaim the good news about Jesus even to the Gentiles, meaning anyone who was not Jewish.

These are great lessons for any of us who want to experience more of God in our lives, and for anyone who wants to serve Him more fully.

If you've already put your faith in Christ, today's a good day to thank God for what happened in Caesarea! And if you've never put your faith in Christ, today's a good day to do that, too! Let God's Spirit fall upon you as it fell upon all who heard Peter's message that day when he said:

> *"All the prophets testify about Him [Jesus] that everyone who believes in Him receives forgiveness of sins through His name" (Acts 10:34-36,43).*

Let's pray:

Father, thank You for speaking to people so specifically about events that were about to change their lives so dramatically. We pray that You would speak to us again today, so that we may hear from You and do all that is on Your heart for us to do. In Jesus' name, Amen.

LESSON 3: WHAT HAPPENED ON MOUNT CARMEL?   JUNE 14

As we continue our devotional tour of the Holy Land, we're heading further north along the Mediterranean coast, this time to the top of Mount Carmel. It's a beautiful spot where a powerful story took place about 3,000 years ago.

To hear a summary of the story in under two minutes, including how it applies to your life today, click the link to the video below. Then continue reading the rest of the message below that to learn how God can answer your prayers in extraordinary ways, even though you may feel like just an "ordinary person."

Watch "What Happened on Mount Carmel?" (or on ericelder.com).

So what happened on Mount Carmel? That's where Elijah challenged the prophets of Baal and Asherah to a dramatic showdown. Many of the Israelites had strayed from God, worshiping Baal and Asherah instead. The situation had gotten so bad that God told Elijah to go to the Israelite king, Ahab, and tell him:

> *"…there will be neither dew nor rain in the next few years except at my word" (1 Kings 17:1b).*

So Elijah told this to Ahab and the rain stopped. All of Israel began to suffer. But neither Ahab nor the people turned back to God. After three and a half years, God told Elijah to go back to Ahab and tell him that the rain was about to come again.

Elijah went to Ahab and told him to meet him on Mount Carmel, where the dramatic showdown took place, and where God would answer Elijah's prayers in a way that convinced the Israelites to turn their hearts back to God. It was after this that Elijah climbed to the top of Mount Carmel, bent down to the ground to pray, and by the end of the day, the rain poured down.

It's one of the coolest stories in the Old Testament, and if you haven't read it yet, or haven't read it in a while, I'd like to encourage you to read the whole thing sometime this week. You'll find it in the book of 1 Kings, chapters 17-19.

While there are tons of helpful and encouraging lessons from these chapters—ranging from how God can provide for your needs even during a famine to how God can give you the courage you need to do some very difficult things—the lesson I'd like to focus on today deals with the question of why God sometimes answers your prayers and other times doesn't—or at least not in the way you expected.

Sometimes God can knock your socks off with His answers to your prayers, like He did with Elijah's prayers on Mount Carmel. The book of James even holds up Elijah's story as an example of just how powerful prayer can be. James says:

"The prayer of a righteous man is powerful and effective. Elijah was a man just like us. He prayed earnestly that it would not rain, and it did not rain on the land for three and a half years. Again he prayed, and the heavens gave rain, and the earth produced its crops" (James 5:16b-18).

So Elijah was human, just like us, and God heard and answered his prayers in a powerful way. Yet did you know that not long after this event, Elijah prayed another prayer—one that he seems to have prayed as earnestly as the one before—yet God didn't do what Elijah asked?

This other prayer took place after the showdown at Mount Carmel, when Elijah had to run for his life because Ahab's wife had vowed to hunt Elijah down until he was dead. So Elijah ran as far as he could until he was thoroughly exhausted. The Bible says,

"He came to a broom tree, sat down under it and prayed that he might die. 'I have had enough, Lord. Take my life; I am no better than my ancestors'" (1 Kings 19:4b).

Then he lay down under the tree and fell asleep.

But God didn't answer this prayer, at least in the way that Elijah wanted Him to answer it. God didn't take his life. God wanted Elijah to live, for God still had more for Elijah to do with his life.

So God sent Elijah an angel. The angel woke him up and gave him something warm to eat. After eating two of these angel-cooked meals, Elijah gained enough strength to travel another forty days and forty nights until he reached Horeb, the mountain of God. And it was there on Mount Horeb that God Himself appeared to Elijah in a very personal way,

"…in a gentle whisper" (1 Kings 19:12b).

God didn't give Elijah what he wanted, but He gave him something much better: an angel of encouragement, strength for the journey, and a one-on-one visit with Elijah himself.

I want to encourage you today that God can answer your prayers as dramatically and powerfully as He answered Elijah's prayers for rain. But God can also answer your prayers like He answered Elijah's second prayer, not necessarily giving you what you want or expect, but giving you something truly better.

God loves you. He cares about your life. And He has things that He truly wants to do in and through your life. Keep praying earnestly that God's will would be done here on earth, through you, just as God's will was done through Elijah's prayers at Mount Carmel.

Let's pray:

Father, thank You for Elijah's example of what it means to pray earnestly for Your will to be done. Give us Your wisdom and insight into the situations in our lives today so that we can pray for Your will to be done in them as well. We love You and thank You for hearing our prayers. In Jesus' name, Amen.

LESSON 4: WHAT'S GOING TO HAPPEN AT MEGIDDO? JUNE 15

You may have never heard of Megiddo before, but it's more than likely you've heard about what is going to happen there one day. And with a little help from the Hebrew language, you may realize that you have heard of Megiddo before in just a slightly different form. Take a look at the short video below to see this historical place with an important future. Then keep reading below to see how it can affect your life today.

Watch "What's Going to Happen at Megiddo?" (or on ericelder.com).

So what's going to happen at Megiddo? That's where Christ will return for the final battle of all the nations of the world.

The book of Revelation prophecies about this coming battle, saying that the spirits of demons will go out to the kings of the whole world:

> "...to gather them for the battle on the great day of God Almighty. ... Then they gathered the kings together to the place that in Hebrew is called Armageddon" (Revelation 16:14b, 16).

Armageddon comes to us from the Hebrew words "Har" meaning hill, and Megiddo, referring to the city found there. So Har Megiddo means the hill of Megiddo, which translates for us into "Armageddon."

It's an unusual sight to look out and see the cars and trucks and buses going back and forth about their business at the base of the hill, knowing that one day all the nations of the world will gather here for that final epic battle, the one which has been depicted in so many apocalyptic books and movies.

But perhaps more sobering to me is the fact that since God has fulfilled so many prophecies found in the Bible already, it just follows reason that He will one day fulfill the rest as well, including the prophecies about this cataclysmic battle.

And from history, we know that this location has served as a battlefield for many battles before. King Josiah died here about 600 years before Christ in a battle with Pharaoh Neco of Egypt (2 Kings 23:29) and Sir Edmund Allenby of Britain launched a massive attack here during the first World War, to name a few.

The role of Megiddo as a military battlefield was summed up by Napoleon, one of the foremost military leaders of all time when he saw Megiddo in the early 1800's. He is quoted as saying:

> "All the armies of the world could maneuver their forces on this vast plain ... There is no place in the whole world more suited for war than this ... It is the most natural battleground on the whole earth." (The Battles of Armageddon, pg. 142).

And Megiddo is situated in a primary trade route at the north of Israel, a location from which you can see the hills of neighboring countries who are even now poised and ready to do battle here. The inspiring thing about standing on the hill of Megiddo is that it makes me want to do right before God and men.

While God is certainly more forgiving and patient than I or anyone else I know has ever been or would ever be, there is still a limit to His patience. At some point, He must deal with sin, or He wouldn't be a very good judge at all.

As much as I'd rather not think about it, there comes a time when justice must be done, and we will all have to face judgment for what we've done. This day is often referred to in the Bible as the "Day of the Lord." It's a day that is referred to over twenty-five times in the Bible, including both the Old and New Testaments.

Several weeks before writing this message I had a dream in which I got an invitation in the mail. It was an invitation to an "end of the world party" to be held on June 6-7, just a few weeks from then. I don't put much stock in the dream as anything prophetic, as even Jesus Himself said that no one knows the day or hour when these things will happen, but only the Father (Matthew 24:36). But the dream did help me to think a little more clearly that day when I woke up!

I wondered: What would I do differently if I knew that the world was really going to end in just a few weeks? How would I spend my time? Who do I still need to talk to and what would I say? How can I help more people come into a relationship with Christ so that when the final battle does come they're on the winning side?

And today I wonder: How would it affect your life if you knew that the end were just a few weeks away? It reminds me of a quote from Stephen Levine:

"If you were going to die soon and had only one phone call you could make, who would you call and what would you say? And why are you waiting?"

God wants more than anything else to have a relationship with each one of us, including you and those around you. He knows how sin affects our lives in ways that we could never even understand. And He wants us to be freed from those sins.

That's why He sent Jesus to earth, to die for our sins, so that all who put their faith in Him will be forgiven of their sins and spend eternity with Him in heaven.

If you've never put your faith in Christ, I encourage you to do it today. Don't wait any longer, for no one knows the day or hour when He will return. And if you've already put your faith in Christ, share that faith with someone today.

Give them a call. Write them a letter. Send them a text, an email, or a link to this video and devotional. Remind them that:

"The Lord is not slow in keeping His promise, as some understand slowness. He is patient with you, not wanting anyone to perish, but everyone to come to repentance." (2 Peter 3:9).

Let's pray:

Father, thank You for fulfilling so many of the prophecies of the Bible already and we trust that You will fulfill the rest in due time. Lord, help us to live our lives in such a way that they become shining testimonies to You and help us to encourage those around us to put their faith in Christ so they can be on the winning side in the final battle as well. In Jesus' name, Amen.

LESSON 5: WHAT HAPPENED IN NAZARETH? JUNE 16

Our next stop on this devotional tour of the Holy Land is a city that wasn't known as one of the hot spots of Israel. In fact, the Bible quotes Nathanael as saying,

"Nazareth? Can anything good come from there?" (John 1:46).

But something good did come from there. To hear what happened there, take a look at this short video that I shot while at the Nazareth Village in Israel, a re-creation of what the city might have looked like back in Jesus' day. Then read on below to find out how God can work in your life through even the most difficult situations to accomplish His plans.

Watch "What Happened in Nazareth?" (or on ericelder.com).

So what happened in Nazareth? This is where Jesus grew up. It was also the hometown of Mary and Joseph and the place where the angel Gabriel came to Mary and said:

> "Do not be afraid, Mary, you have found favor with God. You will be with child and give birth to a son, and you are to give Him the name Jesus" (Luke 1:30-31).

But Jesus wasn't born in Nazareth. In fact, His route to ending up here seemed rather circuitous.

Because of the Roman census, Mary and Joseph had to return to Bethlehem at the time of Jesus' birth. Then after Jesus' birth, Herod found out that a new "King of the Jews" may have been born in Bethlehem and began a killing spree of all the newborn boys there, so Mary and Joseph fled to Egypt. After Herod died, Mary and Joseph returned again to Israel and went back to their hometown of Nazareth.

It may have seemed like Jesus and his parents were being yanked around by governments and kings, making their lives difficult at critical times. I try to imagine Mary being nine months pregnant, having to ride on a donkey to Bethlehem, then finding no place to stay and give birth to her child. I try to imagine their having to flee that city because a crazed king wanted to kill their young Son. I try to imagine their having to move to a foreign country when Jesus was small, with all the changes such a move from family and friends must have entailed.

Yet I'm encouraged to think that each stop along the way was not random. Each move was part of God's divine plan for both Jesus and His parents. Hundreds of years earlier each stop along the way had already been foretold.

Getting to Bethlehem was the first stop in fulfilling the prophecies concerning the Messiah. When the chief priests and teachers of the law were asked where the Messiah was to be born, they replied:

> "In Bethlehem in Judea, for this is what the prophet has written: 'But you, Bethlehem, in the land of Judah, are by no means least among the rulers of Judah; for out of you will come a ruler who will be the shepherd of my people Israel' " (Matthew 2:5-6).

The trip to Egypt fulfilled the next stop. As Matthew said:

> "And so was fulfilled what the Lord had said through the prophet: 'Out of Egypt I called my son'" (Matthew 2:15).

And the return to Nazareth fulfilled the third stop. As Matthew said about His return:

> "So was fulfilled what was said through the prophets: 'He will be called a Nazarene'" (Matthew 2:23).

So rather than a seemingly random chain of events moving Jesus from place to place, God had a plan and a way to use all of those events to bring about His will.

How does all this relate to you and me? I take encouragement from the fact that even when it looks like our lives are being pushed and pulled in various directions by people, governments, or difficult situations, that it may actually be God doing the pushing and pulling to fulfill His plans for our lives! And if it's not God doing the actual pushing and pulling, at least it's no surprise to Him what we're going through. If God was able to foretell and use all of the events and situations that would surround the birth and life of His Son, then He is able to foretell and use all of the events and situations that we'll face in our lives as well.

Rather than being upset at others who sometimes seem to be in control of our lives—whether it's a boss or a job, a government official or a family member, a friend or an enemy—we can trust that God is the one who controls them all. And even if He doesn't control them directly, for He has given each of us free will as well, God does know the hearts of men and women and He can work all things together for good.

Although Nazareth wasn't a hot spot in the Holy Land in Jesus' day, God wasn't bothered by its reputation. It was here where God chose to raise His Son and it was here where the Bible says,

> "Jesus grew in wisdom and stature, and in favor with God and men" (Luke 2:52).

Your life is not random and the places where you live and work and eat and sleep are not arbitrary, regardless of the reputation they may or may not have. God has a plan for you, for your life, and for the situations that you're facing even right now. He wants you to trust Him fully with that plan and follow Him wherever He leads—whether that's staying where He wants you to stay or going where He wants you to go.

Trust Him with every aspect of your life and let Him take control of the direction it takes. It's good to make plans for our lives, but it's also good to let God take control of those plans when He has a better one. As it says in the book of Proverbs:

> "In his heart a man plans his course, but the LORD determines his steps" (Proverbs 16:9).

Let's pray:

Father, thank You for taking the random events of our lives and giving them purpose and meaning in ways that go beyond what we could think or imagine. Lord, we commit to trusting You again today, giving You full control over the course of our lives. In Jesus' name, Amen.

LESSON 6: WHAT HAPPENED ON THE SEA OF GALILEE?   JUNE 17

Today, we're visiting the Sea of Galilee. If you'd like to see—and hear—what the water looks like at the Sea of Galilee today, take a look at the short video below. It's a beautiful spot in the land of Israel and the site of some of Jesus' most memorable miracles. Then read on to see how putting your faith in Christ can help you through some of the toughest situations in your life.

Watch "What Happened on the Sea of Galilee?" (or on ericelder.com).

So what happened on the Sea of Galilee? This is where Jesus spent much of His time after He left His boyhood home of Nazareth. In the coming weeks, I'll be talking about several of the miracles that took place here that touched people's hearts and lives.

But today I'd like to focus on two that took place out on the sea itself: when Jesus walked on water and when He calmed the storm that threatened the lives of His disciples.

Jesus is an expert at walking through storms. The miracle that He did on the Sea of Galilee wasn't the first time He displayed His giftedness for this. Just before coming to the Sea of Galilee, Jesus walked unscathed through another storm that threatened to take His own life.

Maybe you remember that when Jesus lived in Nazareth, He went to the synagogue one day and read from the scroll of Isaiah. At first, all the people spoke well of Him, being amazed at "the gracious words that came from His lips." But after quoting from the words of Isaiah—referring to the Messiah that was to come—Jesus added:

"Today this scripture is fulfilled in your hearing" (Luke 4:21b).

Imagine growing up in the same city with Jesus—the guy down the block who did carpentry with His dad—then He gets up and says that He's the Messiah, the One about whom the prophet Isaiah had written about some 700 years earlier. You'd think that Jesus was either a lunatic or a liar. He couldn't possibly be telling the truth, could He?

So the crowd turned on Him. The Bible says:

"All the people in the synagogue were furious when they heard this. They got up, drove Him out of the town, and took Him to the brow of the hill on which the town was built, in order to throw Him down the cliff. But He walked right through the crowd and went on His way" (Luke 4:28-30).

The crowd went from calm to stormy in a matter of seconds. They went from praising Jesus to taking Him to the edge of a cliff to throw Him off within a matter of minutes. But Jesus wasn't fazed by their words of praise nor their acts of violence. He simply said what He had to say, then "walked right through the crowd and went on His way."

So when the storm came up on His disciples on the Sea of Galilee some time later, Jesus wasn't fazed by it either. He and His disciples had just finished a long day of ministering to thousands, having heard earlier in the day that John the Baptist had just been beheaded. Jesus headed off to a mountainside to pray, telling His disciples to get into the boat and head to the other side.

The story picks up here:

When evening came, He was there alone, but the boat was already a considerable distance from land, buffeted by the waves because the wind was against it.
During the fourth watch of the night Jesus went out to them, walking on the lake.
When the disciples saw Him walking on the lake, they were terrified. "It's a ghost," they said, and cried out in fear.
But Jesus immediately said to them: "Take courage! It is I. Don't be afraid."

That's when Jesus famously called Peter to come out to Him and walk on the water and which Peter did until he saw the wind and the waves and started to sink again. So Jesus reached out His hand and took hold of Peter's and pulled him back up.

The story finishes by saying:

And when they climbed into the boat, the wind died down. Then those who were in the boat worshiped Him, saying, "Truly You are the Son of God" (Matthew 14:23b-33).

There are two things that I'd like to mention about this storm. The first is that Jesus is the one who sent them into it. And the second is that Jesus is the one who brought them out of it.

Just like in Nazareth, Jesus didn't worry about the wind and the waves. In the case of the angry crowd, Jesus had nothing to fear. It was the crowd who was fearful by what Jesus was saying and acted wrongfully because of it. Jesus did what was right and when He was done, He simply walked through the crowd and went on His way.

In the same way, when Jesus needed to get to the other side of the lake, He wasn't fazed by the fact that strong waves lay ahead. He sent His disciples into the waves and He went into them Himself afterward. Jesus wasn't afraid of the storm. Jesus just kept doing what He needed to do, and His disciples did what He told them to.

There are times when I've felt like I was being thrown into a storm—and it seemed like it was Jesus who was throwing me into it! I've learned that the best thing to do in those times is to hold onto Jesus as tight as I can. I know that Jesus knows best how to walk through them, whether I'm facing an angry crowd or some wind and some waves.

You may find yourself in the middle of a storm right now, too. The circumstances of your life may be buffeting against you. You may be facing things that are threatening your health, your family, your relationships, your job, your career, your finances or your friends. The threats may be very real, and the prospects ahead may look very grim.

I want to encourage you to hold onto Jesus as tight as you can. Keep walking through the wind and the waves. Keep walking towards Jesus, the Messiah, the Author and Sustainer of your life. And even if you start to sink, know that Jesus is right beside you to take hold of your hands and pull you in close. Hold on tight and never let Him go. He's the One who knows best how to walk through a storm. Let Him speak to you the words He spoke to His disciples that night on the Sea of Galilee:

"Take courage, it is I! Don't be afraid."

Let's pray:

Father, thank You for sending Jesus to help us through the storms we face. Thank You for reminding us that it's sometimes even Jesus who sends us into the storms in the first place. Lord, help us to have the faith to trust in Him, no matter what, and to trust that whether it's Him who sent us into the storm or not, that He's the One who can bring us through it. In Jesus' name, Amen.

LESSON 7: WHAT HAPPENED IN CAPERNAUM?   JUNE 18

I was surprised when I visited the city of Capernaum to learn about all the things that Jesus did there. It shouldn't have been surprising, however, for Capernaum served as the home base for most of Jesus' ministry, having moved there when He left His boyhood home of Nazareth. To hear about some of the things that Jesus did in Capernaum, take a look at the forty-second video below. Then read on to see how Jesus is still working today in the same ways that He did in Capernaum.

Watch "What Happened in Capernaum?" (or on ericelder.com).

So what happened in Capernaum? This is where Jesus healed many people. Here's a sampling of the healings that took place there:

- He healed the centurion's servant
- He healed the paralytic and forgave him of his sins
- He healed the woman who had been bleeding for twelve years
- He healed Jairus' daughter, raising her from the dead
- and He healed two blind men.

The common thread running through each of these stories is that the people were healed by faith in Christ.

In the story of the centurion's servant, Jesus commends his faith, saying:

"I tell you the truth, I have not found anyone in Israel with such great faith…" Then Jesus said to the centurion, *"Go! It will be done just as you believed it would."* And his servant was healed at that very hour (Matthew 8:10b,13).

In the story of the paralytic, Jesus took note of his friends' faith:
When Jesus saw their faith, He said to the paralytic,

"Take heart, son; your sins are forgiven." … Then He said to the paralytic, *"Get up, take your mat and go home."* And the man got up and went home. (Matthew 9:2b,6b-7).

In the story of the woman who had been bleeding for twelve years, Jesus said:

"Take heart, daughter, your faith has healed you." And the woman was healed from that moment (Matthew 9:22b).

In the story of Jairus' daughter, Jesus said:

"Don't be afraid; just believe." … He took her by the hand and said to her, 'Talitha koum!' (which means, 'Little girl, I say to you, get up!'). Immediately the girl stood up and walked around… (Mark 5:36b, 41-42a).

And in the story of the two blind men, before Jesus healed them, He asked them a question:

"Do you believe that I am able to do this?"
"Yes, Lord," they replied.
Then He touched their eyes and said, *"According to your faith will it be done to you"*; and their sight was restored (Matthew 9:28b-30a).

It was this last story that surprised me the most when I read that it took place in Capernaum, for it was this story that inspired me to put my faith in Christ 23 years ago. I had no idea that it took place there in Capernaum until I was preparing for this trip to Israel. It was a detail I had overlooked at the time.

When I had read the story 23 years ago, I was walking along a road in Houston, Texas. I was about 7,000 miles away from Capernaum and it was about 2,000 years later. I was asking

God for a healing in my own life. I felt like Jesus was asking me the same question: "Eric, do you believe I am able to do this, too?"

I thought about everything Jesus had ever done—how He healed the sick, walked on water and raised the dead. I thought if anyone could do it, Jesus could. So I put my hand up in the air, and for the first time in my life, I truly put my faith in Christ. Like the blind men, I said, "Yes, Lord." And like the blind men, I was healed in that moment.

By the next day I had put my faith in Christ for everything in my life. I asked Him to forgive me of my sins and trusted Him to take me to live with Him forever when I died. (If you'd like to read more of this story, you can read it on my website at www.theranch.org.)

The course of my life changed that day, and it was all based on a story that took place in Capernaum. To stand there when we visited Israel and think about what happened then and how it had affected me now was astounding. What a blessing that these stories have been recorded for us and can touch our lives in such life-changing ways.

Faith in Christ is a powerful thing. But you don't have to take my word for it—you can take His word for it! According to His word, it was by faith that the centurion's servant was healed; by faith, the paralytic was forgiven of his sins and healed of his paralysis; by faith, the woman who had been bleeding for twelve years was healed; by faith, Jairus' daughter was raised from the dead; and by faith, the sight of the blind men had restored.

If you need God to do something in your life that you can't seem to do on your own, I'd like to encourage you to put your faith in Christ and keep putting your faith in Him for everything in Your life. You'll be glad you did.

Let's pray:

Father, thank You for the inspiring stories of faith that took place in Capernaum. I pray that You would reach out to us in the same way today, doing the impossible for those who are willing to put their faith in You. In Jesus' name, Amen.

LESSON 8: WHAT HAPPENED ON THE MOUNT OF BEATITUDES?   JUNE 19

The Mount of Beatitudes is one of the many hills that rise up around the Sea of Galilee. It was here that Jesus preached His famous "Sermon on the Mount," blessing thousands of people who had gathered to hear Him speak. But why is it called the Mount of "Beatitudes," and what else did Jesus do on this hill for those who gathered here? Take a look at the short video below to hear more and to get a view of the mountain itself. Then read on to see how Jesus can bless you today—and how you can be a blessing to Him!

Watch "What Happened on the Mount of Beatitudes?" (or on ericelder.com).

So what happened on the Mount of Beatitudes? "Beatitude" means "blessing," and this is where Jesus spoke about the many blessings that God offers to those who believe in Him, such as:

> *"Blessed are the poor in spirit, for theirs is the kingdom of heaven. Blessed are those who mourn, for they will be comforted. Blessed are the meek, for they will inherit the earth. Blessed are those who hunger and thirst for righteousness, for they will be filled..." (Matthew 5:3-6).*

This is also where Jesus demonstrated His blessings to the crowd by multiplying five loaves of bread and two fish into a feast that fed five thousand. The Bible says:

> "Then Jesus directed them to have all the people sit down in groups on the green grass. So they sat down in groups of hundreds and fifties. Taking the five loaves and the two fish and looking up to heaven, He gave thanks and broke the loaves. Then He gave them to His disciples to set before the people. He also divided the two fish among them all. They all ate and were satisfied, and the disciples picked up twelve basketfuls of broken pieces of bread and fish. The number of the men who had eaten was five thousand" (Mark 6:39-44).

It's a remarkable story, and Jesus still does similar things today. I've written about one such story that happened to me recently on our trip to Israel—and even culminated for me at the very spot where Jesus multiplied the loaves and fishes. (I've included this story at the end of this book, in the concluding chapter called "Making A Chance.")

But as practical as Jesus' teachings are, and as remarkable as His ability to multiply loaves and fish is, Jesus doesn't stop there. He goes a step farther and offers us more: an abundant life in Him. But sometimes we're the ones who shortchange what Jesus has to offer us.

I heard a story about a boy who went to his uncle's farm every summer for a few days. When the boy would arrive, his uncle would greet him with pockets full of nickels jingling at his sides. After a few minutes of talking with each other, the uncle reached into his pocket and handed his nephew a nickel.

Throughout the next few days, the uncle did the same thing over and over, spending a few minutes talking with the boy, then handing him a nickel; doing a chore or two, then handing the boy a nickel; taking a walk down the road together then handing the boy a nickel. By the end of those few days, the uncle's pockets were empty, and the boy's pockets were full.

The next summer, the same thing happened. The uncle began with his pockets jangling with nickels and at the end of their time together, the boy's pockets were full of nickels.

After a few summers, the boy got an idea. The next time he visited his uncle at the farm, he was again greeted by his uncle with his pockets full of nickels. The boy said: "Every summer by the end of my time with you, you always give me all the nickels in your pocket. So I've got an idea. Why don't you just give me all the nickels right now, then I can go do what I want, and you can go do what you want without me around to bother you!"

Although the boy's idea had merit at one level, it missed the point entirely at another. The reason the uncle gave the boy the nickels in the first place was because he loved spending as much time with the boy as he could. The uncle wanted to be with his nephew, and their time together always turned out to be precious to them both.

You can almost see this boy's idea start to crop up in the hearts of the people who followed Jesus. The day after Jesus multiplied the loaves and the fishes, more boats arrived at the place where the miracle had occurred, but Jesus was no longer there. The Bible says:

> Once the crowd realized that neither Jesus nor His disciples were there, they got into the boats and went to Capernaum in search of Jesus.
> When they found Him on the other side of the lake, they asked Him, "Rabbi, when did You get here?"
> Jesus answered, "I tell you the truth, you are looking for Me, not because you saw miraculous signs but because you ate the loaves and had your fill. Do not work for food

that spoils, but for food that endures to eternal life, which the Son of Man will give you" (John 6:24-27a).

Jesus went on to remind them that God is eager to provide for their daily needs just as He provided bread from heaven—in the form of manna—every day for forty years while the Israelites wandered through the desert. But then Jesus added:

> "I am the bread of life. Your forefathers ate the manna in the desert, yet they died. But here is the bread that comes down from heaven, which a man may eat and not die. I am the living bread that came down from heaven. If anyone eats of this bread, he will live forever" (John 6:48-51a).

While Jesus is glad to give you practical advice for living, like He did in the Sermon on the Mount, He wants to give you more. And while He's glad to meet your daily needs, as He did for those who ate the feast on the hillside, He wants to give you more.

Jesus wants to give you a relationship with Him, the living bread that came down from heaven. He doesn't want to just give you money for the trip, He wants to be your companion along the journey. He doesn't want to just give you a roadmap to where you're going, He wants to go with you and guide you there Himself. Your relationship with Jesus takes precedence over everything He could ever teach you, or give you, in a lifetime.

I want to encourage you today: come to Jesus for His teachings, for they can change your life; and come to Him for your daily bread, for He's still a God who can provide for all your needs with baskets full left over.

But don't stop there. Don't shortchange all that God wants to do for you today. Come to Him for life, and life abundant. Come to Him for a feast that never ends—eternal life with Him, a life that starts here on earth and goes on forever. As Jesus told those on the hillside:

> "I am the bread of life. He who comes to Me will never go hungry, and he who believes in Me will never be thirsty....If anyone eats of this bread, he will live forever" (John 6:35,51b).

Let's pray:

Father, thank You for blessing us with Your life and Your words. Help us to look to You for our daily bread, but not to stop there. Help us to look to You for bread that will last forever, bread that comes only through an ongoing relationship with You. In Jesus' name, Amen.

LESSON 9: WHAT HAPPENED AT CAESAREA PHILIPPI? JUNE 20

Caesarea Philippi is on the northern edge of Israel in a beautiful region known as Dan. But the things that took place there weren't always so beautiful. To find out more, watch the short video below, then read on to find out how God can do beautiful things for you even if you're in a very dark place.

Watch "What Happened at Caesarea Philippi?" (or on ericelder.com).

So what happened at Caesarea Philippi? This is where God revealed to Peter that Jesus was the Christ, the Son of the living God.

Caesarea Philippi was also home to a cultic temple carved into the side of a massive rock that was called at that time "the gates of hell." It was so named because of the infant sacrifices that took place there in the years leading up to the time of Christ.

With this background in mind, the words that Jesus spoke on this spot are even more meaningful. Here's what happened, as recorded in the book of Matthew:

> When Jesus came to the region of Caesarea Philippi, He asked His disciples, "Who do people say the Son of Man is?"
> They replied, "Some say John the Baptist; others say Elijah; and still others, Jeremiah or one of the prophets."
> "But what about you?" He asked. "Who do you say I am?"
> Simon Peter answered, "You are the Christ, the Son of the Living God."
> Jesus replied, "Blessed are you, Simon son of Jonah, for this was not revealed to you by man, but by My Father in heaven. And I tell you that you are Peter, and on this rock I will build My church, and the gates of hell will not overcome it. I will give you the keys of the kingdom of heaven; whatever you bind on earth will be bound in heaven, and whatever you loose on earth will be loosed in heaven" (Matthew 16:13-19).

I never realized until I went to Israel what a dark place Caesarea Philippi must have been in the days when Jesus was speaking.

The Temple of Pan had been built there a few hundred years earlier, and when people came to worship Pan, they would bring with them an infant child to be offered as a sacrifice. The child was thrown into the water that flowed from the rock on the side of the cliff. If the child went under the water and disappeared, that meant Pan had accepted their sacrifice. If instead, the child was dashed apart under water and its blood flowed into the river below, Pan had rejected their sacrifice. Either way, the child's life was over.

Not only was this area known for this pagan temple, but the Israelites had also rejected God in this region hundreds of years before that. Way back in the days of King Jeroboam, Jeroboam ruled Israel from this area. But for fear that the people would want to leave his kingdom and side with the breakaway kingdom of Judah, he erected two altars in this area instead. He made two golden calves and said to the people:

> "It is too much for you to go up to Jerusalem. Here are your gods, O Israel, who brought you up out of Egypt." One he set up in Bethel and the other in Dan. And this thing became a sin; the people went even as far as Dan to worship the one there (1 Kings 12:28b-29).

So this region of Dan, at the northernmost border of Israel, which is so beautiful and hilly and rich on the outside, had been a place of great darkness spiritually. In Jesus' day, with the Temple of Pan located there, it was an even darker place. Yet this is where God chose to reveal to Peter and the other disciples that Jesus was the Christ. The darkness wasn't a problem for Him, for He was, as He called Himself, "the light of the world." Jesus said:

> "I am the light of the world. Whoever follows me will never walk in darkness, but will have the light of life" (John 8:12).

Perhaps you're in a dark time or a dark place in your life today. Or perhaps you have family or friends who are surrounded by darkness. If so, I want to encourage you to take heart: Jesus can reveal Himself even in the darkest of times and places. In fact, based on the time and place where He made this revelation to Peter, Jesus seems to delight in doing just that.

I also want to encourage you to make sure your faith in Christ is profoundly personal. By that I mean, don't just take someone else's word for it that Jesus is the Christ, the Son of the living God. Make sure that this is something that you believe deeply yourself. If you look at Jesus' questions in the passage above, you'll see that He started by asking His disciples what others said about Him. "Who do people say that I am?" The disciples replied:

> *"Some say John the Baptist; others say Elijah; and still others, Jeremiah or one of the prophets."*

It's sometimes safe and easy to talk about Jesus in terms of what others believe about Him. If asked who He is, some people might say, "Well, my grandmother thinks He's God," or "My parents believe He's the Messiah," or "My friends say that He's their Savior." But after Jesus asked the disciples what others said about Him, He turned to them directly and asked who they thought He was.

> *"But what about you?" He asked. "Who do you say I am?"*

There comes a point in life when you can no longer rely solely on the faith of others to get you through the trials you're facing. You can no longer waver between what others say about Christ. My prayer is that you'll be able to say, like Peter said:

> *"You are the Christ, the Son of the Living God."*

"The Christ" (Greek) and "the Messiah" (Hebrew) both mean the same thing: "the Anointed One."

If you've never put your faith in Jesus, trusting and believing that He is the Christ, the Messiah, the Anointed One, the One who came to die for your sins and bring light into your world, I encourage you to do it today. And if you've already put your faith in Christ, know that He is a Savior who delights in revealing Himself even in the darkest of places. Keep on praying that He will reveal Himself again and again to you, to your family and friends, and to the rest of the world.

Let's pray:

Father, thank You for revealing that Jesus is indeed the long-awaited Messiah, the Savior of all who put their faith in Him. Help us to see that revelation for ourselves in a fresh way today, and help others see Him that way as well, no matter how dark it may seem all around them right now. In Jesus' name, Amen.

LESSON 10: WHAT HAPPENED AT THE JORDAN RIVER?   JUNE 21

For today's message, I'd like to take you to one of the world's most famous rivers, the Jordan River in Israel. The waters of this river flow about 200 miles from the north of Israel to the south, passing through the Sea of Galilee in the north, then continuing its final destination at the Dead Sea in the south. To find out some of the things that took place on this historic river, take a look at the short video below that I shot on the banks of the river itself, then read on to hear about how very much God loves you—and how you can express your love back to Him.

(I've also included in the video an actual baptism at the Jordan River, this one of my son Josiah. You'll note as you watch that there are some overly friendly fish in the river who love nibbling at people's toes! The fish are harmless, but they do make the baptism all the more... uhmm... exciting!)

Watch "What Happened at the Jordan River?" (or on ericelder.com).

So what happened at the Jordan River? This is where John the Baptist baptized Jesus. This is also where John the Baptist baptized thousands of people, as did Jesus' disciples.

The Jordan River has also been the site of many other events over several thousand years of history, such as:

- when Joshua and the Israelites crossed the Jordan River on dry ground as they entered into the Promised Land (Joshua 3:14-17),
- when Naaman was healed of leprosy in the Jordan (2 Kings 5:8-14),
- when Elisha made an ax head float on top of the water (2 Kings 6:1-7),
- and when Elijah was taken up into heaven after crossing the Jordan with Elijah (2 Kings 2:6-12).

But of all the events that took place in the Jordan, perhaps the most famous is the baptism of Jesus. And what makes that event so special to me is not just what Jesus did there, but what God the Father said to Jesus when Jesus was baptized there. Here's the story, as recorded in Matthew chapter 3:

Then Jesus came from Galilee to the Jordan to be baptized by John. But John tried to deter him, saying, "I need to be baptized by You, and do You come to me?" Jesus replied, "Let it be so now; it is proper for us to do this to fulfill all righteousness." Then John consented.
As soon as Jesus was baptized, He went up out of the water. At that moment heaven was opened, and He saw the Spirit of God descending like a dove and lighting on Him. And a voice from heaven said, "This is My Son, whom I love; with Him I am well pleased" (Matthew 3:13-17).

I love the fact that God, the Father, told Jesus, His Son, how very much He loved Him—even before Jesus did one miracle, before He healed anyone of any disease, before He preached any sermon, walked on the water, or raised anyone from the dead.

God, the Father, loved Jesus, not because of all that Jesus had done for Him, but because Jesus was His Son.

And the truth is, God loves you for the same reason, not because of all you've done for Him, but simply because you're His son or daughter, made in His image, and created for a loving relationship with Him from the moment He conceived you (which, by the way, could have been long before the time that your parents conceived you...see Jeremiah 1:5, for example). God loves you. He adores you. He created you. And He has so much in store for you and your life.

The good news is you don't have to go to the Jordan River to let God love on you. He's glad to soak you in His love wherever you may be. How can you feel God's love more in your life? One way is to just take a few minutes to sit and meditate on the truth that He does indeed love you. Read the passage of Jesus' baptism again from Matthew chapter 3 and remember that He loves you just as He loved Jesus, even before Jesus began His ministry.

Remember that you're His child, His little one, His beloved. Remember that He sent Jesus to die for the sins in your life, the messes that you've made, so that you won't have to pay the price for those sins yourself. Remember that His love extends for generations to those who love Him. And remember that you really are special, a wonderful creation of the most loving Father in the world.

And while you're considering this passage on Jesus' baptism, can I also encourage you that if you've never been baptized to consider being baptized soon? There's something special that comes from being obedient to the Lord's command in this area. Jesus' words about baptism were so important that He included them in His final instructions to His disciples before going into heaven. Jesus said:

> *"Therefore go and make disciples of all nations, baptizing them in the name of the Father and of the Son and of the Holy Spirit, and teaching them to obey everything I have commanded you" (Matthew 28:19).*

I've studied the topic of baptism for many years, yet I can honestly say that I still don't understand it fully. But what I do understand is that something powerful takes place when a person is baptized in the name of the Father and of the Son and of the Holy Spirit. I've seen baptism can touch people in so many ways, from realizing that they truly are saved and going to heaven, to feeling like their sins are dripping off of them as they come out of the water, to receiving new giftings from God to help them make the most of their new lives in Christ.

As a follower of Christ, baptism is one of those steps that demonstrate you are willing to follow in His footsteps, being baptized as He was baptized and then living the rest of your life as He lived His.

Let's pray:

Father, thank You for loving us even before we ever did anything for You, and regardless of anything that we've done against You. We pray that You would pour out Your love on us again today in a way that we can hear it, see it, feel it, or otherwise sense it. Lord, we also pray that You would show us ways that we can express our love back to You, whether it is by being baptized ourselves, or in some other way, for our desire is to pour out our love on You as well. In Jesus' name, Amen.

LESSON 11: WHAT WILL HAPPEN AT THE DEAD SEA?   JUNE 22

The Dead Sea was one of my favorite stops on our trip to Israel. Maybe it was because we had some extra time to relax there because of a change in our schedule. Or maybe it was because the land and the water were so unusually beautiful. But I think the main reason I liked it so much is because of what will happen there in the future. To see what it looks like yourself, and to find out what God is going to do there one day, take a look at this short video below. Then read on to find out what God could do in your life in unexpected ways as well.

Watch "What Will Happen at the Dead Sea?" (or on ericelder.com).

So what will happen at the Dead Sea? Everything will come back to life! To understand how dramatic this change will be, you have to understand how dead the Dead Sea really is.

The Dead Sea is the lowest spot on earth at almost 1,400 hundred feet below sea level. It's also the saltiest body of water on earth, with a salinity of 30-33%, which is about six to seven times saltier than the oceans. Because of this, and whatever other reasons God has chosen, nothing is able to live in the Dead Sea whatsoever. There are no fish in the water, so there are no birds in the air. There's no grass along the shoreline, and no algae growing along its edges. The Dead Sea really is dead!

For some reason, I used to picture the Dead Sea as some kind of smelly swamp filled with dead things. But actually there's nothing "dead" in it. There are no dead fish on the shore and the water is as clear as crystal, giving a clear view of millions of shimmering crystals of salt that cover the bottom of the sea itself. In the Bible, it's not called the Dead Sea, but rather the "Sea of Salt," which is perhaps is a bit more descriptive. It's also referred to as the Eastern Sea, as it is on the East side of Israel, and just southeast of Jerusalem.

Given this background of just how desolate the sea is, it's even more remarkable to read about what God is going to do there one day. You can read about it in the book of Ezekiel, chapter 47. God gave Ezekiel a vision of the future, showing him the new temple that would one day be in Jerusalem. And out from beneath this temple, a river would flow—a river of life, all the way to the Dead Sea. Ezekiel says:

> *Then he led me back to the bank of the river. When I arrived there, I saw a great number of trees on each side of the river. He said to me, "This water flows toward the eastern region and goes down into the Arabah, where it enters the Sea [the Dead Sea]. When it empties into the Sea, the water there becomes fresh. Swarms of living creatures will live wherever the river flows. There will be large numbers of fish, because this water flows there and makes the saltwater fresh; so where the river flows everything will live. Fishermen will stand along the shore; from En Gedi to En Eglaim there will be places for spreading nets. The fish will be of many kinds—like the fish of the Great Sea [the Mediterranean]. But the swamps and marshes will not become fresh; they will be left for salt. Fruit trees of all kinds will grow on both banks of the river. Their leaves will not wither, nor will their fruit fail. Every month they will bear, because the water from the sanctuary flows to them. Their fruit will serve for food and their leaves for healing" (Ezekiel 47:6b-12).*

The prophet Zechariah also makes reference to this event, saying:

> *On that day living water will flow out from Jerusalem, half to the eastern sea [the Dead Sea] and half to the western sea [the Mediterranean], in summer and in winter (Zechariah 14:8).*

When you're standing at the edge of the Dead Sea, it's awesome to consider that one day it will be teeming with life—that one day, living water will pour out from underneath the temple in Jerusalem to bring life to all the water touches, even filling this great basin of the Dead Sea with enough fresh water to bring this barren spot back to life.

Having read through many of the other prophecies in the Bible and visited the spots where they've already been fulfilled—such as the destruction of Sodom and Gomorrah that God foretold to Abraham and took place near here, or the birth of the Savior that God told Micah would take place in Bethlehem hundreds of years before Jesus was born—I'm reassured that what has been foretold about the Dead Sea, and its coming back to life again, will take place just as certainly.

And it shouldn't be surprising that God can bring things that have been dead back to life again. I've seen Him do it in my own life, giving me a new birth over twenty years ago when I thought I was headed for death, then giving me an abundant life instead. And I've seen God do the same thing in the lives of countless others as well, breathing new life into marriages that were officially dead, or bringing forth new life from wombs that doctors had declared physically dead.

I think of ministries and churches and corporations that have been on the brink of bankruptcy, without a hope in the world, but through hope in God have come back to life more fully and fruitfully than ever.

God specializes in bringing the dead back to life! This isn't to say that God wants everything to live, for there are some things that should die in our lives, and other things that have run their course and need to pass on so that something fresh and new can be birthed. But there's no doubt that God can breathe life into anything that He intends to bring back to life!

Maybe there's something in your life right now that feels like it is dead or dying and you see no way in the world for it to come back to life. But don't put your hope in the world. Put your hope in the Lord God Almighty, the Author and Sustainer of life itself!

Before you give up on that which may look dead today, consider Him who gives life and breath to every living thing that you see around you today. Be encouraged that the same God who raised Jesus from the dead can give life to your mortal bodies as well. Be encouraged that the same God who breathed life into Adam, who was made out of the dust of the ground, can breathe new life into your family, your business, your marriage, your ministry. Be encouraged that the river of life that will flow into the Dead Sea will bring life to all that it touches.

God loves to bring that which is dead back to life! Let His river of life flow into your life today!

Let's pray:

Father, thank You for showing us how you can breathe life into the most desolate places on earth, and encourage us that Your river of life can touch our lives as well. Lord, help us to have the faith that You can and You will bring new life back into everything that You have said should come back to life. In Jesus' name, Amen.

LESSON 12: WHAT HAPPENED AT SODOM AND GOMORRAH?   JUNE 23

I'm not usually a "fire and brimstone" type of preacher. But if there was ever a time to preach a message on fire and brimstone, it's today, because today we're going to look at the time when God rained fire and brimstone down from heaven on the cities of Sodom and Gomorrah because their wickedness had become so great. To find out what happened there, take a look at this short video below, then read on below to learn how powerful God really is, and how God can use that power in your life today.

Watch "What Happened at Sodom and Gomorrah?" (or on ericelder.com).

So what happened at Sodom and Gomorrah? God destroyed them completely. The destruction that took place at Sodom and Gomorrah was so complete that nothing has grown again in that region for thousands of years.

Compare that to the most powerful destruction men have invented, such as the atomic bombs which destroyed the cities of Hiroshima and Nagasaki during the war with Japan, and you'll see just how powerful God really is.

When the bombs were dropped on those cities, they were almost completely wiped out within seven seconds. But if you visited those cities just forty years later, although you would have found those cities had changed, you would have also found that they were teeming with life again. Buildings, trees, and people had grown up all around them. I'm told that except for the monuments that were erected to remind people of the horrific destruction that took place there years ago, visitors may not even realize the cities were once destroyed.

Sodom and Gomorrah, on the other hand, have never come back to life, and it's not been just forty years, or four hundred years, but more than four thousand years.

While the cities themselves no longer exist, the memory of what happened there is often repeated. Abraham talked about Sodom and Gomorrah, as did Isaiah, Paul, Peter, John, and even Jesus. As for the condition of the land beforehand, we're told that it wasn't always a barren wasteland, but it was at one time *"well-watered, like the garden of the Lord" (Genesis 13:10).* It was such a desirable land that Lot chose to live there when Abraham gave him his choice of where to live.

But as desirable as the land may have been, the people of the land left much to be desired. Their wickedness had become so great that God sent two angels—in the form of men—down to Sodom to destroy it.

Although God's patience is longer than ours, even His patience runs out. And that time had come for Sodom. God didn't want to have to destroy it. He even told Abraham He would spare the entire city if He could find even ten righteous people living there. But when the angels arrived and went to spend the night with Lot and his family, the men of the city showed how far their wickedness had gone. The Bible says:

> *Before they had gone to bed, all the men from every part of the city of Sodom—both young and old—surrounded the house. They called to Lot, "Where are the men who came to you tonight? Bring them out to us so that we can have sex with them" (Genesis 19:4-5).*

Lot pleaded with them not to do this to his guests, but the men of Sodom persisted, saying:

> *"Get out of our way. This fellow came here as an alien, and now he wants to play the judge! We'll treat you worse than them." They kept bringing pressure on Lot and moved forward to break down the door (Genesis 19:9).*

No matter what you might think about the topic of homosexuality, the idea of men forcibly having sex with other men goes against God's beautiful design for sex.

Through a miraculous intervention of the two angels, God whisked away Lot and his family, and finally did what He hoped He wouldn't have to do. Genesis 19:23-26 says:

> *"Then the LORD rained down burning sulfur on Sodom and Gomorrah—from the LORD out of the heavens. Thus He overthrew those cities and the entire plain,*

including all those living in the cities—and also the vegetation in the land. But Lot's wife looked back, and she became a pillar of salt" (Genesis 19:24-26).

Although Lot and his two daughters escaped, Lot's wife looked back, against the clear instruction of the angels who helped them to escape. Perhaps she hesitated and looked back to take one last look at the city where she had spent so much of her life. Or maybe she was just curious and wanted to see for herself just how what such destruction might look like. But whatever the reason, her looking back caused her to suffer the same fate as those who had also so deliberately gone against God's commands—commands that were not designed to restrict or limit them, but commands that would help them to live, and live abundantly.

When Jesus talked about the destruction of Sodom and Gomorrah, He warned people:

"Remember Lot's wife!" (Luke 17:32).

I want to encourage you today to do the same: Remember Lot's wife!

I know that some of you are playing with fire. You're doing things that you know are against God's will for your life. Whether you're doing them because you've always done them, or whether you're just curious and want to see what it's like, you're still playing with fire. And God's fire can burn you seriously—and for eternity.

God may have been patient with you this far and not yet brought the complete destruction upon you that He could bring at any moment. But don't mistake God's patience as His approval of what you're doing. The purpose of His patience is to give you time to turn from your sin so that you can save yourself from the destruction that's coming upon you if you don't.

Remember Lot's wife! Turn from the coming destruction while you still have a chance. Do it today. Don't hesitate. Don't look back. Don't let curiosity kill you. If you've been looking at pornography, stop it today. If you've been considering, or engaged in, and adulterous relationship, end it today. If you've been abusing drugs or alcohol, stop it today. If you've been using God's gift of sex in ways that are selfish instead of ways that lead to an abundant life, stop it today. Remember Lot's wife, and live!

Let's pray:

Father, thank You for reminding us of Your incredible power and Your incredible patience with us. Lord, help us to throw off everything that hinders us from beautiful relationship with You and with those around us. Fill us with Your power to do all that You've called us to do today. In Jesus' name, Amen.

LESSON 13: WHAT HAPPENED AT MASADA?   JUNE 24

In America, the "Fourth of July" is not just a date on the calendar, but to us is a phrase that is synonymous with the word "Freedom!" In Israel, there's a place called Masada that symbolizes for many Jews the fight for freedom as well, a fight that took place there back in 73 A.D.

To find out what happened and take a look at the mountain of Masada yourself, take a look at this short video below. Then read on to find out how taking a stand for freedom can inspire and impact those around you as well.

Watch "What Happened at Masada?" (or on ericelder.com).

So what happened at Masada? This is the place where almost 1,000 Jews committed suicide. As gruesome as it may sound, the truth is that these people were so committed to the idea of staying free that they preferred to die free than to live as slaves.

Although the story of Masada doesn't appear in the Bible, and the suicidal aspects of the story go against traditional Jewish beliefs, what happened at Masada still makes a profound statement about the lengths people are willing to go for freedom. In some ways, it reminds me of Patrick Henry's famous words at the beginning of the American Revolution: "Give me liberty or give me death!"

But while Patrick's Henry's speech was a call to fight for the freedom in which they believed, for the 960 Jewish rebels who had been holed up in the mountain of Masada as a fortress from which they launched their attacks on the Roman Empire, fighting was no longer an option. The Romans had sent thousands of troops to Masada to take back this fortress that King Herod and others had developed over the years. (The word "masada" means "fortress.")

Because of the steep cliffs that protected Masada from its enemies, the Romans could not simply rush into the fortress to take it back. Instead, they moved tons of sand and dirt over the period of three years to build a siege ramp from the base of the mountain to its top. The ramp, as well as the remains of the Roman camps that were built in those days to house the armies for those three years, can still be seen clearly today.

It was a massive undertaking by the Roman government that finally culminated in the year 73 A.D., within a generation after the time when Jesus Christ had lived and died.

But when the Romans finally reached the top of Masada and broke through the gates, they found that the battle for which they had prepared for so long would not have to take place. The 960 rebels had, days earlier, realized that a fight would not be profitable. And rather than giving up their freedom to worship God in the way they believed, they gave up their lives, dying free, rather than living as slaves under Roman rule.

The story of their faith and how they came to their final end was documented by those who lived inside Masada. Interestingly, as a way to avoid committing wholesale suicide which was against their own teachings, each man drew lots and took turns taking the lives of their own families and friends, until finally only one man remained who alone killed himself.

While there's nothing scriptural to justify suicide, this story serves as a reminder of just how precious freedom really is, and to what lengths people will go to get it, rather than to live in slavery any longer.

It was the same sort of commitment the men who signed the U.S. Declaration of Independence made when they wrote:

"...we mutually pledge to each other our lives, our fortunes and our sacred honor"
(from the final sentence of the Declaration of Independence).

And many of those who signed the Declaration of Independence did give up their lives and fortunes because of that pledge of sacred honor to one another.

Christ calls us to do the same.

Jesus frequently invited people to "come and see" what the kingdom of heaven was all about, then challenged them to go deeper and to "come and die" for that kingdom of heaven.

Here are a few of the things that Jesus said about the cost of freedom that could come to those who follow Him:

> "For whoever wants to save his life will lose it, but whoever loses his life for Me and for the gospel will save it" (Mark 8:35).
> "If anyone would come after Me, he must deny himself and take up his cross daily and follow Me" (Luke 9:23).
> "And everyone who has left houses or brothers or sisters or father or mother or children or fields for My sake will receive a hundred times as much and will inherit eternal life" (Matthew 19:29).

Jesus wants us to be as committed to Him and to the freedom that He offers as were those who were committed to freedom at Masada, as were those who were committed to freedom in America.

There's a price to pay for freedom that Christ offers. But when you're following Christ, any price is worth it. And once you're willing to die for Jesus, you'll find it's so much easier to live for Him as well.

Let's pray:

Father, thank You for dying for us to set us free, and help us to be willing to die to set others free as well. And Lord, help us realize that being willing to die for You will free to us to live for You even more. In Jesus' name, Amen.

LESSON 14: WHAT HAPPENED AT THE QUMRAN CAVES?   JUNE 25

The Qumran Caves are the site of what has been called "the greatest archaeological discovery of modern time." To find out what was discovered there, take a look at this short video below. Then read on to see how this tremendous discovery can affect your life in profound ways today, too.

Watch "What Happened at the Qumran Caves?" (or on ericelder.com).

So what happened at the Qumran Caves? That's where the Dead Sea Scrolls were found. And the scrolls found at Qumran aren't just any old scrolls. They contain the oldest hand-written manuscripts of the Hebrew Bible, or the Old Testament, that have ever been found.

Because the scrolls were made of animal skins and parchment, both of which are easily carbon-dated, the ages of these scrolls have been reliably dated as having been written between the years of 200 BC and 68 AD. It was quite a find for the shepherd boy who discovered the caves and the scrolls back in 1947, and for the many scholars and archaeologists who have found more caves and more scrolls in the Qumran area since that time.

Among the thousands of scrolls and scroll fragments that have been found, at least a portion of every book of the Old Testament has been discovered to date, with the exception of the book of Esther. Multiple copies of some of the scrolls have been found, such as the books of Psalms, Genesis, and Deuteronomy, and some of the books have been found in their entirety, such as the book of Isaiah.

What makes this discovery so exciting to researchers is that the books are so very old. For instance, the Isaiah scroll is 1,000 years older than any previously discovered copy of

Isaiah. And even more exciting is the high level of accuracy of today's translations of the Bible when compared to these scrolls from the time of Christ.

Archaeological finds like those at the Qumran Caves continue to shed light and credibility on the Scriptures that we use today. In the words of the book of Isaiah itself:

"The grass withers and the flowers fall, but the Word of our God stands forever" (Isaiah 40:8).

When you look out at the barren mountains that surround Qumran, and see how the grass has withered, the flowers have fallen, and even the people who lived there have faded away, it's an awesome thought to think that the Word of God still stands.

The fact that God's Word has remained true for all this time confirms to me that the same words He spoke to the people back then, God wants to speak to you today.

When God says in the book of Jeremiah,

"I have loved you with an everlasting love," (Jeremiah 31:3).

He meant it then, and He means it today.
When God says in the book of Joshua,

"I will never leave you nor forsake you," (Joshua 1:5),

He meant it then, and He means it today.
When God said in the book of Isaiah,

"…those who hope in the LORD will renew their strength. They will soar on wings like eagles; they will run and not grow weary, they will walk and not be faint" (Isaiah 40:31).

He meant it then, and He means it today.

God loves you, He will never leave you nor forsake you, and He will give you the strength you need to fulfill the purpose for which He created you, if you'll continue to put your hope and faith in Him.

Even though the grass withers and the flowers fade away, the Word of God will stand forever, as evidenced once again by the ancient scrolls that were found in the caves at Qumran. God is faithful and true, and His Word is powerful and reliable.

Keep reading God's Word. Keep hiding it in your heart and memorizing it regularly. Keep meditating on it day and night, as God told Joshua to do in Joshua 1:8. Don't let this ancient treasure that has been preserved for so long be wasted. Keep opening up your Bible again and again and let God's Living Word breathe life into your daily walk with Him.

Let's pray:

Father, thank You for preserving these ancient manuscripts of Your Word for all of these years. Thank You for confirming to us that Your Word is reliable and true, and for giving us the inspiration we need to keep reading it, memorizing it and meditating on it day and night, so that we may experience the fullness of the life for which we were created. In Jesus' name, Amen.

LESSON 15: WHAT HAPPENED AT EN GEDI? JUNE 26

In the midst of the barren hills that surround the Dead Sea, there's a surprising oasis of life. It's called En Gedi, where a freshwater spring pours over steep crevices in the rock, creating a series of beautiful waterfalls and pools as the spring winds its way from the top to the bottom. To find out how God used this oasis to protect and provide for one of the most famous characters in the Bible, take a look at this short video below. Then read on to learn how God can help you when you feel you are being treated unjustly.

Watch "What Happened at En Gedi?" (or on ericelder.com).

So what happened at En Gedi? This is where David came to hide from King Saul when Saul was trying to kill David. But Saul wasn't always angry with David. In fact, David was one of Saul's favorites. David was called to come and live at the palace to play the harp for Saul, bringing great relief to the king every time David played.

But when David's fame began to grow as one of the best warriors in Saul's army, Saul became jealous. Fearing that the people would like David more than him, Saul tried to kill David by pinning him to a wall with his spear.

David tried to talk things out with Saul, reminding the king that David had never done anything wrong against him, but the conversations appeased Saul for only a short time. Then Saul was back to trying to kill David again because of Saul's burning jealousy. It soon became apparent that David would die if he stayed in the palace any longer.

So David fled. He went from place to place as Saul and his men tried to hunt him down. One of the places that God provided for David was En Gedi. The book of 1 Samuel says:

> *After Saul returned from pursuing the Philistines, he was told, "David is in the Desert of En Gedi." So Saul took three thousand chosen men from all Israel and set out to look for David and his men near the Crags of the Wild Goats (1 Samuel 24:1-2).*

If you were to visit En Gedi today, you would see why David fled there. It featured an oasis of fresh spring water in the middle of the barren hills that surround the Dead Sea, with many caves in the hills where he could hide. It's an ideal spot to hide and be refreshed at the same time, and wild goats still climb the steep cliffs today, probably descendants from the wild goats for which the area was named back in David's time.

It was in one of these caves that Saul stopped for a bathroom break. In God's timing, it happened to be the very cave in which David and his men were hiding. The Bible says:

> *He [Saul] came to the sheep pens along the way; a cave was there, and Saul went in to relieve himself. David and his men were far back in the cave. The men said, "Today the LORD is saying, 'I will give your enemy into your hands for you to deal with as you wish.' Then David crept up unnoticed and cut off a corner of Saul's robe (1 Samuel 24:3-4).*

But after cutting off the corner of Saul's robe, David was conscience-stricken that he should not do anything to harm the one that God had chosen as king, nor would he let any of his men attack Saul. When Saul left the cave, David followed after him and called out to Saul:

> *"My lord the king!" When Saul looked behind him, David bowed down and prostrated himself with his face to the ground. He said to Saul, "Why do you listen when*

men say, 'David is bent on harming you'? This day you have seen with your own eyes how the LORD delivered you into my hands in the cave. Some urged me to kill you, but I spared you; I said, 'I will not lift my hand against my master, because he is the LORD's anointed.' See, my father, look at this piece of your robe in my hand! I cut off the corner of your robe but did not kill you. Now understand and recognize that I am not guilty of wrongdoing or rebellion. I have not wronged you, but you are hunting me down to take my life. May the LORD judge between you and me. And may the LORD avenge the wrongs you have done to me, but my hand will not touch you. As the old saying goes, 'From evildoers come evil deeds,' so my hand will not touch you. Against whom has the king of Israel come out? Whom are you pursuing? A dead dog? A flea? May the LORD be our judge and decide between us. May He consider my cause and uphold it; may He vindicate me by delivering me from your hand."

David did three things at En Gedi that I think are worth learning from when we feel we are being treated unjustly

First, he fled from a bad situation. While God may sometimes call you to stay in a bad situation to do all you can to work things out, there are still those times when it's truly OK to flee from it. David did his best to try to talk things out with Saul, but when it became apparent that his very life was in danger if he stayed any longer, he fled. Jesus did the same thing at times, escaping quickly from people and places where people wanted to harm or kill Him, such as escaping from a crowd that wanted to throw Him over the cliff, or fleeing from those who tried to stone Him at the temple, or when He escaped the grasp of those who tried to kill Him as He walked through Solomon's Colonnade (see Luke 4:28-30, John 8:59, and John 10:39).

Second, David trusted God to protect and provide for him. Sometimes you may not want to flee from a bad situation because of the fear that something worse will happen to you. But if God is in it, He can protect and provide for you as well. God can provide a place for you like He provided En Gedi for David. It may not be like the place from which you came, but if it's God's provision, it can be just what you need, and a remarkable place in its own right. God protected and provided for the Israelites in the desert after they fled from their captors in Egypt, giving them manna and meat to eat for forty years. And He did the same for Elijah when Elijah fled from King Ahab, sending bread and meat to Elijah every morning and evening by way of birds who were directed by God to do so (see Exodus 16:35, Numbers 11:31-32, and 1 Kings 17:4-6).

Third, David trusted God to administer justice. Even though you may have a chance to administer justice yourself to those who wrongfully accuse or harm you, you may benefit by taking this lesson from David. He could have killed Saul himself, but then he would have had to face 3,000 angry troops next. By trusting the matter into God's hands, Saul was eventually punished for his wrongdoings, losing his life in battle, and David was brought back to live at the palace, this time as king. Even Jesus, for as many times as He escaped from the hands of His captors, trust God to administer the ultimate justice when God told Him to lay down His life for those who sinned against Him. Because of this, the Bible says:

Therefore God exalted Him to the highest place and gave Him the name that is above every name, that at the name of Jesus every knee should bow, in heaven and

on earth and under the earth, and every tongue confess that Jesus Christ is Lord, to the glory of God the Father (Philippians 2:9-11).

Jesus trusted God to make things right in the end—and make things right He did—just like David trusted God, and just like you and I can do when we feel like others are treating us unjustly.

There are many other things you can do in situations like these, such as forgiving those who mistreat you (see Matthew 18:21-35) or calling for help from others who can step in and help with the situation (see Matthew 18:15-17).

Whether you flee or whether you stay, whether the situation improves or gets worse, know that God can protect and provide for you in the midst of it, and that He can work all things for good in the end. Remember David at En Gedi, and remember what the Bible says:

"… that in all things God works for the good of those who love Him, who have been called according to His purpose" (Romans 8:28).

Let's pray:

Father, thank You for giving us the example of David and Saul, so we can learn from them to see just how much You can do for those who love You. And Lord, help us to keep putting our trust in You that You will always work all things for good in Your way and in Your timing. In Jesus' name, Amen.

LESSON 16: WHAT HAPPENED AT BETHLEHEM? JUNE 27

Today we're headed to Bethlehem, the birthplace of Jesus. If you'd like to go with me into the Church of the Nativity and see for yourself the place underneath the altar of the church that has marked for centuries where they believe Jesus was born, take a look at this short video below. Then read on to learn why God might have chosen this place for the birth of His Son, and why having a heart like God's can bear fruit even hundreds—if not thousands—of years later.

Watch "What Happened at Bethlehem?" (or on ericelder.com).

So what happened at Bethlehem? That's where Jesus was born.

The Church of the Nativity has marked the spot ever since 327 A.D., when the church was built at the request of Helena, the mother of Emperor Constantine. Helena was shown this spot on her visit to the Holy Land as the birthplace of her Savior, and she had a church built there to commemorate it. The spot had already been noted as the birthplace of Jesus for hundreds of years before that time by locals and historians alike, such as Justin Martyr in the 2nd century, and Origen of Alexandria in the 3rd.

It's amazing to think that Jesus was born on this spot, but it's even more amazing to think that Jesus was ever born at all. To think that God, the Father, would love us so much that He would send His Son into the world to live among us, to tell us of His love, and to demonstrate that love by giving up His life for us so we could live with God forever, that's what's really amazing.

As Jesus said so succinctly:

> "For God so loved the world that He gave His one and only Son, that whoever believes in Him shall not perish but have eternal life" (John 3:16).

But why Bethlehem? Why did God want His Son to be born there? As with most things God does, God didn't pick the city of Bethlehem out of a hat of possible locations at the last minute. He had foretold it, hundreds of years earlier, through the prophet Micah:

> "But you, Bethlehem Ephrathah, though you are small among the clans of Judah, out of you will come for me one who will be ruler over Israel, whose origins are from of old, from ancient times" (Micah 5:2).

But why? What was it about Bethlehem that made it so special that God would honor it in this way? I don't know for sure, but I do know that there was another man born in Bethlehem about a thousand years earlier about whom God had said:

> "I have found David son of Jesse a man after My own heart; he will do everything I want him to do" (Acts 13:22b).

God honors those whose hearts are after His own heart: people who love God so much that they will do whatever He wants them to do, whenever He wants them to do it and however God wants them to do it.

And look what God did for David as a result:

> "From this man's descendants God has brought to Israel the Savior Jesus, as He promised" (Acts 13:23).

I don't think it was haphazard that God chose Bethlehem as the birthplace of His Son. It seems to me that because David had honored God with his life, God honored David with the life of His Son, even so many generations later.

Because of David's love for God, God seemed to move heaven and earth, and even the Roman Emperor, to orchestrate things so that this descendant of David's would be born back in David's hometown. As Luke records:

> "In those days Caesar Augustus issued a decree that a census should be taken of the entire Roman world. ...And everyone went to his own town to register. So Joseph also went up from the town of Nazareth in Galilee to Judea, to Bethlehem the town of David, because he belonged to the house and line of David. He went there to register with Mary, who was pledged to be married to him and was expecting a child. While they were there, the time came for the baby to be born, and she gave birth to her firstborn, a son. She wrapped him in cloths and placed him in a manger, because there was no room for them in the inn" (Luke 2:1,3-7).

Even the angels made the connection between Jesus' birthplace and David's, as one of them told the shepherds on the hills of Bethlehem that night:

> "I bring you good news of great joy that will be for all the people. Today in the town of David a Savior has been born to you; He is Christ the Lord" (Luke 2:10b-11).

David was a man after God's own heart, and God honored his heart even a thousand years later. I pray you'll commit today to being a man or woman after God's own heart. You'll be blessed—and so will future generations who will be blessed through your faith.

Let's pray:

Father, thank You for sending Jesus to us here on earth, to live and die for us so that we could live with You forever. Help us commit to being men and women after Your own heart, so that we can bless Your heart, and the hearts of those in generations to come. In Jesus' name, Amen.

LESSON 17: WHAT'S THE CAPITAL OF ISRAEL?   JUNE 28

We've been traveling all around the country of Israel during this study, but now we're going to focus on just one city for the remaining lessons: the capital city of Israel. To take a look this incredible place, and to see what the future holds for it, take a look at this short video below. Then read on to learn what happened there in the past and why what's going to happen there in the future is so important to us all.

Watch "What's the Capital of Israel?" (or on ericelder.com).

So what's the capital of Israel? Jerusalem. Jerusalem became the capital of Israel in the year 993 B.C.—about 3,000 years ago—when King David moved from Hebron to Jerusalem. The Bible says:

> *"David was thirty years old when he became king, and he reigned forty years. In Hebron he reigned over Judah seven years and six months, and in Jerusalem he reigned over all Israel and Judah thirty-three years"* (2 Samuel 5:4-5).

Jerusalem also became the spiritual capital of Israel at that time, for soon after King David arrived, he had the Ark of the Covenant brought into the city as well. If you remember from the book of Exodus, the Ark of the Covenant was an ornate wooden box covered with gold which contained the "covenant" between God and the Israelites in the form of the Ten Commandments, inscribed on two stone tablets by the finger of God Himself. God told the Israelites that He would make a dwelling for His name there above the ark, and that from there He would meet with them and speak with them (see Exodus 25:10-22).

So even though God certainly isn't confined to any one location, there was something special about this ark. When David's son, Solomon, built the temple in Jerusalem to house the Ark of the Covenant, Solomon said:

> *"But will God really dwell on earth? The heavens, even the highest heaven, cannot contain You. How much less this temple I have built! Yet give attention to Your servant's prayer and his plea for mercy, O LORD my God. Hear the cry and the prayer that Your servant is praying in Your presence this day. May Your eyes be open toward this temple night and day, this place of which You said, 'My Name shall be there,' so that You will hear the prayer your servant prays toward this place. Hear the supplication of Your servant and of Your people Israel when they pray toward this place. Hear from heaven, Your dwelling place, and when You hear, forgive"* (1 Kings 8:27-30).

Throughout the Bible, God said that He would choose a place for His Name, a place where His presence would rest, and that people should seek Him in that place and worship Him there. For instance, in Deuteronomy 12, God told the Israelites:

> *"You must not worship the LORD your God in their way. But you are to seek the place the LORD your God will choose from among all your tribes to put His Name there for*

His dwelling. To that place you must go; there bring your burnt offerings and sacrifices, your tithes and special gifts, what you have vowed to give and your freewill offerings, and the firstborn of your herds and flocks. There, in the presence of the LORD your God, you and your families shall eat and shall rejoice in everything you have put your hand to, because the LORD your God has blessed you" (Deuteronomy 12:4-7).

So when Solomon built the temple in Jerusalem, people came to worship there from all over, and continued to come for the next thousand years until the time of Christ.

But when Jesus came, things changed. Jesus was, of course, Emmanuel, which means, "God with us." God, through His Son Jesus Christ, came to dwell among His people in real live flesh and blood. As the apostle John said so eloquently:

"The Word became flesh and made His dwelling among us" (John 1:14a).

And God's plan to dwell among His people didn't stop there. He said that He would continue to dwell among His people wherever they lived, even after Jesus' death and resurrection. Jesus talked about these coming changes in a conversation with a woman from Samaria. The woman said:

"Our fathers worshiped on this mountain, but you Jews claim that the place where we must worship is in Jerusalem" (John 4:20).

Jesus responded:

"Believe me, woman, a time is coming when you will worship the Father neither on this mountain nor in Jerusalem. You Samaritans worship what you do not know; we worship what we do know, for salvation is from the Jews. Yet a time is coming and has now come when the true worshipers will worship the Father in spirit and truth, for they are the kind of worshipers the Father seeks. God is spirit, and His worshipers must worship in spirit and in truth" (John 4:21-24).

Less than forty years after Jesus said these words, in the year 70 A.D., Jerusalem was attacked by the Romans and the temple was completely destroyed, never to be rebuilt again.

Jesus foresaw this coming destruction of Jerusalem, and when He did, He wept over the city. The Bible says:

"As He approached Jerusalem and saw the city, He wept over it and said, 'If you, even you, had only known on this day what would bring you peace—but now it is hidden from your eyes. The days will come upon you when your enemies will build an embankment against you and encircle you and hem you in on every side. They will dash you to the ground, you and the children within your walls. They will not leave one stone on another, because you did not recognize the time of God's coming to you'" (Luke 19:41-44).

Although the city was destroyed as Jesus foretold, and the temple along with it, God was not done making His dwelling among men. God said that He would send His Holy Spirit to live within all those who put their faith in Christ. And so it is that now through God's Holy Spirit He makes His dwelling among us. Now all of us can worship Him "in spirit and in truth," just as Jesus said, from anywhere in the world. As the apostle Paul said, now we are God's temple, and God's Spirit lives within each of us (see 1 Corinthians 3:16-17).

But back to Jerusalem, there is no doubt that God still has a special place in His heart for this Holy City, and that He has special plans for it still to come. God showed the apostle John what's to come in the future. John wrote:

"Then I saw a new heaven and a new earth, for the first heaven and the first earth had passed away, and there was no longer any sea. I saw the Holy City, the new Jerusalem, coming down out of heaven from God, prepared as a bride beautifully dressed for her husband. And I heard a loud voice from the throne saying, "Now the dwelling of God is with men, and He will live with them. They will be His people, and God Himself will be with them and be their God. He will wipe every tear from their eyes. There will be no more death or mourning or crying or pain, for the old order of things has passed away" (Revelation 21:1-4).

It seems that God's greatest desire is to dwell among His people, to live with them, talk with them, walk with them, and make His home with them.

From the beginning of its days as the capital of Israel, Jerusalem has a long history of being the place where God dwelt among His people. And according to the Bible, the New Jerusalem will be a place where God will continue to dwell among His people—for the rest of eternity!

Here in the meantime, praise God that, through His Holy Spirit, He can still dwell among us anywhere, anytime, at any moment, day or night, when we put our faith in His Son, Jesus Christ.

If you've already put your faith in Christ and invited His Holy Spirit to come and live within you, I want to encourage you to make the most of it. Worship God in spirit and in truth. Walk with Him. Talk with Him. Meet with Him every day and throughout your day. Recognize that God is with you right now and at all times. Remember that your body is a temple of the Holy Spirit and treat it with the utmost honor and respect. Then let God's Holy Spirit flow freely through your life into the lives of others, letting God use your hands, feet, eyes, ears, and heart as His to those around you. God loves you and He loves the fact that you would let Him come in and make His dwelling within you. Make the most of it!

And if you've never put your faith in Christ, do it today! God wants to make His dwelling within you, as well and give you access to His unlimited love and joy, peace and wisdom, from this day forward. Put your faith in Christ today. Ask Him to forgive you of your sins. Then invite His Holy Spirit to live within you starting today and on into eternity.

Let's pray:

Father, thank You for wanting to come and live with us. It's overwhelming to think that You would want to do that, yet we know that is Your greatest desire. Please, Lord, continue to make Your presence real to us again today, and know that we look forward to living with You forever one day in the New Jerusalem. In Jesus' name, Amen.

LESSON 18: WHAT HAPPENED ON MOUNT MORIAH?   JUNE 29

Mount Moriah sits on what is perhaps the most valuable piece of real estate in the world. If it were for sale, I'm sure the price would be higher than anyone could pay. On some maps, it is marked as the center of the world, out of which everything else emanates. And in some ways, that's probably true. For it was here on Mount Moriah that some of the most important events of history took place—and will take place again in the future. To find out what happened here, take a look at the short video below. Then read on to see how what happened here can make a difference in what can happen in your life as well.

Watch "What Happened on Mount Moriah?" (or on ericelder.com).

So what happened on Mount Moriah? This is where Abraham was going to sacrifice his son Isaac.

It's one of the first stories recorded in the Bible where someone expressed their great faith in God, even in the face of great obstacles.

God had promised Abraham that his descendants would be as numerous as the sand on the seashore and as the stars in the sky. But there was one problem. Abraham didn't have any children. Not even one. And he and his wife believed that all hope was gone. At least until God spoke to them.

But how could God fulfill a promise like this? Yet Abraham believed Him, and God began to deliver on His promise by giving Abraham and Sarah a son from their own bodies.

But then, the tide seemed to turn. After believing God, and seeing the fulfillment of His promise begin, it seemed like God was about to go back on his promise. God told Abraham:

> "Take your son, your only son, Isaac, whom you love, and go to the region of Moriah. Sacrifice him there as a burnt offering on one of the mountains I will tell you about" (Genesis 22:2).

It must have seemed ridiculous. If Abraham did what God said, not only was Abraham's son going to be dead, but so was God's promise. But if Abraham felt any of that, the Bible doesn't record it. It simply says that early the next morning, Abraham saddled his donkey, cut some wood to make the offering, took two servants and his son Isaac, and set off for the place God had told him to go.

As he reached the spot, he built an altar, bound his son and put him on it. He took the knife in his hand, and just as he was about to slay his son, an angel of the Lord called out:

> "Abraham! Abraham!"
>
> "Here I am," he replied.
>
> "Do not lay a hand on the boy," he said. "Do not do anything to him. Now I know that you fear God, because you have not withheld from me your son, your only son." Abraham looked up and there in a thicket he saw a ram caught by its horns. He went over and took the ram and sacrificed it as a burnt offering instead of his son. So Abraham called that place The LORD Will Provide. And to this day it is said, "On the mountain of the LORD it will be provided."
>
> The angel of the LORD called to Abraham from heaven a second time and said, "I swear by myself, declares the LORD, that because you have done this and have not withheld your son, your only son, I will surely bless you and make your descendants as numerous as the stars in the sky and as the sand on the seashore. Your descendants will take possession of the cities of their enemies, and through your offspring all nations on earth will be blessed, because you have obeyed me" (Genesis 22:11b-18).

Abraham had proved himself faithful. And so did God. When all hope seemed to be gone, Abraham still believed God could fulfill His promise, somehow, someway, sometime. And because of Abraham's faith, and God's faithfulness, Abraham's descendants are now counted in the millions, including those living today, and those who have lived over the past 4,000 years since this dramatic event on Mount Moriah.

The Dome of the Rock now stands on Mount Moriah over the massive rock where Abraham prepared to sacrifice Isaac.

It wasn't the only event that took place there. About a thousand years later, King David bought the threshing floor on Mount Moriah to build an altar and stop a plague that God had sent upon the people. When God saw David's faith, He proved Himself faithful again by stopping the plague after three days, just as He said He would.

About a thousand years after that, Jesus walked up to the steps of the temple to teach the multitudes, a temple that was built over this very place where Abraham and David had expressed their faith. He, too, eventually expressed his faith here, by willingly being sentenced to death in the chambers of the Antonia Fortress at the base of the Temple Mount and carrying His cross from there to the hill where He died for all of our sins.

And it was there that Jesus picked up his cross, and carried it to his death, the ultimate sacrifice that stopped the ultimate plague called "sin."

So you can see how this spot has been the site of many acts of faith, from Abraham 4,000 years ago, to David 3,000 years ago, and to Jesus 2,000 years ago. And you can see why this spot has also become priceless to millions, whether their heritage is Jewish, Muslim or Christian.

One day, the Bible says that a river of life will spring up from this spot. It will bring life to all that it touches, even the Dead Sea twenty miles away.

While Mount Moriah may not have been a very peaceful spot over the years, it has been a spot where many acts of faith have played out, and where God has proven Himself to be faithful—over and over again, and where He will one day prove Himself to be faithful yet again.

How does this all relate to you? God loves it when people put their trust in Him, people whose hearts are fully committed to Him, in spite of how things might look around them.

Here's what the Bible says about Abraham:

> "By faith Abraham, when God tested him, offered Isaac as a sacrifice. He who had received the promises was about to sacrifice his one and only son, even though God had said to him, 'It is through Isaac that your offspring will be reckoned'" (Hebrews 11:17-18).

Here's what the Bible says about David:

> "I have found David son of Jesse a man after My own heart; he will do everything I want him to do" (Acts 13:22).

Here's what the Bible says about Jesus:

> "Therefore God exalted Him to the highest place and gave Him the name that is above every name, that at the name of Jesus every knee should bow, in heaven and on earth and under the earth, and every tongue confess that Jesus Christ is Lord, to the glory of God the Father" (Philippians 2:9-11).

And here's what the Bible says about me and you, as written in Hebrews 11:6:

> *"And without faith it is impossible to please God, because anyone who comes to Him must believe that he exists and that He rewards those who earnestly seek Him" (Hebrews 11:6).*

God wants you to have faith in Him, even when everything you see might tell you otherwise. God wants you to believe in Him, to trust in Him, to keep putting your faith in Him, no matter what, at all times, in all situations, believing that He exists, and that He rewards those who earnestly seek Him.

Keep putting your faith in God, and He'll prove Himself faithful to you, just like He proved Himself faithful to Abraham, David, and Jesus, right there on Mount Moriah.

Let's pray:

Father, thank You for showing your faithfulness to those who showed their faithfulness to You. Help us to be faithful to You today as well, believing that You exist, and that You will reward those who earnestly seek You. In Jesus' name, Amen.

LESSON 19: WHAT'S HAPPENING AT THE WESTERN WALL? JUNE 30

The Western Wall, also called the Wailing Wall, is one of the most famous places on earth, but not because of all that has happened there. The Wall is famous because of how close it is to something else. To find out what it's near, and what goes on there every day and why, take a look at this short video below. Then read on to find out how you can do the same thing they're doing at the Western Wall every day, wherever you are on the face of the planet.

Watch "What's Happening at the Western Wall?" (or on ericelder.com).

So what's happening at the Western Wall? People are praying. They come here to pray from all over Jerusalem, from all over Israel, and from all over the world.

I was visiting a friend in New York before my first trip to Israel who said, "When you get to the Western Wall, will you say a prayer for me?" I said I would, even though I knew I could pray for him just as well right there in New York, which I did.

But I also knew why he wanted me to pray for him there, in that spot: because the Western Wall is the closest spot to the Holy of Holies, the place where God chose—out of all the earth—as a dwelling place for His name.

You may have heard this famous quote from the Bible before:

> *"...if My people, who are called by My name, will humble themselves and pray and seek My face and turn from their wicked ways, then will I hear from heaven and will forgive their sin and will heal their land" (2 Chronicles 7:14).*

But you may not remember the context in which those words were spoken. The context was just after Solomon had finished building the Temple in Jerusalem as a place for God's name to dwell. Here's what God said to Solomon when the temple was completed:

> *"When Solomon had finished the temple of the LORD and the royal palace, and had succeeded in carrying out all he had in mind to do in the temple of the LORD and in his own palace, the LORD appeared to him at night and said:*

> *"I have heard your prayer and have chosen this place for Myself as a temple for sacrifices. When I shut up the heavens so that there is no rain, or command locusts to devour the land or send a plague among My people, if My people, who are called by My name, will humble themselves and pray and seek My face and turn from their wicked ways, then will I hear from heaven and will forgive their sin and will heal their land.*
> *Now My eyes will be open and My ears attentive to the prayers offered in this place. I have chosen and consecrated this temple so that My name may be there forever. My eyes and My heart will always be there'"* (2 Chronicles 7:11-16).

So it's easy to see why people would want to go to the Temple Mount to pray still today. God promised that His eyes would be open and His ears attentive to the prayers offered in this special place.

And it's easy to see why the Temple Mount is still such a sought after property in the world: people want to be as close to God as they can get. They want Him to hear their prayers. They want Him to pay attention to their needs. People want God to answer their prayers, so they still try to get as close to the Temple Mount as they can to pray.

And that brings us to why the Western Wall is so important. The Temple Mount has changed hands many times over the years. Solomon's Temple was destroyed and rebuilt again, only to be destroyed again in 70 A.D. The domed building that now stands above the rock of Abraham was at one time a Christian church, with a cross atop the dome. There was also a time when an Israeli flag flew upon the Temple Mount. The dome is now adorned with a golden moon, the symbol of the Muslims who control the Temple Mount today. And as the third holiest site in Islam, it is forbidden for Jews or Christians to pray anywhere upon it—and if they are seen to be praying, they are asked to leave.

So today, the closest spot to the place where the Holy of Holies once was, and where Jews can pray, and Christians as well, for that matter, is the Western Wall, a 187 foot expanse of the wall that can be seen on the southwestern edge of the Temple Mount (the walls of the Temple Mount are not to be confused with the city walls that encircle the entire old city of Jerusalem, which Nehemiah rebuilt, and which are further out).

But what many people don't realize is that the Western Wall extends along the full length of the Temple Mount and can be visited today in its entirety by descending into the rabbinical tunnels, an extensive network of tunnels that are said to extend underneath the entire Temple Mount as well. The tunnels along the Western Wall have been excavated in recent years, and you can go down underground and walk along the entire length of the Western Wall, down to what would have been the street level during the time of Jesus!

It is spectacular to walk along this massive wall at its base, with its huge foundation stones, and there is one spot along the wall that garners particular attention: the spot that is said to be directly across from where the Holy of Holies once stood, the place where the Ark of the Covenant was located (and is shown in the picture at the right, and in video above). It is remarkable to stand there and imagine that this is the closest we can get to the place where God chose for His name to dwell.

Having said all of that, there is a closer spot still where God has since chosen for His name to dwell: within the hearts of all those who have put their faith in His Son, Jesus Christ. As the apostle Paul told the Ephesians:

> "I pray that out of His glorious riches He may strengthen you with power through His Spirit in your inner being, so that Christ may dwell in your hearts through faith" (Ephesians 3:16-17).

If you've put your faith in Christ, God's Spirit lives within you, just as Jesus told the disciples He would:

> "If you love me, you will obey what I command. And I will ask the Father, and He will give you another Counselor to be with you forever—the Spirit of Truth. The world cannot accept Him, because it neither sees Him nor knows Him. But you know Him, for He lives with you and will be in you" (John 14:15-16).

We all long to be close to God. We want to be with Him and know that He is close enough to hear our prayers. A new worship song by Dennis Jernigan, called "Breathe," expresses this strong desire for intimacy with God by saying:

> *"Lean so close that I feel You breathe*
> *Lean so close You quench this thirst in me*
> *Lean so close You loose these chains in me*
> *Set me free… So I can breathe…"*

Imagine, leaning so close to God that you could feel Him breathe! The good news is that if you want to be this close to God, to talk to Him and to be sure that His eyes are upon you and His ears are attentive to your prayers, all you need to do is to put your faith in Christ. If you've already done that, you need look no further than within your own heart to find the place where the Spirit of God Himself now dwells.

Lean close to God today. Feel his breath on your cheek. Let Him whisper the words He longs to tell you, and the words you're probably longing to hear from Him as well: "My child, I love you." Then respond to that love with a few words of your own.

Let's pray:

Father, thank You for coming to dwell among us, both at the Holy of Holies and now within the temple of our own hearts. Lean so close to us so we can hear You, see You, feel You, touch You, and thank You for being there so we can lean upon You as well. In Jesus' name, Amen.

LESSON 20: WHAT HAPPENED AT THE NORTH GATE?   JULY 1

I'd like to tell you a very personal story today. It's about what happened to me at the North Gate of the Temple Mount. But before I tell you my story, I'd like to tell you Ezekiel's story, and what he saw, in a vision from God, at the North Gate of the Temple Mount. It's a beautiful picture of what it will be like when Jesus returns. Take a look at the short video below to see where the northern gates of the Temple once stood.

Watch "What Happened at the North Gate?" (or on ericelder.com).

So what happened at the North Gate? That's where Ezekiel saw a vision of a river of life flowing out from the Temple, bringing life to all that it touched. It was a vision for him, but it will be a reality for us one day, when Jesus returns. You may remember some of Ezekiel's story from when we talked about the Dead Sea, when God showed Ezekiel this river flowing from the Temple and said:

> "Fruit trees of all kinds will grow on both banks of the river. Their leaves will not wither, nor will their fruit fail. Every month they will bear, because the water from the sanctuary flows to them. Their fruit will serve for food and their leaves for healing" (Ezekiel 47:12).

But that wasn't the only vision Ezekiel had of what would happen at the Temple. God had brought him there many times over his years as a prophet to show him what would happen, ranging from bringing judgment on those who had forgotten God, to bringing blessings to those who continued to wait on Him.

God used one of Ezekiel's visions to speak to me one day. I'd like to share that story with you to encourage you that God still speaks today as He did in the days of Ezekiel.

It happened just shortly after I quit my secular job to go into full-time ministry. I felt God was calling me to do something full-time for Him, but I didn't know what. It was only a week or so after I had quit when I felt God calling me to the Holy Land for the first time. As I prayed about the trip, I felt there were two places I should visit in particular: the place where the Temple used to be and the place where Jesus died. I asked God why He wanted me to go to these two places, and I felt He said: "I will reveal Myself to you there."

So I had just finished writing these things down in my journal, which I was using during my prayer time with God and was about to stand up to go on with my day, when I felt God say He wasn't done yet. "Open your Bible," He seemed to say. So I opened it up and began to read the words I saw on the page. It was a passage from Ezekiel, chapter 8:

> "In the sixth year, in the sixth month on the fifth day, while I was sitting in my house and the elders of Judah were sitting before me, the hand of the Sovereign LORD came upon me there. I looked, and I saw a figure like that of a man. From what appeared to be his waist down he was like fire, and from there up his appearance was as bright as glowing metal. He stretched out what looked like a hand and took me by the hair of my head. The Spirit lifted me up between earth and heaven and in visions of God he took me to Jerusalem, to the entrance to the north gate of the inner court, where the idol that provokes to jealousy stood. And there before me was the glory of the God of Israel, as in the vision I had seen in the plain" (Ezekiel 8:1-4).

There I was, thinking about going to the place where the Temple used to be in Jerusalem, and I felt like God was giving me very specific instructions about where to go on the Temple Mount. In Ezekiel's vision, he was picked up and transported to Jerusalem, between earth and heaven (by the hair of his head, no less!), and dropped him off at the entrance to the north gate of the inner court of the temple. It was there that God revealed His glory to Ezekiel.

I pictured my own upcoming flight to Israel, where I would be transported to Jerusalem, between earth and heaven (by plane, thankfully!) and heading to the Temple Mount as well. I felt like God was telling me for some reason to go specifically to the place where the north gate of the inner court of the temple would have been. Although the temple itself no longer exists, the location of the north gate of the inner court was quite likely just to the north of the rock of Abraham, inside the Dome of the Rock, and where the Holy of Holies would have been located.

I stood up with renewed interest in whatever God wanted to reveal to me on this trip, and on that spot in particular. I went home and told my wife about what I felt God was saying, and that if she needed to find me in Israel, to look for me at the north gate on the Temple Mount!

You can imagine my frustration when I finally got to Jerusalem to find out that the Temple Mount was closed. It was the Muslims holy month of Ramadan, and I was told that the Temple Mount was closed off to non-Muslims. Each day of my trip, I went into Jerusalem and tried to get in, but each day I was turned away.

As I sat outside the walls of the city of Jerusalem one day, I read in my Bible about people who were anointed with oil when they went into service for God. I began to wonder if God could somehow anoint me with oil as I was going into service for Him as well. But where could I find someone who would anoint me with oil? I couldn't just walk up to someone on the streets of Jerusalem and ask if they'd do it!

The next morning, however, as I was talking to a shopkeeper about my desire to see the Temple Mount, but my frustration that I kept getting turned away, he told me that if I went to a certain door before 9 a.m., I could get in, for tourists could get in for a few hours that morning if they went before 9. It was just before 9 a.m. when he told me, so I took off running for the door he had described. After a quick search of my backpack, the men watching that door let me in. I had made it onto the Temple Mount!

I headed for the Dome of the Rock and ran into a group of tourists who were going inside. One woman was staying behind to watch their pile of backpacks, shoes, and cameras, as none of those things could be brought into the Dome. She said she would watch my things, too, and I stepped inside the Dome.

I went to the north side of the wide rock inside, where Abraham was supposed to sacrifice Isaac, and I stood and thanked God for bringing me there. I asked Him to reveal anything that He wanted to reveal to me. I was ready to hear it. I noticed a man to my right who had climbed up on the short base of a pillar inside the door to get a better view of the rock from above. I continued my conversation with God, and after waiting a bit longer for anything He might say, but hearing nothing more, I went back outside.

I returned to the woman who was watching our pile of things, and she started to ask me a series of questions: why I had come, what I was doing there, what kind of church did I go to. I tried to politely answer her questions, but I was in a bit of a hurry to go and explore more of the Temple Mount. I was, after all, waiting for God to show up!

But she kept asking questions, and finally said, "My husband's a pastor, and he would love to hear all of this, but he's still inside the Dome. Could you wait till he comes out and tell him what you're doing?" So I waited.

When her husband came out, I saw that he was the same man I had seen inside the Dome on the north side of the rock of Abraham. I shared with him why I had come to Israel, and about some of my recent experiences, such as praying for the healing of a woman who had cancer. He asked, "When you pray for people, do you anoint them with oil?" He said he found it helpful to anoint people with oil when he prayed for them, as it says to do in the book of James.

I was stunned. I had just been praying the day before that God would send someone to anoint me with oil as I began my ministry, and here stood someone who just might do it, right at the place where the north gate of where the inner courts of the Temple would have been! I told them about my prayer and asked if they might pray for me and anoint me with oil for my service to God. They said they'd be glad to, and although they didn't have any with them, they said we could buy some at one of the shops nearby. Then, when their group took their next break from their tour, they'd pray for me.

I followed them as they left the Temple Mount, walking through the actual northern gates of the Temple Mount that are there today. We walked along the Via Dolorosa, the path through the streets that Jesus was said to have taken when He carried His cross to His death. We ended up at the Church of the Holy Sepulcher, the traditional spot where Jesus was said to have been crucified. Then their group took a break.

We went to a nearby shop and bought a small bottle of "Anointing Oil from the Holy Land," and went back inside the church to pray. It was there, at the place where Jesus died, that they—and God—anointed me with oil for the service I had recently begun for Him.

It was a holy moment, as I realized what God had done: He had brought me to the two places He put on my heart to come: the place where the Temple used to be and the place where Jesus died. And it was in those two spots where God revealed Himself to me in a very personal way, showing me how clearly He speaks, and how clearly He answers prayers. And it was in that moment that God ordained me for the ministry that I've now been doing for the past fifteen years.

As I flew home the next day, I thanked God again for speaking so clearly and personally to me, just as He has spoken to people throughout the ages. What an awesome God we serve!

I want to encourage you today to listen carefully for God's voice. He still speaks today, not just about "big" things, but about the everyday things as well. But it takes time to hear Him clearly, and it takes faith to believe that what He says to you is true. Know, however, that God loves those who seek Him, and when you ask for wisdom, He will give it to you generously. As it says in the Bible:

> "If any of you lacks wisdom, he should ask God, who gives generously to all without finding fault, and it will be given to him. But when he asks, he must believe and not doubt, because he who doubts is like a wave of the sea, blown and tossed by the wind" (James 1:5-6).

Take some time to listen to God today. Quiet your heart, open your Bibles, and ask Him your questions. Then get ready to receive whatever He has to say.

Let's pray:

Father, thank You for speaking to Ezekiel centuries ago, and thank You for speaking to us still today, through Your Word and by Your Holy Spirit. We pray that You would again answer the questions that are on our hearts today, and that we would have the faith to believe You when the answers come. In Jesus' name, Amen.

LESSON 21: WHAT HAPPENED AT THE SOUTHERN STEPS?   JULY 2

Neil Armstrong was the first man to walk on the moon, yet he said that walking on the southern steps of the Temple Mount was even more exciting. Why? To find out, take a look at this short video below, then read on to learn how you can have exciting moments like this every day.

Watch "What Happened at the Southern Steps?" (or on ericelder.com).

So what happened at the southern steps? That's where Jesus walked.

When Neil Armstrong visited Israel in 1994, he asked his host if there was a place where Jesus would have walked—without a doubt—2,000 years ago. His host, Archaeologist Meir Ben Dov and the excavator of the Temple Mount and southern walls in Jerusalem, answered that the southern steps were, for sure, the steps that Jesus would have used when He walked up to the Temple.

Mr. Armstrong bent down and kissed the ground, saying that this was an even more exciting moment for him than walking on the moon. If you were to go to Israel today and wanted to walk where you knew Jesus would have walked, you would go to the southern steps.

That's because the southern steps, which have been excavated in recent years, served as the main entrance to the entire Temple Mount complex. And we know from Scripture that Jesus went to the Temple several times throughout His life. The Temple itself has since been destroyed, and the Temple Courts are buried under years of civilization and rebuilding. But the southern steps can still be walked upon today.

The Bible says that Jesus first visited the Temple as a child, when Mary and Joseph brought Him here to be consecrated to the Lord (see Luke 2:21-40). The family then came back to Jerusalem year after year, as was their custom, for the yearly Feast of the Passover (Luke 2:41).

It was on one of these trips that Mary and Joseph lost Jesus as they were traveling back home, thinking that He was traveling back with relatives or friends. After searching for Him for three days, they finally found Him, back in Jerusalem in the Temple Courts. He was sitting among the teachers, listening to them, and asking them questions. Upon hearing that His parents had been anxiously searching for Him, Jesus replied:

> *"Why were you searching for me? Didn't you know I had to be in my Father's house?"* (Luke 2:49).

Then as an adult, Jesus often taught crowds of people there at the Temple Courts. The Bible says that during the final week of His life:

> *"Each day Jesus was teaching at the Temple, and each evening He went out to spend the night on the hill called the Mount of Olives, and all the people came early in the morning to hear Him at the Temple."* (Luke 21:37-38).

If just walking where Jesus walked sounds exciting—like it was to Neil Armstrong—imagine what it would have been like to hear Him speak! Imagine being there in person, back in 33 A.D., and listening to the words that Jesus spoke, coming from His own mouth!

Imagine hearing Jesus tell some of His parables for the very first time, right there in the Temple Courts: the parable of the two sons, or of the ungrateful tenants, or of the wedding banquet of a king.

Imagine Jesus answering people's questions, whether honest and practical questions, or those that were asked by people in order to trap Him, with words that astonished all who heard them and silenced His critics.

Imagine hearing Jesus answer the question about whether or not it was right to pay taxes to Caesar, and then hearing Jesus ask you to take out a coin with Caesar's image on it and saying:

> *"Give to Caesar's what is Caesar's and give to God what is God's"* (Matthew 22:21).

Or imagine Him answering the question about the resurrection of the dead, and whether or not people would really live again after they died, and hearing Jesus say:

> *"Have you not read what God said to you, 'I am the God of Abraham, the God of Isaac, and the God of Jacob'? He is not the God of the dead but of the living"* (Matthew 22:31b-32).

Or imagine Jesus being asked what He thought was the greatest commandment in the law, and hearing Jesus say for the first time:

> *"'Love the Lord your God with all your heart and with all your soul and with all your mind.' This is the first and greatest commandment. And the second is like it: 'Love your neighbor as yourself'"* (Matthew 22:37-38).

Or imagine watching, along with Jesus, as a poor widow passed in front of you and put two very small coins into the Temple offering, and hearing Jesus say:

> *"I tell you the truth, this poor widow has put in more than all the others. All these people gave their gifts out of their wealth; but she out of her poverty put in all she had to live on"* (Luke 21:2-4).

All of these things took place at the Temple Courts. No wonder the Bible says that all those who heard Jesus speak there—even when He was just twelve—were *"...amazed at His understanding and His answers"* (Luke 2:47).

No wonder the Bible says that the crowds who heard Jesus speak at the Temple Courts as an adult were *"...astonished at His teaching"* (Matthew 22:33b).

No wonder the Bible says that when He spoke during the feast that *"...all the people came early in the morning to hear Him at the Temple"* (Luke 21:38).

Maybe you wish you could have been one of those people who got up early in the morning to hear the wisdom of Jesus. The truth is, you *can* be one of those people!

If you'd like to sit at the feet of Jesus and listen to Him speak His words to you, words that are practical and words that answer the honest questions on your heart, you can still do it today. You can pick up a copy of the Bible and read the words of Jesus, as recorded in the books of Matthew, Mark, Luke, and John, recorded by people who heard Him speak those words in person—Matthew, Mark and John—and Luke, who personally and thoroughly researched the stories by asking eyewitnesses who heard Jesus speak to verify their authenticity, people who were still living at the time he wrote his book. Some of you may even have "red-letter Bibles," where the words of Jesus are highlighted in red so that you can find them easier, underscoring the words of this master teacher that were spoken 2,000 years ago.

Thankfully, the words that Jesus spoke back then are just as applicable to our lives today. Jesus isn't a teacher who is now dead and silent. He's just as alive and eager to speak to you today as He was back then. As the Bible says:

> *"Jesus Christ is the same yesterday and today and forever"* (Hebrews 13:8).

What a blessing it is to be able to walk where Jesus walked, as Neil Armstrong did, and what a blessing it would have been to hear Him teach in person at the Temple Courts. But what a blessing it is that we can still come to Him every day, whether early in the morning, throughout the day, or late in the day, and hear the wisdom of God as spoken through Jesus Christ Himself.

Come to Christ again today—and every day—and let Him speak His words of life to you. Let's pray:

Father, thank You for sending Jesus to speak to the crowds at the Temple, and thank You for those who recorded His words so we can continue to hear Him speak to us today. Open our hearts to hear those words as we come to You again today and every day. In Jesus' name, Amen.

LESSON 22: WHAT HAPPENED AT THE POOLS OF BETHESDA? JULY 3

The Pools of Bethesda, just outside the Temple in Jerusalem, were said to have healing powers. But one day, when a man who had been ill for thirty-eight years went to the pools for healing, he discovered the Source of all true healing. To find out what happened that day, take a look at this minute-and-a-half video shot on location at the remains of the pools themselves. Then read on for encouragement that God still heals today. Here's the video...

Watch "What Happened at the Pools of Bethesda?" (or on ericelder.com).

So what happened at the Pools of Bethesda? That's where Jesus healed a man who had been ill for thirty-eight years.

The man had apparently come to the Pools of Bethesda looking to be healed by the waters there. According to local tradition, there were times when an angel of the Lord would stir up the waters in the pools and the first one into the water after such a disturbance would be healed. As a result, the Bible says,

"Here a great number of disabled people used to lie: the blind, the lame, the paralyzed" (John 5:3).

On one of Jesus' visits to Jerusalem, He went to the pools and saw this man lying there who had been sick for thirty-eight years. Jesus asked:

"Do you want to get well?" (John 5:6b).

The man didn't know who was asking him this question, for he simply replied that he had no one to help him into the pool when the water was stirred. Little did he know that he was talking to the One who is the Source of all healing! But he was about to find out. In the next moment, Jesus did for him the miracle that he had waited so long to receive:

"Then Jesus said to him, 'Get up! Pick up your mat and walk.' At once the man was cured; he picked up his mat and walked" (John 5:8).

Jesus is known for many things, but His ability to heal ranks right at the top. The Bible says,

"And wherever He went—into villages, towns or countryside—they placed the sick in the marketplaces. They begged Him to let them touch even the edge of His cloak, and all who touched Him were healed" (Mark 6:56).

As the "Author of life," as Peter called Him, Jesus is the One who knows best how to heal a life. When God designed our bodies, He designed them with healing in mind, knowing that we wouldn't go through life unscathed. When doctors stitch up a wound or administer an antibiotic, they are often using techniques that simply tap into the body's God-given ability to heal itself, helping to stimulate, accelerate, or otherwise facilitate the body's built-in healing processes.

That's why God said to Moses:

"...for I am the Lord who heals you" (Exodus 15:26).

And God is a healing God not just of our bodies, but of our hearts, minds, and souls as well. After healing the man at the pools, Jesus later found him again at the Temple and said to him:

"See, you are well again. Stop sinning or something worse may happen to you." (John 5:14).

Jesus wanted the man to be fully healed, not just in part, but the whole; not just in body, but in heart, mind and soul.

Jesus' healing power extends to all aspects of our lives. In Paul's letter to the Corinthians, he talks about people in the church there who had, in the past, suffered from all kinds of problems: sexual immorality, idolatry, adultery, prostitution, homosexuality, thievery, greediness, drunkenness, slandering and swindling. But Paul goes on to say,

"And that is what some of you were. But you were washed, you were sanctified, you were justified in the name of the Lord Jesus Christ and by the Spirit of our God" (1 Corinthians 6:11).

They were changed, healed, renewed, restored. How? In the name of the Lord Jesus Christ and by the Spirit of our God. All healing—whether physical, mental, spiritual or emotional—comes from God, in the name of the Lord Jesus Christ and through His Holy Spirit.

Even those healings performed by doctors or nurses, psychologists or psychiatrists, mothers or fathers, or friends or family, ultimately come from the God who designed our hearts, souls, minds and bodies.

If you need a healing in your life today, or know someone who does, I want to encourage you, and to encourage them, to come to Jesus, the Author and Sustainer of life itself.

Remember the man who was healed at the pools of Bethesda. Jesus touched him and said, *"'Get up! Pick up your mat and walk.' At once the man was cured; he picked up his mat and walked" (John 5:8).*

Remember the woman who had been bleeding for twelve years, who had run out of money and doctors and all other options. She came to Jesus and said, *"If I just touch His clothes, I will get well."* Then she touched His cloak, her bleeding stopped, and Jesus said, *"Daughter, your faith has healed you. Go in peace and be freed from your suffering" (Mark 5:28, 34).*

Remember King David, who suffered much at the hands of other men—and from his own sins, yet he wrote in the Psalms, "Praise the LORD, O my soul, and forget not all His benefits—who forgives all your sins and heals all your diseases..." (Psalm 103:2-3).

Remember James, the brother of Jesus, who called on those who were sick to come to Jesus in prayer for their healing: "Is any one of you sick? He should call for the elders of the church and have them pray over them, anointing them with oil in the name of the Lord. And their prayer offered in faith will heal the sick, and the Lord will make them well" (James 5:14-15a).

Remember Peter, who healed a crippled man who was begging for money outside the Temple by saying, *"Silver or gold I do not have, but what I have I give you. In the name of Jesus Christ of Nazareth, walk"* (Acts 3:6). Then taking the man by the hand, he helped him up to his feet, which became strong again, and the man went walking and leaping and praising God.

Peter knew that it wasn't his own power or strength that healed the man. He knew that he was just a conduit who reached out to the One True Source of healing: Jesus.

After the healing, Peter said,

> *"Men of Israel, why does this surprise you? Why do you stare at us as if by our own power or godliness we had made this man walk? ... You killed the Author of life, but God raised Him from the dead. We are witnesses of this. By faith in the name of Jesus, this man whom you see and know was made strong. It is Jesus' name and the faith that comes through Him that has given this complete healing to him, as you can all see"* (Acts 3:12,16).

If you're sick, come to Jesus. If you're worn out, come to Jesus. If you've run out of money and doctors and all other options, come to Jesus.

If you're wrestling with unhealthy thoughts, words, or deeds, come to Jesus. If you're worried sick and your emotions are shot, come to Jesus.

As Peter said,

> *"It is Jesus' name and the faith that comes through Him that has given this COMPLETE healing to him, as you can all see."*

"Do you want to get well?" Come to Jesus. Let Him do His healing work in your life. Let's pray:

Father, thank You for being a God who heals. Thank You for wanting to make us whole and complete. Thank You for designing our bodies to heal themselves when possible, for giving us wisdom to facilitate that healing power when not, and for sending us Jesus who we believe can heal us supernaturally at any moment—even after thirty-eight years. In Jesus' name, Amen.

LESSON 23: WHAT'S GOING TO HAPPEN ON THE MOUNT OF OLIVES? JULY 4

The Mount of Olives is only a short walk from the Temple Mount, and from there you can get a beautiful view of the city of Jerusalem. Jesus spent His nights there during the last week of His life, praying, sleeping, and teaching His disciples. But something else is going to happen on the Mount of Olives one day. To find out what, take a look at this short video below. Then read on to find out what you can do today to prepare for what's going to happen there in the future.

Watch "What's Going to Happen on the Mount of Olives?" (or on ericelder.com).

So what's going to happen on the Mount of Olives? That's where Jesus will return.

Jesus often went to the Mount of Olives with His disciples when He was in Jerusalem, perhaps because it was so close to the Temple. It is just across the valley from the Temple

Mount, and only a Sabbath's day's walk from the city (just over half-a mile away, the maximum distance that Jews were allowed to walk on the Sabbath).

It was a convenient spot for Jesus and His disciples to retreat to after teaching at the Temple during the day. The Bible says:

> "Each day Jesus was teaching at the Temple, and each evening He went out to spend the night on the hill called the Mount of Olives..." (Luke 21:36-38).

But Jesus' affinity for the Mount of Olives may not have been simply because of its proximity to the Temple. The Mount of Olives is also the site where the prophet Zechariah said the Lord would appear one day, redeeming those who honored Him and destroying those who didn't:

> "On that day His feet will stand on the Mount of Olives, east of Jerusalem, and the Mount of Olives will be split in two from east to west, forming a great valley, with half of the mountain moving north and half moving south" (Zechariah 14:4).

And it was from the Mount of Olives that Jesus eventually ascended into heaven after His death and resurrection here on earth. As He rose into the sky, two angels appeared to the disciples and said:

> "Men of Galilee, why do you stand here looking into the sky? This same Jesus, who has been taken from you into heaven, will come back in the same way you have seen Him go into heaven." Then they returned to Jerusalem from the hill called the Mount of Olives, a Sabbath day's walk from the city (Acts 1:11-12).

So the Mount of Olives has become famous as the place where the Messiah will first appear, and over 150,000 people have been buried there on that hill—including the prophet Zechariah—in order to be on hand the moment the Messiah arrives.

But you won't have to be on the Mount of Olives to know that Jesus has come back. Jesus taught His disciples what that day would be like, the signs that would precede it, and what they could do now to prepare for it.

Listen to the words of Jesus that He spoke while still here on the earth, words that He spoke, in fact, right there on the Mount of Olives just a few days before His death:

> As Jesus was sitting on the Mount of Olives, the disciples came to Him privately. "Tell us," they said, "when will this happen, and what will be the sign of Your coming and of the end of the age?"
> Jesus answered: "Watch out that no one deceives you. For many will come in My name, claiming, 'I am the Christ,' and will deceive many. You will hear of wars and rumors of wars, but see to it that you are not alarmed. Such things must happen, but the end is still to come. Nation will rise against nation, and kingdom against kingdom. There will be famines and earthquakes in various places. All these are the beginning of birth pains.
> "Then you will be handed over to be persecuted and put to death, and you will be hated by all nations because of me. At that time many will turn away from the faith and will betray and hate each other, and many false prophets will appear and deceive many people. Because of the increase of wickedness, the love of most will grow cold, but he who stands firm to the end will be saved. And this gospel of the kingdom will

be preached in the whole world as a testimony to all nations, and then the end will come....

"At that time if anyone says to you, 'Look, here is the Christ!' or, 'There He is!' do not believe it. For false Christs and false prophets will appear and perform great signs and miracles to deceive even the elect—if that were possible. See, I have told you ahead of time.

"So if anyone tells you, 'There He is, out in the desert,' do not go out; or, 'Here He is, in the inner rooms,' do not believe it. For as lightning that comes from the east is visible even in the west, so will be the coming of the Son of Man....

"No one knows about that day or hour, not even the angels in heaven, nor the Son, but only the Father. As it was in the days of Noah, so it will be at the coming of the Son of Man. For in the days before the flood, people were eating and drinking, marrying and giving in marriage, up to the day Noah entered the ark; and they knew nothing about what would happen until the flood came and took them all away. That is how it will be at the coming of the Son of Man. Two men will be in the field; one will be taken and the other left. Two women will be grinding with a hand mill; one will be taken and the other left.

"Therefore keep watch, because you do not know on what day your Lord will come. But understand this: If the owner of the house had known at what time of night the thief was coming, he would have kept watch and would not have let his house be broken into. So you also must be ready, because the Son of Man will come at an hour when you do not expect Him" (Matthew 24:1-14, 23-27, 36-44).

When I was young, I remember hearing a lot of stories about Jesus. But for some reason, I missed the fact that one day He was going to come back again! When I realized that He was really coming back, my heart leapt! Wow! The same Jesus who had done so many miraculous things was going to be coming again! What a day that would be!

But this wasn't going to be "gentle Jesus, meek and mild" (not that He was ever was that way when He first came either, but that was my impression as a child). This Jesus was going to be coming in power and might, redeeming those who loved Him and destroying those who didn't.

There will be no question on that day about whether Jesus is the Christ or not. His reappearance will be visible simultaneously and instantaneously all around the world. As Jesus said, *"For as lightning that comes from the east is visible even in the west, so will be the coming of the Son of Man."* You won't have to be on the Mount of Olives to know that Jesus is back. You'll know it—no matter where you are in the world!

And when that day comes, Christ wants you to be ready. After teaching His disciples to look for the signs of His coming, Jesus then told three parables, stories that describe what will happen to those who are prepared for His return, and what will happen to those who aren't. If you haven't read them lately, you might want to read them again this week. You can find them in Matthew chapter 25: the parables about the ten virgins, the talents, and the sheep and the goats.

Jesus summarized them like this:

"Who then is the faithful and wise servant, whom the master has put in charge of the servants in his household to give them their food at the proper time? It will be good for that servant whose master finds him doing so when he returns. I tell you the truth, *he will put him in charge of all his possessions. But suppose that servant is wicked and says to himself, 'My master is staying away a long time,' and he then begins to beat his fellow servants and to eat and drink with drunkards. The master of that servant will come on a day when he does not expect him and at an hour he is not aware of. He will cut him to pieces and assign him a place with the hypocrites, where there will be weeping and gnashing of teeth"* (Matthew 24:45-51).

When Jesus returns, He wants to find you with your hearts firmly committed to Him, ready and eagerly desiring His coming, as a bride eagerly desires the coming of her groom.

He wants to find you using the talents He has given you, not squandering away the resources and abilities He has given you, but using them to make a good return on His investment.

He wants to find you doing the things that He's called all of us to do, both spiritually and physically: giving food to the hungry, drink to the thirsty, inviting in strangers, clothing the naked, caring for the sick, and visiting those in prison.

I want to encourage you today to get ready for His return. If your heart's not fully committed to Jesus, make that commitment today. If you know someone whose heart's not fully committed to Jesus, send this message to them and encourage them to make that commitment today.

And if your heart *is* fully committed to Jesus, get ready for His return! Look forward to it! Look forward to the day when He stands again on the Mount of Olives, in the fullness of His glory, coming back to take you to be with Him forever! Fill your hearts with faith today, make a good return on the gifts He has given you, and serve one another wholeheartedly. Remember, as Jesus said, *"...he who stands firm to the end will be saved"* (Matthew 24:13).

Let's pray:

Father, thank You for the reminder that Jesus is coming back again, and that He will one day take us to be with Him forever. Lord, fill our hearts with faith again today, faith that Jesus will indeed come back for us, and faith that will inspire us to keep doing Your work here on earth right up until that day comes. We put our faith, hope and trust in You again today. In Jesus' name, Amen.

LESSON 24: WHAT HAPPENED AT THE GARDEN OF GETHSEMANE?   JULY 5

The Garden of Gethsemane is made up of a grove of olive trees found at the foot of the Mount of Olives. The word "gethsemane" means "oil press," and this garden likely served as the location of an ancient olive press, a device used to squeeze the oil out of olives. But another kind of pressing took place on the night before Jesus died. It was, perhaps, His most difficult trial on earth. To find out what happened that night, and how He faced it, take a look at this short video below. Then read on to find out how God can give you the strength to pass the trials you face as well.

Watch "What Happened at the Garden of Gethsemane?" (or on ericelder.com).

So what happened at the Garden of Gethsemane? This is where Jesus went to pray the night He was betrayed.

If you remember the story, the trial He faced that night was so difficult that He told His disciples He was *"overwhelmed with sorrow to the point of death"* (Mark 14:34a).

When Jesus tried to get His disciples to stay awake with Him during the night, they couldn't do it. This was a trial He was going to have to face without them.

But He didn't have to face it alone. He faced it together with God His Father in prayer. The words Jesus prayed that night are an encouragement to me, as they have been to people for thousands of years, people who have faced trials of many kinds. Jesus said:

> "My Father, if it is possible, may this cup be taken from Me. Yet not as I will, but as You will" (Matthew 25:42).

You may have heard these words so many times that they've lost their freshness, but I'd like to remind you today of the power contained within them. They are words that can bring you peace and restore life to your soul once again no matter what kind of situation you might be facing.

First, know that when you face a trial of any kind, you're not facing it alone. When you get to that point where you feel so alone that even your closest friends seem unable to walk with you through it any further, know that God is still there to walk through it with you.

When Jesus prayed that night, He went to His Father not just once or twice, but three times. Before each time of prayer, He asked His disciples to stay awake and keep watch for Him. But the fact that they couldn't do it didn't mean that His friends didn't love Him, or that they didn't want to help Him. They wanted to do whatever He asked, but in the end, they simply couldn't do it. Jesus knew their hearts were still with Him nonetheless, and He said:

> "The spirit is willing, but the body is weak"
> (Matthew 26:41).

But even though Jesus' disciples fell asleep, God never did. The Bible says that God never slumbers nor sleeps (see Psalm 121:4). Each time Jesus found the disciples sleeping, He returned to God in prayer.

Second, know that it's not unspiritual to plead with God for that which you think is best. Three times, Jesus said:

> "My Father, if it is possible, may this cup be taken from Me."

Jesus didn't want to face what lay ahead of Him. He pleaded with God to take it away, to change His course, or to show Him another path. It wasn't that Jesus wanted to disobey His Father's will, but neither did He hide the fact that He'd rather do it another way if possible!

The anguish that Jesus faced that night was intense, so intense that Luke says:

> "His sweat was like drops of blood falling to the ground" (Luke 22:44).

The pressure of it all, the squeezing that He felt must have been nearly unbearable. The pain and twisting he felt may have been mirrored in the gnarled and twisted olive trees found in the Garden of Gethsemane itself, some of which are over 1,000 years old—and some could have even been alive at the time of Christ, as olives tree can, remarkably, live several *thousand* years.

Jesus knew that the pain ahead could be severe, and He didn't hesitate to pray that His Father would make another way. If it wasn't "unspiritual" for Jesus to pray this way, then I wouldn't think it would be unspiritual for you to ask for it either.

But third, know that whatever happens in the end, you can trust God to work all things for good, when you truly commit your will to His. Madame Guyon was a Christian who suffered much during her lifetime in France in the 1700's. Yet through it all she was able to find the peace of God by surrendering her will to God's. She wrote:

> *"All your concerns go into the hand of God. You forget yourself, and from that moment on you think only of Him. By continuing to do this over a long period of time, your heart will remain unattached; your heart will be free and at peace! How do you practice abandonment? You practice it daily, hourly and by the moment. Abandonment is practiced by continually losing your own will in the will of God—by plunging your will into the depths of His will, there to be lost forever!" (Madame Guyon, Experiencing the Depths of Jesus Christ).*

While it is important to remember that God has given us free will—the will or desire do that which we want—it's also important to remember that God has a will, too. While God wants to give you the desires of your heart, He also has desires on *His* heart, desires which often go way beyond ours!

I am a firm believer that God wants to bless you, to prosper you, and to make you healthy and wealthy and wise. The Scriptures are full of stories of how God has come through for His people, blessing them with healing and prosperity, both physically and spiritually, and pouring out His wisdom upon them. But I am also a firm believer that God's blessings can often exceed our own, but sometimes we can only see them as blessings when we look at them through eyes of faith.

I once heard a long-time and well-respected Christian leader say that when he looked back on his life, it turned out that the times he thought were his mountaintop turned out to be the valleys, and the times he thought he was going through the valleys turned out to be the mountain tops. God has a way of bringing good from every situation, when we trust Him to do His will in all things.

Know that God wants to bless you, that He wants to bless others through you, and that you can trust Him in all things, at all times, to work His will, in His ways. Know that when He calls you to face your own Garden of Gethsemane, you won't face it alone. You'll be in good company, the likes of which includes Jesus Christ Himself, the One who trusted His Father inherently and said with His whole heart:

> *"My Father, if it is possible, may this cup be taken from Me. Yet not as I will, but as You will."*

I pray that you'll be able to do the same.

Let's pray:

Father, thank You for never leaving us alone, thank You for giving us our own free will, and thank You for giving us the confidence that Your will always is always better than our own. Help us to come to You with complete abandonment so that we can experience the fullness of Your peace, Your joy, and Your life that will come to us when we do. In Jesus' name, Amen.

LESSON 25: WHAT HAPPENED AT THE HOUSE OF CAIAPHAS?   JULY 6

Caiaphas was the high priest at the time when Jesus was betrayed, and it was to Caiaphas' house that Jesus was brought and accused of blasphemy against God. To see the dungeon of this house, and the adjoining pit where prisoners were lowered into by a rope to prevent them from escaping, take a look at this short video below. Then read on to find out what else happened that night at Caiaphas' house, and how God can restore, redeem, and forgive you, too, if you've ever felt that you've done something against Him.

Watch "What Happened at the House of Caiaphas?" (or on ericelder.com).

So what happened at the House of Caiaphas? That's where Peter denied Jesus three times.

After Jesus was betrayed by Judas in the Garden of Gethsemane, the guards brought Jesus to the house of Caiaphas, the high priest. Jesus was taken inside and tried for blasphemy, while Peter waited in the courtyard outside to find out what was going to happen.

But while Peter was waiting, some people in the crowd recognized him as having been with Jesus. Apparently overcome by fear, Peter denied that he even knew Jesus, not just once or twice, but three times. The Bible says:

> *Now Peter was sitting out in the courtyard, and a servant girl came to him. "You also were with Jesus of Galilee" she said.*
> *But he denied it before them all. "I don't know what you're talking about," he said.*
> *Then he went out to the gateway, where another girl saw him and said to the people there, "This fellow was with Jesus of Nazareth."*
> *He denied it again, with an oath: "I don't know the man!"*
> *After a little while, those standing there went up to Peter and said, "Surely you are one of them, for your accent gives you away."*
> *Then he began to call down curses on himself and he swore to them, "I don't know the man!" (Matthew 26:69-74).*

This was, perhaps, the worst night in Jesus' life. But it was also probably the worst night in Peter's life as well. When Peter realized what he had done, the Bible says, *"he went outside and wept bitterly."*

Looking back on the situation, we can forgive Peter for what he did that night—for under the same circumstances, who knows what any of us might have done? And yet I think it would have been harder for Peter to forgive himself. For it was Peter who, just a few hours earlier, at the Passover dinner, said to Jesus:

> *"Even if all fall away on account of You, I never will…. Even if I have to die with You, I will never disown You" (Matthew 26: 33, 35).*

But Jesus knew what Peter was going to do, and mercifully He told Peter ahead of time, speaking words of restoration to Peter even before he sinned. What a gracious Friend and Lord.

Here's what Jesus said to Peter, also known as Simon, earlier in the night:

> *"Simon, Simon, Satan has asked to sift you as wheat. But I have prayed for you, Simon, that your faith may not fail. And when you have turned back, strengthen your brothers" (Luke 22:31, 32).*

Jesus knew that all the disciples would fall away from Him that night, including Peter. But Jesus came to Peter specifically to let him know that He was praying for Him that his faith wouldn't fail. Then He encouraged Peter to strengthen his brothers when he did turn back.

A church has now been built over the House of Caiaphas. It has been named in honor of Saint Peter and is called "The Church of Saint Peter in Gallicantu"—although I'm not sure that Peter would prefer the honor, since "gallicantu" means "cock-crow" in Latin, a reminder of the words Jesus spoke to Peter earlier that night:

> "I tell you the truth, this very night, before the rooster crows, you will disown me three times" (Matthew 26:34).

But then again, Peter may truly appreciate the honor, for even though it showed his weakness, it also showed Christ's strength: to restore those who have fallen far, far from their faith. Jesus' restoration of Peter continued a short time later on the beach at the Sea of Galilee when, after Jesus died and rose again from the dead, He appeared yet again to the disciples.

Taking Peter aside for a very personal conversation, Jesus asked Peter three times if Peter loved Him. The Bible says:

> When they had finished eating, Jesus said to Simon Peter, "Simon son of John, do you truly love me more than these?"
> "Yes, Lord," he said, "You know that I love You."
> Jesus said, "Feed My lambs."
> Again Jesus said, "Simon son of John, do you truly love me?"
> He answered, "Yes, Lord, You know that I love You."
> Jesus said, "Take care of My sheep."
> The third time He said to him, "Simon son of John, do you love me?"
> Peter was hurt because Jesus asked him the third time, "Do you love me?" He said, "Lord, You know all things; You know that I love You."
> Jesus said, "Feed My sheep" (John 21:15-17).

It's as if Jesus was giving Peter a chance to redeem himself, saying that He loved Jesus three times, perhaps to counteract the three times had Peter denied Him. And the restoration took hold, for Peter went on to feed Jesus' sheep in a powerful way, leading the church in Jerusalem for the rest of his life, proclaiming Jesus' name everywhere he went, and facing threats of death without fear from those who opposed his message.

Perhaps you've felt like Peter before on the night that he denied Jesus. Perhaps you've felt you've done something so horrible, at least in your mind, that you believe Jesus could never forgive you. Maybe you've cheated or lied or stolen. Maybe you've had an affair or betrayed your family or friends. Maybe you've denied Christ in ways that only you and He could fully comprehend.

If so, you might wonder if Jesus could ever forgive you, restore you, and use you ever again.

If that's the case, I want to remind you today that Jesus knew about Peter's sins even before he committed them. And He knows about yours and mine. And still, He was willing to die for Peter and you and me, even while we were still involved in our sins. That's the way that the Bible says God demonstrates His love for us:

> "But God demonstrates His own love for us in this: While we were still sinners, Christ died for us" (Romans 5:8).

If you're wrestling with the idea of forgiveness, and whether or not God can or will forgive you of your sins, I pray today that God will show you His unsurpassing love. I pray that these words from the Bible will wash over you. And I pray that you'll know that if you ask God for forgiveness, and put your faith in Christ, that He will indeed forgive you, removing your sins from you as far as the east is from the west, and remembering them no more.

As the Bible says:

> "If we confess our sins, He is faithful and just and will forgive us our sins and purify us from all unrighteousness" (1 John 1:9).
>
> "…as far as the east is from the west, so far has He removed our transgressions from us" (Psalm 103:12).
>
> "For I will forgive their wickedness and will remember their sins no more" (Hebrews 8:12).

While the House of Caiaphas may stand as a reminder of Peter's worst possible sin in his life, it also stands as a beacon of hope for all those need a reminder that Christ can restore, redeem, and forgive them, too.

Let's pray:

Father, thank You for making a way for us to come back to You when we've sinned. Give us the boldness to come back to You again today, leaving our past behind, and walking ahead in the calling that You have on each one of our lives. In Jesus' name, Amen.

LESSON 26: WHAT HAPPENED ON THE VIA DOLOROSA? JULY 7

The Via Dolorosa is a path that winds its way through the streets of Jerusalem, and upon which millions have walked over the years. Why? Because another Man walked this path one day—the most painful day of His life. To see what the path looks like today, and find out why it's called the Via Dolorosa, take a look at this short video below. Then read on to find out how God can give you the strength to get through the painful days in your life as well.

Watch "What Happened on the Via Dolorosa?" (or on ericelder.com).

So what happened on the Via Dolorosa? That's the path that Jesus took as He carried His cross to His crucifixion.

The words "via dolorosa" are Latin for "the way of suffering." And while the Via Dolorosa is a path that many people have taken over the years, not many people ever really want to take the "way of suffering" in life. Suffering goes against human nature, and pain is usually a God-given indicator to let you know that something is wrong and needs to be fixed.

But there are times when God may call you to take a path that leads directly into pain—not because He wants you to suffer, but because He has something better in mind for you on the other side of the pain.

Examples abound:

– Like a pregnant woman who has to endure nine months of labor and the pain of childbirth in order to experience the joy of holding her newborn baby in her arms,

– Or like a teenage girl who has to break up with her boyfriend because she wants to remain pure for her future husband,

– Or like a man with a gash in his arm who has to endure the cleansing and stitching of the wound so that his flesh can eventually be healed.

Jesus showed us the key to making it through times of suffering like these: by keeping your eyes on the prize. As the Bible says:

> "Let us fix our eyes on Jesus, the Author and Perfecter of our faith, who for the joy set before Him endured the cross, scorning its shame, and sat down at the right hand of the throne of God. Consider Him who endured such opposition from sinful men, so that you will not grow weary and lose heart" (Hebrews 12:2-3).

It was for the joy set before Jesus that He was able to endure the cross. If there was any other way, Jesus would have taken it. He said as much in the Garden of Gethsemane the night before He had to walk down the Via Dolorosa. He prayed:

> "My Father, if it is possible, may this cup be taken from Me. Yet not as I will, but as You will" (Matthew 25:42).

While none of us wants to enter into pain and suffering voluntarily—not even Jesus—He showed us how to do it when the time comes for us to enter into it.

He kept His eyes on the prize. When the guards came to take Him away, He went. When they asked Him to carry His cross, He carried it. And when He could carry it no longer by Himself, God sent someone else to carry it for Him:

> "Carrying His own cross, He went out to the place of the Skull (which in Aramaic is called Golgotha)". (John 19:17). "As they were going out, they met a man from Cyrene, named Simon, and they forced him to carry the cross" (Matthew 27:32).

You can still see the place marked on the Via Dolorosa where Simon of Cyrene may have taken up Jesus' cross for Him. It's one of fourteen "stations of the cross" that are marked out along the path, stations that are replicated in many churches throughout the world. If people want to remember all that Jesus did for them in those last few hours of His life, they can walk around the perimeter of the church and stop to meditate at any of these fourteen stations, just as they can on the real Via Dolorosa in Jerusalem.

Walking along the Via Dolorosa is a reminder not only of the suffering that Jesus endured for us, but also of the suffering that He sometimes calls us to endure for Him. As Jesus told His disciples:

> "If anyone would come after Me, he must deny himself and take up his cross daily and follow Me. For whoever wants to save his life will lose it, but whoever loses his life for Me will save it" (Luke 9:23-24).

Although no one ever wants to suffer, Jesus' words are a reminder that some things are worth suffering for, that there is a prize awaiting those who endure it to the end, and that God wants you to have it.

The best way to go through suffering is to make sure you set your eyes on the prize. But it's also important to make sure you're setting your eyes on the right prize. There's nothing worse than enduring pain and suffering, only to find that what you've been waiting for all along has been lost in the process.

If your hope is set on having the perfect family, and then something happens to destroy that perfection, you'll be disappointed. If you're working your hardest to get a promotion, then the promotion doesn't come, you'll be upset. If you give up your dreams in order to help someone else fulfill theirs, but then they blow it and waste all that you've given up for them, you might wonder if it was worth it.

Sometimes these disappointments come because our eyes weren't on the right prize in the first place. Even Peter, who may have expected Jesus to ride into Jerusalem, overthrow the Romans and setup His new kingdom, was willing to die for Jesus as He ascended to His throne. But when Peter found out that Jesus had been arrested, and was likely going to be sentenced to death, his disappointment was evident. Instead of standing up for Jesus anymore, he denied that he even knew him. Perhaps it was because his eyes were on the wrong prize for the moment.

But God honored Peter still, just like He honors all those who love Him and who are called according to His purpose. He eventually showed Peter that Jesus reigned in a kingdom whose authority went beyond Jerusalem, beyond the Romans, and extended over the entire earth. It was better than Peter could have ever expected. We're told that Peter eventually did give up his life for Jesus, being crucified on a cross upside-down. But this time he had his eyes on the right prize, and he was willing to walk down the path of suffering to get it.

As much as God wants to relieve you of much of the suffering you'll face in life, He also wants you to know that some things are achieved only by going through it.

God wants you to trust Him. He wants you to trust that He is able to do *"immeasurably more than all we could ask or imagine"* (Ephesians 3:20a). Keep your eyes on the prize, and if you can't see the prize, then keep your eyes on Jesus. In the end, it will all be worth it.

Let's pray:

Father, thank You for Jesus' example, that we can follow in His steps. Help us to trust that the suffering in our life is worth it, when we entrust our lives completely to You. Help us to take up our cross daily and be willing to die for you, so that we can find the life that You've wanted us to have all along. In Jesus' name, Amen.

LESSON 27: WHAT HAPPENED AT GOLGOTHA? JULY 8

Golgotha means "the place of the skull." It's not a very happy-sounding name, and what took place here was most likely even more gruesome than the name suggests. But on the other hand, what took place here at Golgotha is what has made it the holiest site in all of Christendom. To find out what happened here, and why it matters to so many people, take a look at this short video below. Then read on to find out how God can use the sadness of what happened at Golgotha to bring incredible joy to your life today.

Watch "What Happened at Golgotha?" (or on ericelder.com).

So what happened at Golgotha? That's where Jesus died, was buried, and rose again from the dead.

When Jesus was arrested and sentenced to death, He and those who were to be executed with Him walked through the streets of Jerusalem, carrying their crosses when they could, and having others carry their crosses for them when they couldn't. Eventually they came to the execution site. The Bible says:

> They came to a place called Golgotha (which means The Place of the Skull). There they offered Jesus wine to drink, mixed with gall; but after tasting it, He refused to drink it. When they had crucified Him, they divided up His clothes by casting lots. And sitting down, they kept watch over Him there (Matthew 26:33-36).

Golgotha was undoubtedly a horrific place, just outside the walls of the city at the time of Christ. It seems to have gotten its name either because of all the crucifixions that took place there, or because the hill itself actually resembled a skull. Either way, the hill called Golgotha was a picture of death.

But the day that Christ died there, something changed. When Christ died on the cross, Golgotha became a picture of life, filled with the beauty of sacrificial love.

There's a song that explains how Golgotha—and the cross of Christ—could come to represent such an unusual mixture of death and life. George Bennard said it this way in his song, *The Old Rugged Cross*:

> *On a hill far away stood an old rugged cross,*
> *the emblem of suffering and shame;*
> *and I love that old cross where the dearest*
> *and best for a world of lost sinners was slain.*
> *In that old rugged cross, stained with blood so divine,*
> *a wondrous beauty I see,*
> *for 'twas on that old cross Jesus suffered and died,*
> *to pardon and sanctify me.*

This is why crosses are so prevalent in jewelry, churches, and other holy places. It's not because Christians have some perverse fascination with death, like wearing little guillotines around their necks on a chain. Jesus didn't express His love to us by dying on a guillotine. He expressed it by dying on a cross. And it's the love that Christ expressed for us when He died on the cross that we celebrate as Christians, and that's why we make so much of His cross.

It is both an "emblem of suffering and shame," and also a "wondrous beauty" to behold, all at the same time.

There are two spots in Jerusalem that are considered potential locations of Christ's crucifixion. One is the Garden Tomb, which was discovered in 1848 and which I highlighted in the introduction of this book. The other is the Church of the Holy Sepulchre ("sepulchre" means "tomb" in Latin) and has been the traditional site of the crucifixion since the 1st and 2nd century. Today I'd like to focus on the Church of the Holy Sepulchre.

For those interested, the church itself was first built and dedicated in 335 A.D. by Helena, the mother of Constantine, after she had been shown this site by the believers in Jerusalem at that time. The church has undergone many changes over the years, but the location has remained the same.

When I walked into the Church of the Holy Sepulchre for the first time, and up the stairs to the right that led to the top of the small hill called Golgotha over which the church was built, I was overcome with emotion. It wasn't because of anything I saw there—for it was filled with candles and tourists and objects that glittered with gold. I was overcome with emotion because of what had happened there.

I dropped to my knees. I thanked God for all He had done for me there. And I cried.

I knew that Jesus wasn't the One who should have died on the cross that day. He was totally innocent. It should have been me. It was me who had sinned, and it was me who should have had to pay the price for those sins. But Jesus did it for me, of His own free will, as a demonstration of His love for me.

He could have called twelve legions of angels to rescue Him if He had wanted, as He told Peter in the Garden of Gethsemane (see Matthew 26:53). But He didn't.

The fact that Jesus stepped in to pay for my sins with His life has been, and still is, the greatest expression of love I have ever felt in my life. While others have loved me dearly, like my family and friends, Jesus is the only one who could have stepped in and did for me what He did: fully forgiving me of my sins.

When I got back up from my knees, I walked downstairs again and to the other side of the massive church, to the spot where they believe Jesus was buried in a tomb nearby. The walls and ceiling of the tomb have been destroyed over the years, as the church has changed hands and been ransacked many times since then. Only a plain slab of rock remains of the place where they believe He was lain, and that is housed in a small chapel under the great dome of the church.

While there's little to see there, of course, for neither Christ nor much of the tomb are there, the site is vivid enough in the memories of those who are familiar with the story to recreate in their minds the scene of what happened there. As it says in the Bible:

> "Later, Joseph of Arimathea asked Pilate for the body of Jesus. Now Joseph was a disciple of Jesus, but secretly because he feared the Jews. With Pilate's permission, he came and took the body away. He was accompanied by Nicodemus, the man who earlier had visited Jesus at night. Nicodemus brought a mixture of myrrh and aloes, about seventy-five pounds. Taking Jesus' body, the two of them wrapped it, with the spices, in strips of linen. This was in accordance with Jewish burial customs. At the place where Jesus was crucified, there was a garden, and in the garden a new tomb, in which no one had ever been laid. Because it was the Jewish day of Preparation and since the tomb was nearby, they laid Jesus there." (John 19:38-42).

And then, a few days later:

> After the Sabbath, at dawn on the first day of the week, Mary Magdalene and the other Mary went to look at the tomb.
> There was a violent earthquake, for an angel of the Lord came down from heaven and, going to the tomb, rolled back the stone and sat on it. His appearance was like lightning, and his clothes were white as snow. The guards were so afraid of him that they shook and became like dead men.
> The angel said to the women, "Do not be afraid, for I know that you are looking for Jesus, who was crucified. He is not here; He has risen, just as He said. Come and see the place where He lay. Then go quickly and tell His disciples: 'He has risen from the dead and is going ahead of you into Galilee. There you will see Him.' Now I have told you" (Matthew 28:1-7).

So you can see why this place has become such a sacred spot to those who claim Jesus as their Lord. While the ravages of time, battles, earthquakes, and fires have taken their toll on the Church of the Holy Sepulchre, the events that made this place so holy are no less compelling today than they were when they first took place.

It is not the church itself that has brought millions of people like me here to visit it. It is the realization that what happened here was real, and that God really did love us so much that He sent His one and only Son to die for us so that we could put our faith in Him and live forever.

As incredible it is to be able to be able to go to Jerusalem and touch the ground where Jesus died and rose again, if there was one thing that I could encourage you to do in your lifetime, it wouldn't be to go to Jerusalem. It would be to go to Jesus, to put your faith in Him who died on the cross for your sins, rose again from the dead, and who now calls you to live your life for Him, following Him here on earth and on into heaven.

If there's sin in your life, drop it now at the foot of His cross. If you're involved in lying or stealing, gossiping or cheating, pre-marital or extra-marital or any other kind of sinful sex, turn away from it today and turn back again. If you're burying your gifts in the sand, saving them for no one and nothing in particular, dig them out and put them to work for the kingdom of God. You'll be blessed when you do and so will those around you.

Most of all, you'll be able to express your love back to Christ, the One who expressed His love for you—and for all to see—there on the hill called Golgotha.

Let's pray:

Father, thank You for sending Jesus to die for our sins, and for giving us the chance to be forgiven when we put our faith in Him. Thank You for filling us with Your Holy Spirit, to enable us to do the work here on earth that You've called us to do. And thank You for promising to take us to be with You in heaven when our life on earth is over, where we can live with You forever. In Jesus' name, Amen.

LESSON 28: WHAT HAPPENED AT THE UPPER ROOM? JULY 9

The Upper Room is perhaps best known as the location of Jesus' last supper with His disciples. But something else happened in the Upper Room just fifty days after Jesus rose from the dead, something Jesus told them to expect and to wait for. To find out what happened, take a look at this short video below. Then read on to find out what God wants you to do with all the things that you've learned about Him!

Watch "What Happened at the Upper Room?" (or on ericelder.com).

So what happened at the Upper Room? That's where the Holy Spirit came at Pentecost. God's Spirit flowed into the people gathered there, causing them to praise God in all kinds of languages. As a result of this outpouring of the Holy Spirit, over 3,000 people put their faith in Christ.

It wasn't something that Peter and the other disciples could have done on their own, but God used their voices to reach out to people, who came from all over the world at the time, so that they could hear all that Christ had done for them.

After Jesus rose from the dead, He appeared again to the disciples and over five hundred others throughout Jerusalem for a period of forty days. On one of these occasions, Jesus said:

"Do not leave Jerusalem, but wait for the gift My Father promised, which you have heard Me speak about. For John baptized with water, but in a few days you will be baptized with the Holy Spirit. ... You will receive power when the Holy Spirit comes

on you; and you will be My witnesses in Jerusalem, and in all Judea and Samaria, and to the ends of the earth" (Acts 1:4-5, 8).

So when Jesus went up into heaven, the disciples went back to the room where they were staying. Luke called it an "upper room" (Acts 1:13, KJV), just as he had done when describing the place where they had eaten their last supper (see Luke 22:12). It was here, apparently, that:

> "They all joined together constantly in prayer, along with the women and Mary the mother of Jesus, and with His brothers" (Acts 1:14).

About ten days later, on the fiftieth day since Jesus rose from the dead (and the day of Pentecost, which comes from the Greek word for "fifty"), God sent His Holy Spirit, just as Jesus promised:

> "When the day of Pentecost came, they were all together in one place. Suddenly a sound like the blowing of a violent wind came from heaven and filled the whole house where they were sitting. They saw what seemed to be tongues of fire that separated and came to rest on each of them. All of them were filled with the Holy Spirit and began to speak in other tongues as the Spirit enabled them" (Acts 2:1).

As they spoke, others began to hear them praising God in their own languages, people from all different parts of the world who had come to Jerusalem for the festivals. Some were amazed, but others thought they had just been drinking too much wine.

Peter, who had denied Jesus just a few weeks earlier, stood up with the other disciples, and spoke to the crowd:

> "Fellow Jews and all of you who live in Jerusalem, let me explain this to you; listen carefully to what I say. These men are not drunk, as you suppose. It's only nine in the morning!" (Acts 2:14-15).

He went on to say that this was the work of the Holy Spirit, whom the prophet Joel said would be poured out on the people in the last days.

Peter spoke about Jesus and how, even though Jesus had done many signs and wonders and miracles in their presence, they still handed Him over to be crucified. After telling them at length from the Scriptures who Jesus was and what they had done to Him, they were all cut to the heart. They cried out to Peter and the other apostles:

> "Brothers, what shall we do?"
> Peter replied, "Repent and be baptized, every one of you, in the name of Jesus Christ for the forgiveness of your sins. And you will receive the gift of the Holy Spirit. The promise is for you and your children and for all who are far off—for all whom the Lord our God will call."
> With many other words he warned them; and he pleaded with them, "Save yourselves from this corrupt generation." Those who accepted his message were baptized, and about three thousand were added to their number that day (Acts 2:37-41).

It's a powerful story on many fronts:

- *What Jesus said would happen did happen,*

- *The same Peter who denied Jesus earlier now proclaimed His name to thousands,*
- *The Spirit came in a way that was both astounding and perplexing to those who saw it,*
- *About 3,000 put their faith in Christ and were baptized in a single day.*

And that was just the beginning. In the days that followed, the disciples continued to do more wonders and miraculous signs:

> "And the Lord added to their number daily those who were being saved" (Acts 2:47b).

Soon, those who followed Christ were taking the gospel beyond Jerusalem to Judea and Samaria and to the ends of the earth, just as Jesus said they would.

What does this all mean to you? Well, if you've never put your faith in Christ, do it today, just like those who heard the message on the day of Pentecost did! And if you've already put your faith in Christ, tell others about it so they can put their faith in Christ, too!

When we were in Israel, we had a local Israeli guide who took us from place to place and taught us many things about the places that we were seeing. On the final day, our guide said, "Today, my job is finished. Tomorrow, yours begins. Your job is to go back and tell others what you have learned."

Isn't that the way God loves to work? God could, if He wanted to, put some kind of cosmic loudspeakers in the sky, telling everyone that He exists, that He loves them, and that He wants them to leave their sins and come back into a relationship with Him. (And in many ways, He has already done this—see Psalm 19:1-4 or Romans 1:18-20.)

But God's preferred method is to use the voices of people—yours and mine—to tell others about His love for them, and to share with them everything they have heard and learned and known to be true.

As we near the end of this devotional tour of Israel, I wanted to remind you of why God wanted to teach you all that you've learned about Him so far. First of all, it's for you, so that You will know Him better and fall in love with Him more deeply. But secondly, it's for you to share with others, so they may know Him better and fall in love with Him more deeply, too.

As our Israeli guide said to us, I want to say to you: "Today, my job ends. Tomorrow, yours begins!" If you're not sure how to share what you've learned with others, here are a few ideas.

1) *Ask God to pour out His Holy Spirit upon you in ways that you may have never known before, so that You can proclaim His name to those around you. How can this help? The same way it helped Peter, who went from being afraid to even tell anyone that He knew Christ to being able to proclaim His name before thousands.*

2) *Study your Bible deeply, every day, so that you may know with confidence the truth of what you believe. Find a good study Bible, with footnotes and commentary if possible, to help you grow in the knowledge of all that God wants to say to you. Remember, too, that it's not just a time to study, but a time to spend with the One who created you, who knows you best, and who loves you more than anyone else in the world.*

3) Start sharing what you've learned so far about Christ. Whether it's sharing a simple comment or two on someone's Facebook page about God's love for them, or taking an evangelism class at a local church so that you can sharpen what and how you share with others, look for and take the opportunities God gives you to let others know about your own relationship with Him so that they can grow in their relationship with Him.
4) Share the messages in this book with others! Point them to our website at www.theranch.org, or give them copies of this book! These resources were created to help bring the Bible to life for as many as people as possible.

While I loved going to Israel so that I could learn more about Christ for myself, I also loved going to Israel so that I could share more about Christ with others. My prayer is that you will do the same.

Whether you go to Israel in person, or experience it through the Bible and books like these, I pray that you will be filled with God's Holy Spirit to the point of overflowing, so that whatever God pours out onto you will be flow out onto to others, bringing joy and life to you, to them, and to the God who created us all.

Let's pray:

Father, thank You for pouring out Your Holy Spirit on those who gathered together for prayer in Jerusalem. We pray that You will pour out Your Holy Spirit on us again today so that we may lead others into a deeper relationship with You as well. Give us the wisdom to do it, the courage to do it, and the way to do it. Then help us take the steps of faith we need to take to proclaim Your name throughout the earth. In Jesus' name, Amen.

CONCLUSION: MAKING A CHANCE — JULY 10

Thanks for joining us on this devotional tour of the Holy Land. To see a few highlights of our trip together, take a look at this short video below, as our worship leaders from the trip, Lucas Elder and Gary Marini, lead us in a closing song. Then read on to hear a touching story of God's faithfulness to those who put their faith in Him.

Watch "Conclusion: Making a Chance" (or on ericelder.com).

I was telling a group one time that they should try to go to Israel if they ever got a chance. My son Lucas added: "Don't just wait till you get a chance. Make a chance! Do whatever you can do to get there. It's worth it!" He's right.

So I'd like to tell you just one more story as we close, a story about "making a chance." While I usually try to shorten stories to make them as concise as possible, I think this one is best told with all the details intact. I believe God has several things He might want to speak to you through this story, so I pray that you'll be blessed as you read it.

As we began talking about going on this trip to Israel, a woman from Malawi named Esther had written to me, saying that she wondered if I thought God would ever make a way for her to visit Israel someday. She said she simply began crying every time she read the word "Israel" in some of the devotionals I had written and shared over the Internet. Knowing that she lived in Malawi, and knowing the situation for many who live there, I wasn't sure what to say. I began to pray about how to respond to her email, thinking that I'd say, "I believe that God can make a way, but I'm sorry I can't help you myself." As soon as I said those words in my mind, however, I felt God say, "Yes, you can help her." I said, "No, I can't." He said, "Yes you can." I said, "No, I can't!"

I had been planning this trip to Israel for the past three years, and our whole family had been working and saving money so that my wife and I and our four oldest kids could go with us. We barely had enough money at that time for just one of us to go, let alone six. So when God said I could help Esther get there, too, I really didn't know what to do. So I wrote back to her and said simply that I believed God could make a way, and I'd be praying along with her.

As the summer went on, I kept reading the words of Jesus to His disciples from Matthew 14:13-21, when 5,000 people were gathered together on a hillside at dinnertime. Jesus told His disciples: "You give them something to eat." I could imagine what the disciples must have felt. They said that not even eight months wages would give everyone even one bite, so how could they feed them? All they had were five loaves of bread and two fish from a boy's lunch.

Yet I was puzzled why Jesus would ask them to do something impossible if He didn't think they could do it. Unless, of course, they could do it, and they just didn't know how. I kept asking God, "How? How did Jesus do it? And how can we do it when You ask us to do something that seems impossible to us?"

So I studied that passage over and over, trying to see how Jesus did it. He simply gave thanks to God, broke the bread, and had the disciples start passing it out. Somehow there was enough food for all 5,000 to eat till they were satisfied and still have twelve baskets full left over.

As I shared this dilemma one week with a youth group, some of them came up to me afterwards and said they'd like to help with Esther's ticket. I tried to decline their money, because I didn't want them to think I was telling them the story in order for them to give money for the trip. I was just sharing with them the puzzle of how to do what God asks us to do when we think it is impossible. Several of them insisted, however, saying that they felt God really wanted them to give the money to help with Esther's trip. By the end of that week, I had received just over $300—enough to make the deposit on the trip for Esther to come with us. But I still needed more than 10 times that amount to pay for her whole trip, plus I still had to pay for my own family to go. I didn't tell Esther about the money yet, nor the deposit. I just told her that I was still praying for her and asked if she could get her passport information to me in case God were to make a way for her to come with us.

As the trip got closer, I just couldn't let go of the idea that God wanted me to help Esther get to Israel, but I still didn't know how. So I sent out a note to some others who also read my weekly devotionals on the Internet, letting them know about the situation. We received about a third of the total needed for her trip from that appeal. Another man donated about a third of the cost to cover her airfare from Malawi, and Lana and I put in the final third, as God was also working at the same time to help the six of us going from our family to pay for our trips, too. I told Esther the good news, that God had made a way for her to join us. By the time we left, everyone's ticket was completely paid for! This was astounding!

But then we got to Israel. We were supposed to meet Esther at the airport, as she was to arrive on a flight about twelve hours earlier. But when we got there, we couldn't find her. We paged her several times over the airport intercom, we checked for phone messages and email messages, looked in all the waiting areas, but couldn't find anything about where she might be, or if she even made it on her flights. We finally had to leave the airport, knowing that I had at least sent her the names of the hotels where we'd be staying at before we left, and hoped that she would catch up with us.

But she didn't. She called us the next day from an airport in Addis Ababa, Ethiopia. Although she had made it all the way to the airport in Israel, they had denied her entry into Israel, saying that it was too questionable about how she came to know us through our Internet ministry, and why the rest of the group wasn't there to meet her in Israel when she arrived. Although she tried to explain it to them several times, and she was even still in the airport when our flight finally landed twelve hours later, she wasn't allowed to call or email or make any contact with us. (To the credit of the airport security in Israel, they run a very tight ship and for very good reasons. We appreciate that they take their job so seriously or otherwise no one would be able to travel in and around Israel at all.) But since Esther did not travel together with us into the country with the group, she was questioned more strictly and finally put on a plane headed back to her home.

I couldn't believe it when she told me the story over the phone, and I began trying to think of anything else I could do. We had come too far in getting her to this point that I didn't want to give up on it, even though she was already headed on her flights back home, now waiting in Ethiopia to change planes back to Malawi. I called the immigration office at the Addis Ababa airport to ask if she could be put back on the plane to Israel, that we would meet her at the airport when she arrived and try to provide whatever documents they needed to verify that she was on our tour, but they said there was nothing they could do for her. She had been officially deported, and they were to put her on a flight back to Malawi the next morning. After several calls to several different people at the immigration office, I couldn't get any farther. I went to bed that night wondering why God had brought her so far, only to have her turned back in the end. It was 4 in the morning by this time, and I couldn't think of anything else to do, so I finally slept.

When I woke up a few hours later, I updated my wife Lana on the situation, and asked if she could think of anything else we could do. She remembered that a friend of ours had a daughter who had just come home from serving a year in Ethiopia as a missionary, and maybe she would have a contact who could help us out. I didn't know what they could even do, but I felt I had to pursue any possible option that was still open to us, as I felt it was the Lord who had put it on my heart to try to get her there in the first place. So we texted our friend's daughter back in Chicago, who texted us back with the phone number of a pastor she knew in Addis Ababa. I was astounded that we knew someone who knew someone who lived in Addis Ababa at all!

And I couldn't believe it when we called him and he immediately said that he would do whatever we needed him to do, just let him know. It was such a surprise that my wife and I both cried at the thought that someone would take a call from complete strangers and would be willing to drop everything and go to the airport right away. He was a busy man with a large congregation, and they had just gotten out of some special weekday services they were holding. It was beyond what we could have imagined someone doing for us in this situation. It still makes me cry to think of it—a brother in Christ willing to help out another brother, simply because we have the same Father. So he went to the airport that night, along with a pilot friend from his congregation. Unfortunately they weren't able to find Esther there. We were all disappointed, but we didn't know what else to do.

In the meantime, I had also talked to the tour company who helped us arrange the whole trip, and they said they could try to fax a letter to immigration in Addis Ababa, saying that Esther was indeed part of our tour, and that she was an invited guest as part of our group. I called the immigration office again, saying that we'd try to get a letter to them if they could just let Esther stay at the airport another five or six hours, as it was the middle of the night back in the States, and the tour offices wouldn't be open yet for another several hours. They granted our request and didn't make her get on the next-scheduled flight to Malawi.

So we got their fax number and the tour company tried several times to fax the letter—but the fax wouldn't go through. As the day went on, the rest of our group in Israel continued on with our tour, now sitting in a garden in the city of Capernaum, a site where Jesus had done some incredible miracles. I updated the group on Esther's situation, and we all prayed that someone would be able to get that letter through to the immigration office. I didn't have the heart to call the pastor in Addis Ababa again, but Lana did, so she tried to call him. None of her calls would go through. We sat down again and prayed. Our time was running out.

At the very moment that we sat down to pray, my phone rang. It was the pastor from Addis Ababa! He said he had just been to the airport again to try one more time to find Esther, taking some of his church members with him, this time one who worked at the airport. They had found Esther! They were calling us to see if there was any possibility we could fax him a letter from the tour company saying that she was with our trip! It was the very thing we were trying to do, but he didn't know it, and I didn't know he had gone back to the airport again! I called the tour company who found a way to finally email to the pastor, who printed it out and took it back to the immigration office at the airport. I also instructed the tour company that if they needed to buy another ticket for Esther to get back to Israel, to go ahead and buy it and charge it to my account, up to $1,000, without having to try to call me. We didn't have time to wait for any more calls. I just wanted the ticket waiting for her at the airport if she needed it. I didn't have $1,000 to spend on her ticket, but that's the number that came into my mind while I was on the phone, and what I felt I should say.

The pastor was able to get the documents to Esther, and the immigration office said she could get on a plane back to Israel. The tour company agency found the cheapest ticket they could—it was $992, just $8 under the limit I had given them, so they bought it and had it waiting for her at the airline counter.

As I went to bed that night, exhausted not only from the recent days' activities, but also from the months leading up to this moment, I went to lay down and felt God said, "You passed the test. Enjoy the rest of the trip." I wasn't sure exactly what test I had passed, but I was thankful that it was all working out. Even though Esther wasn't yet back in Israel, I felt like I had done the utmost of what I could possibly do to get her to Israel, as God had called me to do.

The next morning, our first stop on our tour "just happened" to be the site where Jesus multiplied the loaves and the fish to feed the 5,000—the place where Jesus had told the disciples to give the people something to eat, and the passage which had so inspired me all along. There we were standing on the same hill where that miracle from God took place. As I was looked up the passage again to read to our group that morning, I saw that it was told in several of the gospels, so I looked at each version to see which one to read. When I read John's version of the story, I couldn't believe it! In his version, when Jesus asked Philip where they could get food for all these people to eat, John added:

> "He asked this only to test him, for he already had in mind what He was going to do" (John 6:6).

It was a test! And just as Jesus had tested the disciples by asking them to give the people something to eat,—when it seemed utterly impossible—God had tested me to help someone else in need when it seemed impossible, too. And God had told me the night before that I had passed the test. Hallelujah! And now He had brought me to the hillside where Jesus had given the disciples their test! God couldn't have spoken more clearly to me if He had appeared in front of my eyes!

Later that afternoon, Esther arrived again at the airport in Israel, and this time she was allowed to enter the country. (The security people at the airport had asked her, "Why have you come back again when someone who is deported isn't allowed to attempt to come back into the country again for five years, and now you're trying to come back after only three days later!" Had I known that, I don't know that I would have even tried to get her back in. Only God could have opened that door for her to return!) She met us at the hotel for dinner that night.

Over dinner with our group, Esther and I shared with each other all that God had been doing to make this moment possible. And that's when the real clincher came.

Esther told me that from the very first day that I responded to her email, saying that I felt God could make a way for her to visit Israel someday, she said God spoke to her and told her she'd be coming this year, with us. Even when she was being turned away at the airport, she said she was praising God, that those had been the best few days of her life so far. Her mom had even called me during all of this to say that she wasn't discouraged, that they were just going to thank God in all things in order to shame the devil. Esther said that from the very beginning, when she first started thinking about the trip, she wanted to pray that God would make a way for her to go, but that God had stopped her from praying. She said that God told her not to pray for the trip, but to simply give thanks for it. She was puzzled, but did what God said. In fact, as time went on she was tempted to ask others to start praying for her to be able to go on the trip, too, but that God had stopped her from telling even one person about the trip or to pray for her, but simply to continue to give thanks for it. She said she didn't feel she was supposed to tell anyone about the trip until it was set. When she got my email asking for her passport information, and before I had even told her that people had begun to give money for her to come, she said she knew on that day that everything was set, and she could finally begin telling others about it.

I was stunned by what she said. Wasn't that exactly what Jesus did on the hillside when He multiplied the loaves and the fish? He simply gave thanks to God, broke the bread, and asked the disciples pass it out. He didn't plead for it. He just gave thanks for it! I looked at Esther and thanked her for being obedient to what God had told her to do. It had spoken volumes to me, answering a question that had been on my heart for months as I studied that passage trying to see what Jesus had done. I told her what God said to me about passing the test, and that I felt that she had passed her test, too, because of her obedience. We both knew that while God would still use the rest of the trip to speak to us in many ways, that He had already done His greatest work in us already, that of increasing our faith in Him.

As if to confirm all that had just happened that day, when I got back to my hotel room that night and having shared all of this with Esther—even the part about authorizing the purchase of her second ticket for anything up to $1,000 when I didn't know how I'd be able to pay for it—I checked my email before heading for bed. In my inbox was a note saying that a friend of ours back in the States had unexpectedly made an online donation of $1,000 to our ministry while we were at dinner that night! It was as if God were putting the icing on the cake, covering even the final detail of her trip.

I still don't know how to interpret it all. On the one hand, it seems it wouldn't have happened had we not prayed fervently and worked feverishly towards the goal, even day and night near the end. But on the other hand, God wanted to teach us something through what He called Esther to do: to simply give thanks for what He was going to give her. Or as my wife said while we were going through the whole ordeal, she felt that we were like the workers who helped to dig Hezekiah's tunnel to bring water into the City of David. One team started digging from one side, and the other team started digging from the other side, and miraculously both teams were able to meet in the middle to complete the tunnel!

In any case, I hope that God will speak to you through at least some portion of this story. And for some reason, I don't think this is the end of the story. It could very well be the beginning of some new ones! Thanks again for joining us on this incredible trip to the Holy Land!

Let's pray:

Father, thank You for all the remarkable things we've learned from this trip to the Holy Land, and all the remarkable things you still want us to learn in the future. Give us the faith to step out and trust you completely for everything in our lives, giving You thanks, even in advance, for Your love and faithfulness to us. Thank You for sending Your Son to lead us in Your ways and keep giving us the faith we need to follow Him every day, until one day He leads us on into heaven. In Jesus' name, Amen.

The Top 20 Passages in the Bible

20 inspiring devotionals based on the top 20 passages in the Bible

INTRODUCTION TO "THE TOP 20 PASSAGES IN THE BIBLE"   **JULY 11**

Scripture Reading: 2 Timothy 3:16-17

 The Bible is the most quoted book in the world. Why? Maybe it's because the Bible has been around so long. Or maybe it's because the Bible is so big. But most likely it's because the Bible contains wisdom that has touched the lives of so many people throughout the ages and throughout the world.

 When I saw a list one day of the top 20 passages in the Bible—those passages in the Bible that people turn to again and again, more frequently than any others—I was intrigued. I wondered, *What makes these passages so special? Are they words of comfort or words of conviction? Words of encouragement or words of challenge? Words of utter simplicity or words of profound depth?*

 As I've looked through these passages, I've seen that they contain elements of all of these things. And I know from personal experience, having read each chapter many times over the years and at different stages of my life, that they contain some of the most inspiring, convicting, encouraging, and faith-building passages I've ever encountered. I can see why they have bubbled up to the top 20 passages of the Bible.

 In the weeks ahead, I'd like to explore each of these top 20 passages with you as well, starting with number 20—the Christmas story from Luke chapter 1—and working our way to number 1, which just might surprise you!

 Whether you've been an avid Bible reader for years, or you're brand new to discovering the life-changing power of its words, I think you'll truly enjoy this study—not just for the insights you'll learn about the passages, but because I believe that each passage can speak directly to your heart.

 To be honest, I believe any passage from the Bible could speak to you just as profoundly. I couldn't count how many times I've had something on my mind and opened the Bible, only to find that God had something to say to me about it on the words on the pages before me.

 How does God do this? I believe it's because the Word of God is "living and active," as it says in Hebrews 4:12. God has inspired the words on the pages by instilling them with His Spirit, and it is that same Spirit that brings them to life for you. All Scripture is literally "God-breathed," as it says in 2 Timothy 3:16.

So whether you turn to a top 20 passage or to one of the less celebrated ones, know that God can speak to you through His Word, if your heart is open to hearing from Him. No wonder the Bible is the best-selling, most translated, and most quoted book in the world!

I want to encourage you to pick up your Bible again today and read through it, praying as you go, and listening for God to speak. There's no doubt in my mind that the God who created you has things He'd love to speak to you, and things that you won't want to wait to hear.

Then join me in the pages ahead as we look at the top 20 passages from the Bible that people turn to again and again. I'm certain that God has things He wants you to know, things He wants you to do, and mysteries He wants to reveal.

P.S. As we go through this series, I'll also include a prayer and a memory verse from the passage we're studying, to encourage you in your personal prayer time with God, and to have something to memorize as we go along. Hiding God's Word in your heart is one of the best ways to recall it later when God wants to remind you of it. Here's today's prayer and memory verse.

Prayer: Father, thank You for giving us Your words in the form of the Bible. Speak to us as we read from it today and in the days ahead, just as You spoke to those who first recorded these words for us to hear. In Jesus' name, Amen.

Memory Verse:

> *"All Scripture is breathed out by God and profitable for teaching, for reproof, for correction, and for training in righteousness, that the man of God may be competent, equipped for every good work" (1 Timothy 3:16-17, ESV).*

NUMBER 20: THE CHRISTMAS STORY   JULY 12

Scripture Reading: Luke 1

We're looking at the Top 20 passages in the Bible—those chapters that people turn to again and again for God's wisdom—and we're starting today with number 20, the beginning of the Christmas story from Luke chapter 1 (it continues in chapter 2).

When you read Luke 1, you can see that it is filled with all the wonders of Christmas—miracles, angels, signs, and wonders—yet it was written by a man who was well-grounded in reality. Luke was a medical doctor, as noted by the Apostle Paul in Colossians 4:14, who set out to write an "orderly account" of the life of Christ for his friend Theophilus. Luke wrote:

> *"It seemed good to me also, having followed all things closely for some time past, to write an orderly account for you, most excellent Theophilus, that you may have certainty concerning the things you have been taught" (Luke 1:3-4).*

Luke had carefully investigated these stories and had personally interviewed eyewitnesses of the accounts. He had traveled with Paul on his missionary journeys, and later documented their travels in the book of Acts.

Yet with all of Luke's detailed research and careful thought that he put into all of his writings, he still had room in his heart to try to convey—and not shy away from—the truly miraculous events that surrounded the birth of Christ and the events that followed throughout His life.

As a medical doctor, Luke—of all people—would have understood that it was nothing short of miraculous for Mary to give birth to a Son, even though she had never lain with a man. Yet Luke, of the four writers of the life of Christ (Matthew, Mark, Luke, and John), includes more details about Christ's birth than any of the others.

Perhaps it was precisely *because of* his experience as a doctor that Luke includes the miraculous aspects of this story. Having likely witnessed many births himself—as I have with my own six children—he would have known that every birth is a miracle from the hand of God. So it would have been no stretch of the imagination for him to see that the miraculous events surrounding Christ's birth were from the hand of God as well.

Luke 1 also contains one of the most encouraging verses in all of Scripture about the power of God. It comes after the angel Gabriel announces to Mary that she's going to have a child. When Mary asks how this will happen, Gabriel says,

> *"The Holy Spirit will come upon you, and the power of the Most High will overshadow you. So the Holy One to be born will be called the Son of God. Even Elizabeth your relative is going to have a child in her old age, and she who was said to be barren is in her sixth month. For nothing is impossible with God" (Luke 1:35-37).*

And Gabriel would know. This is the same Gabriel who appeared to the prophet Daniel about 500 years earlier, revealing to him the exact timing of the Messiah's birth (see Daniel 9:21-27). And this is the same Gabriel who appeared to Elizabeth's husband, Zechariah, telling him that his wife would soon become pregnant. When Zechariah doubted, Gabriel said,

> *"I am Gabriel. I stand in the presence of God, and I have been sent to speak to you and to tell you this good news" (Luke 1:19).*

It's as if Gabriel was saying, "Maybe you don't realize who I am...but I'm Gabriel, and I stand in the presence of God. Believe me when I say that when God makes a promise, He will fulfill it!"

Just as God fulfilled His promises to Zechariah and Elizabeth, to Joseph and Mary, to Daniel and a host of others in the Bible, God will fulfill His promises to you, too. Whatever you're facing, know that God can work miracles in your life. Nothing is impossible with Him. He can do anything!

He can restore your marriage, heal your sickness, bring you out of your financial troubles. He can restore relationships that are troubled in your life, He can find a new job for you that fits your giftings, He can even bring that child into your life that you've been longing for. Know that God will do whatever's best for you in every situation, but never doubt His miraculous power.

Read Luke chapter 1 for yourself and realize that nothing is impossible with God. Then put your faith in Him again today for everything in your life—even for those things which may seem impossible in your eyes.

Prayer: Father, thank You for inspiring Luke to take the time to carefully investigate and document the miraculous life of Christ so that we, too, would know the certainty of what we have been taught. Lord, fill us with faith again today so that we can truly believe in our hearts that nothing is impossible with You. In Jesus' name, Amen.

Memory Verse:

"For nothing is impossible with God" (Luke 1:37)

NUMBER 19: MAKING THE BEST USE OF THE TIME — JULY 13

Scripture Reading: Ephesians 5

How do you make the best use of the time God has given you here on earth? That's what we're going to learn today as we look at Ephesians chapter 5—the 19th most frequently read of the top 20 passages in the Bible.

When Billy Graham was asked what surprised him most about life, he responded, "The brevity of it."

Life is short, and God wants you to make the best use of the time that He's given you here on earth. He doesn't want you to waste it on sinful activities that, while possibly providing some momentary pleasure, will eventually end up wasting—and even destroying—your life and the lives of others.

In Paul's letter to the Ephesians, Paul writes:

"Look carefully then how you walk, not as unwise but as wise, making the best use of the time, because the days are evil" (Ephesians 5:15-16).

There are a lot of ways you can spend your days, and Paul takes the rest of chapter 5 to compare and contrast several of them with practical examples. Here are a few:

In talking about living a life of purity, Paul says:

"Be imitators of God. And walk in love, as Christ loved us and gave Himself up for us...." (Ephesians 5:1-2a).

He goes on to say that we shouldn't have even a hint of sexual immorality, impurity, or covetousness, and adds:

"Let there be no filthiness nor foolish talk nor crude joking, which are out of place, but instead let there be thanksgiving" (Ephesians 5:3-4).

In talking about drinking, Paul says:

"And do not get drunk with wine, for that is debauchery, but be filled with the Spirit, addressing one another in psalms and hymns and spiritual songs, singing and making melody to the Lord with your heart, giving thanks always and for everything to God the Father in the name of our Lord Jesus Christ" (Ephesians 5:18-20a).

In talking about relationships, Paul says not to abuse any authority God may have given you—whether it's between husbands and wives, children and parents, or workers and bosses—but to submit to one another out of love, being willing to give up your life for those God has put in your care, as Christ laid down His life for us (see Ephesians 5:22-33 and 6:1-9).

What do you want to be remembered for in life? And how might God want you to use your life to make a mark on this world for Him?

You may have heard of the famous Nobel Peace Prize, named after Alfred Nobel. But you may not have heard that Alfred Nobel was one of the wealthiest arms and weapons manufacturers in the world. When Alfred's brother died, a French newspaper mistakenly printed an obituary of Alfred instead, with the heading, "The merchant of death is dead." The paper went on to say that, "Dr. Alfred Nobel, who became rich by finding ways to kill more people faster than ever before, died yesterday."

Alfred was so disturbed by this assessment of his life that he decided to change the way he lived it—and the way he would be remembered throughout history. He donated the bulk of his estate to establish the Nobel Prizes, given annually to those who have made an outstanding contribution to the world in the areas of physical science, chemistry, medical science, literature, and finally "peace." This man who might have been remembered as one of the most notorious "merchants of death" is now remembered as one of the most famous encouragers of peace.

Henry Manning, a priest back in 1884 wrote:

"Next to grace, time is the most precious gift of God. Yet how much of both we waste."

God doesn't want you to waste the days He's given you. He wants you to make the best of them. If you're not sure how to do that, read Ephesians 5 and look for specific things that God might want you to start—or stop—doing in your life. Then do what Paul encouraged the Ephesians to do:

"Look carefully then how you walk...making the best use of the time..."

Prayer: Father, thank You for giving us the time we have here on the earth. Help us to make the best use of time that we can. Keep us from destroying ourselves and others by the things we think and say and do and help us to bless You and bless others instead. In Jesus' name, Amen.

Memory Verse:

"Look carefully then how you walk, not as unwise but as wise, making the best use of the time, because the days are evil" (Ephesians 5:15-16, ESV).

NUMBER 18: GOD'S LOVE FOR YOU   JULY 14

Scripture Reading: Ephesians 1

One of the most difficult things to do in the world is to grasp God's love for you. Your view of His love may be impaired because of difficult circumstances you're facing, or particular sins—whether past or present, or because of poor examples of how a loving Father acts and behaves based on some faulty earthly models, or for a hundred other reasons.

If any of these are the case for you, I'd encourage you to take a close look at chapter 1 of Ephesians (and chapters 2 and 3 if you can), asking God as you read to open the eyes of your heart to His great love.

Paul felt so passionately about this topic that he spent the first half of his letter to the Ephesians telling them of God's great love for them—and the grace that God was eager to extend to them in Christ.

In chapter 1, he prays for them that God,

> "...may give you a spirit of wisdom and of revelation in the knowledge of Him, having the eyes of your hearts enlightened, that you may know what is the hope to which He has called you, what are the riches of His glorious inheritance in the saints, and what is the immeasurable greatness of His power toward us who believe..." (Ephesians 1:17b-19a).

In chapter 2, he says,

> "For by grace you have been saved through faith. And this is not your own doing; it is the gift of God, not a result of works, so that no one may boast. For we are His workmanship, created in Christ Jesus for good works, which God prepared beforehand, that we should walk in them" (Ephesians 2:8-10).

And in chapter 3, he prays,

> "...that you, being rooted and grounded in love, may have strength to comprehend with all the saints what is the breadth and length and height and depth, and to know the love of Christ that surpasses knowledge, that you may be filled with all the fullness of God" (Ephesians 3:17b-19).

God loves you deeply, yet grasping it can be one of the hardest things you'll ever do in your life. But grasping it will also bring you more joy than you've ever known in your life.

Paul seems to have discovered what it meant—at the deepest level—to be "adopted" by God. While some who are adopted find it hard to get over their feelings of abandonment, others realize that being adopted means that that they don't belong to someone by chance, but by choice. Paul clearly had this latter view, as he reminded the Ephesians:

> "In love He predestined us for adoption as sons through Jesus Christ, according to the purpose of His will, to the praise of His glorious grace, with which He has blessed us in the Beloved" (Ephesians 1:5-6).

Mother Teresa, who took in and cared for thousands of children during her lifetime, seemed to capture the heart of God towards those who feel "unwanted" in a beautiful way when she said,

> "There is no such thing as an unwanted child. If you don't want them, give them to me. I want them."

God feels the same way about you. Although you may feel like others have abandoned you, God never has. He *has* always loved you, *will* always love you, and *still* loves you today as much as He ever has. Why? Because you are His beloved child. You are made in His image. You are His own precious creation. He loves you deeply and wants more than anything in the world to have an intimate relationship with you.

If I could do one thing for you today, it would be to do what the Apostle Paul did for the Ephesians: to get down on my knees and pray that God would open the eyes of your heart, and that you would be able to comprehend the breadth and length and height and depth of God's love for you in Christ. And that's just what I'm going to do, if you'd like to pray with me…

Prayer: Father, I pray that every person reading these words would be able to grasp Your incredible love for them in a deeper way than ever before. Open the eyes of their heart, that they would be able to comprehend the breadth and length and height and depth of God's love for them in Christ. In Jesus' name, Amen.

Memory Verse:

> "In love He predestined us for adoption as sons through Jesus Christ, according to the purpose of His will, to the praise of His glorious grace, with which He has blessed us in the Beloved" (Ephesians 1:5-6).

NUMBER 17: THE GOSPEL IN A NUTSHELL — JULY 15

Scripture Reading: John 3

If you were to look at a list of the top 100 verses in the Bible, you'd find that a verse from John chapter 3 at the very top. It's the most quoted verse in the Bible, and the most quoted verse of Jesus. Speaking of Himself, Jesus said:

> "For God so loved the world, that He gave His only Son, that whoever believes in Him should not perish but have eternal life" (John 3:16).

John 3:16 contains the gospel in a nutshell, the good news of Jesus in compact form: that if anyone who wants to be free from the penalty of sin and death, they can do so by putting their faith in Jesus.

Jesus expanded on why this is such good news in the rest of John. He did so in the context of a conversation that took place between Himself and Nicodemus, a member of the Jewish ruling council, who came to Jesus one night to learn more from this controversial, but impressive, teacher.

Jesus told Nicodemus: "You must be born again," to which Nicodemus responded:

> "How can a man be born when he is old? Can he enter a second time into his mother's womb and be born?" (John 3:4).

Jesus answered him:

> "Truly, truly, I say to you, unless one is born of water and the Spirit, he cannot enter the kingdom of God" (John 3:5).

Nicodemus must have taken what Jesus said to heart, for after Jesus died on the cross, Nicodemus, along with Joseph of Arimathea, risked his life and position on the Jewish council by asking Pilate for Jesus' body in order to give Jesus a proper burial (see John 19:38-40). May God give us all that kind of boldness in our faith!

Jesus also mentioned in his conversation with Nicodemus something significant that had happened to the Israelites about 2,500 years earlier. When the Israelites were wandering in the desert, they sinned. As a result, God sent fiery serpents to attack them, and many Israelites died from the bites. Those who were still alive repented of their sins and Moses prayed to God on their behalf. God said to Moses:

> "'Make a fiery serpent and set it on a pole, and everyone who is bitten, when he sees it, shall live.' So Moses made a bronze serpent and set it on a pole. And if a serpent bit anyone, he would look at the bronze serpent and live" (Numbers 21:8-9).

God heard their prayers and saw their repentant hearts and provided a way for them to be saved. Referring to this story, Jesus told Nicodemus:

> "And as Moses lifted up the serpent in the wilderness, so must the Son of Man be lifted up, that whoever believes in Him may have eternal life" (John 3:14-15).

This story has become such a symbol of healing that today, the symbol of a snake wrapped around a pole is still displayed on many of our medical buildings, ambulances, and doctor's insignias.

But it's more than just a symbol of healing. It's a symbol of forgiveness, a symbol of a loving God who will go to the great lengths to extend forgiveness to His people, if only they would turn from their sins and put their faith in Him.

It is in the context of this ancient story of God's forgiveness and healing that Jesus said His most famous quote in John 3:16:

> "For God so loved the world, that He gave His only Son, that whoever believes in Him should not perish but have eternal life" (John 3:16).

I bring this up because John 3:16 is not only the gospel in a nutshell, it's the whole Bible in a nutshell! God has always been wooing His people into a relationship with Him, and offering them forgiveness if they truly desire it, so that they can come back into a relationship with Him. And that's what God has offered to us, by sending His only Son to die for us so we can live.

God loves you, and He doesn't want you or anyone else to be destroyed by sin. He's willing to go to the greatest lengths possible—and He already has—to see that you will be healed, forgiven, and brought back into a new life with Him.

If you've already put your faith in Christ, Hallelujah! Let someone know about it who needs to hear this good news! But if you've never put your faith in Christ—been "born again," to use Jesus' words—there's no better time than right now!

Prayer: Father, thank You for loving me so much that You would send Your only Son to die for me so that I could live. I want to live again. I want to be born again spiritually so I can live with You forever. Forgive me for my sins, for the wrong things I've done. I am putting my faith in Christ right now. Fill me with Your Spirit so that I can live the life You've called me to live, both here on earth, and on into heaven forever. In Jesus' name, Amen.

Memory Verse:

> "For God so loved the world, that He gave His only Son, that whoever believes in Him should not perish but have eternal life" (John 3:16, ESV).

NUMBER 16: THE POWER OF GOD FOR SALVATION — JULY 16

Scripture Reading: Romans 1

If I had to choose one passage from the Bible that God has used most to change *my* life, it would be Romans chapter 1. It's not my favorite passage in the Bible, because Romans 1 is not particularly cheery or uplifting. In fact, it contains some of the worst news I've ever heard in my life!

But the truth is the gospel is often "bad news" before it's "good news." There's no reason to put your faith in a Savior unless you realize that there's something in your life from which you need to be saved. And that was the case with me: I didn't realize there was anything in my life I needed saving from until I read Romans chapter 1. Then I realized that I, too, needed a Savior.

The book of Romans is actually a letter that the Apostle Paul wrote to the believers who lived in Rome. Paul longed to see them so they could mutually encourage one another in their faith, and so he could reap a harvest among them, bringing still more people to faith in Christ. He loved preaching about Christ, even though it had landed him in prison many times. He said:

> *"For I am not ashamed of the gospel, for it is the power of God for salvation to everyone who believes, to the Jew first and also to the Greek" (Romans 1:16).*

Paul then began to describe the gospel that he loved to preach, starting with the "bad news" that God was revealing His wrath from heaven against all ungodliness and unrighteousness.

As I read through Paul's words in chapter 1, I was struck by the fact that God's wrath wasn't so much that He was raining fire down from heaven or causing calamity among the people. His wrath was quite simply this: giving people up to follow their own sinful desires and choices, and then letting the natural consequences of those choices overtake them.

Three times in Romans 1, Paul describes God's wrath in similar terms:

> *"Therefore God gave them up in the lusts of their hearts to impurity, to the dishonoring of their bodies among themselves..." (Romans 1:24).*
>
> *"For this reason God gave them up to dishonorable passions..." (Romans 1:26a).*
>
> *"And since they did not see fit to acknowledge God, God gave them up to a debased mind to do what ought not to be done..." (Romans 1:28).*

As I read through this list of things people did to dishonor God, I realized that I had done many of them myself. I had, as Paul described it so eloquently, "exchanged the truth about God for a lie" (Romans 1:25). And I, too, was "without excuse" (Romans 1:20b), for I knew in my heart that what I was doing was wrong, if only from the evidence of the natural order of God's creation itself.

It was the worst news I had ever heard. I had sinned against God and His wrath was now bearing down heavily upon me, a wrath that threatened to manifest itself in ways that were simply the natural result of the sinful choices I had made.

That's when I finally realized the "good news" of the gospel: that God already knew about my sins and had sent His Son to save me from them, if I would put my faith in Him.

Within 24 hours of reading Romans chapter 1, I decided to put my faith in Christ for everything in my life. I asked Him to forgive me of my sins and to fill me with His Holy Spirit so I could live the life He wanted me to live. He did exactly what He promised and I'm now on a new path, a path of life that leads on into eternity.

The whole book of Romans is incredibly thought-provoking, and we'll revisit some more passages from it later in this series. I hope you'll take a chance to read through all of Romans yourself, starting with chapter 1, inviting God to speak to you as you read. It's turned me into a *believer*, and it's *saved* me—just as Paul said it would. The gospel of Jesus Christ really is, "the power of God for salvation to everyone who believes."

Prayer: Father, thank You for loving us enough to give us the free will to choose Your path or choose our own. But Father, we pray that You would fill us with Your Spirit again today so that we will always choose to follow You in everything we do, avoiding the wrath that we would otherwise bring upon ourselves. We put our faith in Christ again today for everything in our lives. In Jesus' name, Amen.

Memory Verse:

> "For I am not ashamed of the gospel, for it is the power of God for salvation to everyone who believes, to the Jew first and also to the Greek" (Romans 1:16, ESV)

NUMBER 15: WALK IN A MANNER WORTHY OF YOUR CALLING — JULY 17

Scripture Reading: Ephesians 4

One of the benefits of reading the Bible is that it acts as a counselor of sorts, giving you advice on how to handle the situations you face in life. In fact, the Holy Spirit is often called *the Counselor*, and He does some of His best counseling work as you read through the pages of the Bible.

Ephesians 4 is one of those passages that can help you in various ways, including when you're feeling frustrated or angry with those around you. God knows what you're feeling, and so does the Apostle Paul, who wrote the letter to the Ephesians.

Having been unjustly imprisoned for his faith, Paul could have easily given in to the temptation to be bitter and angry with those around him. But instead he chose another path—and he encouraged the Ephesians to do the same:

> "I therefore, a prisoner for the Lord, urge you to walk in a manner worthy of the calling to which you have been called, with all humility and gentleness, with patience, bearing with one another in love, eager to maintain the unity of the Spirit in the bond of peace" (Ephesians 4:1-3).

How could Paul do it? How could he turn off the anger that might otherwise have boiled up within him—and perhaps even consumed him? To answer that question, I think we need to look closer at the little word he uses at the beginning of the chapter: "therefore." Whenever you see a "therefore" in the Bible, it's a good idea to read the words leading up to it so you'll know what the "therefore" is there for!

If you look back at what Paul was writing prior to this chapter, you'll see that he spent the entire first three chapters of the book trying to help the Ephesians understand just how much God really loved them. He even got down on his knees and prayed for them to understand the depth of God's love. Paul knew that once they understood God's unconditional love for them, then they would be able to extend that same love to those around them.

There's a "Dennis the Menace" cartoon in which Dennis and his friend Joey are walking away from the Wilson's house with their hands full of cookies. Joey asks, "I wonder what we did to deserve this?" Dennis tells his friend, "Joey, Mrs. Wilson gives us cookies not because *we're* nice, but because *she's* nice."

The same can be said of God. The reason He treats us with so much love and kindness is not necessarily because *we're* good, but because *He's* good. That's how Paul was able to treat others with kindness even though they were mistreating him, and that's how we can treat others with kindness even though they may be mistreating us. Paul was able to "be nice" to them because God had "been nice" to him. As Paul renewed his mind with this reminder of God's love, he was able to extend that love to others, regardless of how they treated him. Paul told the Ephesians:

"...put off your old self, which belongs to your former manner of life and is corrupt through deceitful desires, and to be renewed in the spirit of your minds, and to put on the new self, created after the likeness of God in true righteousness and holiness" (Ephesians 4:17-24).

If you're struggling to love those around you with the love that God has expressed to you, I'd encourage you to read through all of Ephesians chapter 4 (and keep on reading, if you'd like, through chapters 5 and 6 as well!) You'll find some of the most practical words of advice from the best Counselor in the world. Here are just a few of His pieces of wisdom:

"Be angry and do not sin; do not let the sun go down on your anger, and give no opportunity to the devil" (Ephesians 4:26-27).
"Let no corrupting talk come out of your mouths, but only such as is good for building up, as fits the occasion, that it may give grace to those who hear" (Ephesians 4:29).
"Be kind to one another, tenderhearted, forgiving one another, as God in Christ forgave you" (Ephesians 4:32).

These aren't generic platitudes; they're life-changing attitudes—attitudes that will change how you act.

As a Christian, God has put a great calling on your life. Invite God to renew Your mind, and then do as Paul urged the Ephesians to do:

"...to walk in a manner worthy of the calling to which you have been called, with all humility and gentleness, with patience, bearing with one another in love, eager to maintain the unity of the Spirit in the bond of peace."

Prayer: Father, thank You for Your incredible love for us. Help us to understand just how wide and long and high and deep it is, so that we can extend that love to those around us. Help us to walk in a manner worthy of the calling that You have put upon our lives, and may our walk impact those around us in powerful ways as well. In Jesus' name, Amen.

Memory Verse:

"I therefore, a prisoner for the Lord, urge you to walk in a manner worthy of the calling to which you have been called, with all humility and gentleness, with patience, bearing with one another in love, eager to maintain the unity of the Spirit in the bond of peace" (Ephesians 4:1-3)

NUMBER 14: GOD KNOWS YOU   JULY 18

Scripture Reading: Psalm 139

If you've ever wondered if God knows what you're going through—if "He can see into your heart and know what you're thinking and feeling and experiencing in your life, then you'll want to read Psalm 139.

The word "psalm" means "song,"—or a poem set to music—so the book of Psalms is the songbook of the Bible. Although the tunes aren't recorded for us, the words themselves sing of the wonders of God. And in Psalm 139, they sing of just how deeply God knows each one of us—including you.

Even though this song was written by King David about 3,000 years ago, you can still hear God's voice to you today as you read his opening words. Listen to hear just how deeply God knows you and knows what you're going through in your life.

> *"O LORD, You have searched me and known me!*
> *You know when I sit down and when I rise up;*
> *You discern my thoughts from afar.*
> *You search out my path and my lying down*
> *and are acquainted with all my ways.*
> *Even before a word is on my tongue,*
> *behold, O LORD, You know it altogether.*
> *You hem me in, behind and before,*
> *and lay Your hand upon me.*
> *Such knowledge is too wonderful for me;*
> *it is high; I cannot attain it.*
> *Where shall I go from Your Spirit?*
> *Or where shall I flee from Your presence?*
> *If I ascend to heaven, You are there!*
> *If I make my bed in Sheol, You are there!*
> *If I take the wings of the morning*
> *and dwell in the uttermost parts of the sea,*
> *even there Your hand shall lead me,*
> *and Your right hand shall hold me."*
> *(Psalm 139:1-10)*

These words are especially meaningful to me today as I'm headed to the airport as I write this. I'm sending my son off to college in Sydney, Australia, and my daughter off to college in Lynchburg, Virginia. What a joy and comfort to know that God will be going with both of them as they "take the wings of the morning" and fly so far from home, even dwelling in "the uttermost parts of the sea!"

Just as I know from Psalm 139 that God is with me and will be with my kids wherever they go, I also know that God is with you and will be with your loved ones wherever they go. For there's no place in the world that you can go where God is *not* there!

As David went on to say in Psalm 139:

> "If I say, 'Surely the darkness shall cover me,
> and the light about me be night,'
> even the darkness is not dark to You;
> the night is bright as the day,
> for darkness is as light with You."
> (Psalm 139:11-12)

Even if it looks dark all around you, know that God is still right there with you. The darkness doesn't matter to Him. In His eyes, "the night is as bright as the day." You're not alone. God loves you. He sees you. And He knows what you're going through.

I can say this with confidence because no one knows you better than Him. He created you. He saw what you looked like before anyone else did, while He was still forming you in your mother's womb. And even before you lived a single day of your life, God had a plan for every one of them.

As David sang:

> "For You formed my inward parts;
> You knitted me together in my mother's womb.
> I praise You, for I am fearfully and wonderfully made.
> Wonderful are Your works;
> my soul knows it very well.
> My frame was not hidden from You,
> when I was being made in secret,
> intricately woven in the depths of the earth.
> Your eyes saw my unformed substance;
> in Your book were written, every one of them,
> the days that were formed for me,
> when as yet there was none of them."
> (Psalm 139:13-16)

God knows you. He loves you. And He has an incredible purpose for your life, just as He loves and knows and has an incredible purpose for the lives of everyone around you. Read Psalm 139 sometime today and let the truth of God's words sink deep into your heart.

Prayer: Father, thank You for the reminder today of how great Your love is for each one of us. Thank You that there's nothing hidden from You and that there's no place we can go where You aren't there with us. In Jesus' name, Amen.

Memory Verse:

> "O LORD, You have searched me and known me! You know when I sit down and when I rise up; You discern my thoughts from afar" (Psalm 139:1, ESV).

NUMBER 13: LIKE A TREE PLANTED BY WATER — JULY 19

Scripture Reading: Psalm 1

Several years ago I was praying about what I could do with my life for God. I wanted to serve Him in some great way and was willing to go wherever He wanted me to go and do whatever He wanted me to do.

One day a friend of mine was praying for me. As he prayed, he said he saw me as if I were a tree, not necessarily going or doing anything at all, but standing still and growing tall. He said that as I grew, people would come and rest under the shade of my branches.

It was a great picture, but it wasn't quite what I had in mind. I wanted to go and do something spectacular for God, but it sounded like God wanted me to stay where I was and keep growing in Him. It reminded me in a way of the passage that we're looking at today, Psalm 1. It's a passage that describes just such a man:

> "He is like a tree
> planted by streams of water
> that yields its fruit in its season,
> and its leaf does not wither.
> In all that he does, he prospers."
> (Psalm 1:2)

As I read that passage, all of a sudden, it didn't sound so bad to me. How awesome it would be to be like a tree planted by streams of water. To dig my roots deep into the ground and soak up all I could of the life-giving water nearby. To be able to yield fruit when it was time. To know that my leaves would never wither. And to know that in all I did I would prosper.

I wanted to be like that tree, so I looked at the rest of Psalm 1 where it showed me how:

> "Blessed is the man
> who walks not in the counsel of the wicked,
> nor stands in the way of sinners,
> nor sits in the seat of scoffers;
> but his delight is in the law of the LORD,
> and on His law he meditates day and night"
> (Psalm 1:1-2)

Rather than entering into the ways of the wicked and sinners and scoffers, God wanted me to dig deep into His Word—to take delight in reading it and meditating on it day and night. In the process, I would grow stronger and taller in my faith and in my life. And as I grew, I would be blessed and so would those around me, as a natural byproduct of my own growth.

I felt both relief and exhilaration at the same time. Instead of having to try to figure everything out right away, I could focus simply on meditating on God's Word, letting God bring the fruit "in its season."

There's something spectacular about reading and meditating on God's Word. A monk named Thomas Merton said:

> "By reading the scriptures I am so renewed that all nature seems renewed around me and with me. The sky seems to be a pure, a cooler blue, the trees a deeper green. The whole world is charged with the glory of God and I feel fire and music under my feet."

If you want to serve God in a powerful way, I encourage you to take the words of Psalm 1 to heart. Don't take the path of the wicked and sinners and scoffers. Take the path instead of meditating on God's Word day and night. Send your roots deep into His life-giving words. And as you and your faith grow, you will be blessed—and so will those around you. You'll have a new outlook on life, and others will gather around just to rest in the shade of your tree.

Prayer: Father, thank You for giving us Your Word so that we can read it, meditate on it, and grow in our faith and in our lives. Help us to grow strong and tall as we read Your Word, so that we can bear fruit "in its season," blessing others along the way. In Jesus' name, Amen.

Memory Verse:

> "Blessed is the man who walks not in the counsel of the wicked, nor stands in the way of sinners, nor sits in the seat of scoffers; but his delight is in the law of the LORD, and on His law he meditates day and night" (Psalm 1:1, ESV).

NUMBER 12: DON'T BE ANXIOUS — JULY 20

Scripture Reading: Philippians 4

If you're feeling anxious or worried about anything today, Philippians 4 is a good place to look for help.

I like this passage because the Apostle Paul, who wrote these God-inspired words, doesn't just tell you *not* to be anxious, he tells you *why* you don't need to be anxious; he doesn't just tell you *not* to dwell on your problems, but he tells you *what* to dwell on instead.

And I especially like this passage because Paul didn't write these words while sitting on a grassy hillside at a mountaintop retreat. He wrote them while being held in chains in a first century prison cell, having been beaten, flogged, and facing possible death at any moment. If Paul could learn how to be free from anxiety in a situation like that, then we might be able to learn from him how to deal with our anxious thoughts as well.

Here's what Paul said:

> "Rejoice in the Lord always; again I will say, Rejoice. Let your reasonableness be known to everyone. The Lord is at hand; do not be anxious about anything, but in everything by prayer and supplication with thanksgiving let your requests be made known to God. And the peace of God, which surpasses all understanding, will guard your hearts and your minds in Christ Jesus" (Philippians 4:4-7).

Twice he says to "rejoice in the Lord."

Notice that he doesn't say you have to rejoice about the difficult situation your facing, but to rejoice *in the Lord*. Rather than trying to minimize what you're facing, Paul is trying to maximize who you're facing them with: the Lord.

That's also the reason *why* you don't need to be anxious—because "The Lord is at hand." He's not a God who has taken off to some distant land, but He's actually very close at all times—"at hand"—within an arm's reach.

A woman once told me about a time when she was laying in pain on a hospital bed when she looked up to see a cross on the wall. It wasn't an empty cross—which has a special significance of its own—but it was a cross depicting the agonizing crucifixion of Jesus. While it might seem gruesome to look into the face of a man who is experiencing excruciating pain, for this woman it turned out to be one of the greatest comforts of her life. She was suddenly filled with the realization that Jesus was right there with her—that He knew exactly what she was going through—and He brought her immediate comfort and peace.

Paul also told the Philippians *what* to focus on in the midst of their troubles:

> "Finally, brothers, whatever is true, whatever is honorable, whatever is just, whatever is pure, whatever is lovely, whatever is commendable, if there is any excellence, if there is anything worthy of praise, think about these things. What you have learned and received and heard and seen in me—practice these things, and the God of peace will be with you" (Philippians 4:8-9).

It reminds me of the song that Julie Andrews sang in the Rodgers and Hammerstein musical, *The Sound of Music*. When the children were afraid of the thunder and lightning outside, she sang: "When the dog bites, when the bee stings, when I'm feeling sad, I simply remember my favorite things, and then I don't feel so bad." For her, some of her favorite things were, "Raindrops on roses and whiskers on kittens, bright copper kettles and warm woolen mittens."

What about you? What are some of your favorite things? Or, as Paul asked, what are some things you can think about that are true? Honorable? Just? Pure? Lovely? Commendable? Excellent? Worthy of praise? Think about such things—not just as a technique to distract you from your situation, but as a practical way to put your situation into perspective. For as hard as life can be, there are still things in life which are beautiful and glorious.

Paul learned the secret of being content in every situation, whether he had plenty or was in want. How? By continually *rejoicing in the Lord,* by remembering that *God is at hand,* and in everything, *making his requests known to God*. In one of the most famous verses of the Bible—found at the end of this chapter in Philippians—Paul said:

> "I can do all things through Him who strengthens me" (Philippians 4:13).

If you're feeling anxious and worried today, read Philippians chapter 4. Learn from Paul and put into practice what you learn. As you do, may the God of peace be with you—and may *His* peace be yours.

Prayer: Father, thank You for giving us practical ways to face the things that cause us to be anxious. Help us to remember that You are near, and to dwell on those things that are true, honorable, just, pure, lovely, commendable, excellent, and worthy of praise. In Jesus' name, Amen.

Memory Verse:

> "Do not be anxious about anything, but in everything by prayer and supplication with thanksgiving let your requests be made known to God" (Philippians 4:6, ESV).

NUMBER 11: A LIVING SACRIFICE — JULY 21

Scripture Reading: Romans 12

What are some things that you feel passionate about—things that you like to do that bring joy to you and to those around you? Chances are, God has gifted you in a special way to do those very things. And when you do them, you bring joy to His heart as well.

A man named Eric Liddle loved God. He also loved to run. He wanted to spend his life as a missionary, but he also had a chance to run in the Olympic games. Torn between running or being a missionary, he eventually did both. As he told one of his friends: "When God created me, He made me fast, and when I run, I feel His pleasure."

God has created and gifted each one of us uniquely. To some He has given the gift of teaching, to others, serving, to still others, the gifts of leading or healing or giving or showing mercy. God wants you to use your gifts to the fullest. In Romans 12, the Apostle Paul talks about how you can do just that:

> "I appeal to you therefore, brothers, by the mercies of God, to present your bodies as a living sacrifice, holy and acceptable to God, which is your spiritual worship. ... Having gifts that differ according to the grace given to us, let us use them: if prophecy, in proportion to our faith; if service, in our serving; the one who teaches, in his teaching; the one who exhorts, in his exhortation; the one who contributes, in generosity; the one who leads, with zeal; the one who does acts of mercy, with cheerfulness" (Romans 12:1, 6-8).

The word sacrifice in this context comes from the Greek word "thusia," which means "to make an offering." A living sacrifice, then, is someone who "makes an offering" of their life to God. It's also the basis for our English word "enthusiasm," which means "infused with the Divine Spirit"—a passionate drive that has been given to us by God.

In the movie, *Amazing Grace*, you can see what this kind of passionate drive from God looks like in action. The movie tells the true story of William Wilberforce, a British man who "found God" while he was serving as a member of parliament. Wilberforce considered giving up his position in politics to go into pastoral ministry. But he also had a passion to abolish the slave trade in England, a passion which few people shared at the time, for slavery was firmly entrenched in the economy and culture of many English outposts.

Upon hearing that Wilberforce was facing such a dilemma, his good friend and soon-to-be prime minister of England, William Pitt, arranged a meeting between Wilberforce and some of the other passionate abolitionists. One of them, a pastor, said, "Mr. Wilberforce, we understand you're having problems choosing whether to do the work of God or the work of a political activist." Another added, quietly, "We humbly suggest that you can do both."

Rather than *leave* politics, Wilberforce spent the next thirty years as a member of parliament, using his God-given gifts of eloquence, wisdom, and faith to help bring about the end of slavery throughout the entire British Empire.

What about you? What kinds of gifts might God want you to use for Him? By thinking about those things which you feel most passionate about, it can help you identify what gifts God may most want to use within you.

Someone recently asked me, "If you could be the best in the world at one particular skill, what would it be, and why?" The first thing that came to my mind was "preaching," because I like the idea of being able interact and shape the lives of people God has brought into my life. But the second thing that came to my mind was "writing," because as much as I love personally interacting with people, I know that by writing down the thoughts and ideas that God is putting into my mind, I can influence people's lives for generations to come. Thinking about these two passions in my life has helped me to focus on those things that God has gifted me to do as well.

A Jesuit priest named John Powell talks of an old Christian tradition that says,

> "God sends every person into the world with a special message to deliver, with a special song to sing for others, and a special act of love to bestow. No one else can speak your message, or sing your song, or offer your act of love. These are entrusted only to you."

When you think about your own gifts, your own passions, your own special skills that you could use to "make an offering" to God, what comes to mind? What do you feel passionate about? How has God gifted or empowered you? How has He infused His Divine Spirit within you in a particular way?

If you're not sure what your spiritual gifts might be, read through some of the gifts God has poured out on his people as recorded in Romans 12, 1 Corinthians 12, and Ephesians 4 and try to identify some of those which you feel most passionate about.

If you put even one or two of these gifts into use in your own life this week, I think you'll find out even more what it means to be "a living sacrifice, holy and pleasing to God."

Prayer: Father, thank You for giving us spiritual gifts, gifts that we can use to bless You and bless those around us. We pray that You would help us to understand our gifts even better, so that we can live our lives in such a way that we are truly "living sacrifices," holy and pleasing to You. In Jesus' name, Amen.

Memory Verse:

> "I appeal to you therefore, brothers, by the mercies of God, to present your bodies as a living sacrifice, holy and acceptable to God, which is your spiritual worship" (Romans 12:1, ESV).

NUMBER 10: THE REALITY OF HEAVEN — JULY 22

Scripture Reading: John 14

I'd like to share a conversation I had with a man on a small plane in the Philippines. My wife and I were on a missions trip, flying between two of the islands, and an elderly man was seated next to us. His wife, unfortunately, had recently passed away.

When he found out we were on a missions trip, he asked us a very heartfelt question. He said that he missed his wife greatly and wondered where she was now. He wanted to know if she was OK.

I asked him, "Was she a Christian? Did she believe in Jesus?"

He answered, "Yes, she was, and yes, she believed in Him very deeply."

I said, "Then let's take a look at what Jesus said about where she is now." Then I opened my Bible and read to him these words of Jesus from John chapter 14:

> "Let not your hearts be troubled. Believe in God; believe also in Me. In My Father's house are many rooms. If it were not so, would I have told you that I go to prepare a place for you? And if I go and prepare a place for you, I will come again and will take you to Myself, that where I am you may be also" (John 14:1-3).

As I read Jesus' words, the man began to weep. Suddenly, he knew where his wife was. He knew she was in heaven. He knew she was with Jesus.

Jesus had many other things to say to His disciples in John chapter 14, just as He still has much to say to us today.

He assured them that even though He was going to heaven, He would still be able to hear their prayers. More than that, He assured them that He would answer them, if they asked for anything in His name:

> "Whatever you ask in My name, this I will do, that the Father may be glorified in the Son. If you ask Me anything in My name, I will do it" (John 14:13-14).

And then, as you would expect from any good relationship, Jesus said that He had things He wanted them to do as well:

> "If you love Me, you will keep My commandments. … If anyone loves Me, he will keep My word, and My Father will love him, and we will come to him and make our home with him. Whoever does not love Me does not keep My words. And the word that you hear is not mine but the Father's who sent Me." (John 14:15).

He also assured them that He wasn't going to leave them alone, because the Father was going to send His Holy Spirit to them. He said:

> "These things I have spoken to you while I am still with you. But the Helper, the Holy Spirit, whom the Father will send in My name, He will teach you all things and bring to your remembrance all that I have said to you. Peace I leave with you; My peace I give to you. Not as the world gives do I give to you. Let not your hearts be troubled, neither let them be afraid" (John 14:18-20, 25-27).

There's a note I've seen that summarizes the message of John 14 quite simply. It says:

> "Gone to My Father's house to prepare a place for you. Be back soon—Love, Jesus"

You don't get to heaven by plane or train, by car or bus, or even by rocket ship. You get to heaven by putting your faith in Christ and letting Him take you there Himself. As Jesus told His disciples, when they asked Him how to get there, He said:

> "I am the way, and the truth, and the life. No one comes to the Father except through Me" (John 14:6).

If you need assurance today that heaven is real, that Jesus hears your prayers (and will answer them!), and that He has not left you here alone, I'd encourage you to read the rest of John 14 for yourself. Just as the man seated next to us on the plane in the Philippines found the answers to His questions in these words from Jesus, so can you.

Prayer: Father, thank You for Your reassuring words that You've already gone ahead of us into heaven, and that You're preparing a place for us even now. Help us to continue to put our trust in You that we will be in heaven with you forever, and continue to fill us with Your Holy Spirit, so that we can do all that You've called us to do here on earth. In Jesus' name, Amen.

Memory Verse:

> *"Let not your hearts be troubled. Believe in God; believe also in Me. In My Father's house are many rooms. If it were not so, would I have told you that I go to prepare a place for you?" (John 14:1, ESV).*

NUMBER 9: NEED WISDOM? ASK GOD! JULY 23

Scripture Reading: James 1

When people write to me asking for prayer about what to do in a particular situation, I'll often include in my reply a quote from James chapter 1. That's because James states clearly and emphatically that God loves to pour out His wisdom on those who ask for it.

And because people are facing so many decisions in their lives—whether it's in regards to their relationships, careers, health, finances, ministries, and so on—I find myself quoting James quite a bit. Here's what James says:

> *"If any of you lacks wisdom, let him ask God, who gives generously to all without reproach, and it will be given him" (James 1:5).*

This is a simple, yet beautiful verse. It's simple, because it contains a very basic message: if you need wisdom, ask God. It's beautiful, because it gives you assurance that your prayers are not in vain, that God *will* give you His wisdom, generously and without reproach—meaning He will not rebuke you for asking. He knows that your wisdom is limited, and that's OK.

But believe it or not, as much as you might want to know God's will for your life, God wants you to know it even more. He has a vested interest in your decisions, and He is more than willing to help you make them—if you're willing to ask.

James goes on to say that the *way* you ask for wisdom will help to ensure that you'll receive it: he says to ask for it *in faith*:

> *"But let him ask in faith, with no doubting, for the one who doubts is like a wave of the sea that is driven and tossed by the wind. For that person must not suppose that he will receive anything from the Lord; he is a double-minded man, unstable in all his ways" (James 1:6-8).*

God wants you to come to Him in faith, believing that He will answer you, and believing that His answer is truly the best for you. Some people come to God wanting to hear His thoughts on a matter first, *then* they decide whether or not they want to take His advice. But God wants you to come to Him in faith, with your answer being, "Yes! I'll do it!" even before He tells you what to do! He wants to know that you trust Him, that you believe in your heart that He really does know what's best for you.

What does faith like this look like in real life? If you keep reading in the book of James, you'll find out:

"What good is it, my brothers, if a man claims to have faith but has no deeds? Can such faith save him? Suppose a brother or sister is without clothes and daily food. If one of you says to him, 'Go, I wish you well; keep warm and well fed,' but does nothing about his physical needs, what good is it? In the same way, faith by itself, if it is not accompanied by action, is dead" (James 2:14-17).

The best kind of faith is faith that is put into action, because faith like this demonstrates to God and to those around you that you really do believe what He says is true.

If you're wrestling with a decision in your life, I want to encourage you to ask God for wisdom, whether it's about who to marry, where to live, how to live, how not to live, or any other question that's on your heart. Come to God with an expectant heart. He won't rebuke you for asking for wisdom. Instead, He'll pour out His wisdom on you generously without finding fault.

I'd also encourage you to read through the rest of James chapter 1—and all 5 chapters of the book of James if you can—for his letter contains some of the best wisdom from God on topics like persevering through trials, dealing with temptation, caring for those in need, taming your tongue, praying for healing, and praying in faith.

It might even contain the specific answers to the questions on your heart. If you need wisdom, ask God. And when you ask, ask in faith!

Prayer: Father, thank You for assuring us that You love to pour out Your wisdom on us when we ask for it in faith. Please answer the prayers on our hearts and give us the wisdom we need to make the best decisions we can in the situations we face. In Jesus' name, Amen.

Memory Verse:

"If any of you lacks wisdom, let him ask God, who gives generously to all without reproach, and it will be given him" (James 1:5, ESV).

NUMBER 8: WILL GOD REALLY REWARD YOU?   JULY 24

Scripture Reading: Matthew 6

I got a letter in the mail one day from Isaac Asimov, the famous science fiction writer, back when he was still alive. It wasn't a personal letter, but rather a fund raising letter he had written for an atheistic organization. The letter began by saying: "You'll get your reward in heaven!" Asimov then followed up that quote with his own words: "We've all heard *that* empty promise before."

Asimov didn't believe in God, or heaven, or hell. He went on to say in his letter that if you wanted to get anything out of life, you'd better get it here and now for, according to him, there was no hereafter.

But Jesus said something completely different. And although Jesus never wrote a single book, his words have been recorded for us in a book that has sold more copies than any other book in the history of the world. Let's take a look at what Jesus said about God's rewards in Matthew chapter 6:

In talking about giving, Jesus said:

> *"But when you give to the needy, do not let your left hand know what your right hand is doing, so that your giving may be in secret. And your Father who sees in secret will reward you" (Matthew 6:3-4).*

In talking about praying, Jesus said:

> *"But when you pray, go into your room and shut the door and pray to your Father who is in secret. And your Father who sees in secret will reward you" (Matthew 6:6).*

In talking about fasting, Jesus said:

> *"But when you fast, anoint your head and wash your face, that your fasting may not be seen by others but by your Father who is in secret. And your Father who sees in secret will reward you" (Matthew 6:17-18).*

Jesus followed this up by saying that the rewards God has in store for us don't come just here on earth, but in heaven as well. As Jesus continues in Matthew 6, He says:

> *"Do not lay up for yourselves treasures on earth, where moth and rust destroy and where thieves break in and steal, but lay up for yourselves treasures in heaven, where neither moth nor rust destroys and where thieves do not break in and steal. For where your treasure is, there your heart will be also" (Matthew 6:19-21).*

I know a pastor who could have made a tremendous amount of money from the conferences at which he has spoken and the books that he has written. But instead, he and his wife have chosen to take only a minimal salary, living in an extremely humble house, and declining or giving away the rest of the millions he could have earned.

His friends have challenged him for the way he lives, claiming he has a poverty mentality. But he counters their claims by saying that nothing could be further from the truth. He wants to get rich more than anyone else he knows. The difference is that he wants to store up his riches in heaven, where they will last forever, rather than cashing in on them here where they will rot or rust.

What about you? What do you believe? Will God really reward you for the things you do for Him, and for others, even those things you do in secret? Jesus says He will, and I for one—along with millions of others—believe Him. I pray that you do, too, for God knows it will affect everything you think and do here on earth, as well as what God does for you in eternity.

You can trust Jesus: God really will reward you when you put Him first in your life. As Jesus said at the end of Matthew 6:

> *"Therefore do not be anxious, saying, 'What shall we eat?' or 'What shall we drink?' or 'What shall we wear?' For the Gentiles seek after all these things, and your heavenly Father knows that you need them all. But seek first the kingdom of God and His righteousness, and all these things will be added to you" (Matthew 6:31-33).*

Put your trust in God. He really will reward you!

Prayer: Father, thank You for promising to reward us when we seek first Your kingdom and Your righteousness. Help us to trust You, and not to worry about what we'll eat or drink or wear, but to focus on Your kingdom, storing up our riches in heaven instead. In Jesus' name, Amen.

Memory Verse:

> "But seek first the kingdom of God and His righteousness, and all these things will be added to you" (Matthew 6:33, ESV).

NUMBER 7: WHERE SHOULD I START? — JULY 25

Scripture Reading: John 1

If someone had never read the Bible before and they were to ask you where they should start, what would you tell them? For many people, their answer would be to start with the book of John—and for good reason.

John is one of the most beloved books in the Bible. It contains some of the Bible's most famous verses, including John 3:16, and it focuses on God's love for His children perhaps more than any other book. It's short enough that you can read a chapter a day and finish in just 21 days, but it's long enough to give you a good look at the life of Christ—and why you should put your faith in Him. In fact, John says that's why he wrote the book, as he notes at the end of chapter 20:

> "Now Jesus did many other signs in the presence of the disciples, which are not written in this book; but these are written so that you may believe that Jesus is the Christ, the Son of God, and that by believing you may have life in His name" (John 20:30-31).

John saw, with his own eyes, many of the stories that he recorded in his book. While Jesus had many followers, He had twelve who spent three and a half years with Him eating, sleeping, praying, talking, and ministering. And of those twelve, three were especially close to Jesus: Peter, James, and John (see Mark 5:37, Mark 9:2, Mark 13:3, and Mark 14:33). And of those three, John was perhaps the closest, referring to himself in his book as, "the disciple whom Jesus loved" (see John 13:23, 20:2, 21:7, and 21:20).

Perhaps it was because of John's close friendship with Jesus that John talks about the love of God so much, using the word "love" in his gospel more than any of the other gospel writers combined. Here are just a few of those references, all direct quotes that John recorded Jesus as saying:

> "For God so loved the world, that He gave His only Son, that whoever believes in Him should not perish but have eternal life" (John 3:16).
>
> "A new commandment I give to you, that you love one another: just as I have loved you, you also are to love one another. By this all people will know that you are my disciples, if you have love for one another" (John 13:34-35).
>
> "If anyone loves Me, he will keep My Word, and My Father will love him, and We will come to him and make Our home with him" (John 14:23).
>
> "As the Father has loved Me, so have I loved you. Abide in My love" (John 15:9).
>
> "Greater love has no one than this, that someone lay down his life for his friends" (John 15:13).

If you need some encouragement that God really loves you, read the book of John. If you need some encouragement that you can trust Christ with everything in your life, read the book of John. If you'd like to read the Bible but don't know where to start, read the book of John. Or if you'd just like a fresh reminder of God's love for you and all the things that are possible when you put your faith in Him, read the book of John.

Start in chapter 1, and you'll find that salvation through Jesus wasn't just an afterthought in the mind of God, but that Jesus was with God in the beginning. John said, referring to Jesus as "the Word":

"In the beginning was the Word, and the Word was with God, and the Word was God. He was in the beginning with God. ... And the Word became flesh and dwelt among us ..." (John 1:1-3, 14a).

You'll also find in chapter 1 that Jesus is "the Lamb of God," who came to take away our sin:

"Behold, the Lamb of God, who takes away the sin of the world!" (John 1:29b).

And lastly in chapter 1, you'll find that Jesus calls you to follow Him, just as He called the first disciples to do, saying:

"Follow Me" (John 1:43b).

Then keep on reading the rest of the book, whether it takes you a few hours, a few days, or 21 days, reading just a chapter a day. Even if you've read it many times before, I pray that God will speak new things to you as you do.

Prayer: Father, thank You for the words of Your great love for us that You've recorded for us in the Bible, and Your desire for us to return that love to You and to share it with others. Thank You for John's life and for inspiring him to record these words for us so we can keep putting our faith in Jesus. It's in His name we pray, Amen.

Memory Verse:

"In the beginning was the Word, and the Word was with God, and the Word was God" (John 1, ESV).

NUMBER 6: THE BEST SERMON EVER — JULY 26

Scripture Reading: Matthew 5

I've just been reading what is perhaps the best sermon ever. It was delivered by Jesus to a crowd of thousands on a hillside near the Sea of Galilee. Because of its location, this sermon is often called "The Sermon on the Mount." It spans three chapters in the book of Matthew, starting in chapter 5.

When you read Jesus' famous sermon, you'll see why it's so popular. It's like reading a *Cliff's Notes* version of the entire Bible. You'll also probably recognize many of the famous quotes that come from this passage. Here are just a few from chapter 5:

> *"Blessed are the poor in spirit, for theirs is the kingdom of heaven. Blessed are those who mourn, for they shall be comforted. Blessed are the meek, for they shall inherit the earth"* (Matthew 5:3-5).
>
> *"You are the light of the world. A city set on a hill cannot be hidden. Nor do people light a lamp and put it under a basket, but on a stand, and it gives light to all in the house. In the same way, let your light shine before others, so that they may see your good works and give glory to your Father who is in heaven"* (Matthew 5:14-16).
>
> *"You have heard that it was said, 'You shall not commit adultery.' But I say to you that everyone who looks at a woman with lustful intent has already committed adultery with her in his heart"* (Matthew 5:27-28).
>
> *"You have heard that it was said, 'An eye for an eye and a tooth for a tooth.' But I say to you, Do not resist the one who is evil. But if anyone slaps you on the right cheek, turn to him the other also"* (Matthew 5:38-39).
>
> *"You have heard that it was said, 'You shall love your neighbor and hate your enemy.' But I say to you, Love your enemies and pray for those who persecute you …"* (Matthew 5:43-44).

Reading through the Sermon on the Mount is like reading through the best-of-the-best quotes from *Bartlett's Familiar Quotations*. It even includes the Golden Rule and the Lord's Prayer!

But I'd also like to point out that even the best sermons in the world are only fruitful if those who hear the words put them into practice. As Jesus said at the end of His sermon:

> *"Everyone then who hears these words of mine and does them will be like a wise man who built his house on the rock. And the rain fell, and the floods came, and the winds blew and beat on that house, but it did not fall, because it had been founded on the rock. And everyone who hears these words of mine and does not do them will be like a foolish man who built his house on the sand. And the rain fell, and the floods came, and the winds blew and beat against that house, and it fell, and great was the fall of it"* (Matthew 7:24-27).

I wrote a book a few years ago called *What God Says About Sex*. My purpose was to share what I had learned about this precious gift from God and to spare others from the heartache that often comes from misusing this gift. Many people have read the book over the years, and I've been amazed at the results—some good, and some not so good.

Some people have read it eagerly, taking the words to heart, putting them into practice, and being blessed beyond measure. Others have picked it up with interest at first, only to set it down later and ignore what they read, ending up with unplanned pregnancies, untreatable diseases, and unnecessary pain. Then there are those who have gotten a copy of the book but didn't crack it open—until it was too late.

I know of one man who had it sitting on his bedroom dresser—unopened and unread—when he got his girlfriend pregnant. They broke up soon afterwards, but when their precious baby was born, they entered into a lengthy and heart-wrenching custody battle.

The man later said that he wished he had read my book *before* this all happened.

When I hear stories like these, I get a small glimpse into what God must feel when people read—or don't read—His Book, and the various results that come when they put His Words into practice—or don't.

I'd like to encourage you to take some time this week to read the "Sermon on the Mount" and see for yourself why it is perhaps "The Best Sermon Ever." You'll find it in Matthew chapters 5, 6, and 7. It only takes about 20-30 minutes to read, but if you put what you read into practice, you'll be blessed for a lifetime!

My hope and my prayer is that you will take time to read these chapters and that you'll be a light shining for Christ—and, as Jesus said, when others see your good works, they'll "give glory to your Father who is in heaven."

Prayer: Father, thank You for giving us Your wisdom in the words of the Bible. Help us to read Your word daily, take it to heart, and put it into practice in our lives. In Jesus' name, Amen.

Memory Verse:

> "You are the light of the world. A city set on a hill cannot be hidden. Nor do people light a lamp and put it under a basket, but on a stand, and it gives light to all in the house. In the same way, let your light shine before others, so that they may see your good works and give glory to your Father who is in heaven" (Matthew 5:14-16, ESV).

NUMBER 5: GOD'S PROTECTION JULY 27

Scripture Reading: Psalm 91

There's a difference between "believing in God" and "believing God." You can believe in God yet still keep Him at a distance. But when you believe God—when you take Him at His Word and put what He says into practice in your life—you enter into a relationship with Him, a relationship that is up close and personal; a relationship where every step you take is wise and purposeful because you're keeping in step with Him.

Psalm 91 describes one of the great benefits of this kind of close relationship with God: you enter into His divine protection. Here are some of the things God will do for you when you dwell "in the shelter of the Most High":

> "He who dwells in the shelter of the Most High
> will abide in the shadow of the Almighty.
> I will say to the LORD, 'My refuge and my fortress,
> my God, in whom I trust.'
> For He will deliver you from the snare of the fowler
> and from the deadly pestilence.
> He will cover you with His pinions,
> and under His wings you will find refuge;
> His faithfulness is a shield and buckler.
> You will not fear the terror of the night,
> nor the arrow that flies by day,
> nor the pestilence that stalks in darkness,
> nor the destruction that wastes at noonday.
> A thousand may fall at your side,
> ten thousand at your right hand,

but it will not come near you"
(Psalm 91:1-7).

Moses, who many Jewish scholars believe authored this Psalm, saw his share of trouble. He saw plagues of locusts and plagues of death, threats of famine and threats on his life. But Moses also saw God's divine hand of deliverance.

When the angel of death passed through the streets of Egypt, thousands fell, but Moses and his people were saved. Not only did they believe *in* God, but they also *believed* God. They did what He told them to do, putting the blood of a lamb on the doorframes of their homes so the angel of death would "pass over" and spare the lives of those inside (see Exodus 12).

Jesus is *our* Passover lamb, and when you put your faith in Him—staying close to Him and holding on tight—then He's able to take you under His protective wings. It's hard for God to protect you, though, if you keep running back and forth to Him, coming to Him only *after* disaster strikes. He wants you to be in a close relationship with Him at all times, dwelling with Him, living with Him, taking up residence in His protective refuge. When you do, listen to a few more of the ways you'll be blessed:

"Because you have made the LORD your dwelling place—
the Most High, who is my refuge—
no evil shall be allowed to befall you,
no plague come near your tent.
For He will command His angels concerning you
to guard you in all your ways.
On their hands they will bear you up,
lest you strike your foot against a stone.
You will tread on the lion and the adder;
the young lion and the serpent you will trample underfoot.
Because he holds fast to Me in love, I will deliver him;
I will protect him, because he knows My Name.
When he calls to Me, I will answer him;
I will be with him in trouble;
I will rescue him and honor him.
With long life I will satisfy him
and show him My salvation"
(Psalm 91:9-10, 14-16).

It's good to believe in God, but it's even better to believe God, drawing near to Him and dwelling in His shelter. How do you do that? By calling out to Him when you wake up each morning. By reading His Word and listening to His Spirit so you can hear back from Him. By holding on tight to Him throughout the day and taking care to do what He says, stepping where He says to step (and *not* stepping where He says *not* to step!). And when the day is done, being sure to say goodnight again, entrusting Him to hold you tight throughout the night.

God loves you and wants to protect you, shield you, and deliver you. Just be sure to stay under His protective wings.

Prayer: Father, thank You for loving us and offering us Your strong hand of protection. Help us to come closer and closer to You so that we can see what Moses saw, and experience Your deliverance first-hand. In Jesus' name, Amen.

Memory Verse:

> "Because he holds fast to Me in love, I will deliver him; I will protect him, because he knows My Name" (Psalm 91:14, ESV).

NUMBER 4: GOD WORKS FOR YOUR GOOD — JULY 28

Scripture Reading: Romans 8

God is for you. He loves you. And He can work all things together for good, when you love Him and are called according to His purpose. These concepts are found throughout the Bible. But they're also stated clearly and succinctly in Romans chapter 8.

Although the Apostle Paul wrote this letter to the believers living in Rome, Italy, about the year 54 A.D., Paul's words apply just as much to you today, wherever you happen to live in the world, if you, too, are a believer in Christ. Here are a few of the things Paul said.

He wants you to be free from the guilt and shame that you might feel because of your sins:

> "There is therefore now no condemnation for those who are in Christ Jesus" (Romans 8:1).

He wants you to know that you aren't alone in your struggle against sin, for the life-giving power of the Holy Spirit lives within you:

> "If the Spirit of Him who raised Jesus from the dead dwells in you, He who raised Christ Jesus from the dead will also give life to your mortal bodies through His Spirit who dwells in you" (Romans 8:11).

He wants you to know that if you are experiencing any suffering in this world, that it will hardly compare to the glory you will see one day:

> "For I consider that the sufferings of this present time are not worth comparing with the glory that is to be revealed to us" (Romans 8:18).

Or as Samuel Rutherford, a Scottish writer in the 1600's, paraphrased it: "Our little time of suffering is not worthy of our first night's welcome home to Heaven."

Paul wants you to know that even when you are at a loss as to how to pray for yourself, the Holy Spirit will pray for you:

> "Likewise the Spirit helps us in our weakness. For we do not know what to pray for as we ought, but the Spirit Himself intercedes for us with groanings too deep for words" (Romans 8:26).

And in one of the most famous verses in the Bible, Paul wants you to know that God will work all things for good for those who love Him and are called according to His purpose:

> "And we know that for those who love God all things work together for good, for those who are called according to His purpose" (Romans 8:28).

I often quote this verse—both to myself and to others—because it's a great reminder that God can bring good out of any difficulty that we face.

There's a concept in karate called "borrowed force" that's useful when someone throws a punch at you. Instead of taking the hit and letting the punch knock you out, you can take hold of the punch with your hands, add your own strength to it, and throw your opponent to the ground behind you. Instead of letting the punch defeat you, you can use it for good.

When life, or people, or your job, or the economy, throws a punch at you that could probably knock you out, God wants you to put your faith in Him. When you do, He can help you to take hold of the punch that was meant for evil and turn it into something good something even better than you may have been able to do on your own.

If you remember the story of Joseph and his brothers, you'll see how Joseph was able to see God's hand at work, even after his brothers sold him as a slave into Egypt. God one day raised Joseph up to be second in command in Egypt, giving him wisdom to store up food during years of plenty for an upcoming famine, resulting in saving many people in Egypt as well as his own brothers. Joseph said:

> "As for you, you meant evil against me, but God meant it for good, to bring it about that many people should be kept alive, as they are today" (Genesis 50:20).

God is for you, too. He loves you. And if you'll trust in Him with everything that you're going through today, He really can and will work all things together for good.

I hope you'll read the rest of Romans 8 today—especially the last section in verses 31-39. They're some of the most uplifting words in the whole Bible. If God is for you, who can be against you!

Prayer: Father, thank You for loving us so fully, and for promising us that You will indeed work all things for good in our lives when we love you and are called according to Your purpose. Help us to trust You and Your promises completely, as we face the challenges in our lives today. In Jesus' name, Amen.

Memory Verse:

> "And we know that for those who love God all things work together for good, for those who are called according to His purpose" (Romans 8:28, ESV).

NUMBER 3: FROM COVER TO COVER   JULY 29

Scripture Reading: Genesis 1

A young preacher once invited an older preacher to his church to share a sermon with his congregation. The sermon was powerful, and many people were touched deeply by the message. Afterwards, the younger preacher asked the older preacher the secret of his success.

The older preacher asked him, "How many times have you read the Bible, from cover to cover?"

The younger preacher said, "I've read a lot of it, but I've never read the whole thing all the way through even once yet."

The older preacher then pointed at his Bible and said: "When you've read this book twenty times, from cover to cover, then you'll be able to preach like that."

I know this is a true story, because the man who told it to me was that younger preacher, many years ago, and he went home and did exactly what the older preacher suggested. By the time I heard him tell the story, he was quite old. Although he didn't tell me how many times he'd read the Bible from cover to cover since he first got that advice, if I were to judge from the message I heard him preach that day, I would say he well exceeded the suggested twenty! He was a powerful preacher!

What's good for powerful preaching is also good for powerful living.

The most pivotal time in my life came when I started reading the Bible from cover to cover for myself. I had been in a Bible study for a few months with a small group of men from our church and decided to go out and buy a good study Bible—with lots of footnotes included in it so I could understand better what I was reading.

I started at Genesis, Chapter 1. As I began to read, I tried to immerse myself in the story, reading it not just as ancient history, but more like a newspaper, describing the events of the day as if they were actually taking place while I was reading them. I found that when I read the Bible this way, the stories came alive, starting with the story of the creation of the world:

> "In the beginning, God created the heavens and the earth" (Genesis 1:1).

As I read that passage, I began to picture what it must have been like for God to create something out of nothing.

When God said, "Let there be light," and there was light, I tried to picture what it would have been like to be in total darkness, and then watch as God's light burst onto the scene. As I continued reading, I could see water flowing, waves crashing, plants growing, fish swimming, birds flying, animals moving, and then—as the climactic event—God creating the first two human beings in His own image. I felt like Thomas Merton must have felt when he wrote:

> "By reading the scriptures I am so renewed that all nature seems renewed around me and with me. The sky seems to be a pure, a cooler blue, the trees a deeper green. The whole world is charged with the glory of God and I feel fire and music under my feet."

After a few weeks of reading the Bible like this, I sensed God's love for me in a new and deeper way. I also began to see my need for a Savior. I put my faith in Christ shortly thereafter and I've never looked back. I honestly don't know how many times I've read the Bible since then, either. But I do know that as I've read and reread this precious book over the years, it has changed me, challenged me, comforted me, and most of all increased my faith in Him who spoke its words into existence. As D.L. Moody said:

> "I prayed for faith and thought it would strike me like lightening. But faith did not come. One day I read, 'Now faith comes by hearing, and hearing by the Word of God.' I had closed my Bible and prayed for faith. I now began to study my Bible and faith has been growing ever since."

If you'd like to increase your faith, I'd encourage you to read the Bible, from cover to cover, starting in Genesis chapter 1. Make it a goal for yourself—not just to get through the whole Bible—but to let the whole Bible get through you. You'll be glad you did.

Prayer: *Father, thank You for giving us Your words in the pages of the Bible. Help us to read them and apply them to our lives daily so that we can grow closer and closer to You, and in the process, grow to look more and more like Your Son, Jesus Christ. It's in His name we pray, Amen.*

Memory Verse:

"In the beginning, God created the heavens and the earth" (Genesis 1:1, ESV).

NUMBER 2: SAVORING EVERY WORD — JULY 30

Scripture Reading: Psalm 23

Last time I talked about the value of reading the entire Bible from cover to cover. This time I'd like to focus on another approach to reading the Bible: savoring every word. For the goal of reading the Bible is not just to get all the way through it, but to let it get all through you!

One way to do that is to go slowly and meditate on the words you're reading—to think deeply about them and the implications they may have on your life.

For instance, let's take a close look at just a few verses from Psalm 23, the second most popular passage in the Bible. Because Psalm 23 is such a popular passage, you might be tempted to read it so quickly that you miss the flavor and nutrients offered by each of its words. But by slowing down and meditating on every word, you can better digest what you're reading.

Here's what happened to me as I spent time meditating on the first few verses of Psalm 23 this week, which starts like this:

"The LORD is my shepherd; I shall not want. He makes me lie down in green pastures. He leads me beside still waters. He restores my soul." (Psalm 23:1-2a).

As I started with the words, "The Lord is my shepherd," I thought about how God isn't just "a" god or "one god out of many," but that He is "THE God, THE Lord, THE One and Only Creator of the universe, THE Author and Sustainer of my life, with all of my life's intricate complexities.

As I thought about the little word "is" in "The Lord is my shepherd," I thought about the fact that the Lord IS my shepherd—not that He *was* my shepherd, or that He *will* be my shepherd, but that He IS my shepherd, taking care of me, protecting me, and nourishing me, right here and right now.

As I looked at the word "my," in "The Lord is my shepherd," I realized that the Lord is not just our shepherd, or the shepherd of the whole world, but that He's also MY shepherd. He knows me by name (see John 10:3 and 11), and if I ever strayed away, I know He would leave the rest of the flock behind in safety in order to find me and rescue me from danger (see Matthew 18, 12-14).

With the Lord as my shepherd, it's no wonder the verse continues with the words: "I shall not want."

But it was when I read, "He makes me lie down in green pastures," that God began to speak personally and specifically to me about a situation in my life that happened about a year ago, when we were considering launching out into a whole new aspect of our ministry. At the last minute, God redirected our steps and moved us out to where we're living now at Clover Ranch. As I read about the green pastures this week, I was watching my son mow the green grass in our front yard for the first time this year.

Although a year ago it seemed like God was pulling the rug out from under our feet in some ways, the truth was that He was "making us lie down in green pastures." He was leading us beside His still waters. He was restoring our souls. I was reminded of the quote from Daniel Defoe, the author of Robinson Crusoe, who said,

"God will often deliver us in a manner that seems initially to destroy us."

Oh, how thankful I was—and am—to have the Lord as my shepherd!

I didn't make it through the rest of Psalm 23 that day, but what a sweet time I had with God by just meditating on a few of His words.

As much as I love encouraging people to read through their whole Bibles many times, I love it, too, when they can savor every word. I'd encourage you to read through the rest of Psalm 23 for yourself today, stopping and meditating on those words or phrases that seem to stand out to you. Let them sink deep into your heart and mind, and let God restore *your* soul.

Prayer: Father, thank You for the richness of Your Word, and for using it to speak into our hearts and lives. Help us to read it thoroughly, to think about it deeply, and to let it impact the way we live our lives here on earth. In Jesus' name, Amen.

Memory Verse:

"The LORD is my shepherd; I shall not want" (Psalm 23:1, ESV).

NUMBER 1: THE LOVE TEST — JULY 31

Scripture Reading: 1 Corinthians 13

There's a philosophy in ethics called "enlightened self-interest." It's the intriguing idea that many of the "good deeds" we do are not motivated entirely for the benefit of others, but somehow serve our own self-interests as well.

Giving to charity, for instance, is a noble endeavor. But if our giving is solely dependent on whether or not we get a tax-deduction for our gift, then our giving really falls in the category of enlightened self-interest. We're glad to give—as long as our giving benefits us back in some way.

Not that there's anything wrong with enlightened self-interest in and of itself, as the idea of giving, and getting something in return, is the basis of economies all over the world. It only becomes a problem when we mistake enlightened self-interest for selfless love, thinking that what we're doing is truly loving, when in reality it could be simply selfishness masquerading as love.

Today we're looking at a passage in the Bible that deals almost entirely with love. Pure love. A love that is selfless and unadulterated. A love that gives without expecting anything in return. It's found in chapter 13 of the Apostle Paul's first letter to the believers who were living in the city of Corinth. Paul wrote the letter as a reminder to the Corinthians that no matter how important all of their gifts and abilities might be, they were meaningless without love. Paul wrote:

> "If I speak in the tongues of men and of angels, but have not love, I am a noisy gong or a clanging cymbal. And if I have prophetic powers, and understand all mysteries and all knowledge, and if I have all faith, so as to remove mountains, but have not love, I am nothing. If I give away all I have, and if I deliver up my body to be burned, but have not love, I gain nothing" (1 Corinthians 13:1-3).

Paul knew that God wants love to be at the core of everything we do. In the end, as Oliver Thomas said, "Authentic religion is not a theology test. It's a love test." As important as theology is—and moving mountains and giving sacrificially and every other good thing in which we engage—love must pervade them all, or else we've failed the test.

Paul continues his letter by writing one of the most beautiful definitions of love found in all of literature. Because of this, 1 Corinthians 13 is frequently read at wedding ceremonies throughout the world. Paul says:

> "Love is patient and kind; love does not envy or boast; it is not arrogant or rude. It does not insist on its own way; it is not irritable or resentful; it does not rejoice at wrongdoing, but rejoices with the truth. Love bears all things, believes all things, hopes all things, endures all things. Love never ends" (1 Corinthians 13:4-8a).

Paul's words serve as a checklist of sorts to help us determine how truly loving we are towards those around us. While many times we might think we're acting in love, if we compare our love to the love described in this passage, we'll get to the heart of what truly motivates us. Is it pure love? Or just some form of "enlightened self-interest," giving to others with the hope that we might get some kind of benefit in return?

There are times when we buy cards or gifts, or do favors for people, which seem selfless on the surface. But when we don't get the desired response in return for our efforts, our selfishness is exposed. Perhaps we weren't being truly as loving or generous as we thought. When thinking about some of the relationships in your own life, you can ask yourself these questions, based on 1 Corinthians 13:

> Is my love for this person patient and kind?
> Is it envious or boastful?
> Is it arrogant or rude?
> Does it insist on its own way?
> Is it irritable or resentful?
> Does it rejoice at wrongdoing? Or does it rejoice with the truth?
> Does it bear all things, believe all things, hope all things, endure all things?
> Does my love for them never end?

If you're like me, just reading through this list can be convicting. But Paul didn't write these words to dash us to pieces. He wrote them to lift us up, to encourage us to do what's right, and to begin loving others for all the right reasons again.

Let love motivate everything you do—not selfishness, and not selfishness masquerading as love. As you put these words into practice, you'll see why Paul closes this famous chapter on love by saying that of all the incredible gifts, that God has given you,

> "... the greatest of these is love" (1 Corinthians 13:13b).

Prayer: Father, thank You for loving us with a selfless love. We pray that You would help us show that same kind of love to those around us. Help us to be patient and kind, not envious or boastful. Keep us from arrogance or rudeness, or insisting on our own way, or being irritable or resentful. Help us to never rejoice at wrongdoing, but to always rejoice with the truth. Thank You for Your never ending love for us and help us to love others in the exact same way. In Jesus' name, Amen.

Memory Verse:

> "Love is patient and kind; love does not envy or boast; it is not arrogant or rude. It does not insist on its own way; it is not irritable or resentful; it does not rejoice at wrongdoing, but rejoices with the truth. Love bears all things, believes all things, hopes all things, endures all things. Love never ends" (1 Corinthians 13:4-7, ESV).

CONCLUSION: THE ULTIMATE LOVE AFFAIR — AUGUST 1

Scripture Reading: John 5:39-40

Some people wonder why Christians have such a love affair with the Bible. The truth is that we're not just in love with the words on the pages. We're in love with the One who is portrayed by those words.

It's like carrying around a picture of your beloved in your purse or wallet. When you take out that picture, looking fondly at the image, and maybe even brushing the picture up against your cheek, or giving it a kiss with your lips, it's not that you're in love with the picture on the paper. You're in love with the one whose image is displayed on the paper.

In the same way, those who love their Bibles aren't just in love with the Bible. They're in love with the One who is displayed on its pages.

Yet as wonderful as this kind of love affair with the Bible can be, there's a surprising danger in it. There are times when you might fall so much in love with the words on the pages that you miss having a relationship with the Word Himself, Jesus Christ, who is described on those pages. Even Jesus warned of this danger when He said to some of the religious leaders of His day:

> "You search the Scriptures because you think that in them you have eternal life; and it is they that bear witness about Me, yet you refuse to come to Me that you may have life" (John 5:39-40).

The Message translation of the Bible paraphrases these same words of Jesus like this:

> "You have your heads in your Bibles constantly because you think you'll find eternal life there...These Scriptures are all about me! And here I am, standing right before you" (John 5:39-40, MSG).

Imagine holding a picture of your beloved in your hands, treasuring it, pulling it close to your heart, and even gazing at it longingly, all the while not even realizing or acknowledging that your beloved is standing right there next to you the whole time!

As much as I love the Bible—and it is my favorite book in the world—I have to remind myself from time to time that the Trinity is not made up of "the Father, the Son, and the Holy Scripture." But rather, the Trinity is made up of "the Father, the Son, and the Holy Spirit," three aspects of the same singular God who loves you and wants to be involved actively in your life today!

Keep reading your Bible, but don't forget: Jesus is STILL alive! When His Holy Spirit prompts you to give, then give! When you ask Him a question in prayer, then wait and listen for His answer! When you're feeling stressed and start meditating on God's Word, remember that God's Word—Jesus Christ—is standing right there with you, too!

The words of the Bible are like love letters to you from your beloved, scented with the perfume of heaven, and sealed with a kiss from the Creator of the universe. He loves you more than you could know, and He demonstrated that love by sending His Son Jesus to live and die and rise again from the dead, so you can live and die and rise again from the dead with Him one day, too. If you're going to have a love affair, make sure you have it not just with the words on the pages of the Bible, but have it with the One who is described by those words: Jesus Christ!

Prayer: Father thank You for showing us who you are on the pages of the Bible. Help us to read Your Word as love letters from You and help us to remind ourselves that our relationship is with You—a real and living Person. We invite you to speak into our lives again today and continue to speak to us throughout our lives and on into heaven, when we will be with You forever. In Jesus' name, Amen.

Memory Verse:

"You search the Scriptures because you think that in them you have eternal life; and it is they that bear witness about Me, yet you refuse to come to Me that you may have life" (John 5:39-40).

Romans: Lessons in Renewing Your Mind

40 inspiring devotionals based on one of the most life-changing books in the Bible

ABOUT THIS BOOK

God has used the book of Romans to change many lives since it was written almost 2,000 years ago, including Saint Augustine's back in the 4th century, Martin Luther's in the 16th, John Wesley's in the 18th–and mine in the 20th! So I've written this study guide to help you reap the benefits from this life-changing book, too.

Each lesson in this study focuses on a different aspect of renewing your mind, based on different passages from the book of Romans. Some days you'll read just a verse or two, while other days you'll read whole chapters. But if you'll keep reading through the suggested passages each day, by the end of this study you'll have read through the entire book of Romans.

At the end of each chapter, I've included some "Questions for Reflection" that you can use for personal reflection or group discussion. The study is divided into 40 lessons (counting the Introduction and Conclusion), so you can complete the study by doing one lesson a day for 40 days, or five lessons a week for eight weeks, or a lesson a week for 40 weeks, whichever suits you or your group best.

At the end of this book, I've included four additional devotionals that I wrote, plus one that my wife Lana wrote, after Lana's diagnosis with Stage 4 cancer, which took place midway through writing this series. I've included these special messages to highlight the importance of keeping your mind focused on God's perspective on your life at all times. May God bless you as you seek to renew your mind, day by day, and may your life be transformed in the process.

INTRODUCTION: GOD WOULD LOVE TO RENEW YOUR MIND AUGUST 2

Scripture Reading: Romans 12:1-2

God would love to renew your mind. He would love to replace any thoughts you have that are pulling you down with thoughts that will pull you up. He would love to give you new thoughts, *His* thoughts, thoughts that will change the trajectory of the rest of your life.

How do I know? Because God has given me new thoughts, His thoughts, and thoughts that have changed the trajectory of my life as I've read the book of Romans for the first time as an adult twenty-five years ago.

I wasn't in the pit of despair. I didn't hate myself or my life. I didn't even know I was headed in the wrong direction with my life. But as I began reading through the book of Romans, starting with chapter 1, God began answering questions that had been on my heart for a long time. He began speaking to me through the words on the pages in such a clear and convincing way that I knew it was God who was speaking to me.

The things I read caused me to reevaluate my life, what I had been doing so far, and what I wanted to do in the future. In the weeks that followed, God had so changed my thinking that I came to the point that I wanted to put my faith in Christ for everything in my life: for the forgiveness of my sins, for the direction of my life, for my job, my body, my finances, my future. Everything that was a part of me, I gave to Him.

Now, twenty-five years later, I am in a totally different place than I would have been had I stayed on the path I was on. Even though I didn't realize at the time the direction my life *could* have taken, God knew—and He wanted to spare me from it. He picked me up, turned me around, and put me on a new path—a path that was headed toward an abundant and eternal life.

How did this life-change all get started? It started with an idea. A thought. A thought that maybe God was right, and I was wrong. A thought that maybe if I were to truly follow God with my whole heart, that no matter where He led me, He would take me places that I could never have gone on my own. A thought that if I trusted Him completely, that He really loved me, that He really cared for me deeply, and that He really knew what was best for me, then He would always lead me down a path that was in my best interest and His—even if I didn't understand it at the time.

Ideas are powerful. In the Academy Award-nominated movie, *Inception*, the main character asks an intriguing question:

"What is the most resilient parasite? A bacteria? A virus? An intestinal worm?"

Then he answers his own question with these words:

"An idea. An idea is like a virus. Resilient, highly contagious. Once an idea has taken hold in the brain it's almost impossible to eradicate."

Later on in the movie, he adds:

"And the smallest seed of an idea can grow. It can grow to define…or destroy you."

Ideas have started revolutions of all kinds—both good and bad. The United States was started with an idea back in 1776. But so were the terrorist attacks that killed so many of our people on September 11th, 2001.

Some of the ideas that have been planted in our minds are great. They should be nourished and fed. But other ideas have taken root that aren't so great. They should probably be rooted out and destroyed, before they destroy us.

I've been talking with some friends who grew up having had seeds of faith planted deep within them when they were younger—seeds which were watered regularly as they got older. But somewhere along the way, other people have planted doubts in their minds, doubts that have cropped up and overshadowed their faith. Doubts that have grown so large that you can hardly tell that they ever had a seed of faith at all. Unfortunately, they have begun watering and nurturing these doubts—by the books they read, the shows they watch, and the people with which they have surrounded themselves.

And yet I know they once had seeds of faith. I was there when some of those seeds were planted. I was there as they were being watered. I even did some of the watering myself. I believe they are still there!

But sometimes things happen along the way, both things that happen to us and things that we do to ourselves, that cause those *good* seeds within us to get crowded out and wither, letting the *bad* seeds grow up wild and unhindered.

It might seem like there's no way out once this cycle begins. It might seem sometimes that people have gone too far down the wrong path—that they'll never be able to change. But that's a lie!

The truth is, God can change people's hearts and minds in an instant. He can turn a life around on a dime. He can restore the years that have been wasted and put people back on the right path—*His* path—the path that leads to an abundant and eternal life.

But how? How can God do it? How can He transform you into the person that He wants you to be— into the person that you truly want to be, too?

The apostle Paul gave us an idea in the book of Romans—several ideas, in fact! Ideas that can turn your life around and help you look at everything that happens to you differently. Paul wrote the book of Romans as letter to those who believed in Jesus Christ in the city of Rome, almost 2,000 years ago. He wrote it about 25 years after Jesus died and rose again from the dead. At one point in his letter, Paul said:

> "Do not conform any longer to the pattern of this world, but be transformed by the renewing of your mind. Then you will be able to test and approve what God's will is—His good, pleasing and perfect will" (Romans 12:2).

God is saying the same thing to us today: He doesn't want us to be conformed to the pattern of this world—the worldly way in which things are done. Instead, He wants us to be transformed by the renewing of our minds. Why? Because then we'll be able to know His will for our lives—His good, pleasing and perfect will–and to test it out and approve it for ourselves! To know God's will for our lives–how awesome would that be?

In the lessons ahead, I'll be exploring with you several of Paul's many ideas for how to renew your mind, from how you think about yourself, to how you think about God–and the people and situations that God has placed in your life.

For some of you, this will be a new and exciting venture into unexplored territory. For others of you, this may be a new look at something you've tried to tackle before but haven't yet found the secret of success. In either case, take courage: God is still in the life-changing business and He would love to change your life by renewing your mind!

I remember seeing some flowers that my friend and neighbor Mary Lou had planted in her front yard. The flowers were called impatiens, which grew into huge bushes, bursting with color. My wife and I decided to plant some in our yard. But even though we planted them in the perfect spot and watered them regularly, they hardly grew more than a few inches tall, while Mary Lou's impatiens were flowing over and out of her planter boxes.

We couldn't figure out what was wrong. Then we asked her what her secret was. It turns out it wasn't a secret, she just used Miracle Grow (a type of fertilizer that helps plants grow to their fullest potential)!

My goal in this study is to give you a bit of Miracle Grow for your faith to help you grow to your fullest potential.

Sometimes we try doing things by ourselves. We may be doing the exact same things that other people around us, but you would hardly know it by the results. The difference may not be what we're doing, but what we're feeding on while we're doing it. My goal is to give you a key ingredient of faith! Faith to believe that God can really do all that He says

He can do in our lives! As Jesus said, just a little bit of that stuff has the power to move mountains!

For some of you, moving a mountain may be just what you need right now. So as we go through this study, I'll be sharing some stories from my own life—as well as some stories from the Bible and from Christians throughout the ages—that I pray will boost your faith. I pray they'll give you the burst of life that you need to keep pressing forward and keep moving in the direction that God has in mind for you.

For today, let me encourage you to simply begin by seeking the Lord for His wisdom. When you ask God for wisdom, He's glad to give it to you, pouring His thoughts into your mind. As He says in the book of Isaiah:

> "Seek the LORD while He may be found;
> call on Him while He is near.
> Let the wicked forsake his way
> and the evil man his thoughts.
> Let him turn to the LORD,
> and He will have mercy on him,
> and to our God, for He will freely pardon.
> "For My thoughts are not your thoughts,
> neither are your ways My ways,"
> declares the LORD.
> "As the heavens are higher than the earth,
> so are My ways higher than your ways
> and My thoughts than your thoughts.
> As the rain and the snow
> come down from heaven,
> and do not return to it
> without watering the earth
> and making it bud and flourish,
> so that it yields seed for the sower
> and bread for the eater,
> so is My Word that goes out from
> My mouth:
> It will not return to Me empty,
> but will accomplish what I desire
> and achieve the purpose for which I
> sent it."
> (Isaiah 55:6-11)

God would love to renew your mind. He would love to pour out His wisdom upon you like rain from heaven, refreshing your soul as He does. He would love to feed and nourish those ideas that will one day define you and root out and destroy any ideas that could possibly destroy you.

In the lessons ahead, I pray that God will transform your life by renewing your mind. I pray that God will use this time to renew your mind in powerful ways, transforming your life all along the way. I'm looking forward to it myself, and I hope you are, too!

Will you pray with me?

Father, thank You for giving us ways to transform our lives by renewing our minds. Thank You for the seeds of ideas that You've planted within us, those that are good and godly. Help us to feed and nurture them so that we can grow to our fullest potential. At the same time, we pray that You would help us root out any ideas that have been planted in our minds that are not from you, ideas that could be destroying us, even without our knowledge, so that we can live the life that You desire for us to live. We pray this all in Jesus' name, Amen.

Questions for Reflection:

1) Read Romans 12:1-2. What are some of the benefits of renewing your mind?
2) Read Isaiah 55:1-14. What are some ways you could renew your mind, based on this passage?
3) Read Philippians 4:8. What seeds have been planted in your life that God might want you to nourish?
4) Read Ephesians 5:1-20. What seeds have been planted in your life that God might want you to root out?

LESSON 1: BELONGING TO JESUS   AUGUST 3

Scripture Reading: Romans 1:1-7

One of the best places to start when renewing your mind is with how you identify yourself. For how you look at yourself affects how you look at everything around you.

Let's take a look at how Paul identified himself in the opening words of his letter to the Romans. Paul introduced himself by saying:

"Paul, a servant of Christ Jesus..." (Romans 1:1a).

It's a simple, but powerful statement. In the original Greek language—which Paul used to write this letter—the word *servant* is more like our word for *slave*.

We bristle at a word like that today. No one wants to be a slave. But it all depends on who your master is. When you serve a master who loves you, cares for you, feeds you, clothes you, and would die for you, what better person to serve?

Some people might not like the idea of *belonging* to someone else, but Paul didn't mind. He was glad to be a servant of Christ Jesus.

The truth is, we all serve something or someone. We're either slaves to sin, slaves to work, slaves to others, or slaves to ourselves—who may be the worst master of all. As for me, I'd rather serve Jesus!

Paul went on to say that not only did *he* belong to Jesus, but he wanted the Romans to belong to Jesus as well. After introducing himself, Paul said:

"And you also are called to belong to Jesus Christ" (Romans 1:6).

I love the way Paul said this, that he wanted them "to belong to Jesus Christ." It makes me think about my own life, and how I identify myself. As I read Paul's words to the Romans, I felt like God was saying to me:

"Eric, from what do you get your identity? Your family? Your ministry? Your website? I don't want you to get your identity from anything but Me. Not that your family isn't

great…or your ministry…or your website. But I don't want you to draw your strength from them. I want you to draw your strength from Me. I want you to draw your life from Me. I am your Source. I am your Life. I am your All in All."

Hearing this made me want to stand up and shout: "I belong to Jesus!" He bought me. He paid the price for me. And I know that He's willing to do whatever's best for me—something that He's already proven true by doing the most extreme thing that He could possibly do for me: giving up His life.

It reminded me of the saying:

"Sometimes you don't realize that Jesus is all you need until Jesus is all you have."

Thankfully you don't have to lose everything you've got in order to realize that Jesus is all you need.

I remember going to a training class several years ago to work with AIDS patients. The teacher of the class tried to help us understand what life was like for a person who was dying of AIDS.

During one of the exercises, the teacher asked each of us to write down, on three slips of paper, the three most important things in our lives—whether it was a person, a car, a house, a job, our health, our money, or whatever!

So we took a few minutes to write down those things that were most important to us.

A few minutes later, the teacher came around the room and took from each of us the paper on which we had written our third most important thing. Then he asked: "How does that feel?"

Well, it felt like a punch in the stomach. On my paper, I had written down, "my family." And to have my family taken away gave me a horrible, sinking feeling. He went on to say that this is what AIDS patients often feel when they lose those things that are most important to them.

Then he came around a second time and took away our second most important thing. On my paper, I had written the name of my wife, "Lana." Again, when the paper was taken away, and again he asked: "How does that feel?" Again, I had that horrible, sinking feeling. The whole room was silent as everyone considered what it would be like to lose this second most important thing in our lives.

Finally, he started to walk around the room the third time to take away our last piece of paper—the most important thing in our lives. As he walked towards me, I began to smile. I couldn't help it. I almost burst out laughing, I was so happy!

As the teacher walked up to me and asked for my paper, I didn't know what to say. All I could say was, "You can't take it away!"

He said, "Yes, I can. Give me the paper."

I said, "Well, you can take away the paper, but you can't take away what's written on it!"

On my last piece of paper, I had written the name of the most important thing to me in life: "Jesus."

If your identity is in anything other than Jesus, it can all be taken away, whether it's your spouse, your family, your job, your car, or anything else that's important to you. But if your identity is in Jesus Christ, His love for you can never be taken away!

As Paul says later in the book of Romans:

"For I am convinced that neither death nor life, neither angels nor demons, neither the present nor the future, nor any powers, neither height nor depth, nor anything else in all creation, will be able to separate us from the love of God that is in Christ Jesus our Lord" (Romans 8:38-39).

When you belong to Jesus, nothing in all creation can separate you from His love!

My daughter, Karis, recently wrote a blog post about how finding her identity in Christ is helping her to live the fullest life possible, even during her single years. Here's an excerpt from what she wrote:

> *A few weeks ago, I was at school praying about what to major in, what I should be doing with my life and just what God would want me to do after I finish college.*
> *Then as I was praying, I felt the Holy Spirit whisper to me, "What if you were single the rest of your life? What if all you had was Me? Would I be enough?"*
> *Wait.*
> *Pause.*
> *What?*
> *I know I've read stories of women who have had this happen to them, but never would I have thought that would be me. A life of singleness? Ha, not me.*
> *But as I sat there, I realized... I could honestly answer, "Yes."*
> *And as soon as I did, I had such peace. I realized that all my ideas of what I was going to do with my life after I left school, how I pictured my life in ministry, everything, it was all with a husband, like I planned my life around him (and I don't even have a boyfriend!). Which isn't wrong at all, but I feel like I could use my single years so much better if I focused on God wholeheartedly, not holding anything back.*
> *Sometimes a girl will completely wrap her identity around a guy that she likes and without him she doesn't even know what to do. He is everything to her, she spends all her time with him, her identity is in him, her source of satisfaction, and contentment, and just everything. And in a human relationship that is not healthy.*
> *But towards God, our identity should be Him. A woman's love for a guy should come from her love for Christ. And I want my identity to be found in Him. I definitely believe that if you're not content with who you are, being in a relationship isn't going to make it better.*
> *When I decided I was just going to live totally in love with Jesus, being content with Him no matter what happens, and doing the things I want to do even if I don't have a husband, it felt so perfect. I felt so free.*
> *And it's not that I still don't want a husband, not at all!*
> *But if I never do find a guy, I'll be perfectly content with the love of Jesus.*

As you can tell from just these two stories—my own and my daughter's—how you identify yourself can make a huge difference in how you view everything else around you. This is why finding your identity in Christ is such a great place to start if you're wanting to renew your mind.

Paul could have identified himself as a tentmaker, because he *did* make tents for a living. I'm sure making tents was a great thing to do and I'm sure it helped a lot of people. But that's not how he *identified* himself. His identity was in Christ.

How about you? How do you identify yourself—in your mind, at least, if not publicly? Are you a mother, husband, doctor, lawyer, teacher, nurse, janitor, assistant, homemaker, pastor, president, king? There's no higher title than to say that you're a servant of Jesus Christ, the King of all kings, the Giver of all good gifts, the Doer of all good things.

Jesus wants you to belong to Him.

If you already belong to Jesus, then draw your strength from Him. Draw your life from Him. He's your Source. He's your Life. He's your All in All.

And if you don't belong to Jesus, is there anything holding you back from giving your life fully to Him? He really does love you and He really does want to make things right between you and God again. Turn away from anything that's holding you back from Him so you can put your full faith and trust in Him.

As Paul would tell you—and I would concur—there's nothing better in life than belonging to Jesus!

Will you pray with me?

Father, thank You for Paul's reminder to us of the importance of belonging to Jesus. Help us to remember that we do belong to Him. Help us to find our identity in Him. Help us to draw our strength from Him, realizing that He is our Source, He our Life, and He is our All in All. In Jesus' name, Amen.

Questions for Reflection:

1) Read Romans 1:1-7. How does Paul identify himself?
2) What was Paul called to do?
3) How do you identify yourself?
4) How might your life be different if you identified yourself—whether publicly or privately—as someone who "belonged to Jesus Christ"?

LESSON 2: ENCOURAGING ONE ANOTHER　　　　　　　　AUGUST 4

Scripture Reading: Romans 1:8-17

In our first lesson in this study on renewing your mind, we talked about the importance of belonging to Jesus—of finding your identity in Him. He is our All in All and the ultimate source of our strength. But God has also given us something to help us. He's given us one another.

One of the best ways to renew your mind is to fellowship with other believers, to encourage one another in your faith, so you can give each other a fresh perspective on your life and the situations that you face.

This is what the Apostle Paul longed to do with the Christians living in Rome when he wrote his letter to them in about 57 A.D. If you know anything about this time period in Roman history, you'll know that those were the days of the gladiators, the colosseums, and fights-to-the-death in huge arenas.

It was only seven years after Paul's letter to the Romans—in 64 A.D.—that the mad Emperor Nero blamed the Christians for setting fire to Rome, a fire that many historians believed that Emperor Nero himself set so that he could rebuild the city more to his liking. This newly emerging group of Christians was an easy scapegoat. They were already looked down upon by the people because they chose to follow Christ rather than pay honor to the official Roman gods—one of which included Emperor Nero himself.

The Roman historian Tacitus—who lived in Rome at the time—says that after the fire, Nero arrested a vast number of Christians and had them tortured in the most heinous ways. Tacitus writes:

> "In their very deaths they were made the subjects of sport: for they were covered with the hides of wild beasts, and torn to death by dogs, or nailed to crosses, or set on fire, and when the day waned, burned to serve for the evening lights. Nero offered his own gardens for that spectacle..." (Tacitus, Annals 15.44, circa 100 A.D.)

Just in case you missed what Tacitus was saying in that last statement, he was saying that Christians were set on fire to serve as human torches to light Nero's gardens after the sun had gone down.

It is into this setting, just seven years earlier, that the Apostle Paul wrote his letter to the Romans. For quite some time, he had wanted to visit them in person so that they could encourage one another in their faith. But being prevented from coming in person once again, Paul wrote them a letter instead, a letter that has survived to this day and still encourages Christians around the world.

Listen to Paul's heartfelt love for his Christian brothers and sisters:

> "First, I thank my God through Jesus Christ for all of you, because your faith is being reported all over the world. God, whom I serve with my whole heart in preaching the gospel of his Son, is my witness how constantly I remember you in my prayers at all times; and I pray that now at last by God's will the way may be opened for me to come to you.
>
> "I long to see you so that I may impart to you some spiritual gift to make you strong—that is, that you and I may be mutually encouraged by each other's faith. I do not want you to be unaware, brothers, that I planned many times to come to you (but have been prevented from doing so until now) in order that I might have a harvest among you, just as I have had among the other Gentiles" (Romans 8:8-13).

Life is hard for all of us at times. And it's in those times that we need one another even more than ever. We need one another's perspectives on the situations that we face, just as Paul gave his perspective to the Roman Christians. Although they were being ridiculed and persecuted—and they could have felt that God was treating them unfairly—Paul helped them to see their situation in another light. He thanked God for them, because their faith was being reported throughout the world.

Rather than seeing their situation as lowly and humiliating, Paul saw that their stars of faith were shining brightly—stars that illuminated the darkness around them.

Amazingly, Paul was eager to join them in this dark place. While Paul could have been hesitant for many reasons to go to Rome, he wasn't. As a natural-born citizen of Rome and one of the greatest intellectual thinkers of his day, he could have been embarrassed to align himself with those who followed Christ—a man who was mocked by the Roman leaders and crucified under the Roman governor, Pontius Pilate.

But Paul *wasn't* ashamed. He didn't flinch at the possibility that he could be ridiculed, beaten, jailed, or killed for his faith. Why? Because Paul knew the life-changing power of the gospel that he preached—the "good news" of Christ.

Paul knew that the gospel had the power to save those who responded to it. He was eager to go to Rome and to have a harvest among those who were yet to believe. Paul said:

> *"I am not ashamed of the gospel, because it is the power of God for the salvation of everyone who believes: first for the Jew, then for the Gentile. For in the gospel a righteousness from God is revealed, a righteousness that is by faith from first to last, just as it is written: 'The righteous will live by faith'"* (Romans 1:16-17).

We could all use a few more Pauls in our lives, people who believe so much in the power of the gospel that their faith rubs off on us.

If you need a new perspective on your life—and the situations you're facing in it—can I encourage you to find some other believers and to be honest with them about the struggles you're facing? You can't go it alone, and God doesn't want you to. Even though Jesus may be all you need, the reason He's all you need is because He provides you with all you need—like believing friends who can help you through this life.

Let me encourage you to seek out and engage other Christians in heartfelt conversations. It's risky. It's hard. But it's so worth it. Ask them to tell you if they see anything in your life that you might not be able to see on your own. Ask them what God may be doing in and through the situations you're facing. Open up the Word of God with them to see how God has brought others through situations like the ones you're facing. And if you think your situation is so unique that God's Word doesn't address it, that's most likely because you haven't read enough of God's Word!

God has so much to say to you, but sometimes it takes others to help you see it. If you don't have church home, find one that strongly believes that the Bible is God's Word. Get involved with a group of other Christians. Join a chat room or an Internet forum where you can lift each other up with your prayers and concerns.

Or, if you want, ask another Christian to go through this study of the book of Romans with you, whether you get together in person or share with each other electronically, halfway around the world.

One of my own kids is in Sydney, Australia, right now and I'm thankful that we're still able to encourage one another in our faith from literally half-way around the world! He shares with me what he's learning, and I share with him what I'm learning, and we both encourage one another with the new things we're learning about life from God's Word. The same thing happens with my wife and our other kids here in the house, and with our church and small group that we attend regularly. As iron sharpens iron, so one man or woman can sharpen another.

You may not be getting thrown to the lions, but you'll still benefit from surrounding yourself with other believers. Seek them out. Share your story with them. Ask them to give you a boost in your faith and give them a boost in their faith while you're at it.

And if you're the one who's feeling particularly strong right now, can I encourage you to take some time to write or call, email or text, or just stop by and visit someone who could use your perspective on their life today? As Paul longed to be with the Romans so they could be *"mutually encouraged by each other's faith"*—God wants you to do the same with those around you. You'll be glad you did.

Will you pray with me?

Father, thank You for reminding us that even though Jesus is all we need, that we still need each other, and that our fellowship with other believers is one of the great blessings that Jesus wants to give us. Lord, for those who have such a fellowship, thank You. For those who need such a fellowship, I pray that You would answer their prayers. Help them to reach out to those around them and share honestly the struggles they're going through in life. Then provide them with the fresh perspective and practical help they need to help them through this time with a faith that shines brightly for You. In Jesus' name, Amen.

Questions for Reflection:

1) Read Romans 1:8-17. Why was Paul thankful for the Romans?
2) Why did he long to see them? And what was he praying for them constantly?
3) Do you have a group of Christians with whom you can enjoy the benefits of fellowship? If so, what are some of the benefits of fellowship. If not, where could you start to find such a group?
4) Why was Paul not ashamed of the gospel?

LESSON 3: GIVING THANKS   AUGUST 5

Scripture Reading: Romans 1:18-23

One of the quickest ways to get a new perspective on life is by giving thanks—by taking a few minutes to thank God for the things in your life for which you are truly grateful. But giving thanks doesn't always come naturally.

You can sometimes get so caught up in the heat of the battles you're facing that all of your thoughts, prayers and attention are focused on the battles only. Then, when you get so consumed by the battles that you stop giving thanks for the good things that are happening in your life, you head down a path that can lead to destruction.

I've heard it said that "rebellion against God doesn't begin with a clenched fist, but with a heart that refuses to give thanks."

When you stop giving thanks for the things in your lives that are good and meaningful to you, you can oftentimes find yourself slipping into anger and frustration with the world–and with the God who created it. Your fists may begin to clench, and you may feel like rebelling against anything else that God might want to say to you or want you to do.

The Apostle Paul cited this refusal to give thanks as the beginning of the end for the citizens of Rome, as many people there were already engaging in all kinds of evil. He said:

"The wrath of God is being revealed from heaven against all the godlessness and wickedness of men who suppress the truth by their wickedness... For although they knew God, they neither glorified Him as God nor gave thanks to Him, but their thinking became futile and their foolish hearts were darkened" (Romans 1:18, 21).

If it feels like you're thinking has become futile and your heart seems to have darkened, perhaps it's time to reverse that cycle by giving thanks.

In her book, *The Hiding Place*, Corrie Ten Boom tells the story of a time when she and her sister were in a concentration camp in Germany during the Holocaust. When they were thrown into a bunkhouse that was infected with fleas, her sister remembered that they needed to give thanks in *all* circumstances—even for the fleas. But Corrie said it was too much. She said, "There's no way even God can make me grateful for a flea."

But as the weeks went on, she discovered that the women in her barracks were being given an unusual amount of freedom. They could read to each other from a Bible they had hidden, and they could pray with one another. One day they discovered why when Betsy overheard the guards say that they wouldn't step foot into their barracks. Why not? "That place is crawling with fleas!" the guard said. It was then that Corrie remembered her sister's prayers of thanks even for the fleas.

The movie, *Fireproof*, also talks about the importance of giving thanks. The story is about a fireman whose wife wants out of their marriage. She's fed up with him, and he's equally fed up with her. But as they head towards divorce, the fireman's father steps in and challenges his son to try something he calls "The Love Dare" for forty days. He hands his son a hand-written journal in which he's written specific steps the son can take each day to try to repair his relationship with his wife.

After 20 frustrating days of trying to do it on his own, the fireman has a heartfelt conversation with his dad. His dad encourages him to put His faith in Christ and ask Him for help, but the son refuses, saying he doesn't need a crutch to get through life. The dad responds by saying that Jesus is more than just a crutch—He's the most significant part of his life. The son still doesn't get it, so the dad continues:

> DAD: "If I ask you why you're so frustrated with Catherine, what would you say?"
> SON: "She's stubborn. She makes everything difficult for me. She's ungrateful. She's constantly griping about something."
> DAD: "Has she thanked you the last 20 days?"
> SON: "No. And you'd think after I washed the car, I've changed the oil, do the dishes, clean the house, that she would try to show me a little bit of gratitude. Well, she doesn't. That is what really ticks me off. Dad, for the last three weeks, I have bent over backwards for her. I have tried to demonstrate that I still care about this relationship. I bought her flowers, which she threw away. I have taken her insults and her sarcasm, but last night was it. I made dinner for her, I did everything I could to demonstrate that I care about her, to show value for her, and she spat in my face. She does not deserve this, Dad. I am not doing it anymore. How am I supposed to show love to somebody over and over and over who constantly rejects me?"
> DAD: "That's a good question."
> SON: (after a long pause) "Dad, that is not what I'm doing."
> DAD: "Isn't it? Son, you just asked me: 'How can someone show love over and over again when they're constantly rejected?' You can't love her, because you can't give her what you don't have."

You'll have to see the movie to find out how it ends. But the Dad made his point: What does it feel like to God, when He shows His love to us over and over and over again, yet we refuse to, or forget to, or get so overwhelmed with life that we no longer want to give Him thanks?

For me, I've found it helpful to be intentional about giving thanks to God. I keep a prayer journal handy and try to write in it at least every few days. I used to begin by writing down all the prayers that were on my heart, which felt good to get them down on paper. But I began to realize that I wasn't taking as much time to stop and give thanks to God for all the prayers that He had already answered.

So I changed my approach several years ago and began starting every entry with these words, "Father, thank You…" and then listing something for which I am *sincerely* thankful, something specific that has happened in the past day or two, or even those things that were particularly hard or challenging, but that I was trying to view from God's perspective to see how He might be using them for good.

I've found that as I start my prayer time with thanks, it changes the rest of my prayer time. I now have more expectancy, more eagerness to see how God might answer my prayers, and more hope that God really can bring something good out of even the bad things that I might be facing.

Rather than waiting to see how things turn out before I thank God for them, I've found it much better to thank Him up front.

I remember eating an incredible fish dinner up in Boise, Idaho one time on a business trip. Our hosts had taken us out to a fancy restaurant. I'm sure it was the best fish I had ever eaten. After the meal, when the waitress came to our table to ask how everything was, I could hardly contain myself in thanking her for the great meal.

But as I was thanking her, I realized that she didn't cook the fish, she just brought it to the table, so I asked her to please give my thanks to the chef. But as she walked away, I realized that the chef didn't make the fish, he just prepared it. The one I really needed to thank was God who created the fish! So before I got up from the table, I said a heartfelt prayer of thanks, saying, "Thank You, Lord, for this food!"

Then it hit me. Wasn't that the same prayer I said *before* I ate it: "Thank You Lord, for this food"? But somehow it meant so much more to me now that I realized it really had come from Him! I made a mental note that the next time I prayed before a meal, I'd try to make it just as heartfelt as I felt that day afterwards.

It reminded me of the prayer that Jesus prayed before His meal with over 5,000 people on the hillside in Galilee, when all He had was two loaves of bread and five pieces of fish. The Bible says:

> "Taking the five loaves and the two fish and looking up to heaven, He gave thanks and broke the loaves. Then He gave them to the disciples, and the disciples gave them to the people. They all ate and were satisfied, and the disciples picked up twelve basketfuls of broken pieces that were left over" (Matthew 14:19b-21).

Jesus could have waited till the end of the meal to give thanks for His Father's incredible provision, but He didn't. He gave thanks up front, even though the meal in front of Him may have looked quite meager. His Father in heaven took His prayer of thanks and super-sized their meal right in front of their eyes!

You don't have to wait to give thanks to God till you see the answers to your prayers. Give thanks to Him up front for what you have been given and trust Him to take the next step.

The Romans, because of their refusal to give thanks to God, found that their thinking had become futile and their hearts were darkened. If you want your thoughts to be more purposeful and your hearts to become brighter, do what Paul suggested: begin by giving thanks to God.

Come to the Father today with your prayers. Come to Him with thanksgiving in your heart. Thank Him for those things in your life for which you're truly grateful. Thank Him for those things—even fleas—that may be hard to give thanks for right now, but which God can use in your life for good. And thank Him for the answers to your prayers that haven't even come yet, but by faith you believe *will* come in a way that goes beyond all you can ask or imagine.

Let God renew your mind today by giving thanks to Him.

Will you pray with me?

Father, thank You for the answers to so many prayers that we have prayed in the past. Thank You for those things which we're struggling through today, for as hard as they may seem, we trust that You can work all things for good, for those who love You and are called according to Your purpose. Thank You in advance for the answers to prayer that are yet to come. We trust that You can super-size those answers in just the right way and at just the right time. In Jesus' name, Amen.

Questions for Reflection:

1) Read Romans 1:18-23. What did Paul say happened to the thinking of those who refused to give glory and thanks to God?
2) Why do you think their refusal to give thanks caused them to fall into some of the sins listed in this passage?
3) According to verse 32, what is the ultimate outcome for those who head down this path?
4) What are some things in your life for which you can truly give thanks to God?

LESSON 4: ASKING GOD FOR HIS TRUTH   AUGUST 6

Scripture Reading: Romans 1:24-32

Of all the passages in the Bible, the one that has changed my thinking and the direction of my life more than any other is the one that we're looking at today—a passage at the end of Romans chapter 1.

It's a little hard for me to talk about, though, because what God spoke to me through this passage was very personal and specific to me. While this passage may not speak to you as personally, the principle that I learned from reading it that day *does* apply to every one of us: if you ask God for His Truth—and listen for His honest answer with an open heart and ears to hear—God *will* answer you!

What happened to me was that I had just been reading another passage in the Bible that puzzled me. It said that all of us had sinned and that the penalty for sin was death. Therefore, all of us would eventually die because of our sins (see Romans 3:23 and 6:23).

I thought this was a little strong because I felt I had been a pretty good kid all my life. I hadn't done anything that I felt I would even get put in jail for, let alone die from. But the Bible seemed to say otherwise. So I shared my question about these verses with the guys in my small group Bible study. One of them suggested that I ask God what *He* thought about how good I had been.

I thought that was a fair question, so I went home that night and got ready to pray. But before I did, I started to wonder: *What if it was true? What if I really had done something that could possibly kill me?* I wondered if I really wanted to hear God's answer to that question or not.

But as I thought through what He might say, I decided that what I wanted more than anything was God's truth. Either what the Bible said was true and what I thought was wrong, or what I thought was true, and the Bible was wrong. Both couldn't be true. So I asked God to show me the truth.

Within two weeks, God answered my prayer. He brought me to Romans chapter 1, where I read Paul's words about what happened when people "exchanged the truth of God for a lie" (Romans 1:25a). God had my attention, for that's just what I was wondering, if I had ever exchanged God's truth for a lie. As I read the words that followed, I was amazed to see that Paul, writing almost 2,000 years ago, described the same path that I had taken in life a just few years earlier. Paul said:

> *"They exchanged the truth of God for a lie and worshiped and served created things rather than the Creator—who is forever praised. Amen.*
> *"Because of this, God gave them over to shameful lusts. Even their women exchanged natural relations for unnatural ones. In the same way the men also abandoned natural relations with women and were inflamed with lust for one another. Men committed indecent acts with other men and received in themselves the due penalty for their perversion.*
> *"Furthermore, since they did not think it worthwhile to retain the knowledge of God, He gave them over to a depraved mind, to do what ought not to be done. They have become filled with every kind of wickedness, evil, greed and depravity. They are full of envy, murder, strife, deceit and malice. They are gossips, slanderers, God-haters, insolent, arrogant and boastful; they invent ways of doing evil; they disobey their parents; they are senseless, faithless, heartless, ruthless. Although they know God's righteous decree that those who do such things deserve death, they not only continue to do these very things but also approve of those who practice them"* (Romans 1:25-32).

Even though I felt I had been pretty good all my life, there was one area that I had kept secret from most people. When I went off to college, I became sexually involved in a series of relationships with other men on campus. While on one level I felt that what I was doing was wrong, on another level it seemed so "right" because it seemed to fill a legitimate need that I had in my life for close male friends.

What I didn't know was that I was trying to meet that need in a way that could have possibly killed me. AIDS was just beginning to surface at the time, but it didn't seem like that real of a threat to me. I never even considered the possibility that I might die from what I was doing.

But as I read this passage in Romans, I began to see what I had been doing in a whole new light. I began to see that not only did homosexuality go against the way that God had designed my reproductive organs to work—they would never produce life in this way—but it could have actually led to my death instead. Instead of giving me abundant life, it could have lead to my imminent death. And God didn't want me to die. He wanted me to live! But because of the decisions that I had made, I was afraid I might already be carrying within me the seeds of my own destruction.

I didn't want to die. I wanted to live. But I wondered how I could possibly *undo* what I had done. I couldn't take it back. I also wondered how I could possibly change my thoughts and feelings and emotions regarding other guys. I couldn't think of any way to change them myself, and I didn't see how anyone else could change me either—not my family, or my friends, or a counselor—no one.

But then I read another story in the Bible about Jesus and how two blind men came to Him for healing. They called out to Jesus: "Have mercy on us!"

Instead of just touching their eyes or telling them to dip in a particular pool of water, as He did when He healed others, this time Jesus asked the men a question. He said:

> *"Do you believe that I am able to do this?" (Matthew 9:28b)*

It seemed as if Jesus was asking me the same question. I didn't want to live my life in a way that could possibly kill me, but I didn't know how to change it either. As I read this passage, I felt like Jesus was asking me: "Eric, do you believe that I am able to do *this*, too?"

I thought about everything that I had ever heard about Jesus—how He healed the sick, walked on water, and raised the dead. I thought to myself, *If anyone can do this, Jesus can.*

As I thought about this, I just put my hand up in the air and said, "Yes, Lord, I believe."

And as soon as I said those words, Jesus reached out to me just like He did to the blind men. He touched me. He healed me. He changed my life forever.

The next day I went to a church service where I heard about how Jesus came to die for our sins so that we wouldn't have to. For the first time in my life, I realized that I was a sinner and needed a Savior. I went home that night and knelt down on my bed. With my head on my pillow, I asked God to forgive me for everything I had done that had gone against Him and His plans for my life. I put my faith in Him and asked Him to fill me with His Holy Spirit so that I could live the life *He* wanted me to live.

I woke up the next morning with a whole new perspective on life. Even though I got up and ate breakfast and went to work just the same as the day before, I knew that God had given me a new shot at life. He picked me up off the path of death and put me on the path of life instead.

On this new path, God has given me a wife, six children of my own, and the promise of eternal life with Him forever. I'm now on a path of life and life abundant! It's been twenty-four years since that day, and I've never looked back.

I took a risk when I asked God to reveal His Truth to me. But it was the best risk I've ever taken in my life. Because of that risk, I realized that God was right, and I was wrong, that I *had* exchanged the truth of God for a lie. I put my faith in Him and His Word from that day on. It's changed my life and the lives of my wife and kids–who wouldn't be here otherwise–forever.

Maybe you have days when you feel like God is distant—that He doesn't seem to care about you or what you're going through—that He's simply not interested in the details of your life or the direction that it takes. But nothing could be further from the truth! God loves you so much! The truth is that God wants you to know His will for your life even more than you want to know it! He'd love to reveal His Truth to you if you're willing to ask Him.

I want to encourage you to ask God to renew your mind today. Ask Him to reveal His Truth to you on those topics that are close to your heart. Ask Him to pour His thoughts into your thoughts. Ask Him to give you a new way of thinking about your life and the direction that you're headed. If you're on course, God will tell you. But if you're not, God will tell you that, too—if you'll listen for His voice with an open heart and ears to hear.

If you want to renew your mind, ask God your questions, open His Word, and listen for His answers.

Will you pray with me?

Father, thank You for letting us come to You with our honest questions. We pray that You would give us Your honest answers, too. We do want to know Your Truth. We do want to know how to live our lives in ways that we can have life abundant. Open our ears so that we can hear You clearly and open our hearts to Your Word that You've given to us on the pages of the Bible. Help us to put our faith and trust in You for everything in our lives, including the forgiveness of our sins and the promise that we can live with You forever when we put our faith in Christ. In Jesus' name, Amen.

Questions for Reflection:

1) Read Romans 1:24-32. Looking at this passage, what are some ways that the people in Rome got off track when they "exchanged the truth of God for a lie"?
2) What are some ways they might get back on track if they wanted to?
3) Why is it sometimes hard for us to hear God's Truth in our lives?
4) After reading this passage and hearing this story, is there any particular Truth from God that you'd like Him to reveal to you?

LESSON 5: LISTENING TO YOUR CONSCIENCE   AUGUST 7

Scripture Reading: Romans 2:1-16

When Steve Jobs finished designing the first Macintosh computer, he did something special: he asked everyone who helped him design that first revolutionary machine to sign a large piece of paper. He then took that paper and turned it into an engraving template. When those first Macs finally rolled off the assembly line, the names of their creators were engraved inside every case.

You couldn't see the signatures from the outside—and most people never even knew they existed on the inside because few people had any reason to open up a computer in those days. But if you did open one up and looked deep inside, you'd see them—the signatures of their creators, including "steven jobs."

But Steve Jobs wasn't the first one to sign his creation on the inside. God did it, too, when He created you. He's written His name deep inside you. And if you take a closer look, you'll find that it's not just His name that's written there, but also His laws—His words of instruction to help you live the fullest life possible.

As God said in the book of Hebrews:

> "I will put My laws in their minds
> and write them on their hearts.
> I will be their God,
> and they will be My people"
> (Hebrews 8:10b)

The Apostle Paul echoes these thoughts in his letter to the Romans, saying that your conscience "bears witness" to the fact that God has written the requirements of His laws upon your heart.

> *"Indeed, when Gentiles, who do not have the law, do by nature things required by the law, they are a law for themselves, even though they do not have the law, since they show that the requirements of the law are written on their hearts, their consciences also bearing witness, and their thoughts now accusing, now even defending them"* (Romans 2:14-15).

Your conscience has been implanted in your mind by God. It helps you to consider your options and the outcomes of your actions. It helps you to regulate your passions and desires, comparing them to God's passions and desires for you. When your passions and desires are different than God's, your conscience kicks in to let you know that something is amiss and needs to be addressed.

But your conscience is a warning indicator only. You can override it. You can ignore it. You still have free will. But God has put your conscience within you to help you make decisions, if you're willing to listen to it. Your conscience is a warning indicator to let you know you'd better check something out before proceeding.

How do you check it out? By comparing what you're wanting to do with God's Word.

Even though God has written His Word on your heart, sometimes you can't read the writing so clearly. Your vision gets blurred by your own thoughts and desires.

That's why God has also given you His Word in black and white—on the pages of the Bible—so you *can* read it clearly. That's why He's given you His Word in the flesh—in the form of His Son Jesus—so you can know exactly what He says about it. That's why He's given you His Holy Spirit—which Jesus said He would send to His followers after He was gone—to remind you of all the things He has already spoken to you.

I can think of times in my own life—and maybe you can think of times in yours—when I've done some things that felt so "right" on one level, but on another level felt so "wrong." At those times when I've ignored the warning lights and overridden them, I've ended up in places that God never wanted me to go.

But at those times when I *have* taken notice of God's warning lights and decided to check out what I was doing and compare it to what God wanted me to do according to His Word, I've found that it's way better to do what's right—even if it means laying down some things that I personally desire. Whenever I've done what I've felt God wanted instead, I've found that His plans for me are so much better than the plans I had in mind, giving me peace of mind and life abundant. As someone has wisely said:

> *A clear conscience makes a soft pillow.*

If you'd like to sleep on a soft pillow tonight, I'd encourage you to listen to your conscience. If there's something on your heart or mind that has turned on the warning lights, check it out.

Take a look in God's Word, as written on the pages of the Bible in black and white, and compare what you're doing with what God wants you to do. If they don't match up, a change is in order. Just thank God for His warning lights and do what's right, whatever it takes. As Paul said:

> *"For it is not those who hear the law who are righteous in God's sight, but it is those who obey the law who will be declared righteous"* (Romans 2:13).

As I was thinking about the idea of Steve Jobs engraving his name inside his computers—and God engraving His Word upon our hearts—I was inspired to write a haiku. A haiku is a short Japanese poem that doesn't usually rhyme but is often made up of just 17 syllables—five in the first line, seven in the second, and five in the third.

So here's my haiku, from God to you:

My name is written
upon your heart awaiting
… rediscovery

God loves you so much that He's taken the time to write His name on your heart. He's written His instructions for you there, too, to help you live the fullest life possible.

If you'd like to renew your mind today, listen to your conscience. Check out what your conscience is saying and compare it to God's Word. Listen to His Son. Obey His Holy Spirit. If you do these things, you'll live! If you don't, you risk losing everything, even those things you love the most.

Listen to your conscience—and live!

Will you pray with me?

Father, thank You for writing Your Words on our hearts, and thank You for giving us a conscience to help us know when what we're doing is different from what You want us to do. Help us to listen to You, to follow Your Words, and to live the life that You've created us to live. Fill us with Your Holy Spirit to help us to stop doing anything that doesn't bring glory and honor to You, and to start doing those things that do. In Jesus' name, Amen.

Questions for Reflection:

1) *Read Romans 2:1-16. Can you remember a time when your conscience warned you that something you were doing was amiss? What were the results when you either did or didn't do what your conscience warned you about?*
2) *Read Hebrews 8:7-13. While some people might think that their consciences are formed based solely on the conditions in which they were raised, what does this passage in Hebrews, and the above passage in Romans, suggest is the true basis for your conscience?*
3) *What reason does Paul give for God being so kind, tolerant and patient towards us in Romans 2:4?*
4) *After reflecting on today's message, are there any changes you'd like to make in your own life, or any warning indicators that you need to check out according to God's Word?*

LESSON 6: GETTING TO THE HEART   AUGUST 8

Scripture Reading: Romans 2:17-29

I have thought for some time now that someone should make a movie about two men engaged in an epic battle with each other. In some ways, it would be like every other movie: the hero and villain would be at war throughout the movie, with the hero having the upper hand at some points, and the villain gaining the upper hand at others. Near the end, the hero would deliver the fatal blow that sends the villain to his doom forever.

But the difference in this movie would be that just before the closing credits begin to roll, the camera would back up from the final battle scene, revealing to the audience that the hero and the villain were one and the same person, fighting inside the brain of a man's head. Having achieved the victory in his mind, we would then see the man finally stand up and walk forward to do what's right. No longer bound by the thoughts that were raging within him, he would finally be free to live the life he was called to live.

An audience of such a movie might think that they had been tricked into thinking that the whole battle was "real" for the entire movie, when it was only being played out inside the man's head. But to those who saw what was taking place at a deeper level, they would realize that what took place inside the man's head was no *less* real than what took place after he stood up at the end.

The victory in your mind is often just as critical as the victory in the physical world. In fact, you often need to secure the victory in your mind first before you can secure the victory in the physical world.

There are, however, ways to cover up your true thoughts and feelings with words and actions that make it *look* like you've got it all together on the inside. This kind of activity might deceive men, but it never deceives God. God wants you to win the victory in your mind *and* in the physical world. When there's a disconnect between what's going on inwardly and what's going on outwardly, God wants you to get to the heart.

Paul addressed this disconnect in his letter to the Romans. The Jews were priding themselves on the outward signs of their faith, like the fact that they were circumcised, whereas the Gentiles, or non-Jews, weren't. But Paul said:

> "A man is not a Jew if he is only one outwardly, nor is circumcision merely outward and physical. No, a man is a Jew if he is one inwardly, and circumcision is circumcision of the heart, by the Spirit, not by the written code. Such a man's praise is not from men, but from God" (Romans 2:28-29).

In some ways, the Jews could have seen circumcision as one of the symbols of their salvation. It was a physical sign imprinted on their bodies that showed that they belonged to God, that they were children of a special covenant between God and His people. But Paul said that if their circumcision was external only, then it would only merit praise from men, not from God.

God wanted their circumcision to be a "circumcision of the heart, by the Spirit, not by the written code." Paul said that the Gentiles, who didn't have the law of God written down for them, would be more honoring to God than the Jews if the Gentiles kept the requirements of the law by doing what's right. Paul said:

> "If those who are not circumcised keep the law's requirements, will they not be regarded as though they were circumcised? The one who is not circumcised physically and yet obeys the law will condemn you who, even though you have the written code and circumcision, are a lawbreaker" (Romans 2:26-27).

This isn't to say that circumcision and the rest of the laws were of no value to the Jews, as we'll find out next time in chapter 3 of Paul's letter. But it is to say that God wants our inward reality to match up with our outward reality. And when we get to the heart first, the outward actions will flow much more naturally.

I got an email from a friend who has been struggling with pornography for years, thinking of himself as an addict. He hasn't been sure if he will ever break free. Although I believe he can and will break free one day, it's hard for him to believe it, because of the length and the strength of his battle.

Yet in his most recent email, he said he had just been to a counselor who asked him many in-depth questions about his struggle. After reviewing the situation, the counselor said that he doesn't think my friend has an addiction and gave him several reasons why. This was news to my friend because he's been feeling like an addict for years! It changed my friend's thinking about his situation. He's already had some small victories in his battle since then!

My friend's actions are beginning to change because he has changed the way he thinks about his problem. He now sees that there really is a possibility that he can be free from this battle that has dogged him for so long.

God cares about what's going on inside your brain. He cares about what's going on inside your heart. And He cares about what you do as a result of what's going on inside your brain and heart. What happens internally is just as important—and just as real—as what happens externally.

I remember a book in which the main character in the book has a dreamlike conversation with one of his mentors who had unfortunately died the previous year. As their conversation comes to a close, the main character asks:

> "Tell me one last thing. Is this real? Or has this been happening inside my head?"

His mentor replies:

> "Of course it is happening inside your head, but why on earth should that mean it is not real?"

Sometimes we think that the thoughts in our head are separate from, and unrelated to, the actions that we take in our lives. We treat the two as different realities. But the truth is that our thoughts influence our actions. Both are real and God cares about both.

God wants you to have the victory on the inside so you can have the victory on the outside.

He doesn't want you to be obedient just so you can *say* you have faith in Him. He wants you to have faith in Him so that you can *be obedient*, for that's the way you can live your life to the fullest potential.

While there *can* be value in just doing things because you know they're right, even if you don't feel like doing them, there's *much more* value if what you do on the outside matches up with what you think and feel on the inside. When they match up, you'll feel better about what you're doing, others will feel better about what you're doing, and God will be honored by what you're doing.

As God said to Samuel when Samuel was trying to discern who should be the next king of Israel:

> "Do not consider his appearance or his height, for I have rejected him. The Lord does not look at the things man looks at. Man looks at the outward appearance, but the Lord looks at the heart" (1 Samuel 16:7-8).

Ask God to renew your heart and mind today. Ask Him to reveal anything within you that is improperly motivated, or that seeks for anything other than the good of others and the glory of God. Then, if God reveals anything to you that needs to be changed internally, ask Him for help to know how to change it. Ask Him to remake you from the inside out. Give Him permission to do that work inside you, whatever it takes.

Then, when God is done remaking you on the inside, you'll be able to stand up, move forward, and do what's right. No longer bound by the thoughts that were raging inside you, you'll finally be free to live the life you were called to live!

Will you pray with me?

Father, thank You for caring about what goes on inside us—our thoughts and feelings—just as much as you care about what we do on the outside. Thank You for the reminder that both are real, and both are really important to You. Fill our minds and hearts with Your will for our lives and help us to believe and act on Your will. We pray that doing so will make a tremendous difference to us and to those around us in the weeks and months and years ahead. In Jesus' name, Amen.

Questions for Reflection:

1) Read Romans 2:17-29. What was the problem that Paul was addressing with the Jews in this passage?
2) What did Paul mean when he said that "circumcision is circumcision of the heart"? How can someone be circumcised in their heart?
3) In what ways do your thoughts and feelings sometimes differ from your actions? And in what ways are they related?
4) Are there any areas in your life where your thoughts and feelings are disconnected from your actions? What might you do today to help them line up more closely?

LESSON 7: BECOMING CONSCIOUS OF SIN   AUGUST 9

Scripture Reading: Romans 3:1-20

Some people have no problem recognizing sin in their life. In fact, they magnify their faults in their minds, whether real or imagined, thinking less of themselves than they ought to think.

Yet other people have the problem of *not* recognizing sin in their life. They magnify their strengths instead, whether real or imagined, thinking better of themselves than they ought to think.

Most of us fall somewhere in between: we magnify some weaknesses out of proportion, while minimizing others.

God wants us to have an honest and objective look. For those of you who think you're perfect, I'm sorry to be the bearer of bad news today. And for those of you who don't think you're perfect, I don't want you to magnify what I'm about to say and make you feel worse about yourselves. But here's the truth, according to what God says through Paul in his letter to the Romans:

> *"There is no one righteous, not even one;*
> *there is no one who understands,*
> *no one who seeks God.*
> *All have turned away,*
> *they have together become worthless;*
> *there is no one who does good,*
> *not even one" (Romans 3:10-12).*

The truth is, the gospel—or good news—of Jesus Christ is often bad news before it's good news. If you're not aware of your sinfulness, you'll never be aware of your need for a Savior. And if you don't recognize your need for a Savior, you'll never find salvation.

God didn't give you the laws of the Bible—the ten commandments and the six hundred and some additional laws that followed in the Old Testament—to crush you. He gave them to help you and protect you. And to the extent that you keep those laws, you'll be blessed. But when you fall short of being able to keep those laws, God sent Jesus to make up the difference—to fill the gap between the best that you can do and the best that God wants for you.

And since the Bible says that "there is no one righteous, not even one," that means that God sent Jesus for each one of us. If you want to renew your mind and get a new perspective on life, it's important to see your sins as God sees them. For when you see how short you've fallen compared to God's righteousness, you can see what needs to happen to make up the difference: put your faith in Christ!

This is not a message just for non-Christians to encourage them to put their faith in Christ. This is just as much a message for Christians, who need God's grace just as much *after* being saved as before. As professor and philosopher Dallas Willard says:

> *"The sinner is not the one who uses a lot of grace. The saint uses more grace. The saint burns grace like a 747 burns fuel on takeoff, because everything they do is a manifestation of grace. But we have to learn how to use it. It means we no longer trust just our efforts to manage our lives."*

Throughout the book of Romans, Paul addressed the differences and similarities between Jews and Gentiles—the non-Jews. What good is it being a Jew, some have asked, if both Jews and Gentiles both can be saved by grace? Here's what Paul said:

> *"What advantage, then, is there in being a Jew, or what value is there in circumcision? Much in every way! First of all, they have been entrusted with the very words of God"* (Romans 3:1-2).

God gave His words in the form of the Scriptures to the Jews, and to the extent that they heeded those words they were blessed. But to the extent that they didn't heed those words, there was a gap.

God gave them ways to fill that gap, through sacrifices of atonement that they and their leaders could make. But as good as this was, it was never enough to completely fill the gap. Paul said that it was only because of God's forbearance—His patience, self-control, and restraint—that He never brought upon them the full punishment they deserved for their sins. Paul said:

> "Because in His forbearance, He had left the sins committed beforehand unpunished" (Romans 3:25b).

But when the time was right, God provided a way to fill the gap completely, once and for all. He filled it by offering His own Son Jesus Christ as a sacrifice for our sins. That's the gospel, or good news of Jesus Christ. Even though none of us are righteous on our own, we can *become* righteous by putting our faith in Jesus Christ.

If you feel like a sinner today, hallelujah! When you become conscious of your sins, you've hit upon a truth of God. That means you can also recognize your need for a Savior—someone who can save you from your sins! And that means you can be saved, if you recognize Jesus as your Savior! It really is great news!

Becoming conscious of sin is one of the main purposes of the laws that God gave us. As Paul said:

> "Therefore no one will be declared righteous in His sight by observing the law; rather, through the law we become conscious of sin" (Romans 3:20).

If you want to renew your mind today, ask God to help you become conscious of sin in your life. Then, when you become aware of what needs changing in your life, invite Jesus in to do His work. Remember, God's grace is just as much available to you after you've become a Christian as before.

At the same time, as you ask God to help you to become conscious of sin in your life, don't let Satan magnify your weaknesses out of proportion.

I had a friend this week who shared with me that she was struggling to hear from God. She felt like God wasn't answering her prayers and she wondered what she might be doing wrong. At one point in our conversation, she confessed to me this that she felt God wasn't answering her prayers because she had gone off a special diet she had started for her health. She had eaten some candy bars. She was squirming as she told me, and she said she hadn't told anyone else what she was thinking. But from the way she said it, I knew she was dead serious and completely distraught. I looked at her and said:

> "Satan is lying to you. The truth is that God loves you so much that He has already paid the ultimate price for you—by sending Jesus to die for your sins. There's nothing He wouldn't do for you if it's in His will for your life. There may be a good reason for you to be careful about what you eat for the sake of your health. But that's a different issue. I don't believe that God is holding anything back from you because you ate some candy bars. If you believe that God wants for you what you're praying for, then keep on praying for it! Believe that God will answer your prayers and don't let anything stop you from praying for it."

My friend listened intently to what I was saying, and when I was finished, she asked if I could repeat it all for her one more time, which I did. Sometimes it's hard to get your mind around God's grace. And I admit that I fall into the same mental trap at times, too, and maybe you do as well. Maybe you've had thoughts like these:

> – "I don't have enough money because I haven't made enough contacts this week—God must not love me, or He thinks bad about me, and He's not answering my prayers because of it." (Maybe there's a connection between your contacts and

your money, but maybe not. Your work matters to God, but don't let Satan lie to you that it's because God doesn't love you because you haven't done enough. If you fall short in what you can do, ask God for forgiveness and let Jesus fill the gap.)

– "My kids are a mess because of a sin I committed in high school and now they're just following in my footsteps, even though I've repented a thousand times for it since then." (No, don't let Satan lie to you. If you've confessed it, you're forgiven. God has wiped the slate clean and starts all over again with your kids on their own.)

– "I've been praying for a husband or wife, but no one will marry me. It must be because of my ____." (Fill in the blank: nose, temper, scar, income, freckles, hair, lack of hair, etc. No, don't let Satan lie to you, either. There are plenty of people who have gotten married in spite of having a multitude of traits that seem to be ignored, and even adored, by their devoted spouse. While there may be qualities or characteristics about yourself that God does want you to work on, that's likely a different issue. Trust God that He is answering your prayers and working on your behalf, behind the scenes. At the proper time, you will see the fruit of your prayers.)

If there's a gap between you and perfection, there's good news for you—even as a Christian. Jesus came to fill the gap!

God want to renew your mind. He's given you His law so you can become conscious of sin. But once you're aware of it, don't wallow in it! Put your faith in Christ and let Him make things right again. If you've confessed it, God has forgiven it.

As the Apostle John said:

> "If we confess our sins, He is faithful and just and will forgive us our sins and purify us from all unrighteousness" (1 John 1:9).

Will you pray with me?

Father, thank You for helping us to become conscious of our sins, so that we can see our need for a Savior, so that we can find salvation! Thank you for the good news of Jesus Christ, who came to fill in the gap between the best that we can do and the best that God has in store for us. We ask that You would fill the gaps in our lives today where we fall short, as we put our faith in Jesus Christ. In Jesus' name, Amen.

Questions for Reflection:

1) Read Romans 3:1-20. Why does Paul say, in verse 20, that no one can become righteous by observing the law, but through the law we become conscious of sin?
2) Read 1 John 1:8-10. How do John's words compare with Paul's?
3) In your own life, do you think you tend to magnify, or minimize, your sins? How might God help you to get His perspective on them?
4) Have you ever experienced the good news of Jesus Christ for yourself, putting your faith in Him for the forgiveness of your sins? If not, why not ask Him to fill the gap for you today in prayer? And if so, why not ask Him for extra grace today to fill any other gaps in your life where you feel like you're falling short?

LESSON 8: BEING REDEEMED BY JESUS — AUGUST 10

Scripture Reading: Romans 3:21-31

The great evangelist D.L. Moody was once confronted by a woman who said she didn't like his method of evangelism. D. L. Moody responded, "I don't particularly like my method either. What's yours?"

The woman said, "I don't have one."

To which D.L. Moody replied, "Then I like mine better!"

There are many methods for sharing your faith, such as "The Four Spiritual Laws" from Campus Crusade, "Steps to Peace with God" from Billy Graham, "The Two Questions" from Evangelism Explosion, or "The Ten Commandments" from The Way of the Master. As someone has said, sharing your faith is like prayer: there's probably only one *wrong* way to do it, and that's to not do it at all!

Still, I'd like to give you a method of sharing your faith today that I hope will make it easier for you to do it. It's called "The Roman Road," and it begins with a Scripture that's found in the passage we're looking at today in the book of Romans, chapter 3.

But before I start, I'd like to remind you that sharing your faith is not about a method, but about a person, Jesus Christ. Remember that it is not a *method* that saves people, but *Jesus*—and He would love to work through you to touch the lives of those around you. When you remember this, it takes the pressure off of you and your method. It's Jesus who will save people!

I'd also like to remind you to *pray for opportunities* to share with others. Sometimes we don't share with others because we don't spend time praying for opportunities to share. But if you'll pray for God to open doors for you to share your faith, He'll open your eyes to those who need to hear His good news today. Pray for opportunities to share, and trust that God will help you share as He opens up those opportunities to you!

And third, a practical way to get into a spiritual conversation with someone is to ask if you can pray for them, perhaps for their health or a situation in their life where they might need God's intervention. As they share with you their need, you can pray for that need specifically, and afterwards share how God may have helped you or someone you know with a similar need. You can let them know that we can trust God for all of our needs because of what He has already done for us through Jesus. This can lead naturally into a conversation about the needs we all have in life, and the way that Jesus can meet those needs.

Having said that, let's take a look at "The Roman Road," a way of walking people through a few passages in the book of Romans, like walking them down a road and pointing out highlights along the way.

While there are many Scriptures that are included in the various versions of "The Roman Road," I'd like to give you just four to make it as easy as possible for you to remember. Since we're in this series on renewing your mind, I think it's helpful to commit these verses to memory so you can have them at the forefront of your mind, for your own sake, as well as for the sake of those people that God brings your way.

The Roman Road starts with Romans, chapter 3, verse 23:

> "For all have sinned and fall short of the glory of God..." (Romans 3:23).

We've all sinned. None of us has a perfect moral scorecard. Unfortunately, sin has consequences. The consequences of sin are stated clearly in Romans chapter 6, verse 23:

> "For the wages of sin is death..." (Romans 6:23).

The wages, or what we've earned for our sins, is death. Death is a natural outcome of what happens when we go against God's will for our lives. God wants us to have an abundant life, but when we go against His plan for us, we head in the opposite direction and head down a path that leads to death instead.

The good news is that Jesus came to put us back on track and to save us from the penalty of death, as described in Romans chapter 5, verse 8:

> "But God demonstrates His own love for us in this: While we were still sinners, Christ died for us" (Romans 5:8).

God loves us so much that He doesn't want us to die, so He made a way for us to be free from sin and free from facing an eternity of death and separation from Him. When Christ died on the cross, He took our sins upon Him to pay the penalty for us with His own life.

Although God makes this offer available freely to anyone, He doesn't force it on anyone. He wants us to come to Him of our own free will, confessing with our mouth that 'Jesus is Lord' and believing in our heart that God raised Him from the dead. When we do that, God will save us, as described in Romans 10:9:

> "That if you confess with your mouth, 'Jesus is Lord,' and believe in your heart that God raised Him from the dead, you will be saved" (Romans 10:9).

When you put your faith in Christ, you'll be saved and given a new life, both here on earth and on into heaven forever.

While there are many other passages from the book of Romans that you could use to share God's good news with people, these four verses make up the core of the gospel: addressing the fact that we've all sinned (Romans 3:23), that the penalty for sin is death (Romans 6:23), that God loved us so much that He made a way for us to be freed from our sins (Romans 5:8), and that by putting our faith in Jesus we can be saved from our sins and given eternal life (Romans 10:9).

While it may sound simple, don't underestimate what God can do in someone's life through a few verses from the book of Romans.

It was while reading the book of Romans that a man named Augustine put his faith in Christ, back in 386 A.D. He was sitting in the garden of a friend, weeping as he thought about the wickedness of his life. Some children nearby were singing "Tolle, lege. Tolle, lege." which means "Take up and read. Take up and read." A scroll of the book of Romans was laying open next to Augustine, so he "took up and read". The first few verses he saw, in Romans 13:13-14, described the condition of his life—and what to do about it:

> "Let us behave decently, as in the daytime, not in orgies and drunkenness, not in sexual immorality and debauchery, not in dissension and jealousy. Rather, clothe yourselves with the Lord Jesus Christ, and do not think about how to gratify the desires of the sinful nature" (Romans 13:13-14).

Augustine put his faith in Christ that day and became one of the greatest theologians and leaders in the history of the church.

It was while reading the book of Romans that another man named Martin Luther put his faith in Christ, about 1,000 years after Saint Augustine. Luther was an Augustinian monk who was burdened by the weight of trying to do enough good works to get into heaven. But that burden was finally lifted when he read a verse from the book of Romans. Romans 1:17 showed him that he wouldn't be declared righteous by his good works, but by his faith in Christ:

> *"For in the gospel a righteousness from God is revealed, a righteousness that is by faith from first to last, just as it is written: 'The righteous will live by faith'" (Romans 1:17).*

Martin Luther put his faith in Christ that day and went on to lead a reformation that has impacted lives all over the world.

It was while listening to someone reading Luther's notes on the book of Romans that John Wesley put his faith in Christ, several hundred years later. As Wesley listened to Luther's introductory comments about Romans, Wesley's heart was "strangely warmed," as he described it, and he committed his life entirely to Christ. John Wesley, and his brother Charles, went on to found the Methodist movement, also contributing many of the great hymns of the faith that we still sing today.

And Paul's words to the Romans are still affecting people today, almost 2,000 years after they were written, as it was while reading the book of Romans that *I* put my faith in Christ, too. As I was reading Romans 1:18-32, I realized that I was a sinner, too, and needed a Savior. Now here I am today encouraging you from what I've learned from the book of Romans so you can share it with others.

These are just a few of the lives that have been touched by reading just a few verses from the book of Romans! So don't underestimate the power of a few verses from this book to change lives. If you've been redeemed by Jesus, tell others about it, using the Roman Road if you want as a way to help them understand the good news of Christ. And if you haven't yet been redeemed by Jesus, I'd encourage you to keep reading the Bible so you can put your faith in Him today.

If you're up for a challenge, I'd also encourage you to commit to memory these four simple verses from Romans: 3:23, 6:23, 5:8 and 10:9. Memorizing scripture is a great way to renew your mind, and as you keep these particular verses at the forefront of your mind, they'll also help you as you talk with others about how they can be redeemed by Jesus, too.

Perhaps you're reading this today and you're like Augustine, or Luther, or Wesley, or me, and these verses that I've been sharing from the book of Romans have somehow sparked your thinking and moved your heart in a way that *you*, too want to commit *your* life to Christ. If so, put your faith in Him today for everything in your life. Ask Him to forgive you of your sins and invite Him to be your Lord and Savior. Do what Paul encouraged the Romans to do and you'll be saved, too:

> *"That if you confess with your mouth, 'Jesus is Lord,' and believe in your heart that God raised Him from the dead, you will be saved" (Romans 10:9).*

Will you pray with me?

Father, thank You for sending Jesus to redeem us from our sins. Help us to share that life-changing message with those around us. Open our eyes today to those who need to hear this message and open their hearts to be receptive as we share it, so they can put their faith in You as well. In Jesus' name, Amen.

Questions for Reflection:

1) Read Romans 3:21-31. What do you think about Paul's claim that "all have sinned" in verse 23? What evidence do you see in your life or the lives of those around you that argue either for or against this claim?
2) How does Paul say we can be justified in God's eyes and redeemed from this situation, as stated in verses 24-26?
3) What place does boasting have in the life of a Christian, according to verses 27-28?
4) Why not take some time today to write down the four verses mentioned in this message and commit them to memory as a way to keep them at the forefront of your mind? The verses are: Romans 3:23, Romans 6:23, Romans 5:8, and Romans 10:9. After you've memorized them, consider sharing these verses with a friend who has already put their faith in Christ as a way to practice what you've learned, then pray for God to give you opportunities with someone else who still needs to hear this good news!

LESSON 9: BELIEVING GOD   AUGUST 11

Scripture Reading: Romans 4:1-12

I'd like to talk to you today about believing God. Not just believing *in* God. But *believing God*— believing that He will do what He says He will do. The reason I want to talk to you about believing God is because what you believe influences what you do. Or, to put it another way, you do what you believe.

If you believe that people are going to hell if they don't put their faith in Jesus, then you'll do something about it. If you're not doing something about it, then perhaps you're just giving intellectual assent to an idea, but you're not really *believing* it.

I have a friend who went to the doctor for a checkup. The doctor told him, "Your dad had a heart attack by the time he was forty-eight, and you're going to have a heart attack by the time you're forty-eight, unless you start making some changes in your life." My friend had known this was a possibility before, but it wasn't until his doctor told him the truth so directly that my friend finally *believed* it. That day, he began that day to change the way he ate, the way he exercised, and the way he lived his life. And today, he's still going strong. Why? Because he *believed* what his doctor said.

How much more so, when we hear what God says about our lives, should be believe Him and do what He says?

Abraham is an excellent example for all of us of someone who believed God, who heard what God said and took it to heart, and then backed up what he believed with his actions.

If you remember the story, God told Abraham that he would have so many descendants they would outnumber the stars in the sky and the sand on the seashore. This was a pretty lofty idea considering that Abraham was old and childless. But the Bible says:

> *"Abraham believed God and it was credited to him as righteousness"* (Romans 4:3).

Several years later, when God called Abraham to become circumcised as a way of sealing God's covenant with him, Abraham did what God said that very day. Within a year, he and his wife Sarah had their first child—the first of a long line of those promised descendants.

While Abraham's obedience to be circumcised was important and necessary for the fulfillment of God's plan for his life, the apostle Paul notes in his letter to the Romans that it wasn't *after* Abraham was circumcised that he was declared righteous in God's sight, but *before*. In fact, Abraham was declared righteous several *years* before his circumcision. He was declared righteous the moment he believed. (You can read more about this part of Abraham's story in Genesis chapters 15 through 18.)

Abraham's circumcision was a natural outworking of the faith that Abraham had already expressed in his heart to God. His actions were directly influenced by what he believed.

Dallas Willard is one of the spiritual giants of our generation. When asked what he would advise someone to do who wanted to grow spiritually, he said:

> *"Do the next right thing you know you ought to do."*

You might have thought he could have said, "Read the Bible more," or "Pray more," or "Go to church more." But he didn't. He said that the best course of action was to do the next right thing you know you ought to do, because that's likely the very thing that God wants you to do. He said this may very well involve reading the Bible more so you can get clarity on what it is that God really wants you to do. Or it may involve praying more because you'll need God's wisdom for how to do it. Or it may involve going to church more because you'll most likely need the help of others to do what God has put on your heart to do. But in any case, you'll grow tremendously when you do the next right thing you know you ought to do.

My question for you today is this: what's the next right thing *you* know you ought to do?

What is it that God has called you to do that He is wanting you to step out in faith and do next? Maybe it's something regarding your family, your job, your finances, or your health. Maybe it's something regarding your calling, your gifting, your relationships, or the way you use your time. Maybe it's something that is quiet and internal, or maybe it's something that is "out loud" and vocal. Maybe it's something you need to start doing. Or maybe it's something you need to stop doing.

Although I don't know what it might be that God is putting on your heart right now as you read these words, I imagine there are probably one or two things that have already started coming to your mind as "the next right thing you know you ought to do." Whatever it is, I want to encourage you to do it. Believe in your heart that God has called you to it, then step out in faith and let Him help you do it!

You may remember the story of the widow's oil, back in the Old Testament. This widow had lost her husband, and she and her two sons were struggling to live. She was at a point of desperation because her husband's creditors were coming to take away her boys as slaves.

She cried out to Elisha, a man of God, and asked him what to do. Elisha asked what she had left in her house. She said that she had nothing there at all, "except a little oil" (2 Kings 4:5).

So Elisha told her what to do next. He told her to go around to all her neighbors and ask for their empty jars. She and her sons did what Elisha said.

She went all over the neighborhood asking for empty jars and brought them home. Elisha told her to fill them up with the little oil that she had. By faith, she began pouring out the oil into the first jar, and it didn't stop! It just kept flowing and flowing as she poured it into jar after jar, until every jar she had collected was full.

Elisha told her:

> "Go, sell the oil and pay your debts. You and your sons can live on what is left" (2 Kings 4:7b).

I love this story for several reasons, but one that stands out to me today is the fact that the widow *believed* what God was telling her to do through the prophet Elisha, then she went out and *acted* on that belief. She did the next right thing she knew she ought to do.

One way to renew your mind today is to believe God—not just believe in Him—but really believe Him, because what you believe influences what you do.

Abraham wasn't credited with righteousness after he was circumcised, but before, when he first believed God. It was only afterwards that he stepped out in faith and acted on what he believed.

The widow's life didn't start to turn around after she had sold all her jars of oil and got the money for them, but before, when she first believed what God told her to do through the prophet Elisha. It was only afterwards that she stepped out in faith and acted on what she believed.

God wants you to believe Him, too. He wants you believe what He says and then to act on that belief, to do the next right thing that you know you ought to do. For some of you, this might mean picking up a project that you've been putting off for years. You might think, "Not *that*, Lord! It's been on the back burner for so long, I don't think I'll ever get around to it." For others of you, this might mean acting on something you heard just yesterday. You might think, "Not *that*, Lord! I just heard about it yesterday, I need a few more days, or months, or years to think about it."

We can all think of reasons not to do what we know we ought to do. But I want to encourage you today to believe God, and then act on that belief. Don't let doubt and discouragement hold you back from doing "the next right thing" that God has called you to do.

Believe God today, and then act on that belief! One day, like Abraham and Sarah, and like the widow and her sons, people will be telling the story of what happened to *you* when *you* believed God, too.

Will you pray with me?

Father, thank You for creating each of us with special tasks to accomplish here on earth. Help us to have the faith today to believe what You say when You speak to us, and then to act on that belief. Help us today to step out in faith and do the next right thing we know we ought to do. In Jesus' name, Amen.

Questions for Reflection:

1) Read Romans 4:1-12. Why do you think God credited Abraham with righteousness when he first believed God, rather than after he took his famous steps of obedience?

2) Read James 2:15-18. What are some of the differences between believing God and believing in God, based on this passage?
3) What is the relationship between faith and works, as described by the passage in James?
4) What comes to your mind as "the next right thing you ought to do?" What steps could you take to help clarify that those things really are from God, and then to step out in faith to begin doing them?

LESSON 10: BEING FULLY PERSUADED   AUGUST 12

Scripture Reading: Acts 10

I'd like to give you some hope today— hope that God has the power to do what He has promised.

My daughter showed me a great picture a few weeks ago with the word HOPE written on the palm of someone's hand. What was unique about the picture was that the word HOPE on the hand could be seen reflected in a side mirror of a car, with these words written in small print on the bottom of the mirror:

"OBJECTS IN MIRROR ARE CLOSER THAN THEY APPEAR."

I thought it was a great picture of the hope that God offers to each one of us. When God promises to do something, you can take it to the bank. You can trust that He will bring it to pass. Even if the answers to your prayers might look like they are far off, those answers could really be much closer than you think!

After I saw this picture, my wife and daughter were looking for a new car on the Internet. Our van had broken down and could no longer be repaired, so we've been looking for something to replace it. My wife has had her eye on a particular little car that she's really liked for several years. It's not like her to care much for cars at all, but this one seemed to be just right for her and my daughter.

As they looked, they found it: the exact car they were looking for. Everything was perfect about it: the style, the color, even the design on the front. The only thing wrong with it, from my perspective, was the price! (It was the right price for the car, just the wrong price for us!)

A friend of mine told me that when he sent his daughter off to school, he said he sent her off with only his prayers, because he couldn't afford to send her to the school. He told her: "The same God who takes care of me will take care of you."

Through prayer and hard work, his daughter *was* able to make it through that school. God *did* take care of her.

So as I went to bed with my wife that night after looking at the cars, I told her about my friend's words for his daughter. Then I smiled and said, "You've got my prayers! The same God who takes care of me will take care of you!" We both laughed and went to bed.

The next morning, I went to a men's breakfast at 6:00 a.m. As I pulled into the parking lot, someone pulled in right behind me, someone who had never been to the group before. He just happened to be driving the very same car my wife and daughter had been looking at on the Internet: the exact style, color, and even the design painted on the front.

I couldn't believe it! It hadn't even been 8 hours since I had prayed that prayer. I got out and asked him how he liked his car. He said he loved it. I asked if he'd ever consider selling it. He said, "Actually, I'm thinking about it." He said things had recently changed in his life, and he didn't need this car anymore.

We talked some more, and after breakfast, I asked if I could take a look at the car. I started taking a few pictures for my wife, then I got inside. As I looked around, my eyes landed on the mirror on the right-hand side. There reflected in the mirror, I could see the full length of the side of the car, with these words at the bottom:

"OBJECTS IN MIRROR ARE CLOSER THAN THEY APPEAR."

I almost cried. I didn't know if this particular car was God's answer to our prayers or not, but I did see clearly that if God *wanted* to answer them, He could do it in an instant. I took a picture of the car in the mirror, with the words displayed at the bottom, and I repented of my unbelief. I told God that day that I was sorry for being so flippant the night before, saying to my wife, "The same God who takes care of me will take care of you." I know that God can do anything, absolutely anything.

Let me add that it's been a few weeks now and we haven't gotten the car yet. The man's not quite ready to sell and we're not quite ready to buy. We're not even sure if this is even God's answer or if He has another answer in the works. But seeing the car gave me a boost in my faith and was a vivid reminder of the hope we can have in God—even when it seems like the odds are against us.

That's the kind of faith that Abraham had. The Bible says:

> *"Against all hope, Abraham in hope believed and so became the father of many nations, just as it had been said to him, 'So shall your offspring be.' Without weakening in his faith, he faced the fact that his body was as good as dead—since he was about a hundred years old—and that Sarah's womb was also dead. Yet he did not waver through unbelief regarding the promise of God, but was strengthened in his faith and gave glory to God, being fully persuaded that God had power to do what He had promised" (Romans 4:18-21).*

I love the way that starts: "Against all hope, Abraham in hope believed..." And I love the way it ends: "...being fully persuaded that God had power to do what He had promised."

Abraham was fully persuaded that God had the power to do what He had promised. And that's the kind of faith that God wants you to have. How can you do that? How can you become fully persuaded that God has the power to do what He has promised?

I'd like to give you two ideas today to help give you a boost in your faith. By doing these two things, I believe that God will renew your mind and give you hope for your future, too.

The first is to take time to read the stories about how God has been faithful to people in the Bible. Stories like Abraham's in Genesis chapters 15 through 18. Stories like Moses' in Exodus chapter 1 through 4. Stories like Joshua's in the book of Joshua, or Esther's in the book of Esther, or Ruth's in the book of Ruth. The Bible is filled with stories from cover to cover about how God has worked in the lives of ordinary people to do extraordinary things. As you read these stories, you'll be filled with faith that God can do similar things for you.

The second is to look at stories from people living today who have been touched by the hand of God. The same God who worked in the lives of men and women thousands of years ago is still at work in the lives of men and women today. I've posted many such stories on our website at www.theranch.org about people who are living today who have seen God work in their lives in astounding ways. One of those stories is about a woman named Liesl

Alexander, a woman who was locked in a mental institution for years, taking 36 medications a day, and was written off as one of the most hopeless cases in the institution.

Yet when a group of people from a local church came and began to pray for her, her life turned around completely. By the power of Christ, she was set free to live the life that God had created her to live. For the past 20 years, she's been sharing her testimony about how Christ has changed her life, encouraging anyone who will listen to be fully persuaded that "God can do anything, absolutely anything."

God wants *you* to be fully persuaded that He can do what He has promised to do. Take some time this week to read the Bible and look for stories of how God has touched people's lives in powerful ways, then look at our website or other Christian books to see how God has worked in other people's lives today. You'll see that God really can do anything— absolutely anything.

Remember:
"OBJECTS IN MIRROR ARE CLOSER THAN THEY APPEAR."
HOPE is closer than you might think.
Will you pray with me?

Father, thank You for reminding us that You are always at work on our behalf, and that the answers to our prayers could be revealed in an instant. Help us to trust You fully—to be fully persuaded—that You can do anything, absolutely anything. In Jesus' name, Amen.

Questions for Reflection:

1) Read Romans 4:13-25. What does this passage say to you today about hope?
2) While Abraham and Sarah's story might seem unbelievable, for they were old and past the age of child-bearing, how can their story give you hope for any situation that you're praying about right now?
3) What story does Paul refer to, in verses 23-25, to remind us about God's ability to bring life out of death?
4) What are some steps you can take this week to help yourself become more "fully persuaded" that God can do what He has promised to do, whether they are steps suggested by this lesson, or other steps that might not have been mentioned? Consider committing to doing one or two of those things.

LESSON 11: CALLING THINGS THAT ARE NOT AS THOUGH THEY WERE   AUGUST 13

Scripture Reading: Romans 4:16-25

As we're looking at ways to renew your mind, I'd like to draw your attention to one more verse from Romans chapter 4 before moving on to chapter 5. There's a phrase in this verse that is not only extremely quotable and memorable but can also be a powerful force for defining your future, if you'll take it to heart.

In talking about God, Paul described Him as:

> "...the God who gives life to the dead and calls things that are not as though they were" (Romans 4:17b).

I love that phrase: the God who gives life to the dead and calls things that are not as though they were.

If you can believe that God can give life to the dead, which He has proven over and over, and that He can call things into existence that have never existed before, which He has also proven over and over, then you can believe that God can do miracles in your own life that will outshine anything you've ever seen before.

Some people bristle at the idea of "name it and claim it" theology referring to the idea that we can have anything we want if we'll just speak it forth, believe in it hard enough, and start walking in that direction. While there's incredible power in positive thinking–and it's certainly much better than negative thinking–it *can* lead to problems if what we're naming isn't in line with what God wants us to claim. Rather than being a blessing to us, what we're wanting could actually harm us, as every parent knows who has given in to a poorly thought-out request by one of their children.

But when you get your thinking in line with God's and ask Him for things that He would love to give you, then it becomes a different story. When God names it, He *wants* you to claim it! When God puts a desire in your heart, He *wants* you to speak it forth, to believe in it fully, and to start walking in that direction.

This is exactly why God commended Abraham. Abraham was sad and dejected that he had no heirs to whom he could pass on all the blessings he had received in his life. When he expressed that sadness to God, God spoke to Abraham, giving him a promise that seemed unbelievable. God changed Abraham's name from Abram—which means "exalted father"—to Abraham, which means "father of many," saying:

"You will be the father of many nations" (Genesis 17:5).

Abraham's first response was to fall down and laugh! The Bible says:

"Abraham fell facedown; he laughed and said to himself, 'Will a son be born to a man a hundred years old? Will Sarah bear a child at the age of ninety?'" (Genesis 17:17).

But when God assured Abraham that what He had spoken would come to pass, Abraham believed God. He acted on that belief, circumcising himself and his whole family, and God honored him for his faith and obedience.

Within a year of Abraham's conversation with God, Abraham and Sarah had their promised son. They named him Isaac—which means "laughter"—as God had told them to name him. And so began the promised inheritance to Abraham that has continued from one generation to the next until this very day.

Even though Abraham's body was as good as dead, in terms of its ability to bring forth life, and his wife had been barren her whole life, God proved to them both that He is a God "who gives life to the dead and calls things that are not as though they were."

God has been doing the same thing throughout eternity.

God spoke the world into existence with a word. He called Gideon a "mighty warrior" when Gideon saw himself as the least in his family and the weakest family in his tribe. He called David a "king" and a "man after My own heart" even though David was just a shepherd boy at the time and was told he had a wicked heart by his brother.

The Bible is full of stories of God giving life to the dead and calling things that are not as though they were, with the story of Jesus's death and resurrection being chief among them! But the stories of God calling things that are not as though they were didn't end in biblical days. They still continue today!

Let me tell you just one.

About ten years ago I was invited to attend a Billy Graham evangelism conference in Amsterdam. My passport was about to expire, so I had to fill out an application for a new one. On the application, it asked for my occupation. I wasn't sure exactly what to put in the blank, as the ministry I do on the Internet doesn't seem to fit into a neatly defined category.

Yet at the time I was feeling more and more that one of God's callings on my life was to be an author. I loved writing and had written extensively for my own website, filling up hundreds of electronic pages with digital ink. Yet I never considered myself an author, since the only book I had ever published was a devotional booklet I had written the year before and photocopied at home for the people who asked for it.

That hardly seemed to qualify me as an author, yet I felt that's what God was calling me to be. So, as a statement of faith of God's calling on my life, I filled in the "occupation" blank with just one word: "Author."

When I arrived at the airport in Amsterdam, the customs official took a look at my passport, then asked me what I did. I said I was an author. He asked, "What kind of books do you write?"

I thought about my little devotional booklet and said, "Devotional books to encourage people in their faith."

He asked where I was headed, and I told him about the Billy Graham conference. He said, "With a last name like 'Elder' that fits." He smiled, stamped my passport, and waved me on through.

Something in my heart told me that being an author "fit," too. I realized that I wasn't *stretching* the truth when I said I was an author. I was *believing* the truth. From that moment on, it changed both my outlook and my expectations for the future.

Since that time, I've written and published over a dozen books. My weekly messages, like this one that you're reading right now, are being sent by email to over 35,000 subscribers around the world. I'm not sure what the official qualifications would be for someone to be declared an "author." But for me, I believe I became an author the moment I believed it myself, came into alignment with God's plan for my life in that area, and started walking in obedience to that calling.

God has a way of seeing our potential before we do and then speaking it into existence. How? Because God can see an oak tree in an acorn.

If you're willing to open your eyes to see things as God sees them, you'll start seeing oak trees in acorns, too. You'll see the potential in yourself and in the lives of others that you may never have seen before.

I could tell you story after story of people who are alive today whose lives and situations have been changed dramatically because they put their faith in Christ. I could tell you about marriages that have been dead for years and ended in divorce, but which God brought back to life when both people put their faith in Christ. I could tell you about couples who have been declared infertile by doctors, but whom God has said would bear a child within a year—like Abraham and Sarah—and have! I could tell you about people involved in lifestyles that could literally kill them, lifestyles which some people say are impossible to change, but which God *has* changed, giving them new lives instead. As the angel told Mary:

"For nothing is impossible with God" (Luke 1:37).

When you get in line with God's plans for your life, nothing will be impossible for you, either.

If God has spoken into your life about your future, believe Him. Put your faith into action and start walking in the direction He's told you to walk. If you're not sure what God has called you to do, keep seeking Him for His wisdom. Read the Bible. Pray. Ask others what they think about your future. Then when God gives you the next step to take, take it!

Don't be discouraged if what God says about your future doesn't line up with your present.

Remember that God called Abraham "a father of many nations" before he and Sarah had even conceived their first child together. Remember that God called Gideon a "mighty warrior" back when Gideon felt like he was the weakest of the weak. Remember that God called David "a man after My own heart" even when others were saying otherwise. Remember that God sees an oak tree in an acorn.

Put your trust in God and remember who He is. He is:

"… the God who gives life to the dead and calls things that are not as though they were."

Will you pray with me?

Father, thank You for reminding us today of who You are and what You can do. Give us the faith we need to see Your promises come to pass in our lives. Fill us with Your wisdom, Your plans, Your purposes, and Your ways, so that we can take hold of them by faith and begin walking in obedience to Your calling on our lives, starting even today. In Jesus' name, Amen.

Questions for Reflection:

1) Read Romans 4:16-25. What reasons might Abraham have had for why it could have seemed impossible for God to fulfill what He had promised to him?
2) What reasons might you have for why it could seem impossible for God to fulfill what He has promised to you? How might Abraham have overcome His doubts? How might you overcome yours?
3) Read Judges 7:1-7. In reading this part of Gideon's story, what reason does God give for why He sometimes does what seems impossible through us? What hope does this give you for your situation?
4) If God has given you a promise about your calling or your future, what next steps could you take to put your faith into action and start walking in the direction of that future? If you don't feel that God has spoken to you about your future, what next steps could you take to begin learning more about it from Him?

LESSON 12: HAVING PEACE WITH GOD   AUGUST 14

Scripture Reading: Romans 5:1-11

God wants to give you a lift today. He wants to pick you up, brush you off, and give you a new start. In particular, God wants to give you peace—His peace—a deep peace that will renew and restore you and give you the strength to go on.

How can you have the peace of God? It starts by having peace *with* God, by coming to the place where you're reconciled with Him, the place where you know that you are loved, forgiven, and walking in harmony with Him. The apostle Paul tells us that this kind of peace is available to you when you put your faith in Christ:

> "Therefore, since we have been justified through faith, we have peace with God through our Lord Jesus Christ, through whom we have gained access by faith into this grace in which we now stand" (Romans 5:1-2a).

But this message today isn't just for those who need to put their faith in Christ for the first time. It's for everyone who needs a reminder of the peace that God has in store for those who trust in Him. As the Bible says:

> "You will keep in perfect peace
> him whose mind is steadfast,
> because he trusts in You."
> (Isaiah 26:3)

God wants you to trust in Him. He wants you to keep your mind steadfast, resolutely firm and unwavering. And when you trust in Him, keeping your mind steadfast, He will keep you in peace—perfect peace.

Why is it so hard then to have God's peace? Sometimes it's because we make it harder than it really is. Dallas Willard gives a simple and practical definition of what it means to trust Christ:

> "Trusting Christ means you want to be with Him as much as possible."

When you trust someone, you're happy to be with them. And when you realize what Christ has done for you—and what He's still capable of doing for you—it makes it easier to trust Him and to want to be with Him as much as possible. As the apostle Paul continues his letter to the Romans, he gives us some reasons why we can trust Christ so fully—and why we would want to be with Him as much as possible, too. Paul says:

> "You see, at just the right time, when we were still powerless, Christ died for the ungodly. Very rarely will anyone die for a righteous man, though for a good man someone might possibly dare to die. But God demonstrates His own love for us in this: While we were still sinners, Christ died for us" (Romans 5:6-8).

Let me unpack for just a minute, because it will help you understand just how very much God loves you. If you think about it, you'll realize how very rare it is for one person to die for another, even if the person they're dying for is "righteous." Yet in some cases, it's possible that someone *might* die for someone else if the person they're dying for is truly "good." But then think about what Christ has done. He's gone further still, not just dying for those who "deserve" it, but for those who don't deserve it at all—which, as it turns out, happens to be every one of us.

You see, Christ loves you with an overwhelming love—a love that He wants to pour out on you—not just once when you first get saved, but continually for the rest of your life here on earth and on into eternity.

When you realize that Christ loves you this much—and wants to continue loving you this much—you'll see why you can trust Him completely, and why you would want to be with Him as much as possible.

Trusting Christ brings you peace with God. And when you have peace *with* God, this opens the possibility for you to have the peace *of* God in many other areas of your life as well.

I was sitting at a table last week with some men who were discussing how God has brought His peace into their lives. Their stories were not only interesting, but interwoven.

One of the men had gotten out of jail about a year ago. After having lived a life of self-destruction for years, he finally put his faith in Christ while in prison. He found that the hours he spent there alone with God were some of the sweetest hours of his life.

But his greatest fear while he was in prison was what would happen when he finally got out. What would happen when he came back into the reality of this world, facing those whom he had wronged so horribly? What would happen when he had to face his wife and kids again, whom he had led into a destructive lifestyle? What would happen when he had to face his in-laws again, whom he had pushed away over and over?

As it turned out, one of this man's in-laws was seated at the table with us—the father-in-law who knew how much trouble this man had caused for his daughter—the father-in-law who was so upset with this guy that he even paid for a lawyer to help his daughter start divorce proceedings.

Yet when the son-in-law put his faith in Christ in prison, something changed. The father-in-law realized that his son-in-law was now his "brother-in-Christ." Rather than condemning his son-in-law when he got out of prison, he found himself forgiving him instead. He went to visit his son-in-law at home and offered his forgiveness instead of divorce papers. He told his son-in-law that God wanted him to wipe the slate clean between them and was offering them a new start in their relationship.

When God reconciled these two men to Himself through Christ, He also laid the foundation for them to reconcile with each other down the road. Once they each discovered how they could have peace with God, they also discovered they could now have peace with one another. Can you see how having peace *with* God can help you experience the peace *of* God in other areas of your life? God wants you to have both.

God wants you to be at peace, and He says that you can have that peace by keeping your mind steadfast and trusting in Him. If you want to renew your mind and experience God's peace, I want to encourage you to do what Isaiah said to do: keep your mind steadfast and continue to trust in God. Remember:

> *"You will keep in perfect peace*
> *him whose mind is steadfast,*
> *because he trusts in You."*
> *(Isaiah 26:3)*

Also remember that,

> *"Trusting Christ means you want to be with Him as much as possible."*

If you have areas in your own life where you feel unrest, or areas where Satan has tried to steal your peace, can I encourage you to bring those areas to Jesus again today? He really does love you. He is *for* you. And He wants you to experience His peace, not just once in your lifetime, but throughout your lifetime, a peace that "transcends all understanding" (Philippians 4:7).

As you read your Bible this week, I want to encourage you to read it with three thoughts in mind. First, read the text for what it says, filling your mind with God's words. But don't just stop there. Take time to meditate on the words that you're reading, mulling them over in your mind, reflecting on what the words mean and what they might mean to your life today. And third, be sure to pray while you're reading, asking God to speak to you about the words on the page, realizing that His word really is "living and active" (Hebrews 4:12). This is one of the best ways to spend as much time with Him as possible.

Remember that the Bible is not just a textbook on living. It's a textbook that comes with a built-in teacher, the Holy Spirit. It's like taking a class in school and being taught by the author of the textbook himself. While you can learn a lot by just reading the text, you can learn even more when you go to class with the Author, asking Him your questions, letting Him give you more insights into what He's written, and letting Him correct your thinking in those cases where you've possibly misread the text or missed a crucial word here or there. Don't just read the text and miss spending time with the Author! You'll love your classes more, and He'll love spending the extra time with you, too.

I pray this has given you a lift today, and I pray that as you put these words into practice, God will give you His perfect peace.

Will you pray with me?

Father, thank You for offering Your peace to us through faith in Your Son Jesus Christ. Help us to put our faith in Him again today, trusting Him with our salvation and everything else in our lives. Help us to give over anything in our lives that is causing us unrest right now, and truly trust You in that area, too. Forgive us of our sins and lead us into the fullness of life that You offer to us, both here on earth and on into eternity. In Jesus' name, Amen.

Questions for Reflection:

1) Read Romans 5:1-11. How does Paul say we can gain access to the peace that God has to offer us?
2) According to verse 5, what means does God use to pour out His love into our hearts? How might you invite God to pour out His love into your heart in a new way today?
3) How can Paul's illustration of the different kinds of people that someone might possibly die for help you to understand better Christ's love for you and what He has done for you?
4) If you've never put your faith in Christ, trusting that He died for your sins so that you could have peace with God, is there anything holding you back from doing it today? If so, can you confess it to Him and let it go so you can put your faith fully in Him? And if you've already put your faith in God, but are still struggling to experience His peace, is there anything holding you back from trusting Him more fully with every area of your life today? If so, then ask God for His help with those areas, and ask Him to fill you with His peace—a peace that transcends all understanding

LESSON 13: REJOICING IN OUR SUFFERING   AUGUST 15

Scripture Reading: Romans 5:2-4

I'd like to talk to you today about pain. While it may not sound like a very pleasant topic, when I shared this message with a group of men on Friday morning, one of them wrote to me later in the day and said:

> "Thanks for your devotional this morning. I got there in a pretty lousy frame of mind and you had me full of joy before you were done."

It's amazing how getting God's perspective on a subject can give you a whole new attitude towards it–especially a subject like pain. I'd like to give you a new perspective on pain today so that you'll never see it the same again.

Even though we may not like to think about pain, we sometimes like to talk about it. Like a good fish story, we often try to outdo one another with how much pain we've had to endure in life. One person starts talking about their pain and then another chimes in to say, "Aw, that's nothing. You should have seen…"

I had this happen just a few weeks ago. Three of us were talking about what we've gone through to get some warts off the soles of our feet. One guy started by talking about the pain he felt when he dug a knife deep into his skin to get one out. The other guy started talking about the pain he felt when a doctor froze a wart off his foot.

I couldn't resist. I had to add my story, not only because it seemed worse in my eyes than any of the pain that they had described (it was my own pain, after all, which always tends to seem worse, I'm sure), but also because it was such a strange method to me. My doctor, after trying various other painful treatments, finally used one that outdid them all: he applied some juice from something called a blister beetle from South America directly onto my wart. While I felt nothing whatsoever as he put it on, within a few hours, the skin on the bottom of my foot had blistered to the size of a silver dollar, pulling up what felt like every layer of skin that could possibly have been on the sole of my foot–and the wart along with it. The pain while that blister grew was more excruciating and intense than any other treatment I had received on that wart so far.

But as painful as it was, within a few weeks, the wart was gone. The wart that had plagued me for several years, causing me pain every time I walked, was finally gone.

As Daniel Defoe has said:

> "God will often deliver us in a manner that seems initially to destroy us."

How true that is about pain.

In the book of Romans, the apostle Paul describes pain in a surprising similar way, saying that pain–or "sufferings" in this case–is not just something we have to endure, but something that we can actually rejoice in:

> "And we rejoice in the hope of the glory of God. Not only so, but we also rejoice in our sufferings, because we know that suffering produces perseverance; perseverance, character; and character, hope" (Romans 5:2b-4).

Paul says that the pain we experience in life is not without purpose. Rather, it can produce in us perseverance. Perseverance can then produce character. And character produces hope.

Some of the most hopeful people I know are not those who have a Pollyanna, happy-go-lucky view of life who have never experienced deep pain. Instead, the people I know who are the most hopeful are those who have been through the wringer of life and have persevered through it. The pain they've endured has built up their character and given them hope–a hope that they can then pass on to others who need it.

Pain is not without purpose. In fact, pain has been designed by God to let us know that something in our life needs attention. It's a sign that something is broken and either needs to be fixed before it gets worse, or, as in the case of the pain of losing a loved one, serves an indicator of the depth of our deep love for that person. When you can acknowledge that your pain serves a purpose, it can change your whole perspective on it.

I think my perspective began to change when I first read a book by Dr. Paul Brand called, *Fearfully and Wonderfully Made*. In the book, Dr. Brand describes his work among modern-day lepers.

Leprosy is a disease that affects the nervous system. Those who have leprosy often don't feel pain because their nerve endings don't work properly. As a result, lepers' bodies can often become disturbingly deformed, losing fingers or toes, or going blind in their eyes. It's not the leprosy itself that causes these abnormalities. It's the fact that lepers no longer have the benefits of pain.

They don't know if a stove is hot or cold until they've left their hand on it too long, damaging their fingers beyond repair. They don't know they've stubbed their toe on a rock until the bruises and swelling gives them a visual clue that they've hit something far too hard. Believe it or not, they don't realize that they're supposed to blink every few seconds, because they never feel what it's like to have dry, sore eyes. As a result, they often go blind, unless someone teaches them how to blink on a regular basis to give their eyes the moisture they need. Imagine giving thanks for the ability to feel that your eyes are dry and sore!

Yet lepers often wish they had something most of the rest of us wish we didn't have: pain. Lepers, perhaps more than the rest of us, seem to understand that pain–when used in the way for which God intended it–serves a terrific purpose. If lepers could feel pain, they would probably rejoice like the apostle Paul, saying "Praise God, I can feel the pain!" They know that without it, they're in for bigger hurts down the road.

So far, I've been talking about physical pain. But if you'll indulge me to go a little longer than usual with today's message, I'd like to talk for a few minutes about a pain that can often go deeper and last longer than physical pain, and that's the pain we feel in our hearts and minds when we get hurt by someone else.

I was reminded of this again this past month when I read a blog post by a friend. His post left me stunned. He had served with me in my ministry several years ago, encouraging me, mentoring me, giving me opportunities to use my gifts and talents in ways that went beyond what I could do for myself. Yet a day came when he took me out to lunch and said that he was going to have to step back from my ministry. He said his priorities had changed and he needed to refocus his time and attention on some other things.

I was hurt. A lot. I had enjoyed our friendship and our times together, our conversations, and our urging one another on in the Lord. His reasons for stepping back didn't seem to line up. Something was wrong, but I didn't know what. The pain of not knowing, and the feelings of hurt and rejection, have surfaced in my heart from time to time for the last several years.

Yet when I read his blog post a few weeks ago, I finally understood. Something *had* gone wrong.

He had begun to make a shift in his thinking several years ago on a number of topics. He confessed that he lost his job a few years ago at a large ministry because his views and opinions had shifted so radically that they could no longer keep him on staff. As I read his message, my heart began to break for him. It also began to melt for him. I finally started to understand that his stepping back from my ministry was a blessing in disguise, for if he hadn't done so then, it would have become a bigger problem for me and my ministry today than I could have imagined.

In talking with God about it after I read his blog post, I felt like God was saying to me:

"What looked like rejection was really protection—My protection."

It still hurt, but it definitely made the hurt feel better. I'd like to share what I wrote in my journal after I finally knew the truth. Here's what I felt God was saying to me:

"Oh, no doubt about it, Eric, I know it hurt. But there's also no doubt that I allowed that hurt to help you avoid a bigger one in the future. Pain is not without purpose. In fact, I've designed it precisely for that purpose—to make you aware that something is wrong so you can take action before things get worse. If you don't respond to the initial pain, like a toothache, I've designed the pain to escalate in intensity so you will respond. If you don't respond to even that, then, well, the consequences are your own. But the pain itself serves a very good purpose: to spare you from greater pain down the road. If you'll believe that and take it to heart, you'll never see pain as your enemy again. Pain is your friend, if you'll respond to it in My ways."

Again, these words are my paraphrase of what I felt God was saying to me that day. They helped me to understand what Paul was talking about when he said that we could actually "rejoice in our sufferings," for suffering *does* have a purpose. And these words helped me to understand that we have a choice to make regarding the pains that we experience in life.

There's a story that's told in *The Westside Baptist*, that illustrates this well. It goes like this:

There were two young boys who were raised in the home of an alcoholic father. As young men, they each went their own way. Years later, a psychologist who was analyzing what drunkenness does to children in the home searched out these two men. One had turned out to be like his father, a hopeless alcoholic. The other had turned out to be a teetotaler (someone who abstains from alcohol). The counselor asked the first man, "Why did you become an alcoholic?" And the second, "Why did you become a teetotaler?"

And they both gave the same identical answer in these words: "What else could you expect when you had a father like mine?"

It's not what happens to you in life but how you react to it that makes the difference. Every human being in the same situation has the possibilities of choosing how he will react, either positively or negatively.

We all experience pain. Jesus wept. I've wept. I imagine you've wept, too. We would hardly be human if we didn't. Yet pain is not without purpose, and depending on how you respond to it, it can define your future for years to come.

My kids were crying this week because one of our newly born kittens had died. It was only a few weeks old, but they had already become very attached to it. When they found it dead, they couldn't help but cry.

As I talked to them about it, I told them that I was sorry for the kitten and for them, but I was thankful that they were able to cry. It showed me that they really cared. Their tears were an expression that something had gone wrong in the world. Their tears revealed to me that they had already begun to care for one of God's creatures that was given to us for such a short amount of time. Their tears were response enough.

As Charles Robinson has said:

> "Jesus wept once; possibly more than once. There are times when God asks nothing of His children except silence, patience, and tears."

Pain has a purpose, whether it's to reveal something that needs to be addressed, or to reveal a depth of love that we've felt for something or someone we once held close, but now have lost.

Pain hurts, but that doesn't mean that pain has to be your enemy. As lepers have discovered, pain can be a blessing, sparing you from greater pain down the road. Pain can be a blessing if you'll let God use it in your life to work His purposes, responding to it in ways that God wants you to respond.

When pain threatens to get you down, remind yourself (meaning "put it in your mind again") that pain is not without purpose. Ask God to help you persevere through your pain. Ask Him to use it to build up your character. Then ask Him to fill your life with hope–hope for yourself and hope that you can pour into the lives of others.

As Paul said,

> "And we rejoice in the hope of the glory of God. Not only so, but we also rejoice in our sufferings, because we know that suffering produces perseverance; perseverance, character; and character, hope" (Romans 5:2b-4).

I pray that from this day forward you'll never look at pain the same way again.

Will you pray with me?

Father, thank You for Your words in the Bible that challenge our thinking on so many topics, including the topic of pain. Help us to see the purpose of pain from Your perspective and help us to respond to it in ways that You would have us respond. Help us to understand the role of pain in our lives so we cannot just endure it, but somehow, as Paul did, to truly rejoice in the midst of it. In Jesus' name, Amen.

Questions for Reflection:

1) Read Romans 5:3-5. What are the three benefits that Paul says can come when we "rejoice in our sufferings"?
2) By calling us to rejoice in our sufferings, Paul implies that we have a choice in how we respond to pain. What are some other choices—whether good or

bad—that we might make instead? Why do you think Paul encourages us to rejoice instead of some of those other options?
3) Have you ever seen God use a painful situation in your life, whether physical or emotional, for something good in the end?
4) How might recalling how God has used what's painful in the past encourage you in anything painful you might be experiencing right now? If you'd like, why not ask God, and perhaps a few other trusted people in your life, to give you that strength to persevere through any pain that you're facing right now in your life until you gain the character and hope that God has in store for you.

LESSON 14: BEING FREED FROM SIN — AUGUST 16

Scripture Reading: Romans 5:12-21

One of the best depictions I've ever read of the tragedy that took place when sin entered the world was in a fictional book by Ted Dekker called *Black*. Ted spent the majority of his book describing a world where no one had ever sinned. The people knew there was a particular fruit that they were forbidden to eat located across a certain bridge, but no one went there to eat it.

Instead, they lived out their days doing incredible things with each other and with their God who created them. They had children and built homes and gathered daily to enjoy the lives they had been given. But one day, one of the men gave in to his temptations. He crossed the bridge and ate the fruit.

The moment he did, evil was unleashed from the forest beyond. Huge black bats swarmed out of the forest and covered the land in a dark cloud, devouring people and trees and everything in their path. Only those who found shelter of some kind or another escaped the death and destruction that came upon their land.

Through one man's sin, evil was unleashed upon everyone.

As I read about this horde of evil that covered their world, it was one of the saddest moments I've ever felt while reading a book. I couldn't believe it happened. I couldn't believe this guy ate the fruit. I couldn't believe how utterly tragic it was for everyone else and everything else on the planet.

Thankfully, the story didn't end with that book, but I'll have to let you read the series for yourself to find out what happens next.

It turns out that Ted's story was a powerful retelling of another old, old story, one that the apostle Paul talked about in his letter to the Romans. In chapter 5, Paul described what happened to the world when the first man, Adam, sinned. He described how death entered into the world and reigned over it as a result. But that story didn't end there either. Here's what Paul said:

> "... sin entered the world through one man, and death through sin, and in this way death came to all men, because all sinned... But the gift is not like the trespass. For if the many died by the trespass of the one man, how much more did God's grace and the gift that came by the grace of the one man, Jesus Christ, overflow to the many!" (Romans 5:12,15).

I'm sharing this story with you today because I want to give you God's perspective on the world around you. While there was once a time when death reigned over the earth, you're now living in a time when life reigns over the earth—life that has come through God's abundant grace through Jesus Christ. As Paul went on to say:

> "For if, by the trespass of the one man, death reigned through that one man, how much more will those who receive God's abundant provision of grace and of the gift of righteousness reign in life through the one man, Jesus Christ" (Romans 5:17).

You now live in a colorful, life-filled, and joyous world—if you have the eyes to see it. I know that it sometimes takes eyes of faith, but it's the truth. Life reigns because Christ has come. If you've put your faith in Christ, death no longer has mastery over you. You're no longer a slave to sin, because God has sent you a new Master you can serve, Someone who loves you, cares for you, and has given His life for you—Jesus Christ.

I had a friend who died a few years ago, and when he did, a strange thought crossed my mind. As sad as I was for his death, and the loss of his friendship here on earth, I was thankful for one thing. I thought: "You lucky guy. You're finally free from sin."

You see, he had a tremendous ministry that touched the lives of many people. But he also had a private battle with sin—one that he fought valiantly and victoriously, but still a battle nonetheless. When he died, I knew his battle with sin was finally over. It seemed like a strange thought to me, until I remembered that the apostle Paul talked about this very thing.

In Romans chapter 6, Paul said:

> "… because anyone who has died has been freed from sin" (Romans 6:7).

Paul wasn't advocating that people should die in order to be freed from sin! On the contrary, he was saying that people who had put their faith in Christ and were baptized in His name had already died with Him, in order to be raised to live a new life with Him, both here on earth and on into heaven one day.

You don't have to die to be freed from sin. You just have to put your faith in Christ, being baptized into His death, and rising again to live a new life—a new, colorful, joy-filled life.

When I thought about my friend's death in these terms, I realized that He wasn't freed from sin on the day he died physically. He was freed from sin from the moment he put his faith in Christ and was baptized, which was many, many years earlier. From that point on, he had a new view of life, and God had a new view of him.

Sure, he still had battles to face, but he faced them with confidence, knowing that Christ had already freed him from those sins. Temptations would come, as always, but now he knew he could resist them because now he had the power of Christ. He went on to make the most of the rest of his time here on earth, living victoriously and sharing Christ with many others, being a truly positive force in the world for good.

In your battle against sin, you may think a dark cloud surrounds you, a cloud of death and destruction that is constantly hanging over your head, like the swarm of bats from a Ted Dekker novel.

But that's a lie. The truth is, that cloud of darkness was pushed back when Christ died for you on the cross. On that day, color was restored to the world. Joy became available again. Freedom from sin became a reality for everyone who would put their faith in Him.

God doesn't want you to sin. Sin separates you from Him and from those you love. But if you've been baptized into Christ, you've been freed from sin. Sure, you may still have to fight off temptations, but now you can do it from a position of strength, not from a position of defeat.

If you've never been baptized into Christ, I'd encourage you to do so as soon as possible. Being baptized into His death will allow you to be raised with Him to a new life with Him. Baptism can renew not only your mind, but your heart and soul as well. It will change your outlook on life. And it will help you to be freed from sin. You may still have a battle to fight, but you'll be fighting it with Christ, which makes all the difference in the world!

As further encouragement that you can be freed from sin, here and now, let me close with the words of the apostle Paul on the subject.

> "What shall we say, then? Shall we go on sinning so that grace may increase? By no means! We died to sin; how can we live in it any longer? Or don't you know that all of us who were baptized into Christ Jesus were baptized into His death? We were therefore buried with Him through baptism into death in order that, just as Christ was raised from the dead through the glory of the Father, we too may live a new life.
>
> "If we have been united with Him like this in His death, we will certainly also be united with Him in His resurrection. For we know that our old self was crucified with Him so that the body of sin might be done away with, that we should no longer be slaves to sin—because anyone who has died has been freed from sin.
>
> "Now if we died with Christ, we believe that we will also live with Him. For we know that since Christ was raised from the dead, He cannot die again; death no longer has mastery over Him. The death He died, He died to sin once for all; but the life He lives, He lives to God.
>
> "In the same way, count yourselves dead to sin but alive to God in Christ Jesus" (Romans 6:1-10).

If you've put your faith in Christ, you can count yourselves as "dead to sin but alive to God in Christ Jesus," too.

Will you pray with me?

Father, thank You for setting us free from sin by dying for us. Help us to see that death no longer reigns over us, but because of Christ, we can reign in life. Help us to put our faith in You anew today, trusting that the world is gloriously new because of You. Help us to see it the way You see it, so we can enjoy it as You intended us to enjoy it, living valiantly and victoriously while we're here. In Jesus' name, Amen.

Questions for Reflection:

1) Read Romans 5:12-6:10. Why does Paul say "the gift is not like the trespass" in comparing the effects of Adam's sin with the effects of Christ's death and resurrection?
2) What can we do to "reign in life," as Paul says in verse 17?
3) Have you ever thought of baptism as a way of dying to your old self, and being raised to new life? What about this idea might be attractive to you?
4) Have you ever been baptized? If so, what difference does being baptized make in how you view your battle with sin today? If you haven't been baptized, what

difference might baptism make in your battle with sin? If you need further encouragement to be baptized, here are a few more verses you might read: Acts 2:38, Matthew 3:16-17, Mark 16:16, 1 Peter 3:21, John 3:5, and Acts 8:35-38.

LESSON 15: BEARING FRUIT TO GOD   AUGUST 17

Scripture Reading: Romans 6:11-7:6

Is it OK to sin—at least a little bit every once in a while? After all, if we've already put our faith in Christ, He's already forgiven us of our sins. So He'll forgive us again, won't He?

While this is actually a reasonable idea on the surface—at least in terms of being forgiven of your sins by Christ—when you look at it at a deeper level, grasping what happens to your relationship with God and those around you every time you do sin, you'll see that your best bet is to stay as far away from sin as you can, as often as you can, and for as much of your life as you can!

It's like a kid saying, "My dad says not to run out in the road. But I know he'll still love me even if I do run out in the road, so what's the big deal if I do it once in a while?" A kid like that would be missing the point entirely. The point isn't whether or not the dad would still love him just as much if he ran out in the road. The point is that the dad doesn't want him to get hit by a truck!

If the only reason you shouldn't sin is because you think Jesus might be mad at you if you do, then you need to re-adjust your thinking! It's not that Jesus won't love you just as much if you sin—it's that He wants you to live! He wants to protect you from engaging in things that could be dangerous to you and to those around you. Sure, He'll still love you. But that's the reason He doesn't want you to sin… *because* He loves you.

The apostle Paul addressed this issue very clearly in his letter to the Romans, who, having been convinced that Jesus had forgiven them of all their sins, might have been tempted to fall back into sin again, thinking that it no longer mattered if they sinned, because they could still be assured of Christ's love for them. Paul said:

> *"What then? Shall we sin because we are not under law but under grace? By no means! … What benefit did you reap at that time from the things you are now ashamed of? Those things result in death! But now that you have been set free from sin and have become slaves to God, the benefit you reap leads to holiness, and the result is eternal life. For the wages of sin is death, but the gift of God is eternal life in Christ Jesus our Lord"* (Romans 6:15,21-23).

Sin leads to death, but Christ gives you life! If the choice is to sin or to follow Christ, Paul says to follow Christ!

But there's an even greater reason to drop your life of sin and follow Christ. Paul says it's because God wants you to bear fruit—good fruit. When you follow sin, you bear fruit that leads to death. But when you follow Christ you bear fruit for God. Here's how Paul said it in his letter to the Romans.

> *"So, my brothers, you also died to the law through the body of Christ, that you might belong to another, to Him who was raised from the dead, in order that we might bear fruit to God. For when we were controlled by the sinful nature, the sinful passions aroused by the law were at work in our bodies, so that we bore fruit for death. But*

now, by dying to what once bound us, we have been released from the law so that we serve in the new way of the Spirit, and not in the old way of the written code" (Romans 7:4-6).

God didn't abandon His laws when Christ came. His laws are still good and will protect you from sin. What God did was to make an offering on your behalf to pay the penalty for your sins so you wouldn't have to pay it yourself. Now, when you put your faith in Christ, you receive forgiveness of your sins. If you continue to sin, there will still be other consequences—for sin still always has consequences—but the good news is that you will no longer be separated from your relationship with Him because of your sin.

Whenever you sin, even if it's "just a little," it puts a wedge between you and God, as well as between yourself and those around you. God doesn't want that wedge, and neither do you. He loves you too much for *anything* to come between Him and you. And I believe, if you've read this far into the message already, that you love Him too much to put that wedge between the two of you, too.

I was once teaching a class of adults how to use computers. One of the students had been using very colorful language throughout the class, not necessarily swearing, but still they were undoubtedly "off" color. I had introduced myself as a technology expert, which, in my role as their teacher, I was. But it wasn't until later in the day that I mentioned that I was also a pastor. Immediately, this man who had been so colorful with his words all day turned colorfully red in the face, too! He quickly began to apologize for his language in front of me and the rest of the class.

In my attempt to be honest, for I really wasn't bothered by it, I said something that made him turn even redder still. I said, "That's OK. You don't have to apologize to me. I'm not the one who's been watching over you every day anyway." The whole class turned to him with a look that said he was really in trouble now!

The truth is that his language really didn't affect his relationship with me much at all. But by his reaction, it seems like it may have affected his relationship with God quite a bit. It may have seemed like a "little sin" to him, but the fact that he was embarrassed in front of me and the class gave me the impression that it may have been a much bigger deal in his relationship with God.

I didn't say this to the man to make him feel more guilty than he already did for saying those things in front of me. Just like I'm not saying these things to make you feel more guilty of the things you may be doing in your own life. Believe me, I know how hard it is to keep from sinning, even though I've been trying to follow Christ with my whole heart for 24 years. I'm still not, by any means, "sin-free." I wish I were, because I know that whenever I sin, it causes damage. This, in turn, makes me want to stay away from it as much as humanly possible.

And in the bigger picture, I not only see the damage that sin causes, but I also see that it hinders my ability to bear fruit for God. And that is perhaps the biggest damage of all.

God has created you to do good works. He has things He wants you to do in this life. When you sin, you hinder those good works, sometimes more than you can possibly imagine. Believe me when I say that God has good works for you to do. He has created you uniquely, with special gifts and abilities. He's poured unique talents into your life. He's trained you up to be an asset to Him. He wants to use you to reach out into the world, both in large and small ways.

Don't let Satan hinder you from accomplishing all that God has created you to do. Don't follow the path of sin that would keep you from the path God has lined out for you. Don't let yourself become a slave again to those things of which you're now ashamed, things which bore fruit for death. Serve God fully instead, bearing good fruit to Him.

How do you do that? By keeping away from sin as much as possible, and by staying close to Jesus as much is possible. As Jesus said:

> "I am the vine; you are the branches. If a man remains in Me and I in him, he will bear much fruit; apart from Me you can do nothing. If anyone does not remain in Me, he is like a branch that is thrown away and withers; such branches are picked up, thrown into the fire and burned. If you remain in Me and My words remain in you, ask whatever you wish, and it will be given you. This is to my Father's glory, that you bear much fruit, showing yourselves to be My disciples" (John 15:5-8).

God wants you to bear fruit—*much* fruit, as Jesus said. Keep away from sin, even "little sins," as much as possible. Not because God will love you less if you do sin, but because He loves you so much He doesn't want you to leave His side even for a minute. When you stay close to Him, you *will* bear fruit for Him.

Will you pray with me?

Father, thank You for loving us so much that You gave us rules for how to live the best possible lives here on earth. Thank You for saving us from what we have earned because of our sins, and giving us the gift of eternal life instead, if we've put our faith in Christ. Help us to stay as close as possible to Him so that we can bear as much fruit as possible for You. In Jesus' name, Amen.

Questions for Reflection:

1) Read Romans 6:11-7:6. What does Paul say we should offer to God in verses 11-14? How might offering these things to sin lead to death, whereas offering them to God leads to life?
2) In verses 15-18, Paul says that just because we're free from the law, it doesn't mean that we're not still slaves to something else. What is that other thing, and why is it so much better than being a slave to sin?
3) In chapter 7, verses 1-3, what illustration does Paul use to talk about being set free from the law? What does being freed from the law allow us to do?
4) Is anything specific hindering you from bearing as much fruit as possible for God? Is there an action step you can take this week to help you drop whatever is hindering you, and get any closer to Jesus? Ask God, and perhaps a few trusted friends, to help you do it so that you can bear as much fruit for Him as possible.

LESSON 16: SETTING YOUR MIND ON WHAT THE SPIRIT DESIRES — AUGUST 18

Scripture Reading: Romans 7:7-8:11

What is it about rules that makes us want to break them? I was in a church one day when the pastor was talking about the benefits of a new diet he had started. He was telling us how he ate a bowl of oatmeal every morning for breakfast, and how much of a change that was from the way he used to eat. He said he previously used to sit down some nights and eat an entire 2-pound bag of peanut M&M's in one sitting!

As surprised as I was to hear that, as soon as he said it, something sprang to life within me. I began to imagine what it would be like to sit down and eat a whole bag of peanut M&M's, all by myself, in one sitting. It sounded crazy. I'd never even *thought* about the idea before. That's a lot of M&M's! But it sounded really good, too. (And for some of my international readers, peanut M&M's are peanuts dipped in chocolate and covered by a hard candy shell).

The more I thought about it, the more I wanted to do it. Although it seemed wrong, I still wanted to do it. Somehow, his sermon on the benefits of his new diet just made me want to eat more. The very thing he was telling me *not* to do was the very thing I wanted to do—and it was his sermon that sparked the idea in me to do it!

When one of my daughters asked me what I wanted for Christmas that year, only one thing came to mind: a 2-pound bag of peanut M&M's.

What was happening to me? Why was I now desiring something that I had never thought of desiring until I was told that I shouldn't desire it? Wouldn't it have been better if I had never heard that sermon at all? And what could I do about it now that I had?

The apostle Paul described this dilemma in Romans chapter 7 (except for the part about the peanut M&M's), which also includes one of the most tongue-twisting passages in all of Scripture:

> "What shall we say, then? Is the law sin? Certainly not! Indeed I would not have known what sin was except through the law. For I would not have known what coveting really was if the law had not said, "Do not covet." But sin, seizing the opportunity afforded by the commandment, produced in me every kind of covetous desire. For apart from law, sin is dead. Once I was alive apart from law; but when the commandment came, sin sprang to life and I died. I found that the very commandment that was intended to bring life actually brought death. For sin, seizing the opportunity afforded by the commandment, deceived me, and through the commandment put me to death. So then, the law is holy, and the commandment is holy, righteous and good.
>
> "Did that which is good, then, become death to me? By no means! But in order that sin might be recognized as sin, it produced death in me through what was good, so that through the commandment sin might become utterly sinful.
>
> "We know that the law is spiritual; but I am unspiritual, sold as a slave to sin. I do not understand what I do. For what I want to do I do not do, but what I hate I do. And if I do what I do not want to do, I agree that the law is good. As it is, it is no longer I myself who do it, but it is sin living in me. I know that nothing good lives in me, that is, in my sinful nature. For I have the desire to do what is good, but I cannot carry it out. For what I do is not the good I want to do; no, the evil I do not want to do—this I keep on doing. Now if I do what I do not want to do, it is no longer I who do it, but it is sin living in me that does it.
>
> "So I find this law at work: When I want to do good, evil is right there with me. For in my inner being I delight in God's law; but I see another law at work in the members of my body, waging war against the law of my mind and making me a prisoner of the law of sin at work within my members. What a wretched man I am! Who will rescue me from this body of death?" (Romans 7:7-24).

I like the way Paul puts this. He says that the law is good, but that sin is always present, too, ready to spring into life at any moment. And when sin sees an opportunity, it seizes it, producing within us our covetous desires. The law is not the problem–sin is. And sin seems already nearby and ready to seize upon such opportunities.

It seems like a dilemma that could cripple us for life. But Paul doesn't leave us there, and neither does God. Paul asks: "Who will rescue me from this body of death?" Then he continues this passage by answering that question, as well telling how you can win the battle over the sins and temptations that you face in life, too. Paul says:

> "Thanks be to God—through Jesus Christ our Lord! So then, I myself in my mind am a slave to God's law, but in the sinful nature a slave to the law of sin. Therefore, there is now no condemnation for those who are in Christ Jesus, because through Christ Jesus the law of the Spirit of life set me free from the law of sin and death. For what the law was powerless to do in that it was weakened by the sinful nature, God did by sending his own Son in the likeness of sinful man to be a sin offering. And so He condemned sin in sinful man, in order that the righteous requirements of the law might be fully met in us, who do not live according to the sinful nature but according to the Spirit.
>
> "Those who live according to the sinful nature have their minds set on what that nature desires; but those who live in accordance with the Spirit have their minds set on what the Spirit desires. The mind of sinful man is death, but the mind controlled by the Spirit is life and peace; the sinful mind is hostile to God. It does not submit to God's law, nor can it do so. Those controlled by the sinful nature cannot please God. You, however, are controlled not by the sinful nature but by the Spirit, if the Spirit of God lives in you. And if anyone does not have the Spirit of Christ, he does not belong to Christ. But if Christ is in you, your body is dead because of sin, yet your spirit is alive because of righteousness. And if the Spirit of Him who raised Jesus from the dead is living in you, He who raised Christ from the dead will also give life to your mortal bodies through His Spirit, who lives in you" (Romans 7:25-8:11).

Paul says it clearly: the one who can rescue you from the battles you're facing is Jesus Christ our Lord. The same Spirit who raised Jesus from the dead is living within you, if you've put your faith in Him. And that same Spirit can bring you the same life-giving power and victory, if you'll set your mind on what the Spirit desires.

Jesus has already fought the hardest battle on your behalf, dying for your sins so you don't have to. Now your job is to set your mind on what the Spirit desires, letting go of anything that is pulling you back into your sinful desires.

If you can win the battle in your mind, you're well on your way to winning the battle in your flesh, too.

My sweet daughter bought me a 2-pound bag of peanut M&M's for Christmas that year. But when I got the bag and came face to face with the choice I was about to make, I did something I hadn't expected. I changed my mind.

Whereas before I had only imagined what it would be like to indulge my desires, I now thought through what that decision would mean down the road. What if I really did eat the whole bag in one sitting? How sick would I get? How many pounds would I instantly be adding to my already increasing body fat? In a matter of minutes, I had changed my mind.

I decided to just eat just a few. I shared a few more. Then I put the rest away in a cupboard, to be eaten only occasionally as a special treat, or to be served to friends who stopped by.

Instead of being controlled by my fleshly desires, I set my mind on what the Spirit desires instead. And in so doing, I won the victory.

Believe me, I know there are bigger battles in life than facing a 2-pound bag of peanut M&M's. But I also know that God is bigger than any of those battles, too. The choices you make in your mind will affect the choices you make with your body. I want to encourage you today to make good choices—to set your mind on what the Spirit desires, and not on fleshly things.

When tempted to look at someone who's attractive for longer than you should, just look away. Leave them there. And don't look back. When tempted to click on an inappropriate website, just let it go. Don't click that link. Ask yourself, "What does the Spirit desire?"

When tempted to start a bad habit, remember that the best way to stop a bad habit is never to start in the first place. Just don't do it. Don't even get started. When fighting a bad habit that you've already started, just drop it. Let it go. Find a way to redirect your time and energy into something more godly and healthy.

In every battle, call upon the Spirit of Christ who lives within you to help you do what He wants you to do. Remember:

> "And if the Spirit of Him who raised Jesus from the dead is living in you, He who raised Christ from the dead will also give life to your mortal bodies through His Spirit, who lives in you."

Will you pray with me?

Father, thank You for doing the hardest work of all in our battle against sin. Help us to do the hard work we have to do of setting our minds on what Your Spirit desires. Help us in the battles we face today so we can drop whatever might threaten to harm us, and to take hold of that which will lead us to life. In Jesus' name, Amen.

Questions for Reflection:

1) Read Romans 7:7-8:11. Have you ever experienced what Paul described in verse 9 where "sin sprang to life" after hearing about something you shouldn't do?
2) What does Paul say is the cause such experiences? Is the law at fault, or something else?
3) What encouragement do you take from the solution Paul puts forth, that if the Spirit of Christ lives in you—the same Spirit that raised Jesus from the dead—that He can give life to your mortal bodies as well?
4) Is there an area in your life where you could use the help of the Spirit of Christ right now to overcome a battle that you're facing? How could simply setting your mind on what the Spirit desires help you in this area?

LESSON 17: KNOWING WHO THE HOLY SPIRIT IS — AUGUST 19

Scripture Reading: Romans 8:9-11

I used to think that the Holy Spirit was like a light inside my heart. But one day, God helped me to understand that the Holy Spirit is not a substance, but a person—a person who wanted to live and act and move in my life. As Jesus said:

> "And I will ask the Father, and He will give you another Counselor to be with you forever—the Spirit of Truth. The world cannot accept Him, because it neither sees Him nor knows Him. But you know Him, for He lives with you and will be in you. … All this I have spoken while still with you. But the Counselor, the Holy Spirit, whom the Father will send in My name, will teach you all things and will remind you of everything I have said to you. … I have much more to say to you, more than you can now bear. But when He, the Spirit of Truth, comes, He will guide you into all truth" (John 14:16-17, 25-26, and 16:12-13a).

The Holy Spirit really is a person, not just some spiritual substance that flows through your body.

I realized this most clearly when I was worshipping God in the middle of a large sanctuary with hundreds of other people. As I was singing, I was thinking about the beauty of Jesus and how great it could be if I could really see Him with my own eyes. Far away at the front of the sanctuary there was a stained glass window with a picture of Jesus on it.

While everyone else was still standing and singing, I just sat down in my seat and closed my eyes. I began to picture what Jesus would look like in my mind—something like that faraway image of Him in the stained glass window. But suddenly, with my eyes still closed, I pictured two eyes directly in front of mine! They were so close that I couldn't look at both eyes at the same time. I had to look back and forth between them, as you might do when looking close into the eyes of someone you loved.

With my own eyes still closed, I felt that His eyes were coming closer and closer to mine—so close, in fact, that I had to back up in my seat. But when they finally came as close as they possibly could without touching me, the two eyes disappeared. I wondered where they had gone. At the same time, I sensed that they hadn't left me at all. Instead, I realized they had somehow passed right through me and began to turn around inside my head.

I felt my own eyes refocusing, as if Jesus Himself wanted to look through my eyes. I could picture His arm going down inside my arm as if He were putting my arm on like a sleeve. His hand went down inside my hand as if putting on a glove. I could imagine His feet going down into my legs, one at a time, like He was putting on a pair of jeans. His feet slid down into my feet as if putting on a pair of shoes.

My mind began to be flooded with Scriptures about how the Spirit of God really does lives inside us, like the ones I mentioned earlier. I began to understand that He wanted to take up residence within me, live inside me and carry out His will through me—at least to the extent that I allowed Him free reign to do so. I invited Him in and asked Him to push all of me out, so that I could be filled with Him as full as possible, from head to toe and from fingertip to fingertip.

I felt like God was telling me that when I was ready to open my eyes again, He wanted to look through my eyes and help me see the world as He sees it. He wanted to use my hands to do what He wanted them to do. He wanted me to walk where He would walk. He wanted me to hear my ears what He would hear, speak with my mouth what He would speak, and feel with my heart what He would feel with His.

When I finally did open my eyes, I *did* see the world differently. I realized that the Spirit of God *wasn't* just a light inside my heart. He was a person—a person who had literally come to take up residence inside my mortal body, giving life to it, as well as power, wisdom and direction. As Paul said in Romans chapter 8:

> *"You, however, are controlled not by the sinful nature but by the Spirit, if the Spirit of God lives in you. And if anyone does not have the Spirit of Christ, he does not belong to Christ. But if Christ is in you, your body is dead because of sin, yet your spirit is alive because of righteousness. And if the Spirit of Him who raised Jesus from the dead is living in you, He who raised Christ from the dead will also give life to your mortal bodies through His Spirit, who lives in you"* (Romans 8:9-11).

These verses have incredible power if you'll take them to heart.

I saw their power displayed most clearly when my wife Lana was pregnant with our second child. Lana was having some abnormal bleeding early on in the pregnancy, so she went in for a test. They drew her blood on two different days and checked the level of her hormones. If the baby was OK, her hormones would be doubling every day. But if the baby wasn't OK, then her hormones wouldn't be rising, but going down instead. When we got the results, we found that her hormones were dropping rapidly.

The doctor told us this could only mean one of three things: 1) either the baby had died and was about to miscarry on its own, or 2) the baby had lodged in Lana's fallopian tubes instead of her womb, and if the baby wasn't removed, it would burst the tubes and die, possibly killing Lana at the same time. The third option was that the test was wrong.

The only way the doctor would be able to tell for sure was to do an interior ultrasound, which we scheduled for the next day. That night, before the ultrasound, Lana called a friend to pray for her. The friend suggested she read Romans chapter 8. As Lana read these ancient words of the apostle Paul, she was struck in a new way by verse 11:

> *"And if the Spirit of Him who raised Jesus from the dead is living in you, He who raised Christ from the dead will also give life to your mortal bodies through His Spirit, who lives in you"* (Romans 8:11).

She realized that if the Spirit of God was living inside her, the same Spirit who raised Jesus from the dead could raise this baby from the dead, too. We both began to call upon God's Spirit fervently, and asked others to do the same.

The next day, we went to the hospital for the interior ultrasound. The nurse called Lana into the room and I sat in the waiting room outside. After a long and emotional wait, the nurse called me in. I saw Lana laying on the hospital bed. She was crying. The nurse took me over to the ultrasound machine and pointed to a black dot in the middle of it. She said, "Do you see that dot on the screen?"

I could see it, the black dot that was our baby. I was about to burst into tears myself when the nurse said, "Do you see how it's beating? That's your baby's heartbeat!"

Lana wasn't crying because the baby had died! She was crying because the baby was alive! But that couldn't be! Lana's hormones were dropping so rapidly. I realized there weren't just three options, but four, because the Spirit of God who raised Jesus from the dead was now living inside Lana's mortal body as well! We felt like we had just witnessed the "dunamis" power of God, God's dynamite that, when ignited by faith, causes miracles to happen!

Lana went on to carry the baby to full term and give birth to a completely healthy little boy—a little boy who is now nineteen years old and full of faith himself, believing that the same Spirit who raised Jesus from the dead can do all kinds of miracles in the world today.

The Holy Spirit is not just some ethereal substance that flows in and out of your life. He is a person, a person who carries with Him the power of God, and who has taken up residence within you, if you belong to Christ. The Holy Spirit wants to work in your life in powerful ways, too. He wants you to call upon Him and His power by faith.

Whether you're battling with life or death, or battling with a sin that's overwhelming you, God's Spirit can give you power to win those battles. If you're struggling with reading the word of God or struggling to understand how it applies to your life, God's Spirit can help to guide you into all truth. If you're trying to mend a broken relationship or wondering how to go on with life having lost someone who was precious to you, God's Spirit, the Counselor and Comforter, can bring you a wisdom and a peace that passes all understanding.

If you want to renew your mind today, renew your thinking about the Holy Spirit. When you see Him as a person, rather than a substance, it will change the way you talk with Him—and what you can expect of Him.

I know a pastor who says that he always gets super-excited when he sees God's Spirit moving in even a small way in an audience where he is speaking and ministering. He gets excited because He knows that since God's Spirit is a person, that means that if part of Him shows up, then all of Him is there!

If you belong to Christ, then you don't just have a little bit of the Holy Spirit living inside of you, but the *whole* of Him living inside of you—the same Spirit who raised Christ from the dead.

Call on God's Holy Spirit today and invite Him to do His powerful work in your life right now.

Will you pray with me?

Father, thank You for sending Your Holy Spirit to live inside us when we belong to Christ. We call upon Him now to bring life to our mortal bodies, both here on earth, and in heaven forever. Raise to life those things in our lives which seem like they might be dead, so that we can be filled again with the abundant life that You have in store for us instead. We pray this in the strong name of Jesus, Amen.

Questions for Reflection:

1) Read Romans 8:9-11. How have you pictured the Holy Spirit who lives in you, if you belong to Christ and He lives within you?
2) What difference would it make in your life to picture Him as a person, rather than a substance?
3) Are there some particular areas of your life where you could really use the Spirit's power right now? Why not talk to Him right now and invite Him, by faith, to do His life-changing power in your life?
4) If you don't belong to Christ, and don't have the Spirit of God living within you, why not invite Him into your life today? Turn away from any sin in your life and

ask Jesus to forgive you, then invite His Holy Spirit to take up residence within you, giving you His power to do His work in your life.

LESSON 18: RECEIVING THE SPIRIT OF SONSHIP — AUGUST 20

Scripture Reading: Romans 8:12-17

It's only been ten days since Steve Jobs died and I'm still mourning the loss. I've followed his life and career for the last 28 years, ever since I used one of his first computers, an Apple Lisa (the predecessor to the Mac), to write a poem (complete with text and graphics) to my college sweetheart at the time (now my wife of 22 years).

It was an experience that changed my view of computers, and my major in college, and my eventual career. I no longer saw computers as cold, sterile, and unmerciful machines. Instead, I began to see them as devices that could help me give expression to some of my innermost thoughts and feelings.

Today, 28 years later, I'm still using one of Steve Jobs' computers to give expression to my innermost thoughts and feelings, now using them to encourage people all over the world to put their faith in Christ for everything in their lives.

I've written to Steve a couple of times in recent years to thank him for the impact he's had on my life and, by extension, the lives of so many others, as I use his computers to reach out around the world. I've also prayed for him and shared my faith in Christ with him in those letters, hoping to give to him the best blessing I can think of in return for the blessing he's been to me. I don't know if he ever did put his faith in Christ or not, but my hope and prayer is that at some point he did.

Although Steve's time of decision has come and gone, there's still time for you to make yours. If you haven't yet put your faith in Christ for everything in your life, especially for the forgiveness of your sins, I'd encourage you to do it today.

Jesus told the story of a rich man and a beggar, both of whom died about the same time. Jesus said:

> "There was a rich man who was dressed in purple and fine linen and lived in luxury every day. At his gate was laid a beggar named Lazarus, covered with sores and longing to eat what fell from the rich man's table. Even the dogs came and licked his sores.
> "The time came when the beggar died and the angels carried him to Abraham's side. The rich man also died and was buried. In hell, where he was in torment, he looked up and saw Abraham far away, with Lazarus by his side. So he called to him, 'Father Abraham, have pity on me and send Lazarus to dip the tip of his finger in water and cool my tongue, because I am in agony in this fire.'
> "He looked up and saw Abraham far away, with Lazarus by his side. So he called to him, 'Father Abraham, have pity on me and send Lazarus to dip the tip of his finger in water and cool my tongue, because I am in agony in this fire.'
> "But Abraham replied, 'Son, remember that in your lifetime you received your good things, while Lazarus received bad things, but now he is comforted here and you are in agony. And besides all this, between us and you a great chasm has been fixed, so that those who want to go from here to you cannot, nor can anyone cross over from there to us.'

> "He answered, 'Then I beg you, father, send Lazarus to my father's house, for I have five brothers. Let him warn them, so that they will not also come to this place of torment.'
> "Abraham replied, 'They have Moses and the Prophets; let them listen to them.'
> "'No, father Abraham,' he said, 'but if someone from the dead goes to them, they will repent.'
> "He said to him, 'If they do not listen to Moses and the Prophets, they will not be convinced even if someone rises from the dead'" (Luke 16:19-31).

There are times when I wish we could get into heaven based on all the good we've done in our lives. But when I remember how much we've all sinned, I'm thankful that it's *not* based on what we've done in life, for none of us have a perfect moral scorecard. Instead, it's based on our faith in the One who gave us life, and our acceptance of the sacrifice that has been made for our sins. As Jesus said to Martha when her brother died:

> "I am the resurrection and the life. He who believes in Me will live, even though he dies; and whoever lives and believes in Me will never die. Do you believe this?" (John 11:25-26)

It has always been this way. God has always required a sacrifice for our sins in order to escape the penalty that we would have received otherwise. Even in the days when the Israelites were slaves in Egypt, God didn't tell them to write their good deeds on the doorframes of their homes. He told them to put the blood of a lamb on their doorframes, as a sign of their faith in Him. Then, when He saw that sign, He would "pass over" their homes and not bring upon them the destruction that they would have received otherwise (see Exodus 12).

Why then do people *not* put their faith in Christ? Sometimes people have an intellectual block that keeps them from doing it. But other times there's a more practical reason: they simply don't have a good example of what a loving father looks like, which makes it hard for them to believe that there's a loving Father in heaven who cares about them deeply, too.

I don't know much about Steve Jobs' personal life, but I do know that he was given up for adoption at birth. His biological parents were unmarried college students at a time when abortion was still illegal in the U.S. His biological mother left the University of Wisconsin and went to San Francisco to give birth, where Steve was adopted by his new parents.

When Steve eventually discovered who his biological parents were, he made contact with his mother and his biological sister, with whom he later became close friends. But according to his biological father, Steve never did make contact with him, even up to Steve's death.

I'm not a psychologist, but I've heard from some of my friends who have been adopted that they sometimes wrestle with feelings of abandonment and self-worth, wondering why their parents might have given them up for adoption. In some cases, this sense of worthlessness can drive them to prove their worth in other ways.

I have no idea if this was a factor in Steve Jobs' own personal drive, yet if it was, he went after it with gusto. By this time last year, the company he helped to create had become worth more than any other technology company in the world, and just a few months ago, it became the most valuable company of *any* industry, based on the value of its stock. More important than building a thriving company, Steve's life has influenced millions of other lives around the world like a huge tidal wave, touching lives of people who didn't even know who he was until this week.

But Steve Jobs life didn't become more valuable as his stock price and market influence grew. The truth is, his life was worth more than even he could have ever imagined even before he started his famous computer company in his garage. His Father in heaven had placed a value on him before anyone but God Himself even knew he was alive.

It's the same for you. God has loved you since before you were born. Your life is worth more to Him than you can imagine and has had immeasurable value since before you even had a chance to make your mark on the world. God loves you so much He sent His Son to die for your sins so you wouldn't have to, inviting you back into a personal relationship with Him if you'll just put your faith in Christ.

This is perhaps the most important part of today's message: when you put your faith in Christ, God adopts you as *His* son or daughter. When you put your faith in Christ, you become an heir of God, and a co-heir with Christ. You receive from God the "Spirit of sonship," which includes the full rights and privileges of a son or daughter, as well the ability to see God as the truly loving Father that He is. The apostle Paul describes this Spirit of sonship like this:

> *"...those who are led by the Spirit of God are sons of God. For you did not receive a spirit that makes you a slave again to fear, but you received the Spirit of sonship. And by Him we cry, "Abba, Father." The Spirit Himself testifies with our spirit that we are God's children. Now if we are children, then we are heirs—heirs of God and co-heirs with Christ, if indeed we share in His sufferings in order that we may also share in His glory"* (Romans 8:12-17).

What difference does it make to be able to view God in your mind as the loving Father that He is? All the difference in the world. Paul uses the word "Abba" in his description of God, an Aramaic word that means "Daddy." It's a term of endearment. It describes a relationship that is not just a father and a son who are connected by birth, but who are connected by true affection for one another.

My younger kids will often call me "Daddy." It's a truly affectionate term. Every once in a while, even my teenagers will still call me "Daddy," whether it's my nineteen year old son writing an email to me from college, or my seventeen year old daughter using her most playful voice to tell me I'm doing something silly. It always warms my heart when they do this, to think that they not only see me as their father, but also as their "Abba," their "Daddy."

That's the kind of relationship God the Father wants to have with you. He doesn't want to be a distant and formal father, but a close and familiar one–a "Daddy"–a "Daddy" you can trust and run to and lean on whenever you need to.

Although God wants you to make the most of your life here on earth, and to use the gifts and abilities that He's given you to their fullest, you don't have to create a multi-billion dollar corporation to prove your worth to Him and to enter into that sweet relationship with Him. You just have to believe in Him, putting your faith in Christ for the forgiveness of your sins. And when you do, you'll be given the Spirit of sonship, and become adopted as His son or daughter, with all the rights and privileges that go along with it.

If you've already put your faith in Christ, you've already been adopted as His child. Your role now is to believe it and receive it, letting its truth sink deep into your life and heart today. If you've never put your faith in Christ, I'd encourage you to do it today and receive God's Spirit of sonship right now.

Will you pray with me?

Father, thank You for giving us Your Spirit of sonship when we put our faith in Christ. We pray that You will help solidify what that means in our lives today, helping us to know that You really do care about us, that we have worth just by being one of Your children, and that You will strengthen us by that same Spirit in our lives today. Thank You Daddy. We love you. In Jesus' name, Amen.

Questions for Reflection:

1) Read Romans 8:12-17. What images come to mind when you think of the word "Daddy"? How would using the word "Daddy" to describe God change your relationship with Him, compared to other words you could use for Him?
2) What are some of the benefits Paul lists in this passage of receiving the Spirit of sonship?
3) What difference would it make to think of yourself as an heir of God, and a co-heir with Christ?
4) If you've never put your faith in Christ, what benefits do you see of being adopted by God? Why not put your faith in Christ today and receive from God His Spirit of sonship?

LESSON 19: KNOWING THAT IN ALL THINGS GOD WORKS FOR YOUR GOOD AUGUST 21

Scripture Reading: Romans 8:28

I want to encourage you today that God can work ALL things for your good in your life no matter what you're facing. He really is FOR you, even in those things that seem hardest to face, and you can trust that He can work for your good even in those things.

I've been reading the book, *Pollyanna*, this week to my kids. The book was written back in 1913 about an eleven-year-old girl whose contagious optimism transformed an entire town. If you've ever heard someone described as a "Pollyanna," it's a term that came from this book.

But as I read the book this week again, I realized that for all her optimism, Pollyanna was in no way a naive little girl who was ignorant about the real pain that people face in life. Her profound optimism wasn't the result of ignorance, but it was the way she was able to keep sane and healthy in spite of severe losses in her life. Born on the mission field, Pollyanna lost her mother when she was young, then lost her father when she was eleven. She was sent to live with her stern and strict aunt on the East Coast, where she often had to fight back tears at the unfair treatment she received.

Yet with all the bad that was thrown at her, Pollyanna chose to train her mind to try to see the good in life, believing that there was always something she could be glad about. It was something she learned from her father when she was on the mission field. He called it the "glad game."

In talking about the game to a woman named Nancy, Pollyanna said:

> "We began it when some crutches came in a missionary barrel. You see, I'd wanted a doll. But when the barrel came the lady wrote that no dolls came in, just the little crutches. So she sent 'em along. The game was to find something about everything to be glad about, no matter what. We began right then—on the crutches."
> Nancy said, "I can't see anythin' to be glad about gettin' a pair of crutches when you wanted a doll."
> "There is—there is," Pollyanna crowed. "I couldn't see it either at first. Father had to tell it to me. You just be glad because you don't— need— 'em! You see, it's easy when you know how! Only sometimes it's almost too hard, like when your father goes to Heaven."

Rather than being naive about life, it was Pollyanna's disappointments in life that helped her to see things in a whole new light. She went on playing the "glad game" in her new town, helping the people see that no matter what they faced in life, there was always something to be glad about. Without giving away too much of the story, Pollyanna even found a way to be thankful when she *did* have to use crutches by the end of the book.

In a similar way, the apostle Paul is known for saying some of the most optimistic things in his letters in the New Testament. For instance, in his letter to the Philippians he wrote:

> "Rejoice in the Lord always. I will say it again: Rejoice!" (Philippians 4:4).

Some people might think, "Sure, that's easy for Paul to say, as he was one of the most highly educated and influential leaders in the early church." But the truth is, Paul saw more suffering in his lifetime than most of us would ever see in ten or twelve lifetimes, if we were able to live that many. Paul wrote:

> "I have worked much harder, been in prison more frequently, been flogged more severely, and been exposed to death again and again. Five times I received from the Jews the forty lashes minus one. Three times I was beaten with rods, once I was stoned, three times I was shipwrecked, I spent a night and a day in the open sea, I have been constantly on the move. I have been in danger from rivers, in danger from bandits, in danger from my own countrymen, in danger from Gentiles; in danger in the city, in danger in the country, in danger at sea; and in danger from false brothers. I have labored and toiled and have often gone without sleep; I have known hunger and thirst and have often gone without food; I have been cold and naked. Besides everything else, I face daily the pressure of my concern for all the churches. Who is weak, and I do not feel weak? Who is led into sin, and I do not inwardly burn? If I must boast, I will boast of the things that show my weakness" (2 Corinthians 11:23b-30).

Yet in spite of all this, Paul was still able to encourage people to "Rejoice in the Lord always." In his letter to the Romans, Paul explained why we can rejoice always. He wrote:

> "And we know that in ALL things God works for the good of those who love Him, who have been called according to His purpose" (Romans 8:28, emphasis added).

I have quoted this verse more often to myself and to others than perhaps any other verse in the Bible. It's a statement that I've tested for myself over and over again and continue to find to be true. It's not just a "Pollyanna" way of looking at the world. It's a truth that God has given us to hold onto tightly, knowing that no matter how things look in the situations that we're facing, we can trust Him to work in those situations for our good, if we're willing to trust those situations to Him.

But like Pollyanna in the book, there are times when finding the good in a situation seems like a daunting task. But rather than running away from such tasks, Pollyanna relished them. At one point, a sick and bedridden woman challenged Pollyanna to find something in her situation that she could be glad about. Pollyanna sprang to her feet and clapped her hands. She said:

> *"Oh goody, that'll be a hard one—won't it? I've got to go, now, but I'll think and think all the way home. Goodbye, I've had a lovely time!"*

Pollyanna *did* think and think and came up with several ideas, one of which was to encourage the woman to be glad she had her hands and arms. That simple statement made the woman wonder why she didn't *do* something with her hands and arms, so she began to knit little things for fairs and hospitals. She became so *glad* to think she could do something with them.

I think people sometimes view *me* as being a little too "Pollyanna-ish," too, when I tell them to trust God completely in every situation that He can work it for our good. But I've found that sometimes when I tell people stories of God's faithfulness to me in my life, they often don't realize, or don't take seriously when I tell them, how desperately I've had to pray through the situations in which I've been. They only hear the outcome of the stories, knowing that somehow God turned even awful situations into something good.

I think that's the way we sometimes read the stories in the Bible, too. Since we already know how they end, we can sometimes gloss over how dramatic the turnarounds really were.

For instance, when Moses and the Israelites were up against the Red Sea, with nowhere to turn and the chariots from Egypt pressing in, all of a sudden, God opened up the Red Sea so they could pass through on dry ground. It was a near-death experience for them all, yet God delivered them through it. But since it only takes a few paragraphs to read through the whole story, we don't always get the sense of impending doom that the people must have felt. I imagine Moses went through some serious questions for God about how God could possibly work this one out for good. Yet God told Moses to stand firm, that Moses would indeed see God's deliverance… and he did (see Exodus, chapter 14).

Or when Daniel spent the night in the lion's den and came out alive the next day. People may just think that Daniel found a safe place to hide or that the lions just weren't hungry. But if you read the story closely, you'll see that as soon as Daniel was lifted out of the lion's den, those who had falsely accused Daniel were thrown into the den themselves, and the text says:

> *"And before they reached the floor of the den, the lions overpowered them and crushed all their bones"* (Daniel 6:24b).

I imagine Daniel had some serious questions for God about how God could possibly work this one out for good. Yet Daniel was extracted without even a wound on him (see Daniel, chapter 6).

When we hear stories of God's faithfulness to others, we tend to minimize the adversity they faced, and maximize the possibility that God could bring them through it. Yet when we experience our own life-dramas, we tend to maximize the adversity we're facing, and minimize the possibility that God can bring us through it.

Today, I want to stir up your faith. I want to help you see the truth that God can work all things for your good, too. I want to encourage you to keep putting your faith in Christ. Regarding the situations you're facing in life today, ask yourself:

> "What good might God be doing through this? What good might come out of what I'm going through right now? What might God be doing that I can hang onto in faith, and hope for, and pray towards? What good might God be doing on my behalf right now?"

God wants to turn your thinking around today. He wants you to see that He really can—and does—work all things for good for those who love Him and who are called according to His purpose.

This isn't just a "glad game" from a children's story. This is a truth from God, recorded in His Word, in order to help you see your life the way He sees it, full of hope and promise and significance.

God loves you and really can work for your good in ALL things.

Will you pray with me?

Father, thank You for showing us that there are different ways to look at the things we're going through in life. Help us to look at the things we're facing and see them as You see them. Help us to look for and see the good that You're working in those situations so that we can face them with courage and faith. Help us to overcome our weakness so that we can keep putting our trust in You for everything in lives. In Jesus' name, Amen.

Questions for Reflection:

1) Read Romans 8:28 and 2 Corinthians 11:23b-30. How might the trials Paul faced in life have helped him to come to the point of believing that God really could work for his good in ALL things?
2) If faith is like a muscle that gets stronger and stronger the more we use it, what kinds of things might God put someone through to help them grow as strong in their faith as possible?
3) What good might God be doing in the situations you're facing in life right now?
4) Like Pollyanna, what can you find to be glad about in those situations?

LESSON 20: KNOWING THAT GOD IS FOR YOU   AUGUST 22

Scripture Reading: Romans 8:31-39

I have a riddle for you today. Can you answer all seven of the following questions with the same word?

1) The word has seven letters
2) Preceded God
3) Greater than God
4) More evil than the devil
5) All poor people have it

6) Wealthy people need it
7) If you eat it, you will die

I'll give you the answer at the end of today's message. But for now, I'd like to talk to you about Romans chapter 8.

In the last lesson, I talked about how God can work ALL things together for good for those who love Him and who are called according to His purpose. In this lesson, I want share *why* God works all things for your good. It comes because God is, ultimately, FOR you. And if God is FOR you, who can be against you? That's the question the apostle Paul asks at the end of Romans chapter 8:

> *"What, then, shall we say in response to this? If God is for us, who can be against us? He who did not spare His own Son, but gave Him up for us all—how will He not also, along with Him, graciously give us all things? Who will bring any charge against those whom God has chosen? It is God who justifies. Who is He that condemns? Christ Jesus, who died—more than that, who was raised to life—is at the right hand of God and is also interceding for us"*
> (Romans 8:31-34).

It's easy to wonder sometimes if God is really FOR you. You lose your job and it makes you wonder what happened. You get a horrible report from the doctor and you wonder what you did wrong. You open an email from a friend to discover some news you wish you had never read, and you wonder how God could be working in this, too.

Yet the truth is that God IS for you. He loves you deeply and cares about your life more than you could possibly imagine. He is as heartbroken about the things that break our hearts as we are, yet He has a perspective that is greater than ours. He can see the good in situations that we can hardly grasp while we're going through it.

Often it's only through hindsight that we can see what God saw in foresight. That job loss wasn't the worst thing that happened to our career after all, but actually helped us leapfrog forward. That bad report from the doctor turned out to deepen our faith rather than shatter it. And that email from a friend brought situations to light that never could have been dealt with had they stayed in the dark.

If only we could have the foresight that God has, we would be able to weather the storms that come at us much better. If we could see things as He sees them, our minds would be refreshed rather than distraught when seemingly bad news comes along. Today, I'd like to give you a lens through which you can look at everything that comes your way, and to see it in foresight rather than waiting till it's long past to see it in hindsight.

The lens of life comes through looking at everything through the cross of Christ. Rather than be tossed to and fro by the storms of your life that come along, God has settled that matter once and for all when He sent Jesus to die for your sins. He didn't have to come along and rescue you, but He did. God didn't wait until you were cleaned up and doing good for Him to send Jesus to die, but, as Paul said in Romans 5:8:

> *"While we were still sinners, Christ died for us."*

If this question is settled, why then do we still wonder if God loves us when things go wrong in our lives? Why do we wonder why funds seem to have dried up, or job opportunities seem limited, or our health or relationships seem to be falling apart? It's a natural feeling, I know, but it's not the truth. If God loved you when you were still in the muck and mire of sin, why would he then abandon you when you're trying your hardest to follow Him?

My wife and I have felt this before. After giving birth to three healthy children, my wife had a miscarriage. It was a blow to us emotionally and personally. Then she had a second miscarriage. Then a third. Then a fourth. It was as if everything we were doing was falling apart. Yet we felt like we were giving our all for the cause of Christ more than ever before. It was natural to wonder what we were doing wrong.

Yet it was during a time of worship when my wife had a breakthrough. She was listening to a worship CD by Don Moen about the healing power of Jesus when she finally surrendered to whatever God's will was for her in this area of her life.

She wasn't happy about the miscarriages, but she knew that all she could do was to trust Him completely. She had asked herself all the important questions, trying to find out if there was anything she was doing to contribute to these miscarriages. But finding nothing, there was no more she could do but to continue to trust in God. She did, and God gave her the peace that passes understanding that somehow, in some way, He would work all things for her good.

Just after this, she became pregnant again and this time she was able to carry the child to full term, giving birth to our fourth child. Then came a fifth, and eventually a sixth. Whether the turnaround in her heart and mind had anything to do with the turnaround in the situation, we still don't know. But what we do know is that when she came to the end of herself and put her faith in Christ again, she regained the peace that God was indeed FOR her. And regardless of what happened after that, she decided she was going to praise God.

I have felt the same at other time of my life. When I'm praying to God for funding for a special project, or just for our daily needs as we minister to others, it sometimes feels like pulling teeth. Like I'm begging God to do something for me that I know He doesn't have to do, but that I wish He would do for our sake and the sake of those we're trying to reach through our ministry.

Then I think about what God has already done for me through Christ, and it's like I put on a whole new set of glasses. I can finally see what God is wanting me to see. Rather than wondering what I'm doing wrong, I start seeing things from God's perspective. I start seeing that there's nothing that God would withhold from me, if He thought it was for my good. As Paul said:

> "If God is for us, who can be against us? He who did not spare His own Son, but gave Him up for us all—how will He not also, along with Him, graciously give us all things?" (Romans 8:31-32).

I sometimes think I'm asking God for too much when I ask for money—whether it's ten dollars, or a hundred, or a thousand. But then I remember what He's *already* done for me. If someone were to give you ten dollars, or a hundred, or a thousand, they'd be giving up a lot for you. What if they gave you ten thousand, or ten million, then they'd really be paying a price.

But what about someone who's gone to war for you, and lost an arm or a leg for you, so you could be free? If someone gave up their arm for you, that's worth way more than ten million dollars. Now imagine if they gave up their life for you. What price could you put on that? And then, to take it a step further, imagine that they were not only willing to give *their* life for you, but their most cherished possession in the world, their child, so that *you* could live? Now we're talking priceless to the n-th degree. And that's what God has done for us by sending Jesus to die for us. And somehow we wonder if God still loves us if He doesn't send us ten bucks, or a hundred, or a thousand?

The truth is, there's nothing God *wouldn't* do for you. He loves you and He is *overwhelmingly* FOR you. He wants to work all things for good in your life because He created you. He has a purpose for your life. And He wants to see you fulfill that purpose.

Don't ever think that because you don't get what you want, when you want it, that it means that God doesn't love you. It's a lie. There may be other reasons involved, and there may be things that God wants you to change, or redirect, or pray differently about. But it's not because He doesn't love you. He's already settled that point beyond argument. And when you look at what's going on in your present situation through the lens of what He's already done for you in the past, you'll see it clearly too. You'll have the foresight that most people only get in hindsight. Your mind will be fixed on the good that God is doing and wants to do through you, rather than the bad that may seem to be engulfing you. This isn't just positive thinking. This is godly thinking. This is looking at life as God sees it.

Once you see that God is for you, you'll become convinced, like the apostle Paul was, that there is nothing else in life that can separate you from His love. *Nothing!* As Paul said in the conclusion of chapter 8:

> *"Who shall separate us from the love of Christ? Shall trouble or hardship or persecution or famine or nakedness or danger or sword? ... No, in all these things we are more than conquerors through him who loved us. For I am convinced that neither death nor life, neither angels nor demons, neither the present nor the future, nor any powers, neither height nor depth, nor anything else in all creation, will be able to separate us from the love of God that is in Christ Jesus our Lord" (Romans 8:37-39).*

What can separate you from the love of God? It's the same answer as the answer to today's riddle: Nothing!

1) NOTHING *is a word that has seven letters*
2) NOTHING *preceded God*
3) NOTHING *is greater than God*
4) NOTHING *is more evil than the devil*
5) *Poor people have* NOTHING
6) *Wealthy people need* NOTHING
7) *And if you eat* NOTHING,
   you will die!

What can separate you from the love of God? NOTHING!

God loves you and would do anything for you. He's already demonstrated that. Now your role is to believe it and live it out in your life in spite of whatever you might be facing today. Remember: God is FOR you!

Will you pray with me?

Father, thank You for reminding us that You are FOR us. Help us to look at life today through that lens, so that we can have your foresight into the situations we're facing. Help us to know that You are working for our good in ALL things, and that nothing can separate us from Your love. In Jesus' name, Amen.

Questions for Reflection:

1) Read Romans 8:31-39. Have you ever felt like God doesn't love you because of something specific that happened in your life? Do you still feel that way, in light of today's lesson?
2) Why is Jesus' death more valuable than anything else God could do for you?
3) What kinds of struggles did Paul go through, and how do you think those struggles may have helped him become convinced that there is nothing that can separate us from God's love?
4) If God is FOR you, who can be against you?

LESSON 21: TRUSTING IN THE POTTER — AUGUST 23

Scripture Reading: Romans 9:1-33

Perhaps you've heard the story of the three trees, where each one had a glorious dream for their future. One wanted to be crafted into a beautiful treasure chest, covered with gold and filled with precious jewels. Another wanted to be turned into boards for a mighty sailing ship, carrying kings and queens across the sea. The third didn't want to be cut down at all, but wanted to grow as tall as possible, pointing people towards God as they looked up into its branches.

A day came, however, when each of the trees were cut down and taken away. The first was turned into a feeding trough, not a treasure chest. The second was too weak to be used for a mighty ship and was used for a common fishing boat instead. The third was deemed too worthless for much of anything and was cut into pieces and thrown into the scrap pile.

Rather than seeing their dreams fulfilled, each of the trees felt abandoned and without hope. It's a tragic story and one that has been repeated many times, in many lives, over the years. It may even be part of your story.

Maybe you've had dreams of getting married, raising a family, and serving God with your whole heart, only to see your dreams dashed by divorce, adultery, and kids who have all but lost their faith. Maybe you've had dreams of being wildly successful in business, giving generously to the poor and needy, only to find yourself being poor and needy instead. Maybe you've stepped out in faith to start a new ministry, or a new job, or a new life in a place where you really felt God had called you, only to find yourself far from home and wondering why you ever left in the first place.

Rather than seeing your dreams fulfilled, you may feel– like the trees in the story–abandoned and without hope.

If so, I want to encourage you today to keep putting your faith and trust in God. Keep remembering that God is the Potter and you are the clay. Keep trusting that He is molding and shaping you into exactly what He wants you to be. As the apostle Paul said in Romans chapter 9:

> "But who are you, O man, to talk back to God? "Shall what is formed say to Him who formed it, 'Why did You make me like this?'" Does not the potter have the right to make out of the same lump of clay some pottery for noble purposes and some for common use?" (Romans 9:20-21).

Sometimes we bristle at the thought that we don't fully control our own destiny. None of us wants to be like a puppet on a string, pulled this way or that by some unseen puppet master. Yet when you put your faith in God and let *Him* take control of your life, you can trust that He will guide you and direct you in ways that are better than you could have imagined.

I had a friend this week who was wondering if she had been shortchanged when God passed out the BLT's—the Brains, the Looks and the Talents. She wondered why others seemed to have gotten so much more in some of those areas. But the truth is, she wasn't shortchanged at all. First of all, she had actually been given huge amounts of each, but couldn't see it for herself. Secondly, I assured her that God had, in fact, given her everything she needed to fulfill His plan for her life. As Paul said to the Ephesians:

> *"For we are God's workmanship, created in Christ Jesus to do good works, which God prepared in advance for us to do" (Ephesians 2:10).*

If God has prepared good works in advance for you to do, He will give you everything you need for the walk He's called you to walk. And He'll continue to do so, even if it seems like you're going in a direction than you had planned. The key is to keep putting your faith and trust in the Potter, remembering that He is FOR you and will work all things together for your good. When you put your faith in God, you put a smile on His face. As the writer of Hebrews says:

> *"And without faith it is impossible to please God, because anyone who comes to Him must believe that He exists and that He rewards those who earnestly seek Him" (Hebrews 11:6).*

God is pleased when you put your faith in Him, and He will reward you when you earnestly seek Him.

This, after all, is what the whole book of Romans is about. Paul is continually telling the Christians in Rome that it is their *faith* that matters most to God, not their righteous acts or their heritage—whether they were born Jewish or Gentile. In chapter 9, Paul laments the fact that so many Jews have missed the fact that God wants them to come to Him by faith. Paul begins by saying:

> *"I have great sorrow and unceasing anguish in my heart. For I could wish that I myself were cursed and cut off from Christ for the sake of my brothers, those of my own race, the people of Israel. Theirs is the adoption as sons; theirs the divine glory, the covenants, the receiving of the law, the temple worship and the promises. Theirs are the patriarchs, and from them is traced the human ancestry of Christ, who is God over all, forever praised! Amen" (Romans 9:2-5).*

Paul sees the noble heritage that the Jews had been given because of the faith of Abraham. Yet Paul also says that just because someone is a descendant of Abraham doesn't mean they are actually people of faith.

> *"For not all who are descended from Israel are Israel. Nor because they are his descendants are they all Abraham's children. On the contrary, 'It is through Isaac that your offspring will be reckoned.' In other words, it is not the natural children who are*

God's children, but it is the children of the promise who are regarded as Abraham's offspring" (Romans 9:6b-8).

Paul then goes on to describe how God raised up various people for various purposes, whether it was Isaac or Jacob or Moses or Pharaoh. Some were for noble purposes, and some for common use, but all were for His glory.

God wants you to keep putting your faith in Him. And when you do, He'll reward you!

Remember the story of the three trees? It would have been tragic if their story had ended when all their dreams were dashed to pieces. Thankfully, their story doesn't end there. Their dreams *were* eventually fulfilled–but in a way that went beyond all that they could have imagined.

The first tree didn't get to become a treasure chest that it had hoped, covered with gold and filled with precious stones. It became a feeding trough for animals instead. But one day, it was covered with golden straw, and when the most precious treasure of all was laid inside it–the Son of God–the tree realized its dream had been fulfilled.

The second tree didn't get to become the mighty sailing ship that it had hoped, carrying kings and queens across the sea. Instead, it was used for a common fishing boat. But one day, that boat carried a group of men who were caught in a fierce storm on a lake. One of the men stood up and said to the wind and the waves, "Be still," and they obeyed Him. As soon as the tree realized what had been done, it realized that it was carrying no ordinary man, but the King of all kings, the One who had created the whole universe.

And the third tree, the one that didn't want to be cut down at all, but point people to God whenever they looked up into its branches? Eventually its boards were pulled from the scrap pile and used as the cross on which our Savior was crucified. And when Jesus rose from the dead three days later, that tree realized that from then on, whenever anyone thought of the cross, their thoughts would be pointed towards God.

You may feel like your life isn't working out the way you had dreamed. You may feel like you're not in the place that you had hoped to be. But don't give up on God–and don't give up on your dreams. God has a way of fulfilling them beyond what you could imagine.

I know of families who have weathered the storms of divorce and adultery and have come out on the other side praising God and helping many others along the way. I know of people who have lost their businesses and homes and things of this world who are now giving away more than anyone else around them, because they've learned what it means to give everything to God. I know of people who have struggled in faith and sometimes wondered if they were doing the right thing, but eventually discovered that God was in it every step of the way.

Don't give up on your dreams, and don't get upset if things aren't working out the way that you had hoped. Keep trusting in the Potter. Whether He wants to use your life for noble purposes or common use, it's all for His glory. Your Father really does know best.

Will you pray with me?

Father, thank You for reminding us that You are in control, even when our lives seem out of control. Thank You that You are the Potter and we are the clay. Help us to be moldable and shapeable by You today. Help us to continue to trust in You, that You will reward us when we believe in You and earnestly seek You. In Jesus' name, Amen.

Questions for Reflection:

1) Read Romans 9:1-33. How do you feel about letting God be the Potter, and trusting Him to mold you and shape you as He sees fit? What might be appealing or unappealing about this idea?
2) What is it that Paul wished for his Jewish brothers and sisters in this passage?
3) Why does Paul say in verse 6 that "not all who are descended from Israel are Israel"? What's the difference? Consider verses 30-32 in your response as well.
4) Read Hebrews 11:6. What does God seem to want from you more than anything else right now, and what can you expect from Him as a result?

LESSON 22: BELIEVING IN YOUR HEART   AUGUST 24

Scripture Reading: Romans 10:1-13

There were once five frogs on a log. One of them decided to jump off. How many frogs do you think were still on the log? ... Four? ... None? ... Nope. All five. One of them just *decided* to jump off.

There's a difference between deciding to do something and doing it. There's a difference between believing in something in your mind and moving that belief deep down into your heart so that it can take root and spring into action.

Throughout this study of the book of Romans, we've been looking at ways to renew your mind and the difference that can make in your life. But if *all* you do is focus on your mind and never move what you've learned down into your heart so those truths can be put into action, then all of this will just be an intellectual exercise.

God wants you to do both: He wants you to renew your mind *and* believe what you've learned in your heart so that it can make a difference in your life.

In Romans chapter 10, Paul tells the Romans what it takes for someone to be saved. He says:

> "That if you confess with your mouth, 'Jesus is Lord,' and believe in your heart that God raised Him from the dead, you will be saved"
> (Romans 10:9).

This is one of the greatest statements of faith found in the whole Bible. If you can say with your mouth that Jesus is Lord, you're also declaring that no one else is Lord, not even yourself. And when you believe in your heart that God raised Jesus from the dead, you're saying that you believe in the resurrection–and that one day you'll be raised from the dead, too, if you've put your faith in Christ.

This sums up two of the most important ideas of what it means to be a follower of Christ: that Jesus is both your Lord *and* Savior.

Many people want a Savior–someone to save them from their sins. But not everyone wants a Lord, someone who calls the shots in their lives. But the truth is, it's awesome to have Jesus as both Lord *and* Savior. Why? Because when He's your Savior, he'll save you from your sins. And when He's your Lord, He'll put you on a path that keeps you from having to be saved from quite so much in the future!

When I saw at age 24 where I was headed in life, I realized that it would have been better if I had let Jesus call the shots instead of me. I asked Jesus to be my Savior–to forgive me of my sins–and also to be my Lord–to take control of my life from that point on. Now that

I'm 48, I can say that this second half of my life has been *significantly* better than the first half (and I loved the first half, too! I just didn't realize how much trouble I was causing for myself and others along the way!)

Now I have a purpose for my life that propels me forward and I have Someone to go with me along the way, guiding and directing me so I can make the most of the time I have here on earth.

How does this apply to you? Have you come to the place in your life where you've confessed with your mouth, "Jesus is Lord," and believed in your heart that God raised Him from the dead? If so, that's the best decision you could have ever made in your life and it's the starting point for your life with Christ. But it doesn't end there. God wants you to follow through on that decision and take a leap of faith, jumping off the log and jumping into His full-blown plan for your life.

I know of a young man who has put his faith in Christ and is theologically brilliant. He's well-versed in Scripture and has sound doctrine. But he's recently started dating a non-Christian girl, going against God's stated desire for him in his life. As it says in the Bible:

"Do not be yoked together with unbelievers. For what do righteousness and wickedness have in common? Or what fellowship can light have with darkness?" (2 Corinthians 6:14).

Like King Solomon, he's going to find out some day that all the wisdom in the world is worthless if you don't put it into practice. King Solomon was, as the Bible declares, the wisest man who has ever lived. Yet he didn't put that wisdom into practice when it came to his relationships, going against God's clear warning to the Israelites about not taking wives from those that didn't believe in Him. God said:

"You must not intermarry with them, because they will surely turn your hearts after their gods" (1 Kings 11:2).

Yet that's exactly what happened: Solomon married women who didn't believe in God and they led him astray. Wisdom is only valuable if you move it from head knowledge to believing it deep down in your heart and putting it into practice.

Someone in this situation might think: "But I could lead this person to Christ, and God wants me to lead people to Christ, doesn't He?" Yes, that's right. But if it means violating one of God's other pieces of wisdom along the way, then it's more likely to do harm than good. God wants you to follow His plan for your life in all areas, not just the ones that appeal to you.

I know men who are in love with other men. They compare their relationships to the close friendship that Jonathan had with David. They say that God wants them to have close male friendships. And on that point I agree: God does want them to have close male friendships. But then God draws a line—as He does with all relationships outside of a husband and wife committed for life—warning that if you become involved romantically and physically with anyone else, you'll do more damage than good. If God says something is destructive, no matter how good it may seem at the time, in the end, it will be destructive.

Jesus is glad to be your Savior, but as I said before, if you'll let Him be your Lord, too, you won't need saving from quite so much!

Maybe the area you need a Lord today is in your finances, helping you decide where and when to spend your money. Look in the Bible and you'll find your answers. God has great wisdom regarding finances, whether it's saving or spending or giving your money away, like this:

> "Give, and it will be given to you. A good measure, pressed down, shaken together and running over, will be poured into your lap. For with the measure you use, it will be measured to you" (Luke 6:38).

But you'll have to put that wisdom into practice so that you can make good and godly decisions.

Maybe the area you need a Lord today is in your health, helping you to know what to eat and what to drink and how to take care of your body. Again, look in the Bible and you'll find your answers, like this:

> "Everything is permissible"–but not everything is beneficial. "Everything is permissible"–but not everything is constructive (1 Corinthians 10:23).

While you can justify almost anything, that doesn't mean everything is equally good for you! Look closely at God's Word for your answers and then put what He says into practice.

Maybe the area you need a Lord today is in your relationships, helping you know how to act and react to those around you. The Bible contains a wealth of wisdom on this topic, too, like this:

> "For if you forgive men when they sin against you, your heavenly Father will also forgive you. But if you do not forgive men their sins, your Father will not forgive your sins" (Matthew 6:14-15).

Applying a verse like this to your life could bring more healing and wholeness to your relationships than you could ever achieve by any other approach.

I'm sure you're getting the idea. God loves you incredibly much. And He's glad to save you from those things that plague you in your life. If you'll let Him be your Lord, too, and not just your Savior, you won't need saving from quite so much.

If you've never put your faith in Christ, I'd encourage you to do it today. Confess with your mouth that, "Jesus is Lord," and believe in your heart that God raised Him from the dead, and as this verse in Romans says, you will be saved.

If you've already put your faith in Christ, I'd encourage you to follow through on that decision. Keep digging into God's word to find out what He wants you to do with your life. Then don't just decide to do what He says. Jump off the log and do it! Keep believing in your heart that Jesus is both your Lord *and* Savior.

Will you pray with me?

Father, thank You for being so interested in our lives that You're willing to be both our Lord and Savior, saving us from our sins and guiding us into godly living. Help us to make wise decisions so we can follow You in every area of our lives, then to follow-through on those decisions and put them into practice in our lives. In Jesus' name, Amen.

Questions for Reflection:

1) Read Romans 10:1-13. What was Paul's heart's desire for the Israelites? Why did he say in verses 2-4 that they were not able to receive it?

2) What can you do in your life to keep from being like the Israelites Paul mentioned?
3) Why does it seem to be important to both confess with your mouth that "Jesus is Lord," and believe in your heart that God raised Him from the dead?
4) If you've never put your faith in Christ, are you ready to do it today? And if you've already put your faith in Christ, how are you doing at following through on that decision in your life?

LESSON 23: HOLDING THE ROPE   AUGUST 25

Scripture Reading: Romans 10:13-21

When William Carey was raising funds in England to support his missionary work in India, he told people he felt as if there was a man drowning in a well and calling out for help. Carey said he was willing to go down into the well to save the man, but he needed some people to hold the rope for him while he went.

Several men volunteered to help Carey in his work, "holding the rope" for him back home, raising funds and praying so he could do the part God had called him to do.

While the way people do missions has varied throughout the years, the idea of "goers" and "senders" has not. God continues to call people to go and preach His message to people throughout the world, and He continues to call others to help send people on their way.

The apostle Paul talked about this idea in his letter to the Christians in Rome. Paul said:

> *"...for, 'Everyone who calls on the name of the Lord will be saved.' How, then, can they call on the one they have not believed in? And how can they believe in the one of whom they have not heard? And how can they hear without someone preaching to them? And how can they preach unless they are sent? As it is written, 'How beautiful are the feet of those who bring good news!'" (Romans 10:13-15).*

In the past, these verses have conjured up in my mind a vision of missionaries climbing over the top of a mountain in some remote jungle, bringing the good news of Christ to the people in the valley below. As the villagers would hear this good news being proclaimed to them—news that was like music to their ears—they would exclaim, "How beautiful are the feet of those who bring good news!"

When I read that passage today a different vision comes to mind. Why? Because, in many ways, I'm now a missionary myself, writing to people all over the world to encourage them to put their faith in Christ for everything in their lives. The scenery is different, but the principle is the same.

Instead of climbing a misty mountaintop, I'm sitting at my desk in my bedroom, looking out over miles and miles of wide open spaces. I'm on the second floor of a two-story, traditional American farmhouse in the heart of the Great Midwest. There are no mountains to block my view, and only a few other farmhouses dotting the ground in the distance. The corn and soybean fields have been harvested for the year, so all that's left is a clear view of the horizon in every direction.

Yet when I push the "send" button on my computer, I realize that this message I'm writing right now will make its way over the plains, across the country, under oceans, into the sky and back down to the earth again.

Within an instant, this message will show up in places like Papua New Guinea, an island half-way around the world in the South Pacific, where someone just signed up to receive these messages on Monday, saying,

> "I will be very much excited to receive the news & also pray to strengthen each other's faith."

Almost simultaneously, this message will also show up in an inbox in Nigeria, a country in western Africa where someone wrote to me last week saying,

> "I have been far from God. Most times I start and end my day without praising or praying to God. My bible is always beside me and most times I don't open it. How do I strengthen my walk with God, how do I make him priority, and how do I become consistent with my maker???? Please advise me on what steps to take."

At the same time, it will appear on someone's cell phone in the UK, where a woman wrote to me this week saying,

> "You are so right about thinking of Jesus as a saviour and sometimes not having Him as Lord of our lives too. Today's reading made me take stock of what you said, and I recommitted and surrendered my life afresh and asked Jesus to be Lord of my life also as well as being my saviour."

Missions is changing, but the message stays the same. When Jesus told His disciples to "Go into all the world and preach the good news to all creation," (Mark 16:15) He didn't put any limits on where to go, how to go, or to whom we should go. He just said to, "Go!" Jesus wanted His disciples to take the message as far as they could, starting in Jerusalem, spreading out to Judea and finally to the ends of the earth.

As we've been looking at the book of Romans for ways to renew our minds, I want to remind you that the goal of a renewed mind is not simply to renew your thinking but to renew your actions, too. Jumping into God's plan regarding missions is one of those actions that God wants you to take, whether it's as a goer or a sender or both. God wants you to be one of those people about whom it is said: "How beautiful are the feet of those who bring good news!"

For some of you, this may be a reminder of what God has already called you to do. For others of you this may be a confirmation of what God has been stirring in your heart in recent weeks or months. And for some of you, this may be a totally new thought—a totally new direction that God wants you to take in your life. Whatever the case, I want to encourage each of you to get involved in whatever mission God has put in front of you.

I was privileged to see an evangelist this fall named Reinhard Bonnke while he was speaking at a youth conference in Chicago. He's ministered to millions on the African continent, with crowds so large that in just one meeting his team saw over 1 million people fill out decision cards to put their faith in Christ.

Yet, at age 71, he recently got onto Facebook. At first, he wasn't sure if he was interested. But when someone showed him a demonstration of how it worked, the way he could connect with people around the world, and the ease with which he could get a message out, he was sold. He looked at the screen and said, "It's a pulpit!"

Now he personally posts several short thoughts each day on Facebook. Over 381,000 people have "liked" his page and several hundred people now comment and interact with him and his thoughts on a daily basis. His mission is the same as it's been his whole life, it's just taken on a whole new dimension!

A few years ago I read a conversation between David Yongii Cho, the pastor of the largest church in the world–located in Seoul, South Korea–and Rick Warren, the pastor of one of the largest churches in America. As they were talking about their next steps for future growth, they both pointed to the same thing: the Internet. Pastor Cho, who had over 750,000 members in his congregation at that time, said "we are so jammed that we have no way to keep growing except by going into cyberspace!"

Pastor Warren responded, saying, "No matter how much land you have it eventually fills up. We were running over 10,000 in attendance before we built our first building. So we know how to grow and minister without buildings. But what we are trying to learn now is how to do it through the Internet into the homes."

Now, several years later, both churches have strong and vibrant Internet ministries, providing spiritual support and encouragement to members in home groups around the world.

As the world grows, God wants to use every means possible to reach as many as possible before the end comes. Considering that the world has added another *billion* people in the last twelve years and is expected to add *another billion* in the next ten to twenty years, it's no surprise that God is using all kinds of new technologies to reach more people in an instant than ever before.

Amazingly, you don't have to be a famous evangelist or the pastor of a huge church to have an impact on people all over the globe. I'm surprised some days to think of just how many people I reach from my little bedroom office here in central Illinois. To put it in perspective, I read that Reinhard Bonnke once had a tent built for his crusades in Africa that could hold 34,000 people. It was the *largest tent* ever built in the world.

Yet when I finish writing this message tonight and push the "send" button, God will take these words and send them out to more than 35,000 people in more than 160 countries who have signed up for these messages over the years–that's more people than can fit in the world's largest tent! That's amazing!

It's more possible today than ever before to fulfill Jesus' command to "Go into all world and preach the gospel to all creation." And if you're a follower of Christ, God wants you to be part of the process.

Whether you're a goer, a sender, or both, God wants you to be involved in His mission. God doesn't just want to renew your mind–He wants you to put what you've learned into action. As the apostle James said:

> "In the same way, faith by itself, if it is not accompanied by action, is dead" (James 2:17).

Let me encourage you to get involved with God's mission, whether it's going, or sending, or both. Try starting a spiritual conversation with a friend on Facebook. Look into a missions trip with your church or with other groups who are taking the gospel to others.

Consider supporting a missionary, or two, or three, or more with your prayers and your financial gifts.

Without trying to sound self-serving, I'd love to have your help with our ministry as well! We've been richly blessed over the years to have many people come alongside us and support our work so that we can do the part God has called us to do: encouraging as many people as possible to put their faith in Christ for everything in their lives. In many ways, I feel like William Carey as he was going off to India. I'm willing to go down into the well to save as many as I can, but I need some rope-holders to help me as I go.

If you'd like to help "hold the rope" for us, you can learn more about our ministry and make a donation on our website at www.theranch.org. I think you'll enjoy seeing what God is doing through this ministry whether you decide to get involved in our work or not.

But whatever God puts on your heart to do, let me encourage you to *do it*. As Paul said:

"How, then, can they call on the one they have not believed in? And how can they believe in the one of whom they have not heard? And how can they hear without someone preaching to them? And how can they preach unless they are sent?"

When you take part in God's mission, people will be able to say of *you*:

"How beautiful are the feet of those who bring good news!"

Will you pray with me?

Father, thank You for making it more possible than ever before to "go into all the world and preach the gospel to all creation." Show us how we can be involved in Your mission in the world today and in the days ahead and give us the faith to do what You've called us to do. In Jesus' name, Amen.

Questions for Reflection:

1) Read Romans 10:13-21. In verses 13-15, what steps does Paul say are involved for someone to put their faith in Christ?
2) If you've already put your faith in Christ, can you see how each of those steps might have been involved in your own decision-making? If you haven't yet put your faith in Christ, which step do you think might be needed next?
3) What steps could you take in your life right now to get more involved with God's mission in the world?
4) Read Philippians 4:19. Ask God to give you the faith, strength and resources to be involved in His global mission in ways that go beyond whatever you've done so far.

LESSON 24: HEARING THE MESSAGE — AUGUST 26

Scripture Reading: Romans 10:16-21

We're getting ready for Christmas here in Illinois! We've put the tree up this afternoon, and last night went to see our teenage daughter dance in a special Christmas show.

And as we get closer to Christmas, I'd like to encourage you to take this time to get closer to God. Christmas is the time of year when we celebrate that God came so close that we could reach out and touch Him—in the form of Jesus. And it's a great time to remember that God is still very close to us—even closer than you might think. As Paul said to the men of Athens:

> "God did this so that they would seek Him and perhaps reach out for Him and find Him, though He is not far from any one of us" (Acts 17:27).

God has been trying to get His message out to people in as many ways as possible, even using the heavens and the skies. When Paul talked about this in his letter to the Romans, he referred back to Psalm 19 which says:

> "The heavens declare the glory of God;
> the skies proclaim the work of His
> hands.
> Day after day they pour forth speech;
> night after night they display knowledge.
> There is no speech or language
> where their voice is not heard.
> Their voice goes out into all the earth,
> their words to the end of the world"
> (Psalm 19:1-4a).

Yet even with the heavens and the skies proclaiming the glories of God, there are still people who don't listen to them. In Romans chapter 10, Paul laments the fact that so many of his Jewish brothers and sisters had missed what God was trying to say to them. At the end of the chapter, Paul quotes what God said through the prophet Isaiah:

> "All day long I have held out my hands to a disobedient and obstinate people" (Romans 10:21).

What a sad picture to imagine God the Father holding out His hands to His children continually, yet they are unwilling to take hold of it.

At the same time, I realize that it's not always easy to reach out to God, especially when you feel like you've been hurt by Him.

In the Christmas show we saw last night, the main character was a man who had tried hard to push God out of his life. He hadn't always pushed God out, though. At one time in his life, he had a wonderful relationship with God. He had married the woman of his dreams, had a young boy with her, but then tragedy hit: his wife was killed in a car accident.

From that point on, the man kept God at arm's length. Even though God continued to try to talk to him, the man kept pushing God away. He could no longer believe in a God who either would not or could not save his wife from death. It was simply more than he could bear.

Sometimes we're like the man in this play. When life doesn't go the way we think it should, we wonder if God really is who He says He is. We wonder if He really loves us as we thought He did. We wonder if He's really as powerful as He says He is in the Bible. The truth gets muddied in the midst of life.

But what can you do when you start to lose your faith? What can you do to try to get—or get back—that love relationship with God that He says in His word that He wants with you?

Thankfully, Paul gives us the answer to that as well. Paul says:

"Consequently faith comes from hearing the message, and the message is heard through the Word of Christ" (Romans 10:17).

Or as it says in the New King James Version:

"So then faith comes by hearing, and hearing by the Word of God" (Romans 10:17, NKJV).

If you want to increase your faith, one of the best ways you can do it is to immerse yourself in the word of God. When you do, you'll hear the message that God wants you to hear—the message of Christ, the Savior who came into the world at Christmas to demonstrate God's love for you in person.

While God speaks through the heavens and the skies, He has also spoken through many people, as recorded in the Bible. As you read God's words in the Bible. You can hear what God said to people like Adam and Eve in the garden of Eden, or to Moses out in the desert, or to Abraham and Isaac and Jacob throughout their life-long journeys.

You can hear what God said to Sarah and Hannah and Mary and Elizabeth. You can hear what God said to Peter and John and the woman at the well. And as you hear God's words as spoken to others in the Bible, it makes it easier to recognize His voice when He speaks to you as well.

I know as I hear the stories in the Bible, my faith comes alive. I start to ask God how He might work in my life in the same ways. Faith really does come from hearing, and hearing by the word of God.

I also want to encourage you to not just read these stories once and then be done. The word "hearing" in this passage has the meaning of "hearing continually," or in other words, "hearing and hearing and hearing." So then, faith comes by hearing and hearing and hearing–not just by having heard. Read the Bible, and keep reading, then you'll see your faith start to grow. As D.L. Moody said:

"I prayed for faith and thought it would strike me like lightening. But faith did not come. One day I read, 'Now faith comes by hearing, and hearing by the Word of God.' I had closed my Bible and prayed for faith. I now began to study my Bible and faith has been growing ever since."

If you've got a Bible nearby, I hope you'll read it. If you don't have a Bible nearby, I hope you'll get one. There are so many great Bibles these days—and in so many languages of the world–that it would be sad if those who had access to God's Word didn't read it on a regular basis. If you don't have a Bible in print, you can also read it online in multiple languages and translations at places like www.biblegateway.com, or www.blueletterbible.org.

And if you'd like to hear how God is working in people's lives today, I've put dozens of stories that you can read in the story section of *The Ranch* website at www.theranch.org. God is still speaking to people today, and I'd love for you to hear the stories of how God is using His Word to build people up in their faith.

In the show we watched last night, the man who had pushed God away finally reached the breaking point where he could no longer take it. He realized he had to either give up on life or give in to God. He chose to give in to God, to surrender His life to God's plan for it, and in so doing, he found that he was also finally able to hear God speaking to him.

As we get closer to Christmas this year, I hope you'll use this time to get closer to God. Take Paul's words to the Romans as God's words to you for building up your faith:

> "So then faith comes by hearing [and hearing and hearing and hearing], and hearing by the word of God."

Will you pray with me?

Father, thank You for speaking to us in so many ways and so much of the time. Help us to hear Your message to us today, so we can respond to it in the way You want us to respond. In Jesus' name, Amen.

Questions for Reflection:

1) Read Romans 10:16-21. Have you ever sensed God speaking to you through nature, as Paul implies when he quotes from Psalm 19?
2) Why do you think some people still don't listen to God, even when He might seem to be speaking to them clearly?
3) Why do you think Paul is so sad for his fellow Israelites, based on the words he quotes from Isaiah in verse 21?
4) Based on verse 17, what are some steps you can take in your own life to increase your faith? Why not commit to taking them today?

LESSON 25: CORRECTING MISPERCEPTIONS   AUGUST 27

Scripture Reading: Romans 11:1-32

The way we perceive things isn't always the way they are. Yet those misperceptions can persist for years, causing us to miss the truth of what God might be trying to say to us. It doesn't have to be that way, however. God has a way of bringing the truth into our lives, if we're open to it, in a way that can renew our minds and change our perspective on everything.

I had an email from a woman who wondered if Jesus could possibly love her–not because of something she had done, but because of who she was: a Jew. She had always been told that Jesus doesn't love Jews. Yet after reading some of the stories on my website, she was confronted with a new truth and wondered: Is it possible that Jesus might love a Jew?

I don't want to betray her confidence, but I would like to share a portion of her heartfelt letter with you because I feel that her words express something that we all wonder about at times: whether or not God really loves us, too. Here's part of what she said in her letter.

> *I was sent your site by accident and have been reading the stories. The more I read the more questions I have. I've never seen Jesus portrayed as this site does. I should tell you that I'm Jewish and I believe in the one true G-d of Abraham, Isaac, and Jacob.*
>
> *I've read some the stories on your site and have to wonder how they could be true, but I can't stop reading them either, something just feels right about them. My heritage has ingrained in me that Jesus isn't for my people. I can't explain why, but I find some of the stories making me cry and I'm not one that cries easily. It doesn't make sense. I don't even know why I'm writing. I'm just really confused. How can this G-d of*

yours, be the G-d I've grown up with? Would Jesus love someone who hasn't been faithfully reading the Torah for a long time?

I'm sorry, I know this doesn't make any sense, and I've always been told that Jesus doesn't love Jews. But after reading some of the stories I just don't know what to believe. Is it possible he might love a Jew?

How would you answer a letter like that? Could you find enough evidence in the Bible to show that Jesus really did love this woman? And even if you could, how could you convey it to her in a way that she would believe it?

As for me, I shared that I could understand why she might wonder if Jesus loved the Jews. But the truth is that Jesus *was* a Jew. The twelve disciples were Jewish. And the whole New Testament—which talks about Jesus—was written *by* Jews. In fact, Jesus never left the land of Israel to go to any other nation, except for the brief time as a child when His parents took Him to Egypt to avoid being killed by King Herod.

Does Jesus love the Jews? Absolutely! But sometimes it's hard to see the truth through all of the misperceptions that we've been taught or believed for so many years.

The apostle Paul faced similar misperceptions among the people that he ministered to as well. Some of them believed that God had finally given up on the Jews, because Paul and others were now taking the gospel to the Gentiles.

But nothing could have been further from the truth. In Romans 11, Paul said:

"I ask then: Did God reject His people? By no means! I am an Israelite myself, a descendant of Abraham, from the tribe of Benjamin. God did not reject His people, whom He foreknew. Don't you know what the Scripture says in the passage about Elijah—how he appealed to God against Israel: "Lord, they have killed Your prophets and torn down Your altars; I am the only one left, and they are trying to kill me"? And what was God's answer to him? "I have reserved for Myself seven thousand who have not bowed the knee to Baal." So too, at the present time there is a remnant chosen by grace"

(Romans 11:1-5).

God's heart still beat with love for the Jews, and the apostle Paul was one of many of them. Paul himself regularly preached and ministered in the Jewish synagogues *first* whenever he arrived at a new town, just as Jesus did (see Matthew 4:26, 9:35, 12:9, 13:54, Acts 14:1, 17:2, 18:4, 18:19, 19:8).

But Paul, like Jesus, faced a fair amount of opposition in the synagogues. When they were thrown out of the synagogues, they took their message just as zealously to the Gentiles in those areas. After several years of this, it seems that some of the Gentiles began to think of themselves more highly than the Jews around them. But Paul gave them this warning:

"I am talking to you Gentiles. Inasmuch as I am the apostle to the Gentiles, I make much of my ministry in the hope that I may somehow arouse my own people to envy and save some of them. For if their rejection is the reconciliation of the world, what will their acceptance be but life from the dead? If the part of the dough offered as firstfruits is holy, then the whole batch is holy; if the root is holy, so are the branches.

"If some of the branches have been broken off, and you, though a wild olive shoot, have been grafted in among the others and now share in the nourishing sap from the

olive root, do not boast over those branches. If you do, consider this: You do not support the root, but the root supports you. You will say then, 'Branches were broken off so that I could be grafted in.' Granted. But they were broken off because of unbelief, and you stand by faith. Do not be arrogant, but be afraid. For if God did not spare the natural branches, He will not spare you either" (Romans 11:13-21).

Paul wisely warns the Romans not to be arrogant about God's love for them, but to remember that they were grafted into the root because of their faith and that God wants them to stand firm in that faith to the end.

We all have misperceptions at times. Whether we're Jewish and questioning God's love for us, or whether we're Gentiles and becoming arrogant about His love for us. In either case, God wants to bring His truth into our lives and clear up any misperceptions we might have. He wants us to know that He loves us deeply, and to respond to that love in faith.

I was talking recently to a father and his college-age son who felt a barrier had grown up between them. The father seemed to feel the son wasn't interested in a relationship with him because of some of the things that had passed between them. The son, likewise, felt that his father was no longer interested in a relationship with him because of the distance that he felt.

During our talk, the father said that not a day went by when he didn't think about his son, and the son said that he wished he could find ways to spend more meaningful time with his father. Yet these thoughts had gone unspoken for so long that both of them felt the other no longer loved or cared about them. It was only when the Holy Spirit brought out these deep truths through our conversation that they realized that they both eagerly wanted their relationship to be restored, but didn't know how to express it. Tears flowed as they prayed together, having come face to face with the truth. I pray they're on a new path in their relationship with one another.

I also pray for the Jewish woman who wrote to me, that God would continue to speak His truth into her life and help her to respond to that truth in faith. I know He can do it, for He has done it for me and for many, many other people throughout history. I believe He can do it for you, too.

At the end of Romans, chapter 11, Paul breaks out into one of the most beautiful doxologies in the Bible—an eruption of praise to God:

*"Oh, the depth of the riches of the wisdom
and knowledge of God!
How unsearchable His judgments,
and His paths beyond tracing out!
'Who has known the mind of the Lord?
Or who has been His counselor?'
'Who has ever given to God,
that God should repay Him?'
For from Him and through Him and to
Him are all things.
To Him be the glory forever! Amen"
(Romans 11:33-36).*

If you need some of God's deep wisdom and knowledge in your life today, I'd encourage you to call out to Him. Ask Him to reveal more of His truth to you. Ask Him to correct any misperceptions you may have about Him, or about your relationships with those around you. Ask Him to guide you and direct you and point you in the direction He wants you to go, trusting that He will always lead you along a path that is absolutely the best for you.

Then, as He reveals His wisdom to you, I pray you'll respond to it in faith, taking the steps that He wants you to take. When you do, I hope you'll find yourself like Paul, erupting in praise and saying:

> *"Oh the depth of the riches of the wisdom and knowledge of God! … To Him be the glory forever! Amen."*

Will you pray with me?

Father, thank You for reminding us that we don't always have the fullness of Your truth, but that if we come to You, You can pour it out on us in abundance. Lord, reveal Your truth to us this week so we can clear up any misperceptions we have about You and about those around us. In Jesus' name, Amen.

Questions for Reflection:

1) Read Romans 11:1-32. In verses 13 and 14, what does Paul say is one of the benefits he hopes will result from his ministry to the Gentiles?
2) What would you say to someone who's Jewish who wonders if Jesus might possibly love them?
3) In verses 17-21, what reason does Paul give for why some branches were broken off, and why others were grafted in?
4) What misperceptions might you have, whether about God's love for you or about your relationships with others, that God might want to correct? Call out to Him today and ask Him to reveal His truth to you.

LESSON 26: BEING TRANSFORMED ~ PART 1   AUGUST 28

Scripture Reading: Romans 12:1-2

The name of this study, "Romans: Lessons in Renewing Your Mind," comes from the verse we're looking at today from Romans chapter 12:

> *"Do not conform any longer to the pattern of this world, but be transformed by the renewing of your mind"* (Romans 12:2a).

This verse contains two distinct thoughts for how you can transform your life, like two sides of the same coin. On one side of the coin, it says: "Do not conform any longer to the pattern of this world…" On the other side it says: "…but be transformed by the renewing of your mind." They're two different thoughts, but with the same goal, helping you become more and more like Christ.

Today I'd like to focus on the first side of the coin, "Do not conform any longer to the pattern of this world." Next week, we'll look at the other side of the coin, "but be transformed by the renewing of your mind."

When Paul talks about "the pattern of this world," he's talking about what might seem "normal" in the world around us. But the truth is that what's normal in the world around us are thoughts and ideas that pull us in the exact *opposite* direction that God wants for us. This is why Paul didn't want the Romans to conform to the world around them—and why God doesn't want us to conform to the world around us.

But how do you break out of what may seem "normal"? How do you break out of "the pattern of this world"?

Here are a few ideas that others have passed on to me over the years, and I'm glad to pass them onto you. These aren't meant to be legalistic "do's and don'ts" for your life, but they're good ideas that I've tested out and found extremely helpful in my own life. So in that light, here are three ideas that might help you to avoid being conformed to the world around you. And all three have to do with the media that we consume: the TV shows, movies, and other materials we expose yourself to.

I'm not a TV basher, but before my wife and I got married twenty-two years ago, we read a book that encouraged us not to have a TV in our house for the first year of our marriage. The author suggested that having a TV in your house is like having a third partner in your marriage. It's always sitting there, always available for a bit of entertainment or distraction, and could take away significant time from simply enjoying each other's company during the first year of your marriage. The author noted that the first year of marriage sets the stage for patterns that can become habits for the rest of a couple's life, making it important to start good habits early on.

So we gave it a try. It was radical idea among the people we knew. I remember a family that came over one night and one of their kids started running around the house in circles, looking for a TV. When he couldn't find one, he started shouting with a bit of desperation in his voice, saying, "This is a house with no TV! This is a house with no TV!"

But for us, we were so excited about getting married and spending as much time as we could together that it didn't seem like we were giving up that much. It was great to just spend our hours talking to each other, cooking together, and even doing dishes together.

When we finally did get a TV again, we were shocked at how much the programming seemed to have changed in the time that we weren't watching. Looking back, it's hard to know if the programming had gotten so much worse, or if we had just been away from it for long enough to realize that the shows on TV were no longer "normal" for us. It was now easy for us to turn it off and keep it off.

Over the years, we've gone through various seasons where we've watched TV and others where we haven't watched TV. But in general, that first year of marriage set a pattern for us that has held for more than two decades. We've recently moved into the country where we only get three or four channels at most, depending on the weather. For the most part, neither my wife nor I, nor our six kids, seem to miss it too much! Our family has always grown up with TV on the "side burner" of our lives, not at its center, an idea that started for us over twenty-two years ago and has continued to help us avoid being conformed to the pattern of this world.

"Do not be conformed to the pattern of this world," Paul said. And by intentionally limiting the amount and the type of TV shows that we've watched, we've been better able to keep God's view of what's "normal" in plain sight, rather than the world's view of life.

The second type of media that often impacts our worldview are the types of movies that we watch. Prior to becoming a Christian, I would watch all kinds of movies, regardless of their ratings. Someone challenged me, however, that it would be wise to not watch any movie that was rated R or above—an idea that again seemed radical to me at the time. I was over 17, after all, and why cut out what might be good movies, just because they contained more adult content? But I respected the person who told me and began to look more closely at the movies I watched.

I noticed that whenever I would watch an R-rated movie, the images that stayed in my head the longest seemed to be those images that gave the movie it's R-rating. There may have been other redeeming qualities to the movies, but those images that stuck with me the most were those that were most questionable, whether the violence, or the cursing, or the strong sensuality. I began to realize that if the people in Hollywood, whose morals and values were often much more loose than my own, felt that a movie had questionable content for the general public, then perhaps there was a reason for me to stay away from it, too!

A friend of mine recently told me that he, too, used to watch R-rated movies all the time, not thinking anything about it. He thought he could handle it, that it didn't affect him, he said, to watch women in little or no clothing, or to watch gruesome violence, or to listen to people repeatedly take God's name in vain.

But then he got married. When he brought home a stack of movies to watch with his wife, he saw it through new eyes: hers. After trying to watch a few movies with his new wife, she began to say, "Why are you watching that?" She began to wonder what kind of man she had married, who thought that these kinds of shows were normal. Now he chooses his movies much more carefully, not just because of his wife, but because he realized that the movies he watched *were* affecting his view of life and what he considered to be "normal."

"Do not be conformed to the pattern of this world," Paul said. By intentionally putting limits on the types of movies that you watch, whether it's going by the rating systems that Hollywood has put in place, or checking out movie reviews first by people that we trust, such as www.pluggedin.com, you'll find yourself better able to focus on God's pattern for your lives and less on the world's.

The third type of media that I've had to take control over are the things I read—the newspapers and magazines, blogs and books. Words have power, and a writer can steer a person's emotions in ways that can affect us for a lifetime, whether for good or for bad.

I remember a national newspaper that I used to love to read. The stories were always interesting and educational. When I read those stories, I learned so much about topics I had never thought about before. I felt like the paper was keeping me "up" with current events and helping me have the inside scoop on what was going on. But over time, I realized that whenever the paper wrote about topics that I already knew something about in-depth, I found that the authors were surprisingly one-sided in their views, leaving out opposing views or slanting the articles towards conclusions that were the exact opposite of mine.

I continued reading the paper because I was learning so much about other topics, but I began to wonder: If the paper could take such a one-sided view of the topics that I *did* know about in-depth, what other ideas were they skewing in my mind on topics that I knew much less about? As much as I loved the paper—and my company at the time even paid for my subscription—I decided to cancel it. I didn't want my worldview to be shaped by an organization that held such different core beliefs from my own.

This has also carried over into the books I read and the blogs that I follow. My goal isn't just to surround myself with ideas that are only compatible with my own, but to consider carefully what I'm reading and why, rather than just consuming the material because it's interesting or intriguing. Books, newspapers, magazines, and blogs all come with their own slant, no matter how much they say they are trying to remain neutral. The important thing is to find out whether that slant is in line with God's Word or not, then choose what you read based on that.

"Don't be conformed to the pattern of this world," Paul said. And by being careful about what you read, making sure it lines up with God's view of life rather than the world's view of life, you'll find it much easier to resist the pull of the world on your heart and soul.

In all three of these areas–whether it's TV show you watch, the movies you buy or download or rent, or the newspapers or magazines or books or blogs that you read–God wants you to be careful about what you take into your life. You don't have to be a prude and you don't have to be legalistic. Each of these media can have good, useful and redeeming values. But if you want to see your life transformed, you'll find that the process is much easier when you take control over the media that you consume. You'll begin to get your life back, your time back, and be able to see the world with a fresh set of eyes.

"Do not be conformed to the pattern of this world," Paul said. That's not just good advice from a first-century apostle to the Romans of his day. It's good advice for you and me in regards to the world of our day, too.

In the next lesson, I'll share more about the flip side of this coin, with some practical ideas for how to you can "be transformed by the renewing of your mind." In the meantime, I pray that God will use the ideas I've shared with you today to spark new ways that you can avoid being conformed to the pattern of this world.

Will you pray with me?

Father, thank You for helping us realize that You don't want us to conform to the pattern of this world, but to be transformed by the renewing of our minds. Help us to cut out or limit those things that are harmful to us, causing us to conform to the pattern of the world. Give us ideas for how we can do this in practical ways in our lives and in our world. In Jesus' name, Amen.

Questions for Reflection:

1) Read Romans 12:1-2. What relationship is there between offering your body to God as a living sacrifice and not conforming to the pattern of this world?
2) What dangers can you see in your own life that might stem from conforming too much to the pattern of this world?
3) Are there any ideas from today's message that you might want to put into practice in your own life, or has it sparked any other ideas that you might want to try?
4) At the end of verse 2, Paul says that if you don't conform and be transformed, you'll be able to "test and approve" what God's will is for your life. What does Paul mean by this?

LESSON 27: BEING TRANSFORMED ~ PART 2   AUGUST 29

Scripture Reading: Romans 12:1-2

In the last lesson, week we looked at three ways to renew your mind by taking control of the amount and types of media that you consume, from TV and movies to books, magazines, newspapers and blogs. This week, we're going to look at three more ways to renew your mind. All three have to do with increasing how much you consume of something else in your life: God's Word, the Bible.

If I could give you just one idea for how to "be transformed by the renewing of your mind" that far surpasses any other, it would be this: to get as much of God's Word into your mind as you can, as often as you can, and with as much understanding as you can.

When you do this, your mind will be renewed and your life will be transformed, just as the apostle Paul encouraged the Romans to do in his day when he said:

"Do not conform any longer to the pattern of this world, but be transformed by the renewing of your mind" (Romans 12:2a).

So today, I'd like to give you three ways to get more of God's Word into your mind: 1) read God's Word, 2) memorize God's Word, and 3) study God's Word.

First, I want to encourage you to *read* God's Word, and read it often.

Whether you read just one verse a day, one chapter a day, or ten chapters a day, if you'll keep filling your mind with God's Word, you'll find that your mind is renewed on a regular basis.

You need more than just physical food to keep you going. As Jesus said:

"Man does not live on bread alone, but on every Word that comes from the mouth of God" (Matthew 4:4).

God wants you to have spiritual food as much as physical food–and a steady diet of it. The good news is that if you're on a diet of God's Word, there's no limit to how much you can eat! You can feast on God's Word as much as you want, as often as you want! You can never have too much of God's Word!

Yet some people are famished in their spiritual lives because it's been so long since they've had any spiritual sustenance at all. Don't let this happen to you! If you don't have a copy of God's Word in a language that's easy for you to read and digest, then I'd encourage you to get one soon. There are also many websites that contain the entire Bible online for free. One that I often use is called "The Bible Gateway" at www.biblegateway.com. This website contains the entire Bible in over 100 versions and 50 languages.

I'd also encourage you to have a plan in mind for how you want to read the Bible, whether you start at the beginning and read the whole thing from cover to cover, or whether you pick a plan that includes selected readings from various books of the Bible. One website that has several plans for reading the Bible is called YouVersion at www.youversion.com. If you go to their home page, you'll find a variety of reading plans to fit your interest. You can print them off and check them yourself, or have the system highlight a passage or send it to you by email each day.

I've done many plans over the years, both online and on paper, and I've liked each of them for different reasons. My first time through the Bible, I just read it straight through in a year, reading 3 or 4 chapters a day, starting with Genesis and finishing with Revelation. At other times, I've alternated between reading something from the Old Testament and something from the new, plus a reading from the Psalms or Proverbs every day. And at other times, I've taken my time to read each passage as thoroughly as possible, taking three years to read through the entire Bible.

Currently, I'm going through a plan that my daughter tried last year and loved which takes you through the entire Bible in 90 days, called a B90X. Since it takes an average reader about 90 hours to read through the entire Bible, this plan gives you about an hours' worth of reading each day for 90 days. If you read half an hour a day, it'll take 6 months. If you read 15 minutes a day, it'll take a year. I'm actually doing this 90 day plan by *listening* to the Bible for an hour each day on my phone, using an app from the YouVersion website. While I'm not able to get through a full hour every day, I'm hopeful that at least I'll finish sometime this year–if I just keep going!

But whatever way you do it, just be sure to do it. Read God's Word over and over, and you'll find yourself transforming as you do.

Second, I want to encourage you to *memorize* God's Word.

Don't think that you can't memorize it, because you can! Here's a surprisingly easy way to memorize even whole chapters at a time. If you'll read the same passage of the Bible out loud every day for thirty days, you'll often find out that you've actually memorized it by the end of the month, if not before, without even *trying* to memorize it.

My wife has done this with our kids, for instance, reading Psalm 139 to them every day, sometimes once, or twice, or three times a day. Amazingly, the kids all knew the whole chapter word for word within just two weeks, and all they did was listen to it being read to them. And of course, my wife was able to pick it up at the same time, too.

You might also want to try writing out a verse or two on a small card and carrying it with you wherever you go. Then you can pull out the card whenever you're waiting in line, or taking a walk, or riding in a bus or train or car, reading it over and over until you've gotten it stored away in your mind. You'll be amazed at how God can speak to you through just one or two verses from the Bible even while you're memorizing it, and how it will come back to your mind at a later time, especially when you particularly need it. Some people try to memorize the chapter and verse numbers along with the passages so they can easily find them later, while other people just focus on the words themselves. Either way, the important thing is to "hide God's Word in your heart," as the Bible says:

"I have hidden Your word in my heart that I might not sin against you" (Psalm 119:11).

If you'd like a list of some great verses to memorize, I've posted a list on my website called "The Top 100 Verses in the Bible." This is a list that you can read, print out, or write on note cards for yourself. It's free, and you can get it from the link below: https://theranch.org/the-top-100-verses-in-the-bible/

So my second recommendation is to memorize the Bible, so you can recall it to your mind whenever it's needed.

Third, I want to encourage you to *study* God's Word.

While you can get so much from reading the Bible just as it's written, you can get even more out of it when you study it in-depth, whether on your own or in a group with others.

Even people mentioned in the Bible have found it useful to have others help explain to them what it means. When a man from Ethiopia was reading the book of Isaiah, Philip saw him and asked, "Do you understand what you are reading?" The man from Ethiopia replied:

"How can I, unless someone explains it to me?" (Acts 8:31).

So Philip stopped and explained the passage to the man. The man was so moved by what he learned, he put his faith in Christ on the spot and asked Philip to baptize him in some water nearby (see Acts chapter 8).

There's a reason we have pastors and teachers, authors and speakers. They've often spent a fair amount of time studying the Bible themselves, plumbing its depths and testing it out in the face of the reality of life. By learning from their wisdom, you'll be able to see some of the precious jewels they've already discovered, and you'll be better able to apply them to your life as well. Or, as Isaac Newton said:

"If I have seen further it is by standing on the shoulders of giants."

When you take the time to learn from others who have gone before you, you too can stand "on the shoulders of giants," seeing what they've seen and then going further yourself. I'd also recommend talking to others about what you're reading in the Bible. As God said to the Israelites when He gave them His commands:

"These commandments that I give you today are to be upon your hearts. Impress them on your children. Talk about them when you sit at home and when you walk along the road, when you lie down and when you get up. Tie them as symbols on your hands and bind them on your foreheads. Write them on the doorframes of your houses and on your gates" (Deuteronomy 6:6-8).

There's so much to learn from others that I hope you'll make use of the wealth of knowledge that is contained within the books and people around you. Spend some time at a local Christian bookstore, if you have one nearby, or browse for books that might be of interest on websites like www.christianbook.com. I've written several devotional books myself to encourage people in their Bible reading, several of which include study questions at the end of each chapter that you can use for personal reflection or small group discussion, like the questions I've included at end of this message today.

If you'd like any of my books to help you get more out of your Bible reading, you can get them anytime from www.inspiringbooks.com.

The Bible is so important to helping you understand life, which is why every one of my devotional messages contains at least one, and usually several, passages of scripture from the Bible. I know that the most important things I could ever tell you are already contained in the words of the Bible. The rest of what I have to say simply highlights or underscores what can already be found in God's Word.

In conclusion, I want to encourage you to *read* God's Word, *memorize* God's Word, and *study* God's Word.

When you do these things, you'll find that you'll be renewing your mind as you do, transforming your life and discovering God's will along the way. As the apostle Paul said:

"Do not conform any longer to the pattern of this world, but be transformed by the renewing of your mind. Then you will be able to test and approve what God's will is– His good, pleasing and perfect will" (Romans 12:2).

Will you pray with me?

Father, thank You for giving us Your Word, and for those who have preserved it and translated it and helped us to understand it throughout the generations. Help us to read Your

Word on a regular basis, to hide it in our heart when we can, and to study it on our own and with others so we can learn as much as possible. Lord, help us to renew our minds so we can transform our lives. In Jesus' name, Amen.

Questions for Reflection:

1) Read Romans 12:1-2. What are some ways that reading the Bible has helped you to renew your mind? And in what ways has renewing your mind helped in transforming your life?
2) Have you ever read the entire Bible from cover to cover? If so, how has that helped you in your life? If not, in what ways do you think it might help you? Are there any goals you have in mind for reading God's Word this year?
3) What advantage do you think there might be to memorizing verses or passages from the Bible, compared to just reading it? Would you like to try memorizing some more passages of Scripture again this year? Remember, here's a link to the Top 100 verses in the Bible if you'd like some ideas of where to start: https://theranch.org/the-top-100-verses-in-the-bible/
4) What value have you gotten from reading other books about the Bible? What value have you gotten from talking to others about the Bible? Are there any steps you'd like to take this year towards studying God's Word more in depth, whether on your own or with others?

LESSON 28: THINKING OF YOURSELF   AUGUST 30

Scripture Reading: Romans 12:3-8

The way you think of yourself is often affected by what others say about you. One of my favorite stories that shows the power of other people's words over us is a true story told by a woman named Eddie Ogan.

Eddie says that when she was young, the pastor at her church challenged everyone in the congregation to prepare for a special offering to be taken up at the end of the month for a poor family. Eddie, her two sisters and their mother were so excited about what they might do to help that they went home that night and came up with a plan: if they ate only potatoes, turned off the lights, didn't listen to the radio, got odd jobs and sold what they could, they might be able to save enough to help out with this special offering.

It turned out to be one of the best months of their lives. By the time the month was over, they donated all the money they had save to the special offering: $70 in all, made up of three crisp twenties and a ten. They felt rich.

Later that afternoon, the pastor of the church stopped by their house for a visit. He left an envelope with their mother. Their hearts sank as they went back in and opened it. Out fell three crisp twenties, a ten, and seventeen one dollar bills. Suddenly they realized that *they* were the poor family in the church. They had never thought of themselves as poor before, but at that moment, they felt they were and they felt that everyone else must see them that way, too.

The next week, they didn't want to go back to church again, but their mother made them. A missionary was speaking about needing $100 to put a roof on a church building in another country. The pastor asked his congregation if they could take up an offering to help these poor people. Eddie and her family smiled for the first time in a week. They put the contents of their envelope back into the offering. When the money was counted, it was just over $100. The missionary was surprised and said that the church must have some rich people in it to take up such an offering!

When Eddie and her family realized they had put in $87 of that offering, they realized that *they* were the rich family in the church! "Hadn't the missionary said so?"

Eddie says that from that day on, she's never been poor again.

The way you look at yourself can often be shaped by what others say about you… whether for good or bad. But God wants you to look at yourself for who you truly are: a child of His, created to fulfill His purposes here on earth. He doesn't want you to think of yourself any higher, or any lower, than you really are. Pride can ensnare you, but low self-esteem can also keep you from reaching your fullest potential.

How can you think of yourself properly? The apostle Paul gives us some perspective in his letter to the Romans. In chapter 12, Paul says:

> *"For by the grace given me I say to every one of you: Do not think of yourself more highly than you ought, but rather think of yourself with sober judgment, in accordance with the measure of faith God has given you. Just as each of us has one body with many members, and these members do not all have the same function, so in Christ we who are many form one body, and each member belongs to all the others. We have different gifts, according to the grace given us. If a man's gift is prophesying, let him use it in proportion to his faith. If it is serving, let him serve; if it is teaching, let him teach; if it is encouraging, let him encourage; if it is contributing to the needs of others, let him give generously; if it is leadership, let him govern diligently; if it is showing mercy, let him do it cheerfully"* (Romans 12:3-8).

When you realize that God has created you for a specific purpose, you can better see how you fit into the scheme of things here on earth. Albert Einstein is quoted as saying:

> *"Everybody is a genius. But if you judge a fish by its ability to climb a tree, it will live its whole life believing that it is stupid."*

God doesn't compare you to those around you. He compares you to the potential that He has put within you. And that potential is often defined by how you act, or don't act, "in accordance with the measure of faith God has given you."

If God has created you to prophesy, then prophesy in proportion to your faith. If God has created you to serve, then serve in accordance with the amount of faith God has given you. If teaching, teach, if encouraging, encourage, if giving, give generously, if leading, govern diligently, if showing mercy, show it cheerfully.

By living your life in this way, it releases you from the trap of comparing yourself with others and from the pitfalls of both pride and low self-esteem.

But living this way is easier said than done.

I recently finished reading a series of books called *The Hunger Games*. It's a gripping story about a post-war America, in which the leaders of the country pit children against one another in a fight to the death for the entertainment of the rest of the country. As these gruesome games go on year after year, one girl stands up to the games and finds herself at the center of a revolution.

But throughout the book, this one girl, Katniss Everdeen, thinks she's not the right person for the job. She doesn't want to be the face of the revolution. She doesn't see how she could possibly lead the charge. Yet everything about her screams out to those around her that she's exactly the person who can spearhead this effort to make things right again.

At one point in the story, she struggles with a decision about a particular strategy they're considering, so she asks a friend what he thinks. He says:

> "I think... you still have no idea. The effect you can have."

When I read that line, I was considering fasting and praying about some situations in my own life and the lives of some people close to me. But I was wondering if it would make any difference anyway. Just then, I felt God speaking to me and saying, "Eric, I think *you* still have no idea, either, the effect you can have."

God was right. I had no idea. But I was willing to give it a try. I stepped up in faith, began fasting and praying, and over the next few days watched as God unfolded the answers to those prayers.

I felt like Katniss Everdeen, the girl who had no idea the effect she had on those around her, yet who sparked a revolution to change the course of history. I felt no pride, and I felt no lack of self-esteem. I felt like I was simply acting "in accordance with the measure of faith God had given me."

Sometimes we're unable to see ourselves for who we really are, and it takes others to point it out to us. But we have to be careful whose judgments we take into account. As Eddie Ogan found out, had she chosen to believe the words of the person who said her family was poor, she might have felt poor her whole life. But she chose to believe the words of the man who said she was rich instead. Either statement could have been true, depending on how she looked at it. In the end, she chose to believe what *God* said about her: that her family had acted in faith to help someone else in need, and in doing so, were considered rich.

Sometimes we have to let the words of others sink deep into our hearts so that we believe them. Other times, we have to do as Solomon said in the book of Ecclesiastes and let them just pass on by:

> "Do not pay attention to every word people say, or you may hear your servant cursing you—for you know in your heart that many times you yourself have cursed others" (Ecclesiastes 7:21-22).

Not every word someone says about you is true, nor is it the whole truth. Only God has that perspective. Don't think you're stupid if you can't climb a tree if God has created you to swim!

Renew your mind today in the way you think of yourself. Take what others say with a grain of salt, then take it to God for His perspective. Let God tell you exactly what He thinks of you, without getting puffed up and without getting down on yourself, but with sober judgment. Then do what God has created you to do, "in accordance with the measure of faith that He has given you."

Who knows? Perhaps you're like Katniss Everdeen, too. You have no idea...the effect you can have.

Will you pray with me?

Father, thank You for giving us a purpose for our lives and thank You for giving us gifts to carry out that purpose. Help us to put the gifts You've given us to use this week to a degree that we may have never used them before—according to the measure of faith that You've given us. In Jesus' name, Amen.

Questions for Reflection:

1) Read Romans 12:3-8. How have words spoken to you through others either boosted you up or pulled you down? Take those words to God and ask Him to give you His perspective on them.
2) Looking through this short list of gifts in the book of Romans, are there any that stand out that you feel God might have given to you? Is there a way you could step out in faith and use one or two of those gifts in your life this week, this month, or this year?
3) Paul lists some specific adjectives to describe how we are to use our gifts: generously, diligently, and cheerfully. If you were to use those words to measure how well you're doing in using your gifts, how are you doing?
4) How could changing the way you think about your gifts change your approach to using them?

LESSON 29: THINKING OF OTHERS   AUGUST 31

Scripture Reading: Romans 12:9-21

The story's told of two friends who were walking through a desert together when one of the friends slapped the other in the face. The one who was slapped wrote a note in the sand saying:

"Today my best friend slapped me in the face."

But as they walked further along, the one who had been slapped fell into a pool of water and began to drown. This time, his best friend reached down and pulled him out of the water, saving his life. This time, the friend who was rescued etched a note on a stone saying:

"Today my best friend saved my life."

When asked why he wrote one note in the sand and the other note in stone, the one who had written both phrases replied:

"When someone hurts us, we should write it down in sand, where the winds of forgiveness can erase it away. But when someone does something good for us, we must engrave it in stone, where no wind can ever erase it."

Too often, we get this backwards: we write people's offenses in stone rather than sand, perhaps because they've hurt us so much, or perhaps to protect ourselves from being hurt again. Then we write the good deeds that people have done for us in sand, forgetting over time just how significant those good deeds have been in our lives.

But according to the Bible, true love keeps no record of people's offenses at all. As Paul said to the Corinthians:

"Love... keeps no record of wrongs" (1 Corinthians 13:5b).

In the last lesson, we looked at the importance of thinking of ourselves properly, without falling into the traps of either pride or low self-esteem. In this lesson, we're looking at the importance of thinking of others properly, without falling into the traps of either conceit or comparison.

When Paul wrote about love to the Romans, he wrote a simple yet profound statement:

> *"Love must be sincere"* (Romans 12:9a).

While this may seem obvious–that if we love someone, we should love them *sincerely*–it's not so easy to do. For some people, it's easy to fake love.

I know a man who seemed like he was a friend to everyone, describing himself as having "great people skills." Yet in private conversations with him, I discovered that he viewed others with various degrees of disdain, resentment and frustration, often thinking of himself as better than those around him. The love he showed to others was based on keeping up his image in public more so than having true esteem for those around him.

His attempts at love were just a shallow imitation of what real love looks like. Real love is sincere. In Latin, the word "sincere" literally means "without wax," (*sine* meaning without, and *cera* meaning wax). Apparently, if a craftsman carved a statue in stone and accidentally nicked or chipped the carving along the way, he would fill in those spots with wax. On the surface, the statue would look pure and faultless. But after a while in the hot sun, the wax would melt, and the truth would be known: that which appeared pure and faultless at first was in fact quite flawed.

When Paul said that love must be sincere, or "without wax," he was saying that love shouldn't be just for show, but for real.

In the past, I used to think that the word "Sincerely" was just a formal way of signing off on a business letter, as I learned in business school back in college. But in recent years, and knowing the meaning of the word "Sincerely," I find myself using it more and more often.

When I write a note from the depths of my heart, I sign it, "Sincerely, Eric Elder." To me, it's no longer just a formal closing, but a heartfelt statement saying, "I really mean this from the depths of my heart." It's much closer to meaning "Love, Eric Elder" than I ever would have thought. And that's just what Paul said: Love must be sincere.

I find that it's helpful for me to check how sincere I am in my love for others by substituting the words "true affection" for "love." I might be able to say that I love someone, but when I ask myself if I have *true affection* for them, then the flaws in my love for them are revealed.

When this happens, I have to regroup my thinking and try to see them as God sees them: as beloved children of His who have been created for specific plans and purposes here on earth. When I change my thinking, it changes how I view others, and subsequently how I love and interact with them. It doesn't always happen in an instant, but I recognize it much quicker now when I do the "true affection" test!

In Romans 12:9-21, Paul includes more than a dozen statements about what real love looks like when it's sincere. Here are a few of those statements:

- *Be devoted to one another in brotherly love.*
- *Honor one another above yourselves.*
- *Share with God's people who are in need.*
- *Practice hospitality.*

- *Bless those who persecute you; bless and do not curse.*
- *Rejoice with those who rejoice; mourn with those who mourn.*
- *Live in harmony with one another.*
- *Do not be proud, but be willing to associate with people of low position.*
- *Do not be conceited.*
- *Do not repay anyone evil for evil.*
- *Be careful to do what is right in the eyes of everybody.*
- *If it is possible, as far as it depends on you, live at peace with everyone.*
- *Do not take revenge, my friends, but leave room for God's wrath*
- *Do not be overcome by evil, but overcome evil with good.*

If you reframe each of these thoughts as a question, you'll get some good ideas for what you might do this week, this month, or this year to show more love to those around you. For instance:

- *What can you do to show your devotion to another brother or sister in Christ?*
- *What can you do to honor someone else above yourself?*
- *What can you do to share with other Christians who are in need?*
- *What can you do to practice hospitality towards someone you know?*
- *What can you do to bless someone who is persecuting you?*
- *What can you do to rejoice with someone as they rejoice, or to mourn with someone as they mourn?*
- *What can you do to live in harmony with others, rather than provoking continual discord?*
- *What can you do to be humble instead of proud, and to associate with people of low position?*
- *What can you do to avoid being conceited?*
- *What can you do to refrain from repaying anyone evil for evil?*
- *What can you do to do what is right in the eyes of everybody?*
- *What can you do to live at peace with everyone, as far as it depends on you?*
- *What can you do to not take revenge on someone else, but leave room for God's wrath?*
- *What can you do to avoid being overcome by evil, but to overcome evil with good?*

I know that I want to keep my love for others sincere, without wax, as pure and flawless as possible. I want to have true affection for others, whether they're close friends and family or just casual acquaintances or strangers or even enemies.

I want to think of others as God thinks of them: as children of His, created by Him for specific plans and purposes here on earth.

I don't want to be the kind of person who etches in stone those things that others have done wrong. I don't even want to write them in the sand. I want to be able to keep *no* record of wrongs, recalling instead only the good that others have done for me in my life.

But I know that to do all of this it will take more than what I can do on my own. It will take the love of Christ, living in me and working through me, to think of others the way God wants me to think of them. If you want that, too, I hope you'll pray with me today. Pray that

God will help you to love others in ways you could never have done on your own. With His help, you'll be able to express love to others as the apostle Paul encouraged the Romans to do, saying:

"Love must be sincere."

Will you pray with me?

Father, thank You for loving each one of us and giving each one of us a purpose and a plan for our lives. Help us to think of others in the same way that You think of them. And help us to treat them with the love and honor that is due them. In Jesus' name, Amen.

Questions for Reflection:

1) Read Romans 12:9-21. What would it look like for someone to be devoted to someone else in brotherly love?
2) How can you honor one another above yourself, truly honoring them for who they are and who God created them to be?
3) What are some ways you could "share with God's people who are in need," or "practice hospitality" towards those around you? How can doing these things express your love in ways that words alone may not express?
4) What are some reasons God wouldn't want you to take revenge on someone, but to leave it in His hands instead? What are some ways you can bless your enemies or those who may be persecuting you, and what might be the result when you do?

LESSON 30: DOING WHAT'S RIGHT — SEPTEMBER 1

Scripture Reading: Romans 13:1-7

As we continue to look at ways to renew your mind, I'd like to look with you today at the way you view those in authority over you, whether they're a boss, a parent, or even a government authority. If you view authority with contempt, distrust, and disrespect, you'll often find that same contempt, distrust and disrespect coming back to you. But if you view authority with God's perspective, trusting that even ungodly authorities can have a place in God's plan in the world, then you can have much more peace of mind in the midst of struggles.

I remember working for a boss for whom I didn't have much respect. He often asked me to do things that seemed pointless. We were friendly towards each other, but neither of us had much trust or respect for the other.

One day he asked me to fill out a survey that the company said was to be voluntary and anonymous. But my boss required that everyone that worked for him had to fill it out, and because I was working out of town at the time, I was going to have to fax my survey to him, making it obvious that it came from me. When he said I had to fill out the survey, I reminded him that it was supposed to be voluntary and anonymous. Still, he said he expected to see my survey on his desk by the next morning. I was furious. While it may not have seemed like a big deal to him—asking me to fill out what he thought was a harmless survey—I was afraid if I gave my honest responses, it could jeopardize my future standing in the company. And if I didn't answer honestly, I was afraid I would be compromising my own standards of integrity. So I decided I was just going to refuse to turn it in.

But as the day went on, God began to work on my heart, bringing to my mind the biblical view of authority.

The apostle Paul wrote about this view to the Christians living in Rome. And from what I know about the way the Romans treated Christians at the time, I'm sure the Roman Christians had way more problems with their bosses than being asked to fill out inane surveys! They obviously had it much worse than me, and yet here's what Paul said to them:

> "Everyone must submit himself to the governing authorities, for there is no authority except that which God has established. The authorities that exist have been established by God. Consequently, he who rebels against the authority is rebelling against what God has instituted, and those who do so will bring judgment on themselves. For rulers hold no terror for those who do right, but for those who do wrong. Do you want to be free from fear of the one in authority? Then do what is right and he will commend you. For he is God's servant to do you good. But if you do wrong, be afraid, for he does not bear the sword for nothing. He is God's servant, an agent of wrath to bring punishment on the wrongdoer. Therefore, it is necessary to submit to the authorities, not only because of possible punishment but also because of conscience. This is also why you pay taxes, for the authorities are God's servants, who give their full time to governing. Give everyone what you owe him: If you owe taxes, pay taxes; if revenue, then revenue; if respect, then respect; if honor, then honor" (Romans 13:1-7).

Paul encouraged the Roman Christians to "do what's right." He knew that if Christians could respect those in authority over them, the benefits would abound all around, both to those they serve and to themselves.

Any parent knows that when a child is obedient and respectful, that child can often ask for most anything and the parent is happy to oblige. Yet when a child is disobedient and disrespectful, the parent is often unwilling to give in to any type of request, for fear that the child might abuse whatever is given to them. When a child shows respect and honor to a parent, that same respect and honor often returns back to them.

Going back to my earlier story with my own boss, I remember finally coming to the conclusion that it was more important to respect and honor my boss—even though I disagreed with him—because God had called me to respect and honor those in authority over me. My boss wasn't asking me to do anything immoral or illegal. I just disagreed with his approach. After expressing my disagreement, and his insistence that he still wanted me to do it, then I knew what I had to do.

I filled out the survey as honestly as I could and faxed it to him by the next morning. My heart felt at peace. I knew I had done what was right, even if it might cost me something down the road. To my amazement, my relationship with my boss changed starting that very day. I don't know if it was something that changed within me, or something that changed within him—or a combination of the two—but over the next few months, he became my biggest supporter and my strongest advocate for every project I took on. He knew he could count on me to do what he asked me to do and because of this trust, he gave me greater leeway in how I carried out my projects than he had ever given me before.

Like a horse that was finally broken, I felt I could now be useful to him in all kinds of ways.

This doesn't mean that those in authority over us are always right, just as any parent knows full well! Any parent can and will make mistakes–and the same goes for bosses and governments. But just because those in authority over us don't always do the right thing doesn't mean that we can't do the right thing. As Paul said, "he who rebels against the authority is rebelling against what God has instituted, and those who do so will bring judgment on themselves."

Even men in the Bible like Joseph, Nehemiah and Daniel found ways to serve those in authority over them even though the people over them were often ungodly and did the *wrong* things.

Joseph was sold as a slave in Egypt, yet he still treated his masters with respect and honor, doing what was right and earning a place of respect and honor in their households, their prisons, and eventually in service to the king himself, being placed second in command over all the land.

Nehemiah was captured and put into the service of an ungodly king, yet he became the king's cupbearer, a trusted position to ensure that no one poisoned the king's wine. When Nehemiah needed some time and money to go rebuild the walls around Jerusalem, the king honored his request, because Nehemiah had honored the king. Daniel was taken as a slave to Babylon, yet he served the king with integrity in his heart and his attitude, earning the king's respect and becoming one of his top officials.

I'm sure each of these men wanted to rebel against the authorities God had put over them at many points in their lives. And on some occasions, they did have to disobey the ungodly and immoral commands of those in authority over them, rightly claiming that God had a higher authority in those particular instances.

When Potiphar's wife asked Joseph to go to bed with her, Joseph refused. When Nebuchadnezzar's officials asked Daniel and his friends to bow down and worship the king, they refused. In both cases, Joseph and Daniel paid a significant price for their insubordination, but they were willing to do so because they realized that in some cases, it was more important to submit to the authority of God than the authority of men. So there seem to be times when submitting to God's authority trumps submitting to earthly authorities. But those times are much fewer than most of us might like to admit!

The principle remains: when we submit to those in authority over us, whether it's our authorities on earth, or our Authority in heaven, we'll have peace of mind, because we'll know we've done what's right.

If you're wrestling in your mind with something that someone in authority has asked you to do, bring it to God. Ask Him to help you to know what to do, then do it. You'll avoid punishment and your mind will be clear. As Paul concluded:

> "...submit to the authorities, not only because of possible punishment but also because of conscience. Give everyone what you owe him: If you owe taxes, pay taxes; if revenue, then revenue; if respect, then respect; if honor, then honor" (Romans 13:4b-7).

Will you pray with me?

Father, thank You for reminding us of the importance of submitting to those in authority over us. Lord, give us Your wisdom as we weigh how to do that to the best of our ability, not only to avoid punishment, but because of conscience. Help us to renew our minds in the way we think about those in authority over us, changing our hearts and minds and even our relationships with others as we do. In Jesus' name, Amen.

Questions for Reflection:

1) Read Romans 13:1-7. Why do you think Paul wanted the Christians in Rome to respect those in authority over them? What possible benefits could result from this type of submission?
2) In what areas of your life could you benefit from putting Paul's words into action?
3) How could changing the way you view those in authority over you bring you more peace of mind?
4) How could changing the way you interact with those in authority over you bring about a change in your relationships with them?

LESSON 31: THINKING ABOUT SINFUL DESIRES　　　　　　SEPTEMBER 2

Scripture Reading: Romans 13:8-14

My kids and I were window shopping in downtown Chicago last week. We were looking at all the cool things in the Apple store on Michigan Avenue when my wife came up after finishing a doctor's appointment. She said she had seen a man outside in a wheelchair who was asking for money. He didn't look like he was doing very good at all.

She didn't have much to give him, but she gave him what she had: a little pocket change and a prayer. When she asked if she could pray for him, he said:

> "Yes! Pray that God will give me a girl. I think about making love (he used another word for it) with a girl all day long and I can't get the thoughts out of my mind. I'm just so lonely and I can't stop thinking about making love with someone."

After getting her thoughts back together—and refraining from trying to immediately cast something evil out of him—she began to pray for him, asking God to give him what he needed, even if it wasn't the thing that he was asking for.

When my wife told me about it later, it reminded me of the verse that we're looking at today in the book of Romans. The verse says:

> "… do not think about how to gratify the desires of the sinful nature" (Romans 13:14b).

Paul knew that even just thinking about gratifying the desires of the sinful nature could lead to doing them eventually. As the apostle James said in his book:

> "… but each one is tempted when, by his own evil desire, he is dragged away and enticed. Then, after desire has conceived, it gives birth to sin; and sin, when it is full-grown, gives birth to death" (James 1:14-15).

Just as good thoughts can lead to good actions, sinful thoughts can lead to sinful actions. And sinful actions, when pursued in full, can lead to all kinds of destruction, even death.

It doesn't take much imagination to think about what could happen if this man in his wheelchair *did* get a girl and *was* able to do with her whatever he wanted. But if we're honest with ourselves, the thoughts he expressed may not be so far removed from the thoughts any one of us have from time to time. And if we don't keep them in check, all kinds of terrible things could happen if we were to follow-up on our thoughts as well.

I was talking to another man this week who said he was having similar thoughts–although he used more palatable words. He said he was just standing there admiring the beautiful curves of a particular woman he had seen when he suddenly realized what he was doing. Before he let those thoughts overtake him, he reminded himself that he had died to his old sinful nature when he was baptized into Christ. He was lonely, too, just like the man in the wheelchair, and he longed for a lifetime companion. But he also knew he couldn't gratify the desires of his sinful nature in the way that he was imagining. So he took control of his thoughts, brought them back under the authority of Christ, and was able to walk away with a victory in his mind instead of a defeat. What a blessing that was for him and for others who were spared from the destruction that could have ensued.

What my friend was doing was "putting aside the deeds of darkness and putting on the armor of light" as Paul described in the rest of his thoughts to the Romans. Paul said:

> "So let us put aside the deeds of darkness and put on the armor of light. Let us behave decently, as in the daytime, not in orgies and drunkenness, not in sexual immorality and debauchery, not in dissension and jealousy. Rather, clothe yourselves with the Lord Jesus Christ, and do not think about how to gratify the desires of the sinful nature" (Romans 13:12b-14).

It really is possible to take control of your thoughts. When you do, you'll be blessed and so will those around you.

If you look back even further in this passage, you'll see why Paul was so passionate about helping others get control over their thoughts:

> "And do this, understanding the present time. The hour has come for you to wake up from your slumber, because our salvation is nearer now than when we first believed. The night is nearly over; the day is almost here" (Romans 13:11-12a).

Paul wants us to wake up from our slumber, because our salvation is nearer now than when we first believed. For years, people have been saying that Jesus is coming soon, just as Jesus said Himself almost 2,000 years ago. The truth is, His coming is closer now that it's ever been! As Paul said, "The night is nearly over; the day is almost here!" What a great thought and what a great motivator to do what's right!

Don't let the darkness overtake you. Don't give in to dwelling on thoughts that could lead to your destruction. Don't be fooled into thinking that Jesus *isn't* coming back soon, because He is. As Jesus said to the apostle John:

> "Yes, I am coming soon" (Revelation 22:20).

Jesus wants you to live your life to the fullest and the best way to do that is to live your life in the light. This isn't to say that it's easy to overcome temptation. But it is possible, and more than that, God will help you to do it. As Paul said in his letter to the Corinthians:

> "No temptation has seized you except what is common to man. And God is faithful; He will not let you be tempted beyond what you can bear. But when you are

tempted, He will also provide a way out so that you can stand up under it" (1 Corinthians 10:13).

You may have tried various ways to overcome temptation. But Paul mentions something in this passage that we're looking at today that may give you some extra help as you try to break free. If you look back just a little farther still, you'll see that Paul says instead of focusing on our sinful desires, we should focus on how we can express God's love to others:

"Let no debt remain outstanding, except the continuing debt to love one another, for he who loves his fellowman has fulfilled the law. The commandments, 'Do not commit adultery,' 'Do not murder,' 'Do not steal,' 'Do not covet,' and whatever other commandment there may be, are summed up in this one rule: 'Love your neighbor as yourself.' Love does no harm to its neighbor. Therefore love is the fulfillment of the law" (Romans 13:8-10).

There's a big difference between lust and love. Lust, at its core, is all about selfishness and doing whatever you want to others. Love, at its core, is all about selflessness, and doing for others what you would want them to do for you. Instead of thinking about how you can gratify your own sinful desires, Paul says you're to put on the armor of light and think about how you can express God's love to others.

I've shared before about my aunt who got some great advice from her doctor when she was going through some days filled with dark depression: he suggested that instead of thinking about herself, she try to think about ways she could help other people. By focusing on blessing others instead of wallowing in her own thoughts of despair, she was able to pull herself out of the darkness by focusing on others. She began to bake food for friends, bringing them cakes, cookies, pies, or anything she thought they might enjoy. She was able to get out of the pit she was in and, to this day, she continues to bless those around her, now from a place of victory rather than defeat.

The same can happen for those who struggle with sinful desires, which can bring about the same kind of darkness. When tempted to dwell on thoughts that are potentially destructive to yourself or to those around you, you can take those thoughts captive and replace them with other thoughts. Reach out and put on God's armor of light and let the light of Christ shine through you instead. Replace your selfish thoughts with selfless thoughts, and you'll begin to see God turnaround situations that you may have thought were hopeless.

Take a meal to a friend. Write a letter to someone who needs encouragement. Put a check in the mail to someone who could use a financial boost. Call a parent or an aunt or an uncle or a brother or a cousin or a friend you may not have seen or talked to in a long time. It may seem like hard work at first, but soon you'll find that the darkness is fleeing, and the light of Christ is flooding into your soul.

Clothe yourself with Christ today. Let His light shine through you. Let Him use your hands and your feet, your words and your actions, to those around you who could use a touch from Him. Let your mind wander about ways you can love your neighbor as yourself, instead of ways that you can gratify the desires of your sinful nature. If you need some extra encouragement, just remember the words of Paul, who said:

"And do this, understanding the present time. The hour has come for you to wake up from your slumber, because our salvation is nearer now that when we first believed."

Will you pray with me?

Father, thank You for promising that You will come for us soon. Help us to keep that at the forefront of our minds as we consider how to bless those around us instead of how to gratify our own sinful desires. Help us to take our eyes off ourselves and to focus on those things that You want us to do in the world. In Jesus' name, Amen.

Questions for Reflection:

1) Read Romans 13:8-14. Why does Paul say we should let no debt remain outstanding except the continuing debt to love one another?
2) How can loving others help us to overcome sinful thoughts and actions in our lives?
3) What are some practical ways that you could show your love to others, instead of dwelling on how you could gratify the desires of your sinful nature?
4) What are some other ways that you might "clothe yourselves with the Lord Jesus Christ"?

LESSON 32: BEING FULLY CONVICTED IN YOUR OWN MIND   SEPTEMBER 3

Scripture Reading: Romans 14:1-15:13

It's amazing how different people can see things so differently, even when looking at the exact same thing. I recently heard about a Brit, a Frenchman, and a Russian who all looked at the same painting of Adam and Eve frolicking in the Garden of Eden, but came to three different conclusions:

"Look at their reserve, their calm," said the Brit. "They must be British."
"Nonsense," said the Frenchman. "They're naked, and so beautiful. Clearly, they are French."
"Look at them," said the Russian. "They have no clothes, no shelter, and only an apple to eat. Yet they're being told this is paradise. They must be Russian!"

The same thing can happen to each of us as Christians. We can all look at the same exact passage of Scripture, yet come to vastly different conclusions. How can we live in unity with each other, even in the midst of our differences? Here are a few ideas that the Apostle Paul gave the Romans, and which we can apply to our lives today:

"Accept him whose faith is weak, without passing judgment on disputable matters. One man's faith allows him to eat everything, but another man, whose faith is weak, eats only vegetables. The man who eats everything must not look down on him who does not, and the man who does not eat everything must not condemn the man who does, for God has accepted him. Who are you to judge someone else's servant? To his own master he stands or falls. And he will stand, for the Lord is able to make him stand.

"One man considers one day more sacred than another; another man considers every day alike. Each one should be fully convinced in his own mind. He who regards one day as special, does so to the Lord. He who eats meat, eats to the Lord, for he gives thanks to God; and he who abstains, does so to the Lord and gives thanks to God.

For none of us lives to himself alone and none of us dies to himself alone. If we live, we live to the Lord; and if we die, we die to the Lord. So, whether we live or die, we belong to the Lord...

"Therefore let us stop passing judgment on one another. Instead, make up your mind not to put any stumbling block or obstacle in your brother's way. As one who is in the Lord Jesus, I am fully convinced that no food is unclean in itself. But if anyone regards something as unclean, then for him it is unclean. If your brother is distressed because of what you eat, you are no longer acting in love. Do not by your eating destroy your brother for whom Christ died...

"Let us therefore make every effort to do what leads to peace and to mutual edification. Do not destroy the work of God for the sake of food. All food is clean, but it is wrong for a man to eat anything that causes someone else to stumble. It is better not to eat meat or drink wine or to do anything else that will cause your brother to fall...

"Accept one another, then, just as Christ accepted you, in order to bring praise to God" (Romans 14:1-8,13-15,19-21,15:7).

I love reading these verses because they remind me that I don't have the ultimate answer to every question regarding the Bible. I've come to many conclusions over the years and I feel fully convinced in my own mind that those conclusions are right. Yet I'm reminded by these verses that there are some things that are even more important than being "right." Like being loving, caring, considerate and pleasing to God and to others.

In his autobiography, Benjamin Franklin said that he was incredibly tactless in his youth, arguing with others to the point where no one wanted to talk to him anymore. Yet he eventually became known as one of the most diplomatic men who ever lived, even becoming the American Ambassador to France.

What changed? Franklin said it was something an old Quaker friend said to him when he was young. Dale Carnegie, in his book *How to Win Friends and Influence People*, paraphrased what Ben's Quaker friend said that day, saying it went something like this:

"Ben, you are impossible. Your opinions have a slap in them for everyone who differs with you. They have become so offensive that nobody cares for them. Your friends find they enjoy themselves better when you are not around. You know so much that no man can tell you anything. Indeed, no man is going to try, for the effort would lead only to discomfort and hard work. So you are not likely ever to know any more than you do now, which is very little."

Benjamin Franklin took these words to heart and decided to make a change in his life. As Franklin says in his own autobiography:

"I made it a rule to forbear all direct contradiction to the sentiment of others, and all positive assertion of my own, I even forbade myself the use of every word or expression in the language that imported a fix'd opinion, such as 'certainly,' 'undoubtedly,' etc., and I adopted, instead of them, 'I conceive,' 'I apprehend,' or 'I imagine' a thing to be so or so, or 'it so appears to me at present.' When another asserted something that I thought an error, I deny'd myself the pleasure of contradicting him abruptly, and of showing immediately some absurdity in his proposition: and in answering I began by observing that in certain cases or circumstances, his opinion would be right, but in the present case there appear'd or seem'd to me some difference, etc. I soon

found the advantage of this change in my manner; the conversations I engag'd in went on more pleasantly. The modest way in which I propos'd my opinions procur'd them a readier reception and less contradiction; I had less mortification when I was found to be in the wrong, and I more easily prevaile'd with others to give up their mistakes and join with me when I happened to be right.

"And in this mode, which I at first put on with some violence to natural inclination, became at length so easy, and so habitual to me, that perhaps for these fifty years past no one has ever heard a dogmatical expression escape me. And to this habit (after my character of integrity) I think it principally owing that I had earned so much weight with my fellow citizens when I proposed new institutions, or alterations in the old, and so much influence in public councils when I became a member; for I was but a bad speaker, never eloquent, subject to much hesitation in my choice of words, hardly correct in language, and yet I generally carried my points."

Benjamin Franklin realized that there were more important things than being right. And by giving deference to the ideas and opinions of others, he *did* win more friends and influence more people.

We as Christians can do the same. It's important to discover your convictions and hold onto them strongly. But there's a difference between holding strongly to your convictions at the expense of others and holding strongly to your convictions for the sake of others. One strives to be right no matter what, the other strives to build others up no matter what. Which are you trying to do?

I know for me, I still have a long way to go in how I present my beliefs to others and how I listen to others when they share their beliefs with me. In the end, I want the love of Christ to prevail.

It's good to be fully convinced about what you believe. Yet it's also good to give God enough leeway to allow Him to speak into other people's lives, just as He's spoken into yours.

As you work on renewing your mind this week, remember that God is working on the minds of others as well. Give them the grace they need to let God do His work in their lives, just as He's given you the grace you need as He works in yours. As Paul concluded:

"Accept one another, then, just as Christ accepted you, in order to bring praise to God."

Will you pray with me?

Father, thank You for speaking to us and giving us clear direction for our lives. Help us to remember that You are speaking to others and giving them clear directions for their lives, too. Help us to be mindful of the ideas and opinions of others, allowing for the possibility that they may just be right. In the end, help us to accept one another, just as You have accepted us, in order to bring praise to You. In Jesus' name, Amen.

Questions for Reflection:

1) Read Romans 14:1-15:13. Why does Paul say we should not condemn others for what they're doing, when they're doing it in accordance with the measure of their faith?

2) What are some of the benefits that could come from fully convinced of something in your own mind?
3) What are some of the negatives that could result from imposing those beliefs on others, even though you may be fully convinced of them yourself?
4) What motivation does Paul give us in Romans 15:7 for why we should "accept one another"?

LESSON 33: OVERFLOWING WITH HOPE — SEPTEMBER 4

Scripture Reading: Romans 15:13

I'd like to pray for you today that the God of hope would fill you with joy and peace so that you may overflow with hope. This is what the apostle Paul prayed for the Christians in Rome, as recorded in the book of Romans, chapter 15:

> "May the God of hope fill you with all joy and peace as you trust in Him, so that you may overflow with hope by the power of the Holy Spirit" (Romans 15:13).

What a prayer! Paul wanted them to be so filled with joy and peace that they *overflowed* with hope! If there's any day on the calendar that could give you hope, it would be Easter Sunday, Resurrection Day, the day that Jesus overcame death itself. Because Jesus died and rose again, we who have faith in Him can know that when we die, we'll rise again as well. This is what I love about Christianity: even in the face of death, there's always hope!

My wife Lana was filling up a glass for one of the kids this week, but she filled it up too far and the glass overflowed and ran all over the table! That's the kind of hope that God wants to fill you with, too. He doesn't just want to give you a *drop* of hope, or a glass that's *half-full* of hope, or a glass that's even *full* of hope. God wants to give you a glass that *overflows* with hope!

If you remember back in Lesson 10 of this study, you might remember that I wrote about a picture my daughter had given me. The picture showed a hand reflected in the side view mirror of a car. The word "HOPE" was written on the palm of the hand. Below the word "HOPE" were the words on the mirror that said:

"OBJECTS IN MIRROR ARE CLOSER THAN THEY APPEAR."

You might also remember that this picture filled me with hope at the time because Lana had just been praying for another car. Ours was on its last legs and we had to get a new one. But the car she was praying for was twice what we could afford. So I told her that night that I'd pray for the car she wanted, and added, "The same God who takes care of me will take care of you!" It was my way of saying, "Sorry, I can't help you on this one. God's going to have to do it Himself!"

The very next morning, as I drove into a parking lot to go to a men's meeting, a man pulled in right behind me driving the very car that Lana had been praying for! I'd never seen this man or his car ever before!

When I got out of my car, I introduced myself and casually asked if he ever thought about selling his car. He said he had just been thinking about it! He said I could take a look at the car, so I sat down inside it and looked out the window. That's when I saw the side view mirror with the reflection of the car in it, and these words in the mirror:

"OBJECTS IN MIRROR ARE CLOSER THAN THEY APPEAR."

I couldn't believe it. I took a picture of the mirror with my phone and confessed my unbelief to God, reminding myself that God could do anything, absolutely anything.

Over the next few months, I checked back with the man several times about the car. He wasn't quite ready to sell, and I wasn't quite ready to buy. But I kept the picture on the background screen of my phone from the day I first saw that car, as a reminder to myself that with God, there's always hope.

As the months went on, I began to give up on the idea of ever getting the car for Lana. The picture on my phone began to be more discouraging than encouraging, so I changed the background picture on my phone to something else. But a few days later, I decided to put the picture of the car back on my phone. I needed the reminder that with God, there's always hope.

Then one day, a few weeks ago, we got a tax refund in the mail. I had already decided that I would put the money towards a new car, and even though it wasn't enough to get Lana the car she was praying for, I was glad to finally be going shopping for *any* car, as we had been borrowing cars from others and even renting them at times to get where we needed to go.

As I shopped around, I was disappointed in the cars I saw. I tried to think of any way I could get Lana the car she had been praying for. With a bit of desperation, I called a friend to see if she had any ideas, because she had recently bought a car similar to the one Lana wanted. It turned out that she happened to be at the car dealership where they sold this type of car, a place she had only been to once before! She looked around the lot and found a car that was exactly what we wanted. Not only was it the perfect car, it was the perfect price, too!

I drove home, picked up Lana and drove a couple hours to the car dealership to see the car. By the end of the day, Lana was driving home in the car that just a few months earlier, I thought we'd never be able to get!

Now I don't have to look at the picture of the car to give me hope... I can look at the car itself! God continually reminds me that He's the God of hope, and that He wants us to *overflow* with hope, by the power of the Holy Spirit!

God cares about the details of our lives. Now I want to tell you why this answer to prayer is especially meaningful to me at this particular point in my life.

A few months ago, Lana was diagnosed with Stage IV breast cancer, meaning that the cancer has already spread to her lungs, liver and spine. The doctors say it will shorten her lifespan considerably and give us very little hope she'll survive.

But that doesn't mean that we're without hope. If you know my wife, you'll know that she's *overflowing* with hope! Why? Because we serve the God of hope! Even in the face of death, there's always hope! The Bible says:

> *"But as for me, I will always have hope; I will praise You more and more"* (Psalm 71:14).

We recently heard a pastor say that when Satan shoots his fiery darts at you, just say "Thanks for the ammunition!" and throw them right back at him by giving praise to God in the very area that's being attacked. So as for Lana and me, we will always have hope. We'll just keep praising God more and more. By doing this, we're holding up our shield of faith, which, as the Bible says,

"... can extinguish all the flaming arrows of the evil one" (Ephesians 6:16b).

How can you keep renewing your mind, in both the good days and the bad? By putting your faith in Christ for everything in your life. Keep putting your trust and hope in Him. God really can to anything, absolutely anything. Hope is just around the corner. As it says on mirror of Lana's car:

"OBJECTS IN MIRROR ARE CLOSER THAN THEY APPEAR."

Will you pray with me?

Father, thank You for raising Jesus from the dead on Easter Sunday, so many years ago and thank You for promising to raise us from the dead one day, too, if we'll just put our faith in Your Son. I pray for each one reading this message today that the God of hope will fill them with all joy and peace as they trust in Him, so that they may overflow with hope by the power of the Holy Spirit. In Jesus' name, Amen.

Questions for Reflection

If you've never put your faith in Christ, for the forgiveness of your sins and for the assurance that you'll be with Him forever in heaven, I pray you'll do it today. As Jesus said:

"I am the resurrection and the life. He who believes in Me will live, even though he dies" (John 11:25).

Every one of us will die someday. The question is what will happen to you on that day? Jesus said if you'll put your faith in Him, you'll have eternal life:

"For God so loved the world that He gave His one and only Son, that whoever believes in Him shall not perish but have eternal life" (John 3:16).

But if you don't put your faith in Jesus, you'll have to pay the price for your sins yourself, as Jesus went on to say:

"For God did not send His Son into the world to condemn the world, but to save the world through Him. Whoever believes in Him is not condemned, but whoever does not believe stands condemned already because he has not believed in the name of God's one and only Son" (John 3:17-18).

Jesus didn't come to condemn you to hell, but to save you from it. He doesn't want you to die. He wants you to live an abundant life, both here on earth and in heaven forever. Ask Jesus to forgive you of your sins. Invite Him into your life to become your Lord. Then live your life like it'll never end–because if you've put your faith in Him, you'll live forever!

LESSON 34: INSTRUCTING ONE ANOTHER — SEPTEMBER 5

Scripture Reading: Romans 15:14-24

One way to renew your mind is to teach others what you've been learning. It's a way to both review what you've learned, and to bless others at the same time. So today, I'd like to encourage you to consider taking some time to teach others what you've learned in life.

Sometimes we get caught up by the idea that we haven't learned enough to be able to teach anyone else anything. Sometimes we think we need more training, or that others may be more qualified to teach than we are... both of which may be true. But this doesn't mean that there aren't others who could benefit from what we've learned so far!

For some time now I've been praying for a drum teacher for my two younger sons. They've been wanting to play the drums and we have a drum set, but they didn't have anyone to teach them. A few months ago, I ran across a high schooler who played the drums for a worship team in town. I asked if he happened to give drum lessons and he said he did. He pulled out a business card with his name on it. At the top, it said:

"Drum Lessons for Beginners"

That was just what I needed! I signed the kids up and they've been learning and loving the drums ever since. What I loved about this high schooler was that he told us up front exactly what he had to offer: "Drum Lessons for Beginners." He made no claims that he was the best drummer in town, or that he'd be teaching them advanced music theory. But he did have exactly what we needed: a willingness to teach what he had learned so far.

In Paul's letter to the Romans, he told them that he had wanted to come to them many times before, but had so far been hindered from doing so. I'm sure Paul would have been a great teacher for them, and they could have learned a lot from his time with them. But Paul pointed out that they already had people to teach them— they had each other! Paul said:

> "I myself am convinced, my brothers, that you yourselves are full of goodness, complete in knowledge and competent to instruct one another" (Romans 15:14).

Paul was convinced that they were already filled with enough goodness, knowledge and competence to "instruct one another." What a boost that must have been to the Roman Christians! They didn't have to be like Paul or wait for Paul to benefit from godly teaching about the Lord. They had what it took to instruct one another!

Paul knew the power of an encounter with Jesus. He had taken his own advice from the beginning of his ministry. The book of Acts tells that within days after Paul had his life-changing encounter with Jesus on the road to Damascus, he was already telling others what he had learned. The Bible says:

> "Saul spent several days with the disciples in Damascus. At once he began to preach in the synagogues that Jesus is the Son of God. All those who heard him were astonished and asked, 'Isn't he the man who raised havoc in Jerusalem among those who call on this name? And hasn't he come here to take them as prisoners to the chief priests?' Yet Saul grew more and more powerful and baffled the Jews living in Damascus by proving that Jesus is the Messiah" (Acts 9:19b-22).

Even as a brand new Christian, Paul had something to offer. "Bible Lessons for Beginners," so to speak. Yes, he preached to anyone who would listen, including kings and the highest religious leaders in the land. But his heart always beat for sharing the gospel with those who had never heard about Jesus before. That is, in fact, why he was so often hindered from going to Rome, where there were already Christians capable of teaching one another. Paul said:

> "It has always been my ambition to preach the gospel where Christ was not known, so that I would not be building on someone else's foundation. Rather, as it is written: 'Those who were not told about Him will see, and those who have not heard will

understand.' This is why I have often been hindered from coming to you" (Romans 15:20-22).

Several years ago, I was shopping for a new Bible. I like to read the Bible over and over and sometimes like to read it in different versions, because I learn something new when I do. But as I was looking for a new Bible, I felt God was saying to me something like this: "You don't need another Bible, Eric. What you need is to be writing to others what you've learned from the Bible already."

I had already begun writing devotional messages like the ones I send out now each week, like this one. In each message, I simply share a passage from the Bible and share how God has used it to speak into my own life, encouraging others to read their Bibles and let God speak into their lives, too.

I don't make any claims that I'm better at reading the Bible than anyone else, or that there aren't other people who may be way more qualified to teach the Bible than I am. But what I do have, I'm willing to offer to others. What I've learned from God through the Bible has so affected my life that I want to share it with everyone who will listen.

Although it's good to learn as much as you can before teaching others, and to get as much training as you can, and to check and recheck your theology and ideas so that you're not leading people astray, the truth is that the best prerequisite for teaching others about Jesus is that you've spent time getting to know Jesus yourself.

This is just what the Bible says about the first disciples. After Peter and John healed a man, they spoke to the people gathered there who then heard their message and put their faith in Christ. The rulers and elders of the people were astonished. The Bible says:

"When they saw the courage of Peter and John and realized that they were unschooled, ordinary men, they were astonished and they took note that these men had been with Jesus" (Acts 4:13).

Peter and John were ordinary and unschooled men, yet they had one thing that many of you reading these words today have: they had been with Jesus.

If you've been with Jesus, spending time with Him, reading His words, praying and interacting and learning from Him, then it's not surprising that He would want you to share what you've learned with others. As Jesus told His first disciples:

"Therefore go and make disciples of all nations, baptizing them in the name of the Father and of the Son and of the Holy Spirit, and teaching them to obey everything I have commanded you" (Matthew 28:19-20).

One of the characteristics of *being* a disciple is *making* disciples. It simply goes with the package!

Don't let your training–or lack of training–stand in the way of sharing what you've learned with others.

When I first graduated from college, I spent five months in Bangladesh teaching some people at a disease research center how to use a computer program for their work. I didn't know much about the computer program myself, but I had a book about it and was able to read enough as I went along to test out the program and teach them what I learned along the way.

I imagine they might have learned more if they had taken a class from a professor in computer programming, or someone who had worked with the software for years already. But there weren't any professors in computer programming around, nor anyone else who had worked with the software before either! But I was willing to go anywhere and work with anyone, so somehow God sent me. The people I taught were grateful and I was blessed to be able to use my skills, no matter how limited, to help others.

I'd like to encourage you to consider sharing with others whatever God may have shared with you, whether it's drum lessons, Bible lessons, or even these lessons on renewing your mind.

If you've been with Jesus, through the Spirit and through the Word, and have benefited from your time with Him, you can be sure that others can benefit from what you've learned, too! I am convinced, as Paul was convinced about the Christians in Rome, that you yourselves are "full of goodness, filled with knowledge and competent to instruct one another."

Take whatever you've learned and share it with others. You'll be blessed as you review what you've learned, just as you'll be a blessing to those who may be learning it for the very first time.

Will you pray with me?

Father, thank You for teaching us so much about who You are and how You want us to live our lives. Help us to share what we've learned with others so that we can pass on the blessings that You've passed on to us. Help us to overcome our fears of speaking and writing, teaching and preaching, so that we can be like Paul, boldly going where no man may have gone before and proclaiming the good news about Christ to everyone who will listen. In Jesus' name, Amen.

Questions for Reflection:

1) Read Romans 15:14-24. What was the message that Paul said he had been preaching everywhere he went? And to whom had he been preaching that message to?
2) With all of Paul's learning, training and experience, why do you think he still loved preaching to those who were brand new to the message of Christ?
3) What kinds of things has God taught you from which you have greatly benefited?
4) Can you imagine anyone else who might benefit from learning what you've learned? And if so, would you be willing to be the one to teach them?

LESSON 35: ASSISTING OTHERS ON THEIR JOURNEY   SEPTEMBER 6

Scripture Reading: Romans 15:23-29

One of the things I love about the human heart is that it's wired to help others when they're in need. I see this repeated over and over: when a natural disaster strikes a town, or when a terrible wrong is committed against someone who's done right, or when a beloved friend passes away. When people see a need, they often respond with caring hearts.

But even though our hearts are wired to help others in need, sometimes we need a little prompting. Sometimes we need to remind our minds of the blessings we've received from others, and then our minds can nudge our hearts to respond as we should.

The apostle Paul gives two such reminders in his letter to the Romans. The first comes when he tells them that he's planning to visit them in the future when he passes through Rome on his way to Spain, and he hopes they'll help him on his journey there. Paul says:

"But now that there is no more place for me to work in these regions, and since I have been longing for many years to see you, I plan to do so when I go to Spain. I hope to visit you while passing through and to have you assist me on my journey there, after I have enjoyed your company for a while" (Romans 15:23-24).

While mentioning that he is looking forward to enjoying their company for a while, Paul also mentions that he hopes to have them assist him on his journey to Spain. I don't think Paul was trying to "guilt" the Romans into helping him on the next leg of his missionary journey. From what I've read about Paul in his other writings, I believe he simply knew that their hearts would *want* to help him on his journey. After all, his own heart was wired in the same way.

Then in the very next paragraph, Paul mentions that he's on his way to deliver a gift to his Jewish brothers and sisters who were in need in Jerusalem, gifts which he had collected from the churches in Macedonia and Achaia. Paul says:

"Now, however, I am on my way to Jerusalem in the service of the saints there. For Macedonia and Achaia were pleased to make a contribution for the poor among the saints in Jerusalem. They were pleased to do it, and indeed they owe it to them. For if the Gentiles have shared in the Jews' spiritual blessings, they owe it to the Jews to share with them their material blessings. So after I have completed this task and have made sure that they have received this fruit, I will go to Spain and visit you on the way. I know that when I come to you, I will come in the full measure of the blessing of Christ" (Romans 15:25-29).

Paul understood this blessing of giving and receiving, that when someone blesses you in your life, it is good and right and appropriate to share your blessings with them at some point in return, freely and voluntarily.

On a personal level, I know that my heart is often moved to help others on their journey, especially those who have been a blessing to me.

When I first became a Christian, I remember hearing about "tithes and offerings," giving ten percent and more of your income to the work of God in the world. I hadn't tithed before, not because I was against it, but because I simply didn't have this principle in my mind yet. But once I understood this principle in my mind, my heart was glad to respond—thrilled to respond, in fact.

I remember some of the first "big" checks I wrote to support the work of God in the lives of missionary friends I knew (at least they were big checks to me, as I had never done this before). I was thrilled to be able to help my friends in a significant way each month. I didn't feel obligated or guilted into it in any way. I just knew the blessing of hearing about Christ in my own life, and I was glad to help my friends share about Christ with others. It's all part of this idea of giving and receiving—sharing with others the blessings that God has given to us.

Now that I'm in full-time ministry myself, I sometimes have to remind myself that when I share about a need that I have, that God is often prompting others to respond at the same time. I have to remember that it's not an obligation or a burden to others to hear about and respond to my needs. It's the way God has wired our hearts. Knowing this has helped me to be more open about the needs in my own life and I've been thankful to see how people have responded to those needs.

In the past few months, I've been amazed again at the generosity of others, including many of you, who have stepped in and helped my wife and me as we walk through my wife's journey with cancer.

I have been humbled and reminded frequently just how good and kind and caring the human heart really is. Sometimes we miss this truth, especially when we are bombarded with such bad news about the wicked things that people have done in the world.

Of course there's bad in the world. Of course there's wickedness, greed, evil, and depravity. But all of this stems from good hearts that have been corrupted by sin—usually related to some kind of selfishness. But when our hearts are right with God, something else takes over—something called *selflessness*; doing to others what you would have them do to you and giving your life for the sake of others, just as Jesus gave His life for us.

Assisting others on their journey is not foreign to the human heart. But sometimes it does take a little prompting from our minds–and the Holy Spirit–to get our hearts in gear.

This week, I heard about some friends who have been praying about buying a van and a mammogram machine so they can go back to their home villages in Kenya and do cancer screenings for the women there. Perhaps it was because of my wife's recent diagnosis that my ears were especially attentive to their request. My heart wanted to respond. I didn't know what I could do or how I could help, but I was willing to find out.

I called my friends and listened as they talked about their hopes and dreams and prayers for this project. I'm still not sure what I can do yet, but now my heart and mind are both engaged and attuned to the need. As my friends move forward with their plans, perhaps we can find a way to take part along the way.

At the same time, I was surprised this week by a note from one of our readers overseas who asked if there was anything special Lana and I needed at this time. He had been blessed by our ministry and wanted to do something special in return. Although I hesitated to share our personal needs with him, I eventually did share a few things about which we had been praying. Within a few hours, he responded to say that he was sending a gift that would not only cover those needs that I had shared, but would double the amount of what I had shared!

To me, this was a living example of what Paul was talking about in his letter to the Romans, where those who had received spiritual blessings from someone responded by sending a gift of material blessings in return.

The human heart really is wired to respond to the needs of others. Oftentimes the only thing holding us back is making our minds aware of the needs around us so our hearts can respond.

With this in mind, I'd like to encourage you to be on the lookout for ways that God might want to use you this week to bless others, especially those who have been a blessing to you. Perhaps you have a friend or relative who has gone out of their way to spend some time with you. Perhaps you have a spiritual leader or mentor or a particular ministry than has spoken into your life in a special way. Perhaps you have a project or a school or an organization which has been a blessing to you and now you can be a blessing to them in return.

I'm sure your heart is good and eager to assist others on their journey, but sometimes it takes a little reminder like this to jog your memory and bring it to the forefront of your mind.

I pray that as God renews your mind in this way that the natural response of your heart will follow. Don't ignore the promptings that God puts there. Don't put them off until the feelings "go away." Lean into those promptings and see what God may have in mind for you—and for those He wants to bless through you.

Will you pray with me?

Father, thank You for blessing us in various ways through the people around us. Help us to be attentive to their needs as well so that we can be a blessing to them. Refresh our minds again today about practical ways that we can help them, then nudge our hearts to follow through on those thoughts. In Jesus' name, Amen.

Questions for Reflection:

1) Read Romans 15:23-29. In what ways could the Christians in Rome have possibly assisted Paul on his journey to Spain?
2) Read Acts 28:7-10. In what ways did the people of Malta respond to the blessings they received from Paul?
3) Who are some people in your life who have been a blessing to you? In what ways might you be able to bless them in return?
4) In what ways could you open your mind still further to the needs around you in order to meet those needs yourself? Consider praying that God would renew your mind in this area, so He can work His blessings through you.

LESSON 36: ENLISTING OTHERS TO PRAY FOR YOU — SEPTEMBER 7

Scripture Reading: Romans 15:30-33

Are you struggling with something in your life today? If so, I'd like to encourage you to do something special: enlist others to pray for you.

If you think asking for prayer is a sign of weakness, think again! Asking for prayer is one of the strongest things you could ever do—and one of the best ways to keep you strong.

The apostle Paul knew this secret and often called on others to pray for him, as he did near the end of his letter to the Romans. Paul said:

> "I urge you, brothers, by our Lord Jesus Christ and by the love of the Spirit, to join me in my struggle by praying to God for me. Pray that I may be rescued from the unbelievers in Judea and that my service in Jerusalem may be acceptable to the saints there, so that by God's will I may come to you with joy and together with you be refreshed" (Romans 15:30-32).

Paul asked for prayer with boldness. He *urged* the Romans to pray for him, "I urge you, brothers, by our Lord Jesus Christ and by the love of the Spirit." And he didn't just ask for a blanket prayer to cover him in all ways at all times. He asked them to pray for him in specific ways, particularly in those areas where he struggled the most. He asked that he would be rescued from the unbelievers in Judea, that his service in Jerusalem would be acceptable to the saints there, and that he would be able to come to them in Rome with joy and together with them be refreshed.

The dangers that faced Paul on his trip to Jerusalem—and then on to Rome—were real and significant. If you read about his trip in the book of Acts (chapters 21-28), you'll see that Paul was captured, imprisoned and threatened with death on several occasions, not counting the shipwreck that obliterated his ship along the way. Paul needed prayer and I have no doubt that the prayers of the Christians in Rome helped to sustain him all along the way.

But it's not easy to ask others to pray for you. I know. Just last week I was celebrating my 23rd wedding anniversary in New York City with my superb wife, Lana. We had an awesome time, filled with fun, romance and a wonderful walk through Central Park. But on the last day of the trip, I got sick—and not just a little sick, but a violent, wrenching sickness like I haven't experienced in a long time.

At one point, Lana asked if she should call a few people and ask them to pray for me. I said, "No, I'll be all right." I hoped it would just pass quickly, and I didn't want anyone to worry, as they knew we were on our special anniversary trip. But as the hours passed and I was just getting worse and not better, I finally agreed to have Lana made a few calls.

Although the sickness persisted throughout the night and on into the next few days, I felt different immediately just knowing that a few other people were praying for me and checking in on me from time to time. I was also able to see the fact that I was sick in a new way, realizing that my body was doing just what it should do in trying to forcefully expel whatever had maliciously entered into it.

It turned out I had the flu and the healing process that God had begun on that first day finally prevailed. Thankfully, I'm almost back to full strength again. Unfortunately for Lana, she got what I had a few days later, so we had to enlist others once again to pray for her!

The reason I bring this up today is to let you know that I understand what it's like to need prayer, but not want to ask for it—especially at those times when we feel the weakest. But the truth is, without prayer, we'll just get weaker and weaker. *With* prayer, God can give us the strength we need to go on.

I also wanted to tell you this story because prayer not only changes things, it changes the way you look at things. Even though I still had to walk through the rest of my sickness, I was able to realize that the very things that was making me feel sick—the expelling of whatever had made its way into my system— was the very thing that was bringing my healing. By being able to look at what was happening to me differently, I was able to better endure the rest of the time that I had to go through it.

Prayer really can renew your mind, and by enlisting others to pray for you, you can renew your mind even faster.

If there's an area in your life where you're struggling today, I want to encourage you to do as Paul did and enlist others to join you in your struggle—through prayer. As Paul said,

"I urge you... to join me in my struggle by praying to God for me."

There are all kinds of struggles you might be facing right now: whether they're struggles with lust or secret sins, fear or doubts, real or imaginary dangers, hardships, relationships or bothersome thoughts. The list is endless. The beauty of prayer is that it can address every single struggle you could possibly face.

One of my friends and mentors says that everyone needs a prayer team. You don't have to be in full-time ministry, or going through a particular crisis, to ask people to pray for you on a regular basis. You could be an expectant mother or a struggling student, a successful architect or an aspiring teacher. You could be married or single, with kids or without. You could be needing money or managing your money. You could be traveling full-time or at home full-time. Whatever you're doing and whatever you're going through, you can benefit by enlisting others to pray for you.

Not sure who to ask? You might ask a friend, or a co-worker, or a neighbor. You might ask a pastor or a priest. You might even ask someone you don't know, like Lana and I did last week in New York, when we were visiting some churched there. At one church, I sensed the man sitting next to me was truly "a believer." I could tell from his "Amens" that he not only believed *in* God, but he believed in *the power* of God. So after the service, I asked if he would pray for us. He was not only glad to pray, but he invited us to dinner, which we unfortunately had to decline because of our schedule.

At another church, we were talking to a man outside the church before the service. Afterward, we reconnected again. We asked if we could pray for him and then he returned the favor and prayed for us.

For years now, we've been asking for and benefiting from the prayers of others. We've asked for prayer from family and friends, small groups and Sunday School classes. We asked for prayer when we were single, when we were dating, when we got married, and when we started having children.

When Lana was diagnosed with cancer this year, she set up a blog to keep others updated and let them know how they could pray for us. The effects have been tremendous already, as the prayers of others have given us an abundance of strength, wisdom, healing and encouragement.

If you're going through a struggle in your life, you don't have to go through it alone. Enlist others to join you in your struggle by praying to God for you. If you're not sure who to ask for prayer, or just want to get some additional prayers from believers who love to pray, we have a special prayer page at *The Ranch* website setup just for that. Just visit www.theranch.org to find it.

By the way, the apostle Paul did eventually make it to Rome, just as he had asked the Romans to pray for him.

It may not have been exactly the way he expected, or the timing he expected, but he did get there, through God's strength—and the prayers of others. As Luke recorded in the last chapter of the book of Acts:

> *"When we got to Rome, Paul was allowed to live by himself, with a soldier to guard him... For two whole years Paul stayed there in his own rented house and welcomed all who came to see him. Boldly and without hindrance he preached the kingdom of God and taught about the Lord Jesus Christ"* (Acts 28:30-31).

God answers prayer, and He loves when we enlist others to pray with us.

Will you pray with me?

Father, thank You for showing us the value of enlisting others to pray for us. Help us to reach out to others when we're struggling so that we won't become weaker and weaker, but grow stronger and stronger each day through Your strength. In Jesus' name, Amen.

Questions for Reflection:

1) Read Romans 15:30-33. What are some reasons people might be hesitant to ask for prayer?
2) What difference could it make if you enlisted others to pray for you?
3) In what areas are you struggling right now where you could ask others to pray for you?
4) Who are some specific people that might be willing to pray for you?

LESSON 37: BEING WISE AND INNOCENT   SEPTEMBER 8

Scripture Reading: Romans 16:1-20

Once you've worked hard to renew your mind, God wants you to keep it renewed. And one of the best ways to keep it renewed is to be careful of the company you keep.

Believe it or not, there are people out there who don't have your best interests in mind. They'll use smooth talk and flattery to try to lead you astray from the teaching you've learned–teaching that has helped you in many ways in your life.

In the final chapter of his letter to the Romans, Paul warns about such people. Paul says:

"I urge you, brothers, to watch out for those who cause divisions and put obstacles in your way that are contrary to the teaching you have learned. Keep away from them. For such people are not serving our Lord Christ, but their own appetites. By smooth talk and flattery they deceive the minds of naive people. Everyone has heard about your obedience, so I am full of joy over you; but I want you to be wise about what is good, and innocent about what is evil. The God of peace will soon crush Satan under your feet" (Romans 16:17-19).

If you look at this paragraph closely, you'll find some secrets for how to detect when people are trying to lead you astray for the wrong reasons.

First, Paul urged the Romans, "to watch out for those who those who cause divisions and put obstacles in your way that are contrary to the teaching you have learned."

God had taken a great deal of time to teach the Christians in Rome good solid truths about Himself and the Bible, and Paul wanted them to hold onto those truths. In the same way, God may have taken a great deal of time to teach you some good solid truths about Himself and the Bible and God wants you to hold onto those truths, too.

If someone comes along and tries to teach you about a "new" truth, or "higher" way of looking at God and the Bible, be wise about how you listen to them. Take what they say back to God and the Bible to see what He says about it in His Word. While there's value in keeping an "open mind," you don't want to keep it so open that all the good teaching you've already learned falls out!

Be a good student of the Bible, like the people in the city of Berea, who took even what Paul said and examined it carefully according to what they had already learned. The Bible says:

"Now the Bereans were of more noble character than the Thessalonians, for they received the message with great eagerness and examined the Scriptures every day to see if what Paul said was true" (Acts 17:11).

Second, Paul gave the Romans some simple advice about what to do when they came across people who were teaching them things that were contrary to what they had already learned: "Keep away from them."

Why? Because the company you keep matters. If you don't choose your friends wisely, Satan will be glad to choose some for you. Satan knows that one of the best ways to lead you astray is to put people in your life who will pull you over to his side.

Paul gave a similar warning in his letter to the Corinthians when he said:

> "Bad company corrupts good character" (1 Corinthians 15:33b).

How can you know who's "bad company"? By studying not just *what* they're teaching, but by studying *their character* as well. Paul alludes to this when he talks about the motives of those who might try to lead the Romans astray. Paul says: "For such people are not serving our Lord Christ, but their own appetites. By smooth talk and flattery they deceive the minds of naive people."

Although it's not always apparent right away, a little study of the people around you can go a long way in determining their true motives, whether they're doing what they're doing to serve the Lord Christ, or to serve their own appetites.

It makes me think of a girl who falls in love with a boy just because he tells her, "You're beautiful. I love you. And I want to do something special to make you happy." All his smooth talk and flattery may work in his favor, but it may not work in hers. If the girl were wise, she would study not only the words that are being spoken, but the motives of the person who is speaking those words.

If you're wise, you'll do the same: anytime someone tries to speak something into your life that runs contrary to what you've already learned, it's helpful to study not only the words that are being spoken, but the motives of the person who is speaking those words.

I think it's interesting to note that leading up to his warning about those who might lead the Romans astray, Paul begins his chapter by listing some "good characters" and what made them noteworthy or admirable, people that Paul knew personally in Rome. For instance, he says:

> "I commend to you our sister Phoebe... for she has been a great help to many people, including me.
> "Greet Priscilla and Aquila, my fellow workers in Christ Jesus. They risked their lives for me. Not only I but all the churches of the Gentiles are grateful to them...
> "Greet my dear friend Epenetus, who was the first convert to Christ in the province of Asia.
> "Greet Mary, who worked very hard for you" (Romans 16:1a,2b,5b,6).

The list goes on and on, as Paul commends to them person after person:

> "Greet Andronicus and Junias, my relatives who have been in prison with me. They are outstanding among the apostles, and they were in Christ before I was.
> "Greet Ampliatus, whom I love in the Lord.
> "Greet Urbanus, our fellow worker in Christ, and my dear friend Stachys.
> "Greet Apelles, tested and approved in Christ...
> "Greet Tryphena and Tryphosa, those women who work hard in the Lord...

> "Greet Rufus, chosen in the Lord, and his mother, who has been a mother to me, too" (Romans 16:7-10a,12a,13).

If you want to learn something about a person, a personal recommendation like this goes a long way.

In choosing an eye doctor one time, Lana and I talked with a friend who worked for an eye doctor. Our friend told us that when her doctor needed a doctor, he chose a particular man in town, having seen his practice long enough and knowing his character was strong enough that he trusted this other doctor with his own eyes. So when we needed an eye doctor, we were able to benefit from his very personal recommendation.

Contrast this with another eye doctor we went to visit a few weeks earlier who, with his smooth talk and flattery, almost convinced us to come to him. But when we went home and looked into his life and practice a little more, we found out that his credentials weren't quite as good as what he made us believe, and the bad recommendations we read about him just sealed our resolve to search for another doctor.

This isn't to say that we might not be led astray at times by personal recommendations, too. But many times, if we'll take the extra effort to study the person as well as what they're trying to say to us, we can save ourselves from being led astray.

Third, Paul concludes his warning with these words: "Everyone has heard about your obedience, so I am full of joy over you; but I want you to be wise about what is good, and innocent about what is evil."

Paul was full of joy over the obedience of the Romans. Everyone had heard about it, he said, and he didn't want anyone to take that away from them. "Be wise about what is good," he said, "and innocent about what is evil."

Again, these are similar to words he wrote in his letter to the Corinthians:

> "In regard to evil be infants, but in your thinking be adults" (1 Corinthians 14:20b).

Paul wanted the Romans—and the Corinthians—to put their *minds* to work, being wise about what was good. At the same time, he wanted them to be like children in regards to evil, having nothing to do with it and being as innocent as possible.

What's the end result of all of this? As Paul said at the end of his warning:

> "The God of peace will soon crush Satan under your feet."

With all the work that goes into renewing your mind, be sure to keep it renewed by being wise about what is good and innocent of evil. Study the teaching of those around you—and the character of those teaching it—before allowing their teachings into your mind. As you protect your mind, God will protect you, and keep Satan at bay.

Will you pray with me?

Father, thank You for reminding us to stay true to what we've been taught about You and Your Word. Help us to study deeply any ideas, and the people behind those ideas, that are presented to us that conflict with what we've already heard from You. Help us be wise and innocent so we can keep our minds pure. In Jesus' name, Amen.

Questions for Reflection:

1) Read Romans 16:1-20. What are some of the words that Paul uses to describe those whom he trusts in Rome, compared to the words he uses to describe those who might be trying to deceive their minds?
2) Can you think of some times when you've been led astray by smooth talkers who've been serving their own selfish interests?
3) Can you think of other times when you've been blessed by the wisdom and personal recommendations of true friends?
4) What are some ways this week that you can "be wise about what is good and innocent about what is evil"?

LESSON 38: BELIEVING AND OBEYING GOD — SEPTEMBER 9

Scripture Reading: Romans 16:21-27

Today we've reached the conclusion of the book of Romans, the final words of Paul's letter that punctuate his goal for writing it. These words also underscore the purpose for which God wants you to renew your mind: so that you might believe and obey Him. Here's what Paul said:

> "Now to Him who is able to establish you by my gospel and the proclamation of Jesus Christ, according to the revelation of the mystery hidden for long ages past, but now revealed and made known through the prophetic writings by the command of the eternal God, so that all nations might believe and obey Him—to the only wise God be glory forever through Jesus Christ! Amen" (Romans 16:25-27).

Paul often concluded his letters by giving praise to God, just as he did above in this letter to the Romans. Sandwiched in between his words of praise, he also mentions the purpose for which the mystery of Jesus Christ has been revealed: so that all nations might believe and obey Him. This is God's desire for all people in all nations, including you and me—that we would believe and obey Him.

As I've mentioned in some earlier lessons, there's a difference between believing *in* God, and *believing God.* You can believe *in* God, yet still not *believe Him*—still not be convinced about who He is and what He can do in and through your life. God wants you to believe *in* Him, for sure. But He also wants you to *believe Him* when He tells you something regarding your life. Then He wants you to take action based on that belief.

Believing and obeying God is a major part of renewing your mind. God wants you to renew your mind so that you can bring your thinking in line with His. When you do this, you'll be better able to believe and obey Him, regardless of whatever life may throw your way.

I've been praying quite a bit this week for my wife Lana, who, as I've mentioned before, was diagnosed with Stage 4 cancer a few months ago. Apart from a miracle, the doctors say that this type of cancer is incurable and will shorten her life considerably. As you can imagine, our faith has been put to the test on a daily basis regarding what we believe about God and what He is doing through all of this. Yet with all that's going on, we continue to find God's peace in the midst of it.

How? Because God has spent considerable time and effort over the years filling our minds with *His* thoughts about us, that He is *for* us, not against us, and that He will work *all things* for good, even in this.

At the risk of being extra-vulnerable, I'd like to share one of my journal entries with you from earlier this week. I often write down my questions for God in my journal, and then listen for what He might be saying in response. While I'm not always sure if the thoughts I attribute to God are really mine or His, they do give me a starting point for helping me think through what He *might* be trying to say to me. With that disclaimer, here's what I felt God was saying to me earlier this week regarding His will for Lana and her healing, most of which are thoughts that are based firmly in what He's already written in His Word:

> "Eric, you know My will is that she be healed, that she have no more pain, and that she never be separated from you. You also know that in this world you will have trouble. But take heart, I have overcome the world. Peace I give you, peace I leave with you, not as the world gives, but My peace I give you. I know you believe I could heal her in an instant. But I also know that you believe I can work all things for good, ALL THINGS, no matter what happens. Eric, I have prayed for you that your faith may not waver. Yes, I do give, and yes, I do take away, but I know and I trust that you will still praise Me. Your faith is, of course, more precious to Me than gold. Yes, pray for her healing, but also pray for her heart to be at peace. Pray that she will continue to know that I am walking through this with her every step of the way."

At that point, I asked God for a verse that might help me express this dichotomy I feel inside me, that while I trust in God fully for Lana's healing, I also trust Him whatever the outcome may be. The verse that came to mind was from the book of Job.

While I sometimes think it's cliché to think of Job when things are going bad in life, I also realize there's a reason why people turn to Job when things go awry: because no matter what happened to Job, he still gave praise to God!

The Bible says that Job was the greatest man among all the people of the East. He was blessed with seven sons and three daughters, seven thousand sheep, three thousand camels, five hundred yoke of oxen, five hundred donkeys, and a large number of servants.

He was upright and blameless in all he did, even praying for his sons and daughters on a regular basis, offering sacrifices on their behalf in the early morning, just in case they might have sinned and cursed God in their hearts.

Yet for all his faith and all the good that he had done, tragedy struck. In a single day, he lost almost everything with which God had previously blessed him: his sons and daughters, all of his livestock and almost all of his servants. Overwhelmed with grief, Job tore his robe and shaved his head.

But what encourages me about this passage is that through it all, Job still trusted God. After all these terrible things happened to Job, the Bible says:

> "Then he fell to the ground in worship and said: 'Naked I came from my mother's womb, and naked I will depart. The Lord gave and the Lord has taken away; may the name of the Lord be praised.'
> "In all this, Job did not sin by charging God with wrongdoing" (Job 1:20-22).

Even when life turned against him, Job still gave glory to God. I can see why people might lose their faith when tragedy strikes. But I can also see, from this story of Job, that it doesn't have to be that way. Job had no guarantees of what the future held, but he knew who held his future and he trusted Him implicitly.

When Paul wrote his letter to the Romans, he didn't know what his future held, either. As we learn from the book of Acts, Paul's future had a fair share of tragedy as well. But through it all, Paul trusted God implicitly. He knew that God was able to strengthen him through Jesus Christ for whatever he might face and that God would be glorified through it all, no matter what happened. As Paul said in his closing words to the Romans:

> "Now to Him who is able to establish you [to strengthen you] by my gospel and the proclamation of Jesus Christ... to the only wise God be glory forever through Jesus Christ! Amen"

I don't know what you're going through today, but whatever it is, don't let fear and doubt overtake you. Take it all to Christ instead. As Paul wrote to the Corinthians:

> "...take every thought captive to make it obedient to Christ" (2 Corinthians 10:5b).

No matter what comes your way, take it to Christ. No matter what people say, take it to Christ. No matter what life throws at you, take it to Christ. Let Christ speak to you in all situations. Let Him have the last word. Let Him override anything that anyone might say to you that is contrary to His Word.

The truth is that God loves you *very much*. He is *for* you. And He will work *all things* for your good, when you love Him and are called according to His purpose.

Whenever a thought comes your way that goes against what God says in His Word, ask Him to strengthen you through Jesus Christ. Ask Him to renew your mind and to fill your thoughts with *His* thoughts, giving you the faith to believe *His* Words, so you can walk in obedience to whatever *He* calls you to do.

In whatever you do, keep glorifying God and enjoying Him through it all, which, according to the historic Westminster Confession of Faith, is the chief end of man:

> "To glorify God, and to enjoy Him forever."

As Paul said to the Romans, let me say to you:

> "Now to Him who is able to establish you by my gospel and the proclamation of Jesus Christ... so that all nations might believe and obey Him—to the only wise God be glory forever through Jesus Christ! Amen."

Will you pray with me?

Father, thank You for being able to establish us in our faith and help us to be obedient to You. Renew our minds again this week and help us to take every thought captive that sets itself up against You. Fill us with faith, help us to walk in obedience, and may your name be glorified through it all. In Jesus' name, Amen.

Questions for Reflection:

1) Read Romans 16:25-27. What is God's goal for the nations, according to this passage of Scripture?
2) Why is it so important to God that we believe and obey Him? What difference can it make to Him, to us, and to others?
3) In what areas of your life could you use some strengthening in your faith today?

4) *Is there a particular act of obedience that God might be calling you to do this week? Ask Him to give you the strength and faith to do it.*

CONCLUSION: "BRAIN WASHING" IN THE BEST POSSIBLE WAY!   SEPTEMBER 10

Scripture Reading: Romans 12:1-2

My son came home from Bible college a few weeks ago and said some people in his town think that all the kids who go to his school are brainwashed. My son said, "They're right! We are!"

Their brains are washed in the best possible way, washed by God Himself, cleansed by His Holy Spirit, and renewed to look more and more like the mind of Christ every day.

As we wrap up this study of *Romans: Lessons in Renewing Your Mind*, I wanted to give you some final thoughts on how to keep your "brain washed" in the best possible way, too.

First, I want to encourage you to keep reading the Word of God.

My wife has been going through chemotherapy the last few months and spending a lot of time reading and memorizing God's Word. Once in a while she'll read a newspaper or magazine article about cancer and its devastating effects. It always reminds her how much more hope and joy she has whenever she reads the Bible! So she picks up her Bible again and starts reading it instead. We could all do more of that!

As God said to the Israelites:

"These commandments that I give you today are to be upon your hearts. Impress them on your children. Talk about them when you sit at home and when you walk along the road, when you lie down and when you get up. Tie them as symbols on your hands and bind them on your foreheads. Write them on the doorframes of your houses and on your gates" (Deuteronomy 6:6-8).

Some people might think that reading the Bible all the time is like burying your head in the sand and ignoring the problems in your life. But there's a difference between burying your head in the sand and burying your head in God's Word! Sand leads to suffocation and death, whereas the Bible leads to fresh air and life!

If you want to keep your mind as fresh and clean as possible, keep reading God's Word as much as possible, every day, many times a day. A pastor was once asked which version of the Bible was the best. His answer? "The one you read the most." Amen!

Second, I want to encourage you to keep surrounding yourself with other Christ-minded believers so they can "re-mind" you of God's Word, too.

I know that there may be times when you may not feel like going to church. I know that you may not feel like going to Bible studies and getting to know complete strangers. I know that once you've gotten to know those complete strangers, they may do things that annoy you, or irritate you, or make you wonder why you ever bothered going at all.

But for all the potential pitfalls of interacting with others, there's nothing more powerful than having a Christian brother or sister encourage you in your faith and life.

As the writer of Ecclesiastes said:

"Two are better than one,
because they have a good return for their work:
If one falls down,

> *his friend can help him up.*
> *But pity the man who falls*
> *and has no one to help him up!*
> *Also, if two lie down together, they will keep warm.*
> *But how can one keep warm alone?*
> *Though one may be overpowered,*
> *two can defend themselves.*
> *A cord of three strands is not quickly broken."*
> *(Ecclesiastes 4:9-12).*

Renewing your mind is hard work, but God doesn't want you to do it alone. He wants you to rely on Him, and He wants you to rely on His people, the body of Christ, who all share the same head, Jesus Christ.

We got a package in the mail last week that made us cry. It came from a church we used to attend about 20 years ago. In the package were a stack of cards from the church members and a check from the church. We were so overwhelmed by this expression of love and care that we couldn't even open the stack of cards.

When we finally did open them, our tears began to flow again–tears of joy and thankfulness for their thoughts and prayers for us during this time in our lives. It was such a reminder to us of how the body of Christ works to lift us up in our time of need.

While it can be hard at times to invest your time in getting to know other Christ-minded believers, it's an investment that will pay dividends for you and for them for years to come… for all eternity, in fact!

So first, if you want to keep renewing your mind, keep reading God's Word. Second, keep surrounding yourself with other Christ-minded believers so they can remind you of God's Word, too. And third, always remember that God LOVES you, He is FOR you, and He can work ALL THINGS for good in your life!

When I started writing this study almost a year ago, I had no idea what the year might hold. I had no idea how my life was about to change as my wife was diagnosed with cancer. Yet, as I've been rereading the whole book of Romans again this week and rereading each of my messages from this past year, I've been reminded again just how much God loves *me*, is for *me*, and can work all things for good in *my life*, too.

And I'm positive that God loves you, is for you, and can work all things for good in your life. How can I be so sure? You don't take my word for it! You can take His! Here are just a few reminders again of what Paul said in his letter to the Romans:

> *"But God demonstrates HIS OWN LOVE FOR US in this: While we were still sinners, Christ died for us"* (Romans 5:3).
> *"If God is FOR us, who can be against us?"* (Romans 8:31b).
> *"And we know that in ALL THINGS God works for the good of those who love Him, who have been called according to His purpose"* (Romans 8:28).

If you've read with me this far, I'm sure that you love God and are called according to His purpose, too, so these words apply to you just as much as they applied to the Romans to whom Paul was writing! Let God's Word sink deep into your mind today. Let Him speak words of love, words of support, and words of encouragement to you every day.

If you need a good "brain washing," I'd encourage you to take some time to read and reread the whole book of Romans again (then take some more time to read and reread the whole Bible again!) There's nothing better to help you renew your mind than to wash it with the Word of God. Surround yourself with other Christ-minded believers who can speak God's Word into your life as well. And always remember that God LOVES you, is FOR you, and can work ALL THINGS for your good.

As I said at the beginning of this study, one of the most powerful forces in the world in an idea. Revolutions of all kinds have been sparked by mere ideas and even the smallest ideas can grow to either define... or destroy you. That's why it's so important to make sure your ideas are in line with God's ideas.

As Paul encouraged the Romans, let me encourage you:

"Do not conform any longer to the pattern of this world, but be transformed by the renewing of your mind. Then you will be able to test and approve what God's will is – His good, pleasing and perfect will" (Romans 12:2).

Will you pray with me?

Father, thank You for speaking to us through this amazing book called Romans. Thank You for Paul's faithfulness to write down what he learned from You so he could share it with others. Help us to be faithful with what we've learned so we can apply it to our own lives and to help others apply it to theirs as well. Wash our minds, cleanse our hearts, and fill us with Your peace. In Jesus' name, Amen.

Questions for Reflection:

1) Read Romans 12:1-2. The term "brainwashing" is often used in a negative way, referring to someone who has been convinced of something that is untrue. But in light of today's study, how can "washing your brain" with God's Word work in your favor?
2) Who are some people in your life who are so filled with God's Word that it seems to flow out of them whenever they speak? What could you do to spend more time learning from and growing together with them?
3) Read Romans 8:28-39. What verses from this passage stick out in your mind that are particularly helpful to you in your life right now?
4) Skim through the book of Romans again or take an hour or so to read the whole book again. Write down any words or phrases that God may be wanting to speak to you. Hold onto those words and let God use them in the days ahead to continually renew your mind.

APPENDIX ~ MESSAGE 1: LANA'S HEALTH   SEPTEMBER 11

(The following five messages were written in 2012, midway through the writing of this series on renewing your mind. Even though the messages and the prayers shared within them are from a previous season of my life, I've included them here at the end of this series to highlight the importance of keeping your mind focused on God's perspective at ALL times. May God bless you as you read these additional messages, and may He give you the desires of your heart as you keep putting your faith in Him!)

By Eric Elder, February 19th, 2012

I normally use this space to write some words of encouragement to you, but this week I could use some encouragement myself.

A few weeks ago my wife and I received the surprising news that she has breast cancer. Two days ago, we received the even more surprising news that it was not Stage 1 breast cancer with one lump in her breast, but that it is actually Stage 4 breast cancer, with multiple tumors that have already spread to her lungs, liver and spine.

If you know Lana, you know that she's the picture of health… she's at her ideal body weight, she eats well, she runs two to three miles every few days, and her bloodwork is perfect in every way. She feels good and strong and healthy. Other than the lump in her breast that we discovered in December, and some minor pain in her lower back that started soon after that, we wouldn't have even thought to have her tested for anything that could possibly be going wrong inside her body. Even when people do find lumps in their breasts, the majority of the time those lumps turn out to be harmless. But not this time.

I've prayed with many people over the years with many types of cancer. I've seen some people healed naturally, others supernaturally, and still others who haven't been healed in the way that we had fervently hoped or prayed, including my own mother who died of breast cancer twenty-one years ago. But even in those instances where God hasn't healed people in the way that I had hoped, I have seen God use even those situations for good in the end. As good and miraculous as healing is, I know that there is still more that Christ offers us than just the healing that we desire. As the apostle Paul said:

> "If only for this life we have hope in Christ, we are to be pitied more than all men" (1 Corinthians 15:19).

I believe in healing. I've seen people healed with my own eyes and through my own prayers numerous times. God wants us to be healed and He has wired our bodies to heal themselves as much as possible, whether it's the coagulating of blood to heal a scrape on our skin, or the multiplication of white blood cells to fight off a raging infection.

But there's also an enemy at work whose main goal, according to Jesus, seems to be to steal, kill, and destroy. As Jesus said:

> "The thief comes only to steal kill and destroy; …" (John 10:10a).

But Jesus didn't leave it there. He went on to say:

> "… I have come that they may have life and have it to the full" (John 10:10b).

The healings and miracles of Jesus are so numerous that the pages of the Bible can't even contain them all. As the apostle John said:

> "Jesus did many other things as well. If every one of them were written down, I suppose that even the whole world would not have room for the books that would be written" (John 21:25).

And yet as miraculous and amazing and God-ordained as healing is, there are some things that are even more amazing… like forgiveness… and the peace that passes understanding… and eternal life.

When some men in the Bible brought their friend to Jesus to be healed, having pressed through the crowds and cutting through a roof to get their friend to Jesus, Jesus said to the sick man,

> "Take heart, son; your sins are forgiven" (Matthew 9:2b).

The religious leaders were shocked that Jesus would make such a bold statement, knowing that only God Himself had the power to forgive sins. But knowing their thoughts, Jesus said to them:

> "Which is easier: to say, 'Your sins are forgiven,' or to say, 'Get up and walk'? But so that you may know that the Son of Man has authority on earth to forgive sins…" Then He said to the paralytic, "Get up, take your mat and go home." And the man got up and went home" (Matthew 9:5-7).

To Jesus, the forgiveness of sins seems to be just as miraculous, if not more so, than healing. And considering what Jesus had to go through in order to forgive us of our sins, it seems like forgiveness was quite possibly the more difficult of the two.

When Jesus Himself was headed for the cross, way too young and way too innocent, rather than fighting His death, He submitted to the will of His Father in heaven, knowing that His Father's plans were even more glorious than anything anyone could have imagined. Yet Jesus still prayed that if there was any way possible, that His Father would take the cup of death away from Him so that He wouldn't have to drink it. At the same time, He trusted His Father completely, regardless of the outcome, saying:

> "… yet not My will, but Yours be done" (Luke 22:42b).

Jesus sought for the peace of His Father above all else, and He encouraged His disciples to do the same: As Jesus told His disciples,

> "I have told you these things, so that in Me you may have peace. In this world you will have trouble. But take heart! I have overcome the world" (John 16:33).

And ultimately, what could compare to the promise of eternal life? As Lana told a friend this weekend:

> "For me, it's a win-win situation. Either I go to be with Jesus, or I get to stay here and be with Eric and my family."

As Paul said,

> "I eagerly expect and hope that I will in no way be ashamed, but will have sufficient courage so that now as always Christ will be exalted in my body, whether by life or by death. For to me, to live is Christ and to die is gain. If I am to go on living in the body, this will mean fruitful labor for me. Yet what shall I choose? I do not know! I am torn between the two: I desire to depart and be with Christ, which is better by far; but it is more necessary for you that I remain in the body" (Philippians 1:20-24).

Jesus came to give us life to the full, both here on earth and in heaven forever. This is the hope that we have in Christ and this is the hope for which He gave up His life.

So with both of these hopes in mind, can I ask for your earnest prayers on our behalf? We're praying for healing and more–that God would heal Lana's body completely and gloriously—and that through it all, God's name would be glorified in ways that go beyond anything we could ask or imagine. Thank you so much.

Will you pray with me?

Father, thank You for revealing to us this cancer that is at work within Lana's body so we can know what to do next. Lord, we pray for healing and more, that You would heal her body completely and gloriously, and through it all, that Your name would be glorified in ways that go beyond anything we could ask or imagine. In Jesus' name, Amen.

APPENDIX ~ MESSAGE 2: HIT YOUR KNEES! SEPTEMBER 12

By Eric Elder, February 26th, 2012

In my message last week, I shared that I could use some encouragement, and thanks to your prayers and God's help, I got it! I can't tell you how much I appreciate all your prayers and notes and words of encouragement.

In case you missed last week's message, I shared that my wife Lana and I were surprised a few weeks ago to find out that she has breast cancer, and we were even more surprised to find it was not just one lump in her breast, but had already spread, with multiple tumors showing up on CT scans and MRI's throughout her lungs, liver and spine.

This news was devastating, as you can imagine. But within hours of sending out our note asking for your encouragement, prayers started coming in from all over the world–from places like Kenya and Ghana, Malaysia and the Bahamas, Qatar and Dubai and all over the U.S. The prayers of the saints were spreading faster than any cancer ever could!

I heard from a chaplain of a prison in New Mexico who said that all of the inmates in his prison were going to be praying for my wife. I heard from another man in Uganda who said:

> "I bet you or your husband has never been to Uganda. Yet you have. This Day's Thought has been the highlight of my inbox since 2007. I feel like I know you, the picture is more complete with the family photo. Am surely praying for you."

As the week went on, God continued to speak to us, reminding us that Jesus already drank the cup of death for us and that He was holding out a cup of life to us instead! We feel that Jesus wants us to drink from His cup of life, and drink deeply. Whereas I wrote my message last week in part to comfort my own soul in the event that this cancer might take my wife's life, this week I'm writing with full faith and confidence that God could heal her in a moment, completely and gloriously! And I'm thrilled to say that this miracle may have already begun!

The day after we sent our prayer request to you, Lana noticed that the tumor in her breast had shrunk suddenly and significantly. And by 4 o'clock in the morning, she wasn't sure if she could even find it at all! We began to pray hard that this would be just an indicator of what is going on in the rest of her body, that the cancer is being driven out by the power of God and that what was once in the darkness must now flee in the light!

We've been praying toward that end for the rest of the week, and with that in mind, I'd like to ask you to consider praying and fasting along with me and hundreds of others who have already told us they'll be praying with us during a special 24 hour prayer vigil for my wife. You don't have to go anywhere special, just pray wherever you are starting on morning Monday morning, February 27th at 7:00 a.m. Central Time (-6 GMT), through Tuesday morning, the 28th, at 7:00 a.m. We're going to be praying and fasting that God would spare Lana's life, confessing that her life and ministry isn't at the end, but that it's just at the beginning in a whole new way!

We believe that even one prayer, offered in faith, has tremendous power! As the Bible says:

> "And the prayer offered in faith will make the sick person well; the Lord will raise him up. If he has sinned, he will be forgiven. Therefore confess your sins to each other and pray for each other so that you may be healed. The prayer of a righteous man is powerful and effective. Elijah was a man just like us. He prayed earnestly that it would not rain, and it did not rain on the land for three and a half years. Again he prayed, and the heavens gave rain, and the earth produced its crops." (James 5:13-16).

One prayer, offered in faith, can make the sick person well. One prayer, offered in faith, can bring forgiveness. One prayer, offered in faith, can close the heavens and open them again.

And one prayer, offered in faith, can lead us to eternal life. As the apostle Paul said:

> "That if you confess with your mouth, 'Jesus is Lord,' and believe in your heart that God raised him from the dead, you will be saved" (Romans 10:9).

We're praying and believing for Lana's healing, not just because we're afraid she'll die, but because we believe that it pleases the heart of God whenever we pray a prayer offered in faith.

Whereas last week I felt like I needed a cheerleader to keep me up in my spirits, this week I'm feeling like *being* the cheerleader, cheering you all to stand up and clap and shout and make some noise for the Lord.

I remember watching some cheerleaders at a college football game stand in front of one section of a stadium full of people. The cheerleaders would raise their arms and shout to the people to do the same, calling on them to lift their hands, shout and clap, and stomp their feet for the victory that they were hoping would soon come. Then the cheerleaders would move to the next section and call on those people to stand up on their feet and do the same. Then they'd take off running around the stadium, going from section to section, until the people throughout the whole stadium were on their feet, clapping and shouting and stomping!

As this message goes around the world this week, I want to call upon all of you to stand to your feet in prayer and praise, shouting and clapping and making some noise for the Lord! (You don't have to do it out loud, but you can if you want!)

While it may seem selfish of me to call on so many of you to pray so intensely for my wife and my family and me, after reading your notes and letters this week, I know for sure that this is not just about saving her life for my sake or the sake of the kids, but for God's sake and for all that He is wanting to do through this to bring glory to His name. I pray that this is yet another testimony that will bring hope and healing and salvation to people all over the world.

So with that in mind, I want to encourage you to pray with us, and fast with us, for 24 hours this week, that Lana's healing would be complete and glorious, and that God's name would be glorified through it all!

There are times when fasting should be done in secret. But there are other times in the Bible where fasting was done in the light, in full view of everyone, like when Esther was about to make a special request of the king to save her people, but which could have cost her life. Esther said:

> "Go, gather together all the Jews who are in Susa, and fast for me. Do not eat or drink for three days, night or day. I and my maids will fast as you do. When this is done, I will go to the king, even though it is against the law. And if I perish, I perish" (Esther 4:16).

Esther declared her fast, publicly and widely, because she knew that God could use those prayers for the salvation of many, many souls. Esther was placed in a unique position to call this fast and I believe Lana has been placed in a similar position. As Esther's cousin said to her just before she declared her fast:

> "And who knows but that you have come to royal position for such a time as this?" (Esther 4:14b).

If you'd like some ideas for how to fast and pray, I've included a link below that I've found helpful.

http://www.cru.org/training-and-growth/devotional-life/7-steps-to-fasting/index.htm

If you're thinking of joining us, I'd like to encourage you by sharing a note I received this week from a dear friend who had mistakenly, but thankfully, thought that our day of prayer and fasting was *last* Monday instead of this coming one. As she set out to fast and pray for 24 hours, she wrote to us and said:

> "This morning, I pledge a day of fasting and hourly prayer for Lana's healing. I pray for her recovery and the Lord granting her 50 more years of ministry at Eric's side. I pray for the possibility of unbelievers hearing of Lana's healing and following their curiosity to the Gospel. I pledge to pray each hour for Lana's healing not only for the benefit of her family and friends, but for the benefit of the Body of Christ. May God hear my pleas."

Then, when her fast was nearly complete, she wrote:

> "Lana and Eric, Soon—as in fifteen minutes—my day of fasting and prayer will be over, so I wanted you to know how much it meant to me carry you both in my heart and mind all day. During the day and night, I remembered many moments of laughter and friendship, but I thought mostly about how you express your faith. It is inspiring, yes, but also challenging, because your faith makes me—and those who listen to me share about your work—question if we are doing as much, being as faithful. While I know comparison is not the answer, I can't help but think that the Lord uses those moments to nudge me, and others, along. Lana, you are so dearly loved, and I am in your debt for thousands—yes thousands—of little ways you have encouraged my faith. P.S. While praying about whether or not I should commit to doing the fast and prayer day, I went to check the dates so that my prayers could be added to others. I believed I saw 20-21. I was convinced, in fact, so I was shocked to read, this morning, that the prayer vigil is set for next week. So, it is my hope that the Lord directed me to

this day for His purposes, but I will add my prayers to the others on the 27th as well. :)"

I am fully convinced that God directed our friend to pray for us that day and I would love for you to join us in prayer, too, whether it's on the 27th and 28th, or at any other time when you read this message. I sure time zones and dates don't mean nearly as much to an eternal God as they do to us here on earth!

But if you'd like to join us on this special day when hundreds of others will be praying, too, we're starting at 7:00 a.m. Central Time (-6 GMT) on Monday, February 27th through 7:00 a.m. on the 28th. You don't have to go anywhere special to pray. Just pray wherever you are. And if you'd like to post your prayers on Lana's blog, or read the prayers of others, you can do so anytime at lanaelder.wordpress.com.

And at some point during your prayers, can I encourage you to "hit your knees," by kneeling on the ground? As one of our friends said who is organizing this special day of fasting and prayer:

> "Hit your knees when you pray, because we want Satan to feel the earth tremble as we pray for Lana."

I know I'll be hitting my knees several times tomorrow and I'd love for you to do the same. If you need some words to pray for Lana throughout the day, here's a Psalm I've been praying over her, line by line, for the past few days. I pray it encourages you in making your own requests to God as well!

> May the LORD answer you when you are in distress; may the name of the God of Jacob protect you.
> May He send you help from the sanctuary and grant you support from Zion.
> May He remember all your sacrifices and accept your burnt offerings.
> May He give you the desire of your heart and make all your plans succeed.
> We will shout for joy when you are victorious and will lift up our banners in the name of our God.
> May the LORD grant all your requests.
> Now I know that the LORD saves His anointed;
> He answers him from His holy heaven with the saving power of His right hand.
> Some trust in chariots and some in horses,
> but we trust in the name of the LORD our God.
> They are brought to their knees and fall, but we rise up and stand firm.
> O LORD, save the king!
> Answer us when we call!
> (Psalm 20: 1-9)

Thanks again so much! Your words and prayers are already glorifying God in ways that go beyond anything we could ask or imagine!

Will you pray with me?

Father, thank You for what you are already doing in this situation with Lana, both in the healing we believe is taking place in her body, and the glorifying of your name that is taking place around the world. Let this day of prayer and fasting be a testimony to Your power, Your might, and Your victory over darkness, once and for all. We pray for healing and more, that You would heal Lana's body, completely and gloriously, and through it all, that Your name would be glorified in ways that go beyond anything we could ask or imagine. In Jesus' name, Amen.

APPENDIX ~ MESSAGE 3: A PICTURE OF HEALING — SEPTEMBER 13

By Eric Elder, March 4th, 2012

The words "thank you" just don't seem enough to convey to you how very much we appreciate all of your thoughts and prayers and words of encouragement over these past two weeks since I shared with you that my wife was diagnosed with Stage 4 breast cancer.

How could we not cry and be touched when we got letters like this one from a man we've never met, but who is literally rallying the troops to pray for us from a naval ship in Japan…

> *"Hello Eric and Lana,*
> *I just want to start this email off by thanking you for your "this days thoughts" messages. My Mom has been sending these to me daily and your messages have not only been helping me get closer to GOD but also helping keep in contact with my mom. You see I am currently stationed out in Japan and i can say that i do not get to go to services as much as i would like too but your messages help me out in major ways. It is very stressful out here sometimes but i can honestly say that within these last few week things have gotten a lot better for me and i have no doubt that it is because of your messages. So once again. Thank You.*
> *When i read the message about how Lana has breast cancer i immediately stopped what i was doing and began to pray. I can only imagine how difficult it is to for you two to deal with that. I told your story to some of my fellow sailors and soldiers out here and asked them to also pray for you both. They agreed without thinking twice about it. We plan on sending your ministry some donations as well as a little care package for you two. Many times when we are out to sea or deployed we have had many churches and people send us care packages to help lift out spirits. Believe me when i say that it really does lift out spirits. So we decided that we would get some things together from here in japan to lift your spirits. Also i am currently getting the sizes of some people who want to wear the t-shirts(if any are left) and we are going to get a photo of it and send that to you too also.*
> *You said that prayers came from Kenya, Ghana, Malaysia, the Bahamas, Qatar and Dubai. Well you now have prayers from the troops in Japan too. We hope that our efforts encourage you to stay strong. GOD is going to take care of you. I, and the sailors and soldiers, will pray for you every day just as you all pray for our safety day in and day out. Once again thank you for your messages you send out daily! Take Care and God Bless You Both."*

Wow! What a perfect picture of the body of Christ in action… people lifting each other up in their time of need.

Here's another one from a woman from South Wales who was praying for us while waiting for a flight in Hong Kong:

> "I am sitting here in Hong Kong airport waiting for a flight to Bangkok and thought I would check your developments—Lana, your courage and faith take my breath away. I said my prayers for you on the plane yesterday and I keep praying although I am not as familiar with the bible as the other folks! When my holiday is over I am faced with some tests but you have helped me already by your strong commitment to God. As we say in the South Wales valleys (UK) 'fight the good fight with all thy might'. God Bless and keep you safe."

And here's a short note from a man in South Africa whose three short lines spoke volumes to me on our day of prayer and fasting for my wife's healing…

> "Your wife will live. He is Jehovah Rapha [the God who heals]! greetings from South Africa."

My faith was so touched by these words that I wrote them down on a piece of paper and took them to bed with me that night.

Right below those lines on my piece of paper, I added these words from Psalm 21, which another friend here in Illinois had sent me later in the day. She said she had been listening to Psalm 20 on her "Listener's Bible," praying through the words of this Psalm for Lana, as I had asked people to do. She was praying that God would give Lana "the desire of her heart," which is not just to live, but to live long. She said she wasn't paying attention and didn't stop the Bible reading at the end of the chapter. When she heard following verses from Psalm 21, the very next chapter, she shouted for joy. The words record what God did for King David when he first prayed for long life almost 3,000 years ago…

> "How great is his joy in the victories You give! You have granted him his heart's desire and have not withheld the request of his lips.
> "He asked You for life, and You gave it to him–length of days, for ever and ever" (Psalm 21:1, 2, 4).

Then on Tuesday morning, when our 24 hours of prayer and fasting were just ending, I added one more word to my paper that I took to bed with me that night. It was Merriam-Webster's "Word of the Day" for Tuesday February 28th. I've been getting these words of the day in my inbox every day for many years. The words are fairly random each day, but the word for that morning was anything *but* random! The word of the day that day happened to be:

> "LIVELONG"

Praise God! I'm holding onto each of these three thoughts as special reminders to me that my wife *can* live, that God *can* give her the desire of her heart, and that she *can* "live long."

Some people might worry that I'm holding onto false hope. But with God, there is no such thing as false hope. With God, there is infinite hope! As the Bible says:

> "For nothing is impossible with God" (Luke 1:37).

Believe me, I'm not naive enough to think that this cancer doesn't have the power to kill my wife. It does. The first person I prayed for when I started this ministry seventeen years ago died of cancer three weeks later. And twenty-two years ago today, on March 4th, 1990, my own mother died of breast cancer. I know it's a killer disease. Believe me when I say that when I first heard the news, I cried for 24 hours straight

But believe me, too, when I say that God gave me a picture of healing last week that renewed my faith and hope in Him that He *still* could do the impossible in this situation.

When Lana and I first found out the lump in her breast was cancerous, we scheduled an appointment with a surgeon to meet with him and talk about doing surgery. The appointment was three weeks away, as he was going to be out of town and his schedule was full. So we prayed during those three weeks that by the time we met with him, the lump would be gone and Lana wouldn't have to do the surgery at all. Since the biopsy showed that the cancer was a solid mass in her breast, growing aggressively, the chances of the lump shrinking at all, let alone disappearing completely were little to none.

Every day, Lana could feel the lump in her breast, about the size of a marble. And every few days, she would anoint it with oil and pray that God would take it away. But every day, the lump was still there. Then we got the report that the situation was worse than we thought: the cancer had already spread from Lana's breast to her lungs, liver and spine. The oncologist said she was going to cancel our appointment with the surgeon for it was no longer necessary. The tumors were now too numerous for surgery on just one lump to make any difference. The news was devastating.

That's when I sent out my note asking for prayer to all of you and you began to pray for us. The next day, we went in for a bone biopsy and had another conversation with the oncologist. She reconfirmed the diagnosis that she had told us before, reiterating that our appointment with the breast surgeon the next day was no longer necessary.

But later that night, just before going to bed, Lana went to pray for the lump in her breast as she had done all along. But this time when she went to find the lump, it had shrunk to the size of a BB, smaller than a pea. When she woke up again at 4 in the morning, she went to feel it again and couldn't find it at all! One day it was there, and the next it was gone, just as she had prayed it would be. That was the day we were to meet with the surgeon, three weeks after she began praying that prayer!

Lana woke me up to check it out, and I couldn't find it either! Perhaps the words of the oncologist weren't as dire as we had thought, but they were prophetic instead: that our appointment with the breast surgeon really was no longer necessary!

I began to cry and praise God, saying that I wasn't sure if I could even believe it or not. I also didn't know what that meant for the other tumors throughout her body. But it gave me a picture of healing that matched the picture of healing I get from the Bible where the blind see, the lame walk, and the sickness is gone. I began to pray for Lana's whole body, that God would take away every lump from everywhere and that He would complete the incredible work that He was doing.

I also put my hand on my own forehead, where I had had a mild but constant headache for the previous three weeks. I assumed it must be from the stress of the diagnosis, as I rarely get headaches, and if I do, they last for only a few hours at most. But this headache had persisted day and night for three straight weeks. It didn't cause me severe pain, but it was enough to be noticeable and it always got worse whenever I leaned forward or put on my glasses.

After putting my hand on my head and praying for my headache, I returned to praising God with Lana. Unsure if we could really believe that this had just happened, or if we might find the lump again in the morning, or what might be going on with all the other tumors in her body, we finally laid down again to try to get some sleep.

But as I laid down, I took out my Bible and put on my glasses to read for a while. When I put them on, I expected to feel the pain in my eye again. But there was no pain. I leaned forward in the bed, and there was still no pain. I got out of bed and leaned my head way down to my toes and there was still no pain. None whatsoever. The headache that I had felt for three straight weeks was gone, completely gone!

I began to cry again, not because of what God had done for my headache, but because it gave me yet another picture of healing and what that implied about the tumors in Lana's body, too. I finally fell asleep, praising God that no matter what, He had restored my faith that He really *could* do anything, absolutely anything. I finally believed once again that with God, nothing is impossible, even the healing of my wife.

When we woke up the next morning, we felt for the lump again, and after some time searching, we thought we might have found it, although much, much smaller than it had been for almost two and a half months straight. We contacted the doctor to ask if this was normal for the lump to shrink like this. She said that it may have been due to some swelling that could have subsided from a biopsy done three weeks earlier. When I heard those words, the pain in my head returned. I prayed:

"God, no matter what's going on, I thank You for giving me a picture of healing, a picture of what it can be like when You heal someone, suddenly and miraculously. I believe, Lord, that You can heal Lana in an instant, just as You've healed me in an instant of other things in the past and just as I've seen You heal others. Thank You Lord for giving me a picture to hang onto no matter what happens next."

Over the past week, my headache has come and gone, fading in and out, but no longer as continuous as it had been. The lump in Lana's breast has also seemed to come and go, where some days she can find it, although it's still very small and other days she can't seem to find it at all. We've scheduled an ultrasound on the lump for tomorrow (Monday, March 5th) with the doctor who originally did the biopsy to see if the technology confirms what we are seeing: that the tumor has indeed gotten smaller or gone away completely. I, for one, can't wait to see the results!

But I can also say that my faith this week has soared to the point where it doesn't much matter what the doctor's report says. What matters most is that God has shown me that He can do anything, absolutely anything. (Update: The following day, the radiologist said the lump in Lana's breast was measuring 20% smaller than when he first measured it, measuring only 1.2 cm instead of 1.5 cm the month before, and before the biopsy that could have caused any inflammation, and that this *was* unusual. He said he had never seen a lump like this go away or shrink without treatment and that he "didn't have a great explanation for why this is happening.")

If you've been reading my messages for the past several months, you know that we've been studying the book of Romans and looking at the topic of "Renewing Your Mind." While I hope to return to our study of the book of Romans again soon, I must also say that this whole experience has been one intense crash course on the importance of getting our thinking in line with God's. Every time we get a doctor's report, or read an article on the internet, or hear a story from someone else who's died of cancer, we have to take our thoughts captive, asking God to replace our thoughts with His... that He is the only one who truly knows how this will turn out in the end.

It's not like I need God to heal Lana for me to continue to believe in Him. And it's not like He has to keep doing miracles for me to continue to believe in Him. I'm already in. I'm fully committed. I've signed on the dotted line and given my whole life to Jesus. It's not like I'm troubled of what will happen to Lana if she dies. I know she loves Jesus with all of her heart, soul, mind and strength and that she'll be with Him forever in heaven–and that I'll be with her there someday myself.

But what God *has* done for me these past two weeks, thanks to His help and your prayers, has been to renew my mind and believe in Him again that He can do ALL THINGS–that truly *nothing* is impossible with God. I know that God can work all things for good for those who love Him and are called according to His purpose and that God really can give Lana the desire of her heart, at any time and through any means, to live a long and full life here on earth and then on into heaven forever.

What do the coming weeks hold for us? I can't say for sure. But I can say this: I'm looking forward to the weeks ahead more than ever before, because I know I'll be going through them with a God who loves me, and who loves Lana, and who loves you more than any of us could possibly imagine.

I pray this week that you would know this love of God as well, and if you haven't put your faith in Christ, that you would do it now, for the forgiveness of your sins so you can live with Him forever, and for everything else in your life, so you can live the abundant life He's called you to live here on earth. Like the apostle Paul, I pray for you, that you would know God's immeasurable love and His remarkable power. As Paul said:

> *"And I pray that you, being rooted and established in love, may have power, together with all the saints, to grasp how wide and long and high and deep is the love of Christ, and to know this love that surpasses knowledge–that you may be filled to the measure of all the fullness of God.*
> *"Now to Him who is able to do immeasurably more than all we ask or imagine, according to His power that is at work within us, to Him be glory in the church and in Christ Jesus throughout all generations, for ever and ever! Amen"* (Ephesians 3:14-21).

I look forward to sharing another update again with you next week, then I hope to return to our study of Romans after that with renewed vigor, knowing the importance of "renewing our minds."

Will you pray with me?

Father, thank You for being Jehovah Rapha, the God who heals, and for giving us a picture of healing that we can hang onto. Lord, we pray that You would continue to heal Lana's body, completely and gloriously, and through it all, that Your name would be glorified in ways that go beyond all we could ask or imagine. We pray also that You would use this situation to spark our faith to believe once again that nothing is impossible with You, no matter how dire the circumstances and no matter how bleak the reports. We trust and believe that Your report is always good, for You truly can work all things for good for those who love you and who are called according to Your purpose. In Jesus' name, Amen.

APPENDIX ~ MESSAGE 4: LIVING LIKE YOU'RE GOING TO LIVE

By Eric Elder, March 11th, 2012

I'd like to give you one more update on my wife Lana this week, then we'll return next week to our study of the book of Romans and the topic of "Renewing Your Mind."

Although I know my messages these past few weeks have touched many hearts and lives as you've been watching Lana go through this, she's never really liked being the center of attention, so she's ready for me to go back to writing about you instead of her!

But I had one more thought I'd like to share with you before we return to our study of Romans and as I said last week, we've never been so aware of the importance of "renewing our minds" and keeping our thoughts focused on God's thoughts than we have been during this whole experience. It's so much better that way! Given that, here's Lana's most recent update, which she posted on her blog at lanaelder.wordpress.com.

> I just wanted to follow up with everyone on my visit to my oncologist on Wednesday. She put together a treatment plan that would use chemotherapy to help shrink the tumors and would alleviate any symptoms from the cancer that I might have down the road. She also explained that treating Stage 4 cancer is like treating diabetes. You can manage the symptoms of diabetes with insulin, but it is something that you will have the rest of your life. In the same way, the treatments I would have for any symptoms of my cancer would be something I would likely need for the rest of my life. She said I could take a break from the chemo for a couple of months from time to time, but that the tumors will most likely grow back and then I would be back on the chemo to shrink them.
>
> However, currently, I feel very few symptoms and have a lot of hope from the prayers and nutritional changes I've been making. She agreed to let me continue doing what I've been doing and check the status of my tumors in two months. I was so thankful and happy that she agreed to this. I could have kissed her! Thursday I met with a nutritional doctor to help me determine the best way to build up my immune system over the coming months. I have also read many books regarding nutritional approaches to treating cancer. I am currently taking more supplements than anyone I know but I feel very good about this approach and I'm so thankful to be able to treat the cancer this way. I'm praying my tumors will continue to shrink and disappear through prayer and nutrition.
>
> On a funnier side note, as we the left nutritionist yesterday, walking out with a bag chock-full of supplements, Eric said he felt like he was in a scene from the movie "The Princess Bride" when two men take their friend Westley to see Miracle Max. Even though they thought Westley was dead, it turned out he was only "mostly" dead according to Miracle Max, so he made a special pill to bring him back to life. As the two friends left with the pill in their hands and their friend Westley over their shoulders, Miracle Max and his wife Valerie are seen standing at the door waving. Valerie then leans into Miracle Max and says, "Think it'll work?" to which Miracle Max says, "It would take a miracle!" and they just keep waving. (It's a great movie if you haven't seen it.) Apparently, that's how Eric felt leaving the nutritionist yesterday with all these pills, smiling and waving and thinking "It would take a miracle!" Thankfully, he makes me laugh. I credit him for most of the wrinkles on my face! I told Eric I feel like some

people think I am like Westley... that I'm "mostly" dead. But I just want you all to know I'm alive and well. I continue to eat very healthy and exercise (either walking, running, weights, or stretching). I also know it probably will take a miracle to cure me from this disease. But thanks to your prayers, I'm chock-full of faith, too!
So thank you for adding your prayers to mine! I do believe they make a difference. A psalm I read last night that encouraged me is Psalm 121.
"I lift up my eyes to the hills—where does my help come from?
My help comes from the LORD, the Maker of heaven and earth.
He will not let your foot slip—He who watches over you will not slumber; indeed, He who watches over Israel will neither slumber nor sleep.
The LORD watches over you—the LORD is your shade at your right hand; the sun will not harm you by day, nor the moon by night.
The LORD will keep you from all harm—He will watch over your life; the LORD will watch over your coming and going both now and forevermore."
(Psalm 121:1-8)
I am very much aware that my help comes from the Lord. But I also know that God works through His people and I have seen Him working through many of you. Whether it's a word of encouragement, a prayer, a card, or a gift, I sense God working through you all to encourage and strengthen me. You are being the hands, feet and body of Christ to me. So thank you again for everything. May God bless you back abundantly!!

As you can tell from Lana's note, she's planning on living! And I, for one, am thrilled with that plan!

One of the gems that has emerged like a diamond for me through all of the high-intensity pressure of the past few weeks was a comment from a friend that captivated me when I first read it and still captivates me today. At the end of her note she wrote:

"... and for everyone's sake, LIVE like she's going to LIVE!"

Wow! That made me sit up in my chair and think long and hard about how I was going to live in the days, weeks, months, and years ahead. Was I going to live like my wife was dying? Or was I going to live like she was going to live? They seemed like two diametrically opposed paths.

But the truth is, we're all on a path towards death, and have been ever since the day we were born. And at the same time, we're all on a path towards life, too. The only difference in the situation that Lana and I are facing is that we truly believe we've been given a great gift: the gift of seeing both the brevity and fullness of life, simultaneously.

We all have a choice to make each day. We can either live like we're dying, or we can live like we're going to live. Lana has chosen to live like she's going to live, and with that attitude, the chances are good that she could outlive us all! I know I want more of that attitude in my own life, too. When people live like they're going to live, it's contagious.

So many of you have written to say that even though we've been asking for prayer for ourselves through all of this, that you've been blessed by praying for us through it all as well. It's an interesting phenomenon, one that is summed up in this thought by Marianne Williamson:

> "And when we let our own light shine, we unconsciously give other people permission to do the same. As we are liberated from our own fear, our presence automatically liberates others."

Lana's not afraid of dying. She just wants to live! And by choosing to do everything she can to stay healthy and alive as long as possible, she's giving me and many others the inspiration to live our days to the fullest as well.

The truth is, none of us are guaranteed tomorrow. But we can choose how we're going to live today. As the apostle James said:

> "Now listen, you who say, 'Today or tomorrow we will go to this or that city, spend a year there, carry on business and make money.' Why, you do not even know what will happen tomorrow. What is your life? You are a mist that appears for a little while and then vanishes. Instead, you ought to say, 'If it is the Lord's will, we will live and do this or that.' As it is, you boast and brag. All such boasting is evil. Anyone, then, who knows the good he ought to do and doesn't do it, sins" (James 4:13-17).

God has called us to do as much good as possible in the days He's given us here on earth. So while none of us are guaranteed tomorrow, the challenge—and the joy—is to live like we're going to live, while at the same time being fully conscious that at any moment we could die.

Neither Lana nor I are trying to be heroic nor presumptuous about what God might have in store for either of us in the future. But what we do want to do is to be faithful with every day that God gives to us here on earth. Every day really is a gift from God, and as someone has wisely said, that's why today is called "the present."

I want to encourage you today: don't be afraid of dying, but live like you're going to live. As Jesus said,

> "Do not be afraid of those who kill the body but cannot kill the soul. Rather, be afraid of the One who can destroy both soul and body in hell. Are not two sparrows sold for a penny? Yet not one of them will fall to the ground apart from the will of your Father. And even the very hairs of your head are all numbered. So don't be afraid; you are worth more than many sparrows" (Matthew 10:31).

God has created you to do many good things here on the earth, things which He has prepared in advance for you to do (see Ephesians 2:8-10).

So live like you're going to live! That's what Lana is planning on doing, and that's what I'm planning on doing, too. We hope you'll join us!

Will you pray with me?

Father, thank You for giving us another day of life today. Thank You for reminding us of the importance of living every day to the fullest and living in such a way that our lives bring glory and honor to You and to those around us. We pray that Your light would shine through us, even in the darkest of times, so that people can see You more clearly, putting their faith and trust in You for everything in their lives. In Jesus' name, Amen.

APPENDIX ~ MESSAGE 5: THE DIFFERENCE THREE DAYS CAN MAKE   SEPTEMBER 15

By Lana Elder, Palm Sunday, April 1st, 2012

As we approach Holy Week, I want to talk to you about the difference three days can make.

I heard a story recently of a seminary student who was struggling to keep going. He was tired, exhausted and ready to give up. He fell asleep in class one day and didn't wake up until everyone else had gone home–except his teacher.

His teacher gently woke him up and said:

"Go home, eat a good meal, get some sleep and don't make any important decisions in the next three days."

The student followed his advice, regained his strength, and is now leading a worldwide ministry. He said his teacher's advice was some of the best he had ever received.

Three days can often mean the difference between victory and defeat.

I think of the story of King David in the book of 1 Samuel. From almost the moment that David was anointed by Samuel to be the next king of Israel, King Saul, the current king, wanted David dead. If you read in 1 Samuel 17, you'll see that shortly after Samuel anoints David to be the next king, David kills the giant Philistine, Goliath. From then on, King Saul seems to have it in his heart to kill David. Throughout the rest of the chapters in 1 Samuel, Saul pursues David in an attempt to kill him.

Life has got to be difficult when your king wants to kill you. Can you imagine if the President, or the King, or the Prime Minister of your country wanted you dead? But every time King Saul tries to kill David, God continues to protect him.

One of the most devastating times in David's life takes place when David escapes to the land of the Philistines to avoid being destroyed by Saul. While David was gone on one of his fighting expeditions, the Amalekites raided Ziklag, the town where David and his men and their families had settled. The Bible says:

"David and his men reached Ziklag on the third day. Now the Amalekites had raided the Negev and Ziklag. They had attacked Ziklag and burned it and had taken captive the women and all who were in it, both young and old. They killed none of them, but carried them off as they went on their way.

"When David and his men came to Ziklag, they found it destroyed by fire and their wives and sons and daughters taken captive. So David and his men wept aloud until they had no strength left to weep. David's two wives had been captured–Ahinoam of Jezreel and Abigail, the widow of Nabal of Carmel. David was greatly distressed because the men were talking of stoning him; each one was bitter in spirit because of his sons and daughters. But David found strength in the Lord his God" (1 Samuel 30:1-6).

I try to imagine what it must have been like to be David. God had anointed him to be the next king, but at first, his life was nothing like royalty. King Saul was constantly trying to kill him–and then this happens. Everything David owns is burned and his wives have been captured. David and his men weep until they have no strength left. His own followers were now talking of stoning him. All hope seemed lost.

I think I would have given up. Looking at the situation from my human perspective, I would have said, "That guy Samuel the prophet was wrong. I certainly have not been chosen by God to do *anything*. Everyone is against me. God is not for me. If He were for me, my life would not look like this. I am just going to go back to tending sheep."

Thankfully I'm not David. Instead, the Bible says, "David found strength in the Lord his God." David didn't lose his faith in God through all of his trials. If he had, we would never have known about one of the greatest kings this world has ever had.

David persevered. He inquired of the Lord and chose to pursue his enemy. Amazingly, they found an abandoned slave of an Amalekite who was left for dead because he was ill. The slave was able to lead David and his men to their families. The Bible says:

> "David fought them from dusk until the evening of the next day, and none of them got away, except four hundred young men who rode off on camels and fled. David recovered everything the Amalekites had taken, including his two wives. Nothing was missing: young or old, boy or girl, plunder or anything else they had taken. David brought everything back" (1 Samuel 30:17-19).

Okay, now that's why this guy is so famous! David was certainly known to be a fighter, and in this instance, he doesn't disappoint us.

In the very next chapter, just three days after David's most intense battle to save everything dear to him and to those around him, David gets the news: King Saul has died. The Bible says:

> "After the death of Saul, David returned from defeating the Amalekites and stayed in Ziklag two days. On the third day a man arrived from Saul's camp, with his clothes torn and with dust on his head. When he came to David, he fell to the ground to pay him honor.
> "Where have you come from?" David asked him.
> He answered, "I have escaped from the Israelite camp."
> "What happened?" David asked. "Tell me."
> He said, "The men fled from the battle. Many of them fell and died. And Saul and his son Jonathan are dead" (2 Samuel 1:1-4).

In the next chapter, David becomes king of Judah and eventually he becomes king over all of Israel. What's significant to me is that his life really changed in a matter of days–three days to be exact. I think of how downcast David must have been up to that point, "greatly distressed" as the Bible says, when his belongings were burned and his people were captured. Then just three short days later he had it all back again, and not only that, but the king who had been pursuing him was finally dead. Life certainly was looking better for David.

This, of course, reminds me of another story in the Bible when things didn't look too good, but God turned things around in a miraculous way–in just three days. It's the story of Jesus.

Jesus was a man who, much like his great ancestor David, was destined to reign as king. As the angel told Mary in Luke 1:32-3:

> "He will be great and will be called the Son of the Most High. The Lord God will give Him the throne of His father David, and He will reign over the house of Jacob forever; His kingdom will never end."

I wonder how His mother felt on that day the angel visited. And then I wonder what she must have felt on the day she saw him crucified. Here was her beloved son, destined to be king, yet hanging dead on a cross. How could this be? All hope seemed lost.

But for God, time is relative. Hope is eternal.

Jesus had a lifetime of doing incredible things here on earth. He healed the sick. He raised the dead. He walked on water. He encouraged people to forgive and to do what is right.

He told stories to encourage people to use their gifts and talents today, not worry about tomorrow, and not to judge others. He talked about what were the most important matters of the law, like justice, mercy and faithfulness. He criticized hypocrisy. And yet with all of His miracles and powerful teaching, there were still leaders who wanted Him dead. They pursued Him, much like King Saul pursued David, to try and kill him. And in Jesus' case, they succeeded—or so it seemed.

But just like David, Jesus never gave up His faith in His heavenly Father. Jesus trusted His Father to do what was best, even as He prayed in the Garden of Gethsemane on the night before He died. Jesus prayed:

> "Father, if You are willing, take this cup from me; yet not my will, but Yours be done" (Luke 22:42).

Just like David, Jesus "found strength in the Lord His God," even spending His last night on earth in deep and earnest prayer.

And His Father did not disappoint Him. Even though it may have looked hopeless, hope was never lost. It never is. Even after Jesus' death on the cross, hope was just around the corner. Three days later, Jesus rose from the dead!

Jesus' death on the cross turned out to be part of God's plan. As Jesus Himself said:

> "For God so loved the world that He gave His one and only Son, that whoever believes in Him shall not perish but have eternal life" (John 3:16).

I wanted to tell you these stories to encourage you that hope is eternal. Even when things may seem to be at their worst, God can turn them around in a matter of days, hours, or even a moment.

You may be a seminary student and ready to give up. Don't! Go home, eat a good meal, get some sleep and don't make any important decisions in the next three days!

You may have thought you were destined for great things in your lifetime, but now you're hiding in caves. Even the king seems out to get you.

You may think it would be better if you just gave up your dreams and gave in to despair. Don't! Don't lose hope now, as God's most important miracle for your life may be just around the corner.

You may be facing an impossible situation, one that seems irreversible, incurable or unchangeable.

You may be ready to give up on God altogether, perhaps even considering turning away from Him for the rest of your life. Don't! I can't guarantee you what the outcome will be, but

I can guarantee you that God will always be there for you, if you'll keep putting your faith in Him.

Never give up on God. As David said in the Psalms:

> *"Wait and hope for and expect the Lord; be brave and of good courage and let your heart be stout and enduring. Yes, wait for and hope for and expect the Lord" (Psalm 27:14, Amplified Bible).*

Let's pray…

Father, I thank you that we can always come to you even when all hope seems lost. You always have a plan and you know what's best. Help us to trust you in all things. Whether it's three seconds, or three days, or three years or more, help us to trust You today and every day until we see what You have in store for us, just around the corner. In Jesus' name, Amen.

Making the Most of the Darkness

12 inspirational messages to give you hope during your time of loss

INTRODUCTION   **SEPTEMBER 16**

Let me start off by saying, "I'm sorry." If you're about to read this book, chances are good that you've probably lost someone or something that was very precious to you. And for that, perhaps the best thing I can say to you right now is simply, "I'm sorry."

I wish there were something more I could do for you, or say to you, that would help to take away your pain or to ease your burden, even just a little. Although it may not seem like much, perhaps saying, "I'm sorry," is just enough for right now.

Sometimes it's just enough to know that there are other people who care, that there are other people who are aware of your pain and that there are other people who have walked through the darkness as well. I wish I could say I know what you're going through, but I don't. And even though no two losses are the same, sometimes it's nice just to know that other people have walked through the darkness and found something special along the way, something they may have never noticed when they were walking in the light. Stars, for instance, shine brighter when there are no other lights around.

I'm not saying it's easy, or altogether wonderful to walk in the darkness. It's not. But if you read through the words on the following pages, you'll find that there *are* beautiful lights along the way, glimpses of heaven and riches that glisten that you may never have noticed had you not walked this way. Samuel Rutherford, a Scottish pastor in the 1600s, said:

> "Jesus came into my prison cell last night, and every stone flashed like a ruby."

On the pages that follow, I'd like to share with you some of the rubies I saw as I walked through my own period of darkness—my first year of grief after losing my precious wife, Lana. I wrote these 12 messages *while* I was walking through the darkness, not *after* the fear and danger were gone, which always seems to make things look brighter and more obvious than before. I wrote them in the midst of the pain and heartache that I was experiencing, both as a way to help me stay focused on the One who was walking through it with me, and as a way to give hope to others who were walking through their own times of darkness.

At the beginning of my journey, I read a book called *Getting to the Other Side of Grief*. As I was just getting started, I honestly didn't know that there *was* another side of grief and, if there was, if I'd ever get there myself. The pain was just too intense. But the authors of the book had both lost their spouses, they made a compelling case for the fact that there *is* another side of grief, and if I was willing to work through it—and in my case, to walk through it with God—I could get there, too.

I took their words to heart and I began to walk with intentionality, trusting that their words were true. More than that, I had the promise of God's Word in the Bible that says that He will work all things together for our good:

> *"And we know that in all things God works for the good of those who love Him, who have been called according to His purpose" (Romans 8:28).*

I knew this to be true from the previous 26 years of following Him. But I had never had to put it to the test more than in this first year after losing my sweet wife. She was, after Christ Himself, the greatest gift God had ever given me. And losing her was like losing part of myself, too.

On the pages that follow, you'll get to know a little bit more about me and her and my family and our faith in God. Even though we may not have gone through what you're going through right now, I hope that something of what we've gone through will be of help to you. There's something about walking with others through their pain that helps to ease our own pain, even if just a little bit.

On the other hand, you may be hesitant to walk with me through these 12 messages for fear that they might open up some of your own wounds in a deeper way. If that's the case, let me encourage you to keep reading on two fronts:

1) When I decided to put these 12 messages into this book, I was even fearful myself to reread them at first. Having just walked through an entire year of grief, I didn't really want to relive it. Yet as I reread each of the messages, I was surprised at how hopeful I felt after reading each one, and to see that God was indeed walking with me every step of the way—even when I sometimes couldn't see it for myself.

2) There's something cathartic about walking through someone else's pain that brings healing in our own. That's one of the reasons people love watching good movies so much, even sad ones, because people are able to release some of their own emotions as they watch others go through similar struggles, even if they're not exactly the same.

I remember one night some friends invited me to watch a movie with them when I was stopped for the night at their house on a long trip with the kids. This was before Lana had died, but after I had discovered that she may not live much longer. My friends said the movie was about some guys who bought a zoo and that the kids and I might like it.

I had no idea that the movie was about a husband who lost his wife to a serious illness and dealt with the aftermath of that tragic event. As I realized what the movie was about, I started to boil inside, thinking that I would have never watched it if I had known what it was about, and I wouldn't have had my kids watch it either. I didn't want to think about Lana dying, let alone what life might be like once she was gone.

But somehow I stayed in my seat, for as the movie unfolded, I was drawn into the story, drawn into the way the main characters walked through this loss in their life. Although it wasn't all peaches and roses, it wasn't without hope, either. Many of the thoughts and emotions they expressed were the same thoughts and emotions that had flitted through my own mind but never wanted to entertain. Watching now, however, in the context of someone else's pain, somehow seemed to ease my own.

As the movie came to a close, I was so thankful I had watched. It didn't end all neat and tidy, but it *did* end with hope. And while the movie itself wasn't about God, it gave me hope that *with* God somehow He would be able to work it all out in the end. So perhaps reading our story will give you that hope, too.

I also want to let you know you can read these messages at your own pace. I wrote these over the course of a year, so I was at a slightly different place in my grief with each message. One of the books I read on grief during this past year was one that was timed to be read over the course of a year, not all at once (called *Journeying Through Grief*). Grief is a process, and we can't walk through every stage right away, even if we wanted to. In fact, sometimes it can be better if we don't try to rush grief. Bob Deits, the author of several books on grief, said:

"Grief is the last act of love we have to give those who have died."

If you're just trying to avoid pain, you might be tempted to rush through your grief as fast as possible. But if, on the other hand, your grief is a way to express your last act of love to one who has died, you might rather take as much time as you need to make sure you express it well.

There's no hurry or timetable with grief. But I can say there is another side of it. As I mention in the final chapter of this book, I'm thankful now to be able to see it for myself.

There is another side of grief. As Jesus said to His disciples just before He died:

"You will grieve, but your grief will turn to joy" (John 16:20b).

That may have sounded like an outlandish promise to the disciples at the time, except for the fact that it was Jesus who was saying it–the same Jesus whom they had seen heal the sick, walk on water and raise the dead. If anyone could make a promise like that and live up to it, Jesus could.

So with that hope in mind, and with my heartfelt condolences for the loss that you've experienced, I invite you to read the 12 messages that follow. I pray that they give you hope for your future–and that they help you to see the stones along the way flash like rubies.

CHAPTER 1: TWO STORIES AND A CONCLUSION   SEPTEMBER 17

Dear friends, thanks so much for your thoughts and prayers and kindnesses since my sweet wife Lana passed away on November 15th. It's been 4 months now and I wanted to share some thoughts with you on Lana, healing and God's will. I apologize in advance for the length of this message, but if you've been discouraged or having trouble trusting God, especially in the face of significant loss, I hope you'll read this message. This message is really just two stories, with some follow-up comments to help you bring them together and apply them to your lives.

I haven't shared these stories publicly until this week, as they are so personal and intimate that I've just been treasuring them in my own heart. But I feel they're important to share as a way of testifying to what God is doing in my life, and hopefully encouraging you at the same time.

The first story started on the day of Lana's funeral, on November 20th, 2012. Before she died, Lana had asked me to preach at her funeral if it ever came to that. She said I didn't have to do it if I didn't think I could, but if I could, she wanted me to be the one to do it. I did get up and preach, but not without seriously considering backing out several times, even a few times during the service just before I was about to speak. I just wasn't sure if I could do it.

One of the reasons I felt so unsure, apart from the sadness I felt in my heart from already missing her, was that I felt like I had lost so much in the days leading up to her death. I had not only lost my best friend, my encourager, my partner in ministry and, apart from Jesus, the greatest source of joy and delight in my life. We had also depleted all of the money in our bank account during those final months of her battle with cancer. On the morning of her funeral, we had $26.45 in the bank. I felt like I had lost everything. (I hadn't, but I felt like it.)

The morning of the funeral, I prayed that God would give me the strength to do what I wanted to do and needed to do. I also prayed, more as a wish than anything else, that God would give the kids some kind of inheritance from Lana from the gifts that came in. I knew that no amount of money would make up to them for losing their mother, but I wished I had something I could give them as an inheritance from her. $26.45 wasn't going to go very far among the 6 kids.

So I prayed that God would provide enough from the memorial gifts to pay for the funeral and still have some left over for the kids. From past funerals, I knew that the gifts that are received are sometimes just enough to pay for the funeral and that's it, so I wasn't expecting much. But then in my heart, I prayed, "God, if there's any way to give the kids $1,000 each as an inheritance, that would be great." But then from deeper still in my heart, I thought that what I would *really* like for them is if I could put $5,000 into each of their bank accounts. I quickly did the math and $5,000 times 6 kids would be $30,000.

There's no way, I thought. With $26.45 in the bank, I knew it was an outlandish request. But I laid it out before God anyway. Later that day, I got up to preach at Lana's funeral. (If you haven't watched it yet, I'd encourage you to watch it online at lanaelder.wordpress.com. It was like no other service, funeral or otherwise, that I've ever been to before and I think you'll find it both inspiring and helpful. So please watch it if you can!)

Starting that day and the days that followed, people *did* begin sending in memorial gifts for our family in honor of Lana. Some gave $5, some gave $15 and some gave $20 or $100. A few gave $1,000 and some even gave $5,000. By December 4th, just 2 weeks and 1 day after the funeral, we had received just over $30,000 from over 200 different people, none of whom knew about my private prayer to God!

Now keep that date and that astounding answer to prayer in mind as I tell you the 2nd story. For it was on December 4th, just one year earlier, that we had first discovered the lump in Lana's breast, our first indicator that anything was even wrong at all.

It was on that day that we had heard a missionary talk about their work in Kenya, teaching women how to do self-exams for breast cancer. Later that night we checked and discovered the lump. We thought it was probably nothing serious, as is often the case. But over the next few weeks, and after a mammogram, then an ultrasound and finally a biopsy, the doctors confirmed that the lump really was cancerous. At that time, the doctors had no reason to think that the cancer had already spread. They felt that with treatment, they could remove it and all would be fine. We were shocked but felt this was beatable.

A few days later, Lana was listening to a podcast on her phone of a sermon that gave her some encouragement. When she was done listening, she handed her phone to me so I could listen to it, too. But as she handed me her phone, I felt God speak to me as loud and clear as any time I'd ever heard Him speak in my life. Although He didn't speak in audible words, the effect of what He was saying was, "This *is* a good message, Eric. But it's not *My* message for you in this situation. This time I have something else in mind."

As I listened to the message, I found it was all about praying "bold prayers," that we shouldn't just pray for a "C" on a test, but for an "A." That we shouldn't just pray that we would survive a difficult marriage, but that it would thrive. That we shouldn't just pray for a sickness to go away, but for a long and healthy and abundant life instead. It was the kind of message I would normally believe and receive and be encouraged to pray with all my heart in whatever difficult situation I faced.

But if God had really spoken to me, then what was He saying in regards to Lana's healing? With a great sadness in my heart, I felt He was saying, "Eric, I know you have the faith to ask for the moon and get it. But not this time. This time I have something else in mind." God brought to my mind Psalm 23, reminding me that He would be with me, even in the face of death:

> "Even though I walk through the valley of the shadow of death, I will fear no evil, for You are with me…" (Psalm 23:4).

I felt that verse was a little extreme. This cancer was beatable. It didn't have to end in death. Then why was God telling me this? But the following week I found out why.

A few days later, Lana went in for a few more tests. She had started having some other symptoms, some unexplainable bleeding and intense lower back pain. The tests showed that it was worse than the doctors initially thought. The cancer had already spread to her lungs and liver and spine. In addition, the cancer was in a special category called "triple negative," which meant that it wouldn't respond to normal treatments that worked for other types of breast cancers. There was no cure, the doctors said. The best they could do was to treat the symptoms and try to keep her as comfortable as possible for as long as possible, but that the cancer would eventually take her life. Statistically, the doctors said she had about 1 to 3 years to live, depending on how she responded to treatment. The majority of women with Stage 4, triple-negative breast cancer don't make it past 5 years. And only 1 in a hundred ever make it to 10 years.

We were devastated. But having heard God speak to me the week before, even before the doctors told us what was going on, somehow gave me great faith. Not faith that Lana would be healed, although I believed God *could* still heal her in an instant, but faith that He would be with us through it all. This was no news to God. He had already revealed it to me before we, or even the doctors, had an inkling about what was coming.

Knowing that God was with us gave me great peace in my heart. But as comforting as this was, I still didn't know how to walk forward in a practical way, given what I felt God was saying to me. If God had told me that Lana was going to be healed, and to walk in faith and stand on the promise of the words He had spoken to my heart, I knew how to walk that out: read and reread the Scriptures, fast and pray, gather others to fast and pray, and look for answers from any doctor or person of faith who could help us beat this disease. But if I had really heard right, and God was really saying, "I know you have the faith to ask for the moon and get it, Eric, but not this time," how could I walk that out? How could I stand on something that I didn't *want* to believe and didn't *want* to be true?

Was I supposed to just give up on the possibility of healing? Not bother praying at all for her? Not ask others to join us in fasting and prayer? Not go to the doctors to try to get whatever help we could find? I felt that taking any of those paths would be utterly wrong. Lana wanted to live, and I wanted her to live! And who knows? Maybe I had heard wrong. Maybe the doctors were wrong. And even if I *had* heard right, and the doctors were right, maybe God would still heal her miraculously! God's default position on healing is that we *should* be healed, as evidenced by the many ways He has created our bodies to heal themselves, to automatically seal up cuts, fight off infections and repair damaged tissue. God has demonstrated His desire for our healing throughout the Bible, performing miraculous healings from cover to cover. God loves healing and wants us to be healed! There's no doubt that God is a healing God!

So I tried to remember what other biblical characters when they received a word from God that they didn't want to believe either.

I thought of Hezekiah, who was sick and dying when God spoke to him through the prophet Isaiah, saying that Hezekiah's sickness would end in death. Hezekiah wept bitterly and pleaded with God for a different outcome:

"Remember, O LORD, how I have walked before You faithfully and with wholehearted devotion and have done what is good in Your eyes" (2 Kings 20:3a).

God heard Hezekiah's prayers, healed him and gave him an extra 15 years of life.

I thought of King David, who got a word from God through Nathan the prophet saying that the child born to David and Bathsheba would die. But David didn't give up and didn't give in. He fasted and prayed and wept before God every night saying:

"Who knows? The LORD may be gracious to me and let the child live" (2 Samuel 12:22).

In David's case, however, his child still died after 7 days, but not without David pleading with God for a different outcome.

Then I thought of Jesus, who, when faced with His own imminent death, knelt down and prayed so earnestly that His sweat fell like drops of blood:

"Father, if You are willing, take this cup from Me; yet not My will, but Yours be done" (Luke 22:42).

Jesus knew what His Father was asking of Him, yet still He pleaded for another way, that the cup He was about to drink would somehow be taken from Him. Yet Jesus yielded to His Father's will, even over His own.

From these 3 stories of Hezekiah and David and Jesus, I felt I was in good company that even if I had heard right from God, I could still plead with Him, in fasting and prayer and tears, and pour out my heart to Him for what Lana and I both wanted: that she would be healed completely and gloriously and continue to live a long, healthy and abundant life.

So we fasted and prayed and called others to join us in fasting and prayer. We talked to doctors and nurses and researchers and nutritionists, both locally and globally, to see if God had an answer through them. We called the elders of our church, and 2 of our former churches, to anoint us with oil and pray for Lana's healing. We held prayer meetings in our living room and drove and flew to get prayer from some of the most faith-filled men and women of God we knew.

As time marched on, however, the tests continued to come back blacker and bleaker. Either what God had spoken to me at the beginning was true, or God was preparing the way for one of the most miraculous turnarounds of all time. Either way, we felt good about the steps we were taking, about doing everything we could possibly do to bring about her healing and about trusting in God completely, whatever the outcome.

As much as Lana and I, and many of you, wished that the outcome had been different, I can say that when it came time to say our final goodbyes, we had no regrets. We had done everything we could think of doing to keep her alive, and God had kept His promise to be with us through it all.

Let me tie these 2 stories together for you by sharing 2 journal entries from December 4th, 2012, the first of which was written early in the morning as I was remembering the one-year anniversary of finding the lump that took Lana's life, and the 2nd of which was written at midnight that same night, after receiving the checks in the mail that put us over $30,000 in memorial gifts in her honor.

"12/4/12—Father, thank You for revealing to me and Lana the lump in her right breast one year ago today... Lord, any thoughts about this being the one-year anniversary of the day You revealed this lump? 'I've given you a great gift, Eric. A chance to see into the future, and to make your plans accordingly. I have not hidden what is to happen from My prophets. I warned Abraham about the destruction of Sodom and Gomorrah before it happened, just as I told him that he and Sarah would have a child in a year, and just as I told you, Eric, that your friends would have a child in a year. Although I didn't tell you an exact date [regarding Lana], I did tell you what the outcome would be, both by showing you the lump, and by confirming that while you could pray for healing, this wasn't My will in this case. I wanted you to know, Eric, because I wanted you to have time to plan, prepare and say goodbye properly. And you have done marvelously. Your kids, your friends, your family, are all living testaments to that fact. I also gave you test after test, and doctor after doctor, to confirm this to you, for you wanted the truth, and you knew the truth would set you free. They were hard truths to hear, and hard to watch you hear, but they were necessary to help you absorb and understand what I was saying. I've given you a gift Eric, both in what I revealed, and in the fact that I do reveal My knowledge to My children. Lana wanted to live and not die, and she was right to do so, for that's My will [He wants all of us to live forever!]. But I wanted you to know so you could plan, prepare, and say goodbye properly. I wanted you to care for her and love her and be with her to the fullest extent possible, so when she passed through the veil, you would have no regrets, nothing left undone, nothing more you could have done, but love her thoroughly. I did this for you, yes, but also for Me, for I wanted you to be able to care for her on earth as I cared for her from heaven. You were, and still are, My hands and feet and voice to many on earth. You will be sad, no doubt, for to lose the one you love, when you have loved so deeply, is sad. But you will rejoice as well, for you have been given a great and wonderful gift.'"

"12 midnight—Father, thank You for helping us reach the $30,000 mark that I had asked You for, to give $5,000 to each of the kids as an inheritance from Lana. Lord, we only had $26.45 in our bank account the day of the funeral. It was an outlandish prayer, and within a few weeks, You've brought the full amount I extravagantly asked for. 'Open your mouth wide, Eric, and I will fill it.' Thank You, Lord! I love You. By the way, the sunset looked delicious tonight, like rainbow sherbet, and I wanted to lick it. 'Thank You.' Thank You, Lord."

Yes, life can be extremely hard. But it also offers sunsets that look like rainbow sherbet! The trick is to not let the hardest parts of life overshadow the best parts about it. God is at work in both. The Bible says:

> "Friends, when life gets really difficult, don't jump to the conclusion that God isn't on the job. Instead, be glad that you are in the very thick of what Christ experienced. This is a spiritual refining process, with glory just around the corner... So if you find life difficult because you're doing what God said, take it in stride. Trust Him. He knows what He's doing, and He'll keep on doing it" (1 Peter 4:12-13, 19, The Message).

Friends, God loves you and has a unique calling and purpose for your life, just as He had a unique calling and purpose for Lana's life. Don't be discouraged when life doesn't work out the way you think it should. God is still on the job. Keep putting your trust in Him. He knows what He's doing, and He'll keep on doing it.

Thanks for reading these 2 stories, and thanks again for your prayers and kindnesses you've shown to me and my family, especially during this past year. It means so much and is yet one more reminder of all that's good in life. May God bless you and keep you as you keep putting your trust in Him!

CHAPTER 2: KEEPING YOUR EYES OPEN   SEPTEMBER 18

Last week I shared 2 stories and a conclusion with you about how God has been helping me to keep the hardest parts of life from overshadowing the best parts about it. Based on the responses I've gotten, it was one of the most significant messages I've ever shared.

This week, I'd like to follow up on that message and share a few more stories to help you keep trusting in God even in the face of significant loss. I know you may not have lost a spouse like I have, but you may be facing something just as challenging in your own life, whether it's a divorce, a broken relationship, a wayward son or daughter, a job loss, a change in health or the loss of a dream that meant the world to you.

In any case, I want to encourage you to keep your eyes open to what God is doing all around you. Even though you may not see God doing what you expect Him to do in one particular area, if you can see God at work in other areas, it can help you to keep putting your trust in Him.

I believe this is what Jesus did for John the Baptist when John was in prison and facing the very real possibility of death. Up to this point, John had thought that Jesus was the one who was going to save God's people. But perhaps it was something about being in prison that seemed to make John wonder if what he had previously thought was true. John sent his followers to Jesus to ask, "Are You the one who was to come, or should we expect someone else?" (Matthew 11:3) After all, didn't Jesus come to "set the captives free" (Luke 4:18)? And wasn't John a captive, in desperate need of freedom?

But Jesus sent a message back to John, saying,

> "Go back and report to John what you hear and see: The blind receive sight, the lame walk, those who have leprosy are cured, the deaf hear, the dead are raised, and the good news is preached to the poor. Blessed is the man who does not fall away on account of Me" (Matthew 11:4-6).

It's as if Jesus was reminding John of all the things that God was doing all around him. And even if God didn't do what John may have thought He should do, John could still trust God to do what was right. When Jesus said, "Blessed is the man who does not fall away on account of Me," it's almost as if Jesus was saying, "Blessed is the man who does not fall away on account of what they *think* I should or should not be doing." Sometimes we're so focused on one area of our lives that we miss what God is doing in other areas.

It turns out that John wasn't set free, even though others in the Bible were, like Daniel when he was rescued from the lions' den (Daniel 6), or Peter when an angel led him out of jail (Acts 12), or Paul and Silas when an earthquake loosened their chains and caused the prison doors to fly open (Acts 16). In John's case, he only lived long enough to hear back from Jesus that God was indeed still on the job and working in the world.

I believe it was just what John needed to hear in order to face what he had to face: his own imminent death.

It may have seemed like John had lost his faith there at the end. But by coming to Jesus with his doubts, that didn't mean he *lost* his faith. That was an *expression* of his faith. It showed that John still looked to Jesus for answers, even in the face of circumstances he couldn't understand. If this was a test of John's faith, I believe he passed it with flying colors, as Jesus later said of him:

> "I tell you the truth: Among those born of women there has not risen anyone greater than John the Baptist..." (Matthew 11:11a).

I don't know if the trial that my wife Lana just went through was a test, or simply the result of living in a world that's been subjected to sin and sickness and decay. But if it was a test, I believe she passed with flying colors, keeping her faith in Christ to the end. Now I'm praying that I'll be able to pass with flying colors, too.

One of the ways I'm trying to do that is by doing what Jesus told John to do: to keep his eyes open to the work that Jesus was *still* doing in the world and not to base his conclusions on what he *thought* Jesus should or should not be doing.

Let me share just a few brief stories of what I've seen God doing lately, some of which may seem trivial, but in the face of the loss that I've had, even the smallest glimpse of God is worth more than gold to me.

A few weeks ago I was helping my kids do some late-night craft projects: tie-dying a dress with my daughter and making rubbery, squishy bugs with my son. I was already worn out from the day and going back and forth on these 2 projects was wearing me down further. I wanted to help them, but I was definitely missing Lana and the help that she would have been in moments like these.

At one point, I went upstairs to take a break and, as I passed a mirror, I noticed that I was still wearing some old reading glasses, as I had lost my new pair a few weeks earlier. As I looked in the mirror, I decided it was time to order another new pair, as I hadn't been able to find mine. On the way back down the stairs to the basement where my daughter was tie-dying her dress, I paused on the steps and reached my hand up to heaven. I said, "Lana, help me!" (I know it's God that helps us, but I still find myself talking to Lana in heaven, especially at times like these.) Then I continued on down the stairs.

As I got down on my hands and knees on the cold cement floor of the basement to help with the tie-dying project, I happened to look to my left and there, under the basement sink, hanging on some bottles of soap and shampoo, were my reading glasses that had been missing for weeks! Had I *not* been doing these projects with the kids, down on my hands and knees on the cold cement floor of the basement, I never would have found them! And had I *not* remembered the conversation with myself in the mirror upstairs just a few minutes earlier, and my quick call for help from heaven as I walked down the steps again, I wouldn't have put my prayer and the answer together either. My whole outlook on helping the kids for the rest of that night changed in that instant. It was as if a little reward had been dropped out of heaven and was dangling on the bottles of soap in front of me.

That may not seem like a God-moment to you, and it may not have seemed like one to me, either, if this was the first time something like this had happened. But just a few weeks earlier, when I was recovering from the flu and getting ready to start back into homeschooling our 3 youngest kids for the first time since Lana died, I had reached up to heaven as well. After gathering up literally dozens of books from around the house that the kids use for school, we were still missing 2 books. In an act of desperation more than anything else, I looked up to heaven and said, "Lana, help me!" Within minutes we found the 2 missing books. They appeared practically out of thin air.

But more than that, after we found those 2 missing books, one of my sons wanted to take a break and do some kind of "outside project." Even though it was the middle of winter and the temperature was literally below freezing outside, I said, "OK, let's fix that broken pole on the trampoline." It wasn't a very practical idea, as it was too cold to actually jump on the trampoline anytime soon, but it was the first thing that came to my mind that would be quick and easy enough to get outside and back inside before we froze.

So we went out into the freezing cold to start working on the trampoline pole and I happened to look up into the net above us. There, hanging at the top of the net, were my daughter's prescription glasses that had been missing since Lana's funeral more than 2 months earlier! It was as if they had been dropped down from heaven and had gotten caught in the net for us to find!

How they had survived the cold and the wind and the snow for 2 months, I didn't know. But what I did know was that within minutes of calling out to heaven for help, I had found 2 missing schoolbooks AND a pair of missing glasses! All the while trying to help my kids, which was something I needed to do and wanted to do, but was having trouble working up the strength to do. The moment I saw those glasses in the net, my whole perspective on the day changed. I *knew* that God was at work and that I was doing exactly what I should be doing. It gave me the strength to go on.

Just this past week, as the weather has started to get nicer here in Illinois, I was walking around the yard with a friend who's spent years in the landscaping business, asking his advice about where and what kind of trees we could plant around the house. This was a project that Lana and I had been wanting to do for some time. To be honest, it was hard to even think about planting trees, as sometimes it feels like the dreams and plans I had with Lana died when she died. But I have to remember that I didn't die, and that God might still want me to keep some of those shared dreams and plans alive, too.

So there we were, walking around the yard and sharing ideas, when my daughter reached down and found a charm on the ground for a charm bracelet. Then she found another a few feet away, and then a 3rd a few feet from that. They still had the tags on them, as we had bought them for her birthday party the month before, but we had lost them somewhere between the store and the house during a snowstorm that night. Now here they were, out in the middle of the yard, hundreds of feet from the house, as we were trying to plan and continue the dream of planting more trees in the yard!

Again, it may seem trivial to you (and perhaps makes you wonder about us and why we keep losing so many things!) But to me, it was as if God was saying, "Yes, this is exactly what I want you to be doing, walking around the yard and planning where to put trees for the future! Keep moving forward on the dreams that you and Lana shared, and keep going on with all that I have called you to do in your life! You'll be blessed as you do these things, just as will others when you're done doing them!"

I feel like Jesus keeps telling me, as He seemed to be telling John the Baptist, to keep my eyes open to the things that He's doing in the world, and to keep on trusting in Him, even in the face of all that I've lost.

I could share a dozen more stories from the past 4 months since Lana died where I've seen God at work in such small ways that it's changed my outlook on everything else going on around me, but I'll let these suffice to encourage you to keep *your* eyes open to the things God is doing in *your* life and the lives of those around you.

It reminds me of a grandfather who was out fishing with his grandson one day when the grandson asked if his grandfather had ever seen God. His grandfather gazed out across the lake where they were sitting and answered, "The older I get, the more I see Him everywhere I look."

Don't be discouraged when you don't see God at work in your life the way you *think* He should be working. Don't give up on Him because things don't always go your way. Don't think for a minute that He doesn't love you just because you've lost something precious in your life. As the Bible says,

"He who did not spare His own Son, but gave Him up for us all-how will He not also, along with Him, graciously give us all things?" (Romans 8:32).

As we head into Passion Week, this week before Easter when Jesus experienced some of the most intense pain and suffering that this world has to offer, remember that you're not alone. Jesus knows what it's like to suffer and die. He knows what it's like to lose those who are close to you, like He did when He lost his good friends Lazarus and John the Baptist. In the case of Lazarus, Jesus raised him back to life. In the case of John the Baptist, Jesus spoke words of encouragement so John could face death with faith. Regardless of the outcome, Jesus never left them alone.

In all things, remember that God really does love you and has a unique calling and purpose for your life. Keep your eyes open. The more you do, the more you'll see Him everywhere you look.

CHAPTER 3: HAVING FAITH IN THE RESURRECTION — SEPTEMBER 19

(Written Easter Sunday, 2013)

Happy Easter from our house to yours! We could all use a dose of faith, and Easter Sunday is a great day to get one. If you're struggling with trusting in God, even in the face of significant loss, this message is for you.

It's been almost 5 months since we took this picture of me and my 6 kids, not knowing that just 2 weeks later my wife Lana would pass on to be with the Lord (she was inside resting when this picture was taken, as we were in the middle of a 10-hour filming session for a project to give hope to other families facing loss). Since that day, we've had to celebrate 7 major holidays without our beloved Lana: Thanksgiving, Christmas, New Year's Eve, Valentine's Day, 2 birthdays, and now Easter.

Each of these "firsts" without her this year could have easily overwhelmed me with grief if it weren't for my faith in Jesus Christ and the prayers of people like you.

But when Christmas rolled around, God reminded me why we celebrate the holiday at all: Christmas is the celebration of the birth of the baby who would one day defeat death forever! While celebrating Christmas was still hard without Lana, God's reminder of the reason we were celebrating it helped me to keep a balanced perspective on her life and her death...and her new life with Him.

The same holds true for Easter. While there's no doubt it's been hard to go through our Easter traditions this year without Lana, God keeps reminding me of the purpose of *this* holiday, too. Easter is the day we remember that Jesus rose from the dead and, because He rose from the dead, we can be assured that all of us who have put our faith in Him will be raised from the dead, too, including my dear wife, Lana. Without Lana here with me this week, it's already been a different kind of holiday. I found myself videotaping the kids during an Easter egg hunt so that I could come home and show her the tape, only to remember that she wouldn't be there when I got home. But then God reminded me that it's quite likely that Lana's not missing a thing. The Bible says that we are surrounded by "a great cloud of witnesses," witnesses who have kept their faith to the end and who remind us to do the same.

> *"Therefore, since we are surrounded by such a great cloud of witnesses, let us throw off everything that hinders and the sin that so easily entangles, and let us run with perseverance the race marked out for us. Let us fix our eyes on Jesus, the author and perfecter of our faith, who for the joy set before Him endured the cross, scorning its shame, and sat down at the right hand of the throne of God. Consider Him who endured such opposition from sinful men, so that you will not grow weary and lose heart" (Hebrews 12:1-3).*

As sad as it is that I'm having to celebrate Easter without Lana here with me in the flesh, the truth is that without Jesus, there would be no holiday to celebrate at all, and there would be no hope of Lana being raised from the dead either. So in the midst of my heartache, God keeps reminding me of the *whole* truth: not just the truth that she's gone, but the truth that she's gone to be with Jesus and has been raised to a new life in spectacular glory. And having the *whole* truth in mind brings His peace to my heart. As the Bible says:

> *"Brothers, we do not want you to be ignorant about those who fall asleep, or to grieve like the rest of men who have no hope" (1 Thessalonians 4:13).*

We do have hope. True hope. Not a desperate clinging to the mere idea that maybe there's some kind of life after this life, but a firm faith in the reality that there really is a heaven, and that Jesus is really there, with my beloved Lana right alongside Him.

I don't want to try to prove to you today that Jesus rose from the dead, but I would like to remind you of the fact that He *did* rise from the dead and that His resurrection was witnessed by many here on earth. Not only that, but there were others in the Bible who were once dead who were also resurrected to new life and who have also appeared afterward to people here on earth, too!

As for Jesus' resurrection, and His appearance to people on earth, listen to some of these verses from the Bible:

> "When Jesus rose early on the first day of the week, He appeared first to Mary Magdalene, out of whom He had driven seven demons" (Mark 16:9).
>
> "Afterward Jesus appeared in a different form to two of them while they were walking in the country" (Mark 16:12).
>
> "Later Jesus appeared to the Eleven as they were eating; He rebuked them for their lack of faith and their stubborn refusal to believe those who had seen Him after He had risen" (Mark 16:14).
>
> "Afterward, Jesus appeared again to His disciples, by the Sea of Tiberias" (John 21:1).
>
> "This was now the third time Jesus appeared to His disciples after He was raised from the dead" (John 21:14).
>
> "After that, He appeared to more than five hundred of the brothers at the same time, most of whom are still living, though some have fallen asleep. Then He appeared to James, then to all the apostles, and last of all He appeared to me [Paul]..." (1 Corinthians 15:6-8a).

What's even more amazing to me and that I've been reminded of since Lana passed on to be with Jesus, is that I keep reading verses that I've read before, but that strike me now in a new light: that Jesus wasn't the only one who died and rose again and appeared to people here on earth. Listen to this!

> "And when Jesus had cried out again in a loud voice, He gave up His spirit. At that moment, the curtain of the temple was torn in two from top to bottom. The earth shook and the rocks split. The tombs broke open and the bodies of many holy people who had died were raised to life. They came out of the tombs, and after Jesus' resurrection they went into the holy city and appeared to many people" (Matthew 27:50-53).

Not only was Jesus raised from the dead, but many others were raised as well who appeared to many people in Jerusalem. Even Peter, James and John saw people raised from the dead while Jesus was still living, when they saw Moses and Elijah standing on the mountaintop, talking with Jesus:

> "After six days Jesus took with Him Peter, James and John the brother of James, and led them up a high mountain by themselves. There He was transfigured before them. His face shone like the sun, and His clothes became as white as the light. Just then there appeared before them Moses and Elijah, talking with Jesus" (Matthew 17:1-3).

Moses and Elijah were so real that Peter asked Jesus if he should build a shelter for each one of them, even though they had been dead for thousands of years! It was a reminder to them, and to me, that God is not the God of the dead, but the God of the living, as Jesus once told the Sadducees, the group of religious leaders in Jesus' day who didn't believe in the resurrection of the dead. Jesus said:

> "Now about the dead rising-have you not read in the book of Moses, in the account of the bush, how God said to him, 'I am the God of Abraham, the God of Isaac, and the God of Jacob'? He is not the God of the dead, but of the living. You are badly mistaken!" (Mark 12:26-28).

I share all this as a preface to what I'm about to share next. As with some of the other stories I've shared with you recently, I do so with hesitancy as I don't want you to think I've lost my mind. I'm also not sure what to think of them myself, for I realize I'm still in the midst of grief, and perhaps the grief is clouding how I think and see spiritual things right now. Then again, perhaps it's during our most difficult times that we're apt to be the closest to God and that we're able to best see what's really true!

On New Year's Eve, I was praying on my knees during a time of worship at a large Christian conference, celebrating the New Year with over 20,000 other believers. As I knelt there on the floor, I felt as if Lana was leaning down next to me. She whispered in my ear, as she had done many times before in my life: "I love you, Eric Elder." Her voice was as clear and soft and sweet as at any time I'd ever heard her say that to me before. I could almost feel her breath on the side of my face.

The next night I felt her presence again, this time as I lay in bed. I wrote in my journal the following morning:

> "Father, thank You for Lana's love for me and mine for her. I miss her Lord. But how can I be anything but grateful to You for giving her to me to be my wife for so many years. This morning I woke up and literally felt her arms around me and heard her voice talking to me. I couldn't move for several minutes, it was so real, her touch and her words. I even thought I saw her when I turned my head. Thank You, Lord, for her continued presence, even if it is in my dreams, or in that state between dreams and wakefulness. Thank You, Lord, and thank you, Lana."

I've reached up to heaven many times in the last few months and have taken hold of Lana's forearm and felt like she's taken hold of mine, only to find the arms of Jesus taking hold of both of us, as He promised that He would never leave us nor forsake us. He promised us that death would not separate us, for we had put our faith in Him. He promised us that we would live forever, not just at the end of time, but right now, in abundant life.

As Jesus told Martha in the Bible, after her brother Lazarus died:

> "Your brother will be raised up."

To which Martha replied:

> "I know that he will be raised up in the resurrection at the end of time."

To which Jesus replied:

> "You don't have to wait for the End. I am, right now, Resurrection and Life. The one who believes in Me, even though he or she dies, will live. And everyone who lives believing in Me does not ultimately die at all. Do you believe this?" (John 11:23-26, The Message).

Martha said she believed it. Lana said she believed it. And I can say I believe it, too.

As I shared at the celebration of Lana's life back in November, a good friend of mine sent me this text which helped me to see the reality of Lana's new life in heaven:

> "It is so hard to be in this place, but it is good to know Lana is seeing our Father and Jesus face to face. She is touching them and hearing their voices and talking to them about anything and everything she wants to. Somehow you, because you are one, are part of that. It takes my breath away."

When I think about it, really think about it, it takes my breath away, too.

This is the great hope that we have in the resurrection, not only that Jesus was raised from the dead, but that all of us who have put our faith in Him will be raised from the dead as well.

As Jonathan Edwards, the great evangelist, said at the funeral of David Brainerd, the great missionary:

> "True saints, when absent from the body, are present with the Lord" (quoting from the Apostle Paul in 2 Corinthians 5:8).

As Jesus Himself said to the thief on the cross who was dying next to Him and who had just put his faith in Jesus:

> "I tell you the truth, today you will be with Me in paradise" (Luke 23:43).

Jesus really did rise from the dead. And those who put their faith in Him really will rise from the dead, too.

If you've never put your faith in Christ, let me encourage you, as Lana would encourage you, as Jesus Himself would encourage you: put your faith in Him today. Believe that He died for your sins. Believe that He's forgiven you of your sins. And believe that He will raise you to new life with Him, starting right now and forever. As the Bible says:

> "That if you confess with your mouth, 'Jesus is Lord,' and believe in your heart that God raised Him from the dead, you will be saved" (Romans 10:9).

CHAPTER 4: REAPING A HARVEST — SEPTEMBER 20

I'd like to share an incredible story with you today about something that happened to me just last week.

As many of you know, I run a website called The Ranch to encourage people in their faith. On the day of Lana's funeral, the computer that runs our website happened to crash, too, and it's taken the past 10 months to completely rebuild it from scratch.

To be honest, I wasn't even sure if God wanted me to rebuild them. When Lana died, I laid everything down at God's feet, telling Him I was only going to pick up what *He* wanted me to pick up again. It was a good time to re-prioritize my life, to see what was important to Him and to me and to start over again with so many things.

But after a few months of contemplating all of this, I was convinced that I was to keep pressing on with our online ministry.

One of the notes that convinced me came from a Jewish woman who had visited the website several years ago. On May 25, 2010, she wrote:

"I was sent to your site by accident, and have been reading the stories, and the one about Capernaum has me confused even more. The more I read, the more questions I have. I've never seen Jesus portrayed as this site does. I should tell you that I'm Jewish and I believe in the one true G-d of Abraham, Isaac, and Jacob.

"I've read some of the stories on your site and have to wonder how they could be true, but I can't stop reading them either, something just feels right about them. My heritage has ingrained in me that Jesus isn't for my people. I can't explain why, but I find some of the stories making me cry and I'm not one that cries easily. It doesn't make sense. I don't even know why I'm writing. I'm just really confused. How can this G-d of yours, be the G-d I've grown up with? Would Jesus love someone who hasn't been faithfully reading the Torah for a long time?

"I'm sorry, I know this doesn't make any sense, and I've always been told that Jesus doesn't love Jews. But after reading some of the stories I just don't know what to believe. Is it possible he might love a Jew?"

After corresponding with her a few times over the next 3 years, I received this note from her on May 4, 2013:

"Dear Eric,

"I don't know if you will remember me or not, but I'm feeling led to tell you what's happened since we first communicated. I wrote you about 3 years ago, about completely believing in the G-d of my ancestors, but not so sure about the Christians claiming Jesus was the Messiah we've longed for all these millennia. Someone had accidentally forwarded me one of your Daily Thoughts. I couldn't get it out of my head....

"In the time that life has moved on for both of us, I've learned that I can believe Jesus is the Messiah. He truly is the Son of G-d. I've also learned that I don't have to give up my Jewish heritage or traditions. I can be fully Jewish and a believer. I've found a wonderful Messianic Synagogue where I've accepted the Messiah Yeshua (Jesus Christ). I'm learning to read the scriptures and see them in a whole new way. I'm amazed how much of the Tanakh is in the New Testament, and how they complement each other.

"I was telling a friend at lunch today, when I'm quiet I can hear G-d speaking to my innermost being. I see Him working in my life in ways I could have never imagined. It is the most wonderful thing in the world. I truly believe the email that was sent to me by mistake was Divine appointment and no mistake....

"Thank you for your ministry and commitment to the L-rd. You truly have touched lives and made a difference. I'm living proof."

Reading her note made me cry and rejoice at the same time. I wrote back to tell her that her note, along with several other clear indications from God, had helped me to decide to bring the website up again. Even if I never wrote another message, or added one more thing to it, I felt it was important to bring all of the content back online for people to read in the future and have their lives changed, too.

So I began rebuilding the website from the ground up, going back 15 years to when I first broadcast my first live message over the Internet, from my house in Illinois to a friend's house in Texas, back in the days before Skype, before Facebook, before Twitter and Pinterest and Instagram.

When I did my first live webcast, CNN, ABC and Fox News had all just started doing their first live webcasts, too. The pope started broadcasting his weekly prayers from the Vatican the month before, and Billy Graham started broadcasting his evangelistic crusades the month after.

I just read this week that Google is celebrating their 15th anniversary this month, too, having launched their little startup company to index the web the same month that I launched The Ranch.

I tell you this to say that a lot of life has passed in the past 15 years, and I had a lot of content to convert, restore and bring up to date from those early days 15 years ago. But as I've been reading the stories and messages I've posted over all these years, and watching the videos from even those earliest days, I've found myself crying, touched by the way God spoke through those messages to people back then, and how He could still speak to me through those messages today.

To my amazement, my old self was able to minister to my new self, because both of my "selves" were simply sharing and receiving words of life from the Word of God.

In those very first broadcasts, which you can now watch online again on our Video Archives page, I shared about keeping your eyes fixed on the goal, and that we will reap a harvest if we do not give up.

Well, this past year, I've been able to start reaping a harvest from all those years of planting. Notes like the one above from the Jewish woman are glimpses. On my 15th anniversary, I posted another video on my website, sharing another glimpse, this time of several trees that Lana and I have planted over the years which astoundingly have all begun to produce fruit just this year. And last week, I got a glimpse of another harvest of another kind.

For 15 years, I have been producing content to put on The Ranch website, including books, music and videos. From the beginning, I felt it was important to offer these resources to people around the world on our website, free of cost, so they could access them anytime night or day.

But along the way, I've sometimes wondered if I've been shooting myself in the foot financially, *paying* to put these things online, and paying annual fees to keep the music and messages and videos streaming 24/7/365 days of the year when I could possibly be charging for them instead.

In an effort to expand our reach to as many people as possible, I've also started posting our books and music and videos other places online, on places like Pandora and iTunes, Amazon and Barnes & Noble, Spotify, Twitter, Tumblr and Facebook.

About a year and a half ago, some of these services have actually begun to pay me for streaming my content on their sites. On Pandora, for instance, every time someone creates a radio station (by typing in my name) to listen to some of my music, I'm paid .00017 cents per "listen." It takes a lot of listens to earn a full penny! But over the past year and a half, I've been getting checks for $20, $30 or $40 every 3 months, meaning my songs are being played over 70,000 times a month!

I've also helped other people record their music and put it on our website over the years. One of these artists is actually doing phenomenal on Pandora now, and is getting a check for over $2,000 every 3 months. Their songs are being played nearly 5 million times a month!

I've been thrilled for them, and at the same time, just as happy to get my check for $30 or $40 every 3 months for my music, too.

But last week, when I opened my email from the company that pays my streaming royalties, there was not just 1 statement, but 2. In the first statement, they said I had earned $38 from my songs for the quarter, and I said, "Thank You, Lord." But when I opened the 2nd statement, they said they were paying me an additional $14,305!

Apparently, every time this other artist who is doing phenomenal was being paid as the performer of their songs, I was supposed to be paid also as their record label, as I had helped them to record their music and publish it online. So the royalty company was catching up and paying me the royalties for all the time that this artist was being paid as well!

It couldn't have come at a better time, too, as I felt I was being squeezed on every side financially in the past 2 months. I hadn't been able to write any messages while I was rebuilding the website, and I hadn't been able to let anyone know of our financial needs either. At the same time, I felt God was clearly leading me to keep rebuilding the website, keep converting and restoring all of the content, and to continue making it all available free of charge to anyone who came to the website, day or night.

The Bible verse that the kids and I have been memorizing the past 2 weeks happens to be Matthew 6:33, which talks about not worrying about what you will eat or drink or wear, but to seek God first in all things:

> "But seek first His kingdom and His righteousness, and all these things will be given to you as well" (Matthew 6:33).

I just kept putting that verse at the forefront of my mind and kept rebuilding the website. As I was putting some of the final touches on the website on Thursday, that's when the surprise email came. The check was deposited in my bank account overnight. When I woke up early in the next morning, I couldn't believe the money was actually in the bank. What surprised me even more was what happened next.

I had decided to use the money to refill the bank accounts of my kids, as they had been having to use some of their inheritance money from Lana to pay for bills for college. If you'll remember, they had each miraculously received $5,000 in answer to my seemingly impossible prayer on the day of Lana's funeral. As I began to transfer the $14,305 into each of their accounts, I was astounded that I was able to fill their accounts back up to $5,000 each, to within $3.74! It made me cry again, not just the significance of receiving such a large check, but receiving the exact amount needed to bring each of their accounts back up to where they were 2 weeks after Lana's funeral. Of course the money is helpful, but what was even more helpful to me was to know that God was still answering my prayers. After going through such a significant loss, it's easy to wonder sometimes if God even hears us. But this was one more reminder to me that He does hear us...and answers, too. Just because He doesn't answer every prayer the way we hope, we can trust Him and know that He hears us and does answer, sometimes in ways that that go off the charts.

I just wanted to share this incredible story with you as encouragement to you to keep planting. Keep watering. Keep investing in people and projects and activities that bring glory to God. As the Bible says:

"Let us not become weary in doing good, for at the proper time we will reap a harvest if we do not give up" (Galatians 6:9).

I wish Lana were here to see the blessings of what we're reaping right now, such as the Jewish woman who came to Christ or the fruit trees that are now bearing fruit or the music we've recorded being played before millions and blessing us back at the same time.

But I have no doubt she's seeing, enjoying and perhaps even playing a significant role from her new home in heaven in bringing part of heaven to earth as we go along.

Thank You, Lord, that even out of tragedy You're able to bring fruit that lasts. And thank you, friends, for continuing to pray for us, believe in us and minister to us so we can keep on ministering to others.

I truly appreciate it, and I'm truly looking forward to this next season of planting and harvesting, as long as the Lord allows.

CHAPTER 5: KEEPING JESUS AT THE CENTER   SEPTEMBER 21

I spoke Thursday night at to a group of people at our church who gather each week and encourage one another through some of life's toughest struggles.

I shared with them how God had helped me to keep my life from spinning out of control during some of the toughest times as I was in the process of losing my sweet wife, Lana, to cancer last year.

One of the ways God helped me was by reminding me to keep Jesus at the center of my life. I'd like to share with you today what I shared with them on Thursday night. I hope you'll be encouraged to keep Jesus at the center of your life, too, no matter what you may be going through today. Here's the message as I shared it live with our group.

Thanks, Jason, and if you don't know me, my name's Eric Elder, and I've been a part of Care Groups before. I haven't been here for this current season of Care Groups, but I used to lead, 2 years ago, a group for people overcoming homosexuality, and helping them with struggles with same-sex attraction and just how to walk through that.

Last spring, I was unfortunately in a group called GriefShare because my wife passed away last November from breast cancer.

And so I'm back again tonight just to share with you a little bit about my walk and keeping Jesus at the center of my life, even through some of these difficult times.

Let me just encourage you to open your Bible, if you have a Bible with you, and just read along with me. We're going to look at First John, starting in chapter 2. John says, in verse 15:

> "Don't love the world's ways. Don't love the world's goods. Love of the world squeezes out love for the Father. Practically everything that goes on in the world–wanting your own way, wanting everything for yourself, wanting to appear important–has nothing to do with the Father. It just isolates you from him. The world and all its wanting, wanting, wanting is on the way out–but whoever does what God wants is set for eternity" (1 John 2:15-17, The Message).

Keeping Jesus at the center, for me, this past year and a half since we found out my wife had cancer and then she died about 9 months later, you know there were a lot of times when I felt like my world was spinning out of control.

She's been more than just essential to my life. And this is wrong to say this, but in many ways, she was my savior. Of course, Jesus is my Savior. He's the One that redeemed me, saved me and is the One that's going to carry me into heaven when I die.

But because I came out of homosexuality, back 28 years ago, really through an encounter with Christ, but it was also through the help of my wife, who was my girlfriend at the time. We had started dating and I had actually been involved with someone else at the time and I had to confess to her that not only was I involved with someone else at the time that I started dating her, but I was involved with another man.

That was an excruciating 2-hour conversation, of me not saying anything, and her wondering if I was an ax-murderer, or what I had to confess that was so terrible. But as I shared that with her, she loved me so unconditionally, and she was so gracious to me, and she just treated me with such kindness and gentleness. Just the way she walked me through that, and through temptations and through life, I can really say she saved me from a lot.

So I know that Jesus is the center of my life. He has been since I put my faith in Him. As one of my friends said about her husband, she said, "Jesus is like my cake, and my husband is the icing on my Jesus cake."

I said, "Oh, that's really nice. That was Lana for me. Jesus was my cake, and Lana was the icing on my Jesus cake."

But as she started going through cancer and the doctors were saying that it was incurable, and they didn't know how long she had to live, but it wasn't long, I started seeing that maybe Jesus and Lana had sort of merged roles in such a way that the thought of losing her felt like I was losing my cake, too.

I don't know if it's right or wrong, because I know we're supposed to be so intertwined—you know, it would be sad if she died and I felt nothing—so I know God gives us those kinds of relationships for a reason. But there was a time there, just a few months before she died, where we were having some of these hard conversations about what the future would look like, and what I was going to do if she did pass on.

She was talking to me about remarriage and things like that, and I didn't want to hear it. That was the farthest thing from my mind. I was not interested in even entertaining the thought. I just wanted her, and I wanted her alive.

And yet a few weeks into that cycle of conversations, somewhere from the back of my mind, as my life was spinning out of control, and what I thought was my center was being taken away from me, I started gravitating in my mind back to some other things that gave me some peace and some happiness and some comfort, and that included former homosexual relationships from over 25 years earlier.

And I just thought, you know, I have no interest at all in getting married again. But there was a part of me that said, "But if there was a man that came along, what would I do then?" Because it didn't involve the same kind of commitment, the same kind of relationship, the same kind of work, it just was sort of fun. At least that was my memory of it from long ago.

For about 2 weeks, this just really puzzled me, and it just weighed on me, because I was like, "This has been over 25 years since I've had any serious consideration to that at all." God had just broken that off of me in a wonderful way and given me a wife and 6 children of our own. So to have these thoughts again and go, "Wow, why would I even be going there? Why would I go back there?"

I had a conversation with Jason, and he said that it makes some sense, that when your life is being threatened in these ways and something's being threatened to be taken away from you, you sort of gravitate towards what brought you peace and comfort in the past. And I knew he was right, but it bothered me that it was even on my mind and was even– do you know what I mean? I mean it was like, "Oh, my gosh, I don't even want to have that thought again."

It was about 2 weeks of struggling with this and just trying to work it out in my brain.

Then I woke up one Sunday morning, and I just started reading Romans chapter 1, and I read the passage that really changed my life, where Paul talks about homosexuality and talks about how the end of that is not going to be good for us. That is a passage that changed my life, and it was a hinge and a turning point in everything regarding my faith, as well as my sexuality.

So to read that passage again, I was just like, "OK, that's right. That's right. This was in my past. This is not going to be part of my future."

Then I came to church, and Pastor Baker was talking about the topic again that morning, and he just was talking about it and he said, "You can justify it, you can rationalize it, you can go through all kinds of arguments about it"–and I'm paraphrasing him here, I don't want to put words in his mouth, but if you've heard him speak on this, you know where he stands–but he said, "You know, the bottom line is that if God says it's not good for you, then it's not going to go well for you."

He says, "If there's anything in the Bible, whether it's adultery or fornication or sex outside of marriage or before marriage, or any topic in the Bible, if God says this is not good for you, the bottom line is: it's just not going to go well for you."

That was like number 2 that day where I was like, "Whew. That's right, I don't even have to think about this. The Bible is very clear, and it's been very clear in the past."

And then later that night, I had a conversation with a friend and his wife who had a similar diagnosis a few years ago, and he was worried that she might die. He said something that shocked me, he said, "I was wondering if maybe, if God took her, that He was then releasing me, and I could go and pursue homosexuality."

And I was like, "You can't do that!" Somehow hearing it from someone else, the very thoughts that I was considering, but hearing them speak it as if that was what God was really going to say and I was like, "Now I know it's wrong. I just didn't care." You just get to the point where, "God, I know this is wrong, I understand it's wrong, but I don't care. I just want to do what I want to do," which is what John says:

> "The world and all its wanting, wanting, wanting…"

You just want to do what you want to do. But if you do what *God* wants you to do, that's when you'll have eternal life. That's when things will go well for you.

So those 3 things for me: just reading the Word that morning and finding Romans chapter 1 again, just hearing the pastor and coming to church and getting reminded again, "You know, it's just not going to go well for you."

And then hearing my friend just speak the words that I was thinking. Just to verbalize those and say, "Wow."

After 2 weeks of just being perplexed about this, it just cleared up. It totally cleared up and it's not come back again. I just needed that though, I needed to hear from God in some very clear ways.

Then when Lana did pass away, I didn't have that struggle. I didn't have that wrestling anymore, because I had invited God in, and I said, "God, I want to do what *You* want, and

I really want Your will more than anything else. And as bad as this hurt, I am not going to go back into something that would hurt me even more, because You don't want me to do that. You want me to have life, and life abundant."

And sometimes, as we've learned in GriefShare, when someone close to you dies like that, it puts a wall up between you and people around you, because they don't really know what that relationship was like.

They don't know, for instance, this is the first time I've ever shared this publicly, how Lana has been so vital, not just my best friend, my lover, my everything to me, mother of my kids, my homeschool teacher of all my kids. Not just all those important things, but how she helped me in this area of sexuality. And then to lose that, it's hard for me to explain to other people.

And so there's this wall that sort of goes up between you and other people to where you're not really able to let them in, and they're not able to enter in, because they don't know what that has meant to you and what you have lost.

But in GriefShare they said that God knows what it's like to lose someone close to Him. And God lost a son. God knows what it's like to weep. And Jesus lost his best friend in Lazarus. And *they* can enter in with you. And even if other people can't, you can still invite God in, and let Him come into your life. Let Him be with you and fill those lonely places.

God really has done that. I still miss Lana terribly. I wish she was here. I would take her back in a heartbeat. But God has really come in. He really has walked me through this. He really has helped me in so many ways.

I want you to look at another passage with me. Then we'll go to a song, where you can just meditate on what it means to you to keep Jesus at the center. This is in Hebrews, just back a few pages, Hebrews chapter 12, starting in verse 2. The writer of Hebrews says this:

> *"Keep your eyes on Jesus, who both began and finished this race we're in. Study how He did it. Because He never lost sight of where He was headed–that exhilarating finish in and with God–He could put up with anything along the way: cross, shame, whatever. And now He's there, in the place of honor, right alongside God. When you find yourselves flagging in your faith, go over that story again, item by item, that long litany of hostility He plowed through. That will shoot adrenaline into your souls!*
>
> *"... My dear child, don't shrug off God's discipline, but don't be crushed by it either. It's the child He loves that He disciplines; the child He embraces, He also corrects. God is educating you; that's why you must never drop out. He's treating you as dear children. This trouble you're in isn't punishment; it's training, the normal experience of children. Only irresponsible parents leave children to fend for themselves. Would you prefer an irresponsible God? We respect our own parents for training and not spoiling us, so why not embrace God's training so we can truly live? While we were children, our parents did what seemed best to them. But God is doing what is best for us..." (Hebrews 12:2-3, 5b-10a, The Message).*

I felt like, as my life was spinning out of control, that God had to sort of correct me, discipline me, bring me back in. And it was a discipline that I welcomed. I didn't *want* Him to leave me alone. I needed Him. And the truth is, we all need Him.

Maybe you're at a place where you feel like you're either being crushed by God because He's either giving you more than you think you can handle or you feel like you're being disciplined by Him or maybe you feel like you're being punished. I want you just to not think about it that way.

If there's some path that you're not on a good path, God can come in and correct you, if you're willing to let Him, and just let Him help you get back onto the good path.

God has so much for us. He wants us to live. He wants us to live an abundant life. He has great plans and purposes for you and for me. I just want to encourage you to keep Jesus at the center of your life.

Let's pray:

Father, thank You for these words, God, and allowing me to share some of the crazy things that have happened to me over the last year and a half. God, I just thank You for walking me through it. I thank You for keeping me on Your path. I thank You, Lord, when I was tempted to veer, that You brought me back. God, I pray for each person listening to this tonight (and reading and listening later!), that You would keep them on Your good path, Lord. Help them to keep walking with You, Lord. Help them to keep their eyes fixed on Jesus, the Author and Perfecter of their faith. Lord, help them to know Your great love for them. And I pray most of all You'd help them to overcome the world, Lord, and not let the world overcome them. We pray this in Jesus' name, Amen.

CHAPTER 6: LIVING A LIFE WITH NO REGRETS — SEPTEMBER 22

We had a wonderful "Night of Worship" here at The Ranch last night! Thanks to those of you who came and to those of you who prayed for the night to be a blessed one. It was!

Thanks, too, for your gracious notes from places like the Philippines and South Africa, saying you wish you could be here. We hope to make this an annual event, so perhaps in the future we can meet many more of you in person as well.

During the night I shared 3 video clips of my dear wife Lana that were filmed last year on November 1st, 2012, just 2 weeks before she passed away. She had a message that I felt was perfect for the evening.

So as we were worshipping outside by the bonfire, under the stars and with a half-moon shining, we projected the video of Lana onto the side of the barn and enjoyed hearing what she had to say to us about "living a life with no regrets."

I'd like to share those 3 clips with you today as well. I believe they'll be particularly helpful to you if you're wrestling with a big decision and don't know what to do, or if you're just wondering how you can make the most of the life God has given you.

This video was shot by a film team who heard about our situation and offered to spend the day with us at our home, just to capture some memories for us and to offer hope to others who might face a similar loss in the future. Lana agreed, and we spent an amazing day with Drew Waters, Josh Spake and by Skype, Josh's wife Candice.

Although the film team will be putting all the footage they shot that day into another format, editing it for their own purposes as background for an upcoming movie called *Nouvelle Vie* (which means "new life" in French) they've graciously allowed us to use the raw footage for other purposes like this.

I've posted these 3 clips in 1 video on our website at the link below, or you can read the message in the transcript below that.

Here's the link to the video…

Lana Elder—Living Life with No Regrets (or on ericelder.com).

And here's the transcript…

CANDICE: A lot of people in your position are very fearful, very scared, very worried, but you have come at this from a whole stance of hope, which is very, again I use the word profound. Because it's unusual, and it's so–you can just see how God is working and continues to work in your life. And so, describe what that peace is like for you and how it's helped you battle fear, anxiety, being scared and stuff like that.

LANA: Well, I've always tried to live my life with no regrets. And so, whenever I had a big decision to make, I would think–obviously I would pray about it and ask God what's best, and then I would just have to say, "Will I regret having made this decision?" Especially ones like–I went to college, I met my husband Eric in college, and we got married shortly after college and I was pregnant with my first child and had to decide whether I would stay at home or work and staying at home meant a severe cutback in pay. But I wanted to live a life of no regrets, so I decided I would rather stay home and be with my child, than have the money and have some other luxuries. And it's a decision I've never regretted. So I've been a stay-at-home mom all my life–or since college. I know at times some people would wonder why I would get a college degree and then not even use it and stay home. But I remember thinking, even as I was making that decision, if something were to happen to me or one of my children–a death–I would have regretted going to work. So I was really glad–I mean, not glad, but when I found this out–it just made me glad that I hadn't taken my life to go to work and missed seeing my kids grow up. It just changes everything. My kids, I just love to be around them. And so, having made that decision gives me great hope for situations like this that I made the right decision. It made some impact on our finances, but the other impact is, I think, much greater–the impact it had on my kids' lives, because I wouldn't have been able to take them to a lot of the programs like AWANA scripture memorization. I would have been too busy. And my kids, I love them, and they have great hope in God as well and love Jesus, and I think that's because of the way they were brought up.

CANDICE: How do you describe the peace that passes all understanding in your life? What does that feel like? Describe that from your perspective.

LANA: The peace that surpasses all understanding is just really being with God. And when you're reading scripture, or in worship, it's so wonderful to have that peace. And even having made decisions, and seeing how they impact your life over the years, how that decision that impacts your life, and you know that it's a good decision, that just gives you great peace, knowing that you did the right thing.

ERIC: Can I just have her clarify one thing, too, that not everybody chooses to stay home, if she just could talk about that, that this was the vision for what you [Lana] wanted to do, but other people are called to do other things, because she believes that strongly. I just don't want to give the wrong impression. So maybe you could just say something about that.

LANA: Absolutely. Yes, I do want to clarify that. Not everyone is called to stay at home. There are certainly many instances where women are called to go to work, or both parents can go to work, but for me, it was really just what I was called to do. That's just how God created me, just to be a mother and stay home with my kids.

CANDICE: I think that's wonderful. The reason it's wonderful is because I think you mentioned a couple things: One is that you would have been too busy to go to AWANA or scripture memory class and that greatly impacted your kids, and 2, you mentioned that, in situations like this, you've been able to spend your life with your kids. That's what you wanted. And I think it just makes it perfect the point that you are in God's will and right where you need to be, where He has you in this pursuit of what you've dedicated your life to, and so I commend you for that. I think that you have fulfilled that calling beautifully. Another question I had for you is, I wanted to see what some of the messages are that you have for Eric and your kids, so let's start with Eric. What is something that you would like to share with him? What is a message you have for him?

LANA: Eric is just incredible. He's incredibly talented and can play the piano, write music, do carpentry work, he knows everything about the computer, and he's incredibly gifted. So I just want him to press on, keep going with a lot of the projects he's already started. I know he has a couple that he and I have been working on together–the St. Nicholas project, talking about the life of Christ and how much he [Nicholas] was a believer in Jesus and that's how he became so famous as St. Nicholas, our Santa Claus right now. So I just want him to continue to press on with things. I know he will, and God will use him greatly. I love him incredibly much. He's my prince and he takes incredible care of me and the kids. So I'm not worried. That's another thing that makes passing into heaven at this time just so peaceful, because I know the kids are going to be in great hands, with Eric taking care of them.

CANDICE: Thank you for sharing that Lana. What about for the kids? What message do you want to tell the kids?

LANA: My kids have been just wonderful. I was blessed, again, to be able to homeschool, and Eric encouraged me to do that as well [because Lana wanted to try it]. He was a great encouragement, and my kids, I just know that they love Jesus. That's been great comfort to know that they're going to do great in life in whatever God has called them to do. I don't know what they're called to do, each of them yet, but I just know that they'll do well, because everything they do, they do so well. I have no fear of anything going wrong, I just know they're going to be blessed for the rest of their lives. I had 6 blessings. They're awesome. I'm going to miss them.

CANDICE: What dreams do you have for your kids?

LANA: My dreams for my kids is just that they would love the Lord with all their heart, soul, mind and strength. And they do that, and so whatever dreams that they have, I know that God will help them fulfill them, whatever it is. Because if they keep seeking God, they're going to be on the straight path. They'll do what God's called them to do and so that's my dream, that they would do that, they would just keep loving Jesus, and loving each other and loving their neighbors.

CANDICE: Lana, what dreams do you have for Eric?

LANA: Pretty much the same thing. Like I said, he's incredibly talented, and gifted and can do anything, and he has great dreams for some projects that he's working on, and I just pray that he can just continue to fulfill those dreams and do what God's called him to do. I know that God has a unique plan for my family, but for everyone, God has a unique plan, and I know that if they just keep following Jesus, and asking Him for direction, they'll do well. And your dreams [Eric] will come true.

ERIC: They have. They already have.

LANA: I know. Love you, buddy.

DREW: I've got a question for you. What do you hope that people watching this get from it?

LANA: I would hope that the people that are watching this, that they would know that they have a unique calling in life. Everyone God created so uniquely, like everybody has different fingerprints, just so unique. So I would hope that people watching this would know that God created them uniquely, that He has different dreams for them as well. But if they keep following God, or asking God for direction, that God will show them what their unique place is in the world, what they're uniquely designed or created to do, that they would just keep seeking God, and keep seeking the answers to what they feel called to do.

DREW: Lana, I've got another question for you, and this is a very direct question, so I apologize for it, but you don't seem fearful of death. Why is that?

LANA: I'm actually not fearful of death and I believe, the only thing I can attribute it to, is just having followed God for so long, waking up and talking to Him each day, throughout the day, He's helped me through many things. And since I am talking to Him all the day long, death will be just like meeting Him and talking to Him all day long–but without my kids and family [laughter]. I don't know why I don't fear death, but God has been such a loving God to me, and I feel like I've been so blessed throughout my life, like I said earlier, about living my life with no regrets, and just doing everything I've wanted to do. Even the past years, I've gone everywhere I've wanted to go. I wanted to go to Israel and see the Holy Land and I got to go there 5 years ago, and then miraculously got to go 2 years after that. So I've been to Israel twice and I'm so blessed to have done that. So I've done everything I've wanted to do, and I don't have–there's not like one place I'd like to go see still or anything that I still need to accomplish. So I feel like I've done everything, and I can go see Jesus at any time. It would be fine. But I know it's hard for people who I'm leaving behind. Since my diagnosis, I've tried to live my life like I'm going to live. I didn't want to live like I'm going to die. I wanted to live like I'm going to live. So that's all I've done, just keep going on with the normal day. But I know it's hard for the people that are left behind, because I feel their pain. I feel sorry for them, because I would like to be with them as well. But also, I just love Jesus, and I'm looking forward to that day, too.

ERIC [later that day]: They just asked me to say a few words to you, and there's just not enough words to express what you've meant to me. I remember on our wedding day, I just said to you that you were a gift from God to me and I wanted to treat you as a gift. You've been just a super gift, and I feel like I've unwrapped layer after layer of you. You've just given yourself to me in everything. You have sacrificed so much for me, for the ministry, for the kids–just everything. You're a giver, and you've just given your life away. And I can't think of anything better you could do with your life. You don't just live your life, you give your life. That means so much to me, and I know that's going to mean a lot to our kids, just to know that your life was not lived in vain, and that your death won't be in vain if you do die. If you're healed, hallelujah! That won't be in vain, either!

I gave this to Lana–it's a little plaque–for our anniversary back in April this year, and it says, "And they lived happily ever after." It just reminds me of the joy that we've had together. You know, I'm going to cry a lot if you pass away. But I felt like God said, "Tearfulness is OK. Fearfulness is not." So I think it's OK to be tearful, but I'm not fearful, either.

And this just came in the mail today. I just got 2 more tiles for your collection here and I just wanted to unwrap this with you. This is a quote from Alfred Lloyd Tennyson. It says:

> "If I had a flower for every time I thought of you, I could walk through my garden forever."

It's so true. I'm sure there won't be a day that goes by that I don't think about you. And this is really from me, and the kids and from everybody that knows you, and it just says, "You are loved." And you are.

LANA: You're really good at expressing your love to me all the time. You're just always so kind and so generous. He [Eric] makes it easy for me to love him because he's so much like Jesus, always thoughtful and kind and he puts me above himself all the time. He wants to make sure I'm taken care of. So I just appreciate these things, too, his gracious, kind gifts, thoughtful gifts, just incredible.

ERIC: Thanks. And I'm not like Jesus, but I was thinking just last week as you were just lying in bed and the pain was on you, and even in your pain you were writing a message to our subscribers in different countries and giving them hope and encouraging them with your hope. And I was just thinking of Jesus on the cross, just going through the pain and suffering for each one of us, and I thought, "Wow, *you're* like Jesus! I'm married to someone like Jesus!" So I'm just so thankful to you and I just love you so much.

LANA: Thanks, thanks a lot. I love you.

JOSH: Let me ask you a couple questions. To your children, what is your wife's legacy?

ERIC: For my children, just to say what Lana's legacy is, I think her heartbeat is to give. She wants to give, give and give some more. And I think it's hard for her to do. I think she's struggled with it because we have so many needs. We all have needs. The kids have needs, and Lana has needs, and yet she's just given so much. We give money away and we give things away and she gives food away and she just gives away. I feel like she's a giver. I know that's her heart, even for some of the projects we're working on now, just to tell, for instance, the St. Nicholas story, of a man who gave his life away, too, because he was following the One who gave His life for all of us. So I think that's her legacy. I feel like she's following Jesus and that she denies herself many times so that she can give, and I don't think that you can get better than that.

JOSH: How long have you all been married?

ERIC: We've been married 23 years, and we've known each other 28 years, and they've been super, all super. I have no regrets. I can't complain that she's being taken now. How could I complain to God and say, "God, why did you take her?" All I should be able to do is say, "God, thank You! How could You possibly love me so much that You would give me 28 years with her?" So I'm sad. I'm disappointed if you go. But I cannot complain, for one single day.

JOSH: How is she not replaceable?

ERIC: How is she not replaceable? I can't think of how she *is* replaceable. I can't imagine anything–I mean there is nothing that could replace her. She's a unique creation of God–one of a kind. There's no replacing any one of us. We're all here for a reason, we're all here for a purpose, just like Lana. There are lots of people that we love, lots of people that are friends, lots of people that do a lot for us and we're really close to, and I don't think any of us are replaceable.

JOSH: I'm going to ask one more question. So the heart of the story of *Nouvelle Vie* is finding life. And we don't know what's going to happen, right? You know God is a miraculous God and God could really pull through, or He may choose not to, and whatever it is, He's glorified in all things. If God chooses to take your wife from you, how do you persevere? How do you go on?

ERIC: *Nouvelle Vie* means "new life," and for me, as a Christian, I've already been given a new life. And some people say, even if Lana dies, we're going to pray and raise her from the dead. And I love that. I would love to do that. I have prayed that for some of my friends in the past, too. But the truth is, I know what being dead is like, and I've already been dead, and Jesus has already raised me from the dead. I've now got a new life and now I'm going on. I'm going to have a new life forever because of Jesus and what He's done for me. So we could pray that Lana would be raised from the dead, and that might happen, but the truth is that she's already been raised from the dead. She knows what a dead life is like and she's been given a new life already, and that's going to continue on for eternity. So to me, that's part of the hope of *Nouvelle Vie*, that it speaks about the new life that we can have right now, today, starting this very day. You don't have to wait till you die to be raised from the dead. You can be resurrected. You can be redeemed. You can be restored, anytime you choose to just put your faith in Christ, to ask Him to forgive you of your sins. He will take you to be with Him forever in heaven and give you a whole new life here on earth. So that's the hope that I have, and the courage that I have, that your passing [Lana] really is "passing." As the Bible says, it's a sleeping, you fall asleep, then you'll be woken up by Jesus when He comes back for us. It'll be a short sleep for you, and maybe a long few years for us, but in the light of eternity, it'll just be a blink of an eye. And I can't wait to see you again.

CHAPTER 7: BUILDING A SAFETY NET   SEPTEMBER 23

You might think that walking across the Grand Canyon on a tightrope without a safety net is crazy. But there's something crazier still, and that's doing life without a safety net.

I recently spoke at one of our former churches about how you can build a safety net in your own life to keep from losing your faith in God, even in the face of significant loss. I've included a link to the message below, and the text of the message below that just as I gave it that morning.

Here's a link to the audio…

Listen to "Building A Safety Net"

And here's the text of the message…

Thanks, Tony. I made it through the first hour, but I'll tell you, I had to grab a box of Kleenex to do it.

This is the first time I've stood up and preached on a Sunday morning since 10 months ago when I preached at my wife's funeral. Just putting on my suit this morning–this is the same suit and shirt I wore preaching her funeral–and just putting it on again today, I said, "OK, God, I think I'm ready." But can I ask you to pray for me, too, because I need all the help I can get. Let's pray.

"Father, we thank You so much for walking us through the tragedies of life and just being there for us. Thank You for other believers, and especially for people in this room who have walked our family through this as well. I just pray that You would speak to each one of our hearts, Lord, that You would just help remind us that You are there, that You are with us, and that You can walk us through anything we go through. In Jesus' name, Amen."

When Ron asked me to preach and to join in this series that you're doing on "Who We Are," and he asked me in particular to preach on *this* message, "Who We Are as The Church," I was very happy to say yes. Because I am a strong believer in the church. And the church of course is not just the building and the bricks and the place where we gather, the church is the body of believers, the church is you and me, doing life together, that is the church, and that is who we are.

So I just want to talk to you today about the value of the church, the power of the church, and of course, you're here this morning, so that means you're already reaping the benefits of being part of the church. But I also want to encourage you this morning to get involved in a deeper way with some of the people around you. Because when we do life together, with close friendships, that's when we really grow the most, that's when we can support each other the most, and that's when we can be supported when we need help as well.

We're all going to go through losses. You might not have had a loss like I had this past year, but we all suffer losses in all kinds of ways: loss of job, loss of relationship, loss of health, loss of finances, or as in my case, loss of someone that I dearly love. It's a part of life and we're all going to go through it. So my encouragement for you today–this is my bottom line of the whole thing and then I'll expand it–my bottom line is just get plugged in to some other believers so you can be there for them and they can be there for you. And that way you can get through these tragedies without losing your faith in Jesus. OK? Let's start off.

Do you recognize this guy [showing photo of a man walking across a tight rope]?

It's Nik Wallenda, who 3 months ago walked across a gorge near the Grand Canyon, live on international television–without a safety net underneath him.

Just last week, this clip was voted the number one moment on TV for 2013. Of all the different–the final episode of "The Office," or whatever other moments there were–this was the number 1, the moment that people most were riveted by–as they watched this man, live on television, walk across a tiny wire–never been done before–across the Grand Canyon, without a safety net below him.

And you might say, "That guy is crazy." And you would be right! But I'll tell you, there's something crazier, and that's doing life without a safety net. And I want to talk to you this morning about how you can build a safety net under you. Because the truth is, even though he had no physical net, that man had a lot of people around him.

As you watch him do that, and you watch the tape of it, there are people on one side of the canyon, people on the other side, he's been training for years, there were people talking to him in his headset, warning him about the wind, making sure things were going all right, talking to him the entire way. He's talking to God. He's talking to his team. This man was prepared. He did not do life alone, and *you* cannot do life alone. It's even crazier, if you think you can do life on your own, and I'll tell you some stories about me over these last couple years, particularly this last year and a half of walking through and how I just could not make it on my own.

A lot of things helped me through, my faith in Christ being the chief among them, but the believers in the body, coming around me was right up there and really helped make this so that I didn't lose my faith as well.

This reminds me of a little cartoon. My kids love these cartoons and show them to me. I love this one.

CHAPTER 8: LOOKING FORWARD—3 STORIES OF HOPE   SEPTEMBER 24

I'd like to talk to you this morning about hope–capital H-O-P-E–hope. I know you don't want to hear about heartache today. We all have enough of that. You want to hear about hope, and I do too.

So I want to share 3 stories with you about how God has given me hope over the past year. I pray they give you hope, and then you can pass it on to others. The 3 stories I'd like to share with you have to do with a ring, an apple and 3 emails.

The first story is about a ring. Several years ago my wife, Lana, lost her wedding ring one day. She had already been up and going for a while before she realized that her ring was missing from her finger. She never went without it, so she was surprised and disturbed that it was missing.

So we started looking all over the house. We looked by the kitchen sink where she did the dishes. We looked in the bathroom where it might have come off. We looked everywhere we could, but we couldn't find it all day.

By the end of the day, we were going back to bed and she thought to look under the bed. There was her ring on the floor. She said, "You know, I remember waking up this morning and hearing this 'clink, clink, clink.'"

I said, "Well, that would have been good information to know as we were searching for your ring all day!"

She went on to say that at night, when she put her hand under her pillow, she would sometimes play with her ring, spinning it around and taking it on and off. The night before, she must have taken it off and fell asleep, and then it must have fallen to the ground in the morning when she got up.

So that became a little joke between us over the years. Whenever something would go missing, one of us would say, "Did you hear anything go 'clink, clink, clink?'"

So a few months ago I was sitting with a couple at our dining room table. At one point in the conversation, I looked down at my hand and noticed my ring was missing. I've always worn my wedding ring, too, and even though Lana passed away about 8 months before this, I still wore my ring every day. I couldn't bring myself to take it off. Even though I knew there might come a day when I *would* take it off, I couldn't imagine ever *wanting* to take it off. And honestly, I was dreading that day.

So when I noticed my ring was missing, I panicked. I thought, "Where's my ring?" I felt naked and embarrassed in front of this couple, wondering if they noticed it, too. I wondered what they might think of me–if I had taken it off because I wanted to start dating again or something, which I definitely didn't! All these thoughts started racing through my mind, all the time wondering, "Where could my ring be?"

Then I remembered something. Earlier in the year, I had decided to start losing some weight. I'm a stress eater, so when I get stressed, I eat. By January of this year I had gained more weight than I had ever gained in my life. I knew that I needed to stay healthy, for myself and for my kids and I wanted to start losing weight again, but I just didn't have the fortitude to do it at the time. As the year went on, however, I decided to do it, and began losing weight, week by week. The night before I had met with this couple, I was lying in bed and noticed that my ring was loose and could come right off and go back on again. So I laid there in bed, spinning it around and taking it off and on, and then must have fallen asleep with it off.

As I was sat there at the dining table with this couple, I thought to myself, "You know, I do remember hearing this 'clink, clink, clink' when I woke up!"

After saying goodbye to my visitors, I went upstairs, looked under my bed, and there was my ring on the floor. I looked to heaven and said, "OK, Lana, now I get it. Now I can see how you could have overlooked hearing that 'clink, clink, clink' when you lost your ring years ago." And so I had a little smile in that moment in my mind with Lana.

Although I was dreading the day when I would have to take off my ring, having that little smile with Lana made me think: "Well, today's as good a day as any. At least I can look back on it with fondness and a smile, rather than with sadness. So I'll try and just leave it off." So I left it off. I still felt naked for the rest of the day, and even today when I look down and see that it's missing, I feel like part of me is missing, too. But at least I can look down and think about it with a smile now, and with thankfulness for the time that I did have with Lana.

I tell you that story to say that sometimes God gives us those little moments of grace. Moments that we may have been dreading in the future, but when they come, God gives us the grace to get through it–sometimes even with a little smile that says, "It's going to be OK. I love you and I'll walk you through this, too."

In one of the books I read on grief, called *Decembered Grief* by Harold Ivan Smith, I read a quote that has helped me through this new season of my life. The quote is from an unidentified woman and says:

> "It has taken me many months to get to the point where I can say, 'All right, the future is not going to be what you thought it was. It's gone, and you're not going to have it. You just will not have it. Your future went with him. Now you've got to build a new one.'"

I didn't like reading those words at first, but over time I knew they were true for me, too. I've come to realize that the future is not going to be what I thought it would be, either. It's gone, and I'm not going to have it. I just will not have it. Now I've got to build a new one.

Many of you know what this is like in your own life. You've reached those points in your life where you've had to say, "This isn't the direction I thought my life was going to take." And at some point, you've had to let it go and say, "It's not going to happen; they're not coming back," just as I've had to say, "OK, she's not coming back."

And she's not. As much as I hate to say that, I know that God still has a future for me. It reminds me that I just need to keep "fixing my eyes on Jesus, the Author and Perfecter of my faith, who for the joy set before Him endured the cross…" (see Hebrews 12:2).

As much as I wish I had my old life back, I know the best thing I can do now is to keep moving forward–to keep saying, "God, I'm going to fix my eyes on You. I'm going to trust You, no matter what, because I know You'll work it all out somehow for good in the end." And I know He will.

CHAPTER 9: MAKING THE MOST OF THE DARKNESS — SEPTEMBER 25

Some of the scariest times in my life have not been those where things are swirling all around me, but actually in the pitch black, in the silence of night. But I've also found that some of the most amazing things in life can best be seen when it's dark.

Here's a transcript of a message I shared this week on how God can help you overcome fear with His love. It's one of the most important lessons I've learned this past year as I've been walking through my own times of darkness…

Good evening and if you don't know me, I'm Eric Elder. The quick snapshot of my past year has been in some ways some of the darkest times of my life, and in other ways, some of the most enlightening times of my life.

My wife passed away a year ago next week and Jason was here and helped me conduct the service here at the church. She died quickly after 9 months of breast cancer. I've got 6 kids, 3 still at home with me and 3 in college, so it's been—as you can imagine—a difficult year, but an amazing year at the same time.

I just wanted to encourage you tonight that God's love never fails you. God's love never leaves you. Even in your darkest hours, I want to encourage you that God is still with you, and I can tell you He's been with me. I have preached that and taught that for years. Knowing that going into this, I still get into those dark moments and I wonder how it's going to turn out. Then I remember God's great love for me, and I just know it's going to be all right. He's going to work all things for good for those who love Him and are called according to His purpose (see Romans 8:28).

So I just want to continue tonight in the series that Jason has started in 1 John chapter 4. This is a passage that talks about God's great love for us, that the only reason we can love others is because He loved us first and sent Jesus to die for us. It is out of His love that comes down to us that we can then extend that love to others.

I'm not going to read the whole chapter to you, but if you need some encouragement that God loves you this week, I encourage you to read 1 John chapter 4. That's not the gospel of John, not the book of John, but later in the Bible, 1 John. It's a letter that he wrote, and I'm going to look at verses 17 through 19.

> *"God is love. When we take up permanent residence in a life of love, we live in God and God lives in us. This way, love has the run of the house, becomes at home and mature in us, so that we're free of worry on Judgment Day—our standing in the world is identical with Christ's. There is no room in love for fear. Well-formed love banishes fear. Since fear is crippling, a fearful life—fear of death, fear of judgment—is one not yet fully formed in love. We, though, are going to love—love and be loved. First we were loved, now we love. He loved us first"* (1 John 4:17-19, The Message).

As I said, the scariest times in my life have not been those where things are swirling all around me, but actually in the pitch black, in the silence of night. I was at an amusement park and went on an attraction where you just sit in a seat in a theater and they swirl all kinds of things around you. They had little fake rat tails that ran across your feet under the seats and they sprayed water at you and all these things went by you on the screen.

But the scariest time of that whole attraction was when they shut off all the lights completely, and it was totally silent, and you had no idea what was coming next. You didn't know where it was coming from. You couldn't see anything. And I'll tell you, for all the other things that came at me that day, that was the moment when I panicked. Even though I knew I was in a safe environment and they were going to take care of me—I was going to be fine—I just had this moment thinking, "What's it going to be?" because it was pitch black and it was totally silent.

Sometimes that's the way we feel in life. Take kids, for instance. When are they most scared? At night, in their beds, even though there's nothing there. Nothing's going to happen. But because they can't see, they don't know.

And we're the same way, it's when we don't see what's going on, when we don't know what's going to happen, that we can become consumed with fear. And that's when we most need to remember: God loved us first and His love is still there for us, even in the darkness.

I want to encourage you, in those dark times, to make the most of the darkness. Because the truth is, there are some things that can be seen better when it's pitch black outside.

If you've ever walked past a house during the day and you look in the windows but they've got a curtain up, a curtain like this [holding up a curtain], it's really hard to see anything that's going on inside because of the daylight. You can't really see.

I don't know if you can see me behind here [stepping behind the curtain]. Can you tell how many fingers I'm holding up? No? Nothing?

You can't see in. But if you walk by the same house at nighttime—and Jason if you want to turn the lights off—if you walk by the same house again at nighttime and the lights are on inside, it's amazing, especially with sheer curtains like this. When the lights are on in the house, can you see me now? Can you tell how many fingers I'm holding up now? [the people can see and start to respond I hold up different number of fingers: 5, 2, 3, 1.]

Quite a difference, isn't it?

I'll tell you, when Lana died, for those first few days especially, I felt like I could glimpse into heaven like I'd never seen before. It was so dark on my side, but it was so bright on her side. When we were married, we became one, and even death doesn't separate love. And I felt like I could see into heaven, and she was dancing with Christ, and because, in some supernatural way I was one with her, I was there with *Him* as well.

It was dark on my side, but I could see into the windows of heaven better than I could ever see before. Thankfully, I was able to keep my eyes open and say, "OK, I'm going to make the most of this darkness and I want to learn everything I can about heaven while I'm here." And I looked at passages about heaven and when exactly you go there? Is Lana there right now or is she dead in the ground? Is she dancing with Jesus or is she in some waiting zone?

The conclusions I came to may not be the same ones you come to, but I have no reason to believe that Jesus was saying anything other than the truth when He told the thief on the cross:

> *"Today, you will be with Me in paradise" (Luke 23:43).*

Whatever "today" is to God, because He is outside of any constraint of time, Lana is there with Him *today*. She was there the moment she died. She was there with God. God loved her, and God loves me, and all of this reminds me that God is with us all the time. But again, it was *because* of the darkness that I could actually see.

There's another story I want to tell you, too. This was when I was driving in California last year. It was September and we dropped our daughter off in Northern California for school. So our whole family took a road trip and went to see my brother and my sister who live out west. Lana and all of us, we took a big drive.

We dropped my daughter off and then we drove down the coast, down Highway 1 that winds along California along these cliffs with hairpin turns. I had been there before—with its beautiful scenery, it's incredible—so I wanted to take the family on this drive, a couple hour drive to where we were going to spend the night.

But we got a late start for the day and it was getting closer to nighttime. Then the fog rolled in, some rain came up, and all of a sudden it was pitch black. We were practically alone on this road of hairpin turns, because no other car would dare drive on it, except someone random from Illinois who didn't know any other way to go.

I was amazed how dark it was. There were no cities. There were no streetlights. There were no gas stations. We were out in the middle of a desert and mountains, so there were no houses, nothing inland. It's just ocean on the other side, so there was nothing out there—it was pitch black. And it was terrifying. It was probably the most terrifying drive of my life.

It was probably also the longest "2-hour" drive, which actually took 8, I've ever made in my life and just took us forever to get there. My wife was in a lot of pain from the cancer. We were just trying to get to the hotel. I had given up on the "scenic" idea a long time ago, but this was still the quickest way that we knew to get there.

Every once in a while, I would have to pull off to the side of the road. It was so tense. It was so difficult for me to drive and to see. And when I did, the first time I pulled off, I got out of the car and I just sort of "shook off." I said, "OK, God, You're going to have to help me."

Then I looked up. Even though the fog was all around us, it was totally clear above us! The sky was full of stars—more stars than I had ever seen in my life. I live in the country here in Illinois and I thought we had the place that could see the most stars of any place on the planet Earth. But this place had 10-fold–100-fold–what I had ever seen before because there were simply no lights anywhere for miles and miles around. The sky was just filled with stars.

And I thought, as I was driving earlier in the car, that if I just riding and not driving, I would have closed my eyes in fear. But after I stopped and looked up into the sky, I saw a sight I had never seen before. It was incredible. Even though the drive didn't get any better, my attitude sure did! I was actually driving through a wonderland.

I've heard when you're down in a well– even in the daytime–if you go down in a deep, deep well, you can see the stars up above. Of course, normally, you can't see any stars when the sun is shining–except 1 star, the sun–but you can't see any of the others. But down in a well you can see the stars. In fact the deeper you go in the well, the more stars you see.

It's one of those natural phenomena, just like the curtain here, that veil that I showed you, it actually because of the darkness that surrounds you that you can see things you never saw before.

A third story I want to tell you is about a cocoon.

Imagine a cocoon for a caterpillar—my kids and I were walking down the road this morning and we saw a little caterpillar—imagine all those hundreds of legs or however many they have, and they're grounded for life, or so it seems.

They're walking along, as slow as a snail's pace, literally, and then they crawl into here [this cocoon] to die, or so they think. They spin this little cocoon. This is their last hurrah. And they come in here thinking this is it, this is the end.

But the changes and the transformations that take place inside this dark, claustrophobic place are amazing. When that caterpillar comes out again, it doesn't have those hundreds of legs. It's not grounded. Now it can fly, it can flit, it can float. It can go faster than it could have ever gone before. It can go higher than it could have ever imagined.

This is certainly an analogy for our transformation into heaven. In an instant we will be changed, the Bible says. We'll get new bodies. We'll be like the angels, the Bible says (see 1 Corinthians 15:35-58 and Mark 12:25). I can't even imagine what it's going to be like.

But this is also, I think, an analogy for our life here on earth, for the ones who are left behind, as in my case, or for you if you're in a dark place right now.

I read about a woman who had gone through a similar grief. She had lost her mother. And she said she went into like a cocoon-like state for about 2 years. She said it was dark and terrible for her.

But she said that when she came out, she couldn't believe the transformation that had taken place in her while she was inside that cocoon. She said she felt more alive, more radiant, more compassionate, more gracious and more loving than she had ever felt before she had entered that cocoon. She learned that God was able to make the most out of her darkness.

It wasn't necessarily the things that she did, but what *God* did in her, and what God can do in us, if we allow Him to, during those dark times.

C.S. Lewis' wife died of cancer, too. He married her knowing that she had cancer. They said it was terminal, but they still hoped she would be healed. He married her, anyway, and she died. He wrote several things about this, but here's one of the quotes that he wrote that I really love. It says:

"Grace grows best in winter."

Grace grows best in winter. Sometimes we grow more gracious and loving in the winter seasons of our life than we do when the sun is shining. There are a lot of things that grow well in the summer and in the light. But there are certain things that seem to just grow best in winter, in the darkness.

I want to read one more passage for you, and this is from Romans chapter 8, because maybe you're in a dark place right now, or maybe when you go home tonight, you're going to feel like you're in a dark place.

I want to encourage you that God still loves you. In fact, He may be doing a transformation in you that you're not even aware of. Don't give up on Him, because He's certainly not given up on you. So this is Romans chapter 8, near the end of the chapter. Paul says:

> *"I'm absolutely convinced that nothing–nothing living or dead, angelic or demonic, today or tomorrow, high or low, thinkable or unthinkable–absolutely nothing can get between us and God's love because of the way that Jesus our Master has embraced us" (Romans 8:38-39, The Message).*

Paul says nothing–nothing–absolutely nothing can get between us and God's love, because of the way that Jesus our Master has embraced us.

I want to pray for you, that God would embrace you with His love–that you would feel it and that you would make the most of the darkness.

Whether it's the illustration of the veil, and seeing into heaven, or whether it's the illustration of the well and a starry night with fog all around, or the cocoon, where it may be dark, but you can trust that a huge transformation is taking place, I just want to encourage you and remind you just to let God embrace you with His love. Let Him make the most out of your darkness.

Let's pray.

Father, thank You for carrying me through this past year, even those darkest nights, and even those that may be yet to come. I pray that You would help me to remember how much You love me. I pray for those reading these words, God, that You would help them to know that You love them, too. God, I know You're embracing them with Your love. Your love never fails. Your love has been demonstrated in Jesus when He first loved us and came to die for our sins, so we could be free of them. And Lord, that same grace that saved us is the same grace that sustains us. God, I pray that You would embrace each person in this room, and each person reading this later, that You would embrace them with Your love, a love that can overcome fear, a love that never fails, and a love that can never separate us from You. In Jesus' name, Amen.

CHAPTER 10: LEAVING A LEGACY — SEPTEMBER 26

This is one of my all-time favorite pictures. It's a picture of my wife, Lana, giving our oldest daughter, Karis, one big last kiss before sending Karis "off to school" for the first time ever…at age 19!

Since Karis was homeschooled from kindergarten through high school, we had never sent her off to school before. But when Karis decided to move 4 states away to Virginia for her sophomore year of college, we finally got to experience it.

Karis and I had gotten up early in the morning to start the 12-hour drive to drop her off in Virginia, but Lana called me after we had been on the road for about 30 minutes. Lana was crying because, even though she had said goodbye to Karis, she realized she hadn't given her a goodbye kiss. I said I could turn around and meet her half-way if she wanted. Lana said, "Would you?"

So I turned around and drove back towards home. Lana met us half-way, still crying, and pulled over on the side of the road. She jumped out of the van and ran to give Karis one big last kiss. It was one of the sweetest moments I've ever seen in my life.

Looking back on that picture now, I'm so thankful I turned around that day, and so thankful that Lana wanted me to. I had no idea that 18 months later Lana would be diagnosed with terminal cancer, and 9 months after that she would be gone.

As hard as it's been to lose Lana, memories like these remind me of the legacy Lana left us. Her life was filled with love for me and for the kids and for those around her, and that love still helps to fill the holes in our hearts that were created when she passed away.

Some people, because of their great love for others and the investment they've made in their lives, leave a legacy when they die. Others, because of their lack of love or the abuse they've doled out over the years, simply leave a vacancy. It's much easier to fill a hole in your heart that's already been filled with love, than to fill a hole in your heart that's been empty for years.

Thankfully God can fill both kinds of holes! His love is limitless! But I'm thankful, too, for Lana's love, as it has helped me through so much of this past year without her. It inspires me to want to leave a legacy when I leave this life as well.

As we come to the end of the calendar year, and as I come to the end of this first year without Lana, I can honestly say I'm looking forward to the new year ahead. I feel that God has many more things for me to do in my lifetime, and I want to make the most of the days I have left.

Two weeks ago, my daughter Karis turned in her final paper and graduated from college with a 4-year degree in biblical studies. Two weeks before that, my 2nd oldest, Lucas, walked across the stage at his college graduation, graduating with a 3-year advanced diploma in worship in leadership. And next May, my third oldest, Makari, will graduate with a 2-year certificate in transformational ministry.

As much as I wish Lana were here to see these milestones herself, I can't help but be thankful for all the fruit that her years of labor and love have borne.

When Lana left, she left a legacy, not a vacancy. And that inspires me to want to leave a legacy as well. How can I do that? I believe the best way is to do what Lana did, which was the same thing that Jesus called each of us to do: love God and love others as we love ourselves. Jesus said:

> "'Love the Lord your God with all your heart and with all your soul and with all your mind.' This is the first and greatest commandment. And the second is like it: 'Love your neighbor as yourself.' All the Law and the Prophets hang on these two commandments" (Matthew 22:37-40).

I want to leave a legacy in the future, not a vacancy. Of all the goals I could set for myself in the New Year, this one inspires me the most. I pray it inspires you, too.

Will you pray with me?

Father, thank You for helping us through 2013, and I pray that You'll help us through 2014 as well, with love in our hearts for You and for those around us, so that we can leave a legacy of Your love everywhere we go. In Jesus' name, Amen.

CHAPTER 11: HELPING OTHERS REACH THEIR GOALS — SEPTEMBER 27

As you head into a new year, I'd like to encourage you to consider making one of your goals to help someone else reach one of their goals. That way if one of you succeeds, you'll both succeed at the same time! And you may just help someone do something they never could have done on their own.

About 8 years ago, I came to the realization that my wife had some goals for her life that she may never achieve without some help. There were 3 in particular I was concerned about: 1) She wanted to go to Africa and help orphans in need. 2) She wanted to go to Israel and walk where Jesus walked. 3) She wanted to make a movie about St. Nicholas to inspire others in their faith at Christmastime.

Lana had talked about wanting to do each of these things from time to time, but was never able to move forward on them. Raising our kids and helping me reach some of my goals had become her full-time focus. She was happy to do these things, but I felt that some of her dreams got shelved in the process, and I didn't want her to miss out on anything that she felt called to do herself.

So I began to pray to see if there was anything I could do to help her reach her goals. And I'm so glad I did.

The Bible says that each of us has different gifts, and we're to use those gifts for the common good (see 1 Corinthians chapter 12), so God began to show me how I could use my gifts to help her with her goals.

First, I talked to her about her dream of wanting to go to Africa. I asked if she would want to go on a missions trip if we could find one with a reputable group that we could trust was doing good work there. She said that would be great. The very next day, I was in a bookstore looking for a book that I had been waiting to come out for months. The publisher had contacted me a year earlier to ask if the author might mention one of my stories in his book, but I never knew what he decided to do.

That very next day after talking to Lana about going to Africa, I happened to find the book in the bookstore! It had just been published and I quickly began to skim through it to see if there was any mention of my story. There wasn't! But I was enthralled by the vision of the author. After skimming through the first 100 pages, I got to a line that stunned me: the author said he was trying to recruit thousands of American volunteers to come to Africa the following year!

I bought the book and brought it home to Lana. I said, "How would you like to go next year?" Within 24 hours, we had found a reputable group! She said, "Yes!" and we began to save money and raise money for both of us to go to Africa along with our 2 oldest kids and one of their friends.

CHAPTER 12: STORING THE MEMORIES   SEPTEMBER 28

One of the things I look forward to at the end of each year is to look back. I'm often surprised at all that's happened during the year, and it gives me hope for the year to come.

This past year has been no exception. As I was writing my year-end letter for my family and friends this week, I was amazed at all that God helped me to do this year, even though I felt like so much of it was just absorbed in my grief of losing Lana. As God reminded me of all that He has done in my life this year, I was reminded of the words of Jesus:

> "But the Counselor, the Holy Spirit, whom the Father will send in My name, will teach you all things and will remind you of everything I have said to you" (John 14:26).

As I looked through my journal, as I looked through my Facebook posts, as I looked through pictures on my phone and in albums, I was reminded of all that God was doing in my life, even when I wasn't aware of it at the time.

This time of looking back truly has given me hope for the future. I'm in a different place now after a year of grief than I was last year at this time. And in many ways, I'm in a different place now than I've ever been in my life. Things will never be the same.

That's a statement that has often brought a flood of tears. But as I've looked back over all that God has done in my life this past year, I can see that statement in a different light. From here on out, things *will* never be the same. And I praise God for it. It reminds me of the lyrics to a song by Stephen Schwartz called, "For Good," from his popular musical, *Wicked*:

> "It well may be
> That we will never meet again
> In this lifetime
> So let me say before we part
> So much of me
> Is made of what I learned from you
> You'll be with me
> Like a handprint on my heart
> And now whatever way our stories end
> I know you have re-written mine…
> Who can say if I've been changed for the better?

But because I knew you
I have been changed for good."

In the weeks before Lana died, she asked me to put together a picture book of all the work we've done on the house here at Clover Ranch and send it to a friend who helped us so much with the project. As I looked through pictures from the past 7 years, I was amazed at the transformation that I saw had taken place from year to year. It was a lot of work and it took a lot of time, but it was beautiful in the end.

I put together the book and sent it to our friend as Lana had asked. But it was so helpful to me to look back and gave me such hope for the future as I look forward, that I bought an extra album for myself and printed out an extra set of pictures so I could keep a copy, too. It's filled with memories I'll treasure for the rest of my life.

As hard as it was to look back at the past, I've been encouraged by it as I look forward to the future. Perhaps you'll find it encouraging, too.

In closing, I'd like to share with you the year-end letter I wrote to my family and friends this week. As you've been with me on this journey, I certainly consider you my family and friends, too! It's a summation of some of the things you've already read in these messages, but written from the vantage point of one-year down the road. I pray it encourages you that with God's help, whatever your loss, He really can help you get through it. There really is another side to grief, and I'm thankful now to be able to see it for myself.

With that introduction, here's my year-end letter.
January 18th, 2014

Happy New Year to you! I wanted to send you an updated picture of our family, along with an update on how we're doing. I was torn again this year between which Christmas picture to send you, so I'm sending you both.

We took these on Christmas Eve at the Lexington Cemetery, about 7 miles from our home, where we installed a memorial bench for Lana this fall. One picture seems to highlight Lana's beautiful memorial and the other seems to highlight the beautiful faces of our kids. I think Lana's spirit is clearly evident in both!

I kept the first few months of last year as low-key as possible: doing school with the 3 younger kids, finishing projects around the house and working on some behind-the-scenes things for the ministry. I wrote a few messages for The Ranch website and spoke at a few churches, but overall it was nice to spend some time out of public view for a while after our whirlwind year.

In April I drove to Houston in a friend's truck to pick up the granite bench for Lana's memorial. My cousin Joan had found it at a craft shop there and sent us a picture just a few days before Lana passed away. Lana loved it and I did too. It turned out to be cheaper to pick it up myself than to ship it to Illinois, and the road trip gave me some extra time on my own to think and pray.

While I was in Houston, I visited the church where we were married. Of course I cried as I knelt at the front of the church where I said my vows to Lana: "You are a gift from God to me and I plan to treat you as a gift." As I walked through the empty hallways that day, I felt like I was reliving a scene from the *Titanic*. My mind filled in the empty hallways with people and dancing and private moments with Lana (and the photographer) from 24 years ago. I don't think I needed a photographer to remember anything from that day.

We tried to keep things the same as much as possible around the house this year because so much had already changed in our lives. We planted a garden as usual in the spring, and we made Lana's favorite salsa with all the tomatoes and peppers and parsley that we grew. The rest of the garden was overtaken with weeds when our tiller broke, just so you're not left with some picturesque but false view of our life in the country–although we all still love it out here!

The rest of our summer was filled with fun things like Kaleo's dance recital in May, Josiah's week at Boy Scout camp in June, and music festivals and a camping trip to the sand dunes on Lake Michigan in July and August.

In the fall I drove Makari back out to California (in her 1993 convertible 240SX...the best way to head out west!) to start her 2nd year at Bethel College in Redding where she'll finish a 2-year certificate in transformational ministry in May. On the last day of our trip, driving through the mountains with the top down in the beautiful sun, I somehow felt that everything was going to be all right.

It was a turning point for me and, by the time I flew back to Illinois and started school with the 3 younger kids again, I felt like my heart was really on its way to healing. The deep pain of losing Lana was starting to be replaced with so many beautiful memories, and it's just been getting better and better ever since.

In December I flew to Australia to spend 2 weeks with Lucas and watch him graduate after 3 years with an advanced diploma in worship and leadership from Hillsong International Leadership College. It was great to meet Lucas' friends and teachers, see a ballet at the Sydney Opera House, spend a day at the Taronga Zoo and see *The Hunger Games 2* at the world's largest IMAX theater.

Two weeks after Lucas graduated, Karis texted me to let me know she had just turned in her final paper to finish her bachelor's degree in biblical studies from Liberty University Online. She'll have a graduation ceremony in Virginia in May, but as of now I have 2 college graduates! I'm so proud of both of them, and I know Lana would be so pleased at the fruit of all her labors of homeschooling the kids from kindergarten through high school.

We were all together for 2 weeks at Christmas before Makari had to fly back to California for her 2nd semester at Bethel. We're starting to get back into the swing of school here at the house, too, happy to have Lucas home for a while after being so far away for much of the last 3 years. Last weekend we had a movie night here at the house with all the kids (minus Makari) to watch the first of the *Lord of the Rings* movies as Bo had just finished reading the first book.

And that brings us up to today, January 18th, 2014. It's a new year and a new season of life. Psalm 5:3 has become one of my daily prayers:

"In the morning, O LORD, You hear my voice; in the morning I lay my requests before You and wait in expectation."

I never could have made it without God's help and without your love and prayers. Thank you! I appreciate you all so much.

15 Tips For A Stronger Marriage

15 Tips for a Stronger Marriage

Practical tips for newlyweds, nearly-weds or anyone who wants to strengthen their marriage

INTRODUCTION

I was sitting with a couple recently to help them plan their wedding when the bride-to-be asked me to do something impossible: she wanted me to talk at her wedding about marriage and what made my marriage to my wife, Lana, so successful.

She said she admired our relationship and wanted to learn whatever she could to make her marriage the best that it could be.

Here's why her request seemed so impossible: how could I possibly summarize 23 years' worth of thoughts on marriage in such a short message on her wedding day? Yet her question also inspired me because I loved the idea of being able to pass along to them anything that might be helpful. So I began to think of all the tips I had heard before we got married, after we got married and throughout our 23 years of marriage. I quickly came up with 4 or 5 sermons to share at her wedding!

In the end, I only shared 1 simple message with them, based on 3 words, which I felt would help them get through anything they might face in the future. I'll share those 3 words with you in the conclusion of this books as they serve as the glue that holds all the other tips together. But I still wanted to share with this couple all the other great tips that God had brought to my mind. The result is this little book that I'm now sharing with you.

I wish I could say that if you'll just put these 15 tips into practice you'll be guaranteed success in your own marriage, but relationships just don't work like that. Each one of us is unique and each one of our relationships is unique. Yet I still believe each of these tips can be helpful to you in one way or another, even if it's just to talk through them with your spouse, or spouse to be, and then adapt and apply them to your own relationship.

For those of you who are not married, I think you'll find nuggets of gold in these tips that apply to any of your relationships, not just your marriage. In fact, I heard from a single woman who wrote to tell me as I was writing this series to say how surprised she was that God was speaking to her through these marriage tips, even though she's not married. Here's an excerpt from what she wrote, which I share more about in Tip #13:

> "I was hesitant at first to read this devotional as I'm not married. I was just scrolling through and saw a part about Lana and yourself getting a car and about marriage being a calling. So I decided to start from the top, for I believed God wanted me to learn a thing or two and also to be encouraged as I was feeling a bit down and questioning my future. I enjoyed it and it made me laugh how God worked out your

differences, even your breaking up and eventually getting married. That gave me hope since I'm single and struggling relationship wise... Thanks for sharing your testimony. I must read the rest and see what else God wants me to know. God bless!"

At the end of this devotional book (starting on December 27), I've also included a bonus section called "12 Tips on Parenting." I wrote this section in response to another question by some other friends who asked for my thoughts on that topic.

Lastly, you might want to consider going through this book with a few other couples who are newly married, nearly married or just want to strengthen their marriage, no matter how long they've been married. Who knows? This book may be just what they need to make their marriage not just good, but great!

Any way you do it, I pray God will bless you through it, both now and for many years to come.

TIP 1: PRAY WITH EACH OTHER DAILY — SEPTEMBER 29

I've kept these tips short to help you get started as quickly as possible, but I hope you won't rush through them.

We have a game at our house called *Othello*, and the description on the box says the game takes "a minute to learn; a lifetime to master." The same is true for each of these tips. You can probably read each one in just a few minutes, but they could take a lifetime to master!

So I hope you'll take some time to really consider how to apply each one to your own marriage. With that in mind, here's the first of the 15 tips!

Before Lana and I got married, I heard someone say that he prayed every night with his wife before they went to bed. He said this assured them of 2 things every day:

1) This assured them that each of them was being prayed for every single day of their lives. Since I believe in the power of prayer, I was so eager to try this even before I got married that I tried it with a friend who was my roommate at the time. It turned out to be so powerful, and we saw so many answers to our prayers, that I was convinced to keep doing it when I entered into marriage as well.

2) This also assured them that each of them would have a chance to express some of their deepest needs that they may never have shared otherwise. Often I would go through a whole day with Lana, talking and doing life together, and think that I knew what she probably wanted prayer for by the end of the day. But there were often times when I would ask her how I could pray for her and she would surprise me with something that I would have never guessed on my own.

No matter how late it was at night or what kind of mood we were in, we kept this commitment daily, even if it was just praying a blessing over each other in Jesus' name. One of Lana's favorite prayers to pray for me and for the kids was based on this verse from the Bible:

"The LORD bless you and keep you; the LORD make His face shine upon you and be gracious to you; the LORD turn His face toward you and give you peace" (Numbers 6:24-26).

I shared this tip with the couple who inspired me to write this book and they posted a message on Facebook just a few days into their honeymoon:

> "A man filled with great wisdom told us before we got married that every night we should pray together before we fell asleep. So far in our short marriage we have done that. There is nothing more intimate."

I agree! Pray with each other every day.

TIP 2: TAKE OUT THE TV — SEPTEMBER 30

Lack of communication is the #1 cause of divorce. It's amazing how even *having* a TV in the room can impact your communication with your spouse. It's always easier to turn on the TV than to talk to someone else. The TV doesn't talk back; you don't have to listen if you don't want to. You can be delighted and entertained for hours on end without doing any of the heavy lifting of a relationship. Having a TV in the room is like always having a third person in your marriage. Even when it's off, the temptation is still there to turn it on.

Lana and I read a book before we got married called *The First Years of Forever* by Ed and Gaye Wheat which argued convincingly that the patterns you set in the first 2 years of marriage will set the tone for the patterns you'll have in your 7th year and 14th year and so on. So to set your patterns right from the start, make communication a #1 goal. Lana and I put our TV in the back of a closet for the first year of our marriage. The only time we took it out was when we heard that the Berlin Wall was being torn down live on television, 1 of the most significant news events of that year. Then back into the closet it went.

I can't tell you the joy that Lana and I had that first year, just the two of us in our 1-bedroom apartment in Houston, Texas. It freed us up to spend all kinds of time together, whether it was cooking dinner, playing games, cleaning dishes, going out or making love. Someone had given us money to buy a new TV as a wedding present, which we saved to get one when our first year was over. But we enjoyed our life without a TV so much that we kept it that way for several years until we finally decided to buy one so we could watch movies or teach the kids. After 23 years, we still watched very little TV, nor did our kids, because we just never developed the habit. (And when we did start watching TV again, we were shocked at how much more negative the content on TV seemed to have turned in just those few short years.)

Let me add here again that these are suggestions that you'll have to adapt to your own situation, whether it's limiting time on the Internet or social media, or watching only a set number of shows or sporting events per month, or whatever it takes to give you the best shot at increasing your time to communicate. As the Apostle Paul reminded the Corinthians:

> "Everything is permissible"–but not everything is beneficial. "Everything is permissible"–but not everything is constructive (1 Corinthians 10:23).

TIP 3: COMBINE YOUR BANK ACCOUNTS — OCTOBER 1

Communication is the #1 cause for divorce, but finances are a close second. Lana and I were encouraged at the beginning of our marriage to combine our bank accounts and share a checkbook. This meant that we had to talk about our purchases with each other so there were no surprises. This also kept us in check from making whimsical or unnecessary purchases. By combining our bank accounts we were also able to better save our money and make a priority of helping to fulfill each other's dreams, whether it was a special trip for an anniversary or a missions trip to another country or a new vehicle when we needed one.

Because we had to make our decisions together, we simply made wiser decisions. Although it was harder at first because we had to work together, it kept us from having the mentality that "this is my money" and "this is your money." We realized early on that "this is God's money" and we wanted to spend it in the best way possible. As King David said to God:

> "Everything comes from You, and we have given You only what comes from Your hand" (1 Chronicles 29:14b).

This may not apply to every situation or every stage of life, but it's important to do something to make sure your finances enhance your marriage and not take away from it. For instance, I noticed that Lana was supportive whenever I was asked to speak anywhere special, but that doing so cost her in terms of my time and energy. So I began giving her any money I received from these extra speaking engagements, rather than using it for our everyday bills. It was a simple way to make sure the money we received was working *for* our marriage, not *against* it.

TIP 4: NEVER USE THE "D" WORD: DIVORCE   OCTOBER 2

There's a funny line in the movie, *It's a Wonderful Life,* when the house maid Annie gives some money to George Bailey when he's in dire straits. Annie says, "I've been saving this money for a divorce, if ever I got a husband!" It's a funny line for a movie, but it's a terrible line for real life. Sometimes you might be tempted to hold things back from your spouse "just in case things don't work out." But those very things that you're holding back might be the pathway to greater intimacy if they were shared, whether it's money or secrets or simply giving yourself as fully as possible to your spouse.

If you're committed to marriage for life, which God certainly is, never use the word "divorce," especially as a threat. Some people hold onto that option and use it as a weapon in an argument. But it's not a weapon. Jesus said that Moses allowed for divorce only because of the hardness of people's hearts, but that it wasn't always that way from the beginning (see Matthew 19:8).

If you're struggling in your marriage, keep your hearts soft and tender by looking for other ways to deal with your problems, whether you look to God, the Bible, prayer, counselors, friends or perhaps even time away. But not divorce. God says in the Bible:

> "I hate divorce" (Malachi 2:16).

And anyone who's been through one knows why. When I've counseled couples for marriage, I've sometimes told them that I'm glad to bless their marriage, but on one condition: that if they ever consider a divorce, that they have to come back to me first and get my blessing for that, too. Then I let them know that in all my years of counseling people, I have never recommended that a couple divorce, even in some of the most intense situations. (I have, from time to time, let people know they have the freedom to divorce, both scripturally and as part of the free will that God has given us in all things. But I have also seen God work in some of the most intense situations, especially when both people are willing to do so, that I know I am not the one to recommend that option.)

TIP 5: CONFESS YOUR SINS QUICKLY — OCTOBER 3

I heard about a man who walked across America. He said his toughest moments weren't when he was walking through the rain or snow or to the top of a tall mountain. He said his toughest times were when he got tiny grains of sand in his shoes. Unless he stopped to regularly dump out the sand, those tiny grains would rub against his feet until blisters formed and then he would suffer for days or weeks in extreme pain until his feet healed.

I heard this story in a sermon about marriage one Sunday morning, in the context of confessing even those small sins in our lives to our spouse, dumping them out of our shoes before they rubbed enough to cause more severe pain. I immediately thought of a particular friendship I had with someone that I enjoyed, perhaps a little too much. There was nothing sinful going on, but the fact that this friendship came to mind as I heard this story made me wonder if maybe I should confess it to Lana and ask her what to do about it. I didn't want to mention it though, because I was afraid the best solution would be to step back from this friendship all together, and I didn't want to lose the friendship.

But after a few days of praying, I realized that even though this issue seemed like no big deal, as small as a grain of sand, I knew I'd rather dump it out now than let it possibly endanger my marriage down the road. I confessed it to Lana, and we agreed it would be best for me to back off from the friendship. Even though it was a good friendship in my life, I felt so much freer after stepped back and it never caused another problem again. Confess any sins right away, even if they're as small as a grain of sand. As the Bible says,

> "Therefore confess your sins to each other and pray for each other so that you may be healed" (James 5:16).

TIP 6: LOVE YOUR WAY THROUGH ANY "IRRECONCILABLE DIFFERENCES" OCTOBER 4

I once heard about an interviewer who asked several couples who had gotten a divorce how many "irreconcilable differences" they had in their marriage; things that they were simply never able to agree upon. The average answer was 5 or 6 "irreconcilable differences." The interviewer then asked the same question of several couples who were still together after 40, 50 and 60 years. Their answer? 5 or 6! It wasn't the number of irreconcilable differences that made the difference in whether the couples stayed together or not, but their commitment to love each other through them.

We're all unique. We all have different backgrounds and life experiences. It's no surprise that we think differently on various topics as well. It's part of life and it's all part of what makes being married work so much better than being alone for so many people, because they can each bring their best ideas to table. But invariably this means that many other ideas have to be left on the table, even good ones. Lana and I agreed on a lot of things, but there were probably 5 or 6 that we still never agreed on in all our years together.

We're all like porcupines, with our various differences and sins poking out of us all the time. And when we get close enough to each other, there's a good chance we'll get poked. Yet even porcupines find a way to have baby porcupines. How do they do it? Very carefully!

Don't let your sins and differences cause you to lose your commitment to a lifetime of marriage no matter what. Love your way through them instead. As the Bible says:

> "Above all, love each other deeply, because love covers over a multitude of sins" (John 15:13).

TIP 7: INVITE AND ALLOW JESUS TO LOVE YOUR SPOUSE THROUGH YOU — OCTOBER 5

When I married Lana, I knew without a doubt that she was a gift from God to me. But I also realized that if she was a gift from God to me, then perhaps I was a gift from God to her, too. As such, I often wondered what Jesus would want me to do for her if He were here on earth, for the Bible says that we are the body of Christ and He wants to be able to live His life through us to touch others (see 1 Corinthians 12).

So when Lana would lay in bed at night, exhausted from a long day of taking care of everyone else around her, I would think, "What Would Jesus Do?" If Jesus was here, what would He want to say to her? What would He want to do for her? How would He minister to the deepest needs of her heart right now? Then I would try to let Jesus use me to love her, using my words to speak to her, my hands to stroke her head, my ears to listen to what she'd been going through during the day.

WWJD (What Would Jesus Do) might seem like a trite acronym to put on a bracelet or a bumper sticker, but it's only trite if we make it so. If we take it seriously—and realize it's exactly what God *wants* us to ask at all times and in all situations, especially with our spouse—it can change the dynamics of every relationship that we have.

As I was writing this message to you today, I happened to hear from the wife of a couple I had married several years ago. She shared with me that that this was the single most important tip she learned back then, and that it was the #1 thing that was getting her through the mess she and her husband were in right now, inviting and allowing Jesus to love her spouse through her.

Just as God has placed your spouse in your life as a gift to you, He has placed you in your spouse's life as a gift to them. Invite and allow Jesus to love your spouse through you. As the Bible says:

> "Now you are the body of Christ, and each one of you is a part of it" (1 Corinthians 12:27).

TIP 8: BE WILLING TO LIVE FOR YOUR SPOUSE — OCTOBER 6

I spoke to a man who was divorcing his wife. She wanted to move to another state to fulfill some of her dreams, but he didn't want to. They were at a stalemate and this was the last straw.

I asked him, "If someone threatened to kill your wife, would you be willing to die for her?"

"Yes, of course," he replied.

Then I asked, "If you would be willing to die for her, would you be willing to live for her?"

We talked again shortly thereafter, and he put his faith in Christ. He reconciled with his wife and they moved across the country. As Jesus told His disciples:

> "Greater love has no one than this, that he lay down his life for his friends" (John 15:13).

Then Jesus proved His love for His friends by laying down His life for them.

Surprisingly, "laying down your life" doesn't always mean giving up your own dreams and plans, too. For Jesus also said,

> "For whoever wants to save his life will lose it, but whoever loses his life for Me will find it" (Matthew 16:25).

Sometimes it's by helping your spouse achieve their dreams that you'll be better able to fulfill your own dreams. If God is the one who has put special dreams and desires within both you and your spouse, then He'll find a way to accomplish those dreams and desires for both of you, too.

TIP 9: HELP YOUR SPOUSE ACHIEVE THEIR GOALS — OCTOBER 7

This may sound like the previous tip, but the difference is that sometimes you'll have to take the initiative to help your spouse achieve their goals. It may be that God has put you in their life just for this purpose, because He knew they would need your unique help. After God created Adam, He said:

> "It's not good for the Man to be alone; I'll make him a helper, a companion" (Genesis 2:18, MSG).

One of the main purposes for marriage, according to God, is so we won't have to do life alone; that we'll have a helper and a companion along the way.

Lana was both of those things to me: a wonderful companion and a terrific helper. She helped me do things I could never have done on my own, whether it was building a family or launching a ministry or giving me regular feedback and encouragement on my writing and speaking and planning and dreaming. At the same time, I was able to help her achieve some of her goals. Over the years, however, I realized that she still had other dreams and desires for her life which would never be realized if I didn't step in to give her a boost. She wanted to do missions work in Africa, visit the Holy Land and make a movie about the life of St. Nicholas.

But with all of her other responsibilities, those dreams seemed either distant or impossible. So I sat down with her and began to pray about each one, asking God how I could help her achieve her dreams. Within a few years, I was able to help her take a missions trip to Africa, visit the Holy Land twice and write out the story of the life of St. Nicholas, which we planned to use as the basis for a movie someday. When we found out that Lana had cancer, I can't tell you how thankful I was that I had stepped in to help her fulfill those dreams while she was still able to do them—and I'd encourage you to do the same.

TIP 10: REMEMBER YOUR MARRIAGE IS A CALLING TOO — OCTOBER 8

I think a word of caution is in order here, too. Be careful when considering giving up one type of "calling" to follow another. I shared my story with a group one day about quitting my job and going into full-time ministry. A woman came up to me afterwards to tell me how excited she was because God was calling her to do the same thing. After congratulating her for being willing to take this step of faith, I asked her what kept her from doing it before. She said, "Well, my husband won't like it because I'm going to have to move and leave him behind."

"As in divorce?" I asked.

"Yes," she said, and she looked at the floor.

I said, "Don't forsake one type of calling (your marriage) to fulfill another. If this is from God, He'll help you to do both."

Your marriage is a calling just as much as any other kind of "calling." When I quit my job and went into full-time ministry, I knew for me that meant living on faith for all of our financial provision (we all live on faith, actually; it's just that sometimes we're more acutely aware of it than others). But I also knew I was called to my marriage with Lana.

So I wrote Lana a letter, telling her that even though I felt called by God to do this ministry, I also felt called by God to marry her and to take care of her as best I could. I committed to her, right at the beginning of our ministry, that if ever she felt she wasn't being cared for because of the ministry that I was doing, then I would quit doing ministry or I would find another way to do it so that I could care for her better.

I didn't want to shortchange one calling to fulfill another. As the Bible says rather forcefully:

> "Anyone who does not provide for their relatives, and especially for their own household, has denied the faith and is worse than an unbeliever" (1 Timothy 5:8).

Lana never had to exercise her right to pull out the letter and pull me out of ministry, although she came close a few times. And whenever she did, we prayed together, and I filled out applications for other jobs. God always made a way for me to fulfill both callings, however, so I could keep loving her well and keep doing ministry well. I knew that if I had to neglect one calling to fulfill another, then I was probably doing something wrong, and if God had called me to both, He would help me to find a way to do both.

TIP 11: REMEMBER THAT GOD IS THE PROVIDER FOR BOTH OF YOU — OCTOBER 9

If you haven't noticed, each of these tips builds on the others. While there's a lot that you can do for your spouse, you can't do everything! There are some things only God can do. Ultimately, He's the one who provides for you both. As the Bible says,

> "The earth is the LORD's, and everything in it..." (Psalm 24:1a).

When I was first dating Lana, we relied on each other for everything: our conversation, our intimacy, our affirmation, our affection. But when God broke us up for a period of time, we learned to rely on Him as the ultimate source of everything in our lives, including each other. When we finally came back together and eventually got married, we had a new awareness that God was the source of all we needed, even if He used one or the other of us to meet that need. He was still the source of it all.

I was reminded of how much God loved Lana one morning after we had had a funny conversation the day before. Her car had broken down and we needed to find another, but there was no way we could afford one. She told me the kind of car she really wanted to get. She had never cared about makes or models of cars before, just whatever would get her from Point A to Point B. When I looked at the prices of used models online, I thought, "Good luck with that!"

A friend of ours told us when he sent his daughter off to college, the only thing he had to give her were his prayers and these words: "The same God who takes care of me will take care of you." God did His part, my friend did what he could do, his daughter did what she could do, and God did what only He could do. 4 years later she had a college degree!

So that night as I prayed for Lana and the car she wanted, I said at the end, rather jokingly, "Well, you've got my prayers! The same God who takes care of me will take care of you!" Then I rolled over and fell asleep.

The joke was on me, though, when the very next morning I pulled into the parking lot for a men's group at church and a man pulled in right after me–driving the exact car that Lana had told me she wanted. He had never visited the group before, and I had never seen another car like this around town. It was the same exact make, model and color that Lana had wanted!

I told the man that my wife was talking about getting a car just like that and he said he was actually thinking of selling it! I had to shake my head and confess to God that I had forgotten how much *He* loved her, too–even more than I did–and that *He* was the one who provided everything for her, just like He provided everything for me. Although we didn't buy that man's car, God made a way for us to buy another one–the same model, make and color–within just a few months of those feeble prayers. God really does love our spouse even more than we love them, and He loves to surprise and delight them, just as He loves to surprise and delight us.

Sometimes we make the mistake of trying too hard to please our spouse, only to fall short again and again, when what we really need to do is to trust God that He will provide for them, even when we can't. So do your best and trust God with the rest.

TIP 12: CHOOSE WELL (AND REMEMBER WHY YOU CHOSE THE ONE YOU DID)
OCTOBER 10

One of the questions I'm asked most about marriage is "How did you know that Lana was 'the one' for you?" Today I'll share that answer with you in Tip #12 for how to have a stronger marriage.

But don't think that today's tip is only for those who are considering marriage. Even if you've been married a long, long time, today's tip can help to re-energize your marriage as you remember why you chose your spouse in the first place.

With that in mind, here's tip #12 for how to have a stronger marriage.

Next to your decision to follow Christ, choosing who to marry is the 2nd most important decision you'll ever make in your life. It's a decision that will affect you for the rest of your life, and it's a decision that will affect generations of people long after you're gone.

I read a book before I got married that scared me, and for good reason: I wasn't ready to get married. Even though I loved Lana deeply, this book helped me see the enormity of the decision to get married and how it would affect my life from that moment on. The book was called *The Mystery of Marriage* by Mike Mason. Mike said:

> "A marriage, or a marriage partner, may be compared to a great tree growing right up through the center of one's living room. It is something that is just there, and it is huge, and everything has been built around it, and wherever one happens to be going–to the fridge, to bed, to the bathroom, or out the front door–the tree has to be taken into account. It cannot be gone through; it must respectfully be gone around. It is somehow bigger and stronger than oneself. True, it could be chopped down, but not without tearing the house apart. And certainly it is beautiful, unique, exotic: but also, let's face it, it is at times an enormous inconvenience.
>
> So there are many things that can be said about one's life's mate, but finally, irrevocably, the one definite thing that needs to be said is that he or she is always there. And that, while it may be common enough in the world of trees, is among us human beings a rather remarkable state of affairs" (Mike Mason, The Mystery of Marriage, p. 39).

The book goes on to describe how nothing in life does more to expose our pride, failings and weaknesses than being married. Our selfishness is exposed at every turn. As the Bible says:

> "As iron sharpens iron, so one person sharpens another" (Proverbs 27:17).

As helpful as it is for us to be sharpened, the process of chipping away at the ugly and unsightly things in our lives can be painful. I just wasn't ready. I remember going to my brother and sister-in-law's wedding, watching them take their vows for a lifetime and thinking, "I can't do this! I just can't do it!" It wasn't that I didn't love Lana, but that I couldn't imagine giving up the idea of just living my life for myself.

In the months that followed, however, God began to show me all that I would gain by being married. I had recently put my faith in Christ, and I was already seeing the fruit of having invited Him into my life and taking His thoughts into account before acting on my own. I was eventually convinced that marriage could be worth giving up whatever independence I had before. The question then became, "Who does God want me to marry?"

Although the Bible gives us certain baseline criteria for choosing a spouse, such as believers marrying other believers (2 Corinthians 6:14a and 1 Kings 11:2b), not marrying close relatives (Leviticus 18:6-19), and marrying someone who can help God fulfill His recreative design for the world (Leviticus 18:22-23 and Romans 1:26-27), it doesn't tell us which person, specifically, who God wants us to marry. At least I didn't think so. For that, I knew I would have to rely on God's Holy Spirit. And I've found that He is more than happy to help us—as long as we're willing to listen.

So how did I know that Lana was "the one"? For me, my answer came after months of asking God to speak to me clearly if she was the one that He wanted me to marry. I had already come to the conclusion that I wanted to marry her, but I needed to know for sure what God wanted, because I knew that He knew both of us better than we knew ourselves.

One morning I sat down in my bedroom to read my Bible, but didn't know what to read. I had just finished reading my Bible from cover to cover a few days earlier for the first time in my life, and I wasn't sure where to start reading again. So I decided to start over at the beginning.

Lana had come to visit me that morning, as we had already been out to watch a friend run a race in downtown Houston. We decided to take some time to pray on our own before going on with the day, so she sat on the couch in the living room with her Bible, and I went to the bedroom with mine. This was a refreshingly new practice for both of us in that previous year.

I opened up my Bible to the first page and began to read again about how God created the world, and how God created Adam, the first man on earth. God put Adam in a beautiful garden and asked him to take care of it. But God saw that even in the midst of this beautiful setting, surrounded by all kinds of spectacular things, Adam was still alone:

> "The LORD God said, 'It is not good for the man to be alone. I will make a helper suitable for him'" (Genesis 2:18).

So God created Eve and brought her to Adam.

Even though I had heard this story since I was a kid, this was the first time I had seen it from God's perspective. As I read about Adam being alone in the garden, my heart fell as God's must have fallen, when He saw how lonely Adam was. Then my heart rose again, as God's must have risen, when God created Eve and brought her to Adam. I imagined the smile on Adam's face must have been about a mile wide!

As I pictured this scene in my mind, I suddenly had an intense awareness that God was looking down at me just as He had looked at Adam. There I was, surrounded by all kinds of spectacular things, but I was still alone. In that moment, God spoke to my heart. The words seemed to leap off the page, and I felt that God had done the same for me: He had created a woman just for me and He had brought her directly to me. She was sitting in the very next room! After months of praying, I knew that I knew that God really did want to fulfill the desires of my heart and He really did want me to marry Lana.

I got up off the floor and ran down the hall. I didn't stop to look in the mirror as I ran, but I'm sure if I did, the smile on my face would have been about a mile wide. I told Lana what God had told me through the story of Adam and Eve. We talked and we cried, and I asked her to marry me right on the spot. To my delight, she said "Yes!" and we spent the rest of that incredible day together walking and talking and riding paddle boats in the rain at Miller Park.

My eyes still water as I think about it again 25 years later. Even though I didn't have a ring to give her, and we didn't have a candlelight dinner, I had something that was even more precious to me: I had a word from God that Lana was "the one." I can't tell you how many times I've come back to that story over the years, both in good times and in hard times, and how it has re-energized my love for and commitment to Lana.

For Lana, the story was much simpler: she said she knew from the day she met me that God wanted her to marry me. She said that as soon as we met, there on the 2nd floor of David Kinley Hall at the University of Illinois, that these words immediately popped into her mind: "That's the man you're going to marry."

She said it was the wording that made her realize it was from God, and the way that the words came into her mind. She said the words seemed to come into her mind out of the blue, and they were spoken in the 3rd person: "That's the man you're going to marry." She said that if it was her own thought, she would have said to herself, "That's the man I'm going to marry!" But she didn't, and the words were clear: "That's the man you're going to marry." She was so convinced that she went home that night and called one of her best friends to tell her she had just met the man she was going to marry. And she was right!

I tell you these stories not because I think God will speak to you in the exact same way, but to give you confidence that God can speak to you, if you're willing to listen to Him. God's Holy Spirit really is alive and active. And, believe it or not, God wants you to know who to marry even more than you want to know it. He has a bigger stake in the outcome of your life than you do, and He knows you and every other person on the planet even better than you know yourself.

I had been diligently seeking God for months for His answer (after dating Lana for years before finally coming to the place of asking God what He wanted for our relationship). And Lana had been praying ever since she was a child for a man to marry who would be like Jesus to her, not that I was ever close to that, but in her eyes at least, she felt that I was the answer to all those prayers.

Once I knew that Lana was the one for me, I knew there was never any going back. I was committed to planting that tree of marriage right in the center of my living room, and I was happier about it than I can possibly tell you. I never used the D word (Divorce) because I knew that wasn't an option. I knew that for better or worse, neither of us were going away, and we were going to have to work through anything that came our way together. And I couldn't have been happier about it.

Just like the words "God will never leave you alone" can be either a blessing or a curse depending on how you look at it, the idea of being with another person 24/7 for the rest of your life can be a blessing or a curse, too, depending on how you look at it. That's why it's so important to remember why you chose the one you did in the first place, because it can help restore the way you look at your marriage, not as a curse of always having someone else around, but as a blessing of always having someone else around.

If you're still considering who to marry, I want to encourage you to choose well. No decision, other than your decision to follow Christ, is as important. And no decision this important is one that God wants you to take lightly. He would love to help you know who to marry, for He has a vested interest in the outcome of both of your lives.

For those of you who have already made your choice of who to marry and who are now living out that choice, perhaps even wondering if you made the right choice or not, I'd like to encourage you to look back and remember why you made that choice in the first place.

What was it that drew you to your spouse? What made him or her so special to you when you first met or when you first started dating? What did God speak to you about him or her along the way? What feelings or emotions stirred within you that made you want to make this commitment to be together forever? Choosing well is important, but remembering can be just as important to helping you stay committed to your choice. As Nehemiah said about the Israelites who went back on some of their earlier choices:

> "They refused to listen and failed to remember the miracles You performed among them" (Nehemiah 9:17).

They didn't listen to God, and they failed to remember the miracles He performed among them. Don't be like that! Listen to God, and then remember what God has told you.

I'm not saying it's easy to choose who to marry or to stay married after you've made that choice, and I'm not saying that people won't surprise you down the road with actions and decisions that catch us totally off guard. In fact, I'm saying just the opposite. I'm saying that none of us really know what we're getting into when we commit to living with another person for the rest of our lives. None of us really know what's in the hearts of other people living on the planet, let alone what's in our own hearts. But God knows.

God knows what's in our hearts, and He knows how to guide and direct us if we're willing to listen. God also knows how to redeem ANY situation and ANY decision we ever make, even the bad ones. In fact, that's why He sent Jesus to die: to redeem us from the poor choices we make, the sins we've committed along the way, so that we can live a new and abundant life, both here on earth and in heaven forever. No matter how you've arrived at the place you're in right now, you can trust Him to redeem and restore it and to help make it right.

But if you're not married yet, do yourself and everyone else around you a huge favor: Choose well! Listen to God, then remember the miracles He's done among you.

TIP 13: WATCH YOUR TIMING, TONE, AND WORDS — OCTOBER 11

I was going to call this tip "How to Have a Fair Fight," which captures the essence of the message well. But the idea behind this tip isn't to help you fight better; the idea is to help you express your feelings better so you and your spouse can truly hear what each other is saying and do something about it before it becomes a fight.

I think you'll find this tip applies to any of your relationships, not just your marriage. As I mentioned briefly in the introduction, I heard from a single woman who wrote to tell me as I was writing this series to say how surprised she was that God was speaking to her through these marriage tips, even though she's not married. Here's the expanded version of what she wrote:

> "I was hesitant at first to read this devotional as I'm not married. I was just scrolling through and saw a part about Lana and yourself getting a car and about marriage being a calling. So I decided to start from the top for I believed God wanted me to learn a thing or two and also to be encouraged as I was feeling a bit down and questioning my future. I enjoyed it and it made me laugh how God worked out your differences, even your breaking up and eventually getting married. That gave me hope since I'm single and struggling relationship wise. My concern about my future especially is that I really want to change my car and I laughed with tears coming to my eyes when you said about Lana's desires for a car and how you reassured her about God working and providing for you and He will do the same for her. I like the part too about your partner understanding your purpose & dreams and how God can use you to help each other reach their potential and how God can use each other to bring about change & transformation. I have always believed that. Thanks for sharing your testimony. I must read the 7 points from earlier and see what else God wants me to know. God bless!"

So whether you apply this tip to your marriage or to any relationship, I hope you'll read today's tip closely and let God speak to your heart.

Lana and I didn't fight often, and when we did, we tried to do so in private. This may have given others the impression that we never fought, but that's not true. I will say, though, that we were able to avoid many of the all-out fights that others experience simply by following some advice that we learned during pre-marital counseling and some other wisdom that we learned for ourselves from the Bible.

This tip involves 3 aspects of how you express your feelings to each other: your timing, your tone and your words.

First, watch your timing. It's important, of course, to share your feelings and not to stuff them down inside. We all have feelings and we want others to respect our feelings. But it's also important to consider the timing of when to share those feelings. Even Jesus didn't say everything that was on His heart to His disciples, but took into account when they would best receive what He had to say. Jesus said:

> "I have much more to say to you, more than you can now bear" (John 16:12).

Jesus eventually did share everything on His heart, and He told the disciples that He would send His Holy Spirit later to remind them of everything He said. But He did so at a time when He knew they could best receive it.

Lana and I found that if we had something important to share with each other, especially if it was potentially explosive, that it was best to talk about it when we were both fresh and alert and able to talk about it rationally. We seemed to have our worst conversations when one or both of us were tired and worn out or when we had pressing deadlines that had to be met. It was better if we could realize the timing was bad and set a time to talk later when we could truly listen to each other.

Second, it's important to watch your tone. It's easy to jump to conclusions and blame your spouse for things they didn't even know were wrong. In America, we love the idea of being "innocent until proven guilty." But in marriage, we often jump to the conclusion that our spouse is guilty, and we start an argument based on that assumed guilt rather than simply explaining what we're feeling. The Bible talks about the importance of tone when it says:

> "A gentle answer turns away wrath, but a harsh word stirs up anger" (Proverbs 15:1).

When I came to Lana with gentleness, simply sharing something that I was feeling, I was usually met with a gentle response in return. But when I came to her with a harsh or accusatory tone, it stirred up a harsh or angry response. This is a simple law of nature and it's a simple law of communication: "For every action there is an equal and opposite reaction."

Instead of looking straight at your spouse and assuming they are the problem, it's better to turn shoulder to shoulder and address the problem together. It might even help to remind yourself and your spouse, "I know you're not my enemy. I'm fighting for you, not against you." By simply reminding yourselves of this truth, you can often diffuse the bomb that might otherwise explode.

I remember being called to a friend's house late one night. She and her husband were in the middle of an argument—and it was bad. In fact, when I walked in, I wondered if she should have called the police instead of me.

But as I sat down with both of them and listened to what they were arguing about, it turned out that the husband was trying to tell his wife that he wished he could spend more time with her, because she was often out helping other people in need. They were talking past each other, though, because they were talking about 2 different things. The truth was that they both wanted to do something good; they just needed to work on how to achieve those good things together.

Here the wife thought her husband hated her for wanting to help others, when the truth was that he loved her so much he wanted to spend more time with her! And he loved that she wanted to help other people, but he just wished she would spend more of that energy on him, rather than depleting it all before she got home. By talking through both of their desires, without accusation or harsh words, they were able to find a way to move forward and help meet each of their desires more fully.

This story leads to the third aspect of how to have a fair fight, which is to watch the words you choose. Here's a simple phrase you can memorize and, if you start using it today, you'll find your conversations will go much smoother immediately. The phrase is:

> "I feel … when … because … "

This focuses the issue on you and your thoughts and feelings rather than on the other person.

In the story I shared above about the couple fighting, the husband started with an accusatory tone by saying "You're always out helping other people!" To which his wife immediately reacted by saying, "What's wrong with helping other people?!?" Then she started listing all the good and godly reasons to help others. She was also stung by the word "always" and said, "I'm not *always* out helping other people!!!" because she began to recall how many times she stayed home to help him or their family. (It's better just to drop the words "you always" or "you never" from arguments, because the other person can usually think of at least a few times when they did or did not do whatever they're being accused of doing).

But because of the husband's wording (and probably his timing and tone, based on the lateness and intensity of the conversation), he had inadvertently derailed the conversation from the beginning, and they began squabbling over side issues. Rather than starting the sentence with the accusatory words "You always…," consider if he had started by saying, "I feel…," and then filled in the blanks that followed:

> *"I feel hurt when you go out to help others because I'd like to spend more time with you myself."*

That's really what the husband was trying to say, but it came out as anger and jealousy rather than love and affection. By blaming her for wanting to help others, he put her on the defensive from the start, rather than simply expressing what he really wanted, which was to spend more time with her.

Using the words "I feel … when … because…" changes the tenor of your conversations immediately and helps you get closer to meeting your own needs sooner than if you get sidetracked on secondary conversations. You may still need to have those secondary conversations, but you'll realize that they are just that: secondary. The main thing is to be able to express what you're feeling, without blame or accusation, by describing how you feel when the other person does or does not do certain things.

Your choice of words can make all the difference, not only for yourself, but also for the other person. The Bible says:

> *"A word fitly spoken is like apples of gold in settings of silver"* (Proverbs 25:11, NKJV).

Which means that words that are well timed and placed are beautiful to behold.

As an exercise to help you think through your words the next time you need to express something you're feeling, imagine a conversation that you may be currently having with your spouse (or co-worker or friend), whether it's a conversation you've been having out loud or if it's still just in your head, and try to rephrase what you're feeling using the words "I feel... when... because."

Think hard about what you're really feeling and why. Rather than accusing the other person in your head, imagine that you're truly just trying to express your feelings and what triggers those feelings.

> I feel lonely
> I feel frustrated
> I feel hurt
> I feel unappreciated
> when you come home late
> when you move my piles
> when you forget to do what I ask
> when you correct me
> because I want to go to bed with you
> because I don't know where things are when I need them
> because I want to know that you care about me
> because I'm trying hard to do the right thing

You can see how each of these statements could lead to further discussion and exploration of why the person feels what they feel and finding a solution that is beneficial for both people.

You might be thinking, "That sounds like a lot of work," and you'd be right! It is! But the payoff is worth it.

In woodworking there's a saying, "Measure twice; cut once." When you carefully take the time to measure a piece of wood twice and then cut it only once, you save yourself a whole lot of time patching things up later. The same could be said of your words: "Think twice; speak once." As the Bible says:

> "Everyone should be quick to listen, slow to speak and slow to become angry" (James 1:19b).

Although it takes extra time and effort to think through your timing, your tone and your words, you'll save yourself a whole lot of time and effort in patching things up later!

TIP 14: DO SOMETHING TO DELIGHT YOUR SPOUSE ON A REGULAR BASIS OCTOBER 12

Before I married Lana, I promised to give her a back rub every night, which was something that she absolutely loved. It worked out well for both of us, because she loved being touched, and I loved touching her! For 23 years I kept that commitment and it was one of the best things I ever promised to do, both for her and for myself.

Those back rubs also led to other kinds of intimacy, setting the tone for our bedtime conversations and often culminating in physical passion. By blessing Lana in this one way, I received all kinds of blessings back.

I also committed to making breakfast for her every morning, something which she loved at the time we got married, too. But as time and the seasons of life changed, she began to prefer other things instead, like sleeping in a little longer while I made breakfast for the kids after she had spent the night nursing a baby! I say this to say that some of our commitments may change over time, but the point is to intentionally commit to doing *something* to delight your spouse on a regular basis. It smooths out the ebbs and flows of life and ensures there's joy in the midst of anything else that might be going on.

For her part, Lana had made a commitment before we got married, too, but one that she didn't tell me about until many years into our marriage. She just did it. She committed to herself that she would go to bed every night at the same time that I went to bed. She had watched other couples live their lives in separate bedrooms for years and she saw the devastating effects that this had on their relationships. So she told herself she was going to do whatever she could to try to ensure that didn't happen in her marriage.

Of course, this ensured she got her nightly back rub! But even more, it meant that we had time to talk and pray together every night; it meant that we were available for physical intimacy on a regular basis; and it increased the likelihood of having a big family like she always wanted!

You and your spouse may have a different set of things you could do to delight one other. If you're not sure what would delight them, just ask them! Then make a commitment to doing something to delight them in the way they'd love to be delighted on a regular basis. As the Bible says:

> "...love one another deeply, from the heart" (1 Peter 1:22b).

TIP 15: MAKE PHYSICAL INTIMACY WITH YOUR SPOUSE THE BEST THAT IT CAN BE
OCTOBER 13

Tip 15 is perhaps the most significant tip I ever received before getting married. It's also one of the most delicate to talk about because it has to do with physical intimacy.

For the sake of modesty, and for the sake of getting this message through any spam filters when I first sent this message out by email, I've simply used the phrase "physical intimacy" to describe the physical union between a husband and wife, and I've used the term "self pleasure" to describe the act of touching yourself in a way that brings you physical pleasure when you are alone. (Now you can see why this tip is so delicate! But I assure you, what you're going to read today could significantly alter the way you interact with your spouse from this day forward!)

With that preface in mind, here is Tip 15.

After I was engaged to Lana, I set up an appointment to meet with a man who had counseled many, many people through marital issues regarding their physical intimacy. I met with him specifically because I wanted to ensure that I did everything possible to safeguard our physical relationship and to make it the best that it could possibly be.

One of the most important tips he shared with me was to consider making a commitment to myself and to Lana that I would not engage in self pleasure, but that I would only experience physical pleasure when I was with her. Many men, he said, go into marriage thinking that they'll be able to be intimate with their wife any time they want. But the reality is that it just doesn't work that way! And because of that, many spouses decide to simply please themselves whenever they want.

This man told me that he had met with numerous groups of women to discuss issues like this and asked them what they would think if they knew their husbands were pleasing themselves when they weren't together. Nearly every woman in every group said they would feel hurt by this, or they would wonder what they were doing wrong that their husbands would do this, or they would wonder what else their husbands might be doing physically when they weren't together.

Then this man went on to tell me about the blessings couples experienced who had committed to enjoying physical pleasure only when they were together. He said it wasn't necessary that they engage in full physical intimacy every time, but that they were at least to be with each other and enjoy the closeness of their bodies. Couples who made this commitment built up trust, lowered barriers to intimacy and brought about a lifetime of fulfillment for each other, both inside and outside of the bedroom.

Since I had never even considered how this might play out in marriage, I didn't know what to think. But this man had thrown down a gauntlet, a challenge, and I had to decide whether or not I was going to pick it up. After talking some more about this with another friend and then with Lana, I decided it was worth a try. So before Lana and I were married, I committed to her that I would not engage in self pleasure, but reserve all physical pleasure only for when I was with her. If for any reason I fell down in this commitment, I committed to confessing it to her before the day was out.

I can attest to the fact that this one tip alone helped me perhaps more than any of the others. Why? Because each of these tips are interrelated and physical intimacy is at the core of what makes marriage unique among all other relationships. So when there's a breakdown in one area of your relationship, it often affects your physical intimacy as well. In order to ensure I would be able to enjoy the physical pleasures of marriage, I knew I would have to nurture the other areas of my marriage, too. As the saying goes:

> "The grass ain't always greener on the other side; it's greener where you water it."

Here's how some of the tips I've mentioned already helped to water our physical intimacy. For instance, by putting our TV in the closet for our first year, it freed up all kinds of time to have meaningful conversations and enjoy soothing back rubs, which often led to physical intimacy. By going to bed every night at the same time as each other and by praying together before we fell asleep, we were able to draw closer spiritually and that drew us closer physically. By confessing our sins quickly to each other, we built up trust between us and kept guilt and shame at bay. By inviting Jesus to use our hands and eyes and words as if they were His very own, we were able to keep our touches and kisses as tender and life-giving as possible.

This isn't to say that it was easy for me to keep this challenge. Even though my physical intimacy with Lana was incredible from day 1, there were still a few times in our first year of marriage when I fell back into old habits of pleasing myself when I was alone or away from home. It seemed like a quick and easy way to release some of the tension in other areas of my life.

Yet I still wanted to give this idea an honest try, and because of my promise to Lana, I followed through with the rest of it and confessed it to Lana each time before the day was out. The first time I had to confess it to her it was more difficult and embarrassing than I imagined. The second time was even more difficult. So after just a few confessions like this, I was able to break the habit and keep my commitment for the rest of our 23 years of marriage.

I'm not telling you this out of some kind of prudish purity, but simply to let you know that it's possible! And believe me, my passions and temptations are just as strong as any other man's! But until my conversation with this marriage counselor, I had never even thought about the idea.

I also tell you this because I can't describe the multitude of ways this one commitment helped our marriage. Here are just a few:

1) This gave us both confidence that I had control over my body, rather than my body having control over me. This helped Lana to trust me to not cross the line of having physical pleasure with someone else, because I wouldn't even cross it with myself.
2) This kept me from turning on the TV in a hotel room when I was away from home, or from buying a magazine that I shouldn't have bought, or from downloading a video that I shouldn't have downloaded. Even though these things certainly crossed my mind and were ever-present opportunities, there was never any point to engaging in these activities since I knew that they would never culminate in physical pleasure.
3) This ensured that the physical side of our marital relationship was fully alive and vibrant throughout our entire marriage. Roger Staubach, the famous quarterback, was once asked how he felt when one of his teammates always seemed to have a different woman on his arm every night. Roger said, "I'm sure I'm just as sexually active as he is. The difference is that all of mine is with one woman." Touchdown, Roger! The joy of my physical intimacy with Lana, and the trust that we built into our relationship because of this one commitment, was worth anything it might have cost me in terms of giving up fleeting pleasures on my own.

While I can't say if this commitment is something that you should make, or that it will have the same impact on your marriage, I do want to encourage you to do whatever you can to nurture the physical intimacy of your marriage.

By the way, one of the best books we read before getting married that helped us in our sexual relationship throughout our entire marriage was called *Intended for Pleasure* by Ed and Gaye Wheat. The book contains many helpful tips for making your sex life the best that it can be. I highly recommend it for any married couple.

As I mentioned in my own book, *What God Says About Sex*, physical intimacy with Lana was the most consistently exhilarating, off-the-charts experience of my life! So whether or not you choose to follow the path I chose, I pray you'll make a commitment to do *something* to protect your physical intimacy and to keep it alive and active as long as you both shall live. As the Bible says:

> "Marriage should be honored by all, and the marriage bed kept pure..." (Hebrews 13:4a)

Honor your marriage and keep your marriage bed pure. Don't look for other ways to find physical pleasure. Look to your spouse and do whatever you can to nurture your relationship with them.

Tomorrow the conclusion of this series with 3 words that tie all the other tips together.

CONCLUSION OF "15 TIPS FOR A STRONGER MARRIAGE"   OCTOBER 14

Believe it or not, all the tips I've shared with you up till now were just the preface, the introduction, to what I'd like to share with you today about how to have a stronger marriage.

When my friends asked me to talk about marriage at their wedding, and what made my marriage to Lana so special, I began to think through all the tips I've shared with you up to this point.

But as important as each of those tips are, I felt like the most important thought I could share with them was the one I'm going to share with you today. This idea focuses on just 3 words that really serve as the glue to hold all the other tips together.

Although there are a number of great phrases of 3 words I could have chosen (like "I love you," "I was wrong," "I am sorry," "I forgive you," or as one reader suggested, "You're right, dear!"), I chose these 3 because they were 3 words our pastor shared with us at our wedding, and because they conclude a wonderful chapter in the Bible about how we relate to one another. I can honestly say these 3 words carried us through our 23 years together perhaps more than any other advice I've shared with you in this book.

You can read below the words I shared with my friends on their wedding day. You can also watch their wedding online on *The Ranch* website at the link below. It was a beautiful outdoor ceremony, complete with birds chirping and bales of hay on which the guests sat. The ceremony's only about 30 minutes long, so feel free to take a look!

Here's the link to watch:

Watch Korey and Makayla's Wedding

And here's the text of what I shared with this beautiful couple that day...

When I met with Korey and Makayla a few months ago to talk about their wedding, Makayla asked me to share some thoughts about what marriage means and what made my marriage to Lana work so well. She said she looked up to us and just wanted to hear from my heart.

So I'm going to tell you 3 short highlights, 3 little snippets from my life and my marriage that I hope will be helpful to you. Really it's summed up in 3 words; 3 words that I hope you'll remember today; 3 words that I hope you'll be able to put into practice in your own marriage.

You might think these 3 words are "I love you," but they're not. They're these:

> "And be thankful."

There's a passage in the Bible that says many things about loving and caring for one another. The passage talks about all the things that we associate with love, such as:

> "...clothe yourselves with compassion, kindness, humility, gentleness and patience. Bear with each other and forgive whatever grievances you may have against one another. Forgive as the Lord forgave you. And over all these virtues put on love, which binds them all together in perfect unity" (Colossians 3:12b-14).

These are all wonderful things. But then Paul goes on and adds these 3 words to all the rest, words that seem to go beyond even just loving each other. Paul says,

"And be thankful" (Colossians 3:15b).

Then he says it again in a lengthier way at the end of the whole passage:

"And whatever you do, whether in word or deed, do it all in the name of the Lord Jesus, giving thanks to God the Father" (Colossians 3:17).

I just want to tell you 3 little snapshots from my life about giving thanks to God for my wife.

On our wedding day, Lana and I wrote our own vows, like you've written your own vows. In my vows, I said to Lana: "Lana, you are a gift from God to me, and I plan to treat you as a gift." From that day on that's what I tried to do. That was the most amazing day to me, to be able to receive this gift from God and to be able to unwrap it over and over and over again, discovering layers of her that I had no idea about.

On our wedding day I said, "Thank You, Lord, and thank You, Lana, for saying 'Yes!' to marrying me."

Then I just kept saying that throughout my whole 23 years. When I would see how she raised our children, I would say, "Thank You, Lord, for this incredible mother of our children and thank you, Lana, for being a godly mother and wife." When I would see how she cooked meals for us, took care of us, edited my manuscripts for my ministry, I'd say, "Thank You, Lord, and thank you, Lana." Lana was a gift from God, and I was so thankful for her.

Our wedding day was 1 snapshot, but there was another snapshot I'd like to share with you, and you, Makayla, were actually very nearby. We were in Israel and Makayla and Jeanette had come with a few of us in our family to Israel and we were in the hotel at the Dead Sea. We had just had a beautiful night of worship, worshipping God in our room with our whole team. After everyone had left, Lana and I went out on the balcony on a beautiful night, and we had a wonderful, romantic, intimate night together. In the midst of that precious night, I just looked up to heaven and I said, "Thank You, Lord, and thank you, Lana." That was 1 of the most precious memories of my life. I can't count how many wonderful nights I've had like that with her, so often saying in the midst of them, "Thank You, Lord, and thank you, Lana."

Then there's a third moment I'd like to share with you, a little snapshot, and this was just a couple years ago. We were in the car at Walmart, sitting in the parking lot after shopping one night. We were having a really hard conversation; one of those where you say, "Wow, this is hard." We didn't have many of those, but that night we were both feeling very passionate about what we felt and believed, and we just weren't on the same page.

The conversation had to do with what kind of treatment plan we were going to do for her cancer. I had one idea. She had another. And it just got more heated and more passionate. The doctors had told us no matter which path we chose, it wouldn't make any difference in the outcome, but we still wanted to try everything we could.

When were at the peak of that conversation, I had to stop and just say to myself, "Lana is a gift from God to me; she is not the problem here." Then rather than face each other and think that we were each other's problem, we had to put the problem to one side and turn shoulder to shoulder to work on it together.

I just had to back up and say, "Lana, you are a gift from God to me, and the reason I feel so passionate about this is because I just don't want to lose you. I want to do anything

I can to keep you. And I want to remind you, in this conversation, in this heated moment, the only reason I feel so passionate about this is because I love you, so, so much."

That eased the tension. It changed the dynamics of the conversation.

In the end, it turned out the doctors were right, and it wouldn't have mattered which plan we chose. Lana died just a few months later.

But I am so thankful that in those heated moments in the parking lot, I decided not to keep arguing over it, but rather to give thanks in all things and say, "Thank You, Lord, and thank you, Lana." She truly was a gift from God to me and I always wanted to treat her as a gift.

With all the other wonderful things you can do for your marriage, remember these 3 words because they can carry you through your whole life:

"And be thankful."

You understand what it means to forgive. You understand what it means to make a life-long commitment. You understand love and graciousness and kindness and humility and being second and all those things.

I think you understand this, too, but I just want to highlight and emphasize—even beyond just loving each other, which is incredible—to be thankful.

"And be thankful."
"And be thankful."
"And be thankful."

And with those words, I married my friends to each other, and I prayed that they, like you, would have a long, wonderful and thankful life together!

Will you pray with me?

Father, thank You for Your wisdom, which You've given to us through Your Word to help us to love one another in the best way possible. Help us to apply these words to all of our relationships so that we can love one other more fully and be more thankful in all that we do. Fill us with Your Spirit to do everything You've put on our hearts to do today and every day, from this day forward. We pray all this in the strong name of Jesus, who has the power to make all our relationships stronger, too. Amen.

PSALMS
Lessons In Prayer

Psalms: Lessons in Prayer

31 inspiring devotionals based on the oldest prayer book in the world

ABOUT THIS BOOK

The book you're about to read is based on thirty-one of the 150 psalms in the book of Psalms from the Bible. I've chosen these particular psalms because they each highlight different aspects of prayer, such as when to pray, how to pray, what to pray for, and how to hear God's voice during your intimate conversations with Him.

While I've quoted portions of these thirty-one psalms in this book, I'd love for you to read them in their entirety, whether in your own Bible or online at websites like biblegateway.com, blueletterbible.com, or biblestudytools.com. To further aid you in gaining the most from these psalms, I asked my wife, Lana, at the outset of this project, if she would be willing to read and record each of the thirty-one psalms so you could listen to them as well as read them—which she was very glad to do.

To make these readings even more special, my family and I then set each of Lana's readings to music, recording some classical piano pieces from the 17- and 1800s to accompany each psalm. You can listen to the readings here on The Ranch at Lana's Psalms or wherever music is streamed or sold.

INTRODUCTION: CONVERSATIONS WITH GOD

Scripture Reading: Romans 12:1-2

I love talking to God. It's often the highlight of my day.

For some people, like my friend Dan Mountney, waking up and talking with God brings focus to everything else that happens in his day. "It centers me," Dan says.

For others, like Adrian Rogers, talking to God brings clarity to what God wants him to do. When asked by a reporter if God had spoken to Adrian like the reporter had just spoken to him, Adrian replied, "Oh, no! It was much louder than that."

For still others, like Billy Graham, talking with God is like talking with a best friend. "How do you know God exists?" Billy was once asked. "Because I spoke with Him this morning," he replied.

What about you? How would you rate your conversations with God? As much as I love talking with God, I still feel in many ways that I am just scratching the surface of what my conversations with Him *could* be like.

Five years ago, my late wife Lana and I were talking about prayer. Lana said, "I'd like to learn more about prayer."

I was stunned. Lana's prayer life was already deep and rich and full. She prayed continually, in private and out loud, for me, for our family, for our friends, for missionaries, for entire countries. She prayed for breakthroughs and healings and restorations. She prayed for forgiveness and for a greater love for others. Yet with all she had learned about prayer over the years, she still wanted *more*.

For me, that was Lesson #1 in going deeper in my own prayer life, to simply know that there's always *more*.

At that same time, I was wanting to take a closer look at the book of Psalms. What was it about this book that made it one of the most beloved books in the Bible? What secrets did it hold that made publishers often publish it by itself, or pair it as the one Old Testament book to go along with the entire New Testament? Why do people seem to quote so often from the Psalms, as Jesus did, more than any other book in the Bible?

By combining my curiosity about the Psalms with Lana's desire to learn more about prayer, we took a deeper dive together into this book to see what we could discover in its depths. We learned that the book of Psalms is really a book of prayers; in fact, it's the oldest prayer book in the world. The word "psalm" means "song" in Hebrew, the language in which the psalms were originally written. And since they are all songs to God, they are often considered prayers as much as anything else—conversations with Him that came from deep in the author's heart.

We learned that over half of those "conversations with God" were voiced by King David, as specifically noted in the text of those psalms, and even more of those conversations clearly alluded to David's authorship based on the situations described within them. I was personally looking forward to learning all I could from this man whom God described as "a man after My own heart" (see Acts 13:22).

What I wasn't expecting was that the next year of our lives would take such an unexpected twist: soon after we began this deeper dive into the book of Psalms and the topic of prayer, Lana was diagnosed with cancer. Ten days later, we were told it was terminal. And nine months after that, Lana was gone, having passed from this life to the next.

It crushed me, and it crushed a part of my heart at the same time. If I had known this would happen when we first decided we wanted to have a deeper, richer and fuller prayer life, I'm not sure we would have done it.

But I was reminded of this thought again when a friend was telling me how he had recently made a decision to go deeper in his relationship with God. He began by waking up ten minutes earlier each day to read his Bible and pray. The following week, he woke up ten minutes earlier still. And the week after that, he woke up ten minutes earlier still, continuing this pattern until he was now waking up an hour or more earlier than usual so he could have as much time with God as possible.

He then told me about several things that had gotten increasingly harder in his life during this time: his work situation, family's heath and his finances.

It reminded me of the difficulties Lana and I had faced soon after we made our decision to go deeper with God. I was tempted to say something to this effect when my friend said something that stopped me:

> "I am so glad I decided to do this with God," he said, "because if I hadn't, I don't know how I could have gotten through this time in any other way."

My friend was right. He was absolutely right. If Lana and I had not committed ourselves to a deeper walk with God, I don't know how we could have gotten through what we had to go through, either. And how much better is it to be on the path of going deeper with God *before* life throws its worst at you, rather than waiting till it hits you full on? The time I've spent grounding myself in God, and in my relationship with Him, is the one thing above all else that has helped me through some of the most difficult challenges in my life.

So here it is, five years since Lana and I decided to take that deeper dive into the topic of prayer as seen through the lens of the Psalms, and now I'd like to share with you some of the lessons that I've learned. Along the way, I'll also tell you about some of the miraculous answers to prayer I've seen and some of the amazing conversations with God I've had, many of which are no less miraculous or amazing to me than those I read about in the book of Psalms. The same God who walked with David through his highs and lows is the same God who has walked with me through mine—and who will walk with you through yours.

God doesn't just have things He wants you to do. He wants true intimacy with you. He wants to really talk to you, as a friend talks to a friend.

Jesus captured the heart of His Father when He spoke about this idea to His disciples:

"I no longer call you servants, because a servant does not know his master's business. Instead, I have called you friends, for everything that I learned from My Father I have made known to you" (John 15:15).

God truly wants to have a friendship with you. And you would be crazy to turn down a friendship like His. As Robin Williams sang in Disney's classic animation, *Aladdin*:

"You ain't never had a friend like me."

I pray God will speak to you in a special way during your time with Him, both while we're doing this study together, and on your own for the rest of your days. I can think of nothing more incredible than to be able to talk personally with the God who created you, who knows you better than you know yourself, and who loves you like no one else on earth ever could.

I'm looking forward to our time together. I hope you are, too.

Will you pray with me?

Dear Jesus, I am so thankful that we can come to you each and every day, all day, at any time during the day, and have a conversation with You. You are so loving and gracious, so kind and helpful, so wise and so knowledgeable about all things, including me. Help me as I go through this day. Walk me through every situation I face. Help me to learn all that You want me to learn as we walk through this study of the book of Psalms. In Your name we pray, Amen.

LESSON 1: MORNING PRAYERS   OCTOBER 15

Scripture Reading: Psalm 5

As I was reading through the book of Psalms, I was looking for secrets to having a more effective prayer life. I didn't get very far into the book when I found one:

"In the morning, O Lord, You hear my voice; in the morning I lay my requests before You and wait in expectation" (Psalm 5:3).

There's something about morning prayers that make them hopeful. After a night of rest, it's time to start a new day, a fresh day.

I've often prayed in the morning, waking up, taking out my Bible and a journal and a pen, then sitting quietly before God. But what I noticed differently in this Psalm is that the author, David, came to God with a spirit of expectancy.

David didn't just come to God with a list of requests. He came with hope in his heart, expectant that God would answer. David knew the goodness of God. He knew that God was with Him. He knew that God was *for* him, just like He is *for* each one of us.

Our prayers have a purpose—not just because they quiet our hearts or help to organize our thoughts. Our prayers have a purpose because they involve another Person. They involve Someone who knows what you're facing and who has the wisdom and ability to do something about them.

God really does know what you're going through. He really does care. And that's why you can come to God with the pieces of your life and ask God to help you put them together.

I love the way Eugene Peterson paraphrases David's words in *The Message* translation of the Bible:

> *"Every morning you'll hear me at it again. Every morning I lay out the pieces of my life on Your altar and watch for fire to descend" (Psalm 5:3, MSG).*

Those words are so hopeful—so helpful. When I read these words, I began doing this in my mind's eye, with my own prayers. I began laying out the pieces of my life on God's altar, with expectancy in my heart, then watching throughout the day for God's fire to descend—just like it had descended in times past when people offered their sacrifices to God's on an altar.

And I began seeing answers, that very day!

After having just written in my journal about what I should do for the day, I got a text from a neighbor at 7:05 a.m. offering to bring over lunch. Then I received word that an anniversary party was cancelled, which I had been wondering if I should attend or not. Then, after taking a morning walk with my wife and praying with her about a situation our daughter was facing, our daughter texted to say how God had just worked it all out! It was as if God were underscoring the words of David for me about laying out the pieces of his life on God's altar, then waiting in expectation.

It's good to pray at night or at the end of a project, as that allows us time to reflect on what God has done and to give thanks for what's been accomplished. But in order to be most effective, it's also important to offer our prayers up to God on the front end, inviting Him to speak and to work and to be involved in whatever we're facing.

Martin Luther famously said:

> *"I have so much to do that I shall spend the first three hours in prayer."*

God *wants* to be a co-laborer with you. He has things He wants to accomplish in and through you. And when you talk about those things with Him up front, He can help you sort them out and let you know what He can do and what you can do. In that way, you can bring it to pass *together*.

Not every answer comes right away, but that doesn't mean we still can't have expectancy in our heart. The past few weeks, my kids and I have been praying every morning for some royalty checks to be deposited in my account for some music I've written and produced. While I normally receive these checks monthly, and they help to pay for the ministry that we do, the checks were delayed because of a new arrangement between the music companies involved. Every morning we've been praying, and every day we've been hopeful for an answer. At the same time, I've been working with the music companies, sending emails and making phone calls and having online chats, trying to help move the process along. I'm doing everything I can, but I'm trusting God with those things I can't do. So every day we pray for the people involved in this process—the computer programmers, the accountants, and the decision-makers—asking God to give them wisdom as they work out the details.

Then this past Friday night, for the first time in months, I started seeing those deposits coming into my account. One, two, three, four of them! As the night went on, there were more: five, six, seven, eight! The deposits kept coming as the system started working again! I praised God, together with my kids, knowing that relief was on the way!

Come to God in the morning. Sit down with Him and go over your day. Ask Him what He wants you to do. Ask Him to do what you know you can't do. Then be on the lookout for His answers. They may not come that day, but they might! And they may not come the next day, or the next month, as I had hoped while waiting for my missing royalties.

But even if you don't see an answer right away, don't think that God isn't working on your behalf. Remember what God told Daniel, through an angel that God sent to him twenty-one days after Daniel had begun praying:

> "Do not be afraid, Daniel. Since the first day that you set your mind to gain understanding and to humble yourself before your God, your words were heard, and I have come in response to them" (Daniel 10:12).

God hears your prayers the moment you utter them. So why not utter them the first thing in the morning? Invite God into your day. Let Him order your steps. Lay out the pieces of your life on God's altar, then wait in expectation. (Please note the P.S. for today after the prayer.)

Will you pray with me?

Jesus, thank You for loving me the way You do. Thank You for caring for me. Thank You for creating me with a purpose in mind, with good works that You want me to do. Help me, Lord, to accomplish those works today. Help me to know that You'll be with me, working right alongside me, doing what only You can do, while I do whatever I can do. Help me to see the answers to my prayers, whether today, tomorrow, or down the road. Help me to trust You and look to You with a spirit of expectation, knowing that You are good, that You are kind, that You are loving, and that You are ultimately for me. In Jesus' name, Amen.

LESSON 2: MAGNIFYING PRAYERS   OCTOBER 16

Scripture Reading: Psalm 8

I set up a telescope one night to look at the moon and the stars. My kids couldn't believe what they were seeing: how detailed and three-dimensional the moon looked, hanging there in space; how many stars there were—hundreds, thousands, millions—all glittering in the night sky.

They could hardly believe that each star was like our own sun—some bigger, some smaller, spread all throughout space! Each flicker of light that looked like it was no bigger than the head of a pin was, in fact, full of power, warmth, and wonder like our own sun—and there were a shining multitude of them everywhere we looked!

All this revelation, all this insight, all this awe came from simply holding a type of magnifying glass up to what we normally see on a regular basis nearly every day.

As I was reading through the psalms and looking for secrets of effective prayer, these words from Psalm 8 stood out to me:

> "O Lord, our Lord, how majestic is Your name in all the earth! ... When I consider Your heavens, the work of Your fingers, the moon and the stars, which You have set in place, what is man that You are mindful of him, the son of man that You care for him?" (Psalm 8:1a, 3-4).

Something happens inside us when we hold up a magnifying glass to the world around us. It opens us up to seeing the incredible work that God has created in a new way. And that fresh perspective can help us to see our own problems in a new way as well.

King David, who wrote these words from Psalm 8 nearly 3,000 years ago, was struck with the same awe and wonder as my kids on the night I set up a telescope for them. As he considered the heavens, the work of God's fingers, the moon and the stars which God had set in place, he burst out in praise! "O Lord, our Lord, how majestic is Your name in all the earth!"

And that made David look at his own life in a new way, saying, "What is man that You are mindful of him, the son of man that You care for him?"

Yet David realized that God was mindful of him. God did care for him. In fact, the same God who took such care to create the world that David saw created him with the same care—and not only created him with care, but considered him worthy to take care of the incredible creation around him!

God, it seems, has a magnifying glass of His own. When He looks at us, He looks with such detail that He can count the number of hairs on our head (see Luke 12:7). He cares for us so much that He has created us in His own image and given us the task of caring for the rest of His whole creation.

If you wonder if God cares for you, just take out a magnifying glass today, literally, and look at one or two things in God's creation. You'll get a new perspective on your own life almost immediately.

This is what happened to William Wilberforce, a member of parliament who played a major role in ending the slave trade in England in the early 1800s. He came to faith one day, not by looking up into the sky, but by looking down into the majesty of his garden. What he saw there so fascinated him that he plopped down on the wet grass to take a closer look. What he saw was the marvel of a spider's web.

The movie *Amazing Grace* captures this faith-defining moment in the life of Wilberforce like this, as his butler finds him in the garden and wonders aloud what he's found:

> "It's God," said Wilberforce. "I have 10,000 engagements of state today, but I would prefer to spend the day out here getting a wet arse, studying dandelions and marveling at… bloody spider's webs."
> "You found God, sir?" the butler asks.
> "I think He found me," Wilberforce responds. "You have any idea how inconvenient that is? How idiotic it will sound? I have a political career glittering ahead of me, and in my heart, I want spider's webs."

Wilberforce found God by looking closely at a spider's web, or, as he puts it in the movie, "I think He found me."

I learned something new about spider's webs just last week. My son told me that he learned in his biology book that a spider's web is sticky only on certain strands of the silk it weaves, but that other strands aren't sticky at all, so that it doesn't get stuck when scurrying around on its own web. God somehow endowed the spider with the ability to spin different types of silk depending on the need.

I must have missed that fact when I took biology, but it was a little tidbit which enlarged my awe and wonder of God once again. How God instilled in a spider the wisdom and ability to know how to spin a web at all, or which silk to spin for which purpose, made me consider not only how clever the spider is, but how clever the God who created the spider is! And if God did this for a spider, imagine what He's done for me, whom God says He has created as the pinnacle of all He has created on the earth, made in the very image of God Himself!

That thought makes me want to burst out in praise to God as well: "O Lord, our Lord, how majestic is Your name in all the earth!" And it made me look at the situations I'm facing today in a new way as well.

What loomed large and overwhelming to me as I began my prayers suddenly seemed puny in comparison to what God could do in each of those situations. Heal a cut? Mend a relationship? Breathe new life into something in my life that has died?

What seemed improbable just moments before thinking about God's majesty suddenly seemed no problem for the God who placed every star in the sky and knows each one by name (see Psalm 147:4)!

The God who holds creation together can certainly hold my life together as well. By magnifying God and His creation, I can see how small—how manageable—my own problems are in comparison. Whatever I face, God knows how to handle it.

If you're facing problems today that are overwhelming you, take out a magnifying glass. Literally. Take a look at one or two things around you today—your fingerprint, a flower, or even a spider's web. Or take out a telescope and look at the nighttime sky. Or just take a look around you at any ordinary object, but look closely to see the colors, the shapes, the details that you may have overlooked before.

Then marvel and wonder at the God who created all that makes up everything you see. Marvel and wonder that the same God who created each of these things created you with the same care—and has believed in you and trusted in you enough to put you in charge of the care of His incredible creation.

Will you pray with me?

Jesus, thank You for your magnificent creation. Thank You for including me in your plans when You created the world. Thank You for Your promise to finish the work You've begun in me. Help me to sort out the things I'm facing. Bring order to my world. Bring peace to my heart. Bring wisdom to my mind. I ask all this in Your name, Amen.

LESSON 3: RAW PRAYERS — OCTOBER 17

Scripture Reading: Psalm 13

One of the beauties of reading through the psalms is that it touches on so many emotions that you don't have to read very far into it to find something that will match what you're going through. And when you find that something, you can pour out your heart to God in prayer, often using the same words that you're reading on the pages in front of you.

Within just a few psalms, we've already seen David's emotions range from eager expectation to awe-filled wonder to today's psalm, in which he pours out some raw prayers full of pain and sorrow. Psalm 13 starts with these words:

> "How long, O Lord? Will you forget me forever? How long will you hide Your face from me? How long must I wrestle with my thoughts and every day have sorrow in my heart?" (Psalm 13, 5-6a).

This is a man in pain, a man in anguish, a man who's wondering if God is even listening anymore. In The Message translation of the Bible, David's words are paraphrased like this:

> "Long enough, God—You've ignored me long enough. I've looked at the back of Your head long enough" (Psalm 13:5-6a, MSG).

Those are some raw words. They're guttural. And they express the real sorrow in his heart.

Maybe you've felt this way before. Maybe you feel this way right now. If so, let me encourage you to say some raw words of your own to God. The pain you're feeling is real, and it's really okay to express to God how you're really feeling. God can take it, and there are times when you just need to say it like David did.

I was speaking to a group of people a few weeks ago who were going through various tragedies in their lives. They had lost husbands or wives, sons or daughters, friends or family members. They were dealing with divorce. They were trying to find their way out of addictions. They were experiencing pain at its worst, and I was asked to speak to them on the topic Worshipping God in the Hard Times.

I don't usually say certain words. They're not part of my normal vocabulary. But during my talk, in an unscripted moment, I covered the microphone and said out loud what I knew many in the room were feeling. I said, "In some of these dark times, you just say, 'God, this really sucks.'" Nods of agreement began throughout the room.

When the night was over, one of the leaders of the group told me that my talk had really touched the people. And the one thing they said that impacted them the most was the moment when I covered the microphone and said what I said. In that moment, they said, they knew that *I knew* exactly what they were going through, and that opened them up to hear the rest of what I had to say.

Sometimes we need to get really honest with God, too—to say exactly what's on our hearts—even if it's not "pretty," or "religious," or what we think we're "supposed" to say. Sometimes we just need to just let it all out—lay it all out—before God, who sees our pain and knows what's on our hearts already anyway.

Sometimes we read the psalms, or sing them in songs, and they begin to sound so holy, so poetic, so "nice," that we can miss just how raw they really are. Eugene Petersen, who translated the Psalms from the original Hebrew into English for The Message translation, said this in his introduction to the Psalms:

> "In English translation, the Psalms often sound smooth and polished, sonorous with Elizabethan rhythms and diction. As literature, they are beyond compare. But as prayer, as the utterances of men and women passionate for God in moments of anger and praise and lament, these translations miss something. Grammatically, they are accurate. The scholarship undergirding the translation is superb and devout. But as prayers they are not quite right. The Psalms in Hebrew are earthy and rough. They are not genteel. They are not the prayers of nice people, couched in cultured language."

I can only imagine the types of words David and the 400 men with him used while they were hiding out in the caves of the dessert while the king and his army were hunting them down to kill them. The men with David were described as "All those who were in distress or in debt or discontented..." (1 Samuel 22:2a). I can guess that at least a few of their conversations were far from genteel.

And I can believe that at least a few of David's conversations with God sounded just as earthy and rough. I can hear it in the English translation, but only if I really think about what he was really going through and how shocking it is that he really said some of the things he said to God. It's not like David suddenly switched into his "religious" voice when talking to God. He just said it like it was. He told God what He was feeling, in a way that he really felt it.

But then somewhere along the way, while pouring out his pain to God, David begins to praise Him instead. He begins to sing to God that no matter what he's going through, he still trusts in God's unfailing love. No matter what happens, he still praises God for having been so good to him. The psalm ends with these words:

> "But I trust in Your unfailing love; my heart rejoices in Your salvation. I will sing to the Lord, for He has been good to me" (Psalm 13:5-6).

How can a man go from pouring out his pain to pouring out his praise in the matter of a few sentences? We see the same thing happen in the book of Job, where Job, who has just lost nearly everything that was dear to him in a single day, tears his robes and falls to the ground. Yet he didn't just fall to the ground and lie there. The Bible says, "he fell to the ground in worship," saying:

> "Naked I came from my mother's womb, and naked I will depart. The Lord gave and the Lord has taken away; may the name of the Lord be praised" (Job 1:21).

Somehow, Job was able to pour out his pain and pour out his praise, nearly simultaneously. Somehow, like David, Job knew he could still trust in God's unfailing love—no matter what.

If you're in pain today—in anguish—or if things look so bleak you're not sure how you'll be able to stand it, let me encourage you to try doing what David did, what Job did, and what I at times have had to do: pour out your pain to God, in words that are real and raw, then pour out your praise to Him as well, trusting in God's unfailing love for yourself.

You might feel like God is being slow to show up, taking His dear sweet time to answer your prayers. You might wonder if He's even listening at all, because you feel like the only thing you can see is the back of His head. But the truth is, God is listening. He does care. And He *is* answering your prayers, even if you can't see those answers yet, or even for a long time.

Pour out your pain. Keep trusting in His unfailing love. And you might just find yourself like David, pouring out your praise as well, saying, "for He has been good to me."

Will you pray with me?

Jesus, thank You for giving us David's example of how to pray raw prayers, guttural prayers, prayers that truly express what's on our hearts. Thank You for letting us see how David and Job and others have been able to not only fall down when they're in pain, but to still worship You as they fall. Help us to talk to You like they did and help us to trust in You the way they trusted in You. Thank You for being so worthy of our trust and praise. In Jesus' name, Amen.

LESSON 4: PLEASING PRAYERS   OCTOBER 18

Scripture Reading: Psalm 19

In my previous message, I talked about the value of saying "raw prayers," prayers that pour out to God exactly what's on your heart, without regard for whether it sounds pretty, or religious, or even kind. God can take it—and He already knows what's in your heart anyway. Sometimes you just have to say it.

But in today's message, I want to talk about the value of saying "pleasing prayers," prayers that are also honest, but which are intentional about being pleasing to God. As a parent, I'm glad when my kids feel the freedom to come to me and express their raw emotions that they're feeling on their hearts, without holding back for fear of what I might think. While it might sting sometimes, and their perceptions may not always be right, it helps to know what they're honestly thinking so we can work through their thoughts together. But I'm also glad when they intentionally take time to say things which they truly believe, and which they know will please me.

Such is the case in David's prayer today, which he ends with these words:

> *"May the words of my mouth and the meditation of my heart be pleasing in Your sight, O Lord, my Rock and my Redeemer"* (Psalm 19:14).

This entire Psalm is filled with "pleasing words," words which David carefully and intentionally poured out to the God who gave him life.

He starts by talking about how glorious God is, and how His creation declares His glory to the ends of the earth:

> *"The heavens declare the glory of God; the skies proclaim the work of His hands. Day after day they pour forth speech; night after night they display knowledge. There is no*

speech or language where their voice is not heard. Their voice goes out into all the earth, their words to the ends of the world" (Psalm 19:1-4a).

I can see how those words would be pleasing to the God, the Creator, the One who created the earth and everything in it. Then he continues by speaking poetically about how magnificently the sun crosses the sky:

"In the heavens He has pitched a tent for the sun, which is like a bridegroom coming forth from his pavilion, like a champion rejoicing to run his course. It rises at one end of the heavens and makes its circuit to the other; nothing is hidden from its heat" (Psalm 19:4b-6).

Then he launches into a carefully worded *anaphora*, a grammatical technique of emphasizing an idea by repeating that same idea in different ways. The Psalms are some of the first writings in the world to use this technique which has been subsequently used by writers like Shakespeare and speechmakers like Churchill:

"The law of the Lord is perfect, reviving the soul.
The statutes of the Lord are trustworthy, making wise the simple.
The precepts of the Lord are right, giving joy to the heart.
The commands of the Lord are radiant, giving light to the eyes.
The fear of the Lord is pure, enduring forever.
The ordinances of the Lord are sure and altogether righteous."
(Psalm 19:7-9).

When I read this Psalm this week, I thought, "Imagine the care and thoughtfulness David must have put into crafting his words of praise to God in this way. He took a topic that was dear to him and dear to God's heart, and then through repeating phrases, was able to express to God what he was feeling deep inside."

I wondered what it would do for my prayer life if I could be as careful and thoughtful in my prayers to God as David was in this Psalm. It seemed like so much work, though, so I just continued writing in my journal as I normally do. But what came out of my pen next surprised me! It was a fully formed anaphora of my own!

"A desire for alcohol is not only for alcohol, but for relief from pain.
A desire for a person is not only for that person, but for relief from loneliness.
A desire for food is not only for food, but for relief from hunger…."

My poem went on for several more lines, describing the various things that people crave to bring relief from real pains. I was surprised at how easily the thoughts flowed from my mind to the paper in front of me. At the end of my thoughts, and my conversation with God, I wrote:

"Thank You for my mind and the ability You've given me to think. It's remarkable. Thank You."

And as I wrote those words, along with my thanks and praise to God for something I saw that He had created—my mind—I felt a touch of what David must have felt when he wrote his words, giving thanks and praise to God for something he saw that God had created—the heavens and His Word. Any father would be pleased to hear his children think and speak about those things in the world around him which the Father had a hand in creating. It shows honor and respect and true thankfulness.

There's a time and place for "raw prayers," prayers that just pour out whatever's on our hearts to God, however they might sound. But there's also a time and place for "pleasing prayers," prayers that are carefully crafted to express other truths on our hearts that *also* bring pleasure and praise to the God who gave us life.

These aren't words to butter up God to get what we want, but to honestly acknowledge Him for who He is, realizing how good and right and wise and perfect He is in all of His ways, and in all that He's created—including us.

We can trust Him and trust His Word, even when He says things we don't want to hear. We can trust Him that He really does know best.

What words could you speak today that would be pleasing to God? What insights has He given you into His ways or His Word or His creation that could bring out your praise for Him that is truly in your heart?

Why not take some time to voice those thoughts to Him, to write them out with a pen and paper, or type them out on a keyboard or keypad, or voice them out in a song or a poem?

Let the words within you flow out from your heart as a stream of praise to Him, as David's words did when he said:

> "May the words of my mouth and the meditation of my heart be pleasing in Your sight, O Lord, my Rock and my Redeemer" (Psalm 19:14).

Will you pray with me?

Father God, thank You for letting us see that David not only poured out his pain, but also his praise, in a way that ultimately brought pleasure and glory to You. Help us to do the same, being honest and real with our problems and pains, but also with our praise and adoration. Help us to think carefully and intentionally about ways we can bring glory to You, both in our hearts and in our words that flow out of them. Let them be pleasing in Your sight, O Lord. In Jesus' name, Amen.

LESSON 5: COMFORTING PRAYERS　　　　　　　　　　　　　　OCTOBER 19

Scripture Reading: Psalm 23

There are many ways to look at today's psalm, Psalm 23, which is perhaps the most famous psalm in the book of Psalms, and perhaps the most famous passage in the whole Bible. Today, I'm looking at what we can learn from Psalm 23 about praying more effectively.

Prayer often involves asking for God's help or wisdom, and the struggle of knowing to do or how things will work out in a given situation. The beauty of this prayer, however, is that it is simply an invitation to let God comfort you; a chance to put your whole faith and trust in Him; to let Him take full control of your life and your situations; to allow Him to lead you beside still waters, lie down in the green grass, and restore your soul; and to put your trust Him, knowing that no matter what comes your way, He'll be with you.

Listen to the words David wrote:

"The Lord is my Shepherd, I shall not be in want.
He makes me lie down in green pastures,
He leads me beside quiet waters,
He restores my soul.
He guides me in paths of righteousness for His name's sake.
Even though I walk through the valley of the shadow of death,
I will fear no evil, for You are with me;
Your rod and Your staff, they comfort me."
(Psalm 23:1-4).

David was a shepherd, and he knew that good shepherds watch out for their sheep. When David was a shepherd, he had attacked and killed a lion one day and a bear another, all to protect his precious sheep. He knew the care that shepherds take of their sheep. So when he faced troubles of his own, it's not surprising that he talked to God in terms that he understood well: "The Lord is my *Shepherd*."

Sometimes we just need to let God's comfort pour over us—to slow down long enough to let Him speak His soothing words to our hearts.

One way I've found to do this—to slow down and let God speak deeply to *my* heart—is to take time and savor not just every thought in a portion of Scripture, but every *word*.

Take the first sentence of Psalm 23, for instance. It has only five words: "The Lord is my Shepherd." But if you'll focus on each and every word, you'll see how God can use a simple sentence to speak volumes to your heart.

Think about the first word: THE. THE Lord is my Shepherd. Not "a" Lord or "some" Lord or "any" Lord, but THE Lord, THE One and Only God, THE Lord of all creation, THE Author and Perfecter of your life. That's your Shepherd. That's the One you're talking to. That's your Lord. "THE Lord is my Shepherd, I shall not want."

Think about the second word: LORD. The LORD is my Shepherd. What's a lord? A lord is a master, a ruler, a caller of the shots. And if God is *your* lord, that means that you're not! He's got this. And He's not just ANY lord, He's THE Lord, THE Ruler over all, THE One Who's got the whole world in His hands, including you. He's totally trustworthy, because He's THE LORD.

Then think about the third word: IS. The Lord IS my Shepherd. It's not "The Lord WAS my Shepherd, years ago, when I needed Him to save me, or when He showed up that one time in a special way." It's not "The Lord WILL BE my Shepherd, some day in the future when I get my act together or clean things up a bit." But it's "The Lord IS my Shepherd, right now, today in the midst of everything I'm going through." The Lord IS your Shepherd, if He really is. And if He's not, then there's no reason to wait even one more minute—you can make Him your Lord today, right now! Then you'll be you'll be able to say, like David did, "The Lord IS my Shepherd! I shall not want!"

You're getting how this works. Let's do two more, and you can think through them with me.

Think about the fourth word: MY. The Lord is MY Shepherd. What does that say about you, that the Lord is *your* Shepherd? If He's *your* Shepherd, that means He's actually, truly concerned about *you!* Not just the world in general, or the people around you, but *you!* When Jesus told the parable about the good shepherd, what did He say about that shepherd's heart for the one lost sheep—out of the hundred that He had? He said that the shepherd would go after that one sheep because He didn't want even one of His sheep to be lost. God really cares about *you*, personally. He is *your* Shepherd, just like He is *mine*. "The Lord is MY Shepherd, I shall not want."

Now let's finish with the last word: SHEPHERD. The Lord is my SHEPHERD. What's a shepherd's job? To look after the sheep. That's their whole job! They take the sheep out to green pastures to get food. They lead them beside still waters to get water. They let them lie down to take a rest. They protect them from wild beasts. And they bring them back home again when the time is right, leading them through the gate when it's time to sleep. "The Lord is my SHEPHERD, I shall not want."

We've only looked at five simple words in this psalm, but you can see how those simple words can speak volumes when you slowly focus on each one, letting God speak to your heart. And perhaps you can see why David concluded this prayer to God with the words that he did, knowing that the Lord was *his* Shepherd:

> "Surely goodness and love will follow me all the days of my life,
> and I will dwell in the house of the Lord forever" (Psalm 23:6).

If you ever need comfort from the Lord, take your time, and let Him speak to you. Don't hurry through it. Come back to Him and His Word again and again, meditating on a few more words, and a few more until the comfort of God pours over your heart. Let His goodness and love follow you today and tomorrow and all the days of your life.

I think God knew we could all use a bit of comfort now and then. No wonder this is the most famous passage in the Bible!

Will you pray with me?

Father God, thank You for being our Lord and our Shepherd. Thank You for David's example of coming to You and receiving Your comfort and goodness and love. Help us today as we continue to spend time in Your presence, whatever we do next, to know that Your goodness and love will follow us throughout this day today, and all of our days ahead, if we'll keep putting our faith and trust in You. In Jesus' name, Amen.

LESSON 6: REJOICING PRAYERS   OCTOBER 20

Scripture Reading: Psalm 30

Today's psalm reminds me that there are seasons for everything. Here in Illinois, summers are hot, over 100 degrees Fahrenheit many days. Winters are cold, often below 32 degrees for many days, with snowstorms that block us in our homes for hours. Spring and fall are beautiful, with budding flowers and blossoming trees in the spring, and changing leaves and crisp, cool nights in the fall.

As George Carlin says (in what is probably the most accurate weather forecast of all time):

> "The weather will continue to change on and off for a long, long time."

The seasons in our life change, too. And as much as I sometimes wish things would never change, there are definitely times when I wish they would: like living through the pain of losing my wife to cancer, for instance. Thankfully, God promises that the hard times we go through won't last forever, that the pain we may be facing now can one day be behind us.

As King David said in Psalm 30:

> "Sing to the Lord, you saints of His; praise His holy name. For His anger lasts only a moment, but His favor lasts a lifetime; weeping may remain for a night, but rejoicing comes in the morning" (Psalm 30:5).

Sometimes it's hard to believe, but it's true: "Rejoicing comes in the morning."

When I first went through the book of psalms five years ago, looking for ways to pray more effectively, my wife was going through her cancer treatments. Things looked bleak, and they turned out even bleaker, as she passed away just nine months after her initial diagnosis. I couldn't see anything in the future other than blank, gray days of nothingness. There was nothing that I could imagine ahead for me if she were to die.

As I read this psalm back then, I wrote some notes to myself:

> "God says that weeping lasts for but a moment, and in light of eternity He's right, even if it seems longer than a moment here. Rejoicing comes in the morning. Wailing turns into dancing."

I couldn't see far enough ahead at the time to know what was going to happen or to know if that would ever be true for me. But it's been five years now since I first took those notes, and I can look back now and see how true those words were. God was right. He really did bring back my joy. He eventually turned my wailing into dancing.

But in the midst of that painful season, I didn't even *want* to think about rejoicing someday. I didn't *want* to think about dancing some day in the future, or any time in the future. I just wanted things to go back to the way they were *before* tragedy hit, *before* our lives were turned upside down.

At that time, I was asked if I would be willing to film an interview to give people hope who were facing terminal illness. I didn't want to do it. I didn't want to talk about it. I frankly didn't know what I could say. Saying anything was like admitting that the prognosis in our case was, in fact, terminal. But I felt God wanted me to do it, so I did, and the film team called the short interview Eric's Hope. A few months later, and two weeks before my wife died, a couple more people from the team came to our house to film another interview, this time with our whole family. They called it Lana's Hope.

One of the things I remember distinctly at that time was a conversation with the woman who asked me to do the interviews. She was writing a screenplay for a feature film they were going to be making in Hollywood based on a fictional story of a woman facing terminal cancer. She asked me if I wanted to know what happens at the end of the movie. I said, "No, I really don't."

She said, "It's good. You might want to hear it."

I said, again, "No, I really don't."

I didn't want to hear that someday everything would get better for the husband in the movie, or that he got married again or something, and that somehow, some way, everything turned out to be okay. I didn't know how the movie was going to end, but I didn't *want* to know, because whatever it was, it couldn't possibly be better than it was for me and our family before my wife got sick. I couldn't imagine having to live in this world without her, and I didn't want to have to think about it.

But you know what? That Hollywood movie came out last fall in theaters, and online just a few weeks ago, so I watched it Friday night. There were still moments that were hard, but you know what? I realized I no longer had that stabbing pain I once had. And the ending *was* touching, sweet, and hopeful, even if things would never be the same as they were before. (The movie is called New Life, and you can watch it wherever movies are streamed or sold.)

My life isn't the same as it was before our lives took that turn. And it never will be. But I have seen God turn my weeping into rejoicing, my wailing into dancing. Things *do* change, and sometimes, very thankfully so. As Mark Twain is credited as saying:

> "If you don't like the weather in New England now, just wait a few minutes."

I sometimes wish things would never change. But that's as unlikely as wishing the weather would never change.

When praying, keep in mind there are seasons in life, too. Too hot? Just wait. Too cold? Hang on a bit. Weeping? Rejoicing comes in the morning. Wailing? God can turn it into dancing.

No, things may not go back to the way they were before. But the truth is that as much as I sometimes wish things would never change, there are *definitely* times when I am thankful that they do.

> "Sing to the Lord, you saints of His; praise His holy name. For His anger lasts only a moment, but His favor lasts a lifetime; weeping may remain for a night, but rejoicing comes in the morning" (Psalm 30:5).

Will you pray with me?

Father God, thank You for the changing seasons, and thank You for the changing seasons in our lives. I pray that You would give us hope today in the fact that some things DO change, that things WON'T always be the same as they are now, and that there are times when that is the BEST way for You to work in and through our lives the way that You want to. Help us to keep putting our trust and faith in You, for as much as things here on earth may change, You never do. In Jesus' name, Amen.

LESSON 7: SWEET PRAYERS — OCTOBER 21

Scripture Reading: Psalm 34

I love chocolate chip cookies. I especially love them when they're fresh out of the oven, warm and chewy, with the chocolate melting into strands when you pull them apart.

But I know I wouldn't like them as much if a few of the ingredients were missing. If there were no butter, they'd just be a clumpy mass of dough. If there were no baking soda, they'd flatten out on the tray. If there were no salt or vanilla or sugar, they'd be almost tasteless. It takes all of the ingredients, mixed together, to make that delicious, mouth-watering moment when they come out of the oven.

Life does have some very "tasty" moments, but to bring them about, it requires mixing all the right ingredients together. And to be honest, some of those ingredients don't taste so great on their own. I wouldn't want to eat a stick of butter. I wouldn't want to eat a cup of flour. I wouldn't want to eat a spoonful of salt or vanilla, or even a cup of sugar, as sweet as it is, without the other ingredients mixed in.

But sometimes that's what life gives us; the ingredients come to us one by one, then we get frustrated and wonder what in the world is going on. "This isn't what I asked for! This isn't what I prayed about! This isn't the way things were supposed to go!" The beautiful thing about God is this: He mixes it all together for good. Notice the word "together" in Romans 8:28:

> "And we know that all things work together for good to those who love God, to those who are the called according to His purpose" (Romans 8:28, NKJV).

God takes all things and works them *together* for good. He's a Master Chef, and that means God can make something good out of *anything* that life throws our way, even those things that we might think are initially bitter or totally useless on their own.

In Psalm 34, David experiences one of those mouth-watering moments, when everything is mixed together just right. His cookies have just come out of the oven, and he can't help himself from bursting into song, at one point singing:

> "Taste and see that the Lord is good; blessed is the man who takes refuge in Him" (Psalm 34:8).

But what makes this moment so sweet, so mouth-wateringly delicious, are ALL the ingredients that went into it. David sings God's praises because he realizes that only God could turn everything he had gone through into something good.

The heading of Psalm 34 tells us what had just happened:

> "Psalm 34. Of David. When he pretended to be insane before Abimelek, who drove him away, and he left."

David had been on the run from King Saul, who was trying to kill him. Then David found himself in the presence of another king—an enemy—who might have also tried to kill him.

Thinking quickly, David pretended to be insane:

> "So he pretended to be insane in their presence; and while he was in their hands he acted like a madman, making marks on the doors of the gate and letting saliva run down his beard."

King Achish [his proper name, also called Abimelek as in Psalm 34, which is his title] said to his servants:

> "Look at the man! He is insane! Why bring him to me? Am I so short of madmen that you have to bring this fellow here to carry on like this in front of me? Must this man come into my house?" (1 Samuel 21:13-15).

And it worked! Abimelek sent him away. Then David burst into song. Victory never tasted so sweet—which is why he probably sang, "Taste and see that the Lord is good…"

Individually, some of the ingredients that went into David's song were pretty bitter. Facing death from one enemy only to find himself facing death from another. But God worked it all together for good, giving him a way of escape (and eventually making David the king over all the other kings in that land). David got a taste of the sweetness of God that day—and he savored every bite.

There are times in our lives when things come together just right, even for that moment, and we could burst into song as well. My encouragement to you today is this: go ahead and burst into song! Pray a prayer of thanksgiving to God for working all things *together* for good.

Savor every bite. Sing a song of praise. Pour out your heart to Him in thanksgiving. You may not be totally out of the fire yet, as David still had obstacles in his way until he finally became king himself. But take time out along the way to give praise to God for what He's brought you through so far, for what He's already worked out for good in your life.

I had one of those mouth-watering moments myself yesterday, where I had a few minutes before I picked up my kids from an activity. I decided to go to a nearby park, sit on the grass, and write in my journal.

As I sat down, I read through this Psalm again. I began to thank God for all the things that He had worked out recently in my life: I had been driving a car that kept breaking down, but I now had another car that I had found at a reasonable price; I had been working on a new book that has been a challenge for various reasons, but I had now finished 3/4ths of it so far; I had been going through a long winter here in Illinois, but I was now enjoying the spring breeze and the scent of blossoms in the trees; and I had been hungry for just a little something right before I came to the park, and I had found a vending machine a few hundred feet from where I sat which had a small packet of M&M candies in it—Dark Chocolate Mint M&M's at that, a rare treat—and I was savoring them slowly, one or two at a time while I prayed.

That didn't mean that everything in my life was going the way I wanted it to. It wasn't. And it didn't mean that I didn't still have obstacles ahead that I would have to overcome. But in those moments, I was able to taste and see that the Lord was good—and His goodness just so happened to taste like Dark Chocolate Mint M&M's.

What are *you* going through today that God might be mixing together for your good? Maybe you're still having to eat all of the ingredients one at a time, and they don't taste so good. But maybe there are some parts of your life that have already been mixed together for good, and which *could* taste sweet if you took time to stop and think about it for a few minutes. It wasn't so sweet when my car broke down on the freeway for the final time on a cold winter morning, but it made it all the sweeter yesterday when I was able to roll down my windows once again on a warm spring day. What had been a big deal—and a big pain—just a few months ago, had turned into something extra sweet on an otherwise "ordinary" day yesterday.

If you need help thinking through the things God may have done for you lately, take a closer look at David's psalm of thanksgiving, Psalm 34. Take a look at some of the things God had saved him from that made the victory so sweet when it did come. Maybe you'll find a few things about which you can burst out into song to God today, too.

- *I sought the Lord, and He answered me; He delivered me from all my fears. (v. 4)*
- *Those who look to Him are radiant; their faces are never covered with shame. (v. 5)*
- *This poor man called, and the Lord heard him; He saved him out of all his troubles. (v. 6)*
- *The angel of the Lord encamps around those who fear him, and He delivers them. (v. 7)*

- *The eyes of the Lord are on the righteous and His ears are attentive to their cry... (v. 15)*
- *The Lord is close to the brokenhearted and saves those who are crushed in spirit. (v. 18)*
- *A righteous man may have many troubles, but the Lord delivers him from them all... (v. 19)*

Thank You, God, for mixing ALL things together for good.
Will you pray with me?

Thank You, God, for mixing ALL things together for good. Thank You for the victories You've given us, and for the ingredients we needed to make those victories so sweet. I pray that You would help us to have Your perspective on our lives, not only the sweet times, but the bitter, so that we can enjoy them even more when they all come together. In Jesus' name, Amen.

LESSON 8: SWEET PRAYERS — OCTOBER 22

Scripture Reading: Psalm 37

Psalm 37 contains some of my favorite verses in the whole Bible, such as this one in verse 4:

"Delight yourself in the Lord and He will give you the desires of your heart" (Psalm 37:4).

What I love about this verse, and about this psalm is that it talks about the benefits of delighting yourself in the Lord, of enjoying His presence, of enjoying your time with Him. A friend of mine says that when he spends time with the Lord, he often comes away with a smile on his face, even if he didn't enter into his time with the Lord with one. It's like spending time with a dear friend.

Changing a frown into a smile is just one of the benefits, though. God goes further and promises that if you'll delight yourself in Him, He will give you the desires of your heart.

I was sharing with someone yesterday about the first time I fasted and prayed for a period of several days. On the second day of my fast, I was praying for a woman I had dated in college, but we were no longer dating. She was trying to make a decision about a job, and I told her I would pray for her during my time of fasting and prayer that week.

On the second day of my fast, as I was praying for her, I suddenly had an image of her, not in the job that she was praying about, but married and living a different life than the one she was currently living. It struck me that God didn't want her to take that job, but He did have a man in mind for her to marry. I changed my prayers and said, "Yes, Lord, give her a husband."

Before I had even finished saying that prayer, these words came into my mind as clear as any words I had ever heard from Him before: "Why don't you marry her?"

I was stunned! That's not what I was praying about at all! I was just praying for direction for her life—not mine!

I closed my journal and decided I must have been getting delirious from having not eaten. It wasn't that I didn't love her and didn't love dating her. I did. But at the time, I just didn't feel it was right for us to keep dating. It turned out that during our time apart, we both fell in love with Christ and gave our lives to Him, in separate cities, in separate ways.

We were now both fully committed to Him first and foremost, and we were beginning to live new lives for the first time.

Maybe God really was speaking to me. Maybe He really did want me to consider that question: "Why don't you marry her?" We lived over 1,000 miles apart and over four hours away by plane. It didn't seem practical. But the question wouldn't leave me for two weeks. I began to pray more intensely, setting aside the next three months to pray about the question, not telling her anything about it.

By the end of those three months, I could hardly think of anything else but marrying this woman! God had put such a love for her in my heart like I had never felt before.

At the end of the three months, I called her to see how she was doing. She said, "I feel like God wants me to quit my job, so I'm going to quit in the next few months. But I have no idea what I'm going to do next."

I could hardly keep my heart from leaping out of my chest. "I have an idea," I said. I told her what I felt God had spoken to me when I was praying for her three months earlier, and how much I would love to get back together with her again—for life. Now she was the one who went into shock!

She liked her new life in her new city. She liked the new friends she was making. She liked the church in which she had gotten involved. And she liked me, but she wasn't sure she was ready for getting married just yet. Over the course of the next few months, it began to look more and more doubtful that we would ever get together again. But then I read a verse in the Bible, a verse that gave me hope. It was from another Psalm, but with the same theme as the one I quoted above:

> *"May He give you the desire of your heart and make all your plans succeed. We will shout for joy when you are victorious and will lift up our banners in the name of our God. May the Lord grant all your requests" (Psalm 20:4-5).*

As I read those words, they became "living and active" within me, as the Bible says about itself in Hebrews 4:12. Those words filled me with faith that it was okay to ask God for something I wanted, and that if He did ever see fit to answer my request, I would shout for joy! I would lift up my banner in the name of my God! Although I was afraid it might sound a little childish, I prayed, "God, I know I don't deserve it, and I know you won't force someone to do anything against their own free will. But if there was only one gift I could ask from you in my lifetime, it would be to marry Lana."

The prospect of marrying her still looked very bleak before I prayed, and my heart was still very heavy, but in that moment, it lifted. I knew I could trust God with the outcome, whatever that may be. And I knew I would indeed rejoice fully if it ever did come to pass.

As both of us prayed and sought the Lord more and more over the next few months while we were apart, God seemed to just keep bringing our hearts together, closer and closer. A year later we were married, on April 29th, 1989—28 years ago yesterday.

As I read through Psalm 37 again this week, I was reminded of how true God's Word really is.

> *"Delight yourself in the Lord and He will give you the desires of your heart" (Psalm 37:4).*

I had set aside time to fast and pray for the first time in my life, "delighting myself in the Lord," and one of the results of that prayer was that God spoke to me: He put a desire in my heart that I wasn't even considering. He literally "gave me the desire of my heart." He put that desire within me, and then He fulfilled that desire on our wedding day.

I'm not saying that we will always get everything we want. I'm not saying that our lives won't be filled with hard things and hard times. I lost my precious wife to cancer four and a half years ago. But I am so thankful that I delighted myself in the Lord that day when I was praying and fasting. I am so thankful that I asked Him to give me the desire of my heart. I am so thankful that God gave me the 23 years of marriage that we *did* have.

And that gives me renewed confidence to keep asking Him to give me the desires of my heart again today—whatever He desires and wants to put on my heart.

This is just one of the benefits of delighting yourself in the Lord, of spending time with Him. Others are listed all throughout this psalm:

- *"He will make your righteousness shine like the dawn, the justice of your cause like the noonday sun"* (v. 6).
- *"For evil men will be cut off, but those who hope in the Lord will inherit the land"* (v. 9).
- *"Better the little that the righteous have than the wealth of many wicked; for the power of the wicked will be broken, but the Lord upholds the righteous"* (vv. 16-17).
- *"In times of disaster they will not wither; in days of famine they will enjoy plenty"* (v. 19).
- *"I was young and now I am old, yet I have never seen the righteous forsaken or their children begging bread. They are always generous and lend freely; their children will be blessed"* (vv. 25-26).
- *"Consider the blameless, observe the upright; there is a future for the man of peace"* (v. 37).
- *"The salvation of the righteous comes from the Lord; He is their stronghold in time of trouble. The Lord helps them and delivers them; He delivers them from the wicked and saves them, because they take refuge in Him"* (vv. 39-40).

Will you pray with me?

Father, thank You for giving me the desire of my heart, 28 years ago. Thank You for encouraging me again today to keep delighting myself in You, and to keep asking You to give me new desires of my heart, new answers to prayer for the days ahead. Help me to keep delighting in You in prayer, keep delighting in You throughout my days, keep delighting in you even when I'm having to wait patiently for Your answers. I ask all of this in Jesus' name, Amen.

LESSON 9: DEEP PRAYERS   OCTOBER 23

Scripture Reading: Psalm 42

Psalm 42 begins with the words of one of my favorite worship songs when I first became a Christian:

> *"As the deer pants for streams of water, so my soul pants for you, O God"* (Psalm 42:1).

The reason this was one of my favorite worship songs was because it spoke to the deep places of my heart. As a new Christian, I just wanted more and more of God. Thirty years later, I still do.

When you read Psalm 42, you can feel David's deep hunger, his deep thirst for God.

> "My soul thirsts for God, for the living God. When can I go and meet with God? My tears have been my food day and night, while men say to me all day long, 'Where is your God?'" (vv. 2-3).

And as you continue reading, you find out that his deep thirst is borne out of the deep pain in his soul:

> "Why are you downcast, O my soul? Why so disturbed within me? Put your hope in God, for I will yet praise Him, my Savior and my God. My soul is downcast within me; therefore I will remember You from the land of the Jordan, the heights of Hermon—from Mount Mizar" (vv. 4-6).

The beauty of these verses is that it not only describes the problem David is facing, but also the solution he found to his problem: putting his hope in God; praising Him still; and remembering Him from the place where he had taken refuge.

It's the same solution to the problems we're facing. I heard from a friend yesterday morning whose week was filled with more than a few problems: a flooded basement, electrical issues, a tax problem, getting sick—all of which led to feelings of stress and loneliness. But like David, my friend found the solution in the simple act of turning to God, of actively hoping in Him and trusting in Him. He took away the feelings of despair. While the circumstances hadn't entirely changed, my friend's heart and mind changed—by trusting in Him.

Last year, I was able to visit the area in Israel where David most likely wrote this psalm, for he says in verse 5: "I will remember You from the land of the Jordan, the heights of Hermon." At one point, we stopped along the trail where we were walking, as we had come to a pool of water where it was easy to picture deer coming and quenching their thirst.

We sang, "As the deer panteth for the waters, so my soul longeth after Thee..." And we called out to God from the depths of our hearts to the depths of His. It was a sweet time of intimacy with our God who has the solutions to all of our problems.

At another point, we saw the raging headwaters of the Jordan River, one of the three tributaries which give birth to that significant river that travels the length of the country. As the water crashed in upon itself, it was easy to see how the waves turned into a metaphor for David's song, describing both the tumult that was going on in his own heart, as well as the peace he found through prayer:

> "Deep calls to deep in the roar of Your waterfalls; all Your waves and breakers have swept over me. By day the Lord directs His love, at night His song is with me—a prayer to the God of my life" (Psalm 42:7-8).

I don't know what problems you might be facing this week. I don't know what troubles may be besetting your soul. I don't know what waves and breakers are sweeping over you. But I do know what can help you through them. I do know Who can satisfy that deep thirst in your soul. I do know what can change your heart and your attitude so you can keep pressing forward, as it changed the heart and attitude of David 3,000 years ago, and of my friend yesterday morning. David summarized the problem—and the solution—in the final words of his psalm:

> "Why are you downcast, O my soul? Why so disturbed within me? Put your hope in God, for I will yet praise Him, my Savior and my God" (Psalm 42:11).

David spoke to his soul. He asked why it was so downcast and so disturbed. Then he spoke to it again, offering the solution that God is offering you today: Put your hope in God. Sing your praise to Him, your Savior and your God. Bring your deep prayers to the One who knows best how to answer them.

Will you pray with me?

Father, thank You for letting us pour out our hearts to you, from the depths of our hearts to the depths of Yours. Thank You for providing the solutions to our problems, the answers to our prayers. Thank You for giving us Your peace even when the breakers and waves are sweeping over us. We pray that You would bring us that peace again today, right now, throughout the day, and in the days that follow. Help us to keep putting our hope and trust and faith in You, for You are worthy of it all. In Jesus' name, Amen.

LESSON 10: SELAH PRAYERS   OCTOBER 24

Scripture Reading: Psalm 46

If your life is chaotic and you need a little peace, listen to God's advice from Psalm 46:

> "Be still, and know that I am God" (Psalm 46:10a).

This is perhaps one of the most calming verses in the Bible—and it occurs in the middle of a very tumultuous psalm. So much is going on here that by the time you get near the end, those calming words are a welcome respite.

Here are a few of the verses that lead up to those climactic words:

> "…we will not fear, though the earth give way and the mountains fall into the heart of the sea, though its waters roar and foam and the mountains quake with their surging" (vv. 1-3).
>
> "Nations are in uproar, kingdoms fall; He lifts His voice, the earth melts…" (v. 7).

> "Come and see the works of the Lord, the desolations He has brought on the earth. He makes wars cease to the ends of the earth; He breaks the bow and shatters the spear, He burns the shields with fire" (vv. 8-9).

And then comes the verse everyone is waiting for:

> "Be still, and know that I am God" (v. 10).

It's almost like a scene from the musical *Hamilton*, as a whirlwind of chaos swirls around Alexander Hamilton at a critical point in his life. The rest of the actors circle around him, picking up chairs and desks and papers, twirling the objects around him and holding them high. Chaos abounds. Then…everything stops.

Hamilton sings, "In the eye of a hurricane, there is quiet for just a moment…" And there is quiet all around as he sings the rest of the song for the next two and a half minutes.

I love the imagery of that scene. Unfortunately for Hamilton, in that quiet moment he looks *inward*, decides to put his trust in *his own strength*—and it *destroys* him.

The writers of Psalm 46, however, look *upward*, decide to put their trust in *God's strength*—and it *delivers* them.

How can you "be still" with God in a moment like that? How can you experience His presence when life around you is so chaotic? For me, it comes by literally stopping what I'm doing—whether it's for just a few seconds or just a few hours—but long enough to "Be still, and know that He is God."

Ever since taking a typing class in high school almost 40 years ago, I've always been a fast typist. And I've just gotten faster since then as I've worked on computers my entire adult life.

But when I spend quiet time with God, I do it "the old fashioned way." I take out a pen and a journal. I hand write my notes to God. I try to take notes on what I feel He's impressing on my heart from His Word and from His Spirit.

I try to write slowly—but it doesn't always happen. Sometimes I rush, and my letters and words become illegible. But the very act of taking out a pen and a journal to record my thoughts are one way for me to slow down—to "Be still, and know that He is God."

There's also a mysterious word that appears in the psalms which helps me, too. It's mysterious because Bible scholars haven't found a well-defined translation of it in the ancient world. But from the context in which it is often used, as best as they can tell, the word means, "stop and listen." It's the word, "Selah." It's a beautiful word, even without any meaning attached. (It's so beautiful that one of my friends named their daughter "Selah.")

The word "selah" occurs 74 times in the psalms (and only 3 other times in the whole Bible, in the book of Habakuk), and it occurs 3 times in today's psalm, Psalm 46. This psalm is clearly a song, for the Hebrew text at the top of it says, "For the director of music.... A song." The word "selah" then appears 3 times, at the end of verses 3, 7 and 11.

For me, whether it means, "Stop and listen," or as the Amplified Bible translates it, "Pause, and think of that," whenever I see it in the Bible, it causes me to take a few extra moments to reflect on the words that precede it.

I say all of this to encourage you in your own prayer time with God to "stop and listen," to "pause, and think of that." Or as verse 10 says in this psalm, without having to guess at the original meaning of the words, "Be still, and know that I am God."

I'd like to give you a chance to do this right now. I know you're busy. I know you're trying to get through the day and get on to whatever you have to do next. But if you're able, take a few extra moments sometime today and read through Psalm 46. Each time you see the word "selah," stop and listen; pause and think of that; be still, and know that He is God.

Psalm 46
For the director of music, Of the Sons of Korah. According to alamoth (also likely a musical term). A song.
God is our refuge and strength,
an ever-present help in trouble.
Therefore we will not fear, though the earth give way
and the mountains fall into the heart of the sea,
though its waters roar and foam
and the mountains quake with their surging. Selah

> *There is a river whose streams make glad the city of God,*
> *the holy place where the Most High dwells.*
> *God is within her, she will not fall;*
> *God will help her at break of day.*
> *Nations are in uproar, kingdoms fall;*
> *He lifts His voice, the earth melts.*
> *The Lord Almighty is with us;*
> *the God of Jacob is our fortress. Selah*
> *Come and see the works of the Lord,*
> *the desolations He has brought on the earth.*
> *He makes wars cease to the ends of the earth;*
> *He breaks the bow and shatters the spear,*
> *He burns the shields with fire.*
> *"Be still, and know that I am God;*
> *I will be exalted among the nations,*
> *I will be exalted in the earth."*
> *The Lord Almighty is with us;*
> *the God of Jacob is our fortress. Selah*

Will you pray with me?

Father, thank You for letting us be still and know that You are God. Help us to pause throughout our day and throughout our week—especially when things are so chaotic we can't think straight. Help us to know what it means to "stop and listen," to "pause and think of that," to experience those "selah" moments, even with all of the mystery that this word conveys. We love You, Lord, and we thank You for letting us be still and know that You are God again today. In Jesus' name, Amen.

LESSON 11: CLEANSING PRAYERS   OCTOBER 25

Scripture Reading: Psalm 51

Sometimes we think our sins are too big for God to forgive. But Jesus didn't die for only the sins that we feel are "petty." He died for *all* our sins, even those which we feel are the most grievous. A sin that leads to death might seem too hard for God to forgive, but if Jesus didn't die for *those*, He wouldn't have had to die at all.

In Psalm 51, David pours out His heart to God in prayer over what are perhaps the most grievous sins he had ever committed—his adultery with Bathsheba, who was another man's wife, and the subsequent cover-up and murder of her husband.

The consequences David had to face from his actions were real, as the child born to him and Bathsheba died. But the cleansing that God poured out on him was real, too, as David poured out his confession to God. Listen to David's heart as he begins his prayer:

> *"Have mercy on me, O God, according to Your unfailing love; according to Your*
> *great compassion blot out my transgressions. Wash away all my iniquity and cleanse*
> *me from my sin. For I know my transgressions, and my sin is always before*
> *me. Against You, You only, have I sinned and done what is evil in Your sight, so that*
> *You are proved right when You speak and justified when You judge" (Psalm 51:1-4).*

David pleads for God's mercy. He acknowledges the evil of what he's done. And he acknowledges God's right to judge him accordingly. Yet he *pleads* for God's mercy nonetheless.

One of the reasons I find the Bible to be so trustworthy is that it doesn't gloss over or try to cover up the sins of some of the most heroic figures contained within it. If I think of some of my own sins that are most grievous to me, and if you think of some of your own sins that are most grievous to you, can you imagine having them recorded in a book for everyone to see? Yet I am so thankful that David's sins were recorded in the pages of the Bible, giving me hope that the same God who forgave David can also forgive me. If I thought that God could only forgive sins that I thought were petty, or if the Bible only recorded sins that seemed trivial, I might think that I could somehow pay the price for my sins myself, doing a few more good deeds, or giving more generously, or in some other way. But David's words remind me that this is not what God wants. He wants our hearts, broken and contrite:

> *"You do not delight in sacrifice, or I would bring it; You do not take pleasure in burnt offerings. The sacrifices of God are a broken spirit; a broken and contrite heart, O God, You will not despise" (vv. 16-17).*

That is exactly what David offers to God. That is exactly what I offered to God on the night that I put my trust in Him for everything in my life. And that is exactly what every one of us can offer to God, whenever we sin, to whatever extent that we sin, even for those sins which we might feel are the most grievous.

As you pray to God, come to Him and ask for forgiveness for even your biggest of sins. Then let Him forgive you, since the price for those sins has already been paid when Jesus died on the cross in your place. To not accept God's forgiveness—and the joy that is possible from that forgiveness—would be like leaving an Easter basket filled with candy on the counter at the store, a basket for which your father has already paid and which truly belongs to you.

But sometimes we leave our baskets of forgiveness sitting on the counter. We don't pick them up and truly enjoy the healing that forgiveness can bring because we don't feel like we deserve it. We don't! But our Father didn't buy it for us because we deserved it. He bought it for us because He loves us. He doesn't want us to die. He knew we would need it one day, so we could once against feel loved and accepted, cleansed and forgiven—otherwise we might melt in a permanent puddle of shame and regret and guilt, never to rise up again.

None of us has a perfect moral scorecard. But God wants us to know that He will gladly forgive us of any and all of our sins if we will simply acknowledge those sins before Him; pour out our broken and contrite hearts to Him; and trust in Him, that He truly has bought our forgiveness at the price of His Son on the cross.

Don't leave the basket of forgiveness and cleansing and true joy on the counter. That's not why He bought it for you. He bought it because He loves you. He adores you. And He *doesn't* want you to die. By faith, through prayer, God will give to you what He has already purchased for you: forgiveness, cleansing, and true joy.

When David came before God, he acknowledged God's ability to forgive. David said:

> *"Cleanse me with hyssop, and I will be clean; wash me, and I will be whiter than snow. Let me hear joy and gladness; let the bones You have crushed rejoice. Hide Your face from my sins and blot out all my iniquity" (vv. 7-9).*

Then David called out to God to do a mighty work in his heart; a work that he knew he couldn't do on his own; a work that only God, the creator of his heart, could do:

> *"Create in me a pure heart, O God, and renew a steadfast spirit within me. Do not cast me from Your presence or take Your Holy Spirit from me. Restore to me the joy of Your salvation and grant me a willing spirit, to sustain me. Then I will teach transgressors Your ways, and sinners will turn back to You" (vv. 10-13).*

If you need a clean heart today, whether it's the first time you've asked God to do this mighty work in your life or the hundredth time, I'd like to lead you in a prayer of cleansing—a prayer straight from the words King David prayed after committing some of the most grievous sins of his life.

Will you pray with me?

"Have mercy on me, O God, according to Your unfailing love; according to Your great compassion blot out my transgressions. Wash away all my iniquity and cleanse me from my sin. For I know my transgressions, and my sin is always before me. Against You, You only, have I sinned and done what is evil in Your sight, so that You are proved right when You speak and justified when You judge… You do not delight in sacrifice, or I would bring it; You do not take pleasure in burnt offerings. The sacrifices of God are a broken spirit; a broken and contrite heart, O God, You will not despise… Cleanse me with hyssop, and I will be clean; wash me, and I will be whiter than snow. Let me hear joy and gladness; let the bones You have crushed rejoice. Hide Your face from my sins and blot out all my iniquity. Create in me a pure heart, O God, and renew a steadfast spirit within me. Do not cast me from Your presence or take Your Holy Spirit from me. Restore to me the joy of Your salvation and grant me a willing spirit, to sustain me. Then I will teach transgressors Your ways, and sinners will turn back to You" (Psalm 51:1-4, 16-17, 7-13). In Jesus' name, Amen.

LESSON 12: STRONG PRAYERSOCTOBER 26

Scripture Reading: Psalm 62

Sometimes you just need to lean on God's shoulder; you just need to feel the strength of His power; you just need to rest in the fact that no matter what comes your way, everything's going to be okay, because you know that God is holding you close.

When I read Psalm 62, it helps me to do just that: It helps me to lean on God's shoulder; it helps me to feel the strength of His power; it helps me to rest in the fact that no matter what comes my way, everything's going to be okay, because I know that God is holding me close.

I love the way David begins this psalm:

> *"My soul finds rest in God alone;*
> *My salvation comes from Him.*
> *He alone is my rock and my salvation;*

He is my fortress, I will never be shaken."
(Psalm 62:1-2).

God's so strong that when we lean on Him, we can truly find rest. He's our rock. He's our salvation. He's our fortress. We will never be shaken.

As a man, I love being independent: making a way where there is no way, leading the charge through life and helping others whom God has entrusted to my care. That's how I'm wired. Yet, I also realize that I have limits, that I can't do everything on my own, and that there are times when I need—and I want—someone else on whom *I* can rely, someone else to whom *I* can turn, someone else in whom *I* can place my trust. And that "someone else" is often the God who created me—the God who built the rocks on which I stand.

As one man said to another on a TV show called *When Calls the Heart*:

"You're a self-made man, Mr. Coulter, and you should be proud of that. But no one does it alone. We all need help at times."

We *do* all need help at times. David was strong. David was a leader. David took hold of life with a passion. Yet, David realized his limits, too. And when he did, he knew where to turn to find someone stronger than himself. He turned to the God who created the rocks on which he was standing.

I love the way Eugene Peterson paraphrases David's opening words in Psalm 62 in *The Message* version of the Bible:

"God, the one and only—
I'll wait as long as He says.
Everything I need comes from Him,
so why not?
He's solid rock under my feet,
breathing room for my soul."
(Psalm 62:1-2, MSG)

I was reading these words three years ago while sitting on a beach in Cancun—a rare treat for me. I was there for just 48 hours, but they were 48 hours in which I knew I was going to need God's help. It was my 25th wedding anniversary—and I was taking the trip alone.

My wife had passed away just over a year earlier. I didn't know how I would handle it, being all alone—being afraid I might capsize under yet another wave of grief.

But sitting there on the beach, all alone on my anniversary, I came upon Psalm 62. I read David's words, written at a time when he could have easily capsized, too. I took heart when I read how, at such a tenuous time in his life, David leaned on God.

"God, the one and only—
I'll wait as long as He says.
Everything I need comes from Him,
so why not?"

In that moment, I realized that everything really *did* come from God—even my dear wife whom I had lost and was missing so much. I realized that if God was able to provide a wife for me all those years ago—not to mention every other blessing I had ever enjoyed in my life—that I could trust Him to provide anything I might need now or ever in the future.

I wrote in the margin of my Bible:

> "Father, thank You for reconnecting me with this truth; that You are the one and only; that everything I need comes from You—even Lana came from You. You are my source and my strength."

Instead of the wave of grief I had feared, I was overwhelmed by a wave of peace; a wave of love; a wave of rest in the fact *that I knew that I knew* that I could trust God with this, too.

It's hard to wait on God, I know. It's hard to wait when there are bills to pay, people depending on you, or a doctor's report that hasn't yet come in. It's hard to wait when a baby's on the way, a life mate hasn't appeared, or a job offer hasn't been forthcoming. It's hard to wait in a checkout lane, at a traffic light, or for dinner to get done. It's just plain hard to wait when there's so much living to do!

But David knew he could trust God still—"in the waiting."

> "I'll wait as long as He says.
> Everything I need comes from Him,
> so why not?"

If you're facing something today that you're afraid might overwhelm you, I'd like to encourage you to say some "strong prayers" of your own to God, prayers where you truly lean on His strength, rest confidently in His love, and know that He is with you, for you, and is solid as a rock. Take heart from the words of David, which continue in Psalm 62, that what God was able to do for him, He is able to do for you:

> "Find rest, O my soul, in God alone;
> My hope comes from Him.
> He alone is my rock and my salvation;
> He is my fortress, I will not be shaken.
> My salvation and my honor depend on God;
> He is my mighty rock, my refuge.
> Trust in Him at all times, O people;
> Pour out your hearts to Him,
> For God is our refuge."
> (Psalm 62:6-8)

Will you pray with me?

Father, thank You for having such strong shoulders upon which we can lean. Thank You for letting us come to You today and rest in Your arms once again. Thank You for being there for us when we come to the end of ourselves. Take over, Lord, and take us beyond where we could have taken ourselves on our own. Help us to trust in You, to wait on You, and to enjoy this time of waiting while we are with You. You are our rock, our fortress, and our salvation. Help us to never be afraid, knowing that You are for us and with us, now and until the end of the age. In Jesus' name, Amen.

LESSON 13: EARNEST PRAYERS OCTOBER 27

Scripture Reading: Psalm 63

In the play *The Importance of Being Earnest,* a man named Jack pretends to be a man named Earnest—a name he has chosen for himself whenever he wants to hide his real identity. Ironically, a woman falls in love with him and, believing his name to be Earnest, tells him that she loves his name so much she can't imagine marrying a man who *wasn't* named Earnest.

And so begins a journey of discovery for the man who is *pretending* to be Earnest, on his way to learning the importance of *being* Earnest (in more ways than one).

In our prayer lives, it seems that God is wanting us to do the same: not just pretending to be earnest, but truly being earnest, truly seeking Him from our hearts.

As I look through Psalm 63, I see David doing just that: earnestly seeking God from his heart:

> "God, You are my God, earnestly I seek You; my soul thirsts for You, my body longs for You, in a dry and weary land where there is no water" (v. 1).

In the heading for this psalm, it says that David wrote it when he was in the desert of Judah. For many of us, we speak of being in a desert figuratively, when times are tough or circumstances are dry. For David, he was literally thirsty, and his body was literally longing for refreshment, for he was truly in a dry and weary land where there was no water.

How amazing then, that David came to God with his thirst and his longing, intentionally remembering from where his help would come. David lifted up his hands to God and sang:

> "I have seen You in the sanctuary and beheld Your power and Your glory. Because Your love is better than life, my lips will glorify You. I will praise You as long as I live, and in Your name I will lift up my hands" (vv. 2-4).

Here's a man who knows the importance of being earnest. He lifts his hands to God, knowing that God is the one who can answer the prayers on his heart.

God wants us to do the same. He wants us to lift up our hands to God, intentionally remembering that He is the one who can answer the prayers on our hearts. He is the one to whom we can express our thoughts and desires, our hopes and our dreams, and our belief that He will answer us when we call to Him.

It takes great faith to come to God in this way, to pour out our hearts to Him. Yet great faith is what pleases God the most, when we come to Him believing that He exists and that He rewards those who earnestly seek Him. As it says in the book of Hebrews:

> "And without faith it is impossible to please God, because anyone who comes to Him must believe that He exists and that He rewards those who earnestly seek Him" (Hebrews 11:6).

What about you? Do you believe that God exists? Do you believe He rewards those who earnestly seek Him? It's okay if you can't answer those questions right away. It's okay if it takes some time to think them through and come to your own conclusions. But in the end, know that it is your earnest prayers that God wants the most, your earnest seeking of Him, and your honest belief in Him.

I was reminded yesterday morning of God's actual presence once again—not His far-off, distant, presence somewhere "out there," but His manifest presence, right here with me in the very room where I'm writing this message.

I had been pondering a thought yesterday morning that I wanted to send to a friend. So I wrote it out and included a quote that was given to me by another friend 25 years ago. I sent it off.

When my friend wrote back, I had to get down on my knees and praise God. Why? Because my friend had been reading a book at that very moment which included the quote that I had just sent... a quote I had only heard in passing 25 years ago and have never seen in print before or since! To me, it was a sign of God's manifest presence, a sign that He was right there, right then, right with me in my room. My only response was to drop down on my knees and say, "Thank You, Lord. Thank You for being right here with me, right now. Thank You for speaking to me, speaking through me, and speaking to yet another believer in the process."

When David came to God, he came earnestly. He came full of faith. He came knowing that God was there, and that He was the Only one who could truly quench his deep thirst, truly satisfy the longings on his heart. David said:

> "My soul will be satisfied as with the richest of foods; with singing lips my mouth will praise You. On my bed I remember You; I think of You through the watches of the night. Because You are my help, I sing in the shadow of Your wings. My soul clings to You; Your right hand upholds me" (vv. 5-8).

David held on tight to God, and God held on tight to him. What a rich picture of a very rich relationship! I long for that kind of relationship with God, too!

I was thinking of this idea again earlier this week, about the importance of being earnest, as I watched one of the *Pirates of the Caribbean* movies with my kids. There's a point in the third movie where, in order to make something happen, someone must speak these words to a woman named Calypso: "Calypso, I release you from your human bonds."

When one of the characters does so, nothing happens. Another character says, "He didn't say it right. You have to say it right." So this second character leans over to Calypso and whispers in her ear as if to a lover: "Calypso, I release you from your human bonds." He used the same words, but with an entirely different tone. And when he did, all kinds of things began to happen!

I'm not saying that you have to say just the right thing in the just the right way to move the heart of God. But I am saying that God wants you to come to Him full of faith, truly believing that He's there, that He cares, and that He rewards those who earnestly seek Him. Because He is there. He does care. And He does reward those who earnestly seek Him.

How do I know? Not only because the Bible tells me so, but because God Himself has confirmed it's so—over and over and over again—as I've come to Him with my own earnest prayers.

I know He'd love to confirm it to you, too. Come to Him with your earnest prayers and discover for yourself the importance of being *Earnest*.

Will you pray with me?

Father, thank You for letting us come to You, anytime day or night, with those things that are on our hearts. I pray that You would hear our prayers today, answering them as You see fit, giving us a strong sense of Your presence as we do. Lord, we come to You today in faith, truly believing that You exist and that You reward those who earnestly seek You. And Lord, we pray now that You would satisfy those longings on our heart, longings which perhaps only You truly know are deep within us. In Jesus' name, Amen.

LESSON 14: SAVING PRAYERS OCTOBER 28

Scripture Reading: Psalm 69

I'm writing this message from the Caribbean island of Trinidad, where earlier this week a tropical storm swept through and threatened to cancel the men's retreat where I was scheduled to speak. But late Friday night, we finally made it to the retreat center, and even at that late hour, the other men arrived, also, eager to hear about the power of God to rescue and save us when we put our faith in Him.

It is this same power that King David called upon from God in Psalm 69, a time when the flood waters were rising in his own life. Listen to David's cry for help at the beginning of this psalm:

> *"Save me, O God, for the waters have come up to my neck.*
> *I sink in the miry depths, where there is no foothold.*
> *I have come into the deep waters; the floods engulf me.*
> *I am worn out calling for help; my throat is parched.*
> *My eyes fail, looking for my God."*
> *(Psalm 69:1-3)*

David wasn't just crying for help. He was screaming… screaming to the point where he had worn out his voice.

What can we learn about prayer from this psalm? For starters, it's a reminder once again that prayer is not always polite and holy. As my friend who is on this trip with me, Jeff Williams, says, "Drowning men don't whistle. They scream."

If you're going to be honest with God, you can't pretend that everything's okay when it's not. If you're fine, say so. But if you're not fine, it's okay to say that, too.

What also intrigues me about this prayer is that David knows Who to come to for help. He didn't scream into thin air. He screamed to the God Whom he knew could save him. Listen to his cry as it continues:

> *"But I pray to You, O Lord, in the time of Your favor;*
> *in Your great love, O God, answer me with Your sure salvation.*
> *Rescue me from the mire, do not let me sink;*
> *deliver me from those who hate me, from the deep waters.*
> *Do not let the floodwaters engulf me or the depths swallow me up or the pit close its mouth over me.*
> *Answer me, O Lord, out of the goodness of Your love;*
> *in Your great mercy turn to me.*
> *Do not hide Your face from Your servant;*

answer me quickly, for I am in trouble."
(Psalm 69:13-17)

There's something about David's relationship with God that caused him to keep coming back to God over and over again—even when he felt that God was distant and not answering him. The beauty of this is summed up in the words of a new friend I've made here on the island, Pastor Mitchell John, who says, "When we call to someone and they don't answer, we usually give up and try calling someone else. But David doesn't change Who he's calling, Who he's crying out to, Who he is supplicating. He keeps calling out to God."

Why would David call out to the God who he feels isn't answering his prayers? There's a clue in this psalm as to why. David talks to God in a way that calls on His favor, His love, His salvation (v13). David knows what God is like. He knows from his previous interactions with God and from his previous experiences. So when David sees no tangible evidence of God in his present situation, he doesn't give up and call someone else. He calls on the One Whom he knows is there—the only One Who is able to help.

So he keeps calling. He keeps crying out. Even when he's losing hope, he knows that his God is the God of hope. So he continues to call, even after his voice gives out. He's obviously wondering, crying and questioning, but in the end, he knows where to turn for help.

What about you? Who do you call for help? How do you pour out your requests when the waters have come up to your neck, when you're sinking into the miry depths with no foothold, when you're worn out from calling and your throat is parched? I'd like to encourage you to keep calling out to God. Keep calling the only One Who can truly save you. Don't hang up and call someone else. Trust in God's favor, God's love, God's salvation.

Maybe you feel like screaming, but you're not sure if it's okay to do so. But if you're going to explore the width and the depth of prayer, take some queues from David and give it a try. If it was okay for David, I think it would be okay for you. You might even need to truly scream! You might want to close your doors first. Or take a walk. Or sit in your car. Or scream into your pillow. But however you do it, don't cry out into thin air. Cry out to the One Who can truly help you best!

Sometimes you need to get really honest with God.

You don't have to pretend with God. You can tell him how you really feel, remembering to thank Him for the good in your life that you do experience, but being honest about the hurts you feel as well.

I've been mulling over a statement lately from a book written by a woman who lost her husband, and how hard it was for her to make small talk with others while she was still dying inside. She said it's like they were asking her:

"Aside from that, how was the play, Mrs. Lincoln?"

Thankfully, you don't have to make small talk with God. If you're in pain, you can say so. If you need help, you can say so. If you're dying inside, you can say so.

Why? Because God already knows, and because He is the only One Who can truly save you. He is the One Who can rescue you. He is the One Who can reach down into your situation and pull you out of the pit.

Listen to David's words, near the end of this psalm:

"I am in pain and distress; may Your salvation, O God, protect me" (v. 29).

Whether you're drowning or in pain or lonely or heartbroken or suffering or in need of saving, cry out to God. If you've never put your faith in Christ for your salvation, do it today. If you've already trusted God for your eternal life, know that you can trust Him for your life here on earth, too.

Our God is a saving God. Call on Him to save you today.

Will you pray with me?

God, save us! Help us as the flood waters rise around us! Help us as we feel like we're drowning and don't know where else to turn. God, we trust in You, in Your favor, Your love, Your salvation. Help us to be honest with You today. Help us to keep putting our faith and trust in You. And help us to keep looking to You for our salvation. In Jesus' name, Amen.

LESSON 15: PRIMING PRAYERS OCTOBER 29

Scripture Reading: Psalm 100

I live on a farm that has an old hand pump on it. We seldom use it anymore, so to get the water to come out the well, you have to "prime the pump"—meaning you pour a cupful of water down inside the pipe, which moisturizes a leather ring on a cylinder, which creates the suction needed to draw out more water. Just a cupful of water can release a fairly unlimited supply of water!

Sometimes we need to do the same thing in our prayer times with God. Sometimes we're able to come to Him with a song that's already in our hearts; a song we're just bursting to sing to Him. At other times we come to Him with barely a cupful of water, and we need *Him* to pour out a song into *our* hearts.

Thankfully, He can do that, too! All we need to do is to pour out a cupful of praise, thereby "priming the pump," which then can release a fairly unlimited supply of praise in return!

Psalm 100 is one of those psalms that always seems to help me prime my pump, bringing me quickly into an atmosphere of praise. It's a short psalm, just 5 verses long, and it takes just 30-40 seconds to read. Yet for those who take its words to heart, it can release a strong and steady stream of praise.

Listen to the words of Psalm 100, which is subtitled in the Bible as, "A psalm. For giving thanks."

"Shout for joy to the Lord, all the earth.
Worship the Lord with gladness;
come before Him with joyful songs.
"Know that the Lord is God.
It is He Who made us, and we are His;
we are His people, the sheep of His pasture.
"Enter His gates with thanksgiving
and His courts with praise;
give thanks to Him and praise His name.
"For the Lord is good and His love endures forever;

His faithfulness continues through all generations."
(Psalm 100:1-5)

Lana and I put this psalm on the cover of our "Order of Service" for the day we got married, so a copy of this psalm was handed to everyone as they entered the doors of the sanctuary. We felt it was a fitting psalm for a day when we were naturally bursting with praise—and it was! There was no need for priming the pump that day! Our hearts were already overflowing with praise!

But there have been other days that I have pulled up this psalm when my heart wasn't naturally bursting with praise, and I've found there's at least a cupful of praise in this psalm to get things going again. A few of the reasons why we can praise God, even on rainy days, are contained within the psalm itself. It begins with a shout! In my last message, I talked about shouting to God when you're angry or upset. But in this message, I'd like to encourage you to shout out a word of praise to God, joining the rest of the earth in its praise of God as well.

Shout out the word "Hallelujah!" for instance, which simply means "Praise God!" in Hebrew (originally "Halal Yah!"). For some reason, I really love saying it in the original Hebrew! And when I do, it becomes more than just a "Woo-Hoo!" to God; it's a "Halal Yah!" to Him, a praise to the Almighty God Who created me, Who loves me and Who gives me every breath I take. It's a "breathy" word of praise, with no hard consonants, like p's or k's, to interrupt the flow. Just pure praise. Pure breath. Pure worship from my spirit to His. And in return, God has often poured out a good dose of His Spirit back into me—and a fairly unlimited supply at that!

It also helps when I say it with a smile—with gladness, as Psalm 5 says in verse 2. There's something about saying "Halal Yah!" that just makes me smile naturally, too. It's a "whoop-de-doo!" kind of a word to me. "Halal Yah!" It's joyous. It's victorious. And it brings out the true gladness that I know is down in my heart. All of this is from just the first two verses of this worshipful psalm:

"Shout for joy to the Lord, all the earth.
Worship the Lord with gladness;
come before Him with joyful songs."

The next verse gives me a few reasons for praising God. They speak about how He is ours, and we are His:

"Know that the Lord is God.
It is He Who made us, and we are His;
we are His people, the sheep of His pasture."

Now there's a reason to praise God! He's our God! He's the One Who made us, and we are His. We are His people and the sheep of His pasture! He cares for us, because we belong to Him.

The next verse continues, telling us *how* we can come to Him, with thanksgiving and praise, knowing that He is ours and we are His:

> *"Enter His gates with thanksgiving
> and His courts with praise;
> give thanks to Him and praise His name."*

Come to Him with a thankful heart. Come to Him with praise. Then, as you enter His courts, give your thanks to Him; give your praise to His name.

Lastly, this psalm reminds me about some of God's best attributes, as listed in the last verse: His goodness, His enduring love, and His faithfulness which continues through all generations.

> *"For the Lord is good and His love endures forever;
> His faithfulness continues through all generations."*

I've been contemplating rainbows lately, and the powerful imagery they convey. They're more than something for little kids to have on their stickers, or for big movements to have on their flags. They're signs of God's promises to the world He loves.

I saw a rainbow on my way home from Trinidad this week, and it came at a perfect time. Because of a delay at the airport, I missed one of my connecting flights…which meant I would miss my bus later in the day, which meant my plans for the rest of the night would change, too. As everything was getting backed up in my mind, I was tempted to get upset with the airlines and the agents and officials at customs.

I decided to praise God instead, trusting Him in the midst of it. I had done everything I could do, and I had to trust Him to do everything He could do. After running to one of my gates and watching the door close as the agent said, "We're sorry, Mr. Elder, we've just filled the last seat on the plane," I was tempted to be dejected again. Instead, I took a few moments to relax and praise God as I began the long walk to the customer service desk, where I was told I could standby for another flight on the other side of the airport, and I took another deep breath and began another long walk to get there.

When I finally arrived at that next gate, I sat down and saw, out the window in front of me, one of the most beautiful rainbows I've ever seen. It was coming down through the clouds and practically touched the plane that was sitting outside the window in front of me. I walked over to the window, and pointing it out to the others around me, we all looked at it in wonder.

About 45 minutes later, the rainbow was still there! I've never seen a rainbow last so long! They called my name and told me there was one more seat on the plane… THAT plane, the one that we had been looking at for so long! It was that plane that had one more seat on it; a seat with my name on it; a seat with a rainbow of God's promise practically touching it.

Sometimes you come to God with a song of praise that's already on your heart. Other times you need to prime the pump with a cupful of praise to get things going, changing the atmosphere in your heart as well as the atmosphere all around you. Either way, always know that there's an unlimited stream of praise ready and waiting for you to tap into at any moment. Just turn to God. Give Him a shout of praise. Give Him your best "Halal Yah!" Then let Him do the rest.

Will you pray with me?

Father, we praise you! We worship You with thanksgiving in our hearts! Halal Yah! Help us to bring forth the fullness of the praise that we know is deep within us—and even more, that we know is deep within You. Help us to pour out a song of praise from our spirit to Yours, then give us a good dose of Your Holy Ghost in return! Help us to praise You from the depths of our beings, knowing that You are good, that Your love endures forever, and that Your faithfulness continues through all generations. In Jesus' mighty name, Amen.

LESSON 16: REMEMBERING PRAYERS   OCTOBER 30

Scripture Reading: Psalm 77

Some of you might feel like you're hanging on by a thread today. But I want to remind you that God's got a hold of you with His strong arms, and that the ground beneath your feet is much more solid than you think.

I remember as a kid watching an interview about the filming of the movie *Huckleberry Finn*. The actor who played Tom Sawyer said that when they filmed a scene out on a lake, the boat he was in accidentally tipped over, throwing him into the water.

Not knowing how to swim, he struggled for air and began screaming for help. He truly believed he was going to drown. But in the midst of all this, he could hear people screaming back to him from the shore. What were they saying? Why weren't they coming to help him? Didn't they realize he was drowning?

But when their screams finally broke through his own, he could hear them yelling: "Stand up!" He took their advice. He reached his feet for the ground beneath his feet—ground that he thought wasn't there, but it was! He shifted his body and finally stood straight up. He was surprised to see that he was "drowning" in only three feet of water!

The ground beneath his feet was much more solid than he thought.

I'm not saying that the problems you're facing are trivial. I'm not saying that the waters may not be truly deep. They may be. But what I am saying is don't let the water fool you. The ground beneath your feet is much more solid than you think. If you've put your faith in Jesus, then you've put your faith in the most solid rock available to any of us. He is THE ROCK on which we stand.

Reach out your feet for the ground beneath your feet, the ground that you think might not be there. Shift your body and try to stand upright again. Let God reach down with His strong arms and help you do it. Then know that He's got a hold of you, and that the ground beneath your feet is much more solid than you think.

In Psalm 77, we find that the writer, a man named Asaph, was in serious distress, too. He was crying out to God for help, stretching out his hands to God, but he still couldn't find relief:

> "I cried out to God for help;
> I cried out to God to hear me.
> When I was in distress, I sought the Lord;
> at night I stretched out untiring hands
> and my soul refused to be comforted."
> (Psalm 77:1-3)

But by the end of the psalm, Asaph had found his footing again. He was able to stand again on THE ROCK beneath his feet. How did he do it? How was he finally able to stand again?

As best I can tell, he did it by "remembering." He prayed to God, remembering what God had done for His people in the past. Four times in this psalm, Asaph uses some form of the word "remember":

> "I remembered You, O God, and I groaned" (v. 3).
> "I remembered my songs in the night" (v. 6).
> "I will remember the deeds of the Lord;
> Yes, I will remember Your miracles of long ago" (v. 11).

And what did he remember? In his case, he thought back to the times when the Israelites thought they were going to drown, too, yet God saved them from doing so. The armies of Egypt were hot in pursuit of them, and only the waters of the Red Sea stood before them. They had nowhere else to go but to run straight into the sea.

And by God's Spirit—by His very breath, the Bible says—the waters convulsed. They parted to the right and to the left. God's breath dried up the floor of the sea beneath their feet and they were able to walk right through it, on solid ground.

Asaph pictures the scene in his mind as he remembers what God had done:

> "The waters saw You, O God,
> the waters saw You and writhed;
> the very depths were convulsed.
> "The clouds poured down water,
> the skies resounded with thunder;
> Your arrows flashed back and forth.
> "Your thunder was heard in the whirlwind,
> Your lightning lit up the world;
> the earth trembled and quaked.
> "Your path led through the sea,
> Your way through the mighty waters,
> though Your footprints were not seen.
> "You led Your people like a flock
> by the hand of Moses and Aaron."
> (Psalm 77:11-20).

I hope you can listen to this psalm in the recording I've posted to go along with it. The music I've recorded is exactly the same in both the first half and the second half of this psalm, but because the words are different in those two halves, the music in those two halves have an entirely different feel. As the psalm begins, it sounds like one of the saddest, most mournful songs of all time. But by the end of the psalm, Asaph's words of remembrance make the music sound exultant! Triumphant! Victorious! It's the exact same music, but it has an entirely different feel!

What's the difference? The difference is that *Asaph remembers what he knows to be true of God*: God is strong, God can save, and even God's breath can make solid ground appear beneath our feet!

What about you? What can you remember today that God has done for you in the past? Was there ever a time when you felt like you were drowning, but God reached down and saved you? When God helped you as you were in distress? When God made a way for you where there was no way?

As you look back over your life, can you remember any times when it seemed like you couldn't go on, but God helped you through it? When you couldn't see a solution, but God made one appear, as if out of thin air? When it looked like everything around you was conspiring to be your end, but it turned out to be just a beginning of something even better than you could have ever imagined?

If so, think about such things! Picture them in your mind! Let those images flow of God's past victories in your life and let them encourage you now as you face whatever struggle you might be facing now. Let God reach down with His strong arm and lift you up, shift your position, and help you stand again on solid ground.

If you've never put your faith in Christ before, do it today. And if you've already put your faith in Christ, put your faith in Him again today for what you're facing right now, too. Let Him be the SOLID ROCK on which you stand.

Will you pray with me?

God, help us to remember You! Help us to look to You! Help us remember what You've done in the past so we can put our faith and trust in You again today. Jesus, we know that You're our SOLID ROCK. We know You have saved us in the past and You can save us from this, too. Help us when we're drowning. Help us to get our feet back on solid footing once again. Help us to know that You will work in our lives again today as You've worked in our lives in the past. And Lord, let this day be one that we can look back on again in the future, remembering how You saved us in this trial, this struggle, this time of distress, too. In Jesus' mighty name—the SOLID ROCK on which we stand—Amen.

LESSON 17: YEARNING PRAYERS   OCTOBER 31

Scripture Reading: Psalm 84

Have you ever felt your heart *lunging* out of your chest towards something or someone—that feeling that you're being pulled forward by some kind of invisible heartstrings? That's what it means to yearn: "to have an intense feeling of longing for something, typically something that one has lost or been separated from."

If you've ever prayed for something with an intensity of heart like that, you know what a yearning prayer feels like. One of the best examples of a prayer like this is found in Psalm 84:

> "How lovely is Your dwelling place, O Lord Almighty!
> My soul yearns, even faints, for the courts of the Lord;
> my heart and my flesh cry out for the Living God" (vv. 1-2).

In this case, the psalmist's heart is lunging towards God—specifically towards God's dwelling place, that place where the psalmist knew he could meet with God.

I wrote a song one day about my own longing to be with God, to be in His dwelling place, just to know that He was right there with me. The song is called "My Sanctuary," and the words begin like this:

All I want, All I need,
Is to be with You and to know You're near.
All I want, All I need,
Is to talk to You, and to know You'll hear.
And I know There's a place
I can go to feel Your presence,
Oh, Lord, bring me there; bring me home.

At that moment, as I was writing that song, I felt like God had answered my prayer. Suddenly I was right there with Him; in His presence; in His sanctuary. At that moment, it became my sanctuary, too.

I sang:

This is my sanctuary, Oh Lord!
This is the place that I call my home!
This is my sanctuary, Oh Lord!
And I know when I'm here I'm not alone!

God answered that "yearning" prayer on my heart, that intense desire to be *near Him; with Him; close to Him*. I can hardly explain the immense *satisfaction* that I felt in the moments that followed—to be in His presence; to enjoy His peace; to experience His relaxing calm.

Sometimes our hearts long for something or someone, when what we're really longing for is what God alone can provide: His immense satisfaction.

I think it's critical, in those moments when we're yearning for something or someone with a heartache that can't be fulfilled, to turn those yearnings towards God. Why? Because sometimes our deepest longings can only be fulfilled by being in His presence—by being so close to Him that we can truly hear His heart about all of the other things for which we're longing.

I spent a few hours of intense prayer one night at a church in Houston. I was praying to know God's will in regards to a particular woman I was seriously considering marrying. I didn't know what God might want, and I didn't want to make a mistake. All I knew was that I *deeply* wanted to marry this woman—if that's what God would want and what she would want as well.

I took a friend along with me to pray in a small chapel at my church. We knelt on the steps at the front of the sanctuary, pleading with God for His answer.

A few verses from the Bible came to mind about how the Holy Spirit can search out the deep things of God and reveal them to us. The verses say:

"However, as it is written: 'No eye has seen, no ear has heard, no mind has conceived what God has prepared for those who love Him' but God has revealed it to us by His Spirit. The Spirit searches all things, even the deep things of God. For who among men knows the thoughts of a man except the man's spirit within him? In the same way no one knows the thoughts of God except the Spirit of God" (1 Corinthians 2:10-11).

So we leaned into our prayers, asking God's Holy Spirit to search out the deep things of God to see what He might have in store regarding my relationship with this woman. In my mind's eye, I could picture the Holy Spirit taking off from the place where we were praying, then zooming towards the throne room of God. I felt as if my prayers were getting so close to the heart of God that at any minute His Spirit would return to reveal to me His answer.

But just as I thought that answer was about to come, something else happened. It felt as if the Holy Spirit had finally arrived and entered into God's dwelling place, but as soon as He did, an invisible door shut fast behind Him. All of our prayers stopped. Our seeking ended. That yearning feeling that had been so intense on my heart was gone. Somehow I knew that our prayers had touched the very heart of God. Even though I didn't know the answer, I knew that everything was going to be okay.

A complete stillness—a complete calm—overwhelmed us. Although this wasn't the answer I was expecting, it brought a peace to my heart that passed all understanding; a peace that was worth more to me than any other answer I could have been given. I simply knew that God had heard my prayers, and that He had it all under control.

A few months later, God *did* reveal His answer to my prayers, both to me and to this woman I was hoping to marry, with a clear and resounding "Yes!" A year later, we were walking down the aisle in the same church, in a larger sanctuary just around the corner from that chapel where I had been praying.

I tell you this story not as a formula for how to get whatever you want from God in prayer. It just doesn't work like that, for all kinds of reasons. I tell you this story to encourage you to bring your intense longings to God—whatever those intense desires may be that are on your heart. By bringing them to Him and spending time in His presence, you can find a peace and a satisfaction that you won't be able to find anywhere else on earth.

The bottom line is that you'll be blessed! That's exactly what the writer of Psalm 84 says will happen:

"Blessed are those who dwell in Your house; they are ever praising You.
Blessed are those whose strength is in You, who have set their hearts on pilgrimage…

They go from strength to strength, till each appears before God in Zion" (vv. 4-5, 7).

Don't let those unfulfilled longings on your heart frustrate you forever. Instead, turn those longings into prayers to God. Bring them before Him—and keep bringing them before Him. Let your heart yearn for God Himself, for His presence, for His sanctuary.

Then, as you come into His presence, recognize that you're in the presence of your Almighty Father, the One Who loves you more than anyone in the world.

Let His peace overwhelm you. Let His wisdom pour out upon you. Let Him solve the puzzles that you can't solve on your own. Let His comfort, His courage, and His confidence overtake you so that you can stand up once again knowing that "God's got this."

As you do this, I pray you'll come to the same conclusion as the writer of Psalm 84:

"Better is one day in Your courts than a thousand elsewhere;
I would rather be a doorkeeper in the house of my God
than dwell in the tents of the wicked.
For the Lord God is a sun and shield;
the Lord bestows favor and honor;
no good thing does He withhold from those whose walk is blameless.
O Lord Almighty, blessed is the one who trusts in You" (vv. 10-12).

Will you pray with me?

Almighty Father, bring us into Your presence today. Bring us into Your dwelling place. Help us turn our yearnings to You, so You can solve the puzzles we can't solve on our own. Help us to know anything You want us to do or not do. Help us to know what's right and what's wrong in every situation. All we want is what You want, God, for we know and believe that whatever You want for us will be best. In Jesus' name, Amen.

LESSON 18: TEARFUL PRAYERS   NOVEMBER 1

Scripture Reading: Psalm 88

I was asking a friend one day why the book of Psalms seemed to be so appealing to so many people worldwide. I asked him, "Of all the Scriptures, what is it about the psalms that make them so especially beloved?"

He described to me the incredible range of emotions which are expressed in the psalms, then he pointed to Psalm 88 as being one of the deepest, most sorrow-filled passages in the whole Bible. When I read it, I was astounded.

I had read the book of Psalms several times before as part of my regular readings through the entire Bible. But to me, after reading through just a few of them, they all began to blur together. Now, however, after hearing my friend say this, I began to see them in a different light.

My friend said, "Maybe it's because you hadn't yet been through some of the things the writers of the psalms were describing." I knew that he was right. It was only after experiencing some of the deepest pains of life did Psalm 88 really speak to me personally.

While this psalm begins like many of the others, with an appeal to God for help, it doesn't end there. It ends with some of the most poignant words in all of Scripture. Maybe you've prayed a prayer like this before. Here's how the psalmist begins:

> "O Lord, the God who saves me, day and night I cry out before You.
> May my prayer come before You; turn Your ear to my cry.
> For my soul is full of trouble and my life draws near the grave" (vv. 1-3).

Whereas other psalms eventually lift us out of the darkness, this one just gets darker:

> "I am counted among those who go down to the pit;
> I am like a man without strength.
> I am set apart with the dead, like the slain who lie in the grave,
> whom You remember no more, who are cut off from Your care" (vv 4-6).

Then, the psalmist begins to blame God for his troubles:

> "You have put me in the lowest pit, in the darkest depths.
> Your wrath lies heavily upon me; You have overwhelmed me with all Your waves.
>
> You have taken from me my closest friends and have made me repulsive to them" (vv- 6-8).

As unthinkable as blaming God may seem, it's also natural. It's natural to question God's wisdom when things are going wrong. It's natural to question His ways when we're not getting ours. It's natural to doubt His love when we don't feel loved by those around us.

But as *natural* as all those feelings may be, I'm thankful we serve a *supernatural* God. The truth is we serve a God Who truly loves us, Who truly helps us, and Who truly works on behalf of us—even when everything around us seems to be saying just the opposite.

I chose to highlight this psalm precisely because of the depths to which it goes. It's not a rosy, cheery picture of life. It's not even an appeal to a deeper faith. It's simply a tearful cry of help. Sometimes we just need to cry in prayer. And sometimes we just need to know that someone else has been where we are.

I had another friend who always loved symbols of crosses which were empty, crosses which showed that Jesus was no longer on the cross, but rather has been raised to life and is still alive today.

But one time when my friend was in a hospital, lying in bed in excruciating pain, she looked up and saw a cross on the wall in front of her which pictured Jesus hanging on it. He was wearing a crown of thorns on his head and nails were driven through His hands and His feet. My friend said that in that moment, she was comforted in her own pain for the first time. Why? Because she knew there was Someone Who had experienced the depths of the pain and sorrow that she was experiencing.

Sometimes we need to focus on the fact that Jesus has been raised from the dead and was victorious over death. But other times we may need to remember that He suffered immensely. Walking through His suffering with Him can help us as we walk through our own. As the Apostle Paul says, "I want to know Christ and the power of His resurrection and the fellowship of sharing in His sufferings, becoming like Him in His death, and so, somehow, to attain to the resurrection from the dead" (Philippians 3:10-11). Sometimes it's important to know the power of Christ's resurrection as well as sharing in His sufferings.

My friend who loves Psalm 88 finds comfort in knowing that there is someone else who understands his pain; someone else who has experienced his sorrow; someone else who doesn't try to cheer him up or tell him everything's going to be okay, but who simply walks through deep despair just as he has.

If you find yourself in a dark place today, remember that you're not alone. Listen to the author of Psalm 88 as he pours out the final words of his prayer to God. Take heart that you're not alone.

"Why, O Lord, do You reject me and hide Your face from me?
From my youth I have been afflicted and close to death; I have suffered your terrors and am in despair.
Your wrath has swept over me; Your terrors have destroyed me.
All day long they surround me like a flood; they have completely engulfed me.

You have taken my companions and loved ones from me; the darkness is my closest friend" (vv. 14-18).

Remember the suffering of the author of Psalm 88. Remember the suffering of Jesus. And remember the suffering of those who have read and have loved Psalm 88 throughout the centuries because it helps them to know they're not alone.

Will you pray with me?

Father, we don't like suffering. We just don't like it. But Father, we know that somehow we can experience a fellowship with You and a fellowship with Your Son through suffering in a way that we could never experience through any other means. Father, help us to keep turning to you, even with our tears. Help us to know that You understand our suffering more than anyone else could ever understand. Help us to take comfort in the fact that You've been where we are, and that You'll walk with us through this, too. We love You, Lord, and we come again to You today in Jesus' name, Amen.

LESSON 19: PROTECTIVE PRAYERS NOVEMBER 2

Scripture Reading: Psalm 91

If you or someone you love needs God's protection today, I hope you'll read this message.

One of the most frequent types of prayers I pray are prayers for God's protection—for myself and for those I love. While Jesus tells us not to worry, one of the reasons He has to do so is because there's so much to worry about!

My dad had a card he kept on the windowsill by the kitchen sink in our home growing up. It said, "Worrying must work. 90% of the things I worry about never happen."

I'm sure that card was a reminder to him, as it often was to me, that many of the things we worry about are not worth worrying about, as they will simply never happen. As the French philosopher Michel de Montaigne said over 400 years ago: "My life has been filled with terrible misfortune; most of which never happened."

The truth is, however, that there are still plenty of things that can and do happen to us and to those we love. What do we do about those? God gives us His answer in Psalm 91, a prayer that is filled with words of trust in God's protection, no matter what might come against us.

Listen to the psalmist's opening words, as he puts his complete trust in God:

"He who dwells in the shelter of the Most High will rest in the shadow of the Almighty.
I will say of the Lord, 'He is my refuge and my fortress, my God, in whom I trust.'

Surely He will save you from the fowler's snare and from the deadly pestilence.

He will cover you with His feathers, and under His wings you will find refuge;
His faithfulness will be your shield and rampart.
You will not fear the terror of night, nor the arrow that flies by day,
nor the pestilence that stalks in the darkness, nor the plague that destroys at midday.

A thousand may fall at your side, ten thousand at your right hand, but it will not come near you."
(Psalm 91:1-7)

I love the imagery of this psalm, which pictures God as a refuge and a fortress, a safe place in the midst of trouble.

The psalmist imagines himself coming to God as a fledgling bird would come to his father, taking refuge under his father's wings. The psalmist says things like these: "He will cover you with His feathers, and under His wings you will find refuge," "Surely He will save you from the fowler's snare and from the deadly pestilence," and "You will not fear the terror of night, nor the arrow that flies by day."

There is great protection when we put our trust in God. Even though "A thousand may fall at your side, ten thousand at your right hand," this psalm continues by saying, "but it will not come near you."

I would never be able to count the number of times I have prayed a prayer of protection over myself and those I love. Every time I turn on the car and back out of the driveway, I pause to pray out loud that God would be with us, that He would protect us, and that we would be able to bless His name as we go about our day, and that He would bless us as we do. Every time my kids are out late, or someone I know is sick or hurting, or one of my friends is going to be home alone, I pray God's hand of protection over them.

I don't take these prayers for granted, and I don't say them superstitiously, as if somehow by uttering the words versus not uttering the words would act like a magic charm to protect those I love. I say these prayers because I truly believe that prayer works, that when we put our trust in God, we are putting our trust in the One who can truly protect us and dispatch His angels to guard us in all our ways.

The psalmist says as much as he continues:

> "You will only observe with your eyes and see the punishment of the wicked.
> If you make the Most High your dwelling- even the Lord, who is my refuge-
> then no harm will befall you, no disaster will come near your tent.
> For He will command His angels concerning you to guard you in all your ways;
>
> they will lift you up in their hands, so that you will not strike your foot against a stone.
>
> You will tread upon the lion and the cobra; you will trample the great lion and the serpent.
> 'Because he loves me,' says the Lord, 'I will rescue him; I will protect him, for he acknowledges My name.
> He will call upon Me, and I will answer him; I will be with him in trouble, I will deliver him and honor him.
> With long life will I satisfy him and show him My salvation.'"
> (Psalm 91:8-16)

I don't know about you, but as I read these words, a great peace washes over me. A great comfort and calm comes into my heart. A great trust rises within me. I can breathe a little easier, knowing that God's got this. He's got it all under control. Even when life seems out of control, I can rest in the fact that God is bigger than anything else that can come against me. Nothing can touch me or those I love unless there is some greater purpose He has in mind.

A friend of mine describes God's protection like the guardrails along the far edges of the road on each side to keep us (our lives) from careening off the edge. While there are plenty of obstacles, pitfalls, breakdowns, tickets for speeding, flat tires—multiple things that can and will happen on our journey—ultimately the providential protection of God will indeed keep us on the road He has designed for us.

If you're needing God's protection today, don't worry. As Jesus said,

> "Therefore do not worry about tomorrow, for tomorrow will worry about itself. Each day has enough trouble of its own" (Matthew 6:34).

Instead, put your trust in God. Put your trust in Him for *everything* in your life, as well as the lives of those you love.

Pray that God's hand of protection would be with you as you face the terrors of the night or the arrows that fly by day. Trust that He will command His angels to guard you in all your ways. Know that when you call upon Him, He will answer you. Though a thousand may fall at your side, or ten thousand at your right hand, it will not come near you.

God is worthy of your trust. Keep praying and keep putting your full faith and trust in Him.

Will you pray with me?

Father, thank You for being a refuge and a fortress, a God in whom we can trust. Thank You for walking with us through the craziness of life, promising that when we put our trust in You, You will protect us when we do. Father, help us to keep trusting in You, even when we face terrors at night or arrows during the day, knowing that You are our shield and our rampart, a strong wall that protects everyone who take shelter within. Lord, help us not to worry about tomorrow. Help us not to fear what we face today. Instead, help us to pray, and to keep putting our trust in You, all along the way. In Jesus' name, Amen.

LESSON 20: SINGING PRAYERS   NOVEMBER 3

Scripture Reading: Psalm 96

Sometimes you have to sing your prayers. Music gives your prayers an added dimension, an added lift.

As Hans Christian Andersen said: "Where words fail, music speaks."

When we combine our words with music, it takes our words to a whole new level.

Psalm 96 begins with these words:

> *"Sing to the Lord a new song; sing to the Lord, all the earth" (v. 1).*
> *Then it goes on to list a number of things about which we can sing to Him:*
> *"Sing to the Lord, praise His name; proclaim His salvation day after day.*
> *Declare His glory among the nations, His marvelous deeds among all peoples.*
>
> *For great is the Lord and most worthy of praise; He is to be feared above all gods.*
>
> *For all the gods of the nations are idols, but the Lord made the heavens.*
> *Splendor and majesty are before Him; strength and glory are in His sanctuary.*
>
> *Ascribe to the Lord, O families of nations, ascribe to the Lord glory and strength.*
>
> *Ascribe to the Lord the glory due His name; bring an offering and come into His*

courts.
Worship the Lord in the splendor of His holiness; tremble before Him, all the earth.

Say among the nations, 'The Lord reigns'" (vv. 2-10a).

The psalms were originally songs, as the word psalm *means* "song."

Even more specifically, the word psalm comes from the Greek word "psallein," which means "to pluck," or to play a stringed instrument, such as a harp.

When we sing songs to God today accompanied by the piano or guitar, we're actually doing what people have done for thousands of years: putting words to music to give them an added dimension, an added lift.

How can singing lift your prayer life? How can music make your prayer life more effective?

For starters, it can make your prayers more memorable. I have a friend who had trouble remembering anything. But she said that when she was a child, if someone put an idea to music, she remembered it for life.

There's something about a melody that makes ideas more memorable.

Here in the U.S., when I was a kid, I learned the entire preamble to our constitution because School House Rock set those words to music. Most kids in the U.S. in my generation can sing it by memory still to this day: "We the people, in order to form a more perfect union, establish justice and ensure domestic tranquility…"

We also learned about English in the same way, singing songs like "Conjunction Junction": "Conjunction junction, what's your function? Hooking up words and phrases and clauses."

Advertisers, of course, use music to make their products more memorable, and again, here in the U.S., most people in my generation can fill in the blanks in a song like this:

"Oh, I wish I were an ____ ____ ____,
That is what I truly want to be.
For if I were an ____ ____ ____,
Everyone would be in love with me!"

(For those not from the U.S. or not from my generation, the answer is "Oscar Meyer Wiener," a famous brand of hot dogs here.)

But more than just making words more memorable, by putting our words to music, we can make our words more precise, more specific. By adding rhythm and rhyme to our melodies, we can take deep spiritual truths and turn them into "sound bites" which can speak volumes into people's hearts.

John Newton was a former slave trader who renounced his ways when he put his faith in Christ. When he wrote out his testimony, he did so by combining rhythm and rhyme and setting his words to music. By doing this, people all over the world now know his "testimony in a nutshell," which begins like this:

"Amazing grace! How sweet the sound
That saved a wretch like me.
I once was lost, but now am found,
Was blind but now I see."

When you take time to turn your prayers into songs, you can make your prayers more precise, more specific, and more memorable, too.

Has God put a song in your heart? Is there a way you combine that song with a prayer that's on your heart and sing it out to Him?

My encouragement to you today is to try singing out your prayers to God. Try putting a melody to the thoughts that are within you. Try adding some rhythm and rhyme to make them more precise, specific and memorable.

Try singing a new song to God, as the first line of Psalm 96 encourages us to do:

"Sing to the Lord a new song; sing to the Lord, all the earth"

If you need some ideas for topics, you could use some of the topics that are listed in the rest of the psalm. Sing about His salvation, His glory, or His marvelous deeds. Sing about His creation, the heavens, or His glory and strength. Sing about His splendor, or about what it means to you that "The Lord reigns."

Maybe you play an instrument, maybe you don't. Maybe you have a melody that is uniquely your own, or maybe you can borrow a melody from somewhere else. But if you want to take your prayer life farther and deeper—and help others go farther and deeper in their prayer lives, too—consider "singing a new song to the Lord."

When you do, you'll find that the words you speak to God will be more precise, specific and memorable, maybe even being repeated and sung by others to help take their prayer lives farther and deeper as well.

Will you pray with me?

Father, thank You for giving us music and rhythm and rhyme. Thank You for putting songs in our hearts that others have written to take our own prayer lives deeper and farther than we could on our own. Help us to bring out new songs from our hearts as well, so that we can give expression to our thoughts in a way that goes beyond the words themselves. When our words fail or seem to fall short, help us to put them to music to give them an added dimension, a lift. Speak to us, as we consider new ways to speak to You. In Jesus' name, Amen.

P.S. One of the reasons I've been setting the Psalms to classical music this year is to give them an added dimension, an added lift, too. If you haven't listened yet to any of the songs from Lana's Psalms that go with this devotional, I hope you will! I love the result! You can listen anytime at theranch.org or wherever music is streamed or sold.

LESSON 21: PRAISING PRAYERS — NOVEMBER 4

Scripture Reading: Psalm 103

We're looking through the psalms to find ways to make our prayer lives more effective. One of the most powerful ways is to include "praise" in our prayers, to include some words of acknowledgement that God is worthy of our praise. Doing so has benefits for us and for God.

If you've ever been in a conversation with someone that has *not* included any kind of praise and has *not* included any thoughts or words of thankfulness or gratefulness on any level, you know how hard such conversations can be.

But a spoonful of sugar really does help the medicine go down, as Mary Poppins sings. More than that, your words of praise will help to recapture the best of your relationship with God, a relationship built on trust that He is worthy of your praise, and that you are the apple of His eye—no matter what your circumstances may be.

Psalm 103 gives us an example of a prayer filled with praise, a prayer that opens and closes with the words, "Praise the Lord, O my soul." This psalm of David begins like this:

"Praise the Lord, O my soul; all my inmost being, praise His holy name.
Praise the Lord, O my soul, and forget not all His benefits—
who forgives all your sins and heals all your diseases,
who redeems your life from the pit and crowns you with love and compassion,

who satisfies your desires with good things so that your youth is renewed like the eagle's" (Psalm 103:1-5).

One thing I especially love about this psalm is that David's words of praise seem to be truly flowing from the depths of his being. His words aren't simply in the category of saying something just to "fake it till you make it." His words are true words of praise, words of faith. "Faith it till you make it" might be more like it, as David truly puts his trust in God's goodness and God's benefits.

"Praise the Lord, O my soul; all my inmost being, praise His holy name," David says. Then he begins to list God's benefits specifically:

- *who forgives all your sins and heals all your diseases,*
- *who redeems your life from the pit and crowns you with love and compassion,*
- *who satisfies your desires with good things so that your youth is renewed like the eagle's.*

David had seen God do each of these things. He had seen God forgive his sins. He had seen God heal his diseases. He had seen God redeem his life from the pit, crown him with love and compassion, and satisfy his desires with good things. David remembered what God had done in the past, and trusted God to do so again in the future.

If you've noticed my prayers at the end of these messages, you'll see that I often start with the words "Father, thank You…" and then go on to list some of the things for which I am truly grateful to God. I have journals filled with these types of prayers. Not because my days are always so rosy and cheery, but because I've made a commitment to myself to try to begin my prayers with words of thanks to God, no matter what else might be going on in my life.

Sometimes I have to push aside the things that are pressing down on me so I can find some words of praise. I know they're within me. I just have to bring them out. So I'll start by writing the words, "Father, thank You…" and think of something that has happened in the past 24 or 48 hours for which I am truly thankful.

This morning, my prayer would go something like this: "Father, thank you for my daughter coming home for this weekend. Thank You for my family gathering together and eating and laughing and crying and watching movies. Thank You for the sunny days when we could be outside and for the rainy ones when everything was watered well."

If this was all you were to read in my journal, you would think I had a most blissful weekend. All in all, it was quite pleasant. But if you read further, you'd find that there were multiple concerns that were on my heart: accidents and injuries, bills that need to be paid, and relationships that need to be ironed out.

If your life is like mine, it's usually a mixed bag of things which are praiseworthy and things which are difficult. By praising God on the front end, however, and praising God again at the end of the conversation, I find it brings balance to my prayers, encouragement to my soul, and blessings to both God's heart and my own.

If you need some ideas to prime the pump of praise in your prayer life, read through Psalm 103. See if you can say any of the words of that psalm with true praise from the depths of your being. Then let your faith begin to flow, putting your trust in God once again for everything in your life.

I'm going to do this myself today as well. If you'd like, you can pray though the rest of Psalm 103 with me here, as I look through the words of David and turn each line that resonates with my heart into a prayer of praise to God. As I often start in my journal, I'll just start with the words, "Father, thank You..." then I'll begin to list those things from this psalm which I can truly say with words of praise from my heart.

Will you pray with me?

Father, thank You...

- *that You are compassionate and gracious, slow to anger, and abounding in love.*
- *that You will not always accuse, nor will You hold Your anger against us forever.*
- *that You don't treat us as our sins deserve.*
- *that as far as the east is from the west, so far have You removed our sins from us.*
- *that You have compassion on us, as a father has compassion on his children.*
- *that even though our days are like grass and quickly forgotten, Your love is everlasting.*

Thank You for being so worthy of our praise. We praise You Lord, from the depths of our souls. We praise Your holy name. In Jesus' name, Amen.

LESSON 22: AVENGING PRAYERS   NOVEMBER 5

Scripture Reading: Psalm 109

Is it ever okay to ask God to bring vengeance on someone who is acting maliciously toward us? If David's prayers are any indication of what we can or can't ask of God, then the answer is "Yes."

It's not an easy answer, though, as God's viewpoint on our troubles is not always the same as our own. We can sometimes be wrong in our assessment of others, and we can sometimes minimize our own guilt while magnifying the guilt of others.

Still, there are times when the malice of others is so evil, so awful, and so clear, that it is altogether fitting and proper to ask God to intervene on our behalf, to spare us from further harm, and to bring about justice on those who are acting contemptuously.

Listen to David's prayer in Psalm 109 and see what you think. David begins by explaining the problem as he sees it:

> *"O God, whom I praise, do not remain silent,*
> *for wicked and deceitful men have opened their mouths against me;*
> *they have spoken against me with lying tongues.*
> *With words of hatred they surround me; they attack me without cause.*
> *In return for my friendship they accuse me, but I am a man of prayer.*
> *They repay me evil for good, and hatred for my friendship"* (vv. 1-4).

So far, so good. The harder part for me to read is what David says next, when he begins to ask God about very specific ways he wants God to intervene! Listen to David's boldness:

> *"Appoint an evil man to oppose him; let an accuser stand at his right hand.*
> *When he is tried, let him be found guilty, and may his prayers condemn him.*
> *May his days be few; may another take his place of leadership.*
> *May his children be fatherless and his wife a widow.*
> *May his children be wandering beggars; may they be driven from their ruined homes.*
>
> *May a creditor seize all he has; may strangers plunder the fruits of his labor.*
> *May no one extend kindness to him or take pity on his fatherless children.*
> *May his descendants be cut off, their names blotted out from the next generation.*
>
> *May the iniquity of his fathers be remembered before the Lord; may the sin of his mother never be blotted out.*
> *May their sins always remain before the Lord, that he may cut off the memory of them from the earth.*
> *For he never thought of doing a kindness, but hounded to death the poor and the needy and the brokenhearted.*
> *He loved to pronounce a curse- may it come on him; he found no pleasure in blessing- may it be far from him.*
> *He wore cursing as his garment; it entered into his body like water, into his bones like oil.*
> *May it be like a cloak wrapped about him, like a belt tied forever around him.*
> *May this be the Lord's payment to my accusers, to those who speak evil of me"* (vv. 5-20).

Those are some pretty strong words! But there have been occasions in my life where I have felt like saying some strong words like that to God in prayer, too. And if we're going to be honest in our conversations with God, part of being honest means saying things that might not sound as holy or as pious as we think we should sound.

And the truth is, calling on God to bring a stop to wickedness IS holy and pious. Jesus didn't hold back from calling a spade a spade when He said things like,

> *"You snakes! You brood of vipers!"* (Matthew 23:33)

or

> *"You travel over land and sea to win a single convert, and when he becomes one, you make him twice as much a son of hell as you are"* (Matthew 23:15).

There are times when we might need to call a spade a spade, too, asking God to intervene to bring an end to wickedness.

I like calling prayers like these "avenging prayers" because asking God to bring about vengeance is different than taking revenge on someone ourselves. God is the ultimate judge and calling on Him for justice is calling on Him to do one of the things He is fully qualified and fully capable of doing.

Noah Webster, in his 1828 dictionary, said this about the difference between the words avenge and revenge:

> "To avenge and revenge, radically, are synonymous. But modern usage inclines to make a valuable distinction in the use of these words, restricting avenge to the taking of just punishment, and revenge to the infliction of pain or evil, maliciously, in an illegal manner."

Calling on God to take action to do what is right and just is very different than asking someone to do something underhanded and equally evil or malicious in return for what they've done to us.

Like David, when I've come to the place where I've had to call on God to bring an end to something evil or wicked that is happening around me, I've taken careful stock of the situation and the people involved first, then I've asked God to bring about justice on His terms. And, at times, I have seen Him act surprisingly swiftly in response.

In one situation, a man was repeatedly abusing those around him, including me. The man refused to respond to civil requests to cease and desist and refused to back down from his destructive tirades. When I finally got the courage to call on God to bring an end to his swath of destruction, two days later the man resigned from his position and left town. It was as if God had answered my prayer in a way that David wanted God to answer his, when David said:

> "May his days be few; may another take his place of leadership."

God is gracious. God is loving. God is kind. Yet, He does not leave the guilty unpunished. As the Bible says:

> "The Lord, the Lord, the compassionate and gracious God, slow to anger, abounding in love and faithfulness, maintaining love to thousands, and forgiving wickedness, rebellion and sin. Yet He does not leave the guilty unpunished" (Exodus 34:6b-7a).

I sat in a courtroom one day when a friend of mine was on trial. I was there to testify to his good traits, but I was also there to admit that he had made some really bad decisions that were very harmful to others. While I wanted the judge to be lenient in some ways, I also didn't want the judge to ignore the harmful things that had been done.

In reading the verdict, the judge commended my friend for the good he had done, and the judge offered the court's help to turn my friend's life around. Yet the judge also said, wisely:

> "The people in this room who have come to support you think you're a good person, and frankly, I believe you're a good person, too, but one who's made some bad decisions. And this court and our society and those you have wronged are not going to tolerate the commission of crimes. There may have been issues in your life that

contributed to those decisions, but there are always going to be issues. This verdict is to get your attention, to require you to make restitution for the wrongs you've done, and to help you to turn your life around."

I felt the judge's sentence was extremely fair, well-reasoned, and compassionate, yet he did not leave the guilty unpunished.

I am thankful that God, being the best judge, is willing to step in and intervene in situations where it would be dangerous and potentially even more destructive for us to try to take matters into our own hands. That's when avenging prayers come in, calling on God to bring about justice. As the Apostle Paul says in the book of Romans:

"Do not repay anyone evil for evil. Be careful to do what is right in the eyes of everybody. If it is possible, as far as it depends on you, live at peace with everyone. Do not take revenge, my friends, but leave room for God's wrath, for it is written: 'It is mine to avenge; I will repay,' says the Lord" (Romans 12:17-19).

Will you pray with me?

Father, thank You that You are a good Father and a good Judge. Lord, for those who have wronged us, help us to call on You for help in bringing about justice and bringing about a change in their hearts. Help us to step out of harm's way and let You step in to take up our cause. We pray that You would bring an end to the wickedness of those who are acting maliciously against us, and that You would cause Your light to drive out any remaining darkness. In Jesus' name, Amen.

LESSON 23: FEARLESS PRAYERS NOVEMBER 6

Scripture Reading: Psalm 112

Last weekend, I shared my testimony with the largest live audience I've ever shared with before. Needless to say, I was more than a little bit nervous.

But I took comfort from two things that I'd like to share with you today: 1) that a healthy fear of God is more important than an unhealthy fear of people and 2) that fearless prayers lead to incredible blessings.

You'll find these same principles at work in Psalm 112, which begins with these words:

"Praise the Lord. Blessed is the man who fears the Lord,
who finds great delight in His commands.
His children will be mighty in the land;
the generation of the upright will be blessed" (vv. 1-2).

A healthy fear of God leads to all kinds of blessings. Why? Because following God and His ways inevitably leads to an abundant life, both here on earth and in heaven forever. God doesn't give us His wisdom—His commands—to hold us back from the fullest life possible, but to bless us with the fullest life possible.

Listen to the blessings that Psalm 112 says will follow when we fear God and take delight in His commands:

"Wealth and riches are in his house,
and his righteousness endures forever.

> *Even in darkness light dawns for the upright,*
> *for the gracious and compassionate and righteous man.*
> *Good will come to him who is generous and lends freely,*
> *who conducts his affairs with justice.*
> *Surely he will never be shaken;*
> *a righteous man will be remembered forever.*
> *He will have no fear of bad news;*
> *his heart is steadfast, trusting in the Lord.*
> *His heart is secure, he will have no fear;*
> *in the end he will look in triumph on his foes.*
> *He has scattered abroad his gifts to the poor,*
> *his righteousness endures forever;*
> *his horn will be lifted high in honor" (vv 3-9).*

And listen to what happens when we don't take delight in God's ways:

> *"The wicked man will see and be vexed,*
> *he will gnash his teeth and waste away;*
> *the longings of the wicked will come to nothing" (v. 10).*

Does this mean that only good will come to those who follow God, and only bad will come to those who don't? Of course not. A simple look at anyone who has committed their life wholeheartedly to their Father in heaven shows that sometimes bad things happen to the best of people, Jesus being the prime example. But listen to what Jesus has to say about a healthy fear of God:

> *"Do not be afraid of those who kill the body but cannot kill the soul. Rather, be afraid of the One who can destroy both soul and body in hell. Are not two sparrows sold for a penny? Yet not one of them will fall to the ground apart from the will of your Father. And even the very hairs of your head are all numbered. So don't be afraid; you are worth more than many sparrows" (Matthew 10:28-31).*

When I told a friend a few months ago that I was asked to share my testimony in front of this live audience, my friend said, "Aren't you afraid?" I said that I was, but that I loved talking about Jesus more than anything else, for it is in Him that I've found my hope—and I couldn't wait to share that hope with others.

I said, "If telling people about the most closely held secret of my life means that I can also tell people about how Jesus has worked in my life, then it's worth it. It's not that I'm *not* afraid. I am. I'm just compelled to push through my fears to share what Jesus has done for me."

The truth is, there's coming a day when everyone's secrets will be made known. Everyone's sins will be revealed. My hope is that by revealing *now* how Jesus has helped me to deal with my secrets, others will put their faith in Him so they can deal with theirs.

As Jesus said in the same passage I referenced above:

> *"So do not be afraid of them. There is nothing concealed that will not be disclosed or hidden that will not be made known. What I tell you in the dark, speak in the daylight; what is whispered in your ear, proclaim from the roofs.... Whoever acknowledges Me before men, I will also acknowledge him before My Father in heaven. But whoever*

disowns Me before men, I will disown him before My Father in heaven" (vv. 26-27, 32-33).

Just listening to Jesus' words reminds me that the words I speak, and the words I don't speak, are massively important and eternally significant. We can be afraid of those who can kill our bodies, or we can be afraid of the One who can send both body and soul to hell.

As the days got closer for me to share my testimony last week, my fear factor kept increasing. But I took great comfort in the two truths I shared with you at the beginning of this message: 1) that a healthy fear of God is more important than an unhealthy fear of people and 2) that fearless prayers lead to incredible blessings, both for us and for all those around us.

Are there some fearless prayers you need to say today?

And if so, will you pray with me?

Father, thank You for reminding us that we can come to You with our fears, and that as we pray boldly, You can reduce our fears immeasurably, knowing that You will bless those who walk in Your ways. Father, help us to be bold in our witness to You. Help us to share with others the hope we have found in You. Help us to pray fearless prayers, knowing that You will answer those prayers with incredible blessings, both for us and for all those around us. In Jesus' name, Amen.

LESSON 24: DAILY PRAYERS NOVEMBER 7

Scripture Reading: Psalm 118

There are many famous quotes in the Bible, especially in the book of Psalms. But there's one quote in Psalm 118 that helps keep me going each day. The quote is this:

"This is the day the Lord has made; let us rejoice and be glad in it" (v. 24).

I've talked several times in these messages about *special* prayers you can say to God when you're facing *special* problems. But today I'd like to focus on the value of *daily* prayers, *thanking God for each day you're alive.*

Thanking God for each day is not only important when things are going good, but also when things are going bad.

I've mentioned in one of my earlier messages that a few months before my wife died, a film team asked if I would be willing to record a short message to offer hope to others facing terminal illness. I didn't think I could do it, as I was still trying to find my own reason for hope in the face of the most significant loss in my life.

But I agreed to do the interview, and at one point during the filming, God filled me with incredible hope for myself, too. I was finally able to say that even if the unthinkable happened to my wife, I knew God would still have a reason for me to live.

"My role," I said, "is to find that reason, fulfill that reason, and walk in that reason."

While it was a struggle for me to finally get to that point, trying to imagine living life without her, I truly believed those words were true. And here I am, five years later, having found that reason again, fulfilling that reason, and walking in that reason. God has continued to call me to purposeful living, day after day after day.

I know there's a reason that I'm here. And I know there's a reason you're here, too. This *really is* "the day the Lord has made." I am so thankful for today, and I am continuing to rejoice and be glad in it.

What about you? What kind of day are you facing today? What is God speaking to you, calling you to do and think and be? I know it can be hard some days to believe that God has a calling on your life, but God *really does* want you to know your purpose for living even more than you want to know it. And He *really does* wants you to live THIS day to the fullest, too.

Let me encourage you to say a fresh prayer to God again today, committing THIS day to live for Him and saying, "This is the day the Lord has made; I will rejoice and be glad in it." Then say it again tomorrow, and the next day, and the next, and the next, so that you can keep making the most of *every day* the Lord your God gives to you.

If you need some help in your heart to do this, here are a few cues from the writer of Psalm 118 for how he was able to do it, even when life had him on the ropes at times.

He remembered God's love endures forever:

"Give thanks to the Lord, for He is good; His love endures forever.
Let Israel say: 'His love endures forever.'
Let the house of Aaron say: 'His love endures forever.'
Let those who fear the Lord say: 'His love endures forever'" (vv. 1-4).

He remembered how God had set him free:

"In my anguish I cried to the Lord, and He answered by setting me free.
The Lord is with me; I will not be afraid. What can man do to me?" (vv. 5-6).

He remembered that God is God and not anyone else:

"The Lord is with me; He is my helper. I will look in triumph on my enemies.
It is better to take refuge in the Lord than to trust in man.
It is better to take refuge in the Lord than to trust in princes.
All the nations surrounded me, but in the name of the Lord I cut them off.
They surrounded me on every side, but in the name of the Lord I cut them off.

They swarmed around me like bees, but they died out as quickly as burning thorns; in the name of the Lord I cut them off.
I was pushed back and about to fall, but the Lord helped me" (vv. 7-13).

He remembered who gave Him his voice to sing and to praise:

"The Lord is my strength and my song; He has become my salvation.
Shouts of joy and victory resound in the tents of the righteous: 'The Lord's right hand has done mighty things!
The Lord's right hand is lifted high; the Lord's right hand has done mighty things!'

I will not die but live and will proclaim what the Lord has done.
The Lord has chastened me severely, but He has not given me over to death" (vv. 14-18).

He remembered the Lord with thankfulness:

"Open for me the gates of righteousness; I will enter and give thanks to the Lord.

This is the gate of the Lord through which the righteous may enter.
I will give You thanks, for You answered me; You have become my salvation" (vv. 19-21).

He remembered the Lord for doing miracles:

The stone the builders rejected has become the capstone; the Lord has done this, and it is marvelous in our eyes" (vv. 22-23).

And he remembered that THIS is the day the Lord has made:

"This is the day the Lord has made; let us rejoice and be glad in it" (v. 24).

If you need to get your mojo back, do what this psalmist did, and do it daily. Remember that God's love endures forever. Remember that He has set you free. Remember that He is God and not anyone else. Remember that He is the one who gave you your voice to sing and to praise.

Remember the Lord with thankfulness. Remember the Lord for His miracles. And remember that THIS is the day the Lord has made. Let us rejoice and be glad in it.

Will you pray with me?

Father, thank You for giving us another day of life. Thank You for giving us a purpose and meaning for today and hope for our future. Thank You for Your eagerness to reveal that purpose and meaning and hope to each one of us. Help us to walk out the calling that You have in mind for us, living each day to the fullest and fulfilling every single thing You want us to fulfill. In Jesus' name, Amen.

LESSON 25: PEACEFUL PRAYERS   NOVEMBER 8

Scripture Reading: Psalm 122

We have six more lessons in the book of Psalms, as we learn about prayer and how to make our prayer lives more effective. As we pull into this final stretch, I think today is a good time to talk about recognizing God's answers to our prayers when they come.

Sometimes we're praying for something intensely, expecting the answer to come in a certain way. But when the answer *does* come, we sometimes don't recognize it, because it comes in a way we hadn't expected.

Today's lesson highlights this point, as the topic is praying for peace. "Peace" is a funny thing. I've seen people who are in the midst of chaos, with pandemonium all around them, yet who are experiencing true peace. But I've also seen people who are in the midst of extreme calm, with utter stillness all around them, yet who are experiencing true turmoil.

When we pray for peace, we sometimes miss God's answer when it comes, because God makes His peace available to us in ways we don't always grasp.

First, I want to look at the importance of praying for peace in our circumstances and how God can truly answer those prayers. But second, I want to look at the importance of praying for peace *regardless* of our circumstances and how God can truly answer those prayers, too.

In Psalm 122, David encourages people to pray for the peace of Jerusalem. For a man who had lived most of his life fighting battles against his enemies, I'm sure his prayers for peace were heartfelt. In Psalm 122, David says:

> "Pray for the peace of Jerusalem: 'May those who love you be secure.
> May there be peace within your walls and security within your citadels.'
> For the sake of my brothers and friends, I will say, 'Peace be within you.'" (vv. 6-8).

What I love about David's prayer for peace is that God answered those prayers! After years of fighting war after war after war, David *did* experience peace in Jerusalem. As it says in the book of 2 Samuel:

> "...the Lord had given him rest from all his enemies around him" (2 Samuel 7:1b).

And the peace that David prayed for and experienced lasted into the next generation, as his son, Solomon, later said this after he had become king:

> "But now the Lord my God has given me rest on every side, and there is no adversary or disaster" (1 Kings 5:4).

Praise God that He answers our prayers for peace in very physical and tangible ways!

I'd also like to point out, however, that God answers our prayers for peace in ways we sometimes miss because we're expecting that peace to come in another form.

One night, my family was invited by a Jewish man to take part in his family's Seder Meal, the traditional Passover Meal which is celebrated by Jewish people every year.

At the end of the meal, the man who had invited us asked if we had any questions. Since so many of the traditions he talked about referred to the long-awaited Messiah, I asked him what he thought of Jesus—and why he didn't think Jesus *is* that long-awaited Messiah.

He answered, "When the Messiah comes, he will bring peace. As I look around, I don't see peace. So clearly Jesus can't be the Messiah we're looking for."

While I appreciated his answer, I couldn't help thinking that he had missed the fact that was so apparent to me: Jesus *did* bring peace! But the kind of peace this man was expecting wasn't the kind of peace that Jesus brought.

Here's how Jesus described the peace He has offered to each one of us:

> "Peace I leave with you; My peace I give you. I do not give to you as the world gives. Do not let your hearts be troubled and do not be afraid ... I have told you these things, so that in Me you may have peace. In this world you will have trouble. But take heart! I have overcome the world" (John 14:27, 16:33).

The peace Jesus describes is the same peace I experienced when I first put my faith in Him—and which I've continued to experience still, over 30 years later. Had I not experienced this miraculous peace of Christ in my heart, I might still be waiting for another Messiah, too—one who could give me peace as the world gives peace.

But because I've experienced the peace of Christ, I am fully convinced He *is* the Messiah—because no one else could give me the kind of peace that He has given to me.

The Apostle Paul describes this inner peace—and how to get it—like this:

> "Do not be anxious about anything, but in everything, by prayer and petition, with thanksgiving, present your requests to God. And the peace of God, which transcends

all understanding, will guard your hearts and your minds in Christ Jesus" (Philippians 4:6-7).

This peace has carried me through sickness and job loss, anger and fear. It has carried me through tornadoes and hurricanes, mishaps and miscarriages. It has carried me through grief and despair, sorrow and sadness.

Praise God that He answers our prayers for peace in ways that transcend understanding, no matter what is going on in the world around us!

If you need peace today, let me encourage you to pray for it. Put your faith in Christ for everything in your life, from the forgiveness of your sins to the circumstances that you're facing today. Pray for God to bring peace into your heart. Pray for God to bring peace to the world around you. And like David, pray for the peace of Jerusalem, even today.

Know that God *can* and *will* answer each and every prayer you pray. Then don't miss His answer when it does come–as it may come in a way you never expected!

Will you pray with me?

Father, thank You for offering us Your peace–a peace that passes understanding–and for making it available to each and every one of us. Help us to know and to experience Your peace in our hearts. Help us to know and experience Your peace in the world around us. And help us to see Your peace come upon the city of Jerusalem, the city where Jesus the Messiah lived and died and rose again from the dead. We pray all of this in His precious name, Amen.

LESSON 26: BUILDING PRAYERS — NOVEMBER 9

Scripture Reading: Psalm 127

I am a futurist. By that, I mean I spend a good deal of time thinking about the future. In fact, I was employed by a Fortune 10 corporation for about 10 years with the specific purpose of advising them on the future of various computer technologies and how those technologies would impact their corporation.

I worked with researchers at Apple and IBM, MIT and NASA. I read papers, went to conferences, and subscribed to dozens of magazines and mailing lists devoted to the study of the future. In many ways, I am now living in the world that I foresaw 30 years ago when I first began doing this type of research.

The funny thing about the future, though, is that we can only predict so much. We're not omniscient—or all knowing—like God is. Without Him, our predictions about the future are only best guesses based on what we can see and the trends that are taking shape.

If we're going to have any success at predicting the future—and making the most of those predictions—we need God to guide us. There's nothing sadder, as others have wisely said, than to spend your whole life climbing the ladder of success only to find, once you reach the top, that your ladder is leaning against the wrong wall.

King Solomon put it like this in Psalm 127:

"Unless the Lord builds the house, its builders labor in vain. Unless the Lord watches over the city, the watchmen stand guard in vain. In vain you rise early and stay up late, toiling for food to eat…" (Psalm 127:1-2a).

How can we know if our ladder is up against the right wall? How can we know if the Lord is in our building projects, or if we're just spinning our wheels needlessly? As Stephen Covey says:

> *"If the ladder is not leaning against the right wall, every step we take just gets us to the wrong place faster."*

I don't know about you, but I don't want to get to the wrong place faster! I don't want to get to the top of the ladder only to realize my ladder is up against the wrong wall! I want every step I take to move me forward, not backward.

But how can I know if the things I'm doing are really what God wants me to do?

That's where "building" prayers come in: prayers to God to show me if the house I'm working on is the house God *wants* me to work on—or if it's time to move on.

By staying in touch with the Father on a regular and consistent basis, He can guide our steps. He can show us if we're headed down the right path, and He can turn us around if we find we're on the wrong one.

I've worked on many houses over my lifetime—literal houses—cleaning, restoring, remodeling, and renovating them. None of them for pay. All of them for love. I've worked on houses for my own family, for my extended family, and for others to enjoy. Each and every time, I have to ask God, "Is this a project You really want me to take on?" Because it's way too much work to spin my wheels endlessly.

And I can say that each time, I have reached various points where I have seriously questioned if God has really asked me to work on it or not. Each and every time, I've reached points where I've had to return to God, again and again, asking for His guidance, His wisdom, and His strength, because it takes way too much time, effort, and resources if He's *not* in it.

I'd like to say I've never wasted one minute, never wasted one penny, never wasted one ounce of strength. I'd like to say those things, but I can't. I've had to regroup and backtrack too many times for that to be the case.

But what I can say is this: there's not one minute I've spent in prayer that hasn't been well-invested. There's not one penny for God's thoughts that hasn't made a return. There's not one ounce of effort on my knees before God that hasn't given me strength. Even though I've made mistakes along the way, and even though I've begun to climb some ladders God hasn't wanted me to climb, He has always helped to redirect me to the ladders He *has* wanted me to climb.

Sometimes God redirects me in ways that are subtle and gentle, other times in ways that are abrupt and painful. But always, He redirects me in ways that keep moving me forward in the right direction for my life—His direction.

There are times when I've been tempted to think that I've just wasted months of energy—mental, physical, and spiritual energy. But at those times, God has reminded me of this:

Time spent seeking My will with all your heart, soul, mind and strength is never wasted. It's always invested, and it will pay huge rewards for years to come.

What about you? What kinds of "houses" are you building where you need God's guidance? Are you building your job? Your career? Your house? Your health? Are you building a relationship? A friendship? A mentorship? A family? Are there some ladders you're climbing where it would be helpful to know if they're up against the right walls or not?

If so, let me encourage you to pray. Pray some "building" prayers of your own. Ask God for His wisdom, His strength, and His resources to either keep you moving forward or to show if it's time to start climbing another ladder.

One of the most beautiful promises God offers in this psalm comes at the end of the verses I quoted from King Solomon earlier. Here are those verses again, this time with God's promise included at the end of them:

> "Unless the Lord builds the house, its builders labor in vain. Unless the Lord watches over the city, the watchmen stand guard in vain. In vain you rise early and stay up late, toiling for food to eat—for He grants sleep to those He loves" (Psalm 127:1-2).

There have been a few times, even this week, where I have been working on a project and God has simply said, "Now's the time to rest." I've protested: "But I've got so much more to do!" And God has said, "Sometimes the best next thing you can do is to get some rest." And I've literally gone back to bed for a while.

I don't know about you, but I don't want to be building *anything* in vain. I don't want to rise early and stay up late in vain. I want every moment to count. And sometimes that means getting some rest so you'll be fresh to start "building" again.

God has reminded me this past week again that if I'll keep bringing my projects to Him in prayer—keep putting my efforts into His hands—He'll make the most of every one. He'll guide me when I need guidance. He'll redirect my steps when I need redirecting. And He will give me rest when I need rest, too.

Keep coming to God in prayer. Keep asking Him for *His* direction. And keep trusting that the time you spend seeking God's will is never wasted. It's always invested, and it will pay huge rewards for years to come.

Will you pray with me?

Father, thank You for promising to never leave us alone. Thank You for walking with us every step of the way. We pray that You would guide us today as we move forward with the projects that are on our hearts. Show us which ones are on Your heart, too, and help us to work on them, with You, together. Father, we look forward to the future, knowing that we won't be alone there, either, knowing that You will be with us always, even to the end of the age. In Jesus' name, Amen.

LESSON 27: QUIETING PRAYERS — NOVEMBER 10

Scripture Reading: Psalm 131

Susanna Wesley had 19 children, two of whom went on to found the Methodist church. How did she ever find a place to spend quiet time with God?

Easy! She sat in a chair and threw her apron over her head! Her children knew not to disturb her during her prayer time.

My late wife Lana and I had six children. Lana was so encouraged when she heard that story about Susanna Wesley that she decided she could make a quiet place in our home to meet with God, too (she didn't have an apron). She cleaned out a 2-1/2 by 2-1/2 square foot space in our closet and laid some blankets on the floor to make it soft. She added a box of tissues, some worship music, and a bag of Nestle Caramel Treasures.

Whenever she needed some quiet time, she would go into her prayer closet, close the door, and put on her music. She read her Bible, sang, prayed, laughed, cried and even danced in that little space. She found it quieted her soul and gave her strength to go on with the day. Lana later recorded a message, called My Prayer Closet, about why she created this special space and how it helped her in her walk with God.

Today's psalm contains a similar theme. In Psalm 131, David says that he "stilled and quieted his soul." Listen to his words in this, one of the shortest psalms in the Bible:

> *"My heart is not proud, O Lord,*
> *my eyes are not haughty;*
> *I do not concern myself with great matters*
> *or things too wonderful for me.*
> *But I have stilled and quieted my soul;*
> *like a weaned child with its mother,*
> *like a weaned child is my soul within me.*
> *O Israel, put your hope in the Lord*
> *both now and forevermore"* (Psalm 131:1-3).

Although this is a short psalm, it packs a lot of wisdom into those three short verses about quieting your soul.

David begins by saying, "my heart is not proud" and "my eyes are not haughty." It's amazing how pride can cause our souls to become stressed or distressed.

When we worry about how we'll look in the eyes of others, we can quickly lose our peace. Our minds become preoccupied with how to avoid being thought of as "less than" or "a failure" or "dumb." We spend money we don't have to impress others or eat more than we should to make ourselves feel better. We often end up on losing more than we gain, digging ourselves into even deeper difficulties.

If we can take a cue from David instead, we would pray that our hearts would not be proud, and our eyes would not be haughty. With nothing to lose in terms of trying to impress others, we can save ourselves from a great deal of grief. By embracing who we are, and not who we aren't, we can find peace and contentment that can't be found in any other way.

David goes on to say, "I do not concern myself with great matters or things too wonderful for me." This may sound anathema in today's culture, but sometimes we need to lay down our striving for "great things," in order to gain something even greater: our peace. With so much to do and so much to accomplish, we sometimes miss the joy of doing those things along the way. I'm all for trying to make the most out of life, but that also means stopping from time to time and asking God what *His* agenda is for you each day.

I've sometimes been stunned, when praying through my list of things to do, that God will highlight only *one* of them for me to work on for that particular day. "Just do this one thing," God seems to be saying, "and you can have the rest of the day to do whatever else you want." I've found it incredibly freeing, both mentally and physically, to let God set my agenda for the day.

Then David says those words I love the most in this psalm: "But I have stilled and quieted my soul; like a weaned child with its mother, like a weaned child is my soul within me."

One of the most peaceful things I've ever witnessed in my life is my wife nursing our children. She would often nurse them for months and even years until they no longer felt the need to nurse. They knew they could come to their mother any time for the peace and comfort of being held in her arms, even after they had been weaned. That calm and peaceful feeling they had while resting in their mother's arms was available to them long after the nursing was over. There is, perhaps, no picture in my mind that is more peaceful.

How can we have that kind of peace with God? By saying "quieting" prayers. By coming to Him not only when we have a great need, but even at those times when we simply want to rest in His arms, to let Him hold onto us, to let Him pull us in close. Even as I write this, I'm encouraging myself to just let God hold onto me, calming me with His peace. I encourage you to do the same, just like David encouraged his fellow Israelites to do with God in the last words of this psalm:

> "O Israel, put your hope in the Lord both now and forevermore."

Where are you putting your hope today? If you're putting it in yourself, and your ambitions, and your appearance or accomplishments or achievements, you'll find your peace will be elusive and can falter as quickly as any of those things can falter. But if you'll put your hope in the Lord, both now and forevermore, you can find peace, no matter what else happens to you in life.

Like Susanna Wesley, who found peace in the midst of a houseful of children by simply putting her apron over her head, you and I can find peace by coming to God anytime in prayer.

Ask God to quiet your soul today. Ask Him to give you His peace. Keep putting your hope in Him, both now and forevermore.

Will you pray with me?

Father, thank You for David's example of quieting his soul in the midst of his building, ruling, and defending a great nation. Lord, thank You for the examples of people like Susanna Wesley and my wife Lana who were able to carve out spaces and places to find peace in the midst of their own busy lives. Help each one of us to do the same, starting today. Quiet our souls and help us find peace even now as we pray. In Jesus' name, Amen.

LESSON 28: SEARCHING PRAYERS   NOVEMBER 11

Scripture Reading: Psalm 139

One of the most intimate moments I've ever had in a conversation with God came while reading today's psalm, Psalm 139.

I was on a ski trip with my family in northern Illinois. I had just quit my secular job to go into full-time ministry. I had quit my job by faith, knowing that God had called me to do it, but not because I had anything particular lined up ahead of time to do next. I only knew that God wanted me to seek Him, day by day, and to stay as close as possible to Him.

I had no special resources tucked away for this time without a job: only about 10 days' worth of salary in the bank and three kids at home. Because we had planned this trip months in advance with another family and had already paid for it, we decided to go, but I was extra nervous about the idea of skiing as I had also given up my health insurance when I quit. If any of us had any kind of accident on the slopes, we would be completely on our own.

When it came time to ski, I sent my family with the other family to the hills, but I stayed back at the rental house to pray. Although I felt as close to God as I had ever been, my level of anxiety about the future was equally high.

As I began to pray, God showed me my next step—and it petrified me. He wanted me to take the 10 days' worth of salary in the bank and invest it in a trip to Israel, a country I had never visited before, and a country I had never even *considered* visiting before. I felt stretched in my faith beyond anything I had ever known before, and I thought I would break. "This couldn't really be what God is saying, is it?" I thought.

I laid down on the couch to take a break from praying when God spoke to my heart in a way that I can only describe as very personal. He knew my anxiety level was at an all-time high, and He wanted to reassure me that yes, He was with me in this, too. He said, very quietly, "Open your Bible, Eric, and read the third line down."

"Open it to where?" I thought.

"Just open it," He said, "and look at the third line down."

"Are you serious, God? This is not a game! This is not Bible roulette!"

But not knowing what else to do, I did what I felt He was saying. Still lying down on the couch, I opened my Bible and looked at the passage on the page. It began with these words:

"O Lord, You have searched me and You know me.
You know when I sit and when I rise; You perceive my thoughts from afar.
You discern my going out and my lying down; You are familiar with all my ways" (vv. 1-3).

There I was, lying down on the couch, and as I read the third line down, two words leapt out as if they were emblazoned with fire, supported by all the other words I had just read:

"You discern my going out and my LYING DOWN; You are familiar with all my ways."

It wasn't just "like" God was speaking to me, God WAS speaking to me! If you've ever had a moment where you know that you know that God is real, that He is right there with you, and that He has something very, very important to say to you, this was that kind of moment.

Immediately I was flooded with peace. With comfort. With full trust, knowing that as long as I stayed close to God, He would lead me and walk me through anything He ever called me to do.

As I read the rest of the psalm, I saw that God knew me better than I could ever know myself, that there was nothing hidden from Him, and that there was no where I could go where He would not come with me.

Over the following days and weeks, I followed God's leading day by day, going to Israel, seeing Him work and walk with me in ways He had never done before, beginning the ministry that I am still doing today, 22 years later (but that's a story that would take a whole 'nother book).

I share this story with you before sharing the rest of Psalm 139 because I want you to know that God is with you just as much as He is with me. He knows your heart as well as He knows mine.

Although God highlighted two words for me that day in a way that made them leap off the page and into my heart, the experience served to underscore the truth of EVERY WORD in Psalm 139. EVERY WORD in the psalm is true, and EVERY WORD in it applies equally to you as it does to me.

With that in mind, if you're anxious about today, if you're unsure about what God is calling you to do next, or if you're needing some encouragement that God is really with you—and *will be* with you no matter where you are or what you do—read the following words from Psalm 139 and let them sink deep into your Spirit. Invite God to search your heart and know your anxious thoughts, trusting that He can and will lead you in THE WAY everlasting, if you will stay as close to Him as possible:

"O Lord, You have searched me and You know me.
You know when I sit and when I rise; You perceive my thoughts from afar.
You discern my going out and my lying down; You are familiar with all my ways.

Before a word is on my tongue You know it completely, O Lord.
You hem me in behind and before; You have laid Your hand upon me.
Such knowledge is too wonderful for me, too lofty for me to attain.
Where can I go from Your Spirit? Where can I flee from Your presence?
If I go up to the heavens, You are there; if I make my bed in the depths, You are there.

If I rise on the wings of the dawn, if I settle on the far side of the sea,
even there Your hand will guide me, Your right hand will hold me fast.
If I say, 'Surely the darkness will hide me and the light become night around me,'

even the darkness will not be dark to You; the night will shine like the day, for darkness is as light to You.
For You created my inmost being; You knit me together in my mother's womb.
I praise You because I am fearfully and wonderfully made; Your works are wonderful, I know that full well.
My frame was not hidden from You when I was made in the secret place. When I was woven together in the depths of the earth,
Your eyes saw my unformed body. All the days ordained for me were written in Your book before one of them came to be.
How precious to me are Your thoughts, O God! How vast is the sum of them!
Were I to count them, they would outnumber the grains of sand. When I awake, I am still with You.
Search me, O God, and know my heart; test me and know my anxious thoughts.

See if there is any offensive way in me and lead me in the way everlasting."
(Psalm 139:1-18, 23-24)

Will you pray with me?

Father, thank You for knowing us so deeply, so intimately. Thank You that there is nowhere on earth, or off the earth, that we could go and NOT have you with us. Lord, You know us better than anyone else knows us, better even than we know ourselves. Search us,

O God, and know our hearts; test us and know our anxious thoughts. Reveal to us anything that we would ever need to know, anything that is not right and needs to be corrected, and lead us in the way everlasting, the way that leads to an abundant life in every possible area of our lives. In Jesus' name we pray, Amen.

LESSON 29: GUIDING PRAYERS — NOVEMBER 12

Scripture Reading: Psalm 143

If you need guidance in your life, wondering which way you should go, let me encourage you to pray a prayer that David prayed in Psalm 143:

> "Show me the way I should go, for to You I lift up my soul....
> Teach me to do Your will, for You are my God;
> may Your good Spirit lead me on level ground" (vv. 8b, 10).

I was asking God to do this very thing a few weeks ago—to show me the way I should go. (I seem to be asking God to do this nearly every day! But for today, I want to tell you three ways God answered my prayers recently.)

I was on a trip out west with my youngest daughter, as we were visiting my middle daughter for a few days in California. There were several things we planned to do on our trip, but there were a few things we really *dreamed* we could do, but they seemed nearly impossible.

As a backdrop for Story #1, my youngest daughter is a huge fan of *America's Got Talent*. She's been watching the show all season, and when she found out we were going to be in LA the same week as the filming of the final episode of the show, she wondered if she might be able to see the show and some of the performers she had been watching all year.

I checked into the idea, but the show was already sold out. A few days into our trip, however, I was praying that God would do something special for her—and He did! Even though we couldn't see the finals of the show, we decided to go down to Hollywood the day afterward to see some of the sites.

We parked at a friend's house near downtown Hollywood and started walking towards the area we wanted to see. About five minutes into our 15-minute walk to our destination, my daughter noticed a group of guys walking towards us on the other side of the street. She looked at me and said, "Dad, that's Light Balance, the dance group I've been watching on TV!"

I looked closer at the guys across the street and saw they were all wearing matching T-shirts with the letters "LB" printed on them. And just as we were looking at them, they looked as us! There was no one else on either side of the street, and no cars coming in either direction. It was just us and them!

I told my daughter to wave and say "Hi" since they were already looking at us, and she did. They all stopped and waved back!

We crossed the street, said hello in person, and were able to tell them how much we liked watching their performances all season. We asked if we could take a picture with them, which they were very happy to do.

One of them took a picture of us all, we said goodbye, and went on our way—my heart rejoicing! Not because I got to meet Light Balance, although I was very happy to meet them! My heart was rejoicing because God had answered my prayer to do something special for my daughter. It was one of the highlights of our trip, and it felt like God had specifically guided us to that very spot at that very point in time.

You might think this story is just coincidental, and I might, too, except for story #2.

My middle daughter, who lives in LA, really loves a famous singer—and she has for most of her life. One of her hopes has been to meet him someday, to truly hang out and be genuine friends. During our time with her, I had been praying that God would fulfill some of the special desires that she's had on her heart as an encouragement to her that she's at the right place at the right time.

She often attends a mid-week service at a church in LA, so we all went together for the night. The church was meeting that week in a hotel ballroom in Beverly Hills because their normal venue was being used for something else that night.

Just before the service started, the singer she has loved for so long happened to walk in and sit down less than 30 feet away from us!

I told her that God had truly put her in the right place at the right time, and that He would continue to do so as she just kept staying close to Him. Who knew, I said, what God might bring about?

Two weeks later, she happened to be at an event for the church, and not only was this singer there, too, but they had a chance to chat and even share a laugh together about something they both thought was hysterical! It was a brief encounter, but I pray it is the first of many such encounters that will continue to fulfill one of the desires that has been on her heart for many, many years.

You might consider this a chance encounter, too, but the evidence in my mind that it was God who was leading our steps just kept mounting with story #3.

I had a desire on my heart that week in LA, too. I wanted to visit a particular place I had never visited before: a beach about an hour away from where my daughter lived. I didn't think we'd have time to go there, so I didn't mention it. I just asked God that if there *were* a way, that *He* would make it possible.

As the days passed, although it looked like it probably wouldn't work out, I just kept it close to my heart, trusting Him with whatever happened.

And then it happened! I had planned to see another friend who lived there in LA, but his schedule was tight as he was headed out for the weekend. He said he could get together, but it would really help him out if I could give him a ride afterward to a boat dock where he was going to be taking an express boat to his next destination. I looked on the map to see where he needed me to take him, and it was 2 miles from the very place I had been wanting to visit!

I hadn't mentioned it to him. I hadn't mentioned it to my daughters. I had only mentioned it to God in my prayers—a prayer that I thought would be nearly impossible to answer!

I was able to visit my friend, drop him off at the dock, then spend a few precious hours in the spot I only dreamed might possible just a few days earlier! God had done it again, guiding and directing to the right place at the right time.

Individually, any of these stories might seem random or coincidental. But collectively, the fact that each story represented each of the different desires on our hearts and different answers to our prayers—any one of which seemed fairly unlikely and nearly impossible— these stories encouraged me that God really does answer our prayers for guidance and direction. He really can put us in the right place at the right time to fulfill His will as well as our desires.

Maybe you feel dismayed today that God hasn't been answering YOUR prayers. If so, you're not alone. Even David felt this way as he began his prayers for guidance to God:

> "O Lord, hear my prayer, listen to my cry for mercy;
> in Your faithfulness and righteousness come to my relief...
> my spirit grows faint within me; my heart within me is dismayed...
> I spread out my hands to You; my soul thirsts for You like a parched land.
> Answer me quickly, O Lord; my spirit fails.
> Do not hide Your face from me or I will be like those who go down to the pit.
> Let the morning bring me word of Your unfailing love, for I have put my trust in You" (vv. 1, 4, 6-8a).

If that's you, today, let me encourage you to keep praying the rest of David's prayer, too, for God's guidance and direction in your life.

> "Show me the way I should go,
> for to You I lift up my soul....
> Teach me to do Your will, for You are my God;
> may Your good Spirit lead me on level ground" (vv. 8, 10).

Just as God answered David's prayers 3,000 years ago, and just as God answered my prayers a few weeks ago, I trust and pray that God will answer your prayers—even today.

Will you pray with me?

Father, thank You for letting us come to You with our prayers for guidance and direction. Thank You for making a way where the way seems nearly impossible. Thank You for Your love, Your faithfulness, and Your encouragement to us to keep praying for guidance and direction, knowing that You care about even the smallest details of our lives. Show us the way to go. Lead us by Your Holy Spirit. Guide us into Your perfect will for our lives, today and forevermore. In Jesus' name, Amen.

LESSON 30: LIFELONG PRAYERS   NOVEMBER 13

Scripture Reading: Psalm 150

Maybe you've heard about the wife who told her husband: "You haven't told me you love me in years!"

To which her husband replied: "I told you I love you on our wedding day, and if that ever changes, I'll let you know."

Some people approach their relationship with God the same way. Maybe they got saved one day many years ago, but they rarely, if ever, tell Him how much they love Him anymore.

Or maybe they've put off talking to God their entire lives, hoping to do all the living they can before coming to Him. They think "I'm going to live the way I want to live until the last moment, *then* I'll put my faith in God."

What they don't realize is that waiting like this would be like waiting to fall in love until the last moment of life. They'd be missing out on so much "life" that they could have had all along the way.

Today, I'd like to encourage you to make a lifelong commitment to prayer with God. As long as you still have breath, I hope you'll still be praising the Lord.

As the final line of Psalm 150—the final psalm in the book of Psalms—says:

"Let everything that has breath praise the Lord. Praise the Lord" (Psalm 150:6).

As long as you have breath, praise the Lord.

Praise Him wherever you go. Praise Him for His acts of power. Praise Him for His surpassing greatness. Praise Him with instruments and dancing. Just say it, even now: Praise the Lord!

Psalm 150 is an exuberant psalm, filled with praises to God from the first word to the last. Listen to the joy that is expressed in this psalm:

"Praise the Lord. Praise God in His sanctuary; praise Him in His mighty heavens.
Praise Him for His acts of power; praise Him for His surpassing greatness.
Praise Him with the sounding of the trumpet, praise Him with the harp and lyre, praise Him with tambourine and dancing, praise Him with the strings and flute,
praise Him with the clash of cymbals, praise Him with resounding cymbals.
Let everything that has breath praise the Lord. Praise the Lord."
(Psalm 150:1-6)

The beauty of making a commitment to lifelong prayer with God is that your conversations with Him will never end—not even when you take your last breath here on earth.

My wife was interviewed just a few weeks before her imminent passing into heaven. The interviewer said: "Lana, you don't seem fearful of death. Why is that?"

Lana said:

"I'm actually not fearful of death, and the only thing I can attribute it to is just having followed God for so long, waking up and talking to Him each day, throughout the day, He's helped me through many things. And since I am talking to Him all day long, death will be just like meeting Him and talking to Him all day long."

Lana's conversations with God didn't end when she took her last breath, and they have continued ever since—now face-to-face.

What a glorious thing to have a lifelong conversation with God here on earth that lasts into eternity.

I have some friends who, after years of knowing them, I still feel like I'm only now *really* getting to know them. I suppose that's one of the reasons God promises to give us an eternity with Him—it will simply take that long for us to even come close to knowing Him the way we'd want to know Him.

After 30 years of following God with all of my heart, soul and mind, I'm still discovering new things about Him nearly every day—when reading His Word, when interacting with His people, when experiencing a nuance about His grace or forgiveness or love that I've never experienced before. I'm continually surprised that there's still more to learn, more to know, and more to understand about Him and this amazing life He's given us.

As I close today, I'd like to remind you of one of my favorite "breathy" prayers, a prayer that is little more than a breath. I mentioned this back in Lesson 15, half-way through this study, and it's worth mentioning again as we talk about "letting everything that has breath praise the Lord."

The prayer is simply this: "Halal Yah!"

It's Hebrew for "Praise Yahweh," or "Praise the Lord." I call it a "breathy" prayer because there are no hard consonants in the phrase. When you say it out loud, you're just using your breath to say a prayer of praise to God. "Halal Yah!" There are no harsh sounds, no guttural stops in the middle, just a gentle glide of your tongue to the front of your mouth to form the "l" sounds. Otherwise, it's just pure breath.

If you have breath today, try praying this simple breathy prayer yourself: "Halal Yah!"

Say it a few times, over and over. Breathe in deeply of the breath of this life that God has given you today, then breathe out a prayer of praise by saying: "Halal Yah!"

Let this prayer serve as an exclamation point at the end of everything else you have to say to Him, just as the last words of Psalm 150 serve as an exclamation point at the end of everything else that's been said in the book of Psalms:

> "Let everything that has breath praise the Lord! Praise the Lord!"

Take a deep breath, then say it with me: "Halal Yah! Praise the Lord! Praise the Lord!" Will you pray with me?

Father, thank You for letting us come to You today and every day with praises on our lips to You. Thank You for the breath You've given us today, whether it's easy to take those breaths or, for some, perhaps a little harder today than on other days. Yet every day we have breath is a day more that we can still praise You. So we praise You today while we still have breath. Hallal Yah! And Lord, when that day finally comes when we take our last breath here on earth, let us step into eternity with You with praises on our lips, then let us breathe deeply of that heavenly air so we can keep on praising You forever. Thank You, Lord, for inviting us into a conversation that will never end. Halal Yah! Praise the Lord! Praise the Lord! In Jesus' name, Amen.

LESSON 31: AMBER SHELLAC — NOVEMBER 14

Scripture Reading: Psalm 119

Some stories take time to tell. I don't mean they're *long* stories. I mean they're stories that *take a long time* before you can tell them.

Today, I'd like to tell you one of those stories, a story that started five years ago this month. And through this story, I hope to encourage you to keep talking to God in prayer every day for the rest of your life. God loves hearing what's on your heart, and He has so much He wants to say to you.

I've come to really love my conversations with God, every day, all through the day. I feel like I could have written this verse from Psalm 119 that says:

> "How sweet are Your words to my taste, sweeter than honey to my mouth!" (Psalm 119:103).

Even His words that are as simple as "Amber Shellac."

One of the reasons I've waited to tell this story is because it involves my wife Lana's casket. It's not something I could talk about right then, as there were too many other important things going on. But I'd like to share it now as a way to show how intimacy with God can be achieved over time.

As the final days of Lana's life here on earth drew near, it became clear to us that apart from a miraculous intervention from God, Lana was about to experience what we all will experience at some point in our lives: the passing from this life to the next.

Lana and I talked about many things in those final days, some of which involved her wishes for her funeral, including her casket. She didn't want anything elaborate—just a plain wooden box.

She remembered seeing Pope John Paul II's funeral on TV about 10 years earlier and could still see the image in her mind of the plain wooden casket in which he was carried through the streets.

His casket was made of simple wood in a trapezoidal shape. I found a picture of it online and showed it to Lana. She said: "That's it. That's exactly what I want."

I called around locally to see if I could find one, but couldn't. So I searched online and found a man in Provo, Utah, who makes simple wooden caskets just like Lana was wanting.

When I called to talk about our situation, he said he could get one to us within a few days if need be, adding that some people order them years ahead of time just to make it easier for others so there's one less decision they have to make later. Lana thought that was a good idea—and if she didn't have to use it for years, all the better!

With a resolve of strength that only God can give for a moment like that, I placed the order, not sure if we'd be using it within days or, if a miracle occurred, getting to save it away for years. Sadly, it was only a matter of days. Lana passed away on November 15, 2012, and her casket arrived the following day.

I had called a friend when I placed the order, a friend who refinishes furniture, to ask if, when the casket arrived, he could refinish it in a style that matched the pope's casket, as it was shipping to us unfinished. He agreed. So when the casket arrived, he picked it up for me at the shipping office and took it back to his shop.

Now under a deadline to get it ready in time for the funeral, my friend went to the hardware store to buy some stain and finish. But as he looked at all of the options, none of them seemed quite right. He considered all kinds of stains, from cherry to walnut to pine, but each one seemed off for some reason. He walked out of the hardware store with one of the options in his hand, but feeling it just wasn't right. Then it came to him, as if out of the blue: "Amber Shellac!"

He had used it for projects in the past, and he KNEW that this was the answer to the riddle he couldn't solve. Amber Shellac would be the perfect finish! He walked back into the store, found the shellac, and left again knowing he had found the solution. He coated the casket in several thin layers of Amber Shellac, and got it done just in time for the funeral.

Lana's casket was perfect. It was just what she wanted, and just what seemed perfectly fitting for her life: simple, pure, and beautiful. It became the centerpiece of those difficult hours as my family and I stood next to it during the visitation and funeral. From time to time during the visitation, as people came through to talk and pray and offer their condolences, I would reach out and stroke the soft, smooth wood of Lana's casket. It was the closest I could get to caressing Lana herself.

I loved Lana's casket, and I know Lana would have loved it, too. We both loved creating and refinishing furniture ourselves. I have built many things from scratch, including the crib that each of our children slept in as infants and a triple bunk bed each of them used at various times as they got older. Lana refinished everything from desks and tables and rocking chairs to all the wooden trim in nearly every room of our house.

How does this relate to my intimacy with God? That brings us to this week, five years later.

I've been trying to finish a special project this week, creating a prayer room in our house that Lana had envisioned in our then-unfinished attic. We began work on it before she got sick, with family and friends helping us to begin the conversion.

But when Lana got sick, we had to stop our work. When she passed away, I simply lost heart and could hardly bear to think about finishing the room she had envisioned. I would start, then have to stop again. Then start, then stop again.

This year, however, one of the goals I set for myself was to finish the work on the attic that we had started all those years ago. With the help again of some encouraging family and friends, I was able to make progress and see it take final shape before my eyes. I recently added what for me was the pièce de résistance, the pinnacle of this special space: a beautiful fireplace, something which I've always wanted in this home, but have never had.

As I lit the fireplace for the first time a few weeks ago, I praised God that this project which has been so many years in the making was nearly finished. All I needed now was to build a wooden frame and mantel over the fireplace to finish it off.

Loving woodworking and all the options that are available to me, I would normally relish thinking through what kind of wood I would choose and the finish that would go on it. But like a woman in labor, I was also at the point where I just wanted to deliver this baby! I said, "God, help me!" as much out of desperation as out of a true prayer that I believed He would answer.

But as soon as I said, "God, help me!" He did!

I remembered Lana's casket, and the answer God had given my friend five years earlier as he was walking out of the hardware store feeling overwhelmed with options, none of which seemed quite right. And just as God's answer came to my friend as if out of the blue, it came to me the same way, and I knew it was right! The perfect answer to my prayer for help: "Amber Shellac!"

Just last night, after days of designing and cutting and sanding the woodwork around the fireplace, I brushed on my first coat of several to come of Amber Shellac—a beautiful and perfect finishing touch to this project that began so many years ago. I am SO looking forward to sitting in this new space soon, with the fireplace going on a cold winter day and seeking God still more with all of my heart.

It's taken many years—and many prayers—to get to this place. But none of those years and none of those prayers have been wasted, even when I felt like giving up so many times along the way. Those years and those prayers have, in fact, been building an intimacy between God and me that I'm not sure could have been built any other way.

As John Ortberg says in his latest book on the topic of intimacy (and which is subtitled *Getting Real about Getting Close*):

> "Intimacy isn't built on grand, elaborate gestures. It doesn't have to be something deep or dramatic—an elaborate, romantic getaway, a dramatic self-disclosure, or sentimental words. Rather, it's made up of a thousand, everyday moments of interaction" (p. 7).

The same applies to our intimacy with God. Sometimes we think we need to get away for a "special" time of prayer with God to really get close to Him. And there is value and purpose in doing that from time to time. But our intimacy with God isn't built on just those "special" times. It's built, rather, on a thousand, everyday moments of interaction with Him—like calling out for help with a woodworking decision and hearing the words: "Amber Shellac!"

I want to encourage you today, and every day, to take time in prayer with God. Take time to talk to Him. Take time to interact with Him, building your intimacy with Him, moment by precious moment.

I want to encourage you to keep "showing up." Keep walking forward. Keep getting up, again and again. For there's great value in even those little things that you do to keep your faith on track. As my daughter, Karis, said this week in a talk she gave to a group of people at our church who are going through a difficult season in their lives:

> "I was telling a friend recently how proud I was of him for staying steadfast when it would be easy to walk away, for declaring that God will always provide, even when situations aren't easy. I want to start celebrating people for staying planted, for staying steadfast in the midst of storms. We usually celebrate people when they do these great things for the Lord, but we don't always celebrate when people stay, when they show up when it'd be easy to walk away, and I want to start doing that more often because I believe that staying is just as valuable. And I want to tell you that tonight, I'm so proud of you for staying. For coming and hearing this message, for choosing to stay in the house of God, and for placing yourself in a position to hear from Him."

Today, I want to tell you the same. I'm proud of you for reading this message. I'm proud of you for coming back to God again and again. I'm proud of you for sticking it out with Him, no matter what, and returning to Him over and over, even when it might have been easier to walk away.

I hope and pray that this study of the book of Psalms has sparked your interest in going further with God—further than you've ever gone before—so that you can truly enjoy fuller, deeper and richer conversations with Him. May these words be true about your conversations with Him from now on and forevermore:

> "How sweet are Your words to my taste, sweeter than honey to my mouth!" (Psalm 119:103).

Will you pray with me?

Father, thank You for speaking to us in little ways and little words, like "Amber Shellac," words which may not mean much to others, but mean so much to us. Lord, thank You for wanting to have a conversation with us, as much as, and even more than we sometimes want to have one with You. I pray today that You would spark in our hearts a love for You and Your Word that will carry us through every day ahead, for the rest of our lives. In Jesus' name, Amen.

St. Nicholas: The Believer

A new story for Christmas based on the old story of St. Nicholas

INTRODUCTION NOVEMBER 15

There was a time when I almost gave up celebrating Christmas. Our kids were still young and weren't yet hooked on the idea of Santa Claus and presents, Christmas trees and decorations.

I had read that the Puritans who first came to America were so zealous in their faith that they didn't celebrate Christmas at all. Instead they charged fines to businesses in their community who failed to keep their shops *open* on Christmas day. They didn't want anything to do with a holiday that was, they felt, rooted in paganism. As a new believer and a new father myself, the idea of going against the flow of the excesses of Christmas had its appeal, at least in some respects.

Then I read an article by a man who simply loved celebrating Christmas. He could think of no greater way to celebrate the birth of the most important figure in human history than throwing the grandest of parties for Him—gathering and feasting and sharing gifts with as many of his family and friends as possible. This man was a pastor of deep faith and great joy. For him, the joy of Christ's birth was so wondrous that he reveled in every aspect of Christmas, including all the planning, decorating and activities that went along with it. He even loved bringing Santa Claus into the festivities, our modern-day version of the very real and very ancient Saint Nicholas, a man of deep faith and great joy as well who Himself worshipped and adored the Baby who was born in Bethlehem.

So why *not* celebrate the birth of Christ? Why *not* make it the biggest party of the year? Why *not* make it the "Hap-Happiest season of all"?

I was sold. Christmas could stay—and my kids would be much hap-happier for it, too.

I dove back into celebrating Christmas with full vigor, and at the same time took a closer look into the life of the real Saint Nicholas, a man who seemed almost irremovably intertwined with this Holy Day. I discovered that Saint Nicholas and Santa Claus were indeed one and the same, and that the Saint Nicholas who lived in the 3rd and 4th centuries after the birth of Christ was truly a devout follower of Christ himself.

As my wife and I read more and more about Nicholas' fascinating story, we became enthralled with this believer who had already been capturing the hearts and imaginations of believers and nonbelievers alike throughout the centuries.

With so many books and movies that go to great lengths to tell you the "true" story of Santa Claus (and how his reindeer are really powered by everything from eggnog to Coca-Cola), I've found that there are very few stories that even come close to describing the actual person of who Saint Nicholas was, and in particular, what he thought about the Man for whom Christmas is named, Jesus Christ. I was surprised to learn that with all the historical documents that attest to Saint Nicholas' faith in Christ, compelling tellings of those stories seem to have fallen by the wayside over the ages.

So with the encouragement and help of my sweet wife, Lana, we decided to bring the story of Saint Nicholas back to life for you, with a desire to help you recapture the essence of Christmas for yourself.

While some people, with good reason, may still go to great lengths to try to remove anything that might possibly hint of secularism from this holiest day of the year, it seems to me equally fitting to go to great lengths to try to restore Santa to his rightful place–not as the patron saint of shopping malls, but as a beacon of light that shines brightly on the One for whom this Holy Day is named.

It is with deep faith and great joy that I offer you this Christmas novella–a little story. I've enjoyed telling it and I hope you'll enjoy hearing it. It just may be the most human telling of the story of Saint Nicholas you've ever heard.

Above all, I pray that God will use this story to rekindle your love, not only for this season of the year, but for the One who makes this season so bright.

May God bless you this Christmas and always!

PROLOGUE   NOVEMBER 16

My name is Dimitri—Dimitri Alexander. But that's not important. What's important is that man over there, lying on his bed. He's—well, I suppose there's really no better way to describe him except to say—he's a saint. Not just because of all the good he's done, but because he was—as a saint always is—a *Believer*. He believed that there was Someone in life who was greater than he was, Someone who guided him, who helped him through every one of his days.

If you were to look at him closely, lying there on his bed, it might look to you as if he was dead. And in some sense, I guess you would be right. But the truth is, he's more alive now than he has ever been.

My friends and I have come here today to spend his last day on earth with him. Just a few minutes ago we watched as he passed from this life to the next.

I should be crying, I know. Believe me, I have been—and I will be again. But for now, I can't help but simply be grateful that he has finally made it to his new home, a home that he has been dreaming about for many years. A home where he can finally talk to God face to face, like I'm talking to you right now.

Oh, he was a saint all right. But to me, and to so many others, he was something even more. He was—how could I put it? An inspiration. A friend. A teacher. A helper. A giver. Oh, he loved to give and give and give some more, until it seemed he had nothing left to give at all. But then he'd reach down deep and find a little more. "There's always *something* you can give," as he would often say.

He always hoped, in some small way, that he could use his life to make a difference in the world. He wanted, above all, to help people. But with so many needs all around, what could he possibly do?

He was like a man on a beach surrounded by starfish that had been washed up onto the shore. He knew that they would die if they didn't make it back into the water.

Not knowing how to save them all, the man on the beach did what he could. He reached down, picked one up, and tossed it back into the water. Then reached down again, picked up another, and did the same.

Someone once asked the man why he bothered at all—that with so many needs all around, how could he possibly make any difference. He'd just toss another starfish into the water and say, "It made a difference to that one." Then he'd reach down and pick up another.

You see, to the world you may be just one person, but to one person you may be the world.

In many ways, my friend was just like you and me. Each one of us has just one life to live. But if you live it right, one life is all you need. And if you live your life for God, well, you just might touch the whole world.

Did his life make any difference? I already know my answer, because I'm one of those that he reached down and picked up many, many years ago. But how about I tell you his story, and when I get to the end, I'll let you decide if his life made a difference or not. And then maybe, by the time we're finished, you'll see that *your* life can make a difference, too.

Oh, by the way, I haven't told you his name yet, this man who was such a great saint, such a great believer in the God who loved him, who created him, who sustained him and with whom he is now living forever.

His name is Nicholas—and this is his story.

CHAPTER 1   NOVEMBER 17

Nicholas lived in an ideal world. At least that's the way he saw it. As a nine-year-old boy, growing up on the northern coast of what he called the Great Sea—you might call it the Mediterranean—Nicholas couldn't imagine a better life.

He would often walk through the streets with his father, acting as if they were on their way to somewhere in particular. But the real reason for their outing was to look for someone who was struggling to make ends meet, someone who needed a lift in their life. A simple hello often turned into the discovery of a need to be met. Nicholas and his father would pray, and if they could meet the need, they found a way to do it.

Nicholas couldn't count the number of times his dad would sneak up behind someone afterwards and put some apples in their sack, or a small coin or two. As far as Nicholas knew, no one ever knew what his father had done, except to say that sometimes they heard people talking about the miracle of receiving exactly what they needed at just the right time, in some unexpected way.

Nicholas loved these walks with his father, just as he loved his time at home with his mother. They had shown the same love and generosity with him as they had shown to so many others.

His parents had somehow found a way to prosper, even in the turbulent times in which they lived. They were, in fact, quite wealthy. But whether their family was rich or poor seemed to make no difference to Nicholas. All he knew or cared about was that his parents loved him like no one else on earth. He was their only son, and their times together were simple and truly joyful.

Their richest times came at night, as they shared stories with each other that they had heard about a Man who was like no other Man they had ever known. A Man who lived on the other side of the Great Sea about 280 years earlier. His name was Jesus. Nicholas was enthralled with the stories of this Man who seemed to be so precious in the eyes of his parents. Jesus seemed both down-to-earth and larger-than-life, all at the same time. How could anyone be so humble, yet so noble? How could He be so poor that He was born in an animal stable, yet so generous that He could feed 5,000 people? How could He live His life so fully, yet die a death so cruelly? Jesus was, to Nicholas, an enigma, the most fascinating person about whom he'd ever heard. One day, Nicholas thought to himself, he hoped to visit this land on the other side of the sea—and walk where Jesus walked.

For all the love that Nicholas and his parents shared, and which held them together, there was one thing that threatened to pull them apart. It was the one thing that seemed to be threatening many families in their country these days, irrespective of their wealth or poverty, their faith or lack of faith, their love for others or their lack of love.

Nicholas' friends and neighbors called it *the plague*. His parents had mentioned it from time to time, but only in their prayers. They prayed for the families who were affected by the plague, asking God for healing when possible, and for strength of faith when not. Most of all, his parents prayed for Nicholas that regardless of what happened around him, he would always know how very much they loved him, and how very much God loved him.

Even though Nicholas was so young, he had seen enough of life to know that real threats existed in the world. Yet he also had been shielded from those threats, in a way, by the love of his parents and by their devout faith in God. As his father had learned over the years, and had many times reminded Nicholas, "In *all* things, God works for the good of those who love Him." And Nicholas believed him. Up to this point, he'd had no real reason to doubt the words his father had spoken.

But it would be only a matter of months before Nicholas' faith would be challenged and he would have to decide if he really believed those words for himself—that in *all* things, God would truly work for the good of those who loved Him.

Tonight, however, he simply trusted the words of his father, listening to his parents' prayers for him—and for those in his city—as he drifted off into a perfect sleep.

CHAPTER 2   NOVEMBER 18

Nicholas woke to the sounds of birds out his window. The air was fresh, washed clean by the seaside mist in the early morning.

But the news this morning was less than idyllic. A friend of Nicholas' family had contracted the sickness that they had only heard about from people in other cities. The boy was said to be near the point of death.

Nicholas' father had heard the news first and had gone to pray for the boy. Returning home just as Nicholas awoke, his father shared the news with his wife and with Nicholas.

"We need to pray," he said, with no hint of panic in his voice, but with an unmistakable urgency that caused all three of them to slip down to their knees.

Nicholas' father began the prayer: "Father, You know the plans You have for this child. We trust You to carry them out. We pray for Your healing as we love this boy, but we know that You love him even more than we do. We trust that as we place him in Your hands this morning, You will work *all* things together for good, as You always do for those who love You."

It was a prayer Nicholas had heard his father pray many times before, asking for what they believed was best in every situation, but trusting that God knew best in the end. It was the same type of prayer Nicholas had heard that Jesus had prayed the night before He died: "If You are willing," Jesus prayed, "take this cup from Me. Yet not My will, but Yours be done."

Nicholas never quite knew what to make of this prayer. Wouldn't God always want what's best for us? And how could someone's death ever be a good thing? Yet his father prayed that prayer so often, and with such sincerity of heart, that Nicholas was confident that it was the right thing to pray. But how God could answer any other way than healing the boy—and still work it out for good—remained a mystery.

After Nicholas' mother had added her own words to the prayer, and Nicholas himself had joined in, his father concluded with thanks to God for listening—and for already answering their prayers.

As they stood, the news came to their door, as if in direct answer to what they had just prayed. But it wasn't the answer they were hoping for. The boy had died.

Nicholas' mother began to weep quietly, but not holding back on her tears. She wept as she felt the loss of another mother, feeling the loss as if it were her own son who had died.

Nicholas' father took hold of her hand and pulled Nicholas close, saying a quiet prayer for the family of the boy who had died, and adding another prayer for his own family. He gave his wife and son one more final squeeze, then walked out the door to return to the other boy's home.

CHAPTER 3   NOVEMBER 19

The boy's death had a sobering effect on the whole city. The people had known the boy, of course, and were sad for the family.

But his death was more sobering because it wasn't an isolated event. The people had heard stories of how the sickness had been spreading through the cities around them, taking the lives of not just one or two people here and there, but entire families—entire neighborhoods. The death of this boy seemed to indicate that the plague had now arrived in their city, too.

No one knew how to stop it. All they could do was pray. And pray they did.

As the sickness began to spread, Nicholas' parents would visit the homes of those who lay dying. While his parents' money was powerless to offer relief to the families, their prayers brought a peace that no amount of money could buy.

As always, Nicholas' father would pray that death would pass them over, as it had passed over the Israelites in Egypt when the plague of death overtook the lives of the firstborn of every family that wasn't willing to honor God. But this sickness was different. It made no distinction between believer or unbeliever, firstborn or last born, or any other apparent factor. This sickness seemed to know no bounds and seemed unstoppable by any means.

Yet Nicholas watched as his father prayed in faith nonetheless, believing that God could stop the plague at any moment, at any household, and trusting God to work it all out for good, even if their lives, too, were seemingly cut short.

These latter prayers were what people clung to the most. More than anything else, these words gave them hope—hope that their lives were not lived in vain, hope that their deaths were not going unnoticed by the God who created them.

A visit by Nicholas' father and mother spoke volumes to those who were facing unbearable pain, for as the plague spread, fewer and fewer people had been willing to leave their own homes, let alone visit the homes where the sickness had struck. The prayers of Nicholas' father, and the tears of his mother, gave the families the strength they needed to face whatever came their way.

Nicholas watched in wonder as his parents dispensed their gifts of mercy during the day, then returned home each night physically spent, but spiritually strengthened. It made him wonder how they got their strength for each day. But it also made him wonder how long their own family could remain untouched by this plague.

When Nicholas finally found the courage to voice this question out loud, a question that seemed to be close to all of their hearts, his father simply answered that they had only two choices: to live in fear, or to live in love, and to follow the example of the One in whom they had entrusted their lives. They chose to live in love, doing for others what they would want others to do for them.

So every morning Nicholas' father and mother would wake up and pray, asking their Lord what He would have them do. Then, pushing aside any fears they might have had, they put their trust in God, spending the day serving others as if they were serving Christ Himself.

While his father's response didn't answer the immediate question on Nicholas' heart—which was how much longer it might be till the sickness visited their own home—it seemed to answer a question that went much deeper. It answered the question of whether or not God was aware of all that was going on, and if He was, whether or not He cared enough to do anything about it.

By the way that God seemed to be directing his parents each day, Nicholas gained a peace of mind that God was indeed fully aware of all that was going on in the lives of every person in his city of Patara—and that God did indeed care. God cared enough to send Nicholas' parents to those who needed to hear a word from Him, who needed a touch from His hands, who needed a touch from God not just in their flesh, but in their spirits as well.

It seemed to Nicholas to be a more glorious answer to his question than he could have imagined. His worry about when the sickness might visit their own home dissipated as he went to sleep that night. Instead, he prayed that God would use his own hands and words—Nicholas' hands and words—as if they were God's very own, reaching out to express God's love for His people.

CHAPTER 4   NOVEMBER 20

In the coming days, Nicholas found himself wanting to help his father and mother more and more as they delivered God's mercy to those around them.

They worked together to bring food, comfort and love to each family touched by the plague. Some days it was as simple as stopping by to let a mother know she wasn't alone. Other days it was bringing food or drink to an entire family who had taken ill. And still other days it was preparing a place in the hills around their city where they carefully laid the bodies of those who had succumbed to the sickness and whose spirits had passed from this life to the next.

Each day Nicholas' heart grew more and more aware of the temporal nature of life on earth, and more and more in tune with the eternal nature of the life that is unseen. It seemed to Nicholas that the line between the two worlds was becoming less and less distinct. What he had once thought of as solid and real—like rocks and trees, or hands and feet—soon took on a more ethereal nature. And those things that were more difficult for him to touch before—like faith and hope, love and peace—began to become more solid and real.

It was as if his world was turning both upside down and inside out at the same time, not with a gut-wrenching twisting, but as if his eyes themselves were being re-calibrated, adjusting better to see with more clarity what was really going on—focusing more acutely on what really mattered in life. Even surrounded by so much sickness and death, Nicholas felt himself coming alive more fully than he'd ever felt before.

His father tried to describe what Nicholas was feeling by using words that he'd heard Jesus had said, that whoever tried to hold onto this life too tightly would lose it, but whoever was willing to let go of this life, would find true life. By learning how to love others without being constrained by fear, being propelled forward by love instead, Nicholas was starting to experience how it felt to truly live.

Whether that feeling could sustain him through what lay ahead, he didn't know. But what he did know was that for now, more than anything else, he wanted to live each day to the fullest. He wanted to wake up each day looking for how God could use him, then do whatever God was willing to give him to do. To do anything less would be to shortchange himself from living the life God had given him to live—and to shortchange God from the work God wanted to get done.

As the days passed, Nicholas came to know what his father and mother already knew: that no one knew how many more days they had left in this world. His family no longer saw themselves as human beings having a temporary spiritual experience, but as spiritual beings, having a temporary human experience. With eyes of faith, they were able to look into whatever lay ahead of them without the fear that gripped so many of the others around them.

CHAPTER 5   NOVEMBER 21

When Nicholas awoke one day to the sound of his mother coughing, time seemed to stand still.

For all the preparation his parents—and his own faith—had given him, it still caught him off guard to think that the sickness might have finally crossed over the threshold of their own home.

He thought that maybe God would spare them for all the kindness they had shown to others during the previous few months. But his father had cautioned him against such thinking, reminding him that for all the good that Jesus had done in His life—for all the healing that He had brought to others—there still came a time when He, too, had to face suffering and death. It didn't mean that God didn't love Jesus, or wasn't concerned for Him, or hadn't seen all the good He had done in His life. And it didn't mean that Jesus remained indifferent to what was about to take place either. Jesus even told His disciples that His heart was deeply troubled by what He was about to go through, but that didn't mean He shrank back from what lay ahead of Him. No, He said, it was for this very hour that He had come. Greater love, He told His disciples, had no one than this: that they lay down their lives for their friends.

Nicholas' mother coughed again, and time slowly began to move again for Nicholas. He stood to his feet. As he approached his mother, she hesitated for a moment. It was as if she was torn between wanting him to stand still—not to come one step closer to the sickness that had now reached her body—or to get up on her feet, too, and throw her arms around him, assuring him that everything would be all right. But a moment later, Nicholas had made her decision unnecessary, for he was already in her arms, holding on as tight as he could as they both broke down in tears. As Nicholas was learning, having faith doesn't mean you can't cry. It just means that you can trust God, even with your tears.

Nicholas' father had already shed some of his own tears that morning. He had gone outside before the sunrise, this time not to visit the homes of others, but to pray. For him, the place where he always returned when he needed to be alone with God was to the fresh air by the sea, not far from their home. While he knew he could pray anywhere, at any time, it was by the sea that he felt closest to God. The sound of the waves, rhythmically washing up on the shore, seemed to have a calming, mesmerizing effect on him.

He had arrived in time to watch the sunrise off to his left, looking down the shoreline of the Great Sea. How many sunrises had he seen from that very spot? And how many more would he have left to see? He turned his head and coughed, letting the question roll back out to sea with the next receding wave. The sickness had come upon him as well.

This wasn't the first time he had asked himself how many days he had left to live. The difference this time was that in the past, he had always asked it hypothetically. He would come to this spot whenever he had an important decision to make, a decision that required he think beyond the short term. He would come here when he needed to look into eternity, taking into account the brevity of life. Here, at the edge of the sea, it was as if he could grasp both the brevity of life and the eternity of heaven at the same time.

The daily rising of the sun and the swelling, cresting and breaking of the waves on the shore reminded him that God was still in control, that His world would carry on—with or without him—just as it had since God had first spoken the water and earth into existence, and just as it would until the day God would choose for its end, to make way for the new heaven and the new earth. In light of eternity, the lifespan of the earth seemed incredibly short, and the lifespan of man even shorter still. In that short span of life, he knew that he had to make the most of each day, not just living for himself, and not even just living for others, but ultimately living for the God who had given him life. If God, the Creator of all things, had seen fit to breathe into him the breath of life, then as long as he could still take a breath, he wanted to make the most of it.

Coughing again, Nicholas' father remembered that this was no mere intellectual exercise to help him come to grips with a difficult decision. This time—as he looked out at the sunrise once more, and at one more wave rolling in—he realized that this was the final test of everything that he had believed up until this point.

Some of life's tests he had passed with flying colors. Others he had failed when fear or doubt had taken over. But this was a test he knew he wanted to pass more than any other.

He closed his eyes and asked for strength for another day. He let the sun warm his face, and he gently opened the palms of his hands to feel the breeze as it lifted up along the shore and floated over his body. He opened his eyes and looked one more time at the sea.

Then he turned and walked toward home, where he would soon join his precious wife and his beloved son in a long, tearful embrace.

CHAPTER 6 — NOVEMBER 22

Nicholas stood alone. He was on the same stretch of beach where his father had stood just ten years earlier, looking out at the sunrise and the waves on the seashore.

Nicholas' father never made it out to look at the Great Sea again, having finally succumbed to the sickness himself. Nicholas' mother passed away first, within two weeks of the first signs of illness. His father lasted another three days after that, as if holding on as long as he could to make sure his wife passed as peacefully as possible from this life to the next, and making sure Nicholas was as ready as possible to take the next steps in his own life.

Nicholas' father didn't shy away from tears, but he didn't want them wasted on wrongful emotions either. "Don't cry because it's over," his father had said to both his wife and his son. "Smile because it was beautiful."

There was a time and place for anger and disappointment, but this wasn't the time for either. If given the chance to do it all over again, his parents would have chosen to do exactly what they did. It was not foolishness, they said, to be willing to risk their lives for the sake of others, especially when there were no guarantees that they would have survived anyway.

As it turned out, the plague ended up taking the lives of almost a third of the people in Patara before it finally ran its course. The sickness seemed to have a mind of its own, affecting those who tried to shield themselves from it as well as those who, like his parents, had ventured out into the midst of it.

After the death of his parents, Nicholas felt a renewed sense of urgency to pick up where they had left off, visiting those who were sick and comforting the families of those who had died.

Then, almost as suddenly as it came to their city, the plague left. Nicholas had spent most of the next few weeks sleeping, trying to recover from the long days—and even longer nights—of ministering to those who were affected. When he was awake, he spent his time trying to process his own feelings and emotions in light of the loss of the family he loved. In so many ways, his parents *were* his life. His life was so intertwined with theirs, and having them taken so suddenly from him, he hardly knew what to do without them. He went to live with his uncle, a priest who lived in the monastery in Patara, until he was ready to venture out further into the world on his own. Now that time had come, and it was time for Nicholas to make his decision.

Unlike many others who had been orphaned by the plague, Nicholas had been left with a sizable inheritance. The question on his heart wasn't what he would do to make a living, but what he would do to make a life. Through all that he had experienced, and now recognizing the brevity of life for himself, Nicholas now knew why his father had come so often to this shore to pray. Now it was Nicholas' turn to consider his own future in light of eternity.

What should I do? Where should I go? How should I spend the rest of my days? The questions could have overwhelmed him, except that his father had prepared him well for moments like these, too.

His father, always a student of the writings of Scripture and of the life of Christ, had told him that Jesus taught that we needn't worry so much about the trouble down the road as just the trouble for that day. Each day has enough trouble of its own, Jesus said.

As Nicholas thought about this, his burden lifted. He didn't have to figure out what he was going to do with the rest of his life just yet. He only had to decide on his next step.

He had enough money to travel the length of the entire world back and forth three times and still have enough to live on for years to come. But that wasn't really what he wanted to do. He had never had a desire to live wildly or lavishly, for the life he knew up to this point already gave him tremendous satisfaction. But there *was* one place he had always wanted to see with his own eyes.

As he looked out across the sea, to the south and to the west, he knew that somewhere in between lay the place he most wanted to visit—a land that seemed more precious in his mind than any other. It was the land where Jesus had lived, the land where He had walked and taught, the land where He was born and died, and the land where so many of the stories of His life—and almost the entirety of Scripture itself—had taken place.

Nicholas knew that some decisions in life were made only through the sweat and agony of prayer, trying desperately to decide between two seemingly good, but mutually exclusive paths. But this decision was not one of them. This was one of those decisions that, by the nature of the circumstances, was utterly simple to make. Apart from his uncle, there was little more to keep him in Patara, and nothing to stop him from following the desire that had been on his heart for so long.

He was glad his father had shown him this spot, and he was glad that he had come to it again today. He knew exactly what he was going to do next. His decision was as clear as the water in front of him.

CHAPTER 7 — NOVEMBER 23

Nicholas' arrival on the far shores of the Great Sea came sooner than he could have imagined. For so long he had wondered what it would be like to walk where Jesus walked, and now, at age 19, he was finally there.

Finding a boat to get there had been no problem, for his hometown of Patara was one of the main stopovers for ships traveling from Egypt to Rome, carrying people and cargo alike. Booking passage was as simple as showing that you had the money to pay, which Nicholas did.

But now that he had arrived, where would he go first? He wanted to see everything at once, but that was impossible. A tug at his sleeve provided the answer.

"You a Christian?" the small voice asked.

Nicholas looked down to see a boy not more than ten looking up at him. Two other children giggled nearby. To ask this question so directly, when it was dangerous in general to do so, showed that the boy was either a sincere follower of Christ looking for a fellow believer, or it showed that he had ulterior motives in mind. From the giggles of his little friends nearby, a boy and a girl just a bit younger than the one who had spoken, Nicholas knew it was probably the latter.

"You a Christian?" the boy asked again. "I show you holy places?"

Ah, that's it, thought Nicholas. Enough pilgrims had obviously come here over the years that even the youngest inhabitants knew that pilgrims would need a guide once they arrived. Looking over the three children again, Nicholas felt they would suit him just fine. Nicholas had a trusting heart, and while he wasn't naive enough to think that trouble wouldn't find him here, he also trusted that the same God who had led him here would also provide the help he needed once he arrived. Even if these children *were* doing it just for the money, that was all right with Nicholas. Money he had. A map he didn't. He would gladly hire them to be his living maps to the holy places.

"Yes, and yes," Nicholas answered. "Yes, I am indeed a Christian. And if you would like to take me, then yes, I would be very interested to see the holy places. I would love for your friends to come along with us, too. That way, if we meet any trouble, they can defend us all!"

The boy's mouth dropped open and his friends giggled again. It wasn't the answer the boy had expected at all, at least not so fast and not without a great deal of pestering on his part. Pilgrims who arrived were usually much more skeptical when they stepped off their boats, shooing away anyone who approached them—at least until they got their land legs back and their bearings straight. But the boy quickly recovered from his shock and immediately extended his right hand in front of him, palm upraised, with a slight bow of his head. It gave Nicholas the subtle impression as if to say that the boy was at Nicholas' service—and the not-so-subtle impression that the boy was ready for something to be deposited in his open hand. Nicholas, seeing another opportunity to throw the boy off guard, happily obliged.

He gently placed three of his smallest, but shiniest coins into the boy's upraised palm and said, "My name is Nicholas. And I can see you're a wise man. Now, if you're able to keep your hand open even after I've set these coins in it, you'll be even wiser still. For he who clenches his fist tightly around what he has received will find it hard to receive more. But he who opens his hand freely to heaven—freely giving in the same way that he has freely received—will find that his Father in heaven will usually not hold back in giving him more."

Nicholas motioned with his hand that he intended for the boy to share what he had received with his friends, who had come closer at the appearance of the coins. The boy obviously was the spokesman for all three, but still he faltered for a moment as to what to do. This man was so different from anyone else the boy had ever approached. With others, the boy was always trying, usually without success, to coax even one such coin from their pockets, but here he had been given three in his very first attempt! The fact that the coins weren't given grudgingly, but happily, did indeed throw him off balance. He had never heard such a thought like that of keeping his hands open to give *and* receive. His instinct would have been to instantly clench his fist tightly around the coins, not letting go until he got to the safest place he could find, and only then could he carefully inspect them and let their glimmers shine in his eyes. Yet he stood stock still, with his hand still outstretched and his palm facing upward. Almost against his own self-will, he found himself turning slightly and extending his hand to his friends.

Seizing the moment, the two others each quickly plucked a coin from his hand. Within an instant of realizing that they, too, were about to clench their fists around their newly acquired treasure, they slowly opened their fingers as well, looking up at the newly arrived pilgrim with a sense of bewilderment. They were bewildered not just that he had given them the coins, but that they were still standing there with their palms open, surprising even themselves that they were willing to follow this man's peculiar advice.

The sight of it all made Nicholas burst out in a gracious laugh. He was delighted by their response and he quickly deposited two more of his smallest coins into each of their hands, now tripling their astonishment. It wasn't the amount of the gifts that had astonished them, for they had seen bigger tips from wealthier pilgrims, but it was the generous and cheerful spirit that accompanied the gifts that gave them such a surprise.

The whole incident took place in less than a minute, but it set Nicholas and his new friends into such a state that each of them looked forward to the journey ahead.

"Now, you'd better close your hands again, because a wise man—or woman—" he nodded to the little girl, "also takes care of that which they have been given so that it doesn't get lost or stolen."

Then, turning to walk toward the city, Nicholas said, "How about you let me get some rest tonight, and then, first thing in the morning, you can start showing me those holy places?"

While holy places abounded in this holy land, in the magical moments that had just transpired, it seemed to the three children—and even to Nicholas himself—that they had just stepped foot on their first.

CHAPTER 8   NOVEMBER 24

Nicholas woke with the sun the next morning. He had asked the children to meet him at the inn shortly after sunrise. His heart skipped a beat with excitement about the day ahead. Within a few minutes, he heard their knock—and their unmistakable giggles—at the door.

He found out that their names were Dimitri, Samuel and Ruthie. They were, to use the common term, "alumni," children whose parents had left them at birth to fend for themselves. Orphans like these dotted the streets throughout the Roman Empire, byproducts of people who indulged their passions wherever and with whomever they wanted, with little thought for the outcome of their actions.

While Dimitri could have wallowed in self-pity for his situation, he didn't. He realized early on that it didn't help to get frustrated and angry about his circumstances. So he became an entrepreneur.

He began looking for ways he could help people do whatever they needed, especially those things which others couldn't do, or wouldn't do, for themselves. He wasn't often rewarded for his efforts, but when he was, it was all worth it.

He wasn't motivated by religion, for he wasn't religious himself, and he wasn't motivated by greed, for he never did anything that didn't seem right if it were just for the money, as greedy people who only care about money often do. He simply believed that if he did something that other people valued, and if he did it good enough and long enough, then somehow he would make it in life. Some people, like Dimitri, stumble onto godly wisdom without even realizing it.

Samuel and Ruthie, on the other hand, were just along for the ride. Like bees drawn to honey, Samuel and Ruthie were drawn to Dimitri, as often happens when people find someone who is trying to do what's right. Samuel was eight, and like Dimitri, wasn't religious himself, but had chosen his own name when he heard someone tell the story of another little boy named Samuel who, when very young, had been given away by his parents to be raised by a priest. Samuel, the present-day one, loved to hear about all that the long-ago

Samuel had done, even though the other one had lived over 1,000 years before. This new Samuel didn't know if the stories about the old Samuel were true, but at the time he chose his name, he didn't particularly care. It was only in the past few months, as he had been traveling to the holy sites with Dimitri, that he had begun to wonder if perhaps the stories really were true.

Now Ruthie, even though she was only seven, was as sharp as a tack. She always remembered people's names and dates, what happened when and who did what to whom. Giggling was her trademark, but little though she was, her mind was eager to learn, and she remembered everything she saw and everything she was taught. Questions filled her mind, and naturally spilled right out of her mouth.

Dimitri didn't mind these little tag-alongs, for although it might have been easier for him to do what he did by himself, he also knew of the dangers of the streets and felt compelled to help these two like an older brother might help his younger siblings. And to be completely honest, he didn't have anyone else to call family, so finding these two a few years earlier had filled a part of his heart in a way that he couldn't describe, but somehow made him feel better.

Nicholas took in the sight of all three beaming faces at his door. "Where to first?" asked Dimitri.

"Let's start at the beginning," said Nicholas, "the place where Jesus was born." And with that they began the three-day walk from the coast of Joppa to the hills of Bethlehem.

CHAPTER 9   NOVEMBER 25

After two days of walking and sleeping on hillsides, Nicholas and his new friends had just a half day left before they reached Bethlehem. For Nicholas, his excitement was building with every hill they passed, as he was getting closer and closer to the holy place he most wanted to see, the birthplace of Jesus.

"Why do you think He did it?" asked Dimitri. "I mean, why would Jesus want to come here—to earth? If I were already in heaven, I think I'd want to stay there."

Even though Dimitri was supposed to be the guide, he didn't mind asking as many questions as he could, especially when he was guiding someone like Nicholas, which didn't happen very often.

Nicholas didn't mind his asking, either, as Nicholas had done the same thing back home. His parents belonged to a community of believers that had been started about 250 years earlier by the Apostle Paul himself when Paul had visited their neighboring city of Myra on one of his missionary journeys, telling everyone who would listen about Jesus. Paul had lived at the same time as Jesus, although Paul didn't become a believer himself until after Jesus died and rose again from the dead. Paul's stories were always remarkable.

Nicholas got to hear all of the stories that Paul had told while he was in Myra, as they were written down and repeated by so many others over the years.

As a child, Nicholas thought that anything that happened 250 years ago sounded like ancient history. But as he started to get a little older, and now that his parents had passed away, too, it didn't seem that long ago at all. The stories that Nicholas heard were the same stories his father and his grandfather and his great grandfather, back to six or seven generations, had heard, some for the very first time from the Apostle Paul in person. Nicholas loved to hear them over and over, and he asked many of the same questions that Dimitri was now asking him—like why would Jesus leave heaven to come down to earth in person.

"The simple answer is because He loved us," said Nicholas. "But that alone probably doesn't answer the question you're really asking, because God has *always* loved us. The reason Jesus came to earth was, well, because there are some things that need to be done in person."

Nicholas went on to explain the gospel—the good news—to the children of how Jesus came to pay the ultimate price with His life for anything we had ever done wrong, making a way for us to come back to God with a clean heart, plus live with Him in heaven forever.

Throughout the story, the children stared at Nicholas with rapt attention. Although they had been to Bethlehem many times before and had often taken people to the cave that was carved into the hillside where it was said that Jesus was born, they had never pictured it in their minds quite like this before. They had never understood the motivations behind *why* God did what He did. And they had never really considered that the stories they heard about Jesus being God in the flesh were true. How could He be?

Yet hearing Nicholas' explanation made so much sense to them, that they wondered why they had never considered it as true before. In those moments, their hearts and minds were finally opened to at least the *possibility* that it was true. And that open door turned out to be the turning point for each of them in their lives, just as it had been for Nicholas when he first heard the Truth. God really did love them, and God had demonstrated that love for them by coming to the earth to save them from their certain self-destruction.

For Nicholas, when he first heard about the love of the Father for him, the idea was fairly familiar to him because he had already had a good glimpse of what the love of a father looked like from the love of his own father. But to Dimitri, Samuel and Ruthie, who had never had a father, much less one like Nicholas had just described, it was simultaneously one of the most distantly incomprehensible, yet wonderfully alluring descriptions of love they had ever heard.

As they made their way through the hills toward Bethlehem, they began to skip ahead as fast as their hearts were already skipping, knowing that they would soon see again the place where God had, as a Man, first touched earth less than 300 years earlier. They would soon be stepping onto ground that was indeed holy.

CHAPTER 10 — NOVEMBER 26

It was evening when they finally arrived at their destination. Dimitri led them through the city of Bethlehem to the spot where generations of pilgrims had already come to see the place where Jesus was born: a small cave cut into the hillside where animals could easily have been corralled so they wouldn't wander off.

There were no signs to mark the spot, no monuments or buildings to indicate that you were now standing on the very spot where the God of the universe had arrived as a child. It was still dangerous anywhere in the Roman Empire to tell others you were a Christian, even though the laws against it were only sporadically enforced.

But that didn't stop those who truly followed Christ from continuing to honor the One whom they served as their King. Although Jesus taught that His followers were to still respect their earthly rulers, if forced to choose between worshipping Christ or worshipping

Caesar, both the Christians and Caesar knew who the Christians would worship. So the standoff continued.

The only indication that this was indeed a holy site was the well-worn path up the hill that made its way into and out of the cave. Tens of thousands of pilgrims had already made their way to this spot during the past 250 years. It was well known to those who lived in Bethlehem, for it was the same spot that had been shown to pilgrims from one generation to the next, going back to the days of Christ.

As Dimitri led the three others along the path to the cave, Nicholas laughed, a bit to himself, and a bit out loud. The others turned to see what had made him burst out so suddenly. He had even surprised himself! Here he was at the one holy site he most wanted to see, and he was laughing.

Nicholas said, "I was just thinking of the wise men who came to Bethlehem to see Jesus. They probably came up this very hill. How regal they must have looked, riding on their camels and bringing their gifts of gold, frankincense and myrrh. For a moment I pictured myself as one of those kings, riding on a camel myself. Then I stepped in some sheep dung by the side of the road. The smell brought me back in an instant to the reality that I'm hardly royalty at all!"

"Yes," said Ruthie, "but didn't you tell us that the angels spoke to the shepherds first, and that they were the first ones to go and see the baby? So smelling a little like sheep dung may not make you like the kings, but it does make you like those who God brought to the manger *first!*"

"Well said, Ruthie," said Nicholas. "You're absolutely right."

Ruthie smiled at her insight, and then her face produced another thoughtful look. "But maybe we should still bring a gift with us, like the wise men did?" The thought seemed to overtake her, as if she was truly concerned that they had nothing to give to the King. He wasn't there anymore to receive their gifts, of course, but still she had been captivated by the stories about Jesus that Nicholas had been telling them along the road. She thought that she should at least bring Him *some* kind of gift.

"Look!" she said, pointing to a spot on the hill a short distance away. She left the path and within a few minutes had returned with four small, delicate golden flowers, one for each of them. "They look just like gold to me!"

She smiled from ear to ear now, giving each one of them a gift to bring to Jesus. Nicholas smiled as well. *There's always something you can give,* he thought to himself. *Whether it's gold from a mine or gold from a flower, we only bring to God that which is already His anyway, don't we?*

So with their gifts in hand, they reached the entrance to the cave—and stepped inside.

CHAPTER 11   NOVEMBER 27

Nothing could have prepared Nicholas for the strong emotion that overtook him as he entered the cave.

On the ground in front of him was a makeshift wooden manger, a feeding trough for animals probably very similar to the one in which Jesus had been laid the night of His birth. It had apparently been placed in the cave as a simple reminder of what had taken place there. But the effect on Nicholas was profound.

One moment he had been laughing at himself and watching Ruthie pick flowers on the hillside and the next moment, upon seeing the manger, he found himself on his knees, weeping uncontrollably at the thought of what had taken place on this very spot.

He thought about everything he had ever heard about Jesus—about how He had healed the sick, walked on water and raised the dead. He thought about the words Jesus had spoken—words that echoed with the weight of *authority* as He was the Author of life itself. He thought about his own parents who had put their lives on the line to serve this Man called Jesus, who had died for him just as He had died for them, giving up their very lives for those they loved.

The thoughts flooded his mind so fully that Nicholas couldn't help sobbing with deep, heartfelt tears. They came from within his very soul. Somewhere else deep inside him, Nicholas felt stirred like he had never felt in his life. It was a sensation that called for some kind of response, some kind of action. It was a feeling so different from anything else he had ever experienced, yet it was unmistakably clear that there was a step he was now supposed to take, as if a door were opening before him and he knew he was supposed to walk through it. But how?

As if in answer to his question, Nicholas remembered the golden flower in his hand. He knew exactly what he was supposed to do, and he wanted more than anything to do it.

He took the flower and laid it gently on the ground in front of the wooden manger. The golden flower wasn't just a flower anymore. It was a symbol of his very life, offered up now in service to his King.

Nicholas knelt there for several minutes, engulfed in this experience that he knew, even in the midst of it, would affect him for the rest of his life. He was oblivious to anything else that was going on around him. All he knew was that he wanted to serve this King, this Man who was clearly a man in every sense of the word, yet was clearly one and the same with God as well, the very essence of God Himself.

As if slowly waking from a dream, Nicholas began to become aware of his surroundings again. He noticed Dimitri and Samuel on his left and Ruthie on his right, also on their knees. Having watched Nicholas slip down to his knees, they had followed suit. Now they looked alternately, back and forth between him and the manger in front of him.

The waves of emotion that had washed over Nicholas were now washing over them as well. They couldn't help but imagine what he was experiencing, knowing how devoted he was to Jesus and what it had willingly cost Nicholas' parents to follow Him. Each of them, in their own way, began to experience for themselves what such love and devotion must feel like.

Having watched Nicholas place his flower in front of the manger, they found themselves wanting to do the same. If Jesus meant so much to Nicholas, then certainly they wanted to follow Jesus as well. They had never in their entire lives experienced the kind of love that Nicholas had shown them in the past three days. Yet somehow they knew that the love that Nicholas had for them didn't originate with Nicholas alone, but from the God whom Nicholas served. If this was the kind of effect that Jesus had on His followers, then they wanted to follow Jesus, too.

Any doubts that Nicholas had had about his faith prior to that day were all washed away in those timeless moments. Nicholas had become, in the truest sense of the word, a *Believer*.

And from those very first moments of putting his faith and trust fully in Jesus, he was already inspiring others to do the same.

CHAPTER 12   NOVEMBER 28

Once again, Nicholas was standing on a beach, alone. This time, however, it was on the shores of the Holy Land, looking back across the Great Sea towards his home.

In the months following his visit to Bethlehem, Nicholas, along with his young guide and bodyguards, had searched for every holy place that they could find that related to Jesus. They had retraced Jesus' steps from His boyhood village in Nazareth to the fishing town of Capernaum, where Jesus had spent most of His adult years.

They had waded into the Jordan River where Jesus had been baptized and they swam in the Sea of Galilee where He had walked on the water and calmed the storm.

They had visited the hillside where Jesus had taught about the kingdom of heaven, and they had marveled at the spot where He had multiplied the five loaves of bread and two fish to feed a crowd of over 5,000 people.

While it was in Bethlehem that Nicholas was filled with wonder and awe, it was in Jerusalem where he was filled with mission and purpose. Walking through the streets where Jesus had carried His cross to His own execution, Nicholas felt the weight on his shoulders as if he were carrying a cross as well. Then seeing the hill where Jesus had died, and the empty tomb nearby where Jesus had risen from the dead, Nicholas felt the weight on his shoulders lifting off, as Jesus must have felt when He emerged from the tomb in which He had been sealed.

It was in that moment that Nicholas knew what *his* mission and purpose in life would be: to point others to the One who would lift their burdens off as well. He wanted to show them that they no longer had to carry the burdens of their sin, pain, sickness and need all alone. He wanted to show them that they could cast all their cares on Jesus, knowing that Jesus cared for them. "Come to Me, all you who are weary and burdened," Jesus had said, "and I will give you rest."

The stories Nicholas had heard as a child were no longer vague and distant images of things that *might* have been. They were stories that had taken on new life for him, stories that were now three dimensional and in living color. It wasn't just the fact that he was seeing these places with his own eyes. Others had done that, and some were even living there in the land themselves, but they had still never felt what Nicholas was feeling. What made the difference for Nicholas was that he was seeing these stories through the eyes of faith, through the eyes of a Believer, as one who now truly believed all that had taken place.

As his adventures of traveling to each of the holy sites came to an end, Nicholas returned to the spot where he had first felt the presence of God so strongly: to Bethlehem. He felt that in order to prepare himself better for his new calling in life, he should spend as much time as he could living and learning in this special land. While exploring the city of Bethlehem and its surroundings, he found another cave nearby, in the city of Beit Jala, that was similar to the cave in which Jesus had been born. He took up residence there in the cave, planning to spend as much time as he could living and learning how to live in this land where His Savior had lived.

Dimitri, Samuel and Ruthie had gained a new sense of mission and purpose for their lives as well. As much as they wanted to stay with Nicholas, they felt even more compelled to continue their important work of bringing more people to see these holy places. It was no longer just a way for them to provide a living for themselves, but they found it to be a holy calling, a calling to help others experience what they had experienced.

It had been four full years now since Nicholas had first arrived on this side of the Sea. During that time, he often saw his young friends as they brought more and more pilgrims to see what they had shown to Nicholas. In those few short years, he watched each of them grow up "in wisdom and stature, and in favor with God and men," just as Jesus had done in His youth in Nazareth.

Nicholas would have been very happy to stay here even longer, but the same Spirit of God that had drawn him to come was now drawing him back home. He knew that he couldn't stay on this mountaintop forever. There were people who needed him, and a life that was waiting for him back home, back in the province of Lycia. What that life held for him, he wasn't sure. With his parents gone, there was little to pull him back home, but it was simply the Spirit of God Himself, propelling him forward on the next leg of his journey.

Making arrangements for a ship home was harder than it was to find a ship to come here, for the calm seas of summer were nearing their end and the first storms of winter were fast approaching. But Nicholas was convinced that this was the time, and he knew that if he waited any longer, he might not make it home again until spring—and the Spirit's pull was too strong for that kind of delay.

So when he heard that a ship was expected to arrive any day now, one of the last of the season to sail through here on its way from Alexandria to Rome, he quickly arranged for passage. The ship was to arrive the next morning, and he knew he couldn't miss it.

He had sent word, through a shopkeeper, to try to find his three best friends to let them know that he would be sailing in the morning. But as the night sky closed in, he had still not heard a word from them.

So he stood there on the beach alone, contemplating all that had taken place and all that had changed in his life since coming to the Holy Land—and all that was about to change as he left it. The thoughts filled him with excitement, anticipation and, to be honest, just a little bit of fear.

CHAPTER 13   NOVEMBER 29

Although Nicholas' ship arrived the following morning just as expected, the children didn't.

Later that afternoon, when the time came for him to board and the three still hadn't shown up, Nicholas sadly resigned himself to the possibility that they just might miss each other entirely. He had started walking toward the ship when he felt a familiar tug at his sleeve.

"You a Christian?" came the voice once again, but this time with more depth as about four years were added to his life. It was Dimitri, of course. Nicholas turned on the spot and smiled his broadest smile.

"Am I a Christian? Without a doubt!" he said as he saw all three of them offering smiles to him in return. "And you?" he added, speaking to all three of them at once.

"Without a doubt!" they replied, almost in unison. It was the way they had spoken about their faith ever since their shared experience in Bethlehem, an experience when their doubts about God had faded away.

As Nicholas tried to take in all three of their faces just one more time, he wondered which was more difficult: to leave this precious land, or to leave these three precious youth whom he had met there. They all knew that God had called them together for a purpose, and they all trusted that God must now be calling them apart for another purpose, too, just as Nicholas had previously felt he was to move to Bethlehem, and they were to continue their work taking pilgrims from city to city.

But just because they knew what God's will was, it didn't mean it was always easy to follow it. As Nicholas had often reminded them, tears were one of the strongest signs of love in the world. Without tears at the loss of those things that matter most, it would be hard to tell if those things really mattered at all.

A lack of tears wouldn't be a problem today. Once again, Nicholas asked them all to hold out their right hands in front of them. As he reached into his pocket to find three of his largest coins to place into each of their outstretched hands, he found he wasn't fast enough. Within an instant, all three children had wrapped their arms completely around Nicholas' neck, his back and his waist, depending on their height. They all held on as tightly as possible, and as long as possible, before one of the ship's crewmen signaled to Nicholas that the time had come.

As Nicholas gave each of them one last squeeze, he secretly slipped a coin into each of their pockets. Throughout their time together, Nicholas' gifts had helped the children immeasurably. But it wasn't Nicholas' presents that blessed them so much as it was his *presence*—his willingness to spend so much time with them. Still, Nicholas wanted to give them a final blessing that they could discover later when he was gone, as he often did his best giving in secret.

Nicholas wasn't sure whether to laugh or to cry at the thought of this final gift to them, so he did a little of both. Under his breath, he also offered a prayer of thanks for each of their lives, then bid them farewell, one by one. The children's hugs were the perfect send-off as he stepped onto the ship and headed for home—not knowing that their hugs and kind words would also help to carry him through the dark days that he was about to face ahead.

CHAPTER 14   NOVEMBER 30

The wind whipped up as soon as Nicholas' ship left the shore. The ship's captain had hoped to get a head start on the coming storm, sailing for a few hours along the coast to the harbor in the next city before docking again for the night. It was always a longer trip to go around the edges of the Great Sea, docking in city after city along the way, instead of going directly across to their destination. But going straight across was also more perilous, especially at this time of year. So to beat the approaching winter, and the more quickly approaching storm, they wanted to gain as many hours as they could along the way.

Keeping on schedule, Nicholas found out, was more than just a matter of a captain wanting to make good on his contract with his clients. It was also soon to become a matter of life and death for the families of the crew on board, including the family of the captain. Nicholas found out that a famine had begun to spread across the empire, now affecting the crew's home city back in Rome. The famine had begun in the countryside as rain had been sparse in the outlying areas, but now the shortages in the country were starting to deplete the reserves in Rome as well. Prices were rising and even families who could afford to pay for food were quickly depleting their resources to get it.

The ship's captain was not a foolish man, having sailed on these seas for almost 30 years. But he also knew that the risk of holding back on their voyage at a time like this could mean they would be grounded for the rest of the winter. If that happened, his cargo of grain might perish by spring, as well as his family. So the ship pressed on.

It looked to Nicholas like they had made the right decision to set sail. He, too, felt under pressure to get this voyage underway, although it wasn't family or cargo that motivated him. It was the Spirit of God Himself. He wouldn't have been able to explain it to anyone except to those who had already experienced it. All he knew was that it was *imperative* that they start moving.

He had thought he might spend still more time in the Holy Land, perhaps even his entire life. It felt like home to him from the very beginning, as he had heard so many stories about it when he was growing up. He had little family waiting for him elsewhere, and up to this point, he was content to stay right where he was, except for the Spirit's prompting that it was time to go.

The feeling started as a restlessness at first, a feeling that he was suddenly no longer content to stay where he was. He couldn't trace the feeling to anything particular that was wrong with where he was, just that it was time to go. But where? Where did God want him to go? Did God have another site for him to see? Another part of the country in which he was supposed to live? Perhaps another country altogether that he was supposed to visit?

As the restlessness grew, his heart and his mind began to explore the options in more detail. He had found in the past that the best way to hear from God was to let go of his own will so that he could fully embrace God's will, whatever that may be. While letting go was always hard for him, he knew that God would always lead him in the ways that were best. So, finally letting go of his own will, Nicholas began to see God's will much more clearly in this situation as well. As much as he felt like the Holy Land was his new home, it wasn't really his home. He felt strongly that the time had come for him to return to the region where he had been born, to the province of Lycia on the northern coast of the Sea. There was something, he felt, that God wanted him to do there—something for which he had been specifically equipped and called to do, and was, in fact, the reason that God had chosen for him to grow up there when he was young. Just as Nicholas had felt drawn to come to the Holy Land, he now felt drawn to return home.

To home he was headed, and to home he must go. That inner drive that he felt was as strong—if not stronger—than the drive that now motivated the ship's captain and crew to get their cargo home, safe and sound, to their precious families.

Storm or no storm, they had to get home.

CHAPTER 15 — DECEMBER 1

Nicholas' ship never made it to the next harbor along the coast. Instead, the storm they were trying to outrun had outrun them. It caught hold of their ship, pulling it away from the coast within the first few hours at sea. It kept pulling them further and further away from the coast until, three hours later, they found themselves inescapably caught in its torrents.

The crew had already lowered the sails, abandoning their attempts to force the rudder in the opposite direction. They now hoped that by going with the storm rather than against it they would have a better chance of keeping the ship in one piece. But this plan, too, seemed only to drive them into the deepest and most dangerous waters, keeping them near the eye of the storm itself.

After another three hours had passed, the sea sickness that had initially overcome their bodies was no longer a concern, as the fear of death itself was now overtaking all but the most resilient of those on board.

Nicholas, although he had traveled by ship before, was not among those considered to be most resilient. He had never experienced pounding waves like this before. And he wasn't the only one. To a man, as the storm worsened, each began to speak of this as the worst storm they had ever seen.

The next morning, when the storm still hadn't let up, and then again on the next morning and the next, and as the waves were still pounding them, they were all wondering why they had been in such a hurry to set out to beat the storm. Now they just hoped and prayed that God would let them live to see one more day, one more hour. As wave after wave pummeled the ship, Nicholas was simply praying they would make it through even one more wave.

His thoughts and prayers were filled with images of what it must have been like for the Apostle Paul, that follower of Christ who had sailed back and forth across the Great Sea several times in similar ships. It was on Paul's last trip to Rome that he had landed in Myra, only miles from Nicholas' hometown. Then, as Paul continued on from Myra to Rome, he faced the most violent storm he had ever faced at sea, a raging fury that lasted more than fourteen days and ended with his ship being blasted to bits by the waves as it ran aground on a sandbar, just off the coast of the island of Malta.

Nicholas prayed that *their* battle with the wind wouldn't last for fourteen days. He didn't know if they could make it through even one more day. He tried to think if there was anything that Paul had done to help himself and the 276 men who were on his ship with him to stay alive, even though their ship and its cargo were eventually destroyed. But as hard as he tried to think, all he could remember was that an angel had appeared to Paul on the night before they ran aground. The angel told Paul to take heart—that even though the ship would be destroyed, not one of the men aboard would perish. When Paul told the men about this angelic visit, they all took courage, as Paul was convinced that it would happen just as the angel said it would. And it did.

But for Nicholas, no such angel had appeared. No outcome from heaven had been predicted and no guidance had come about what they should or shouldn't do. All he felt was that inner compulsion that he had felt before they departed–that they needed to get home as soon as they could.

Not knowing what else to do, Nicholas recalled a phrase of his father's: "standing orders are good orders." If a soldier wasn't sure what to do next, even if the battle around him seemed to change directions, if the commanding officer hadn't changed the orders, then the soldier was to carry on with the most recent orders given. Standing orders are good orders. It was this piece of wisdom from his father, more than any other thought, that guided Nicholas and gave him the courage to do what he did next.

CHAPTER 16　　　　　　　　　　　　　　　　　　　　　　　　　　　DECEMBER 2

When the storm seemed to be at its worst, Nicholas' thoughts turned to the children he had just left. His thoughts of them didn't fill him with sadness, but with hope.

He began to take courage from the stories they had all learned about how Jesus had calmed the storm, how Moses had split the Red Sea and how Joshua had made the Jordan River stop flowing. Nicholas and the children had often tried to imagine what it must have been like to be able to exercise control over the elements like that. Nicholas had even, on occasion, tried to do some of these things himself, right along with Dimitri, Samuel and Ruthie. When it rained, they lifted their hands and prayed to try to stop the rain from coming down. But it just kept raining on their heads. When they got to the Sea of Galilee, they tried to walk on top of the water, just like Jesus did—and even Peter did, if only for a few short moments. But Nicholas and the children assumed they must not have had enough faith or strength or whatever it might have taken for them to do such things.

As another wave crashed over the side of the ship on which Nicholas was now standing, he realized there was a common thread that ran through each of these stories. Maybe it wasn't their faith that was the problem after all, but God's timing. In each instance from the stories he could remember, God didn't allow those miracles on a whim, just for the entertainment of the people who were trying to do them. God allowed them because God had places for them to go, people they needed to see and lives that needed to be spared. There was an urgency in each situation that required the people to accomplish not only what was on *their* heart, but what was on *God's* heart as well.

It seemed that the miracles were provided not because of their attempts to try to reorder God's world, but in God's attempts to try to reorder their worlds. It seemed to Nicholas that it must be a combination of their prayers of faith, plus God's divine will, that caused a spark between heaven and earth, ignited by their two wills working together, that burst into a power that could move mountains.

When Jesus needed to get across the lake, but His disciples had already taken off in the boat, He was able to ignite by faith the process that allowed Him to walk on water, and thereafter calm the storm that threatened to take their lives when He finally did catch up to them.

"Standing orders are good orders," Nicholas recalled, and he believed with all his heart that if God hadn't changed His orders, then somehow they needed to do whatever they could to get to the other side of the Sea. But it wasn't enough for God to will it. God was looking for someone willing, here on earth to will it, too, thereby completing the divine connection and causing the miracle to burst forth. Like Moses when he lifted his staff into the air or Joshua's priests who took the first steps into the Jordan River, God needed someone to agree with Him in faith that what He had willed to happen in heaven should happen here on earth. God had already told Nicholas what needed to happen. Now it was up to Nicholas to complete the divine connection.

"Men!" Nicholas yelled to get the crew's attention. "The God whom I serve, and who Has given each one of us life, wants us to reach our destination even more than we want to reach it. We must agree in faith, here and now, that God not only *can* do it, but that He *wills* us to do it. If you love God, or even if you think you might want to love God, I want you to pray along with me, that we will indeed reach our destination, and that nothing will stand in the way of our journey!"

As soon as Nicholas had spoken these words, the unthinkable happened: not only did the wind *not* stop, but it picked up speed! Nicholas faltered for a moment as if he had made some sort of cosmic mistake, some sort of miscalculation about the way God worked and what God wanted him to do. But then he noticed that even though the wind had picked up speed, it had also shifted directions, ever so slightly, but in such a distinct and noticeable way that God had gotten the attention of every man on board. Now, instead of being pounded by the waves from both sides, they were sailing straight through them, as if a channel had been cut into the waves themselves. The ship was driven along like this, not only for the next several moments, but for the next several hours.

When the speed and direction of the ship continued to hold its steady but impressively fast course, the captain of the ship came to Nicholas. He said he had never seen anything like this in his whole life. It was as if an invisible hand was holding the rudder of the ship, steady and straight, even though the ropes that held the rudder were completely unmanned, as they had been abandoned long ago when the winds first reached gale force.

Nicholas knew, too—even though he was certainly not as well seasoned as the captain—that this was not a normal phenomenon on the seas. He felt something supernatural taking control the moment he first stood up to speak to the men, and he felt it still as they continued on their path straight ahead.

What lay before them he didn't know. But what he did know was that the One who had brought them this far was not going to take His hand off that rudder until *His* mission was accomplished.

CHAPTER 17   DECEMBER 3

The storm that they thought was going to take their lives turned out to be the storm that saved many more. Rather than going the long way around the sea, following the coastline in the process, the storm had driven them straight across it, straight into the most dangerous path that they never would have attempted on their own at that time of year.

When they sighted land early on the morning of the fifth day, they recognized it clearly. It was the city of Myra, just a few miles away from Nicholas' hometown, and the same city where the Apostle Paul had changed ships on his famous journey to Rome.

It was close enough to home that Nicholas knew in his heart that he was about to land in the exact spot where God wanted him to be. God, without a doubt, had spared his life for a purpose, a purpose which would now begin the next chapter of his life.

As they sailed closer to the beach, they could see that the storm that raged at sea had hardly been felt on shore.

The rains that had flooded their ship for the past several days, and that should have been watering the land as well, hadn't made it inland for several months. The drought that the captain and sailors had told him had come to Rome had already been here in Lycia for two and a half years. The cumulative effect was that the crops that were intended to supply their reserves for the coming winter and for next year's seed had already been depleted. If the people of Lycia didn't get grain to eat now, many would never make it through the winter, and still more would die the following spring, as they wouldn't have seed to plant another crop. This ship was one of the last that had made it out of the fertile valleys of Egypt before the winter, and its arrival at this moment in time was like a miracle in the eyes of the people. It was certainly an answer to their prayers.

But that answer wasn't so clear to the captain of the ship. He had been under strict orders from the keeper of the Imperial storehouses in Rome that not one kernel of grain could be missing when the ship arrived back in Rome. The ship had been weighed in Alexandria before it left Egypt and it would be weighed again in Rome—and the captain would be held personally responsible for any discrepancy. The famine had put increasing pressure on the emperor to bring any kind of relief to the people. Not only this, but the families of the captain and crew themselves were awaiting the arrival of this food. Their jobs, and the lives of their families, relied on the safe delivery of every bit of grain aboard.

Yet without the faith and encouragement of Nicholas, the captain knew that the ship and its cargo would have been lost at sea, along with all of their lives.

While it was clear to Nicholas that God had brought him back to his homeland, he too wasn't entirely certain what to do about the grain. While it seemed that giving at least some of the grain to the people of Myra was in order, Nicholas still tried to see it from God's perspective. Was this city, or any other city throughout the empire, any more in need of the grain than Rome, which had bought and paid for it to be delivered? But it also seemed to Nicholas that the ship had been driven specifically to this particular city, in a straight and steady line through the towering waves.

The whole debate of what they were to do next took place within just a matter of minutes of their arrival on shore. And Nicholas and the captain had little time to think through what they were going to do, as the people of the city were already running out to see the ship for themselves, having been amazed at the way God had seemingly brought it to their famished port. They were gathering in larger and larger numbers to welcome the boat and giving thanks and praise to God at the same time.

Both Nicholas and the captain knew that only God Himself could answer their dilemma. The two of them, along with the rest of the crew, had already agreed the night before—as they were so steadily and swiftly being carried along through the water—that the first thing they would do when they arrived on shore was to go to the nearest church and give thanks to God for His deliverance. Upon seeing where they had landed, Nicholas knew exactly where they could find that church. It was one that his family had visited from time to time as they traveled between these twin cities of Patara and Myra. Telling the people that their first order of duty was to give thanks to God for their safe passage, Nicholas and the captain and his crew headed to the church in Myra.

As they made their way across the city and up into the hills that cradled the church, they had no idea that the priests inside its walls had already been doing battle with a storm of their own.

CHAPTER 18 — DECEMBER 4

Nicholas' next step in life was about to be determined by a dream. But it wasn't a dream that Nicholas had conceived—it was a dream that God had conceived and had put in the mind of a man, a priest in the city of Myra.

In the weeks leading up to Nicholas' arrival in Myra, a tragedy had befallen the church there. Their aging bishop, the head of their church, had died. The tragedy that had fallen upon the church wasn't the bishop's death, for he had lived a long and fruitful life and had simply succumbed to the effects of old age. The tragedy arose out of the debate that ensued regarding who should take his place as the next bishop.

While it would seem that such things could be resolved amicably, especially within a church, when people's hearts are involved, their loyalties and personal desires can sometimes muddy their thoughts so much that they can't see what God's will is in a particular situation. It can be hard for anyone, even for people of faith, to keep their minds free from preconceived ideas and personal preferences regarding what God may, or may not, want to do at any given time.

This debate was the storm that had been brewing for a week now, and which had reached its apex the night before Nicholas' arrival.

That night one of the priests had a dream that startled him awake. In his dream he saw a man whom he had never seen before who was clearly to take up the responsibilities of their dearly departed bishop. When he woke from his dream, he remembered nothing about what the man looked like, but only remembered his name: Nicholas.

"Nicholas?" asked one of the other priests when he heard his fellow priest's dream. "None of us have ever gone by that name, nor is there anyone in the whole city by that name."

Nicholas was, to be sure, not a popular name at the time. It was only mentioned once in passing in one of Luke's writings about the early church, along with other names which were just as uncommon in those days in Myra like Procorus, Nicanor, Timon and Parmenas. It seemed ridiculous to the other priests that this dream could possibly be from God. But the old priest reminded them, "Even the name of Jesus was given to His father by an angel in a dream."

Perhaps it was this testimony from the gospels, or perhaps it was the unlikelihood that it would ever happen, that the priests all agreed that they would strongly consider the next person who walked through their door who answered to the name of Nicholas. It would certainly help to break the deadlock in which they found themselves.

What a surprise then, when they opened their doors for their morning prayers, when an entire *shipload* of men started to stream into the church!

The priests greeted each of the men at the door as they entered, welcoming them into the church. The last two to enter were the captain and Nicholas, as they had allowed all of the others to enter first. The captain thanked the priests for opening their doors to them for their morning prayers, then turned to Nicholas and said, "And thanks to Nicholas for having this brilliant idea to come here today."

The astonished priests looked at one another in disbelief. Perhaps God had answered their prayers after all.

CHAPTER 19 — DECEMBER 5

The captain's concern about what to do with the grain on his ship dissipated when they arrived at the church as fast as the storm had dissipated when they arrived on shore.

Within moments of beginning their morning prayers, he was convinced that it could only have been the mighty hand of God that had held their rudder straight and true. He knew now for sure he wanted to make an offering of the grain to the people who lived there. God spoke to him about both the plan and the amount. It was as if the captain were playing the role of Abraham in the old, old story when Abraham offered a portion of his riches to Melchizedek the priest.

The captain was willing to take his chances with his superiors in Rome rather than take any chances with the God who had delivered them all. He knew that without God's guidance and direction so far on this journey, neither he nor his men nor the ship nor its grain would have ever made it to Rome at all.

When the captain stood up from his prayers, he quickly found Nicholas to share the answer with him as well. Nicholas agreed both to the plan and to the amount. The captain asked, "Do you think it will be enough for all these people?"

Nicholas replied, "Jesus was able to feed 5,000 people with just five loaves of bread and two fish—and what you want to give to this city is much more than what Jesus had to start with!"

"How did He do it?" asked the captain—almost to himself as much as to Nicholas.

"All I know," answered Nicholas, "is that He looked up to heaven, gave thanks and began passing out the food with His disciples. In the end everyone was satisfied and they still had twelve baskets full of food left over!"

"That's exactly what we'll do then, too," said the captain.

And the story would be told for years to come how the captain of the ship looked up to heaven, gave thanks and began passing out the grain with his crew. It was enough to satisfy the people of that city for two whole years and to plant and reap even more in the third year.

As the priests said goodbye to the captain and crew, they asked Nicholas if he would be able to stay behind for a time. The winds of confusion that had whipped up and then subsided inside the captain's mind were about to pale in comparison to the storm that was about to break open inside the mind of Nicholas.

CHAPTER 20   DECEMBER 6

When the priests told Nicholas about their dream and that he just might be the answer to their prayers, Nicholas was dumbfounded and amazed, excited and perplexed. He had often longed to be used by God in a powerful way, and it was unmistakable that God had already brought him straight across the Great Sea to this very spot at this very hour!

But to become a priest, let alone a bishop, would be a decision that would last a lifetime. He had oftentimes considered taking up his earthly father's business. His father had been highly successful at it, and Nicholas felt he could do the same. But even more important to him than doing the work of his father was to have a family like his father.

Nicholas' memories of his parents were so fond that he longed to create more memories of his own with a family of his own. The custom of all the priests Nicholas knew, however, was to abstain from marriage and child-bearing so they could more fully devote themselves to the needs of the community around them.

Nicholas pulled back mentally at the thought of having to give up his desire for a family of his own. It wasn't that having a family was a conscious dream that often filled his thoughts, but it was one of those assumptions in the back of his mind that he took for granted would come at some point in his future.

The shock of having to give up on the idea of a family, even before he had fully considered having one yet, was like a jolt to his system. *Following God's will shouldn't be so difficult*, he thought! But he had learned from his parents that laying down your will for the sake of God's will wasn't always so easy, another lesson they had learned from Jesus.

So just because it was a difficult decision wasn't enough to rule it out. An image also floated through his mind of those three smiling faces he had met when he first landed in the Holy Land, with their heads bowed down and their hands outstretched. Hadn't they seemed like family to him? And weren't there hundreds—even thousands—of children just like them, children who had no family of their own, no one to care for them, no one to look after their needs?

And weren't there countless others in the world—widows and widowers and those who had families in name but not in their actual relationships—who still needed the strength and encouragement and sense of family around them? And weren't there still other families as well, like Nicholas and his parents, who had been happy on their own but found additional happiness when they came together as the family of believers in their city? Giving up on the idea of a family of his own didn't mean he had to give up on the idea of having a family altogether. In fact, it may even be possible that he could have an even larger "family" in this way.

The more Nicholas thought about what he might give up in order to serve God in the church, the more he thought about how God might use this new position in ways that went beyond Nicholas' own thoughts and desires. And if God was indeed in this decision, perhaps it had its own special rewards in the end.

The fury of the storm that swept through his mind began to abate. In its place, God's peace began to flow over both his mind and his heart. Nicholas recognized this as the peace of God's divine will being clearly revealed to him. It only took another moment for Nicholas to know what his answer would be.

The storms that had once seemed so threatening—whether the storm at sea or the storm in the church or the storms in the minds of both the captain and Nicholas—now turned out to be blessings of God instead. They were blessings that proved to Nicholas once again that no matter what happened, God really could work all things for good for those who loved Him and who were called according to His purpose.

Yes, if the priests would have him, Nicholas would become the next bishop of Myra.

CHAPTER 21   DECEMBER 7

Nicholas didn't suddenly become another man when he became a bishop. He became a bishop because of the man he already was. As he had done before with his father so many years earlier, Nicholas continued to do now, here in the city of Myra and the surrounding towns: walking and praying and asking God where he could be of most help.

It was on one of these prayerful walks that Nicholas met Anna Maria. She was a beautiful girl only eleven years old, but her beauty was disguised to most others by the poverty she wore. Nicholas found her one day trying to sell flowers that she had made out of braided blades of grass. But the beauty of the flowers also seemed to be disguised to everyone but Nicholas, for no one would buy her simple creations.

As Nicholas stepped towards her, she reminded him instantly of little Ruthie, whom he had left behind in the Holy Land, with the golden flowers in her hand on the hillsides of Bethlehem.

When he stopped for a closer look, God spoke to his heart. It seemed to Nicholas that this must have been what Moses felt when he stopped to look at the burning bush in the desert, a moment when his natural curiosity turned into a supernatural encounter with the Living God.

"Your flowers are beautiful," said Nicholas. "May I hold one?"

The young girl handed him one of her creations. As he looked at it, he looked at her. The beauty he saw in both the flower and the girl was stunning. Somehow Nicholas had the ability to see what others could not see, or did not see, as Nicholas always tried to see people and things and life the way God saw them, as if God were looking through his eyes.

"I'd like to buy this one, if I could," he said.

Delighted, she smiled for the first time. She told him the price, and he gave her a coin.

"Tell me," said Nicholas, "what will you do with the money you make from selling these beautiful flowers?"

What Nicholas heard next broke his heart.

Anna Maria was the youngest of three sisters: Sophia, Cecilia and Anna Maria. Although their father loved them deeply, he had been plunged into despair when his once-successful business had failed, and then his wife passed away shortly thereafter. Lacking the strength and the resources to pick himself up out of the darkness, the situation for his family grew bleaker and bleaker.

Anna Maria's oldest sister, Sophia, had just turned 18, and she turned a number of heads as well. But no one would marry her because her father had no dowry to offer to any potential suitor. And with no dowry, there was little likelihood that she, nor any of the three girls, would ever be married.

The choices facing their father were grim. He knew he must act soon or risk the possibility of Cecilia and Anna Maria never getting married in the future, either. With no way to raise a suitable dowry for her, and being too proud to take charity from others, even if someone had had the funds to offer to him, her father was about to do the unthinkable: he was going to sell his oldest daughter into slavery to help make ends meet.

How their father could think this was the best solution available to him, Nicholas couldn't imagine. But he also knew that desperation often impaired even the best-intentioned men. By sacrificing his oldest daughter in this way, the father reasoned that perhaps he could somehow spare the younger two from a similar fate.

Anna Maria, for her part, had come up with the idea of making and selling flowers as a way to spare her sister from this fate that was to her worse than death. Nicholas held back his tears out of respect for Anna Maria and the noble effort she was making to save her sister.

He also refrained from buying Anna Maria's whole basket of flowers right there on the spot, for Nicholas knew it would take more than a basket full of flowers to save Sophia. It would take a miracle. And as God spoke to his heart that day, Nicholas knew that God just might use him to deliver it.

CHAPTER 22 — DECEMBER 8

Without show and without fanfare, Nicholas offered a prayer for Anna Maria, along with his thanks for the flower, and encouraged her to keep doing what she could to help her family—and to keep trusting in God to do what she couldn't.

Nicholas knew he could help this family. He knew he had the resources to make a difference in their lives, for he still had a great deal of his parents' wealth hidden in the cliffs near the coast for occasions such as this. But he also knew that Anna Maria's proud father would never accept charity from any man, even at this bleakest hour.

Her father's humiliation at losing his business, along with his own personal loss, had blinded him to the reality of what was about to happen to his daughter. Nicholas wanted to help, but how? How could he step into the situation without further humiliating Anna Maria's father, possibly causing him to refuse the very help that Nicholas could extend to him. Nicholas did what he always did when he needed wisdom. He prayed. And before the day was out, he had his answer.

Nicholas put his plan into action—and none too soon! It just so happened that the next day was the day when Sophia's fate would be sealed.

Taking a fair amount of gold coins from his savings, Nicholas placed them into a small bag. It was small enough to fit in one hand, but heavy enough to be sure that it would adequately supply the need.

Hiding under the cover of night, he crossed the city of Myra to the home where Anna Maria, her father and her two older sisters lived.

He could hear them talking inside as he quietly approached the house. Their mood was understandably downcast as they discussed what they thought was their inevitable next step. They asked God to give them the strength to do whatever they needed to do.

For years, Sophia and her sisters had dreamed of the day when they would each meet the man of their dreams. They had even written love songs to these men, trusting that God would bring each of them the perfect man at the perfect time.

Now it seemed like all their songs, all their prayers and all their dreams had been in vain. Sophia wasn't the only one who felt the impact of this new reality, for her two younger sisters knew that the same fate might one day await each of them.

The girls *wanted* to trust God, but no matter how hard they thought about their situation, each of them felt like their dreams were about to be shattered.

At Anna Maria's prompting, they tried to sing their favorite love song one more time, but their sadness simply deepened at the words. It was no longer a song of hope, but a song of despair, and the words now seemed so impossible to them.

It was not just a song, but a prayer, and one of the deepest prayers Nicholas had ever heard uttered by human tongue. His heart went out to each of them, while at the same time it pounded with fear. He had a plan, and he hoped it would work, but he had no way of knowing for sure. He wasn't worried about what might happen to *him* if he were discovered, but he was worried that their father would reject his *gift* if he knew where it had come from. That would certainly seal the girls' doom. As Sophia and Cecilia and Anna Maria said their goodnights—and their father had put out the lights—Nicholas knew that his time had come.

Inching closer to the open window of the room where they had been singing, Nicholas bent down low to his knees. He lobbed the bag of coins into the air and through the window. It arced gracefully above him and seemed to hang in the air for a moment before landing with a soft thud in the center of the room. A few coins bounced loose, clinking faintly on the ground, rolling and then coming to a stop. Nicholas turned quickly and hid in the darkness nearby as the girls and their father awoke at the sound.

They called out to see if anyone was there, but when they heard no answer, they entered the room from both directions. As their father lit the light, Anna Maria was the first to see it—and gasped.

There, in the center of the room, lay a small round bag, shimmering with golden coins at the top. The girls gathered around their father as he carefully picked up the bag and opened it.

It was more than enough gold to provide a suitable dowry for Sophia, with more to spare to take care of the rest of the family for some time to come!

But where could such a gift have come from? The girls were sure it had come from God Himself in answer to their prayers! But their father wanted to know more. Who had God used to deliver it? Certainly no one they knew. He sprinted out of the house, followed by his daughters, to see if he could find any trace of the deliverer, but none could be found.

Returning back inside, and with no one to return the money to, the girls and their father got down on their knees and thanked God for *His* deliverance.

As Nicholas listened in the darkness, he too gave thanks to God, for this was the very thing Nicholas hoped they would do. He knew that the gift truly *was* from God, provided by God and given through Nicholas by God's prompting in answer to their prayers. Nicholas had only given to them what God had given to him in the first place. Nicholas neither wanted nor needed any thanks nor recognition for the gift. God alone deserved their praise.

But by allowing Nicholas to be involved, using Nicholas' own hands and his own inheritance to bless others, Nicholas felt a joy that he could hardly contain. By delivering the gift himself, Nicholas was able to ensure that the gift was properly given. And by giving the gift anonymously, he was able to ensure that the true Giver of the gift was properly credited.

The gift was delivered, and God got the credit. Nicholas had achieved both of his goals.

CHAPTER 23 — DECEMBER 9

While Nicholas preferred to do his acts of goodwill in secret, there were times when, out of sheer necessity, he had to act in broad daylight. And while it was his secret acts that gained him favor with God, it was his public acts that gained him favor with men.

Many people rightly appreciate a knight in shining armor, but not everyone wants to be rescued from evil—especially those who profit from it.

One such man was a magistrate in Myra, a leader in the city who disliked Nicholas intensely—or anyone who stood in the way of what he wanted.

This particular magistrate was both corrupt and corruptible. He was willing to do anything to get what he wanted, no matter what it cost to others. Although Nicholas had already been at odds with him several times in the past, their conflict escalated to a boiling point when news reached Nicholas that the magistrate had sentenced three men to death—for a crime Nicholas was sure they did not commit. Nicholas couldn't wait this time for the cover of darkness. He knew he needed to act immediately to save these men from death.

Nicholas had been entertaining some generals from Rome that afternoon whose ship had docked in Myra's port the night before. Nicholas had invited the generals to his home to hear news about some changes that had been taking place in Rome. A new emperor was about to take power, they said, and the implications might be serious for Nicholas and his flock of Christ-followers.

It was during their luncheon that Nicholas heard about the unjust sentencing and the impending execution. Immediately he set out for the site where the execution was to take place. The three generals, sensing more trouble might ensue once Nicholas arrived, set out after him.

When Nicholas burst onto the execution site, the condemned men were already on the platform. They were bound and bent over with their heads and necks ready for the executioner's sword.

Without a thought for his own safety, Nicholas leapt onto the platform and tore the sword from the executioner's hands. Although Nicholas was not a fighter himself, Nicholas made his move so unexpectedly that the executioner made little attempt to try to wrestle the sword back out of the bishop's hands.

Nicholas knew these men were as innocent as the magistrate was guilty. He was certain that it must have been the men's good deeds, not their bad ones, that had offended the magistrate. Nicholas untied the ropes of the innocent men in full view of the onlookers, defying both the executioner and the magistrate.

The magistrate came forward to face Nicholas squarely. But as he did so, the three generals who had been having lunch with Nicholas also stepped forward. One took his place on Nicholas' left, another on Nicholas' right and the third stood directly in front of him. Prudently, the magistrate took a step back. Nicholas knew that this was the time to press the magistrate for the truth.

Although the magistrate tried to defend himself, his pleas fell on deaf ears. No one would believe his lies anymore. He tried to convince the people that it was not *he* who wanted to condemn these innocent men, but two other businessmen in town who had given him a bribe in order to have these men condemned. But by trying to shift the blame to others, the magistrate condemned himself for the greed that was in his heart.

Nicholas declared: "It seems that it was not these two men who have corrupted you, sir, but two others—whose names are Gold and Silver!"

Cut to the quick, the magistrate broke down and made a full confession in front of all the people for this and for all the other wrongs he had done, even for speaking ill of Nicholas, who had done nothing but good for the people. Nicholas set more than three prisoners free that day, as even the magistrate was finally set free from his greed by his honest confession. Seeing the heartfelt change in the magistrate, Nicholas pardoned him, forever winning the magistrate's favor–and the people's favor—from that moment on.

When Nicholas was born, his parents had named him Nicholas, which means in Greek "the people's victor." Through acts like these, Nicholas became "the people's victor" both in name and in deed.

Nicholas was already becoming an icon—even in his own time.

CHAPTER 24   DECEMBER 10

Within three months of receiving her unexpected dowry from Nicholas, Sophia had received a visit from a suitor—one who "suited her" just fine. He truly was the answer to her prayers, and she was thankfully, happily and finally married.

Two years later, however, Sophia's younger sister Cecilia found herself in dire straits as well. Although Cecilia was ready to be married now, her father's business had not improved, no matter how hard he tried. As the money that Nicholas had given to the family began to run out, their despair began to set in. Pride and sorrow had once again blinded Cecilia's father to the truth, and he felt his only option was to commit Cecilia to a life of slavery, hoping to save his third and final daughter from a similar fate.

While they were confident that God had answered their prayers once, their circumstances had caused them to doubt that He could do it again. A second rescue at this point was more than they could have asked for or imagined.

Nicholas, however, knowing their situation by this time much more intimately, knew that God was prompting him again to intercede. It had been two years since his earlier rescue, but in all that time the family never suspected nor discovered that he was the deliverer of God's gift.

As the time came closer to a decision on what they should do next, Nicholas knew his time to act had come as well. And in order to make it clear that his gift was to be used first and foremost for Cecilia's dowry, and then after that for any other needs the family might have, he waited until the night before she was to be sold into slavery to make his move.

Once again waiting for the cover of darkness, Nicholas approached their house. Cecilia and Anna Maria had already gone to bed early that night, sent there by their father who had told them not to expect any similar miracle to what happened for Sophia. But somewhere in the depths of his despair, their father still had a glimmer of hope in his heart, a wish perhaps, more than anything else, that Someone really was watching out for him and that his prayers just might still be answered. With that hope, he decided to stay awake and stay close to the window, just in case some angel did appear—whether an earthly one or a heavenly one.

Nicholas knew this might happen, and he knew that Cecilia's father might still reject his gift if he found out that Nicholas had given it. But he also hoped that perhaps her father's proud heart had softened a bit and he would accept the gift even if Nicholas was discovered.

Seeing that the house was perfectly quiet, Nicholas knelt down beside the open window. He tossed the second bag of gold into the room.

The bag had barely hit the ground when the girls' father leapt out of the window through which it had come and overtook Nicholas as he tried to flee. You might have thought that Nicholas had *taken* a bag of gold rather than *given* a bag of gold the way the girls' father chased him down!

Fearing that all his efforts had been wasted, Nicholas' heart was eased as the man didn't rebuke Nicholas but thanked him without even looking at who he had caught.

"Please hear me out," he said. "I just want to thank you. You've done so much already for me and my family that I couldn't have expected such a gift again. But your generosity has opened my eyes to the pride in my heart—a pride that almost cost me the lives of two daughters now."

The girls' father had spoken both breathlessly and quickly to be sure that the stranger would hear him before trying to escape again. But when he looked up to see who he was talking to—Nicholas the priest—the shock on their father's face was evident. How could a priest afford to give such an incredible gift?

In answer to this unasked question, Nicholas spoke: "Yes, it was I who delivered this gift to you, but it was God who gave it to me to give to you. It is not from the church and not from the charity of my own hand. It came from my father who earned it fairly by the work of *his* hands. He was a businessman like you. And if he were alive today, he would have wanted to give it to you himself. I'm sure of it. He, of all people, knew how difficult it was to run a business, just as you do. He also loved his family, just as you do, too."

Nicholas paused to let his words sink in, then continued, "But please, for my sake and for God's sake, please know that it was God Himself who has answered your prayers—for He has. I am simply a messenger for Him, a deliverer, a tool in His hands, allowing Him to do through me what I know He wants done. As for me, I prefer to do my giving in secret, not even letting my right hand know what my left hand is doing."

The look on Nicholas' face was so sincere and he conveyed his intentions with such love and devotion for the One whom he served, that the girls' father could not help but to accept Nicholas' gift as if it had truly come from the hand of God Himself.

But as they said their goodbyes, the girls and their father could hardly contain their thankfulness to Nicholas, too, for letting God use him in such a remarkable way.

As much as Nicholas tried to deflect their praise back to God, he also knew he *did* have a role to play in their lives. Although God prompts many to be generous in their hearts, not everyone responds to those promptings as Nicholas did.

Nicholas would wait to see how the family fared over the next few years to see if they would need any help for Anna Maria, too.

But Nicholas never got the chance. The new emperor had finally come into power, and the course of Nicholas' life was about to change again. Even though Nicholas often came to the rescue of others, there were times when, like the Savior he followed, it seemed he was unable to rescue himself.

CHAPTER 25   DECEMBER 11

Back when Jesus was born, there was a king who felt so threatened by this little baby boy that he gave orders to kill every boy in Bethlehem and its vicinity who were two years old and under. Three hundred and three years later, another king felt just as threatened by Jesus, as well as his followers.

This new king's name was Diocletian, and he was the emperor of the entire Roman Empire. Even though the Romans had killed Jesus hundreds of years earlier, Diocletian still felt threatened by the Christians who followed Jesus. Diocletian declared himself to be a god and he wanted all the people in his empire to worship him.

Although Christians were among the most law-abiding citizens in the land, they simply couldn't worship Diocletian. He considered this an act of insurrection, an act which must be quenched in the strongest way possible. By the time Diocletian had finally risen to his full power, he ordered that all Bibles be burned, that Christian churches be destroyed and that those who followed Christ be imprisoned, tortured and put to death.

While persecution against Christians had been taking place for many years under Roman rule, none of those persecutions compared to that which took place during the reign of Diocletian. Nicholas, for his part, didn't fear Diocletian, but as always, he feared for those in his church who followed Jesus.

Having such a visible role in the church, Nicholas knew that he would be targeted first, and if he were taken away, he feared for what would happen to those who would be left behind. But Nicholas had already made his decision. He knew that even if he was killed, he could trust God that God could still accomplish His purpose on earth whether Nicholas were a part of that or not. It was this foundational faith and trust in God and His purposes that would help Nicholas through the difficult years ahead.

Rather than retreat into hiding from the certain fate that awaited him, Nicholas chose to stand his ground to the end. He vowed to keep the doors to his church wide open for all who wanted to come in. And he kept that vow for as long as he could until one day when those who came in were soldiers—soldiers who had come for him.

CHAPTER 26   DECEMBER 12

Nicholas was ready when the soldiers arrived. He knew that his time for second-guessing his decision to keep the church open was over. Unfortunately, the days for his church were over, too, as the soldiers shut the doors for good when they left.

For all the goodwill that Nicholas had built up with people in his town over the years, even with the local soldiers, these were no local soldiers who came for Nicholas. Diocletian had sent them with demands that his orders be carried out unquestioningly, and that those who didn't carry them out would suffer the same fate as those who were to be punished.

Nicholas was given one last chance to renounce his faith in Christ and worship Diocletian instead, but Nicholas, of course, refused. It wasn't that he *wanted* to defy Roman authority, for Christ Himself taught His followers that it was important to honor those in authority and to honor their laws. But to deny that Jesus was His Lord and Savior would have been like trying to deny that the sun had risen that morning! He simply couldn't do it. How could he deny the existence of the One who had given him life, who had given him faith and who had given him hope in the darkest hours of his life. If the soldiers had to take him away, so be it. To say that a mere man like Diocletian was God, and that Jesus was anything less than God, was unconscionable.

For all his faith, Nicholas was still subject to the same sensations of pain that every human being experiences. His strong faith did not exempt him from the natural fear that others feel when they are threatened with bodily harm. He also feared the idea of imprisonment, having to be isolated from others for so long, especially when he didn't know how long his imprisonment might last–or if he would survive it at all.

Nicholas knew that these fears were healthy, given to him by God, to keep out any danger and to protect him from anything that might possibly harm his body. But right now, as Nicholas was being forcefully taken away, he wished he could suppress those fears.

"God, help me," he called out as the shackles that the soldiers were putting on his wrists cut into them. This was the beginning of a new kind of pilgrimage for Nicholas—a pilgrimage that would last far longer than his years in the Holy Land.

It would be hard to compare these two journeys in terms of their impact on his life, for how could you compare a journey freely taken, where you could come and go as you please and stop the journey at any time, with a journey that was forced upon you against your will, where even venturing out to catch a glimpse of the sun was under someone else's control and not yours?

Yet Nicholas found that he was able to sense the presence of God in a way that equaled, if not surpassed, all that he had experienced in the Holy Land. As he had learned from other believers, sometimes you don't realize that Jesus is all you need until Jesus is all you have.

Over the course of his imprisonment, whenever the door to Nicholas' prison cell opened, he didn't know if the guards were there to set him free or to sentence him to death. He never knew if any given day might be his last. But the byproduct of this uncertainty was that Nicholas received a keen awareness of the brevity of life, as well as a continual awareness of the presence of God.

Nicholas found that by closing his eyes he could sense God's presence in a way he had never sensed it before. This cell wasn't a prison–it was a sanctuary. And all Nicholas wanted to do was to stay in God's presence as long as he could. Soon, Nicholas didn't even have to close his eyes. He simply knew that he was always in the presence of God.

Of course, his time in prison was also filled with the stinging pain of the worst kind of hell on earth. The soldiers were relentless in their attempts to get Nicholas to renounce his faith. The pain they inflicted ranged from prodding him with hot branding irons and squeezing his flesh with hot pincers to whipping him severely, then pouring salt and vinegar in his wounds. As a result, his back was permanently scarred. The unsanitary conditions of the prison caused Nicholas to experience more kinds of sickness than he had ever experienced before. At times he even wondered if death might be better than what he had to endure there.

It was during one of those times, the darkest perhaps, of the five years he had spent so far in prison, that the door to his cell opened. A light streamed in, but as he looked at it closely, it wasn't the light of the sun, for as far as Nicholas could tell in his isolated cell, it was still just the middle of the night.

The light that entered the room was the light of a smile, a smile on the face of Nicholas' young friend, now grown to be a man. It was the light of the smiling face of Dimitri.

CHAPTER 27   DECEMBER 13

Nicholas had seen few faces in his time in prison, and fewer still that gave him any kind of encouragement. To see a smile on someone's face, let alone a face that Nicholas loved so much, was pure joy.

It hadn't been easy for Dimitri to find Nicholas. Dimitri had come to Myra knowing that Nicholas had taken a church there. But it had been years since Dimitri had heard from his friend, a time in which Dimitri himself had been imprisoned. Having only recently been set free, Dimitri made his way across the Great Sea in search of Nicholas. Dimitri had to search hard to find Nicholas, but Dimitri had come too far to give up without seeing his old friend and mentor, the first person who had shown him the love of Christ.

Using the street-smarts that he had acquired as a guide in the Holy Land, Dimitri was able to navigate his way through or around most anyone or anything that stood in his way. Dimitri's tenacity, plus the hand of God's guidance, helped Dimitri to find his friend, and to find this door which he opened that night for this special visit. It was a visit that, to Nicholas, seemed like a visit by an angel from heaven.

After the door closed behind them, and after an extended embrace, Dimitri sat down on the floor next to Nicholas. They sat in silence for several minutes, neither of them having to say a word. In holy moments like these, words were unnecessary.

The darkness in the small cell was so great that they didn't even try to look at one another, but simply sat there side by side. Dimitri's eyes had not yet adjusted to the pitch-blackness enough to see anything anyway, and Nicholas was content to merely know that his friend was right there by him. Nicholas could hear the sound of Dimitri's breath, a sound which increased Nicholas' joy, knowing that his friend was still alive and was right there in the flesh.

Nicholas drew in another deep breath and with it he breathed in a new sense of life. It was a breath of life that his friend couldn't help but bring with him.

CHAPTER 28 — DECEMBER 14

"And how are our two young bodyguards doing?" Nicholas asked at last, referring to Samuel and Ruthie. Nicholas had been praying often for all three of them, as he cared for them as if they were his own young brothers and sister.

Dimitri hesitated. He looked at Nicholas but couldn't say a word. He was eager to tell Nicholas everything that had happened in the years that had passed, about how Samuel and Ruthie continued taking people to the holy places, sharing with others the same good news of Jesus that they had discovered in their days with Nicholas.

Like Dimitri, Samuel and Ruthie had to stop guiding pilgrims when the "Great Persecution" came, as it was now being called. All three of them began spending most of their days seeing to the needs of the other believers in Jerusalem, believers who were facing imprisonment and death, just like Nicholas. Since they were not in a high profile position like Nicholas though, the three of them were able to avoid being caught longer than Nicholas. But eventually, they too were imprisoned, being repeatedly questioned, threatened and tortured for their faith.

Samuel and Dimitri were strong enough to withstand the abuse, but Ruthie was too frail. One day, after being treated particularly harshly, she returned to them and collapsed. Although she had obviously been crying from the pain in her body, somehow she had also managed to keep a smile in her heart.

"How can you do it?" asked Samuel. "How can you possibly still smile, even after all that?"

Ruthie replied, "I feel like I've been walking and talking with Jesus for so long now that even death wouldn't really change that. I'll just keep on walking and talking with Him forever."

Ruthie smiled again and Dimitri couldn't help but smile back at her. But her body was giving out and she knew it. She could sense that she was just moments away from passing from this life to the next.

"You can't go!" said Samuel. "You've got to stay here with me! There's still too much work to be done!" But Ruthie was slipping away.

"If you die, I'll just pray that God will bring you back to life!" Samuel was desperate now to hang onto her. But Ruthie just smiled again. She had truly found the secret of living life to the fullest, and nothing, not even death, could take that away.

She spoke, quietly now, with just a whisper. "You could pray that God would raise me from the dead, but the truth is, I've already been raised from the dead once. When we met Nicholas, and he introduced us to Jesus, I was raised from the dead and given a whole new life. From then on, I knew that I would live forever."

With that, Ruthie passed through the veil and into the visible presence of God. The smile that adorned her face in life continued to shine on her face in death, and Dimitri knew where she was. She was just continuing to do what she had always done, walking and talking with Jesus, but now face to face.

Nicholas sat in silence as Dimitri told him the story, taking it all in. As much as he thought he would be sad, his heart began to soar instead. None of this was new to him, of course, but hearing about Ruthie's faith brought his own back to life again as well.

You would think a man like Nicholas wouldn't need to be encouraged in his faith. He had brought faith to countless others, and he was a bishop no less. But Nicholas also knew in his heart of hearts that it was people like him who sometimes needed the most encouragement in their faith. Great faith, he knew, did not come to those who have no doubts. Great faith came to those who have had their faith stretched so far that it had to grow, or else it would break completely. By continuing to trust God no matter what, Nicholas found that he was able to fill in any gaps in his faith along the way, helping it to grow even further.

As sad as he was for Ruthie's passing, Nicholas couldn't help but smile from deep down in his heart the same way that Ruthie must have done on the day that she died. He longed for the day when he could see Jesus face to face, just as Ruthie was now seeing Him. Yet he loved the work that God had given him on earth to do, too.

"We can't lose, can we?" said Nicholas with a reflective smile. "Either we die and get to be with Jesus in heaven, or we live and get to continue His work here on earth. Either way we win, don't we? Either way we win."

"Yes, either way we win," echoed Dimitri. "Either way we win."

For the next several hours, Nicholas and Dimitri shared stories with each other of what God had done in their lives during their time apart. But nothing could have prepared Nicholas for what Dimitri was about to tell him next. For Dimitri, it seems, had met a girl. And not just any girl, but a girl Nicholas knew very well by now. Her name was Anna Maria.

CHAPTER 29 — DECEMBER 15

In his journey to find Nicholas, Dimitri looked for anyone who might know of his whereabouts. When he got to Myra, he went first to the church where Nicholas had served as bishop. Not finding him there, Dimitri took to the streets to see if he could find anyone who knew anything about him. And who did he find in the streets, but the very girl—now a woman—that Nicholas had found so many years ago, selling her braided flowers to anyone who would buy them.

She was no longer covered in the cloak of poverty. Both her inner and outer beauty were immediately evident to Dimitri. He was so taken by her that he couldn't help but be drawn into a conversation. And she seemed to be just as taken by him. She couldn't believe that a man of his stature and faith was willing to talk to her. He was, she thought, the kindest and most impressive man she had ever met.

When Dimitri mentioned his mission, searching for the bishop named Nicholas, Anna Maria gasped. How could this man, this stranger from the other side of the Great Sea, know anything about Nicholas? Dimitri shared the story of how they met, and Nicholas had rescued him from his poverty of faith. Anna Maria couldn't help but share what Nicholas had done for her family as well, saving her two older sisters from slavery by throwing a bag of gold through the window for each of them on the eve of their 18th birthdays.

But then, Anna Maria's smile faded. It was now only a few days until her own 18th birthday, but Nicholas had been taken away to prison five years earlier. No one had seen nor heard from him in all those years. She didn't even know where he was. Although her father had had a change of heart, and wouldn't dream of selling Anna Maria into slavery, he still had no dowry to offer to any potential suitor. Without a dowry, as Dimitri knew very well, Anna Maria's future was dim. And with Nicholas in prison, there was no chance he would be able to rescue their family a third time. Anna Maria had taken again to selling her flowers in the street, and although they were more impressive than her earlier creations, she could barely earn enough from their sales to help the family with the cost of food from time to time.

Dimitri listened, and like Nicholas before him, he knew within minutes what God was prompting him to do. He could be the answer to Anna Maria's prayers, and with much more than just a dowry. But he also knew that these things take time, so he just treasured these thoughts in his heart, buying a flower from Anna Maria, thanking her for sharing what she knew about Nicholas and continuing on his way, promising to get in touch with her if he ever located their precious friend.

On the eve of Anna Maria's birthday, Dimitri found himself in the very spot where Nicholas had hidden twice before, years earlier, just outside the open window of Anna Maria's home. The conversation inside was subdued, as Anna Maria and her father prayed, knowing that there was no way for Nicholas to appear again. They put out the lights and headed for bed.

Dimitri waited for what seemed to him like hours, knowing that he couldn't dare wake them and risk exposing his plan. For he had saved up enough in his years of working in the Holy Land to easily fill a bag with golden coins suitable for a dowry. But he couldn't just hand them the money, for he had more in mind than just giving them the dowry. He wanted Anna Maria's father to give it back to him someday, as a wedding gift to him! It was a long shot, and he knew he would need more time to be sure she was the one for him. He also felt this was the best way to make it all work out in the end, even if she wasn't the one for him. Something told him, however, that she was. And with that thought in mind, he made his next move.

Carefully and quietly, he reached over the windowsill and let the bag drop quietly down on the floor below. No one heard and no one stirred. Having done his duty to God and to his own heart, he set off again in search of Nicholas. Two weeks later, Dimitri had found Nicholas, and was now sharing with him the story of how he had met the woman of his dreams.

The news couldn't have been any sweeter to Nicholas' ears. And again his heart lightened and soared, for even though he was locked away from the rest of the world in his prison cell, Nicholas saw the fruit of his prayers—prayers that were answered in the most incredible way imaginable. He could still make a difference in the world, even from here in prison, even when the world tried to shut him down.

Before Dimitri left that night, he embraced Nicholas one more time; then he was gone. He disappeared through the prison door as miraculously as he had entered it.

It would be five more years until Nicholas would see Dimitri again. Diocletian's grip continued to tighten around the Christians' necks. But during all those remaining years in prison, Nicholas felt freer in his heart than he had ever felt before. No man could keep Nicholas from worshipping Jesus, and no man could keep Jesus from doing what He wanted done.

When the day finally came for Nicholas to be set free, the guard who opened Nicholas' door looked in and said, "It's time to go. You're free."

Nicholas simply looked at the guard with a smile. He had already been free for quite some time.

CHAPTER 30   DECEMBER 16

Thinking Nicholas must not have heard him, the guard spoke again. "I said you're free, you're free to go. You can get up and go home now."

At the word "home," Nicholas stirred. He hadn't seen his home, or his church, or hardly any other soul than Dimitri for ten years. He stood to his feet and his movements began to accelerate as he responded to the guard's words.

"Home?" Nicholas said.

"Yes, home. You can go home now. The emperor has issued a decree that has set all Christians free."

The emperor he was referring to was a new emperor named Constantine. Diocletian's efforts had failed to constrain the Christians. Instead of quenching their spirits, Diocletian had strengthened them. Like Nicholas, those who weren't killed grew stronger in their faith. And the stronger they grew in their faith, the stronger they grew in their influence, gaining new converts from the citizens around them. Even Diocletian's wife and daughter had converted to Christianity.

Diocletian stepped down from ruling the empire, and Constantine stepped up.

Constantine reversed the persecution of the Christians, issuing the Edict of Milan. This edict showed a new tolerance for people of all religions and resulted in freedom for the Christians. Constantine's mother, Helen, was a devout Christian herself. Even though no one quite knew if Constantine was a Christian, the new tolerance he displayed allowed people to worship whoever they pleased and however they pleased, the way it should have been all along.

As much as Diocletian had changed the Roman world for the worse, Constantine was now changing it for the better. Their reigns were as different as night and day and served as a testament of how one person really can affect the course of history forever—either for good or for evil.

Nicholas was aware, now more than ever, that he had just one life to live. But he was also aware that if he lived it right, one life was all that he would need. He resolved in his heart once more to do his best to make the most of every day, starting again today.

As he was led from his prison cell and returned to the city of Myra, it was no coincidence, he thought, that the first face he saw there was the face of Anna Maria.

He recognized her in an instant. But the ten years in prison, and the wear and tear it had taken on his life, made it hard for her to recognize him as quickly. But as soon as she saw his smile, she too knew in an instant that it was the smile of her dear old friend Nicholas. Of course it was Nicholas! And he was alive, standing right there in front of her!

She couldn't move, she was so shocked. Two children stood beside her, looking up at their mother, and then looking at the man who now held her gaze. Here was the man who had done so much for her and her family. Her joy was uncontainable. With a call over her shoulder, Anna Maria shouted, "Dimitri! Dimitri! Come quickly! It's Nicholas!"

Then she rushed towards Nicholas, giving him an embrace and holding on tight. Dimitri emerged from a shop behind them, took one look at Nicholas and Anna Maria and rushed towards them as well, sweeping his children up with him as he ran.

Now the whole family was embracing Nicholas as if he was a dear brother or father or uncle who had just returned from war. The tears and the smiles on their faces melted together. The man who had saved Anna Maria and her family from a fate worse than death had been spared from death as well! And Dimitri grinned from ear to ear, too, seeing his good friend, and seeing how happy it made Nicholas to see Dimitri and Anna Maria together with their new family.

Nicholas took hold of each of their faces—one at a time—and looked deeply into their eyes. Then he held the children close. The seeds he had planted years ago in the lives of Dimitri and Anna Maria were still bearing fruit, fruit he could now see with his own two eyes. All his efforts had been worth it, and nothing like the smiles on their faces could have made it any clearer to him than that.

Throughout the days and weeks ahead, Nicholas and the other believers who had been set free had many similar reunions throughout Myra. Those days were like one long, ongoing reunion.

Nicholas, as well as the others who had managed to survive the Great Persecution, must have appeared to those around them as Lazarus must have appeared, when Jesus called him to come out of the tomb—a man who had died, but was now alive. And like Lazarus, these Christians were not only alive, but they led many more people to faith in Christ as well, for their faith was now on fire in a whole new way. What Diocletian had meant for harm, God was able to use for good. This new contingent of Christians had emerged with a faith that was stronger than ever before.

Nicholas knew that this new level of faith, like all good gifts from God, had been given to him for a purpose, too. For as big as the tests had been that Nicholas had faced up to now, God was preparing him for the biggest test yet to come.

CHAPTER 31   DECEMBER 17

"And you've still never told her, after all these years?" Nicholas asked Dimitri. It had been twelve years since Nicholas had gotten out of prison, and they were talking about the bag of gold that Dimitri had thrown into Anna Maria's open window five years before that.

"She's never asked," said Dimitri. "And even if I told her it was me, she wouldn't believe me. She's convinced *you* did it."

"But how could I, when she knew I was in prison?" It was a conversation they had had before, but Nicholas still found it astounding. Dimitri insisted on keeping his act of giving a secret, just as Nicholas had done whenever possible, too.

"Besides," added Dimitri, "she's right. It really was you who inspired me to give her that gift, as you had already given her family two bags of gold in a similar way. So in a very real sense, it did come from you."

Nicholas had to admit there was some logic in Dimitri's thinking. "But it didn't start with me, either. It was Christ who inspired me."

And to that, Dimitri conceded and said, "And it was Christ who inspired me, too. Believe me, Anna Maria knows that as much as anyone else. Her faith is deeper than ever before. Ever since she met you, she continues to give God credit for all things."

And with that, Nicholas was satisfied, as long as God got the credit in the end. For as Nicholas had taught Dimitri years earlier, there's nothing we have that did not come from God first.

Changing subjects, Nicholas said, "You're sure she won't mind you being away for three months? I can still find someone else to accompany me."

"She's completely and utterly happy for me to go with you," said Dimitri. "She knows how important this is to you, and she knows how much it means to me as well. I wouldn't miss it for the world."

They were discussing their plans to go to the Council of Nicaea that summer. Nicholas had been invited by special request of the emperor, and each bishop was allowed to bring a personal attendant along with him. Nicholas asked Dimitri as soon as he received the invitation.

The Council of Nicaea would be a remarkable event. When Nicholas first opened the letter inviting him to come, he couldn't believe it. So much had changed in the world since he had gotten out of prison twelve years earlier.

Yet there it was, a summons from the Roman emperor to appear before him at Eastertide. The only summons a bishop would have gotten under Emperor Diocletian would have been an invitation to an execution—his own! But under Constantine's leadership, life for Christians had radically changed.

Constantine had not only signed the edict that called for true tolerance to be shown to the Christians, which resulted in setting them free from prison, but he also had started giving them their property back—property which had been taken away under his predecessor. Constantine was even beginning to fund the building and repair of many of the churches that had been destroyed by Diocletian. It was the beginning of a new wave of grace for the Christians, after such an intense persecution before.

As a further sign of Constantine's new support for the cause of Christianity, he had called for a gathering of over 300 of the leading bishops in the land. This gathering would serve two purposes for Constantine: it would unify the church within the previously fractured empire, and it wouldn't hurt his hopes of bringing unity back to the whole country. As the leader of the people, Constantine asserted that it was his responsibility to provide for their spiritual well-being. As such, he pledged to attend and preside over this historic council himself. It would take place in the city of Nicaea, starting in the spring of that year and continuing for several months into the summer.

When Nicholas received his invitation, he quietly praised God for the changing direction of his world. While the Great Persecution had deepened the faith of many of those who survived it, that same persecution had taken its toll on the ability of many others, severely limiting their ability to teach, preach and reach those around them with the life-changing message of Christ.

Now those barriers had been removed—with the support and approval of the emperor himself. The only barriers that remained were within the hearts and minds of those who would hear the good news and would have to decide for themselves what they were going to do with it.

As for Nicholas, he had grown in influence and respect in Myra, as well as the region around him. His great wealth was long since gone, for he had given most of it away when he saw the Great Persecution coming, and what remained had been discovered and ransacked while he was in prison. But what he lost in wealth he made up for in influence, for his heart and actions were still bent towards giving—no matter what he had or didn't have to give. After giving so much of himself to the people around him, he was naturally among those who were chosen to attend the upcoming council. It would turn out to become one of the most momentous events in history, not to mention one of the most memorable events in his own life—but not necessarily for a reason he would want to remember.

CHAPTER 32 — DECEMBER 18

Although Christians were enjoying a new kind of freedom under Constantine, the future of Christianity was still at risk. The threats no longer came from outside the church, but from within. Factions had begun to rise inside the ranks of the growing church, with intense discussions surrounding various theological points which had very practical implications.

In particular, a very small but vocal group, led by a man named Arius, had started to gain attention as they began to question whether Jesus was actually divine or not.

Was Jesus merely a man? Or was He, in fact, one with God in His very essence? To men like Nicholas and Dimitri, the question was hardly debatable, for they had devoted their entire lives to following Jesus as their Lord. They had risked everything to follow Him in word and deed. He was their Lord, their Savior, their Light and their Hope. Like many of the others who would be attending the council, it was not their robes or outer garments that bore witness to their faith in Christ, but the scars and wounds they bore in their flesh as they suffered for Him. They had risked their lives under the threat of death for worshipping Christ as divine, rather than Emperor Diocletian. There was no question in their minds regarding this issue. But still there were some who, like Arius, felt this was a question that was up for debate.

In Arius' zeal to see that people worshipped God alone, Arius could not conceive that any man, even one as good as Jesus, could claim to be one with God without blaspheming the name of God Himself. In this, Arius was not unlike those who persecuted Jesus while He was still alive. Even some of those who were living then and had witnessed His miracles with their own eyes, and heard Jesus' words with their own ears, could not grasp that Jesus could possibly be telling the truth when He said, "I and the Father are one." And for this, they brought Jesus to Herod, and then to Pilate, to have Him crucified.

As a boy, Nicholas had wondered about Jesus' claim, too. But when Nicholas was in Bethlehem, it all finally made perfect sense to him—that God Himself had come down from heaven to earth as a man to take on the sins of the world once and for all as God in the flesh.

Arius, however, was like the Apostle Paul before he met the Jesus on the road to Damascus. Before his life-changing experience, the Apostle Paul wanted to protect what he felt to be the divinity of God by persecuting anyone who said they worshipped Jesus as God. For no man, according to Paul's earlier way of thinking, could possibly consider himself to be one with God.

Like Arius, Paul could not believe the claims of Jesus and His followers. But on the road to Damascus, as Paul was on his way to round up and kill more Christians in his zeal, Paul met the Living Christ in a vision that blinded him physically, but awakened him spiritually to the Truth. In the days that followed, Paul's physical eyes were healed, and he repented of his misguided efforts. He was baptized in Jesus' name and began to preach from then on that Jesus was not merely a man, but that Jesus' claims about Himself to be one with the Father were completely true. Paul gave his life in worship and service to Christ, and had to endure, like Nicholas had to endure, imprisonment and an ever-present threat of death for his faith.

Arius was more like the religious leaders of Jesus' day who, in their zeal to defend God, actually crucified the Lord of all creation. Arius felt justified in trying to gather support among the bishops for his position.

Nicholas and Dimitri didn't think Arius' ideas could possibly gather many supporters. Yet they would soon find out that Arius' personal charisma and his excellent oratorical skills might actually hold sway over some of the bishops who had not yet given the idea nor its implications full consideration.

Nicholas and Dimitri, however, like the Apostle Paul, the Apostle John and tens of thousands of others in the time since Jesus lived and died and rose again from the dead, had discovered that Jesus was, thankfully and supernaturally, both fully human and fully divine.

But what would the rest of the bishops conclude? And what would they teach as truth to others for the countless generations to come? This was to become one of the pivotal questions that was to be determined at this meeting in Nicaea. Although Nicholas was interested in this debate, he had no idea that he was about to play a key role in its outcome.

CHAPTER 33 — DECEMBER 19

After a grand processional of bishops and priests, a boys' choir and Constantine's opening words, one of the first topics addressed at the council was the one brought forth by Arius—whether or not Jesus Christ was divine.

Arius made his opening arguments with great eloquence and great persuasion in the presence of Constantine and the rest of the assembly. Jesus was, he asserted, perhaps the foremost of all created beings. But to be co-equal with God, one in substance and essence with Him, was impossible—at least according to Arius. No one could be one with God, he said.

Nicholas listened in silence, along with every other bishop in that immense room. Respect for the speaker, especially in the presence of the emperor, took precedence over any type of muttering or disturbance that might accompany other types of gatherings like this, especially on a subject of such intensity. But the longer Arius spoke, the harder it became for Nicholas to sit in silence.

After all, Nicholas' parents had given their lives for the honor of serving Christ their Lord. Nicholas himself had been overwhelmed by the presence of God in Bethlehem, at the very spot where God made His first appearance as Man in the flesh. Dimitri, Samuel and Ruthie had all been similarly affected by that visit to Bethlehem. They had walked up the hill in Jerusalem where the King of kings had been put to death by religious leaders—leaders who, like Arius, doubted Jesus' claims to be one with God.

Nicholas had always realized that Jesus was unlike any other man who had ever lived. And after Jesus died, He had risen from the dead, appeared to the twelve disciples and then appeared to more than 500 others who were living in Jerusalem at the time. What kind of man could do that? Was it just a mass hallucination? Was it just wishful thinking on the part of religious fanatics? But these weren't just fans, they were followers who were willing to give up their lives, too, for their Lord and Savior.

The arguments continued to run through Nicholas' head. Hadn't the prophet Micah foretold, hundreds of years before Jesus was born, that the Messiah would be "from of old, from ancient times"? Hadn't the Apostle John said that Jesus "was with God in the beginning," concluding that Jesus "was God."

Like others had tried to suggest, Arius said that Jesus had never claimed to be God. But Nicholas knew the Scriptures well enough to know that Jesus had said, "I and the Father are one. Anyone who has seen Me has seen the Father… Don't you believe that I am in the Father, and that the Father is in Me?"

Even Jesus' detractors at the time that He was living said that the reason they wanted to stone Jesus was because Jesus claimed to be God. The Scriptures said that these detractors cornered Jesus one day and Jesus said, "I have shown you many great miracles from the Father. For which of these do you stone me?"

They replied, "We are not stoning you for any of these, but for blasphemy, because you, a mere man, claim to be God."

Jesus had certainly claimed to be God, a claim that got Him into hot water more than once. His claim showed that He was either a madman or a liar–or that He was telling the Truth.

Nicholas' mind flooded with Scriptures like these, as well as with memories of the years he had spent in prison—years he would never get back again–all because he was unwilling to worship Diocletian as a god, but was fully willing to worship Jesus as God. How could Nicholas remain silent and let Arius go on like this? How could anyone else in the room take it, he thought? Nicholas had no idea.

"There was nothing divine about him," Arius said with conviction. "He was just a man, just like any one of us."

Without warning, and without another moment to think about what he was doing, Nicholas stood to his feet. Then his feet, as if they had a mind of their own, began to walk deliberately and intently across the massive hall towards Arius. Arius continued talking until Nicholas finally stood directly in front of him.

Arius stopped. This breach of protocol was unprecedented.

In the silence that followed, Nicholas turned his back towards Arius and pulled down the robes from his own back, revealing the hideous scars he had gotten while in prison. Nicholas said, "I didn't get these for 'just a man.'"

Turning back towards Arius and facing him squarely, Nicholas saw the smug smile return to Arius' face. Arius said, "Well, it looks like you were mistaken." Then Arius started up his speech again as if nothing at all had happened.

That's when Nicholas did the unthinkable. With no other thought than to stop this man from speaking against his Lord and Savior, and in plain sight of the emperor and everyone else in attendance, Nicholas clenched his fist. He pulled back his arm and he punched Arius hard in the face.

Arius stumbled and fell back, both from the impact of the blow and from the shock that came with it. Nicholas, too, was stunned–along with everyone else in the room. With the same deliberate and intentional steps which he had taken to walk up to Arius, Nicholas now walked back to his chair and took his seat.

A collective gasp echoed through the hall when Nicholas struck Arius, followed by an eruption of commotion when Nicholas sat back down in his seat. The disruption threatened to throw the entire proceedings into chaos. The vast majority of those in the room looked like they could have jumped to their feet and given Nicholas a standing ovation for this bold act—including, by the look on his face, even the emperor himself! But to others, Arius chief among them, no words nor displays of emotion could express their outrage. Everyone knew what an awful offense Nicholas had just committed. It was, in fact, illegal for anyone to use violence of any kind in the presence of the emperor. The punishment for such an act was to immediately cut off the hand of anyone who struck another person in the presence of the emperor.

Constantine knew the law, of course, but also knew Nicholas. He had once even had a dream about Nicholas in which Nicholas warned Constantine to grant a stay of execution to three men in Constantine's court—a warning which Constantine heeded and acted upon in real life. When Constantine shared that dream with one of his generals, the general recounted to Constantine what Nicholas had done for the three innocent men back in Myra, for the general was one of the three who had seen Nicholas' bravery in person.

Although Nicholas' actions against Arius may have appeared rash, Constantine admired Nicholas' pluck. Known for his quick thinking and fast action, Constantine raised his hand and brought an instant silence to the room as he did so. "This is certainly a surprise to us all," he said. "And while the penalty for an act such in my presence is clear, I would prefer to defer this matter to the leaders of the council instead. These are your proceedings and I will defer to your wisdom to conduct them as you see fit."

Constantine had bought both time and goodwill among the various factions. The council on the whole seemed to agree with Nicholas' position, at least in spirit, even if they could not agree with his rash action. They would want to exact some form of punishment, since not to do so would fail to honor the rule of law. But having been given permission by the emperor himself to do as they saw fit, rather than invoke the standard punishment, they felt the freedom to take another form of action.

After a short deliberation, the leaders of the council agreed and determined that Nicholas should be defrocked immediately from his position as a bishop, banished from taking part in the rest of the proceedings in Nicaea and held under house arrest within the palace complex. There he could await any further decision the council might see fit at the conclusion of their meetings that summer. It was a lenient sentence, in light of the offense.

But for Nicholas, even before he heard what the punishment was going to be, he was already punishing himself more than anyone else ever could for what he had just done. Within less than a minute, he had gone from experiencing one of the highest mountaintops of his life to experiencing one of its deepest valleys.

Here he was attending one of the greatest conclaves in the history of the world, and yet he had just done something he knew he could never take back. The ramifications of his actions would affect him for the rest of his life, he was sure of it, or at least for whatever remained of his life. The sensation he felt could only be understood, perhaps, by those who had experienced it before—the weight, the shame and the agony of a moment of sin that could have crushed him, apart from knowing the forgiveness of Christ.

When Nicholas was defrocked of his title as bishop, it was in front of the entire assembly. He was disrobed of his bishop's garments, then escorted from the room in shackles. But this kind of disgrace was a mere trifle compared to the humiliation he was experiencing on the inside. He was even too numb to cry.

CHAPTER 34   DECEMBER 20

"What have I done?" Nicholas said to Dimitri as the two sat together in a room near the farthest corner of the palace. This room had become Nicholas' make-shift prison cell, as he was to be held under house arrest for the remainder of the proceedings. Dimitri, using his now-extensive skills at gaining access to otherwise unauthorized areas, had once again found a way to visit his friend in prison.

"What have you done?!? What else *could* you have done?" countered Dimitri. "If you hadn't done it, someone else surely would have, or at least should have. You did Arius, and all the rest of us, a favor with that punch. Had he continued with his diatribe, who knows what punishment the Lord Himself might have brought down upon the entire gathering!" Of course, Dimitri knew God could take it, and often does, when people rail against Him and His ways. He is much more long-suffering than any of us could ever be. But still, Dimitri felt Nicholas' actions were truly justified.

Nicholas, however, could hardly see it that way at the moment. It was more likely, he thought, that he had just succeeded in giving Arius the sympathy he needed for his cause to win. Nicholas knew that when people are losing an argument based on logic, they often appeal to pure emotion instead, going straight for the hearts of their listeners, whether or not their cause makes sense. And as much as Arius may have been losing his audience on the grounds of logic, Nicholas felt that his actions may have just tipped the emotional scales in Arius' favor.

The torment of it all beat against Nicholas' mind. Here it was, still just the opening days of the proceedings, and he would have to sit under house arrest for the next two months. How was he going to survive this onslaught of emotions every day during that time?

Nicholas already knew this prison cell was going to be entirely different than the one in which Diocletian had put him for more than a decade. This time, he felt he had put himself in jail. And although this prison was a beautifully appointed room within a palace, to Nicholas' way of thinking, it was much worse than the filthy one in which he had almost died.

In the other cell, he knew he was there because of the misguided actions of others. This gave him a sense that what he had to endure there was part of the natural suffering that Jesus said would come to all who followed Him. But in this cell, he knew he was there because of his own inane actions, actions which he viewed as inexcusable, a viewpoint which he felt many of those in attendance would rightly share.

For decades Nicholas had been known as a man of calm, inner strength and of dignity under control. Then, in one day, he had lost it all—and in front of the emperor no less! How could he ever forgive himself? "How," he asked Dimitri, "could I ever take back what I've just done to the name of the Lord."

Dimitri replied, "Perhaps He doesn't want you to take it back. Maybe it wasn't what you think you did *to* His name that He cares about so much, as what you did *in* His name. You certainly did what I, and the vast majority of those in the room wished they would have done, had they had the courage to do so."

Dimitri's words lingered in the air. As Nicholas contemplated them, a faint smile seemed to appear on his face. Perhaps there was something to be said for his heart in the matter after all. He was sincerely wanting to honor and defend his Lord, not to detract from Him in any way. Peter, he remembered, had a similar passion for defending his Lord. And Nicholas now realized what Peter may have felt when Peter cut off the ear of one of the men who had come to capture Jesus. Jesus told Peter to put away his sword and then Jesus healed the man's ear. Jesus could obviously defend Himself quite well on His own, but Nicholas had to give Peter credit for his passionate defense of his Master.

Nicholas was still unconvinced that he had done the right thing, but he felt in good company with others who had acted on their passions. And Dimitri's words helped him to realize that he was not alone in his thinking, and he took some comfort from the fact that Dimitri hadn't completely forsaken him over the incident. This support from Dimitri acted like a soothing balm to Nicholas' soul, and helped him to get through yet one more of the darkest times of his life.

Although Nicholas was convinced that the damage he had done was irreversible in human terms—and that God was going to have to work time-and-a-half to make anything good come out of this one—Nicholas knew what he had to do. Even in this moment of his deepest humiliation, he knew the best thing he could do was to do what he had always done: to put his complete faith and trust in God. But how? How could he trust that God possibly use this for good?

As if reading Nicholas' mind, Dimitri knew exactly what Nicholas needed to help him put his trust back in God again. Dimitri did what Nicholas had done for him and Samuel and Ruthie so many years ago. Dimitri told him a story.

CHAPTER 35   DECEMBER 21

Dimitri began, "What kind of story would you like to hear today? A good story or a bad story?" It was the way Nicholas had introduced the Bible stories that he told to Dimitri, Samuel and Ruthie during their many adventures in the Holy Land. Nicholas would then begin delighting the children with a story from the Bible about a good character or a bad character, or a good story or a bad story, sometimes which ended the exact opposite way it began.

Nicholas looked up with interest.

"It doesn't matter," Dimitri continued, "because the story I have to tell you today could be either good or bad. You just won't know till the end. But I've learned from a good friend," he said as he winked at Nicholas, "that the best way to enjoy a story is to always trust the storyteller."

Nicholas had told them that he watched people's reactions whenever he told stories back home.

"When people trust the storyteller," Nicholas had said, "they love the story no matter what happens, because *they* know *the storyteller knows* how the story will end. But when people *don't* trust the storyteller, their emotions go up and down like a boat in a storm, depending on what's happening in the story. The truth is, only the storyteller knows for sure how the story will end. So as long as you trust the storyteller, you can enjoy the whole story from start to finish."

Now it was Dimitri's turn to tell a story to Nicholas. The story he chose to tell was about another man who had been sent to jail, a man by the name of Joseph. Dimitri recounted for Nicholas how Joseph's life appeared to go up and down.

Dimitri started: "Joseph's father loved Joseph and gave him a beautiful, colorful coat. Now that's good, right?"

Nicholas nodded.

"But no, that was bad, for Joseph's brothers saw the coat and were jealous of him and sold him into slavery. Now that's bad, right?"

Nicholas nodded.

"No, that was good, because Joseph was put in charge of the whole house of a very wealthy man. Now that's good, right?"

Nicholas nodded again.

"No, that's bad," said Dimitri, "because the wealthy man's wife tried to seduce him, and when Joseph resisted, she sent him to jail. Now that's bad, right?"

Nicholas stopped nodding either way because he knew where this was going.

"No, that's good," said Dimitri, "because Joseph was put in charge over all the other prisoners. He even helped to interpret their dreams. Now that's good, right?"

Nicholas continued to listen carefully.

"No, that's bad, because after interpreting their dreams, Joseph asked one of the men to help him out of prison when he got out, but the man forgot about Joseph and left him behind. Now that's bad, right?"

Nicholas saw himself as the man who had been left behind in prison.

"No! That's good! Because God had put Joseph in just the right place at just the right time. When the king of Egypt had a dream and he needed someone to interpret it, the man who had been set free suddenly remembered that Joseph was still in jail and told the king about him.

The king summoned Joseph, asked for an interpretation and Joseph gave it to him. The king was so impressed with Joseph that he put Joseph in charge of his whole kingdom. As a result, Joseph was able to use his new position to save hundreds of thousands of lives, including the lives of his own father and even his brothers—the very ones who had sold him into slavery in the first place. And that's very good!"

"So you see," said Dimitri, "just as you've always told us, we never know how the story will turn out until the very end. God knew what He was doing all along! You see…

– at just the right time, Joseph was born and his father loved him,
– so that at just the right time his brothers would mistreat him,
– so that at just the right time the slave traders would come along and buy him,
– so that at just the right time he would be put in charge of a wealthy man's house,
– so that at just the right time he would be thrown into jail,
– so that at just the right time he would be put in charge of the prisoners,
– so that at just the right time he could interpret their dreams,
– so that at just the right time he could interpret Pharaoh's dreams,
– so that at just the right time he would become second in command over all of Egypt,
– so that at just the right time Joseph would be in the one place in the world that God wanted him to be so that he could save the lives of his father and brothers and many, many others!

"All along the way, Joseph never gave up on God. He knew the secret of enjoying the story while he lived it out: he always trusted the Storyteller, the One who was writing the story of his life."

All of Nicholas' fears and doubts faded away in those moments and he knew *he* could trust the Storyteller, the One who was writing the story of his life, too. Nicholas' story wasn't over yet, and he had to trust that the God who brought him this far could see him through to the end.

Nicholas looked at Dimitri with a smile of thanks, then closed his eyes. It would be a long two months of waiting for the council's decision. But he knew that if he could trust God in that one moment, and then in the next moment, and then the next, each of those moments would add up to minutes, and minutes would add up to hours. Hours would turn into weeks, then months, then years. He knew that it all began with trusting God in a moment.

With his eyes still closed, Nicholas put his full faith and trust in God again. The peace of God flooded his heart.

Soon, two months had passed by. The council was ready to make their final decisions on many matters, including the decision that had landed Nicholas under house arrest in the first place—and Nicholas was about to find out the results.

CHAPTER 36   DECEMBER 22

"They did it!" It was Dimitri, bursting through the door to Nicholas' room as soon as the palace guard had opened it.

"They did it!" he repeated. "It's done! The council has voted, and they've agreed with you! All but two of the 318 bishops have sided with you over Arius!"

Relief swept over Nicholas' whole body. Dimitri could feel it in his body, too, as he watched the news flood over Nicholas' entire being.

"And furthermore," said Dimitri, "the council has decided not to take any further action against you!"

Both pieces of news were the best possible outcome Nicholas could have imagined. Even though Nicholas' action had cost him his position as a bishop, it had not jeopardized the outcome of the proceedings. It was even possible—though he never knew for sure—that his action against Arius had perhaps in some way shaped what took place during those summer months at that historic council.

Within minutes of Dimitri's arrival, another visitor appeared at Nicholas' door. It was Constantine.

The council's decision about what to do with Nicholas was one thing, but Constantine's decision was another. A fresh wave of fear washed over Nicholas as he thought of the possibilities.

"Nicholas," said the emperor, "I wanted to personally thank you for coming here to be my guest in Nicaea. I want to apologize for what you've had to endure these past two months. This wasn't what I had planned for you and I'm sure it wasn't what you had planned, either. But even though you weren't able to attend the rest of the proceedings, I assure you that your presence was felt throughout every meeting. What you did that day in the hall spoke to me about what it means to follow Christ more than anything else I heard in the days that followed. I'd like to hear more from you in the future, if you would be willing to be my guest again. But next time, it won't be in the farthest corner of the palace. Furthermore, I have asked for and received permission from the council to reinstate you to your position as Bishop of Myra. I believe the One who called you to serve Him would want you to continue doing everything you've been doing up to this point. As for me, let me just say that I appreciate what you've done here more than you can possibly know. Thank you for coming, and whenever you're ready, you're free to go home."

Nicholas had been listening to Constantine's words as if he were in a dream. He could hardly believe his ears. But when the emperor said the word "home," Nicholas knew this wasn't a dream, and the word rang like the sweetest bell in Nicholas' ears. Of all the words the emperor had just spoken, none sounded better to him than that final word: home. He wanted nothing more than to get back to the flock he served. It was for them that he had come to this important gathering in the first place, to ensure that the Truths he had taught them would continue to be taught throughout the land.

After more than two months of being separated from them, and the ongoing question of what would become of them and the hundreds of thousands of others like them in the future who would be affected by their decisions here, Nicholas could finally go home. He was free again in more ways than one.

CHAPTER 37 — DECEMBER 23

Nicholas stood at his favorite spot in the world one last time: by the sea. Eighteen years had passed since he had returned to Myra from the council in Nicaea. In the days since coming home, he continued to serve the Lord as he had always done: with all his heart, soul, mind and strength.

Nicholas had come to the shore with Dimitri and Anna Maria, who had brought with them one of their grandchildren, a young girl seven years old, named Ruthie.

Ruthie had been running back and forth in the waves, as Dimitri and Anna Maria tried to keep up with her. Nicholas had plenty of time to look out over the sea and as he often did, look out over eternity as well.

Looking back on his life, Nicholas never knew if he really accomplished what he wanted to in life: to make a difference in the world. He had seen glimpses along the way, of course, in the lives of people like Dimitri, Samuel, Ruthie, Sophia, Cecilia and Anna Maria.

He had also learned from people like the ship's captain that when the captain arrived in Rome, his ship miraculously weighed exactly the same as before he had set sail from Alexandria—even after giving the people of Myra several years' worth of grain from it. Reminders like these encouraged Nicholas that God really had been guiding him in his decisions.

He still had questions though. He never quite knew if he had done the right thing at the council in Nicaea. He never quite knew if his later private conversations with Constantine might have impacted the emperor's personal faith in Christ.

He was encouraged, however, to learn that Constantine's mother had also made a pilgrimage to the Holy Land just as Nicholas had done. And after her visit, she persuaded Constantine to build churches over the holy sites she had seen. She had recently completed building a church in Bethlehem over the spot where Jesus was born, as well as a church in Jerusalem over the spot where Jesus had died and risen from the dead.

Nicholas knew he had had both successes and mistakes in his life. But looking back over it, he couldn't always tell which was which! Those times that he thought were the valleys turned out to be the mountaintops, and the mountaintops turned out to be valleys. But the most important thing, he reminded himself, was that he trusted God in all things, knowing that God could work anything for good for those who loved Him, who were called according to His purpose.

What the future held for the world, Nicholas had no idea. But he knew that he had done what he could with the time that he had. He tried to love God and love others as Jesus had called him to do. And where he had failed along the way, he trusted that Jesus could cover those failures, too, just as Jesus had covered his sins by dying on the cross.

As Nicholas' father had done before him, Nicholas looked out over the sea again, too. Then closing his eyes, he asked God for strength for the next journey he was about to take.

He let the sun warm his face, then he opened the palms of his hands and let the breeze lift them into the air. He praised God as the warm breeze floated gently through his fingertips.

Little Ruthie returned from splashing in the water, followed closely by Dimitri and Anna Maria. Ruthie looked up at Nicholas, with his eyes closed and his hands raised towards heaven. Reaching out to him, she tugged at his clothes and asked, "Nicholas, have you ever *seen* God?"

Nicholas opened his eyes and looked down at Ruthie, then smiled up at Dimitri and Anna Maria. He looked out at the sunshine and the waves and the miles and miles of shoreline that stretched out in both directions before him. Turning his face back towards Ruthie, Nicholas said, "Yes, Ruthie, I have seen God. And the older I get, the more I see Him everywhere I look."

Ruthie smiled, and Nicholas gave her a warm hug. Then just as quickly as she had run up to him, she ran off again to play.

Nicholas exchanged smiles with Dimitri and Anna Maria, then they, too, were off again, chasing Ruthie down the beach.

Nicholas looked one last time at the beautiful sea, then turned and headed towards home.

EPILOGUE   DECEMBER 24

So now you know a little bit more about me—Dimitri Alexander—and my good friend, Nicholas. That was the last time I saw him, until this morning. He had asked if he could spend a few days alone, just him and the Lord that he loved. He said he had one more journey to prepare for. Anna Maria and I guessed, of course, just what he meant.

We knew he was probably getting ready to go home, to his real home, the one that Jesus had said He was going to prepare for each of us who believe in Him.

Nicholas had been looking forward to this trip his whole life. Not that he wanted to shortchange a single moment of the life that God that had given him here on earth, for he knew that this life had a uniquely important purpose as well, or else God would never have created it with such beauty and precision and marvelous mystery.

But as Nicholas' life here on earth wound down, he said he was ready. He was ready to go, and he looked forward to everything that God had in store for him next.

So when Nicholas sent word this morning for Anna Maria and me and a few other friends to come and see him, we knew that the time had come.

As we came into this room, we found him lying on his bed, just as he is right now. He was breathing quietly, and he motioned for us to come close. We couldn't hold back our tears, and he didn't try to stop us. He knew how hard it was to say goodbye to those we love. But he also made it easier for us. He smiled one more time and spoke softly, saying the same words that he had spoken when Ruthie had died many years before: "Either way we win," he said. "Either way we win."

"Yes, Nicholas," I said. "Either way we win." Then the room became quiet again. Nicholas closed his eyes and fell asleep for the last time. No one moved. No one said a word.

This man who lay before us slept as if it were just another night in his life. But we knew this was a holy moment. Nicholas had just entered into the presence of the Lord. As Nicholas had done throughout his life, we were sure he was doing right now in heaven, walking and talking and laughing with Jesus, but now they were face to face.

We could only imagine what Nicholas might be saying to Jesus. But we knew for certain what Jesus was saying to him: "Well done, My good and faithful servant. Well done. Come and share your Master's happiness."

I have no idea how history might remember Nicholas, if it will remember him at all. He was no emperor like Constantine. He was no tyrant like Diocletian. He was no orator like Arius. He was simply a Christian trying to live out his faith, touching one life at a time as best he knew how.

Nicholas may have wondered if his life made any difference. I know my answer, and now that you know his story, I'll let you decide for yourself. In the end, I suppose only God really knows just how many lives were touched by this remarkable man.

But what I do know this: each of us has just one life to live. But if we live it right, as Nicholas did, one life is all we need.

CONCLUSION   DECEMBER 25

What Nicholas didn't know, and what no one who knew him could have possibly imagined, was just how far and wide this one life would reach—not only throughout the world, but also throughout the ages.

He was known to his parents as their beloved son, and to those in his city as their beloved bishop. But he has become known to us by another name: Saint Nicholas.

The biblical word for "saint" literally means "believer." The Bible talks about the saints in Ephesus, the saints in Rome, the saints in Philippi and the saints in Jerusalem. Each time, the word "saints" refers to the believers who were in those cities. So Nicholas rightly became known as "Saint Nicholas," or to say it another way, "Nicholas, The Believer." The Latin translation is "Santa Nicholas," and in Dutch "Sinterklaas," from which we get the name "Santa Claus."

His good name and his good deeds have been an inspiration to so many, that the day he passed from this life to the next, on December 6th, 343 A.D., is still celebrated by people throughout the world.

Many legends have been told about Nicholas over the years, some giving him qualities that make him seem larger than life. But the reason that so many legends of any kind grow, including those told about Saint Nicholas, is often because the people about whom they're told were larger than life themselves. They were people who were so good or so well-respected that every good deed becomes attributed to them, as if they had done them themselves.

While not all the stories attributed to Nicholas can be traced to the earliest records of his life, the histories that were recorded closest to the time period in which he lived *do* record many of the stories found in this book. To help you sort through them, here's what we do know:

- *Nicholas was born sometime between 260-280 A.D. in the city of Patara, a city you can still visit today in modern-day Turkey, on the northern coast of the Mediterranean Sea.*
- *Nicholas' parents were devout Christians who died in a plague when Nicholas was young, leaving him with a sizable inheritance.*

- *Nicholas made a pilgrimage to the Holy Land and lived there for a number of years before returning to his home province of Lycia.*
- *Nicholas traveled across the Mediterranean Sea in a ship that was caught in a storm. After praying, his ship reached its destination as if someone was miraculously holding the rudder steady. The rudder of a ship is also called a tiller, and sailors on the Mediterranean Sea today still wish each other luck by saying, "May Nicholas hold the tiller!"*
- *When Nicholas returned from the Holy Land, he took up residence in the city of Myra, about 30 miles from his hometown of Patara. Nicholas became the bishop of Myra and lived there the rest of his life.*
- *Nicholas secretly gave three gifts of gold on three separate occasions to a man whose daughters were to be sold into slavery because he had no money to offer to potential husbands as a dowry. The family discovered Nicholas was the mysterious donor on one of his attempts, which is why we know the story today. In this version of the story, we've added the twist of having Nicholas deliver the first two gifts, and Dimitri deliver the third, to capture the idea that many gifts were given back then, and are still given today, in the name of Saint Nicholas, who was known for such deeds. The theme of redemption is also so closely associated with this story from Saint Nicholas' life, that if you pass by a pawn shop today, you will often see three golden balls in their logo, representing the three bags of gold that Nicholas gave to spare these girls from their unfortunate fate.*
- *Nicholas pled for the lives of three innocent men who were unjustly condemned to death by a magistrate in Myra, taking the sword directly from the executioner's hand.*
- *"Nicholas, Bishop of Myra" is listed on some, but not all, of the historical documents which record those who attended the real Council of Nicaea, which was convened by Emperor Constantine in 325 A.D. One of the council's main decisions addressed the divinity of Christ, resulting in the writing of the Nicene Creed—a creed which is still recited in many churches today. Some historians say that Nicholas' name does not appear on all the record books of this council because of his banishment from the proceedings after striking Arius for denying that Christ was divine. Nicholas is, however, listed on at least five of these ancient record books, including the earliest known Greek manuscript of the event.*
- *The Nicene Creed was adopted at the Council of Nicaea and has become one of the most widely used, brief statements of the Christian faith. The original version reads, in part, as translated from the Greek: "We believe in one God, the Father Almighty, Maker of all things visible and invisible. And in one Lord Jesus Christ, the Son of God, begotten of the Father, the only-begotten; that is, of the essence of the Father, God of God, Light of Light, very God of very God, begotten, not made, being of one substance with the Father; By whom all things were made both in heaven and on earth; Who for us men, and for our salvation, came down and was incarnate and was made man; He suffered, and the third day He rose again, ascended into heaven; From thence he shall come to judge the quick and the dead..." Subsequent versions, beginning as early as 381 A.D., have altered and clarified some of the original statements, resulting in a few similar, but not quite identical statements that are now in use.*

- Nicholas is recorded as having done much for the people of Myra, including securing grain from a ship traveling from Alexandria to Rome, which saved the people in that region from a famine.
- Constantine's mother, Helen, did visit the Holy Land and encouraged Constantine to build churches over the sites that she felt were most important to the Christian faith. The churches were built on the locations she had been shown by local believers where Jesus was born, and where Jesus died and rose again. Those churches, The Church of the Nativity in Bethlehem and the Church of the Holy Sepulchre in Jerusalem, have been destroyed and rebuilt many times over the years, but still in the same locations that Constantine's mother, and likely Nicholas himself, had seen.
- The date of Nicholas' death has been established as December 6th, 343 A.D., and you can still visit his tomb in the modern city of Demre, Turkey, formerly known as Myra, in the province of Lycia. Nicholas' bones were removed from the tomb in 1087 A.D. by men from Italy who feared that they might be destroyed or stolen, as the country was being invaded by others. The bones of Saint Nicholas were taken to the city of Bari, Italy, where they are still entombed today.

Of the many other stories told about or attributed to Nicholas, it's hard to know with certainty which ones actually took place and which were simply attributed to him because of his already good and popular name. For instance, in the 12th century, stories began to surface of how Nicholas had brought three children back to life who had been brutally murdered. Even though the first recorded accounts of this story didn't appear until more than 800 years after Nicholas' death, this story is one of the most frequently associated with Saint Nicholas in religious artwork, featuring three young children being raised to life and standing next to Nicholas. We have included the essence of this story in this novel in the form of the three orphans who Nicholas met in the Holy Land and whom he helped to bring back to life—at least spiritually.

While all of these additional stories can't be attributed to Nicholas with certainty, we can say that his life and his memory had such a profound effect throughout history that more churches throughout the world now bear the name of "Saint Nicholas" than any other figure, outside of the original disciples themselves.

Some people wonder if they can believe in Saint Nicholas or not. Nicholas probably wouldn't care so much if you believed in *him* or not, but that you believed in the One in whom He believed, *Jesus Christ*.

A popular image today shows Saint Nicholas bowing down, his hat at his side, kneeling in front of baby Jesus in the manger. Although that scene could never have taken place in real life, for Saint Nicholas was born almost 300 years *after* the birth of Christ, the heart of that scene couldn't be more accurate. Nicholas *was* a true believer in Jesus, and he did worship, adore and live his life in service to the Christ.

Saint Nicholas would have never wanted his story to *replace* the story of Jesus in the manger, but he would have loved to have his story *point* to Jesus in the manger. And that's why this book was written.

While the stories told here were selected from the many that have been told about Saint Nicholas over the years, these were told so that you might believe—not just in Nicholas, but in Jesus Christ, his Savior. These stories were written down for the same reason the

Apostle John wrote down the stories he recorded about Jesus in the Bible. John said he wrote his stories:

> "…that you may believe that Jesus is the Christ, the Son of God, and that by believing you may have life in His name" (John 20:31).

Nicholas would want the same for you. He would want you to become what he was: a Believer.

If you've never done so, put your faith in Jesus Christ today, asking Him to forgive you of your sins and giving you the assurance that you will live with Him forever.

If you've already put your faith in Christ, let this story remind you just how precious your faith really is. Renew your commitment today to serve Christ as Nicholas served Him: with all of your heart, soul, mind and strength. God really will work all things together for good. As the Bible says:

> "And we know that in all things God works for the good of those who love Him, who have been called according to His purpose" (Romans 8:28).

Thanks for reading this special book about this special man, and I pray that your Christmas may be truly merry and bright. As Clement Moore said in his now famous poem, *A Visit from St. Nicholas:*

> "Happy Christmas to all, and to all a good night!"

15 Tips For A Stronger Marriage

Bonus: 12 Tips on Parenting!

Bonus Chapter from "15 Tips for a Stronger Marriage"

INTRODUCTION

As a father of 6 kids, I'm always glad to hear what others are doing to parent their kids. So when some friends of my college-age kids asked me what advice I would give them for raising kids of their own in the future, I put together this list of some of the best pieces of wisdom we gathered over the years that have worked well for us. I thought you might like to read it, too.

Since there are 12 tips and there are 12 months in the year, you might want to focus on trying 1 tip each month. They're not in any particular order, so you can pick a tip for each month that seems most helpful to you at the time.

And even if you don't have kids in your life right now, maybe you know someone who does who might be interested in reading these tips. If so, please pass them along, as each tip includes a special word from God's Word. Even though I'm not a perfect father, I know Someone who is—and His wisdom can't be beat!

With that disclaimer out of the way, here are 2 tips per day from *12 Tips on Parenting!*

TIP 1: RECOGNIZE THAT CHILDREN ARE GIFTS FROM THE LORD   DECEMBER 26

Your attitude towards your children may be the single-most important item in your parenting toolbox. The Bible says that children are blessings, not burdens: "Blessed is the man whose quiver is full of them" (Psalm 127:5a).

You can check your attitude by asking what your heart feels when you hear of someone who already has 2 or 3 children and they tell you they're expecting a 3rd or 4th. Or 5th. Or 6th. Or 7th, etc. If your heart sinks with the addition of each child, you may secretly be viewing children as burdens, not blessings. If the same person had told you God had given them a 3rd or 4th car (or 5th or 6th or 7th, etc.), or a 3rd or 4th house (or 5th or 6th or 7th, etc.) and your attitude is like "Wow! That's incredible!" then you may want to rethink your attitude.

Children do take time and energy and attention, just as cars and houses do, and more children take more time and energy and attention, just as more cars and more houses do (just ask anyone who has more than one of any of these!) With great gifts comes great responsibility. But children, like any gifts from the Lord, are still gifts to be treasured, valued and held in the highest regard. Check your attitude and remember that children really are gifts from the Lord.

TIP 2: LOVE YOUR SPOUSE

This tip may not seem like it has anything to do with parenting, but it's actually one of the best tips on this list! I have a plaque from my dad that says: "The most important thing a father can do for his children is to love their mother." My dad reminded me of this one day when I was feeling particularly inadequate about my parenting. He said, "You have no idea what you're doing for your children just by loving Lana." Looking back over the years, I'm sure he was right.

A genuine love between parents can do more for children than we can imagine. The Bible says, "Husbands, love your wives, just as Christ loved the church and gave Himself up for her… and the wife should respect her husband" (Ephesians 5:25 and 33b). Parents at odds cause children to take sides and respect only one or the other parent (or neither) and kids can play off that to try to get what they want. If you want your children to treat others with love and respect, then treat your husband or wife with love and respect (even if they don't do the same for you). Your children will be blessed as a result.

TIP 3: REALIZE THAT CHILDREN TAKE TIME   DECEMBER 27

Children do take time, but they don't take time away from life. Children take time that enhances life. Trips to the zoo, trips to the beach, sitting down and playing games, setting limits on your workdays and Sundays and weekends so you can be with them, all take time away from other things you could be doing. But the return on your investment is so much greater, both in the moment and in the long run.

For Lana, when she decided to stay home from work so she could homeschool our kids and spend more time with them, it was costly on many levels: financially, personally and professionally. But she never felt like she was wasting her life by doing this, but investing her life. When she was facing death, way too young at the age of 48, she said she was thankful she had spent her time the way she did—with no regrets. Quality time is sometimes only possible because quantity time makes it so.

TIP 4: LET EVERYONE WORK TOGETHER TO MAKE THE HOUSEHOLD WORK

One of the blessings for me of having a larger family has been to see how all the kids can work together to help keep our household running. Doing everything for our kids was never an option because we simply couldn't do it all. Responsibilities were given to each child as soon as they were able, from cooking and cleaning to dishes and laundry, from building and bookkeeping to yardwork and petkeeping.

The Bible says, "If you don't work, you don't eat" (2 Thessalonians 3:10, MSG). We never taught this in a mean-spirited way, but as a matter of getting things done more efficiently (or getting things done at all!) whether it was getting food to the table or chores finished on Saturday. For us, giving kids responsibility was both practical (for keeping our house running) and good training for their future.

TIP 5: DISCIPLINE IN LOVE, NOT IN ANGER — DECEMBER 28

Discipline is simply more effective when it is separated from anger. The Bible says, "Children, obey your parents in the Lord, for this is right…" (Ephesians 6:1) but that is quickly followed by these words: "Fathers, do not exasperate your children; instead, bring them up in the training and instruction of the Lord" (Ephesians 6:4).

I've found it best not to explode at my children, not because I don't want to, but because it's not useful. They can't hear you—or your love for them—when you're screaming. The times I most regret in my parenting are the times when I've disciplined in anger. But I've never regretted disciplining in love because that has set the stage for their future success in life. A simple tip: count to 10 before disciplining children. For teenagers, wait a week! (I'm serious!)

TIP 6: PRAY FOR GOD TO REVEAL THE TRUTH, EVEN IF IT'S PAINFUL TO HEAR

A pastor's kid once said that it wasn't fair that his dad was a pastor, because God always seemed to tell his parents whenever he was doing something wrong. We really can pray that God will show us what's going on in our kids' lives, even when we can't see it ourselves. The Bible says, "He [God] gives wisdom to the wise and knowledge to the discerning. He reveals deep and hidden things; He knows what lies in darkness, and light dwells with Him" (Daniel 2:21b-22).

There have been times when I have prayed that God would show me if there's anything I should know about my kids so I can help them stay on the right path, even if it's something I didn't want to hear. I've been surprised when, soon after a prayer like this, God has revealed something to me—whether in a dream or a phone bill or an unexpected email—that was painful to hear but has opened the door to a conversation where I can help walk my kids through a difficult situation.

TIP 7: LOVE DOESN'T ALWAYS SAY "YES" — DECEMBER 29

A good parent wants to bless and please their children. But some parents say "Yes" to their kids' pleas solely to win their love and friendship, not because it's good or best for them. There are times when your kids need a best friend and there are times when you can be one for them. But there are other times when they need you to be a parent, and only you can do that for them.

Some parents say "Yes" to all things in order to win their children's friendship. But a well-timed or well-reasoned "No" can be just as loving. The Bible says, "A word aptly spoken is like apples of gold in settings of silver" (Proverbs 25:11), which means that certain words we say are beautiful and perfectly fit for the occasion. While this applies to words of any type, it can especially apply to our yes's and no's.

TIP 8: KEEP YOUR WORDS UPLIFTING AND ENCOURAGING

As parents, our words have an extra weight of authority. As such, we have to be extra careful with what we say, especially when it comes to criticism. Some people may say, "They have a face only a mother could love." But what if it's the mother who says, "You're ugly!" or "You can't sing!" or "You're no good at _____ or _____ or _____!"

A good rule of thumb is to give at least 10 positive affirmations for every 1 correction, and then only if it's necessary for their benefit (for instance, to save them from embarrassment in public). Watch your words, especially your words of criticism. The Bible says, "Do not let any unwholesome talk come out of your mouths, but only what is helpful for building others up according to their needs, that it may benefit those who listen" (Ephesians 4:29).

TIP 9: PRAY FOR YOUR CHILDREN, BOTH PRIVATELY AND ALOUD   DECEMBER 30

We've prayed for each of our children from the moment we knew they were in Lana's womb. We've prayed for their lives, their health, their faith, their futures, their callings, their spouses, their children and grandchildren and great grandchildren and so on! We've done this privately in our own quiet times, as well as aloud at nighttime when we tuck them into bed and kiss them good night.

I still do this even for my college-age kids when they're home, putting my hand on their heads and praying for them before they go to bed (or before I go to bed, which is more often the case these days!) It may seem awkward, but I believe in the power of prayer, plus I think it's important that our kids know that we're praying for them, as a matter of love and care. As the Bible says: "Therefore confess your sins to each other and pray for each other so that you may be healed. The prayer of a righteous man is powerful and effective" (James 5:16).

TIP 10: WHEN YOUR KIDS SIN, LOVE 'EM MORE

Sometimes our kids do things that make us frustrated and make us want to pull back from them. But I've found that's the time I need to "love 'em more." Someone once asked the famous evangelist Billy Graham what he would do if he found out one of his children had sinned. He said, "Why, I'd love that one even more." It's not that Rev. Graham would love them more because of their sin, but because he knew that love is the best antidote to sin.

Our kids need love and acceptance, just like we do, and that's why they sometimes seek it out in the wrong places, just like we do. It's at times like these that they need to see our love and forgiveness for them more than ever, just as Jesus did for us when He died on the cross. As the Bible says, "God demonstrates His own love for us in this: While we were still sinners, Christ died for us" (Romans 5:8). When your kids hurt you or mistreat you or disappoint you, don't pull back. Do what Jesus did and "love 'em more."

TIP 11: TAKE BREAKS FOR RAINBOWS   DECEMBER 31

A life with kids is filled with interruptions. But don't take the interruptions as sidelines from life, but as one of the best parts of life itself. We have a painting in our home that says, "The work will wait while you show the children the rainbow, but the rainbow won't wait while you finish the work." Take advantage of those fleeting moments to enjoy your life with your children.

It's OK to stop and smell the roses. The Bible says, "Finally, brothers, whatever is true, whatever is noble, whatever is right, whatever is pure, whatever is lovely, whatever is admirable—if anything is excellent or praiseworthy—think about such things" (Philippians 4:8). When we moved to the country, Lana and I would take walks with our kids at sunset whenever we had the chance. There were always plenty of other things to do, but none of them so memorable to me as those sunset walks.

TIP 12: LET KIDS BE KIDS, BUT DON'T LET THEM BE IN DANGER

There's a fine line between letting kids be kids and letting them be in danger, because a lot of the things kids do can be dangerous! It's one thing if they want to let their hair grow out, but quite another if they want to hang out with dangerous people. It's one thing to let them be adventurous, but quite another to let them do something that's truly life threatening.

I've had to walk that fine line and have had multiple conversations with my kids about each of these things. And God is the one who has had to remind me multiple times to let my kids be kids, especially my teenagers. But I've also had to step in and say, "I'm glad to let you be a teenager, but I won't let you be in danger." That's just wisdom, and knowing which is which often comes only from God, who is happy to let us know the difference. If you're not sure what to do in a situation, ask God who is glad to pour out His wisdom on you. As the Bible says, "If any of you lacks wisdom, he should ask God, who gives generously to all without finding fault, and it will be given to him" (James 1:5).

Thanks for reading these 12 tips on parenting and thanks for passing them along to others who might benefit from reading them. Again, you might want to choose 1 tip each month to focus on with your kids this year or you might want to reread this message from time to time in the years ahead as your kids go through different stages of life. As I've been reminded often, none of us are perfect parents. But with God's help, we can keep trying to be the best that we can be.

May the Lord bless you as you seek to love and bless the children in your life!

There's More!

Thanks for reading!
For more inspirational books,
music, and videos, visit:

theranch.org
ericelder.com
and inspiringbooks.com

Eric Elder

www.ingramcontent.com/pod-product-compliance
Lightning Source LLC
Chambersburg PA
CBHW071654170426
43195CB00039B/2190